# THE
# COMMENTARIES
## OF
## SIR WILLIAM BLACKSTONE, KNT.
### ON THE
## LAWS AND CONSTITUTION
## OF ENGLAND

Elibron Classics
www.elibron.com

Elibron Classics series.

© 2005 Adamant Media Corporation.

ISBN 1-4021-8357-7 (paperback)
ISBN 1-4212-8911-3 (hardcover)

This Elibron Classics Replica Edition is an unabridged facsimile of the edition published in 1796, London.

Elibron and Elibron Classics are trademarks of Adamant Media Corporation. All rights reserved.

This book is an accurate reproduction of the original. Any marks, names, colophons, imprints, logos or other symbols or identifiers that appear on or in this book, except for those of Adamant Media Corporation and BookSurge, LLC, are used only for historical reference and accuracy and are not meant to designate origin or imply any sponsorship by or license from any third party.

# THE COMMENTARIES

OF

Sir *WILLIAM BLACKSTONE*, Knt.

ON THE

## LAWS AND CONSTITUTION

OF

# ENGLAND;

CAREFULLY ABRIDGED,

IN A NEW MANNER,

AND

*Continued down to the prefent Time:*

## WITH NOTES,

CORRECTIVE AND EXPLANATORY.

By *WILLIAM CURRY*,
OF THE INNER TEMPLE.

"It is incumbent upon every Man to be acquainted with the Laws; left he incur the Cenfure, as well as the Inconvenience, of living in Society without knowing the Obligations it lays him under."

INTROD. CCM.

*LONDON:*
PRINTED FOR W. CLARKE AND SON, PORTUGAL-STREET, LINCOLN'S-INN.

1796.

TO

THE HONORABLE

SIR FRANCIS BULLER, BART.

ONE OF THE JUSTICES

OF

HIS MAJESTY's COURT OF COMMON PLEAS,

THE FOLLOWING WORK

IS

(BY HIS OBLIGING PERMISSION)

MOST RESPECTFULLY DEDICATED,

AS A MARK

OF THE HIGH SENSE ENTERTAINED

BY THE EDITOR,

OF

HIS EXALTED CHARACTER AS A LAWYER,

AND A JUDGE.

# PREFACE.

THE Abridgement now submitted to the candour of the Profession, and of the Public, consists of Selections of the most material and essential parts of the justly celebrated Commentaries of Sir Wm. Blackstone, on the Laws and Constitution of England; in preparing which, my object has been to preserve 1. Such parts as seemed necessary to be known by every individual, as a member of the community, and, 2. Such as I apprehended the professional student would wish, in a more particular manner, to inculcate and remember.

By the method adopted of selecting entire passages, in the very words of the author, I imagined I should inevitably acquire the important advantage of preserving the freedom, and spirit of the original, without any possible danger of misrepresenting its genuine sense and construction; an advantage which I could not hope to attain in the common mode of abridgement.

In the notes I have intended to advert to the alterations which have been effected in the legal accuracy of the text, by statutes and cases passed, or decided fince it received the laſt corrections of the author, in which I hope that no material omiſſion will be imputed to me. I have alſo in the very few inſtances where any poſition in the text ſeemed, from its mode of ſtatement either to comprehend caſes to which it in ſtrictneſs did not extend, or to exclude thoſe to which it in truth applied, ſubjoined ſuch remarks as I thought neceſſary to prevent the ſtudent from inferring an erroneous concluſion.

The utility of a ſelection of this ſort it is perhaps unneceſſary to inſiſt upon. No adequate benefit can be derived from the Commentaries of Sir Wm. Blackſtone, unleſs by frequent and attentive peruſals; but the ſtudent, whatever may be his induſtry, will find it no eaſy matter to return with ardor and alertneſs (without which he will read to little purpoſe) to a ſecond and a third peruſal of the ſame volumes, protracted too as they now are (though very properly) by long and numerous Annotations. And if this be true of a profeſſional ſtudier of the laws, how much more forcibly will it apply to thoſe who are occupied in the various purſuits of agriculture and commerce; but theſe are equally liable to the ſevere and juſt animadverſions of the law, if they infringe, however inadvertently, upon its ordinances.

AT a time moreover, when the ſcience of legiſlation and government is ſo generally and ſo warmly discussed, a familiar promulgation of those laws which form the body and bulwark of our glorious and enviable constitution, seems peculiarly expedient and desirable; by which I trust it will be perceived that the laws of England require only to be known, to be respected and revered; and such reverence will naturally induce every one to unite, in one voice, to preserve them inviolate; and that in the regular and only constitutional way which the law itself has delineated.

And here I cannot but remark that these desirable ends might be advantageously promoted, by introducing such a compendium of our laws into the upper forms of our public schools, for which the familiar manner of the Commentaries are admirably adapted: it would imprint upon the juvenile mind, at a period when most easily susceptible of impressions, a veneration for the Laws and Constitution of his Country, and furnish him with a guard against the dangerous principles of innovation and dissoluteness, which unfortunately are at present so industriously propagated, by the enemies of rational freedom. And it would, also, afford him a protection in the common affairs of life, as well against his own natural inadvertency, as the fraud and artifices of others.

I should be doing injustice to my own feelings, to conclude without acknowledging the obligations I am under to Mr. *Christian*, whose truly elegant, and useful Annotations, have afforded me not only much entertainment and improvement, but also some valuable hints in respect to recent inaccuracies of the text, which might otherwise have escaped so young an editor.

The *Errata*, which the reader will perceive at the end of the volume, may, I fear, be thought not a little numerous; but the great distance of my residence from the press, made it impossible for me to have that frequent communication with the publisher which was necessary, in order to render it as free from errors as I could wish.

With, however, all it's imperfections, I cheerfully submit it to the ordeal of a generous Public; particularly relying on the candour and indulgence of the Profession, not to pass too critical a scrutiny on endeavours, which, whatever may be their success, have been exerted with disinterested views for the public service.

*Gosport*,
6th Nov. 1796.

# TABLE OF CONTENTS.

## BOOK I.
### OF THE RIGHTS OF PERSONS.

*Introduction* — — 1

#### CHAP. I.
*Of the abfolute Rights of Individuals* — 13

#### CHAP. II.
*Of the Houfe of Commons* — — 20

#### CHAP. III.
*Of fubordinate Magiftrates* — — 30

#### CHAP. IV.
*Of the People, whether Aliens, Denizens, or Natives* 47

#### CHAP. V.
*Of the Clergy* — — 52

#### CHAP. VI.
*Of Mafter and Servant* — — 65

#### CHAP. VII.
*Of Hufband and Wife* — — 72

#### CHAP. VIII.
*Of Parent and Child* — — 80

## TABLE OF CONTENTS.

### CHAP. IX.
*Of Guardian and Ward* — 87

### CHAP. X.
*Of Corporations* — 93

# BOOK II.
## OF THE RIGHTS OF THINGS.

### CHAP. I.
*Of Corporeal Hereditaments* — 102

*Of Incorporeal Hereditaments* — 105

### CHAP. III.
*Of the Modern English Tenures* — 119

### CHAP. IV.
*Of Freehold Estates of Inheritance* — 122

### CHAP. V.
*Of Freeholds not of Inheritance* — 131

### CHAP. VI.
*Of Estates less than Freehold* — 142

### CHAP. VII.
*Of Estates upon Condition* — 149

### CHAP. VIII.
*Of Estates in Possession, Remainder, and Reversion* — 156

### CHAP. IX.
*Of Estates in Severalty, Joint-Tenancy, Coparcenary, and Common* — 164

## CHAP. X.
Of the Title to Things real in general — 171

## CHAP. XI.
Of Title by Descent — 173

## CHAP. XII.
Of Title by Purchase; and first by Escheat — 183

## CHAP. XIII.
Of Title by Occupancy; and by Prescription — 188

## CHAP. XIV.
Of Title by Forfeiture — 191

## CHAP. XV.
Of Title by Alienation — 201

## CHAP. XVI.
Of Alienation by Deed — 205

## CHAP. XVII.
Of Alienation by Matter of Record — 225

## CHAP. XVIII.
Of Alienation by special Custom — 235

## CHAP. XIX.
Of Alienation by Devise — 239

## CHAP. XX.
Of Things personal; and first, of Property in Things personal, 244

## CHAP. XXI.
Of Title to Things personal, by Occupancy; Prerogative; and Forfeiture — 249

## CHAP. XXII.
*Of Title by Custom* — 255

## CHAP. XXIII.
*Of Title by Succession; Marriage; and Judgment* 259

## CHAP. XXIV.
*Of Title by Gift, Grant, and Contract* — 264

## CHAP. XXV.
*Of Title by Testament, and Administration* — 293

# BOOK III.
# OF PRIVATE WRONGS.

## CHAP. I.
*Of the Redress of Private Wrongs by the mere Act of the Parties* — 307

## CHAP. II.
*Of Redress by the mere Operation of Law* — 320

## CHAP. III.
*Of Wrongs and their Remedies, respecting the Rights of Persons* — 321

## CHAP. IV.
*Of Injuries to Personal Property* — 335

## CHAP. V.
*Of Injuries to Real Property; and first of Dispossession, or Ouster of the Freehold* — 350

## CHAP. VI.
*Of Dispossession, or Ouster of Chattels real* — 354

## TABLE OF CONTENTS.

### CHAP. VII.
Of Trespass — 357

### CHAP. VIII.
Of Nusance — 363

### CHAP. IX.
Of Waste — 367

### CHAP. X.
Of Subtraction — 370

### CHAP. XI.
Of Disturbance — 372

### CHAP. XII.
Of Injuries proceeding from or affecting the Crown — 380

### CHAP. XIII.
Of Trial by Jury. — 387

### CHAP. XIV.
Of Judgment, and its Incidents — 401

### CHAP. XV.
Of Proceedings in the Nature of Appeals — 407

### CHAP. XVI.
Of Execution — 410

# BOOK IV.
## OF PUBLIC WRONGS.

### CHAP. I.
Of the Nature of Crimes, and their Punishment — 420

## TABLE OF CONTENTS.

### CHAP. II.
Of the Persons capable of committing Crimes — 423

### CHAP. III.
Of Offences against God and Religion — 427

### CHAP. IV.
Of Offences against the Law of Nations — 437

### CHAP. V.
Of High Treason — 440

### CHAP. VI.
Of Felonies injurious to the King's Prerogative — 449

### CHAP. VII.
Of Misprisions and Contempts affecting the King and Government — 452

### CHAP. VIII. IX.
Of Offences against Public Justice — 458

### CHAP. X.
Of Offences against the Public Peace — 467

### CHAP. XI.
Of Offences against Public Trade — 478

### CHAP. XII.
Of Offences against the Public Health, and the Public Police and Oeconomy — 483

### CHAP. XIII.
Of Homicide — 491

## CHAP. XIV.
*Of Offences against the Persons of Individuals* — 504

## CHAP. XV.
*Of Offences against the Habitations of Individuals* – 507

## CHAP. XVI.
*Of Offences against Private Property* ——— 512

## CHAP. XVII.
*Of Trial and Conviction* ——— 529

## CHAP. XVIII.
*Of the Benefit of Clergy* ——— 537

## CHAP. XIX.
*Of Judgment, and its Consequences* — 539

## CHAP. XX.
*Of Reversal of Judgment* ——— 543

## CHAP. XXI.
*Of Reprieve and Pardon* ——— 545

## CHAP. XXII.
*Of Execution* ——— 549

# ERRATA.

**B. I. Ch. II.** *for* PARLIAMENT *read* HOUSE OF COMMONS.
Page 15. *n.* (a) *for* gentium *read* gentibus.
    18. line 9. *for* rigut *read* right.
    Ibid. *n.* (a) *for* 30 Geo. III. *read* 36.
    36. *n.* (a) *for* vivum *read* visum.
    38. *for* Didimus *read* Dedimus
    Ibid. *for* c. 11. *read* c. 18
    Ibid. *n.* (a) *for* fon *read* fons.
    61. *n.* (b) *for* names *read* named.
    62. l. 18. *for* feffion *read* ceffion.
    78. *n.* (a) *for* fhe *read* he.
    85. laft l. *for* then *read* there.
    116 *for* difinition *read* definition
    118 l. 17. *for* thefe *read* there.
    120 *for* alien *read* aline.
    154 *n.* (a) *for* and *read* an.
    Ibid. *n.* (b) *for* covert *read* coverts.
    375. l. 8. *for* thefe *read* there.
    434. laft l. *for* freery *read* forcery.
    458. *for* ch. viii. *read* ch. viii and ix.

# INTRODUCTION.

## OF THE
## LAWS OF ENGLAND.

THE municipal law of England, or the rule of civil conduct prescribed to the inhabitants of this kingdom, may with sufficient propriety be divided into two kinds; the *lex non scripta*, the unwritten, or common law; and the *lex scripta*, the written, or statute law.

The *lex non scripta*, or unwritten law, includes not only *general customs*, or the common law properly so called, but also the *particular customs* of certain parts of the kingdom; and likewise those *particular laws* that are by custom observed only in certain courts and jurisdictions.

When I call these parts of our law *leges non scriptæ*, I would not be understood as if all those laws were at present merely *oral*, or communicated from the former ages to the present solely by word of mouth; but because their original institution and authority are not set down in writing, as acts of parliament are, but they receive their binding power, and the force of laws, by long and immemorial usage, and by their universal reception throughout the kingdom.

This unwritten, or common law, is properly distinguishable into three kinds: 1. General customs; which are the universal rule of the whole kingdom, and form the common law, in its stricter and more usual signification. 2. Particular customs; which for the most part affect only the inhabitants of particular districts. 3. Certain particular laws;

which by custom are adopted and used by some particular courts, of pretty general and extensive jurisdiction.

I. As to general customs, or the common law, properly so called; this is that law, by which proceedings and determinations in the king's ordinary courts of justice are guided and directed. This, for the most part, settles the course in which lands descend by inheritance; the manner and form of acquiring and transferring property; the solemnities and obligation of contracts; the rules of expounding wills, deeds, and acts of parliament; the respective remedies of civil injuries; the several species of temporal offences, with the manner and degree of punishment; and an infinite number of minuter particulars, which diffuse themselves as extensively as the ordinary distribution of common justice requires. Thus, for example, that there shall be four superior courts of record, the chancery, the king's bench, the common pleas, and the exchequer; that the eldest son alone is heir to his ancestor; that property may be acquired and transferred by writing; that a deed is of no validity unless sealed and delivered; that wills shall be construed more favourably, and deeds more strictly; that money lent upon bond is recoverable by action of debt; that breaking the public peace is an offence, and punishable by fine and imprisonment. All these are doctrines that are not set down in any written statute or ordinance, but depend merely upon immemorial usage, that is, upon common law, for their support.

II. The second branch of the unwritten laws of England are particular customs, or laws which affect only the inhabitants of particular districts.

These particular customs, or some of them, are without doubt the remains of that multitude of local customs beforementioned, out of which the common law, as it now stands, was collected, at first by King Alfred, and afterwards by King Edgar and Edward the Confessor: each district mutually sacrificing some of its own special usages, in order that the whole kingdom might enjoy the benefit of one uniform and univerfal fyftem of laws. But, for reafons that have been now long forgotten, particular counties, cities, towns, manors, and lordfhips, were very early indulged with the privilege of abiding by their own cuftoms, in contradiftinction to the reft of the nation at large: which privilege is confirmed to them by feveral acts of parliament.

Such is the cuftom of gavelkind in Kent and fome other parts of the kingdom (though perhaps it was alfo general till the Norman conqueft), which ordains, among other things, that not the eldeft fon only of the father fhall fucceed to his inheritance, but all the fons alike: and that, though the anceftor be attainted and hanged, yet the heir fhall fucceed to his eftate, without any efcheat to the lord.—Such is the cuftom that prevails in divers ancient boroughs, and therefore called borough-englifh, that the youngeft fon fhall inherit the eftate, in preference to all his elder brothers.—Such is the cuftom in other boroughs, that a widow fhall be entitled, for her dower, to all her hufband's lands; whereas, at the common law, fhe fhall be endowed of one third part only.—Such alfo are the fpecial and particular cuftoms of manors, of which every one has more or lefs, and which bind all the copyhold and cuftomary tenants that hold of the faid manors.—Such likewife is the cuftom of holding divers inferior courts, with power of trying caufes, in cities and trading towns; the right of holding which, when no royal grant can be fhewn, depends entirely upon immemorial and eftablifhed ufage.—Such, laftly, are many particular cuftoms within the city of London, with regard to trade, apprentices, widows, orphans, and a variety of other matters. All thefe are contrary to the general law of the land, and are good only by fpecial ufage, though the cuftoms of London are alfo confirmed by act of parliament.

To this head may moft properly be referred a particular fyftem of cuftoms ufed only among one fet of the king's subjects, called the custom of merchants, or *lex mercatoria*: which, however different from the general rules of the common law, is yet ingrafted into it, and made a part of it; being allowed, for the benefit of trade, to be of the utmost validity in all commercial transactions: for it is a maxim of law, that "*cuilibet in sua arte credendum est.*"

The rules relating to particular customs regard either the *proof* of their existence; their *legality* when proved; or their usual method of *allowance*. And first we will consider the rules of *proof*.

As to gavelkind, and borough-english, the law takes particular notice of them, and there is no occasion to prove that such customs actually exist, but only that the lands in question are subject thereto. All other private customs must be particularly pleaded, and as well the existence of such customs must be shewn, as that the thing in dispute is within the custom alleged. The trial in both cases (both to shew the existence of the custom, as " that in the manor of Dale " lands shall descend only to the heirs male, and never to the " heirs female;" and also to shew " that the lands in question " are within that manor") is by a jury of twelve men, and not by the judges; except the same particular custom has been before tried, determined, and recorded in the same court.

The customs of London differ from all others in point of trial: for, if the existence of the custom be brought in question, it shall not be tried by a jury, but by certificate from the lord mayor and aldermen by the mouth of their recorder; unless it be such a custom as the corporation is itself interested in, as a right of taking toll, &c. for then the law permits them not to certify on their own behalf.

When a custom is actually proved to exist, the next enquiry is into the *legality* of it; for, if it is not a good custom, it ought to be no longer used. " *Malus usus abolendus est*," is an established maxim of the law. To make a particular custom good, the following are necessary requisites.

1. That it have been used so long, that the memory of man runneth not to the contrary (a). So that, if any one can shew the beginning of it, it is no good custom. For which reason no custom can prevail against an express act of parliament; since the statute itself is a proof of a time when such a custom did not exist.

2. It must have been *continued*. Any interruption would cause a temporary ceasing: the revival gives it a new beginning, which will be within time of memory, and thereupon the custom will be void. But this must be understood with regard to an interruption of the *right*; for an interruption of the *possession* only, for ten or twenty years, will not destroy the custom. As if the inhabitants of a parish have a customary right of watering their cattle at a certain pool, the custom is not destroyed though they do not use it for ten years; it only becomes more difficult to prove: but if the *right* be any how discontinued for a day, the custom is quite at an end.

3. It must have been *peaceable*, and acquiesced in; not subject to contention and dispute. For as customs owe their original to common consent, their being immemorially disputed, either at law or otherwise, is a proof that such consent was wanting.

4. Customs must be *reasonable*; or rather, taken negatively, they must not be unreasonable. Which is not always, as Sir Edward Coke says, to be understood of every unlearned man's reason, but of artificial and legal reason, warranted by authority of law. Upon which account a custom may be good, though the particular reason of it cannot be

---

(a) But "if there be any sufficient proof of record, or writing to the contrary, albeit it exceed the memory or proper knowledge of any man living, yet it is within the memory of man: for memory or knowledge is two-fold; first, by knowledge by proof, as by record or sufficient matter of writing; secondly, by his own proper knowledge."—— Co. Lit. 115. a.

affigned; for it fufficeth, if no good legal reafon can be affigned againſt it. Thus a cuſtom in a pariſh, that no man ſhall put his beaſts into the common till the third of October, would be good; and yet it would be hard to ſhew the reafon why that day in particular is fixed upon, rather than the day before or after. But a cuſtom, that no cattle ſhall be put in till the lord of the manor has firſt put in his, is unreafonable, and therefore bad: for peradventure the lord will never put in his; and then the tenants will lofe all their profits.

5. Cuſtoms ought to be *certain*. A cuſtom, that lands ſhall defcend to the moſt worthy of the owner's blood, is void; for how ſhall this worth be determined? But a cuſtom to defcend to the next male of the blood, excluſive of females, is certain, and therefore good. A cuſtom to pay two-pence an acre in lieu of tithes, is good; but to pay fometimes two-pence, and fometimes three-pence, as the occupier of the land pleafes, is bad for its uncertainty. Yet a cuſtom, to pay a year's improved value for a fine on a copyhold eſtate, is good; though the value is a thing uncertain: for the value may at any time be afcertained; and the maxim of law is, *id certum eſt, quod certum reddi poteſt*.

6. Cuſtoms, though eſtabliſhed by confent, muſt be (when eſtabliſhed) *compulfory*; and not left to the option of every man, whether he will ufe them or no. Therefore a cuſtom, that all the inhabitants ſhall be rated toward the maintenance of a bridge, will be good; but a cuſtom, that every man is to contribute thereto at his own pleafure, is idle and abfurd, and indeed no cuſtom at all.

7. Laſtly, cuſtoms muſt be *confiſtent* with each other: one cuſtom cannot be fet up in oppofition to another. For if both are really cuſtoms, then both are of equal antiquity, and both eſtabliſhed by mutual confent: which to fay of contradictory cuſtoms is abfurd. Therefore, if one man prefcribes that by cuſtom he has a right to have windows looking into another's garden; the other cannot claim a right by cuf-

tom to stop up or obstruct those windows: for these two contradictory customs cannot both be good, nor both stand together. He ought rather to deny the existence of the former custom.

Next, as to the *allowance* of special customs. Customs, in derogation of the common law, must be construed strictly. Thus, by the custom of gavelkind, an infant of fifteen years may, by one species of conveyance, called a deed of feoffment, convey away his lands in fee simple, or for ever. Yet this custom does not impower him to use any other conveyance, or even to lease them for seven years: for the custom must be strictly pursued. And, moreover, all special customs must submit to the king's prerogative. Therefore, if the king purchases lands of the nature of gavelkind where all the sons inherit equally; yet, upon the king's demise, his eldest son shall succeed to those lands alone. And thus much for the second part of the *leges non scriptæ*, or those particular customs which affect particular persons or districts only (*a*).

III. The third branch of them are those peculiar laws, which by custom are adopted and used only in certain peculiar courts and jurisdictions. And by these I understand the civil and canon laws.

By the civil law, absolutely taken, is generally understood the civil or municipal law of the Roman empire, as comprized in the Institutes, the Code, and the Digest of the Emperor Justinian, and the novel constitutions of himself and some of his successors.

The canon law is a body of Roman ecclesiastical law, relative to such matters as that church either has, or pretends

---

(*a*) The general rules which our Author has here collected concerning customs, are learnedly considered, explained, and applied, in *Tanistry's* Case reported, Davies, 31. b. to which we beg leave to refer the reader.

to have, the proper jurisdiction over. This is compiled from the opinions of the ancient Latin Fathers, the decrees of general councils, and the decretal epistles and bulls of the holy see.

There is also a kind of national canon law, composed of *legatine* and *provincial* constitutions, and adapted only to the exigencies of this church and kingdom.

At the dawn of the Reformation, in the reign of King Henry VIII. it was enacted in parliament (*a*) that a review should be had of the canon law; and, till such review should be made, all canons, constitutions, ordinances, and synodals provincial, being then already made, and not repugnant to the law of the land or the king's prerogative, should still be used and executed. And, as no such review has yet been perfected, upon this statute now depends the authority of the canon law in England.

There are four species of courts, in which the civil and canon laws are permitted (under different restrictions) to be used. 1. The courts of the archbishops and bishops, and their derivative officers, usually called in our law, courts christian, *curi. christianitatis*, or the ecclesiastical courts. 2. The military courts. 3. The courts of admiralty. 4. The courts of the two universities. In all, their reception in general, and the different degrees of that reception, are grounded entirely upon custom; corroborated in the latter instance by act of parliament ratifying those charters which confirm the customary law of the universities. The more minute consideration of these will fall properly under that part of these commentaries which treats of the jurisdiction of courts. It will suffice at present to remark a few particulars relative to them all, which may serve to inculcate more strongly the doctrine laid down concerning them.

---

(*a*) By statute 25 Hen. VIII, c. 19; revived and confirmed by 1 Eliz. c. 1.

## INTRODUCTION.    9

1. And, first, the courts of common law have the superintendency over these courts; to keep them within their jurisdictions, to determine wherein they exceed them, to restrain and prohibit such excess, and (in case of contumacy) to punish the offender who executes, and in some cases the judge who enforces, the sentence so declared to be illegal.

2. The common law has reserved to itself the exposition of all such acts of parliament as concern either the extent of these courts or the matters depending before them. And therefore if these courts either refuse to allow these acts of parliament, or will expound them in any other sense than what the common law puts upon them, the king's courts at Westminster will grant prohibitions to restrain and controul them.

3. An appeal lies from all these courts to the king, in the last resort; which proves that the jurisdiction exercised in them is derived from the crown of England, and not from any foreign potentate, or intrinsic authority of their own. And, from these three strong marks and ensigns of superiority, it appears beyond a doubt, that the civil and canon laws, though admitted in some cases by custom in some courts, are only subordinate, and *leges sub graviori lege*; and that, thus admitted, restrained, altered, new-modelled, and amended, they are by no means with us a distinct independent species of laws, but are inferior branches of the customary or unwritten laws of England, commonly called the king's ecclesiastical, the king's military, the king's maritime, or the king's academical laws.

Let us next proceed to the *leges scriptæ*, the written laws of the kingdom; which are statutes, acts, or edicts, made by the king's majesty, by and with the advice and consent of the lords spiritual and temporal and commons in parliament assembled. The oldest of these now extant, and printed in our statute-books, is the famous *magna carta*, as confirmed in parliament 9 Hen. III. though doubtless there were many acts before that time, the records of which are now lost, and the determinations of them perhaps at present currently received for the maxims of the common law.

Statutes are either *general* or *special, public* or *private*. A general or public act is an universal rule that regards the whole community: and of this the courts of law are bound to take notice judicially and *ex officio*; without the statute being particularly pleaded, or formally set forth by the party who claims an advantage under it. Special or private acts are rather exceptions than rules, being those which only operate upon particular persons, and private concerns: such as the Romans entitled *senatus-decreta*, in contradistinction to the *senatus-consulta*, which regarded the whole community: and of these (which are not promulgated with the same notoriety as the former) the judges are not bound to take notice, unless they be formally shewn and pleaded.

Statutes also are either *declaratory* of the common law, or *remedial* of some defects therein. Declaratory, where the old custom of the kingdom is almost fallen into disuse, or become disreputable; remedial when made to supply such defects, and abridge such superfluities, in the common law, as arise either from the general imperfection of all human laws, from change of time and circumstances, from the mistakes and unadvised determinations of unlearned (or even learned) judges, or from any other cause whatsoever. And this being done, either by enlarging the common law where it was too narrow and circumscribed, or by restraining it where it was too lax and luxuriant, hath occasioned another subordinate division of remedial acts of parliament into *enlarging* and *restraining* statutes.

These are the several grounds of the laws of England: over and above which, equity is also frequently called in to assist, to moderate, and to explain them. What equity is, and how impossible in its very essence to be reduced to stated rules, hath been shewn in another place. I shall therefore only say here, that (besides the liberality of sentiment with which our common law-judges interpret acts of parliament, and such rules of the unwritten law as are not of a positive kind) there are also peculiar courts of equity established for the benefit of the subject; to detect latent frauds and concealments, which the process of the courts of law is not adapted to reach; to enforce the execution of such matters of trust and confidence as are binding in conscience, though not cognizable in a court of law; to deliver from such dangers as are owing to misfortune or oversight; and to give a more specific relief, and more adapted to the circumstances of the case, than can always be obtained by the generality of the rules of the positive or common law. This is the business of our courts of equity, which however are only conversant in matters of property. For the freedom of our constitution will not permit, that in criminal cases a power should be lodged in any judge, to construe the law otherwise than according to the letter. This caution, while it admirably protects the public liberty, can never bear hard upon individuals. A man cannot suffer *more* punishment than the law assigns, but he may suffer *less*. The laws cannot be strained by partiality to inflict a penalty beyond what the letter will warrant; but, in cases where the letter induces any apparent hardship, the crown has the power to pardon.

# COMMENTARIES
## ON THE
# LAWS OF ENGLAND.

## BOOK THE FIRST.
## OF THE RIGHTS OF PERSONS.

### CHAPTER I.
#### OF THE ABSOLUTE RIGHTS OF INDIVIDUALS.

THE abfolute rights of man, confidered as a free agent, endowed with difcernment to know good from evil, and with power of choofing thofe meafures which appear to him to be moft defirable, are ufually fummed up in one general appellation, and denominated the natural liberty of mankind. This natural liberty confifts properly in a power of acting as one thinks fit, without any reftraint or control, unlefs by the law of nature; being a right inherent in us by birth, and one of the gifts of God to man at his creation, when he endued him with the faculty of free-will.

And thefe rights may be reduced to three principal or primary articles; the right of perfonal fecurity, the right of perfonal liberty, and the right of private property; becaufe as there is no other known method of compulfion, or of abridging man's natural free will, but by an infringement or diminution of one or other of thefe important rights, the prefervation of thefe, inviolate, may juftly be faid to include the prefervation of our civil immunities in their largeft and moft extenfive fenfe.

I. The right of personal security consists in a person's legal and uninterrupted enjoyment of his life, his limbs, his body, his health, and his reputation.

Life is the immediate gift of God, a right inherent by nature in every individual; and it begins in contemplation of law as soon as an infant is able to stir in the mother's womb. For if a woman is quick with child, and by a potion or otherwise, killeth it in her womb; or if any one beat her, whereby the child dieth in her body, and she is delivered of a dead child, this, though not murder, was by the ancient law homicide or manslaughter. But the modern law doth not look upon this offence in quite so atrocious a light, but merely as a heinous misdemesnor *(a)*.

An infant *in ventre sa mere,* or in the mother's womb, is supposed in law to be born for many purposes. It is capable of having a legacy, or a surrender of a copyhold estate made to it. It may have a guardian assigned to it; and it is enabled to have an estate limited to its use, and to take afterwards by such limitation as if it were then actually born *(b)*.

---

*(a)* It is to be observed, however, that if the child be born alive, and afterwards die in consequence of the injury it received in its mother's womb, it may still be murder as it was by the ancient common law. 3. *Inst.* 50. and see *Beale v. Beale,* 1 *P. Wms.* 245.

*(b)* It may also take land by descent, 3 *Wils.* 526. but in this case the presumptive heir is entitled to all intermediate profits of the estate, from the time of the ancestor's death till the birth of the child; which, as is observed by Mr. *Christian* in his valuable edition of our Author, seems to be the only interest it loses by its situation, for it is now become an established rule, " that infants in *ventres ses meres* shall be considered as in *esse,* in all cases, for their benefit, though not to their disadvantage." See *Burnet v. Mann,* 1 *Vez.* 157, *Millar v. Turner, ibid.* 86; also *Wallis v. Hodson,* 2 *Atk.* 114. *Hill v. Chapman,* 3 *Brown. Ch. Ca.* 391. The authority of this observation was however somewhat shaken by two successive determinations to the prejudice of posthumous children, by

Both the life and limbs of a man are of such high value, in the estimation of the law of England, that it pardons even homicide, if committed *se defendendo*, or in order to preserve them. For whatever is done by a man, to save either life or member, is looked upon as done upon the highest necessity and compulsion (*a*). And the law not only regards life and member, and protects every man in the enjoyment of them, but also furnishes him with every thing necessary for their support. For there is no man so indigent or wretched, but he may demand a supply sufficient for all the necessities of life from the more opulent part of the community, by means of the several statutes enacted for the relief of the poor, of which in their proper places.

Besides those limbs and members that may be necessary to a man, in order to defend himself or annoy his enemy, the rest of his person or body is also entitled, by the same natural right, to security from the corporal insults of menaces, assaults, beating, and wounding; though such insults amount not to destruction of life or member.

The preservation of a man's health from such practices as may prejudice or annoy it, and

The security of his reputation or good name from the arts of detraction and slander, are also rights to which every man is entitled, by reason and natural justice; since without these

---

Kenyon, M. R. in *Pierson* v. *Garnet*, 2 *Brown Ch. Ca.* 47. and *Cooper* v. *Forbes*, ibid. 63. grounded on the reasoning of Lord Hardwicke in *Ellison* v. *Airey*, 1 *Vez.* 111. but it has at length been completely recognized and established in the case of *Clarke* v. *Blake*, 2 *Brown Ch. Ca.* 320. 2 *H. Black. Rep.* 399, 2 *F. Vez.* 673, and *Lancashire* v. *Lancashire*, 5 *Term. Rep.* 49.

(*a*) *Hoc et ratio doctis, et necessitas barbaris, et mos gentium, et feris natura ipsa præscripsit, ut omnem semper vim, quacunque ope possent, à corpore, à capite, à vitâ suâ propulsarent.*—Cic. in Orat. pro Milone.

it is impossible to have the perfect enjoyment of any other advantage or right. But these three last articles (being of much less importance than those which have gone before, and those which are yet to come) it will suffice to have barely mentioned among the rights of persons, referring the more minute discussion of their several branches to those parts of our commentaries which treat of the infringement of these rights, under the head of personal wrongs.

II. Next to personal security, the law of England regards, asserts, and preserves the personal liberty of individuals. This personal liberty consists in the power of loco-motion, of changing situation, or removing one's person to whatsoever place one's own inclination may direct; without imprisonment or restraint, unless by due course of law.

The confinement of the person, in any wise, is an imprisonment. So that the keeping a man against his will in a private house, putting him in the stocks, arresting or forcibly detaining him in the street, is an imprisonment. But if a man be lawfully imprisoned, this is no duress of imprisonment. To make imprisonment lawful, it must either be by process from the courts of judicature, or by warrant from some legal officer having authority to commit to prison; which warrant must be in writing, under the hand and seal of the magistrate, and express the causes of his commitment, in order to be examined into (if necessary) upon a *habeas corpus*. If there be no cause expressed, the gaoler is not bound to detain the prisoner.

A natural and regular consequence of this personal liberty is, that every Englishman may claim a right to abide in his own country so long as he pleases, and not to be driven from it unless by the sentence of the law. The law is in this respect so benignly and liberally construed for the benefit of the subject, that though *within* the realm the king may command the attendance and service of all his liegemen, yet he cannot fend any man *out of* the realm, even upon public fervice; excepting failors and foldiers, the nature of whofe employment neceffarily implies an exception : he cannot even conftitute a man lord deputy or lieutenant againft his will, nor make him a foreign embaffador. For this might in reality be no more than an honourable exile.

III. The third abfolute right, inherent in every Englifhman, is that of property: which confifts in the free ufe, enjoyment, and difpofal of all his acquifitions, without any control or diminution, fave only by the laws of the land.

So great is the regard of the law for private property, that it will not authorize the leaft violation of it; no, not even for the general good of the whole community. If a new road, for inftance, were to be made through the grounds of a private perfon, it might perhaps be extenfively beneficial to the public; but the law permits no man, or fet of men, to do this without confent of the owner of the land. In this and fimilar cafes the legiflature alone can, and indeed frequently does, interpofe, and compel the individual to acquiefce; not by abfolutely ftripping the fubject of his property in an arbitrary manner, but by giving him a full indemnification and equivalent for the injury thereby fuftained. And even this is an exertion of power which the legiflature indulges with caution, and which nothing but the legiflature can perform *(a)*.

In the three preceding articles we have taken a fhort view of the principal abfolute rights which appertain to every Englifhman. But in vain would thefe rights be declared, afcertained, and protected, by the dead letter of the laws, if the conftitution had provided no other method to fecure their actual enjoyment. Thefe are *(principally)*,

---

*(a)* So it formerly was; but now by 13 Geo. III. c. 78. two juftices are empowered under certain regulations and reftrictions, to widen or divert any highway over the private property of others upon rendering to the perfons injured fuch adequate amends as fhall be affeffed by a jury.

That of applying to the courts of juſtice for redreſs of injuries. For ſince the law is in England the ſupreme arbiter of every man's life, liberty, and property, courts of juſtice muſt at all times be open to the ſubject, and the law be duly adminiſtered therein. But if there ſhould happen any uncommon injury, or infringement of the rights before-mentioned, which the ordinary courſe of law is too defective to reach, there ſtill remains another ſubordinate right, appertaining to every individual, the right of petitioning the king, or either houſe of parliament, for the redreſs of grievances. Care only muſt be taken, leſt, under the pretence of petitioning, the ſubject be guilty of any riot or tumult; as happened in the opening of the memorable parliament in 1640: and, to prevent this, it is provided by the ſtatute 13 Car. 2. ſt. 1. c. 5. that no petition to the king, or either houſe of parliament, for any alteration in the church or ſtate, ſhall be ſigned by above twenty perſons, unleſs the matter thereof be approved by three juſtices of the peace, or the major part of the grand jury, in the country; and in London by the lord mayor, aldermen, and common council: nor ſhall any petition be preſented by more than ten perſons at a time (a). But, under theſe regulations, it is declared by the ſtatute 1. Will. and Mary, ſt. 2. c. 2. that the ſubject hath a right to petition; and that all commitments and proſecutions for ſuch petitioning are illegal.

The laſt auxiliary right of the ſubject, that I ſhall at preſent mention, is that of having arms for their defence, ſuitable to their condition and degree, and ſuch as are allowed by law. Which is alſo declared by the ſame ſtatute 1. Will. and Mary, ſt. 2. c. 2. and it is indeed a public allowance under due reſtrictions, of the natural right of reſiſtance and

---

(a) But ſee further regulations and reſtrictions on the right of petitioning, 30 Geo. III. c. 8.

self-preservation, when the sanctions of society and laws are found insufficient to restrain the violence of oppression.

In these several articles consist the rights, or, as they are frequently termed, the liberties of Englishmen: liberties, more generally talked of than thoroughly understood; and yet highly necessary to be perfectly known and considered by every man of rank or property, lest his ignorance of the points whereon they are founded should hurry him into faction and licentiousness on the one hand, or a pusillanimous indifference and criminal submission on the other. And we have seen that these rights consist, primarily, in the free enjoyment of personal security, of personal liberty, and of private property. So long as these remain inviolate, the subject is perfectly free; for every species of compulsive tyranny and oppression must act in opposition to one or other of these rights, having no other object upon which it can possibly be employed. To preserve these from violation, it is necessary that the constitution of parliament be supported in its full vigour; and limits, certainly known, be set to the royal prerogative. And, lastly, to vindicate these rights, when actually violated or attacked, the subjects of England are entitled, in the first place, to the regular administration and free course of justice in the courts of law; next, to the right of petitioning the king and parliament for redress of grievances; and, lastly, to the right of having and using arms for self-preservation and defence. And all these rights and liberties it is our birthright to enjoy entire; unless where the laws of our country have laid them under necessary restraints. Restraints in themselves so gentle and moderate, as will appear upon farther inquiry, that no man of sense or probity would wish to see them slackened. For all of us have it in our choice to do every thing that a good man would desire to do; and are restrained from nothing, but what would be pernicious either to ourselves or our fellow citizens. So that this review of our situation may fully justify the observation of a learned French author, who indeed generally both thought and wrote in the spirit of genuine freedom; and who hath not scrupled to profess, even in the very bosom of his native country, that the English is the only nation in the world, where political or civil liberty is the direct end of it's constitution. Recommending therefore to the student in our laws a farther and more accurate search into this extensive and important title, I shall close my remarks upon it with the expiring wish of the famous father Paul to his country, "ESTO PERPETUA!"

## CHAPTER II.

### OF THE PARLIAMENT.

WE are next to treat of the rights and duties of persons, as they are members of society, and stand in various relations to each other. These relations are either public or private: and we will first consider those that are public.

The most universal public relation, by which men are connected together, is that of government; namely, as governors and governed, or in other words, as magistrates and people.

In a free state every man, who is supposed a free agent, ought to be in some measure his own governor; and therefore a branch at least of the legislative power should reside in the whole body of the people. And this power, when the territories of the state are small and it's citizens easily known, should be exercised by the people in their aggregate or collective capacity. But this will be highly inconvenient, when the public territory is extended to any considerable degree, and the number of citizens is encreased. In so large a state as ours it is therefore very wisely contrived, that the people should do that by their representatives, which it is impracticable to perform in person; representatives, chosen by a number of minute and separate districts, wherein all the voters are, or easily may be, distinguished. The counties are therefore represented by knights, elected by the proprietors of lands: the cities and boroughs are represented by citizens and burgesses, chosen by the mercantile part, or supposed trading interest of the nation. The number of English representatives is 513, and of Scots 45; in all 558. And every member, though chosen by one particular district, when elected and returned serves for the whole realm. For the end of his coming thither is not particular, but general; not barely to advantage his constituents, but the common wealth; to advise his majesty (as appears from the writ of summons) "*de commu-ni consilio super negotiis quibusdam arduis et urgentibus, regem, statum, et defensionem regni Angliæ et ecclesiæ Anglicanæ concernentibus.*" And therefore he is not bound, like a deputy in the united provinces, to consult with, or take the advice, of his constituents upon any particular point, unless he thinks it proper or prudent so to do.

With regard to the elections of knights, citizens, and burgesses; we may observe, that herein consists the exercise of the democratical part of our constitution: for in a democracy there can be no exercise of sovereignty but by suffrage, which is the declaration of the people's will. In all democracies therefore it is of the utmost importance to regulate by whom, and in what manner, the suffrages are to be given. In England, where the people do not debate in a collective body but by representation, the exercise of this sovereignty consists in the choice of representatives. The laws have therefore very strictly guarded against usurpation or abuse of this power, by many salutary provisions; which may be reduced to these three points, 1. The qualifications of the electors. 2. The qualifications of the elected. 3. The proceedings at elections.

1. As to the qualifications of the electors. And first those of electors for knights of the shire. 1. By statute 8 Hen. VI. c. 7. and 10 Hen. VI. c. 2. (amended by 14 Geo. III. c. 58.) the knights of the shire shall be chosen of people, whereof every man shall have freehold to the value of forty shillings by the year within the county; which (by subsequent statutes) is to be clear of all charges and deductions *(a)*, except parliamentary and parochial taxes. The knights of shires are the representatives of the landholders, or landed interest of the kingdom: their electors must therefore have estates in lands or tenements within the county represented: these estates must be freehold, that is, for term of life at least; because beneficial leases for long terms of years were not in use at the making of these statutes, and copyholders were then little better than villeins, absolutely dependent upon their lords: this freehold must be of forty shillings annual value; because that sum would then, with proper industry, furnish all the necessaries of life, and render the freeholder, if he pleased, an independent man. The other less important qualifications of the electors for counties in England and Wales may be collected from the statutes; which direct, 2. That no person under twenty-one years of age shall be capable of voting for any member. This extends to all sorts of members as well for boroughs as counties; as does also the next, *viz.* 3. That no person convicted of perjury, or subornation of perjury, shall be capable of voting in any election. 4. That

---

*(a)* Considerable doubts have arisen, as to whether the estates being mortgaged for a sum, of which the interest reduces the annual value to less than 40s. adeems the qualification of voting; the *Bedfordshire* committee, in 1785, determined by a large majority against the mortgagor; whilst the *Cricklade* committee, sitting at the same time, were unanimously of a different opinion. See this matter ably discussed in *Sim. Elec.* 84. where, in the opinion of the present editor, the latter decision is shewn to be most consonant both to law and to reason.

no person shall vote in right of any freehold, granted to him fraudulently to qualify him to vote. Fraudulent grants are such as contain an agreement to reconvey, or to defeat the estate granted; which agreements are made void, and the estate is absolutely vested in the person to whom it is so granted. And, to guard the better against such frauds, it is farther provided, 5. That every voter shall have been in the actual possession, or receipt of the profits, of his freehold to his own use for twelve calendar months before; except it came to him by descent, marriage, marriage settlement, will, or promotion to a benefice or office. 6. That no person shall vote in respect of an annuity or rentcharge, unless registered with the clerk of the peace twelve calendar months before (a). 7. That in mortgaged or trust estates, the person in possession, under the above-mentioned restrictions, shall have the vote. 8. That only one person shall be admitted to vote for any one house or tenement, to prevent the splitting of freeholds (b). 9. That no estate shall qualify a voter, unless the estate has been assessed to some land-tax aid, at least twelve months before the election (c). 10. That no tenant by copy of court

---

(a) Unless the same shall have come by descent, demise, marriage, marriage settlement, presentation to a benefice, or promotion to an office within the year; in which case, it is sufficient if a certificate thereof be procured, and entered, upon oath, at any time before the commencement of the election. 3 Geo. III. c. 24.

(b) This must be understood with some restriction. See *Heyw. Elec.* 99. *Sim.* 98. from which, and the cases there cited, it appears to apply to those cases only where the freehold is split *for the express purpose of multiplying votes*, and not to those where no such object was in view.

(c) This period is now, by 20 Geo. III. c. 17, shortened to *six* months, unless the estate come by descent, marriage, or other means enumerated in the former note; when it is required to have been assessed within *two years* previous to the election.

roll shall be permitted to vote as a freeholder *(a)*. Thus much for the electors in counties.

As for the electors of citizens and burgesses, these are supposed to be the mercantile part or trading interest of this kingdom. The right of elections in boroughs is various, depending entirely on the several charters, customs, and constitutions of the respective places, which has occasioned infinite disputes; though now by statute 2 Geo. II. c. 24. the right of voting for the future shall be allowed according to the last determination of the house of commons concerning it *(b)*. And by statute 3 Geo. III. c. 15. no freeman of any city or borough (other than such as claim by birth, marriage, or servitude) shall be entitled to vote therein, unless he hath

---

*(a)* A further disqualification has been since added by 22 Geo. III. c. 41. which renders all persons employed in collecting or managing the duties of excise, customs, stamps, salt, windows, houses, or the revenue of the post-office, incapable of voting for representatives in parliament; such persons being supposed, from the nature of their appointments, to be too much under the influence of the crown to vote with due freedom and probity. On the construction of this statute, see *Sim. Elec.* 54.

*(b)* Questions relative to the right of elections are now determined (according to the provisions of Mr. Grenville's act, 10 Geo. III. c. 16.) by select *committees* of the house, and not by the house at large as formerly; the method of determining such questions is now therefore materially different from that which prevailed at the time referred to in the text; and, by 28 Geo. III. c. 52. (the last act on this subject) it is provided, that committees appointed to try the right of any election, shall require the counsel of each party to give in a statement of their respective rights; upon which the committee shall report their judgment to the house; and if no petition be preferred against the said judgment, within a twelvemonth, or fourteen days after the commencement of the next sessions, it shall be conclusive. And that should any such petition be preferred, the decision of a second committee thereon shall be absolutely final.

been admitted to his freedom twelve calendar months before *(a)*.

2. Next, as to the qualifications of persons to be *elected* members of the house of commons. Some of these depend upon the law and custom of parliaments, declared by the house of commons; others upon certain statutes. And from these it appears, 1. That they must not be aliens born, or minors. 2. That they must not be any of the twelve judges, because they sit in the lords' house; nor of the clergy, for they sit in the convocation *(b)*; nor persons attainted of treason or felony, for they are unfit to sit any where. 3. That sheriffs of counties, and mayors and bailiffs of boroughs, are not eligible in their respective jurisdictions, as being returning officers; but that sheriffs of one county are eligible to be knights of another. 4. That, in strictness, all members ought to have been inhabitants of the places for which they are chosen: but this, having been long disregarded, was at length entirely repealed by statute 14 Geo. III. c. 58. 5. That no persons concerned in the management of any duties or taxes created since 1692, except the commissioners of the treasury, nor any of the officers following, *(viz.* commissioners of prizes, transports, sick and wounded, wine licences, navy, and victualling; secretaries or receivers of prizes; comptrollers of the army accounts; agents for regiments; governors of plantations and their deputies; officers of Minorca or Gibraltar; officers of the excise and customs; clerks or deputies in the

---

*(a)* And, by 26 Geo. III. c. 100. it is further required, that he should have been resident six calendar months prior to his tendering his vote.

*(b)* Mr. Christian (12 ed. *Blac. Com.* 175. n. 37.) denies this to be the reason of their exclusion; and, with great plausibility of argument, grounded on 2 *Inst.* 3. 121. and 2 *Black.* 101. maintains that it arose from their being *exempted*, by the frank almoign-tenure of their glebe lands, and by their holy order, from all *secular* services; which exemption has since grown into an exclusion by usage.

several offices of the treasury, exchequer, navy, victualling, admiralty, pay of the army or navy, secretaries of state, salt, stamps, appeals, wine licences, hackney coaches, hawkers, and pedlars) nor any persons that hold any new office under the crown created since 1705, are capable of being elected or sitting as members. 6. That no person having a pension under the crown during pleasure, or, for any term of years, is capable of being elected or sitting. 7. That if any member accepts an office under the crown, except an officer in the army or navy accepting a new commission, his seat is void; but such member is capable of being re-elected. 8. That all knights of the shire shall be actual knights, or such notable esquires and gentlemen as have estates sufficient to be knights, and by no means of the degree of yeomen. This is reduced to a still greater certainty, by ordaining, 9. That every knight of a shire shall have a clear (a) estate of freehold or copyhold to the value of six hundred pounds *per annum*, and every citizen and burgess to the value of three hundred pounds: except the eldest sons of peers, and of persons qualified to be knights of shires, and except the members for the two universities: which somewhat balances the ascendant which the boroughs have gained over the counties, by obliging the trading interest to make choice of landed men: and of this qualification the member must make oath, and give in the particulars in writing, at the time of his taking his seat. But, subject to these standing restrictions and disqualifications *(b)*, every subject of this realm is eligible of common right.

3. The third point, regarding elections, is the method of proceeding therein. This is also regulated by the law of

---

*(a)* See *ante*, p. 22, n. *(a)*
*(b)* There have since been *other* disqualifications created by the legislature; for by 22 *Geo.* III. c. 45. all contractors with government are disabled from sitting in the house of commons.

parliament, and the several statutes, all which I shall blend together, and extract out of them a summary account of the method of proceeding to elections.

As soon as the parliament is summoned, the lord chancellor (or if a vacancy happens during the sitting of parliament, the speaker, by order of the house; and without such order, if a vacancy happens by death, or the member's becoming a peer, in the time of a recess for upwards of twenty days) sends his warrant to the clerk of the crown in chancery; who thereupon issues out writs to the sheriff of every county, for the election of all the members to serve for that county, and every city and borough therein. Within three (a) days after the receipt of this writ, the sheriff is to send his precept, under his seal, to the proper returning officers of the cities and boroughs, commanding them to elect their members: and the said returning officers are to proceed to election within eight days from the receipt of the precept, giving four days notice of the same; and to return the persons chosen, together with the precept, to the sheriff.

But elections of knights of the shire must be proceeded to by the sheriffs themselves in person, at the next county court that shall happen after the delivery of the writ. The county court is a court held every month or oftener by the sheriff, intended to try little causes not exceeding the value of forty shillings, in what part of the county he pleases to appoint for that purpose: but for the election of knights of the shire it must be held at the most usual place. If the county court falls upon the day of delivering the writ, or within six days after, the sheriff may adjourn the court and election to some other convenient time, not longer than sixteen days, nor shorter than ten; but he cannot alter the place, without the consent

---

*(a)* Unless in the case of the cinque ports, of which the officer is allowed *six* days, in which to send his precept. See 10 and 11 *Will.* III. c. 7.

of all the candidates: and, in all such cases, ten days public notice must be given of the time and place of the election (a).

And as it is essential to the very being of parliament that elections should be absolutely free, all undue influences upon the electors are illegal, and strongly prohibited. As soon therefore as the time and place of election, either in counties or boroughs, are fixed, all soldiers quartered in the place are to remove, at least one day before the election, to the distance of two miles or more; and not to return till one day after the poll is ended. Riots likewise have been frequently determined to make an election void. By vote also of the house of commons, to whom alone belongs the power of determining contested elections, no lord of parliament, or lord lieutenant of a county, hath any right to interfere in the election of commoners; and, by statute, the lord warden of the cinque ports shall not recommend any members there. If any officer of the excise, customs, stamps, or certain other branches of the revenue, presumes to intermeddle in elections, by persuading any voter or dissuading him, he forfeits 100*l*, and is disabled to hold any office.

Thus are the electors of one branch of the legislature secured from any undue influence from either of the other two, and from all external violence and compulsion. But the greatest danger is that in which themselves co-operate, by the infamous practice of bribery and corruption. To prevent which it is enacted that no candidate shall, after the date (usually called the *teste)* of the writs, or after the vacancy, give any money or entertainment to his electors, or promise

---

(a) The law has since been altered in this respect, by 25 *Geo.* III. c. 84. which provides, that the sheriff shall, within *two* days after the receipt of the writ, cause proclamation to be made, at the usual place of election, of a *special* court to be holden for the sole purpose of such election, at a time not earlier than the 10th, nor later than the 16th day after such proclamation.

to give any, either to particular perfons, or to the place in general, in order to his being elected: on pain of being incapable to ferve for that place in parliament. And if any money, gift, office, employment, or reward be given or promifed to be given to any voter, at any time, in order to influence him to give or withhold his vote, as well he that takes as he that offers fuch bribe forfeits 500*l*, and is for ever difabled from voting and holding any office in any corporation; unlefs, before conviction, he will difcover fome other offender of the fame kind, and then he is indemnified for his own offence.

Undue influence being thus (I wifh the depravity of mankind would permit me to fay, effectually) guarded againft, the election is to be proceeded to on the day appointed; the fheriff or other returning officer firft taking an oath againft bribery, and for the due execution of his office. The candidates likewife, if required, muft fwear to their qualification; and the electors in counties to theirs; and the electors both in counties and boroughs are alfo compellable to take the oath of abjuration and that againft bribery and corruption. And it might not be amifs, if the members elected were bound to take the latter oath, as well as the former; which in all probability would be much more effectual, than adminiftering it only to the electors.

The election being clofed, the returning officer in boroughs returns his precept to the fheriff, with the perfons elected by the majority: and the fheriff returns the whole, together with the writ for the county and the knights elected thereupon, to the clerk of the crown in chancery; before the day of meeting, if it be a new parliament, or within fourteen days after the election, if it be an occafional vacancy; and this under penalty of 500*l*. If the fheriff does not return fuch knights only as are duly elected, he forfeits, by the old ftatutes of Henry VI. 100*l*; and the returning officers in boroughs for a like falfe return 40*l*; and they are befides liable to an action, in which double damages shall be recovered, by the later statutes of king William: and any person bribing the returning officer shall also forfeit 300*l*. But the members returned by him are the sitting members, until the house of commons, upon petition, shall adjudge the return to be false and illegal. The form and manner of proceeding upon such petition are now regulated by statute 10 Geo. III. c. 16. (amended by 11 Geo. III. c. 42. and made perpetual by 14 Geo. III. c. 15. (*a*) which directs the method of chusing by lot a select committee of fifteen members (*b*), who are sworn well and truly to try the same, and a true judgment to give according to the evidence. And this abstract of the proceedings at elections of knights, citizens, and burgesses, concludes our inquires into the laws and customs more peculiarly relative to the house of commons.

## CHAPTER III.

### OF SUBORDINATE MAGISTRATES.

THE magistrates and officers, whose rights and duties it will be proper in this chapter to consider, are such as are generally in use, and have a jurisdiction and authority disperfedly throughout the kingdom: these are, principally, sheriffs; coroners; justices of the peace; constables; surveyors of highways; and overseers of the poor.

I. The sheriff is an officer of very great antiquity in this kingdom, his name being derived from two Saxon words, importing the reeve, bailiff, or officer of the shire.

---

(*a*) But more particularly by 25 *Geo.* III. c. 84. and 28 ibid, c. 52. See *ante*, p. 24. n. (*b*)
(*b*) Now thirteen, by the last cited acts.

## SUBORDINATE MAGISTRATES.

Sheriffs were formerly chosen by the inhabitants of the several counties. In confirmation of which it was ordained, by statute 28 Edw. I. c. 8. that the people should have election of sheriffs in every shire, where the shrievalty is not of inheritance. For antiently, in some counties, the sheriffs were hereditary; as I apprehend they were in Scotland till the statute 20 Geo. II. c. 43; and still continue in the county of Westmorland to this day: the city of London having also the inheritance of the shrievalty of Middlesex vested in their body by charter (a). The reason of these popular elections is assigned in the same statute, c. 13. "that the com-"mons might chuse such as would not be a burthen to "them." But these popular elections growing tumultuous, were put an end to by the statute 9 Edw. II. st. 2. which enacted, that the sheriffs should from thenceforth be assigned by the chancellor, treasurer, and the judges; as being persons in whom the same trust might with confidence be reposed. And the custom now is (and has been at least ever since the time of Fortescue, who was chief justice and chancellor to Henry the sixth) that all the judges, together with the other great officers and privy counsellors, meet in the exchequer on the morrow of All Souls yearly, (which day is now altered to the morrow of St. Martin by the last act for abbreviating Michaelmas term) and then and there the judges propose three persons, to be reported (if approved of) to the king, who afterwards appoints one of them to be sheriff.

However, it must be acknowledged, that the practice of occasionally naming what are called pocket sheriffs (b), by

---

(a) In virtue of this charter the city of London is entitled to the election of two sheriffs; but it is to be observed, that they both constitute but one magistrate; so that in case either of them die, the other is incapable of exercising his official capacity till another be elected. See 4 *Bac. Abr.* 447.

(b) By a pocket-sheriff is meant, one who is nominated at the sole instigation of the crown, not being one of the three

the sole authority of the crown, hath uniformly continued to the reign of his present majesty; but in which, I believe, few (if any) *compulsory* instances have occurred.

Sheriffs, by virtue of several old statutes, are to continue in their office no longer than one year: and yet it hath been said that a sheriff may be appointed *durante bene placito*, or during the king's pleasure; and so is the form of the royal writ. Therefore, till a new sheriff be named, his office cannot be determined, unless by his own death, or the demise of the king; in which last case it was usual for the successor to send a new writ to the old sheriff: but now by statute 1 Ann. st. 1. c. 8. all officers appointed by the preceding king may hold their offices for six months after the king's demise, unless sooner displaced by the successor. We may farther observe, that by statute 1 Ric. II. c. 11. no man that has served the office of sheriff for one year, can be compelled to serve the same again within three years after (*a*).

We shall find it is of the utmost importance to have the sheriff appointed according to law, when we consider his power and duty. These are either as a judge, as the keeper of the king's peace, as a ministerial officer of the superior courts of justice, or as the king's bailiff.

In his judicial capacity he is to hear and determine all causes of forty shillings value and under, in his county court, of which more in it's proper place: and he has also a judicial power in divers other civil cases. He is likewise to decide the elections of knights of the shire, (subject to the control of the house of commons) of coroners, and of verderers; to judge of the qualification of voters, and to return such as he shall determine to be duly elected.

---

proposed in the exchequer: this prerogative, however, it affords us satisfaction to remark, has of late been rarely exercised.

(*a*) Unless (by the same statute) there be no other legally qualified for the office.

As the keeper of the king's peace, both by common law and special commission, he is the first man in the county, and superior in rank to any nobleman therein, during his office. He may apprehend, and commit to prison, all persons who break the peace, or attempt to break it: and may bind any one in recognizance to keep the king's peace. He may, and is bound, *ex officio*, to pursue, and take all traitors, murderers, felons, and other misdoers, and commit them to gaol for safe custody. He is also to defend his county against any of the king's enemies when they come into the land: and for this purpose, as well as for keeping the peace and pursuing felons, he may command all the people of his county to attend him; which is called the *posse comitatus*, or power of the county: and this summons every person above fifteen years old, and under the degree of a peer, is bound to attend upon warning, under pain of fine and imprisonment. But though the sheriff is thus the principal conservator of the peace in his county, yet by the express directions of the great charter, he, together with the constable, coroner, and certain other officers of the king, are forbidden to hold any pleas of the crown, or, in other words, to try any criminal offence. Neither may he act as an ordinary justice of the peace during the time of his office.

In his ministerial capacity the sheriff is bound to execute all process issuing from the king's courts of justice. In the commencement of civil causes, he is to serve the writ, to arrest, and to take bail; when the cause comes to trial, he must summon and return the jury; when it is determined, he must see the judgment of the court carried into execution. In criminal matters, he also arrests and imprisons, he returns the jury, he has the custody of the delinquent, and he executes the sentence of the court, though it extend to death itself.

As the king's bailiff, it is his business to preserve the rights of the king within his bailiwick; for so his county is frequently called in the writs. He must seise to the king's use all lands devolved to the crown by attainder or escheat; must levy all fines and forfeitures; must seise and keep all waifs, wrecks, estrays, and the like, unless they be granted to some subject; and must also collect the king's rents within his bailiwick, if commanded by process from the exchequer.

To execute these various offices, the sheriff has under him many inferior officers; an under-sheriff, bailiffs, and gaolers; who must neither buy, sell, nor farm their offices, on forfeiture of 500*l*.

The under-sheriff usually performs all the duties of the office; a very few only excepted, where the personal presence of the high-sheriff is necessary. But no under-sheriff shall abide in his office above one year; and if he does, by statute 23 Hen. VI, c. 8. he forfeits 200*l*. a very large penalty in those early days. And no under-sheriff or sheriff's officer shall practise as an attorney, during the time he continues in such office: for this would be a great inlet to partiality and oppression. But these salutary regulations are shamefully evaded, by practising in the names of other attorneys, and putting in sham deputies by way of nominal under-sheriffs (*a*).

Bailiffs, or sheriff's officers, are either bailiffs of hundreds, or special bailiffs. Bailiffs of hundreds are officers appointed over those respective districts by the sheriffs, to collect fines therein; to summon juries: to attend the judges and justices at the assises, and quarter sessions; and also to execute writs and process in the several hundreds. But, as these are generally plain men, and not thoroughly skilful in this latter part of their office, that of serving writs, and making arrests and executions, it is now usual to join special bailiffs with

---

(*a*) However objectionable these practices may seem in theory, it is presumed no inconvenience has actually arisen from the exercise of them, as attorneys filling this office are now always men of respectability, and frequently of eminence, in their profession.

them. The sheriff being answerable for the misdemesnors of these bailiffs, they are therefore usually bound in an obligation with sureties for the due execution of their office, and thence are called bound-bailiffs; which the common people have corrupted into a much more homely appellation.

Gaolers are also the servants of the sheriff, and he must be responsible for their conduct. Their business is to keep safely all such persons as are committed to them by lawful warrant: and, if they suffer any such to escape, the sheriff shall answer it to the king, if it be a criminal matter; or, in a civil case, to the party injured. And to this end the sheriff must have lands sufficient within the county to answer the king and his people. The abuses of gaolers and sheriff's officers, toward the unfortunate persons in their custody, are well restrained and guarded against by statute 32 Geo. II. c. 28. and by statute 14 Geo. III. c. 59 (a). provisions are made for better preserving the health of prisoners, and preventing the gaol distemper.

The vast expence, which custom had introduced in serving the office of high-sheriff, was grown such a burthen to the subject, that it was enacted, by statute 13 and 14 Car. II. c. 21. that no sheriff (except of London, Westmorland, and towns which are counties of themselves) should keep any table at the assises, except for his own family, or give any presents to the judges or their servants, or have more than forty men in livery: yet, for the sake of safety and decency, he may not have less than twenty men in England and twelve in Wales; upon forfeiture, in any of these cases, of 200*l.*

II. The coroner's is also a very antient office at the common law. He is called coroner, *coronator*, because he hath principally to do with pleas of the crown, or such wherein the king is more immediately concerned. And in this light the lord chief justice of the king's bench is the principal co-

---

*(a)* And 24 Geo. III. c. 54.

roner in the kingdom, and may (if he pleafes) exercife the jurifdiction of a coroner in any part of the realm. But there are alfo particular coroners for every county of England; ufually four, but fometimes fix, and fometimes fewer (a).

The coroner is chofen by all the freeholders in the county court. He ought to have an eftate fufficient to maintain the dignity of his office, and anfwer any fines that may be fet upon him for his mifbehaviour; and if he hath not enough to anfwer, his fine fhall be levied on the county, as a punifhment for electing an infufficient officer.

The coroner is chofen for life: but may be removed, either by being made fheriff, or chofen verderor, which are offices incompatible with the other; or by the king's writ *de coronatore exonerando*, for a caufe to be therein affigned, as that he is engaged in other bufinefs, is incapacitated by years or ficknefs, hath not a fufficient eftate in the county, or lives in an inconvenient part of it. And by the ftatute 25 Geo. II. c. 29. extortion, neglect, or mifbehaviour, are alfo made caufes of removal.

The office and power of a coroner are alfo, like thofe of the fheriff, either judicial or minifterial; but principally judicial. This confifts, firft, in inquiring, when any perfon is flain, or dies fuddenly, or in prifon, concerning the manner of his death. And this muft be "*fuper vifum corporis*;" for, if the body be not found, the coroner cannot fit. He muft alfo fit at the very place where the death happened; and his inquiry is made by a jury from four, five, or fix of the neighbouring towns, over whom he is to prefide (b). If

---

(a) But though there be many coroners in the county, an inquifition, *fuper vivum corporis*, may be taken by any one of them.

(b) And by 3 Edw. I. c. 10. and 4 Edw. I. ft. 2. if the coroner have notice, and come not in convenient time to view the body, and take his inquifition, upon the death of

any be found guilty, by this inqueſt, of murder or other homicide, he is to commit them to priſon for farther trial, and is alſo to inquire concerning their lands, goods and chattels, which are forfeited thereby: but, whether it be homicide or not, he muſt inquire whether any deodand has accrued to the king, or the lord of the franchiſe, by this death: and muſt certify the whole of this inquiſition (under his own ſeal and the ſeals of the jurors) together with the evidence thereon, to the court of king's bench, or the next aſſiſes. Another branch of his office is to inquire concerning ſhipwrecks; and certify whether wreck or not, and who is in poſſeſſion of the goods. Concerning treaſure-trove, he is alſo to inquire who were the finders, and where it is, and whether any one be ſuſpected of having found and concealed a treaſure.

The miniſterial office of the coroner is only as the ſheriff's ſubſtitute. For when juſt exception can be taken to the ſheriff, for ſuſpicion of partiality, (as that he is intereſted in the ſuit, or of kindred to either plaintiff or defendant) the proceſs muſt then be awarded to the coroner, inſtead of the ſheriff, for execution of the king's writs.

III. The next ſpecies of ſubordinate magiſtrates, whom I am to conſider, are juſtices of the peace; the principal of whom is the *cuſtos rotulorum*, or keeper of the records of the county.

The king's majeſty is, by his office and dignity royal, the principal conſervator of the peace within all his dominions; and may give authority to any other to ſee the peace kept, and to puniſh ſuch as break it: hence it is uſually called the king's peace. The lord chancellor or keeper, the lord treaſurer, the lord high ſteward of England, the lord

---

him that dies ſuddenly; and upon a preſentment by the grand inqueſt, of a death by miſadventure, if the like preſentment be not found in the coroner's roll, he ſhall be fined and impriſoned.

marefchal, and lord high conftable of England (when any fuch officers are in being) and all the juftices of the court of king's bench (by virtue of their offices) and the mafter of the rolls (by prefcription) are general confervators of the peace throughout the whole kingdom, and may commit all breakers of it, or bind them in recognizances to keep it: the other judges are only fo in their own courts. The coroner is alfo a confervator of the peace within his own county; as is alfo the fheriff; and both of them may take a recognizance or fecurity for the peace. Conftables, tythingmen, and the like, are alfo confervators of the peace within their own jurifdictions; and may apprehend all breakers of the peace, and commit them, till they find fureties for their keeping it.

They were only called confervators, wardens, or keepers of the peace, till the ftatute 34 Edw. III. c. 1. gave them the power of trying felonies; and then they acquired the more honorable appellation of juftices.

Thefe juftices are appointed by the king's fpecial commiffion under the great feal. When any juftice intends to act under this commiffion, he fues out a writ of *didimus poteftatem*, from the clerk of the crown in chancery, empowering certain perfons therein named, to adminifter the ufual oaths to him; which done, he is at liberty to act.

Touching the qualifications of thefe juftices; it is enacted by ftatute 5 Geo. II. c. 11. that every juftice, except as is therein excepted, fhall have 100*l*. (*a*) *per annum*, clear of all

---

(*a*) This 100*l. per annum* muft confift of lands, tenements, or hereditaments, fituated either in England or Wales; and if leafehold, muft have been originally created for the term of twenty-one years at the leaft. See 18 Geo. II. c. 20. by which ftatute alfo a remainder or reverfion after one or more lives of the value of 300*l. per annum* is rendered a qualification. The exceptions alluded to in the text are in favor of lords of parliament and their eldeft fon or heirs apparent;

deductions; of which he muſt now make oath: and, if he acts without ſuch qualification, he ſhall forfeit 100*l.* Alſo it is provided by the act 5 Geo. II. that no practiſing attorney, ſolicitor, or proctor, ſhall be capable of acting as a juſtice of the peace.

As the office of theſe juſtices is conferred by the king, ſo it ſubſiſts only during his pleaſure; and is determinable, 1. By the demiſe of the crown; that is, in ſix months after: but if the ſame juſtice is put in commiſſion by the ſucceſſor, he ſhall not be obliged to ſue out a new *dedimus*, or to ſwear to his qualification afreſh; nor, by reaſon of any new commiſſion, to take the oaths more than once in the ſame reign. 2. By expreſs writ under the great ſeal, diſcharging any particular perſon from being any longer juſtice. 3. By ſuperſeding the commiſſion by writ of *ſuperſedeas*, which ſuſpends the power of all the juſtices, but does not totally deſtroy it; ſeeing it may be revived again by another writ, called a *procedendo*. 4. By a new commiſſion, which virtually, though ſilently, diſcharges all the former juſtices that are not included therein; for two commiſſions cannot ſubſiſt at once. 5. By acceſſion to the office of ſheriff or coroner.

The power, office, and duty of a juſtice of the peace depend on his commiſſion, and on the ſeveral ſtatutes which have created objects of his juriſdiction. His commiſſion, firſt, empowers him ſingly to conſerve the peace; and thereby gives him all the power of the antient conſervators at the common law, in ſuppreſſing riots and affrays, in taking ſecurities for the peace, and in apprehending and committing felons and other inferior criminals. It alſo empowers any two or more to hear and determine all felonies and other offences; which is the ground of their juriſdiction at ſeſſions,

---

perſons qualified to be knights of the ſhire, certain officers of ſtate within the range of their particular juriſdictions, and heads of colleges in the two univerſities, within the counties where thoſe ſeminaries ſtand, *Ibid.* 9 Ann. c. 5.

of which more will be faid in it's proper place. And as to the powers given to one, two, or more juftices, by the feveral ftatutes, which from time to time have heaped upon them fuch an infinite variety of bufinefs that few care to undertake, and fewer underftand, the office; they are fuch and of fo great importance to the public, that the country is greatly obliged to any worthy magiftrate, that without finifter views of his own will engage in this troublefome fervice. And therefore, if a well-meaning juftice makes any undefigned flip in his practice, great lenity and indulgence are fhewn to him in the courts of law; and there are many ftatutes made to protect him in the upright difcharge of his office; which, among other privileges, prohibit fuch juftices from being fued for any overfights without notice beforehand; and ftop all fuits begun, on tender made of fufficient amends (*a*). But, on the other hand, any malicious or tyrannical abufe of their office is ufually feverely punifhed; and all perfons who recover a verdict againft a juftice, for any wilful or malicious injury, are entitled to double cofts.

It is impoffible, upon our prefent plan, to enter minutely into the particulars of the accumulated authority, thus committed to the charge of thefe magiftrates. I muft therefore refer myfelf at prefent to fuch fubfequent parts of thefe commentaries, as will in their turns comprize almoft every object of the juftices' jurifdiction (*b*).

---

(*a*) This is, by the 24 Geo. II. c. 24. the words of which are, that "no writ fhall be fued out againft, nor copy of any procefs ferved, on any juftice of the peace, for any thing by him done in the execution of his office, until notice, in writing, of fuch writ or procefs fhall have been delivered or left at his ufual place of abode, at leaft one calendar month before fueing out or ferving the fame, fpecifying the caufe of action. And that it fhall be lawful for fuch juftice, within one calendar month after fuch notice by him received, to tender amends to the party complaining."

(*b*) See *Index*, Title "Justice."

I shall next confider fome officers of lower rank than thofe which have gone before, and of more confined jurifdiction; but ftill fuch as are univerfally in ufe through every part of the kindom.

IV. Fourthly, then, of the conftable. Conftables are of two forts, high conftables, and petty conftables. The former were firft ordained by the ftatute of Winchefter; are appointed at the court leets of the franchife or hundred over which they prefide, or, in default of that, by the juftices at their quarter feffions; and are removable by the fame authority that appoints them. The petty conftables are inferior officers in every town and parifh, fubordinate to the high conftable of the hundred, firft inftituted about the reign of Edw. III. They are chofen by the jury at the court leet; or if no court leet be held, are appointed by two juftices of the peace.

The general duty of all conftables, both high and petty, is to keep the king's peace in their feveral diftricts; and to that purpofe they are armed with very large powers, of arrefting, and imprifoning, of breaking open houfes, and the like. One of their principal duties, arifing from the ftatute of Winchefter, which appoints them, is to keep watch and ward in their refpective jurifdictions. Ward, guard, or *cuftodia*, is chiefly applied to the day time, in order to apprehend rioters, and robbers on the highways; the manner of doing which is left to the difcretion of the juftices of the peace and the conftable: the hundred being however anfwerable for all robberies committed therein, by day light, for having kept negligent guard. Watch is properly applicable to the night only, and it begins at the time when ward ends, and ends when that begins: for, by the ftatute of Winchefter, in walled towns the gates fhall be clofed from funfetting to funrifing, and watch fhall be kept in every borough and town, efpecially in the fummer feafon, to apprehend all rogues, vagabonds, and night-walkers,, **and make** them give an account of themselves (a). The constable may appoint watchmen, at his discretion, regulated by the custom of the place; and these, being his deputies, have for the time being, the authority of their principal.

V. We are next to consider the surveyors of the highways. Every parish is bound of common right to keep the high roads, that go through it, in good and sufficient repair; unless by reason of the tenure of lands, or otherwise, this care is consigned to some particular private person. And indeed now, for the most part, the care of the roads only seems to be left to parishes; that of bridges being in great measure devolved upon the county at large, by statute 22 Hen. VIII. c. 5. If the parish neglect these repairs, they may be indicted for such their neglect.

These surveyors were, originally, appointed by the constable and church-wardens of the parish; but now they are constituted by two neighbouring justices, out of such inhabitants or others as are described in statute 13 Geo. III. c. 78. and may have salaries allotted them for their trouble.

Their office and duty consists in putting in execution a variety of laws for the repairs of the public highways; that is, of ways leading from one town to another: all which are now reduced into one act by statute 13 Geo. III. c. 78. which enacts, 1. That they may remove all annoyances in the highways, or give notice to the owner to remove them; who

---

(a) In pursuance of this statute, watch and ward is now regularly established in many places, under the appointment and authority of the justices at the quarter sessions of the county.

The duties of constables, and other inferior officers of police, are judiciously collected and explained, under their respective titles, in "*Williams's Justice of the Peace,*" and also in the "*Laws respecting Parish Affairs;*" a book much superior in point of composition and arrangement to most anonymous publications of a similar kind.

is liable to penalties on non-compliance. 2. They are to call together all the inhabitants and occupiers of lands, tenements, and hereditaments within the parish, six days in every year, to labour in fetching materials or repairing the highways: all persons keeping draughts (of three horses, &c.) or occupying lands, being obliged to send a team for every draught, and for every 50*l.* a year, which they keep or occupy; persons keeping less than a draught, or occupying less than 50*l.* a year, to contribute in a less proportion; and all other persons chargeable, between the ages of eighteen and sixty-five, to work or find a labourer: but they may compound with the surveyors, at certain easy rates established by the act. And every cartway leading to any market-town must be made twenty feet wide at the least, if the fences will permit; and may be increased by two justices, at the expence of the parish, to the breadth of thirty feet (*a*). 3. The surveyors may lay out their own money in purchasing materials for repairs, in erecting guide-posts, and making drains, and shall be reimbursed by a rate, to be allowed at a special sessions. 4. In case the personal labour of the parish be not sufficient, the surveyors, with the consent of the quarter sessions, may levy a rate on the parish, in aid of the personal duty, not exceeding, in any one year, together with the other highway rates, the sum of 9*d.* in the pound; for the due application of which they are to account upon oath. As for turnpikes, which are now pretty generally introduced in aid of such rates, and the law relating to them, these depend principally on the particular powers granted in the several road acts, and upon some general provisions, which are extended to all turnpike roads in the kingdom by statute 13 Geo. III. c. 84. amended by many subsequent acts.

VI. I proceed, lastly, to consider the overseers of the poor; their original, appointment, and duty.

---

(*a*) See *ante*, p. 17, n. (*a*)

The poor of England, till the time of Henry VIII. subſiſted entirely upon private benevolence, and the charity of well-diſpoſed chriſtians. But, by ſtatute 43 Eliz. c. 2. overſeers of the poor were appointed in every pariſh.

By virtue of the ſtatute laſt mentioned, theſe overſeers are to be nominated yearly in Eaſter-week, or within one month after, (though a ſubſequent nomination will be valid) by two juſtices dwelling near the pariſh. They muſt be ſubſtantial houſeholders, and ſo expreſſed to be in the appointment of the juſtices.

Their office and duty, according to the ſame ſtatute, are principally theſe: firſt, to raiſe competent ſums for the neceſſary relief of the poor, impotent, old, blind, and ſuch other, being poor, as are not able to work: and ſecondly, to provide for ſuch as are able, and cannot otherwiſe get employment: (but this latter part of their duty, which, according to the wiſe regulations of that ſalutary ſtatute, ſhould go hand in hand with the other, is now moſt ſhamefully neglected.) However, for theſe joint purpoſes, they are impowered to make and levy rates upon the ſeveral inhabitants of the pariſh, by the ſame act of parliament; which has been farther explained and enforced by ſeveral ſubſequent ſtatutes.

The law of ſettlements, in regard to the poor, may be reduced to the following general heads; 1. By *birth*; for, wherever a child is firſt known to be, that is always *prima facie* the place of ſettlement, until ſome other can be ſhewn. This is alſo generally the place of ſettlement of a baſtard child; for a baſtard having in the eye of the law no father, he cannot be referred to *his* ſettlement, as other children may. But, in legitimate children, though the place of birth be *prima facie* the ſettlement, yet it is not concluſively ſo; for there are, 2. Settlements by *parentage*, being the ſettlement of one's father or mother: all legitimate children being really ſettled in the pariſh where their parents are ſettled, until they get a new ſettlement for themſelves.

A new settlement may be acquired several ways; as, 3. By *marriage*. For a woman, marrying a man that is settled in another parish, changes her own settlement: the law not permitting the separation of husband and wife. But if the man has no settlement, her's is suspended during his life, if he remains in England and is able to maintain her; but in his absence, or after his death, or during (perhaps) his inability, she may be removed to her old settlement. The other methods of acquiring settlements in any parish are all reducible to this one, of *forty days residence* therein: but this forty days residence (which is construed to be lodging or lying there) must not be by fraud, or stealth, or in any clandestine manner; but made notorious, by one or other of the following concomitant circumstances. The next method therefore of gaining a settlement, is, 4. By forty days residence, and *notice*; for if a stranger comes into a parish, and delivers notice in writing of his place of abode, and number of his family, to one of the overseers (which must be read in the church and registered) and resides there unmolested for forty days after such notice, he is legally settled thereby (a). But there are also other circumstances equivalent to such notice: therefore, 5. *Renting* for a year a tenement of the yearly value of ten pounds, and residing forty days in the parish, gains a settlement without notice; upon the principle of having substance enough to gain credit for such a house. 6. Being charged to and paying the public *taxes* and levies of the parish; (excepting those for scavengers, highways, and the duties on houses and windows) and, 7. Executing, when

---

(a) Residence by notice was amongst the provisions of 13 and 14 Car. II. respecting the poor; but so much of that statute as relates to this subject is now repealed by 35 Geo. III. c. 101. whereby it is enacted, that " no person coming into any parish, township, or place, after the passing of that act, shall be enabled to gain any settlement therein, by delivery and publication of any notice in writing."

legally appointed, any public parochial *office* for a whole year in the parish, as church-warden, *&c*; are both of them equivalent to notice, and gain a settlement, if coupled with a residence of forty days. 8. Being *hired* for a year, when unmarried and childless, and *serving* a year in the same service; and 9. Being bound an *apprentice*, give the servant and apprentice a settlement, without notice, in that place wherein they serve the last forty days. This is meant to encourage application to trades, and going out to reputable services. 10. Lastly, the having an *estate* of one's own, and residing thereon forty days, however small the value may be, in case it be acquired by act of law, or of a third person, as by descent, gift, devise, *&c.* is a sufficient settlement: but if a man acquire it by his own act, as by purchase, (in it's popular sense, in consideration of money paid) then unless the consideration advanced, *bona fide*, be 30*l.* it is no settlement for any longer time, than the person shall inhabit thereon. He is in no case removable from his own property; but he shall not, by any trifling or fraudulent purchase of his own, acquire a permanent and lasting settlement.

All persons, not so settled, may be removed to their own parishes, on complaint of the overseers, by two justices of the peace, if they shall adjudge them likely to become chargeable to the parish, into which they have intruded: unless they are in a way of getting a legal settlement, as by having hired a house of 10*l. per annum*, or living in an annual service; for then they are not removable. And in all other cases, if the parish to which they belong will grant them a certificate, acknowledging them to be *their* parishioners, they cannot be removed merely because *likely* to become chargeable, but only when they become *actually* chargeable (*a*). But such certified person can gain no settlement

---

(*a*) The same is now law, though no certificate be granted; so much of the statute of Car. II. before referred to, as

by any of the means above-mentioned; unless by renting a tenement of 10*l. per annum*, or by serving an annual office in the parish, being legally placed therein: neither can an apprentice or servant to such certified person gain a settlement by such their service.

These are the general heads of the laws relating to the poor, which, by the resolutions of the courts of justice thereon within a century past, are branched into a great variety (*a*).

## CHAPTER IV.

OF THE PEOPLE, WHETHER ALIENS, DENIZENS, OR NATIVES.

HAVING, in the preceding chapter, treated of persons as they stand in the public relations of *magistrates*, I now proceed to consider such persons as fall under the denomination of the *people*. And herein all the inferior and

---

enables the justices to remove persons *likely* to become chargeable, being repealed by 35 Geo. III. c. 101. which enacts, that from thenceforth " no poor person shall be removed by virtue of any order of removal from the parish or place where such poor person shall be inhabiting, until he or she shall have become *actually* chargeable;" unless in the case of unmarried women with child, who shall be deemed to be persons actually chargeable within the meaning of the said act.

(*a*) For a more particular account of the laws, at present subsisting, relative to the poor, the reader is referred to Mr. *Bott*'s book on that subject, as edited by Mr. *Const*; an epitome also of those laws, as far as concerns the head of settlements, is contained in the little treatise we before noticed under the title of " Laws respecting Parish Matters;" to which we would refer those who are not professionally accustomed to the perusal of law treatises.

subordinate magistrates, treated of in that chapter, are included.

The first and most obvious division of the people is into aliens and natural-born subjects. Natural-born subjects are such as are born within the dominions of the crown of England; that is, within the ligeance, or as it is generally called, the allegiance of the king: and aliens, such as are born out of it.

An alien born may purchase lands, or other estates: but not for his own use; for the king is thereupon entitled to them (*a*). If an alien could acquire a permanent property in lands, he must owe an allegiance, equally permanent with that property, to the king of England; which would probably be inconsistent with that which he owes to his own natural liege lord: besides that thereby the nation might in time be subject to foreign influence, and feel many other inconveniences. Yet an alien may acquire a property in goods, money, and other personal estate, or may hire a house for his habitation (*b*): for personal estate is of a transitory and moveable nature; and, besides this indulgence to strangers, is necessary for the advancement of trade. Aliens also may trade as freely as other people; only they are subject to certain higher duties at the custom-house. Also an alien may bring an action concerning personal property, and may make a will, and dispose of his personal estate. When I mention these rights of an alien, I must be understood of alien-friends only, or such whose countries are in peace with ours; for alien-enemies have no rights, no privileges, unless by the king's special favour, during the time of war.

When I say, that an alien is one who is born out of the king's dominions or allegiance, this also must be under-

---

(*a*) Viz. If the estate be of a freehold nature; but if copyhold it will escheat to the lord. *Co. Lit.* 2.<sup>b</sup> n (4). *Dy.* 2. *Marg.* but see 1 *Mod.* 17. *Allen*, 14.

(*b*) See *Co. Lit.* 2.<sup>b</sup> n. (7) & *post.*

stood with some restrictions. The common law indeed stood absolutely so; with only a very few exceptions: so that a particular act of parliament became necessary after the restoration, " for the naturalization of children of his majesty's " English subjects, born in foreign countries during the late " troubles." (a) Yet the children of the king's embassadors born abroad were always held to be natural subjects: for as the father, though in a foreign country, owes not even a local allegiance to the prince to whom he is sent; so, with regard to the son also, he was held (by a kind of *postliminium*) to be born under the king of England's allegiance, represented by his father, the embassador. To encourage also foreign commerce, it was enacted by statute 25 Edw. III. st. 2. that all children born abroad, provided *both* their parents were, at the time of the birth, in allegiance to the king, and the mother had passed the seas by her husband's consent, might inherit as if born in England: and accordingly it hath been so adjudged in behalf of merchants. But by several more modern statutes these restrictions are still farther taken off: so that all children, born out of the king's ligeance, whose *fathers* (or *grandfathers* by the father's side) were natural-born subjects, are now deemed to be natural-born subjects themselves, to all intents and purposes; unless their said ancestors were attainted, or banished beyond sea, for high treason; or were at the birth of such children in the service of a prince at enmity with Great Britain. Yet the grandchildren of such ancestor shall not be privileged in respect of the alien's duty, except they be protestants, and actually reside within the realm; nor shall they be enabled to claim any estate or interest, unless the claim be made within five years after the same shall accrue.

---

(a) This act was 29 Car. II. c. 6.

The children of aliens, born here in England, are, generally speaking, natural-born subjects, and entitled to all the privileges of such.

A denizen is an alien born, but who has obtained *ex donatione regis* letters patent to make him an English subject: a high and incommunicable branch of the royal prerogative. A denizen is in a kind of a middle state, between an alien and natural-born subject, and partakes of both of them. He may take lands by purchase or devise, which an alien may not; but cannot take by inheritance: for his parent, through whom he must claim, being an alien, had no inheritable blood; and therefore could convey none to the son (a). And, upon a like defect of hereditary blood, the issue of a denizen, born *before* denization, cannot inherit to him; but his issue born *after*, may. A denizen is not excused from paying the alien's duty, and some other mercantile burthens. And no denizen can be of the privy council, or either house of parliament, or have any office of trust, civil or military, or be capable of any grant of lands, &c. from the crown.

Naturalization cannot be performed but by act of parliament; for by this an alien is put in exactly the same state as if he had been born in the king's ligeance; except only that he is incapable, as well as a denizen, of being a member of the privy council, or parliament, holding offices, grants, &c. No bill for naturalization can be received in either house of parliament, without such disabling clause in it: nor without a clause disabling the person from obtaining any immunity in trade thereby, in any foreign country; unless he shall have resided in Britain for seven years next after the commencement of the session in which he is naturalized.

---

(a) But by 11 and 12 Wm. III. c. 6. and 25 Geo. II. c. 39. this does not extend to a natural-born subject, *though claiming through an alien*, so that he be born at the time of his ancestor's death.

Neither can any person be naturalized or restored in blood, unless he hath received the sacrament of the Lord's supper within one month before the bringing in of the bill; and unless he also takes the oaths of allegiance and supremacy in the presence of parliament. But these provisions have been usually dispensed with by several acts of parliament, previous to bills of naturalization of any foreign princes or princesses.

These are the principal distinctions between aliens, denizens, and natives: and moreover, by 7 An. c. 5. every foreign seaman, who in time of war serves two years on board an English ship by virtue of the king's proclamation, is *ipso facto* naturalized under the like restrictions as in statute 12 Wm. III. c. 2. and all foreign protestants, and Jews, upon their residing seven years in any of the American colonies, without being absent above two months at a time, and all foreign protestants serving two years in a military capacity there, or being three years employed in the whale fishery, without afterward absenting themselves from the king's dominions for more than one year, and none of them falling within the incapacities declared by statute 4 Geo. II. c. 21. shall be (upon taking the oaths of allegiance and abjuration, or in some cases, an affirmation to the same effect) naturalized to all intents and purposes, as if they had been born in this kingdom; except as to sitting in parliament or in the privy council, and holding offices or grants of lands, &c. from the crown within the kingdoms of Great Britain or Ireland.

## CHAPTER V.

### OF THE CLERGY.

THE people, whether aliens, denizens, or natural-born subjects, are divisible into two kinds; the clergy and laity: the clergy, comprehending all persons in holy orders, and in ecclesiastical offices, will be the subject of the present chapter.

This venerable body of men, being separate and set apart from the rest of the people, in order to attend the more closely to the service of almighty God, have thereupon large privileges allowed them by our municipal laws. A clergyman cannot be compelled to serve on a jury, nor to appear at a court-leet or view of frank pledge; which almost every other person is obliged to do: but if a layman is summoned on a jury, and before the trial takes orders, he shall notwithstanding appear and be sworn. Neither can he be chosen to any temporal office; as bailiff, reeve, constable, or the like: in regard of his own continual attendance on the sacred function. During his attendance on divine service he is privileged from arrests in civil suits (a): in cases also of felony, a clerk in orders shall have the benefit of his clergy, without being branded in the hand; and may likewise have it more than once: in both which particulars he is distinguished from a layman. But as they have their privileges, so also they have their disabilities, on account of their spiritual avocations. Clergymen, we have seen (b), are incapable of sitting in the house of commons; and by statute

---

(a) And this privilege extends to the time of his going to, and returning from the place of worship. 12 *Co.* 100 b.
(b) *Ante*, p. 25.

21 Hen. VIII. c. 13. are not (in general) allowed to take any lands or tenements to farm, upon pain of 10*l. per* month, and total avoidance of the leafe ; nor upon like pain to keep any tanhoufe or brewhoufe ; nor fhall engage in any manner of trade, nor fell any merchandize, under forfeiture of treble the value.

In the frame and conftitution of ecclefiaftical polity there are divers ranks and degrees: which I fhall confider in their refpective order, merely as they are taken notice of by the fecular laws of England; without intermeddling with the canons and conftitutions by which the clergy have bound themfelves. And under each divifion I fhall confider, 1. The method of their appointment ; 2. Their rights and duties ; and 3. The manner wherein their character or office may ceafe.

An arch-bifhop or bifhop is elected by the chapter of his cathedral church, by virtue of a licence from the crown, which is always to be accompanied with a letter miffive from the king, containing the name of the perfon whom he would have them elect : and, if the dean and chapter delay their election above twelve days, the nomination fhall devolve to the king, who may by letters patent appoint fuch perfon as he pleafes. This election or nomination, if it be of a bifhop, muft be fignified by the king's letters patent to the archbifhop of the province; if it be of an arch-bifhop, to the other arch-bifhop and two bifhops, or to four bifhops ; requiring them to confirm, inveft, and confecrate the perfon fo elected : which they are bound to perform immediately, without any application to the fee of Rome. After which the bifhop elect fhall fue to the king for his temporalties, fhall make oath to the king and none other, and fhall take reftitution of his fecular poffeffions out of the king's hands only. And if fuch dean and chapter do not elect in the manner by this act appointed, or if fuch arch-bifhop or bifhop do refufe to confirm, inveft, and confecrate fuch bishop elect, they shall incur all the penalties of a *præmunire*.

An arch-bishop is the chief of the clergy in a whole province; and has the inspection of the bishops of that province, as well as of the inferior clergy, and may deprive them on notorious cause. The archbishop has also his own diocese, wherein he exercises episcopal jurisdiction; as in his province he exercises archiepiscopal. As arch-bishop, he, upon receipt of the king's writ, calls the bishops and clergy of his province to meet in convocation: but without the king's writ he cannot assemble them. To him all appeals are made from inferior jurisdictions within his province; and, as an appeal lies from the bishops in person to him in person, so it also lies from the consistory courts of each diocese to his archiepiscopal court. During the vacancy of any see in his province, he is guardian of the spiritualties thereof, as the king is of the temporalties; and he executes all ecclesiastical jurisdiction therein. If an archiepiscopal see be vacant, the dean and chapter are the spiritual guardians, ever since the office of prior of Canterbury was abolished at the reformation. The arch-bishop is entitled to present by lapse to all the ecclesiastical livings in the disposal of his diocesan bishops, if not filled within six months. And the archbishop has a customary prerogative, when a bishop is consecrated by him, to name a clerk or chaplain of his own to be provided for by such suffragan bishop; in lieu of which it is now usual for the bishop to make over by deed to the archbishop, his executors and assigns, the next presentation of such dignity or benefice in the bishop's disposal within that see, as the arch-bishop himself shall choose; which is therefore called his *option*: which options are only binding on the bishop himself who grants them, and not on his successors. It is likewise the privilege, by custom, of the arch-bishop of Canterbury, to crown the kings and queens of this kingdom. And he hath also by the statute 25 Hen.

VIII. c. 21. the power of granting difpenfations in any cafe, not contrary to the holy fcriptures and the law of God, where the pope ufed formerly to grant them: which is the foundation of his granting fpecial licences, to marry at any place or time, to hold two livings, and the like: and on this alfo is founded the right he exercifes of conferring degrees, in prejudice of the two univerfities.

The power and authority of a bifhop, befides the adminiftration of certain holy ordinances peculiar to that facred order, confift principally in infpecting the manners of the people and clergy, and punifhing them in order to reformation, by ecclefiaftical cenfures. To this purpofe he has feveral courts under him, and may vifit at pleafure every part of his diocefe (a). His chancellor is appointed to hold his courts for him, and to affift him in matters of ecclefiaftical law; who, as well as all other ecclefiaftical officers, if lay or married, muft be a doctor of the civil law, fo created in fome univerfity. It is alfo the bufinefs of a bifhop to inftitute, and to direct induction, to all ecclefiaftical livings in his diocefe.

Archbifhopricks and bifhopricks may become void by death, deprivation for any very grofs and notorious crime, and alfo by refignation. All refignations muft be made to

---

*(a)* The bifhop of every diocefe hath a confiftory court, for caufes ecclefiaftical, which is holden before his chancellor in his cathedral church, whofe authority and jurifdiction is over the whole diocefe; but when the diocefe is large, in places of it fo far remote and diftant that the chancellor cannot call people to the confiftory, without great trouble, and vexation, there the bifhop hath his commiffaries, whofe authority and jurifdiction extends no farther than fome particular places of the diocefe, and who are therefore called in law, *judices*, or *officiales foranei*, that is. judges limited and confined to one certain forum, or court in the diocefe— *(Vide* 4 *Coke's Inft. c.* 74. *and Sir Thomas Ridley's View of the Civil Law, p.* 156.

some superior. Therefore a bishop must resign to his metropolitan; but the arch-bishop can resign to none but the king himself.

A dean and chapter are the council of the bishop, to assist him with their advice in affairs of religion, and also in the temporal concerns of his see.

All antient deans are elected by the chapter, by *conge d' eslire* from the king, and letters missive of recommendation; in the same manner as bishops: but in those chapters, that were founded by Henry VIII. out of the spoils of the dissolved monasteries, the deanery is donative, and the installation merely by the king's letters patent. The chapter, consisting of canons or prebendaries, are sometimes appointed by the king, sometimes by the bishop, and sometimes elected by each other.

The dean and chapter are, as was before observed, the nominal electors of a bishop. The bishop is their ordinary and immediate superior; and has, generally speaking, the power of visiting them, and correcting their excesses and enormities.

Deaneries and prebends may become void, like a bishoprick, by death, by deprivation, or by resignation to either the king or the bishop. Also I may here mention, once for all, that if a dean, prebendary, or other spiritual person be made a bishop, all the preferments of which he was before possessed are void; and the king may present to them in right of his prerogative royal. But they are not void by the election, but only by the consecration.

An arch-deacon hath an ecclesiastical jurisdiction, immediately subordinate to the bishop, throughout the whole of his diocese, or in some particular part of it. He is usually appointed by the bishop himself; and hath a kind of episcopal authority, originally derived from the bishop, but now independent and distinct from his. He therefore visits the clergy; and has his separate court for punishment of offenders, by spiritual censures, and for hearing all other causes of ecclesiastical cognizance.

The next, and indeed the most numerous, order of men in the system of ecclesiastical polity, are the parsons and vicars of churches: in treating of whom I shall first mark out the distinction between them; shall next observe the method by which one may become a parson or vicar; shall then briefly touch upon their rights and duties; and shall, lastly, shew how one may cease to be either.

A parson, *persona ecclesiæ*, is one that hath full possession of all the rights of a parochial church. He is called parson, *persona*, because by his person the church, which is an invisible body, is represented; and he is in himself a body corporate, in order to protect and defend the rights of the church (which he personates) by a perpetual succession. He is sometimes called the rector, or governor, of the church: but the appellation of *parson*, (however it may be depreciated by familiar, clownish, and indiscriminate use) is the most legal, most beneficial, and most honourable title that a parish priest can enjoy; because such a one, (sir Edward Coke observes) and he only, is safe, *vicem seu personam ecclesiæ gerere*. A parson has, during his life, the freehold in himself of the parsonage house, the glebe, the tithes, and other dues. But these are sometimes *appropriated*; that is to say, the benefice is perpetually annexed to some spiritual corporation, either sole or aggregate, being the patron of the living; which the law esteems equally capable of providing for the service of the church, as any single private clergyman.

The distinction of a parson and vicar is this: the parson has for the most part the whole right to all the ecclesiastical dues in his parish; but a vicar has generally an appropriator over him, entitled to the best part of the profits, to whom he is in effect perpetual curate, with a standing salary.

The method of becoming a parson or vicar is much the same. To both there are four requisites necessary: holy orders; presentation; institution; and induction. The method of conferring the holy orders of deacon and priest, according to the liturgy and canons, is foreign to the purpose of these commentaries; any farther than as they are necessary requisites to make a complete parson or vicar. By statute 13 & 14 Car. II. c. 4. no person is capable to be admitted to any benefice, unless he hath been first ordained a priest; and then he is, in the language of the law, a clerk in orders. But if he obtains orders, or a licence to preach, by money or corrupt practices (which seems to be the true, though not the common, notion of simony) the person giving such orders forfeits 40 l. and the person receiving, 10 l. and is incapable of any ecclesiastical preferment for seven years afterwards.

Any clerk may be presented (*a*) to a parsonage or vicarage; that is, the patron, to whom the advowson of the church belongs, may offer his clerk to the bishop of the diocese to be instituted. Of advowsons, or the right of presentation, being a species of private property, we shall find a more convenient place to treat in the second part of these commentaries. But when a clerk is presented, the bishop may refuse him upon many accounts. As, 1. If the patron is excommunicated, and remains in contempt forty days. Or, 2. If the clerk be unfit: which unfitness is of several kinds. First, with regard to his person; as if he be a bastard(*b*), an outlaw, an excommunicate, an alien, under age, or the like. Next, with regard to his faith or morals; as for any particular heresy, or vice that is *malum in se:* but if the bishop al-

---

(*a*) A layman may also be presented; but he must take priest's orders before his admission. 1 *Burn.* 103. A.

(*b*) Mr. *Christian*, in his late edition of our author, has observed, that though this is classed in the books among the causes of refusal, yet no one need apprehend that his preferment would now be impeded by any demerit but his own; and such we may venture to add, is not only the *justice* but the *law* of the case at the present day.

leges only in generals, as that he is *fchifmaticus inveteratus*, or objects a fault that is *malum prohibitum* merely, as haunting taverns, playing at unlawful games, or the like; it is not good caufe of refufal. Or, laftly, the clerk may be unfit to difcharge the paftoral office for want of learning. In any of which cafes the bifhop may refufe the clerk. In cafe the refufal is for herefy, fchifm, inability of learning, or other matter of ecclefiaftical cognizance, there the bifhop muft give notice to the patron of fuch his caufe of refufal, who, being ufually a layman, is not fuppofed to have knowledge of it; elfe he cannot prefent by lapfe: but, if the caufe be temporal, there he is not bound to give notice.

If an action at law be brought by the patron againft the bifhop for refufing his clerk, the bifhop muft affign the caufe. If the caufe be of a temporal nature and the fact admitted, (as, for inftance, outlawry) the judges of the king's courts muft determine it's validity, or whether it be fufficient caufe of refufal: but if the fact be denied, it muft be determined by a jury. If the caufe be of a fpiritual nature, (as, herefy, particularly alleged) the fact if denied fhall alfo be determined by a jury; and if the fact be admitted or found, the court upon confultation and advice of learned divines fhall decide it's fufficiency. If the caufe be want of learning, the bifhop need not fpecify in what points the clerk is deficient, but only allege that he is deficient: for the ftatute 9 Edw. II. ft. 1. c. 13. is exprefs, that the examination of the fitnefs of a perfon prefented to a benefice belongs to the ecclefiaftical judge. But becaufe it would be nugatory in this cafe to demand the reafon of refufal from the ordinary, if the patron were bound to abide by his determination, who has already pronounced his clerk unfit; therefore, if the bifhop returns the clerk to be *minus fufficiens in literatura*, the court fhall write to the metropolitan, to re-examine him, and certify his qualifications; which certificate of the archbifhop is final.

If the bishop hath no objections, but admits the patron's presentation, the clerk so admitted is next to be instituted by him; which is a kind of investiture of the spiritual part of the benefice: for by institution the care of the souls of the parish is committed to the charge of the clerk. When a vicar is instituted, he (besides the usual forms) takes, if required by the bishop, an oath of perpetual residence; for the maxim of law is that *vicarius non habet vicarium*. When the ordinary is also the patron, and *confers* the living, the presentation and institution are one and the same act, and are called a collation to a benefice. By institution or collation the church is full, so that there can be no fresh presentation till another vacancy, at least in the case of a common patron; but the church is not full against the king, till induction: nay, even if a clerk is instituted upon the king's presentation, the crown may revoke it before induction, and present another clerk. Upon institution also the clerk may enter on the parsonage house and glebe, and take the tithes; but he cannot grant or let them, or bring an action for them, till induction.

Induction is performed by a mandate from the bishop to the arch-deacon, who usually issues out a precept to other clergymen to perform it for him. It is done by giving the clerk corporal possession of the church, as by holding the ring of the door, tolling a bell, or the like; and is a form required by law, with intent to give all the parishioners due notice, and sufficient certainty of their new minister, to whom their tithes are to be paid. This therefore is the investiture of the temporal part of the benefice, as institution is of the spiritual. And when a clerk is thus presented, instituted, and inducted into a rectory, he is then, and not before, in full and complete possession, and is called in law *persona impersonata*, or parson imparsonee.

The rights of a parson or vicar, in his tithes and ecclesiastical dues, fall more properly under the second book of these commentaries: and as to his duties, they are principally of ecclefiaftical cognizance; thofe only excepted which are laid upon him by ftatute. And thofe are indeed fo numerous, that it is impracticable to recite them here with any tolerable concifenefs or accuracy. Some of them we may remark, as they arife in the progrefs of our inquiries, but for the reft I muft refer myfelf to fuch authors as have compiled treatifes exprefsly upon this fubject *(a)*. I fhall only juft mention the article of refidence, upon the fuppofition of which the law doth ftile every parochial minifter an incumbent. By ftatute 21 Hen. VIII. c. 13. perfons wilfully abfenting themfelves from their benefices, for one month together, or two months in the year, incur a penalty of 5l. to the king, and 5l. to any perfon that will fue for the fame: except chaplains to the king, or others therein mentioned, during their attendance in the houfhold of fuch as retain them *(b)*: and alfo except all heads of houfes, magiftrates, and profeffors in the univerfities, and all ftudents under forty years of age refiding there, *bona fide*, for ftudy. Legal refidence is not only in the parifh, but alfo in the parfonage houfe, if there be one: for it hath been refolved, that the ftatute intended refidence, not only for ferving the cure, and for hofpitality; but alfo for maintaining the houfe, that the fucceffor alfo may keep hofpitality there: and, if there be no parfonage houfe, it hath been holden that the incumbent is bound to hire one, in the fame or fome neighbouring parifh, to anfwer the purpofes of refidence. For the more effectual promotion of which important duty among the

---

*(a)* Thefe are very numerous: but there are few which can be relied on with certainty. Among thefe are bifhop Gibfon's *codex*, Dr. Burn's *ecclefiaftical law*, and the earlier editions of the *clergymen's law*, publifhed under the name of Dr. Watfon, but compiled by Mr. Place a barrifter. A.

*(b)* This feems to be incorrect in regard to the king, though true in refpect to the other perfons names in the text. See 3 *Burn. Ec. Law.* 290.

parochial clergy, a provision is made by the statute 17 Geo. III. c. 53. for raising money upon ecclesiastical benefices, to be paid off by annually decreasing installments, and to be expended in rebuilding or repairing the houses belonging to such benefices.

We have seen that there is but one way, whereby one may become a parson or a vicar: there are many ways, by which one may cease to be so. 1. By death. 2. By cession, in taking another benefice. For by statute 21 Hen. VIII. c. 13. if any one having a benefice of 8*l. per annum*, or upwards (according to the present valuation in the king's books) accepts any other, the first shall be adjudged void, unless he obtains a dispensation; which no one is entitled to have, but the chaplains of the king and others therein mentioned, the brethren and sons of lords and knights (*a*), and doctors and bachelors of divinity and law, *admitted by the universities* of this realm. And a vacancy thus made, for want of a dispensation, is called session. 3. By consecration; for, as was mentioned before, when a clerk is promoted to a bishoprick, all his other preferments are void the instant that he is consecrated. But there is a method, by the favour of the crown, of holding such livings *in commendam*. *Commenda*, or *ecclesia commendata*, is a living commended by the crown to the care of a clerk, to hold till a proper pastor is provided for it. This may be temporary for one, two, or three years; or perpetual: being a kind of dispensation to avoid the vacancy of the living, and is called a *commenda retinere*. There is also a *commenda recipere*, which is to take a benefice *de novo*, in the bishop's own gift, or the gift of some other patron consenting to the same; and this is the same to him as institution and induc-

---

(*a*) By mentioning *knights*, and other *inferior* dignities, the reader would naturally be lead to imagine, that the *superior* dignity of baronet would confer the same right; but this title was not then in existence.

tion are to another clerk. 4. By refignation. But this is of no avail, till accepted by the ordinary, into whofe hands the refignation muft be made (*a*). 5. By deprivation; either, firft, by fentence declaratory in the ecclefiaftical courts, for fit and fufficient caufes allowed by the common law; fuch as attainder of treafon or felony, or conviction of other infamous crime in the king's courts; for herefy, infidelity, grofs immorality, and the like: or, fecondly, in purfuance of divers penal ftatutes, which declare the benefice void, for fome nonfeafance or neglect, or elfe fome malefeafance or crime. As, for fimony; for maintaining any doctrine in derogation of the king's fupremacy, or of the thirty-nine articles, or of the book of common-prayer; for neglecting after inftitution to read the liturgy and articles in the church, or make the declarations againft popery, or take the abjuration oath; for ufing any other form of prayer than the liturgy of the church of England; or for abfenting himfelf fixty days in one year from a benefice belonging to a popifh patron, to which the clerk was prefented by either of the univerfities; in all which and fimilar cafes the benefice is *ipfo facto* void, without any formal fentence of deprivation.

A curate is the loweft degree in the church; being in the fame ftate that a vicar was formerly, an officiating temporary minifter, inftead of the proper incumbent. Though there are what are called *perpetual* curacies, where all the tithes are appropriated, and no vicarage endowed, (being for fome particular reafons exempted from the ftatute of Hen. IV.) but, inftead thereof, fuch perpetual curate is appointed by the appropriator. With regard to the other fpecies of cu-

---

(*a*) It has been greatly doubted, and the queftion ftill remains undecided, whether the ordinary can, of his own *mere will*, (though he certainly may for fufficient caufe) refufe to accept a refignation when offered. See *Fytche* v. *Bp. London, Cun. Sim.* 52.

rates, they are the objects of some particular statutes, which ordain, that such as serve a church during it's vacancy shall be paid such stipend as the ordinary thinks reasonable, out of the profits of the vacancy; or, if that be not sufficient, by the successor within fourteen days after he takes possession: and that, if any rector or vicar nominates a curate to the ordinary to be licenced to serve the cure in his absence, the ordinary shall settle his stipend under his hand and seal, not exceeding 50*l. per annum*, nor less than 20*l*. and on failure of payment may sequester the profits of the benefice.

Thus much of the clergy, properly so called. There are also certain inferior ecclesiastical officers of whom the common law takes notice; and that, principally, to assist the ecclesiastical jurisdiction, where it is deficient in powers. On which officers I shall make a few cursory remarks.

Churchwardens are the guardians or keepers of the church, and representatives of the body of the parish. They are sometimes appointed by the minister, sometimes by the parish, sometimes by both together, as custom directs. They are taken, in favor of the church, to be for some purposes a kind of corporation at the common law; that is, they are enabled by that name to have a property in goods and chattels, and to bring actions for them, for the use and profit of the parish. Yet they may not waste the church goods, but may be removed by the parish, and then called to account by action at the common law: but there is no method of calling them to account, but by first removing them; for none can legally do it, but those who are put in the place. As to lands, or other real property, as the church, churchyard, &c. they have no sort of interest therein; but if any damage is done thereto, the parson only or vicar shall have the action. Their office also is to repair the church, and make rates and levies for that purpose: but these are recoverable only in the ecclesiastical court. They are also joined with the overseers in the care and maintenance of the poor. They are to levy a shilling forfeiture on all such as do not repair to church on sundays and holidays, and are empowered to keep all persons orderly while there; to which end it has been held that a churchwarden may justify the pulling off a man's hat, without being guilty of either an assault or trespass. There are also a multitude of other petty parochial powers committed to their charge by divers acts of parliament (a).

Parish clerks and sextons are also regarded by the common law, as persons who have freeholds in their offices; and therefore though they may be punished, yet they cannot be deprived, by ecclesiastical censures. The parish clerk is generally appointed by the incumbent, but by custom may be chosen by the inhabitants; and if such custom appears, the court of king's bench will grant a *mandamus* to the archdeacon to swear him in; for the establishment of the custom turns it into a temporal or civil right.

## CHAPTER VI.

#### OF MASTER AND SERVANT.

HAVING thus commented on the rights and duties of persons, as standing in the *public* relations of magistrates and people, the method I have marked out now leads me to consider their rights and duties in *private* œconomical relations.

The three great relations in private life are, 1. That of *master and servant*; which is founded in convenience, where-

---

(a) See the principal of these collected in *Williams's Justice*, and in the publication before referred to, under the title of "*The Laws respecting Parish Affairs.*"

by a man is directed to call in the affiftance of others, where his own fkill and labour will not be fufficient to anfwer the cares incumbent upon him. 2. That of *hufband and wife;* which is founded in nature, but modified by civil fociety: the one directing man to continue and multiply his fpecies, the other prefcribing the manner in which that natural impulfe muft be confined and regulated. 3. That of *parent and child,* which is confequential to that of marriage, being it's principal end and defign: and it is by virtue of this relation that infants are protected, maintained, and educated. But, fince the parents, on whom this care is primarily incumbent, may be fnatched away by death before they have completed their duty, the law has therefore provided a fourth relation; 4. That of *guardian and ward,* which is a kind of artificial parentage, in order to fupply the deficiency, whenever it happens, of the natural. Of all thefe relations in their order.

In difcuffing the relation of *mafter and fervant,* I fhall, firft, confider the feveral forts of fervants, and how this relation is created and deftroyed: fecondly, the effect of this relation with regard to the parties themfelves: and, laftly, it's effect with regard to other perfons.

1. The firft fort of fervants, acknowledged by the laws of England, are *menial fervants*; fo called from being *intra mœnia,* or domeftics. The contract between them and their mafters arifes upon the hiring. If the hiring be general without any particular time limited, the law conftrues it to be a hiring for a year; upon a principle of natural equity, that the fervant fhall ferve, and the mafter maintain him, throughout all the revolutions of the refpective feafons; as well when there is work to be done, as when there is not: but the contract may be made for any larger or fmaller term. All fingle men between twelve years old and fixty, and married ones under thirty years of age, and all fingle women between twelve and forty, not having any vifible livelihood, are

compellable by two juftices to go out to fervice in hufbandry or certain fpecific trades, for the promotion of honeft induftry: and no mafter can put away his fervant, or fervant leave his mafter, after being fo retained, either before or at the end of his term, without a quarter's warning; unlefs upon reafonable caufe, to be allowed by a juftice of the peace (a): but they may part by confent, or make a fpecial bargain.

2. Another fpecies of fervants are called *apprentices* (from *apprendre*, to learn) and are ufually bound for a term of years, by deed indented, or indentures to ferve their mafters, and be maintained and inftructed by them. This is ufually done to perfons of trade, in order to learn their art and myftery; but it may be done to hufbandmen, nay to gentlemen, and others. And children of poor perfons may be apprenticed out by the overfeers, with confent of two juftices, till twenty-one years of age, to fuch perfons as are thought fitting; who are alfo compellable to take them; and it is held, that gentlemen of fortune, and clergymen, are equally liable with others to fuch compulfion: for which purpofes our ftatutes have made the indentures obligatory, even though fuch parifh-apprentice be a minor. Apprentices to trades may be difcharged on reafonable caufe, either at the requeft of themfelves or mafters, at the quarter feffions, or by one juftice, with appeal to the feffions; who may, by the equity of the ftatute, if they think it reafonable, direct reftitution of a ratable fhare of the money given with the apprentice:

---

(*a*) An exception, however, is to be admitted in refpect to incontinence, or any other moral turpitude, for which a fervant may be difcharged without application to a juftice, *Cald. C*. 11. 14. 134. and fo too, if he be prevented from doing the duties of his fervitude by being apprehended and detained in cuftody on fufpicion of having committed any illegal offence. *Ibid* 129.

and parish-apprentices may be discharged in the same manner, by two justices. But if an apprentice, with whom less than ten pounds hath been given, runs away from his master, he is compellable to serve out his time of absence, or make satisfaction for the same, at any time within seven years after the expiration of his original contract.

3. A third species of servants are *labourers*, who are only hired by the day or the week, and do not live *intra mœnia*, as part of the family; concerning whom the statutes before cited have made many very good regulations; 1. Directing that all persons who have no visible effects may be compelled to work: 2. Defining how long they must continue at work in summer and in winter: 3. Punishing such as leave or desert their work: 4. Empowering the justices at sessions, or the sheriff of the county to settle their wages: and 5. Inflicting penalties on such as either give, or exact, more wages than are so settled.

4. There is yet a fourth species of servants, if they may be so called, being rather in a superior, a ministerial, capacity; such as *stewards*, *factors*, and *bailiffs*: whom however the law considers as servants *pro tempore*, with regard to such of their acts as affect their master's or employer's property. Which leads me to consider,

II. The manner in which this relation, of service, affects either the master or servant. And, first, by hiring and service for a year, or apprenticeship under indentures, a person gains a settlement in that parish wherein he last served forty days. In the next place, persons serving seven years as apprentices to any trade, have an exclusive right to exercise that trade in any part of England. No trades are held to be within the statute, but such as were in being at the making of it. For trading in a country village, apprenticeships are not requisite: and following the trade seven years without any effectual prosecution (either as a master or a servant) is sufficient without an actual apprenticeship.

A master may, by law, correct his apprentice for negligence or other misbehaviour, so it be done with moderation: though, if the master or master's wife beats any other servant of full age, it is good cause of departure. But if any servant, workman, or labourer assaults his master or dame, he shall suffer one year's imprisonment, and other open corporal punishment, not extending to life or limb.

By service all servants and labourers, except apprentices, become entitled to wages: according to their agreement, if menial servants; or according to the appointment of the sheriff or sessions, if labourers or servants in husbandry: for the statutes for regulation of wages extend to such servants only (a); it being impossible for any magistrate to be a judge of the employment of menial servants, or of course to assess their wages.

III. Let us, lastly, see how strangers may be affected by this relation of master and servant: or how a master may behave towards others on behalf of his servant; and what a servant may do on behalf of his master.

And, first, the master may *maintain*, that is, abet and assist his servant in any action at law against a stranger: whereas, in general, it is an offence against public justice to encourage suits and animosities, by helping to bear the expence of them, and is called in law maintenance. A master also may bring an action against any man for beating or maiming his servant: but in such case he must assign, as a special reason for so doing, his own damage by the loss of his service; and this loss must be proved upon the trial. A master likewise may justify an assault in defence of his ser-

---

(a) This is said on the authority of 2 *Jones*, 47. and, according to the words of the statutes, seems, in strictness, to be true; but the practice, I believe, has always been otherwise, justices of the peace interfering in disputes relative to servants of every description.

vant, and a servant in defence of his master. Also if any person do hire or retain my servant, being in my service, for which the servant departeth from me and goeth to serve the other, I may have an action for damages against both the new master and the servant, or either of them: but if the new master did not know that he is my servant, no action lies; unless he afterwards refuse to restore him upon information and demand. The reason and foundation, upon which all this doctrine is built, seem to be the property that every man has in the service of his domestics; acquired by the contract of hiring, and purchased by giving them wages.

As for those things which a servant may do on behalf of his master, they seem all to proceed upon this principle, that the master is answerable for the act of his servant, if done by his command, either expressly given, or implied: *nam qui facit per alium, facit per se*. Therefore, if the servant commit any trespass by the command or encouragement of his master, the master shall be guilty of it: though the servant is not thereby excused, for he is only to obey his master in matters that are honest and lawful. If an innkeeper's servants rob his guests, the master is bound to restitution: for as there is a confidence reposed in him, that he will take care to provide honest servants, his negligence is a kind of implied consent to the robbery (a); *nam, qui non prohibet, cum prohibere possit, jubet*. So likewise if the drawer at a tavern sells a man bad wine, whereby his health is injured, he may bring an action against the master: for although the master did not expressly order the servant to sell it to that person in particular, yet his permitting him to draw and sell it at all is, impliedly, a general command.

---

(a) And it is the same though the robbery be not committed by the *servant* of the innkeeper, (unless it be by some one belonging to the guest) for he is bound to take care of the goods committed to his charge. *Calye*'s Case, 8 *Co.* 32.

In the same manner, whatever a servant is permitted to do in the usual course of his business, is equivalent to a general command. If I pay money to a banker's servant, the banker is answerable for it: but if I pay it to a clergyman's or physician's servant, whose usual business it is not to receive money for his master, and he embezzles it, I must pay it over again. If a steward lets a lease of a farm, without the owner's knowledge, the owner must stand to the bargain; for this is the steward's business. A wife, a friend, a relation, that use to transact business for a man, are *quoad hoc* his servants; and the principal must answer for their conduct: for the law implies, that they act under a general command; and without such a doctrine as this no mutual intercourse between man and man could subsist with any tolerable convenience. If I usually deal with a tradesman by myself, or constantly pay him ready money, I am not answerable for what my servant takes up upon trust; for here is no implied order to the tradesman to trust my servant: but if I usually send him upon trust, or sometimes on trust and sometimes with ready money, I am answerable for all that he takes up; for the tradesman cannot possibly distinguish when he comes by my order, and when upon his own authority.

If a servant, lastly, by his negligence does any damage to a stranger, the master shall answer for his neglect: if a smith's servant lame a horse while he is shoeing him, an action lies against the master, and not against the servant. But in these cases the damage must be done, while he is actually employed in the master's service; otherwise the servant shall answer for his own misbehaviour. By statute 6 Ann. c. 3. however, no action shall be maintained against any, in whose house or chamber any fire shall accidentally begin; for their own loss is sufficient punishment for their own or their servant's carelessness. But if such fire happens through negligence of any servant (whose loss is commonly very little) such servant shall forfeit 100*l*. to be distributed among the sufferers; and, in default of payment, shall be committed to some workhouse and there kept to hard labour eighteen months. A master is, lastly, chargeable if any of his family layeth or casteth any thing out of his house into the street or common highway, to the damage of any individual, or the common nuisance of his majesty's liege people : for the master hath the superintendance and charge of all his houshold(a).

## CHAPTER VII.

### OF HUSBAND AND WIFE.

THE second private relation of persons is that of marriage, which includes the reciprocal rights and duties of husband and wife ; or, as most of our elder law books call them, of *baron* and *feme*. In the consideration of which I shall in the first place inquire, how marriages may be contracted or made ; shall next point out the manner in which they may be dissolved ; and shall, lastly, take a view of the legal effects and consequence of marriage.

I. Our law considers marriage in no other light than as a civil contract. And, taking it in this civil light, the law treats it as it does all other contracts : allowing it to be good and valid in all cases, where the parties at the time of making it were, in the first place, *willing* to contract; secondly,

---

*(a).* Numerous other cases and descriptions in addition to those noticed in the preceding pages, relative to the laws respecting masters and servants, may be found in a small (and we believe the only) treatise lately compiled on that subject, by the author of the *Parish Law*, and who, by collecting in a single volume of " *Law Selections*," some of the most useful and important heads of our law, will probably be considered by many as having done no inconsiderable service to the public.

*able* to contract; and, lastly, actually *did* contract, in the proper forms and solemnities required by law.

First, they must be *willing* to contract. "*Confenfus non concubitus, faciat nuptias,*" is the maxim of the civil law in this cafe: and it is adopted by the common lawyers, who indeed have borrowed (efpecially in antient times) almoft all their notions of the legitimacy of marriage from the canon and civil laws.

Secondly, they muft be *able* to contract. In general, all perfons are able to contract themfelves in marriage, unlefs they labour under fome particular difabilities, and incapacities. What thofe are, it will be here our bufinefs to inquire.

Now thefe difabilities are of two forts: firft, fuch as are canonical, and therefore fufficient by the ecclefiaftical laws to avoid the marriage in the fpiritual court; but thefe in our law only make the marriage voidable, and not *ipfo facto* void, until fentence of nullity be obtained. Of this nature are precontract; confanguinity, or relation by blood; and affinity, or relation by marriage; and fome particular corporal infirmities. But fuch marriages not being void *ab initio*, but voidable only by fentence of feparation, they are efteemed valid to all civil purpofes, unlefs fuch feparation is actually made during the life of the parties. For, after the death of either of them, the courts of common law will not fuffer the fpiritual court to declare fuch marriages to have been void; becaufe fuch declaration cannot now tend to the reformation of the parties. By ftatute 32 Hen. VIII. c. 38. it is declared, that all perfons may lawfully marry, but fuch as are prohibited by God's law; and that all marriages contracted by lawful perfons in the face of the church, and confummate with bodily knowledge, and fruit of children, fhall be indiffoluble. And it is declared by the fame ftatute, that nothing (God's law except) fhall impeach any marriage, but within the Levitical degrees; the fartheſt of which is that between uncle and niece.

The other ſort of diſabilities are thoſe which are created, or at leaſt enforced, by the municipal laws. Theſe civil diſabilities make the contract void *ab initio*, and not merely voidable. And, if any perſons under theſe legal incapacities come together, it is a meretricious, and not a matrimonial, union.

1. The firſt of theſe legal diſabilities is a prior marriage, or having another huſband or wife living: in which caſe, beſides the penalties conſequent upon it as a felony, the ſecond marriage is to all intents and purpoſes void.

2. The next legal diſability is want of age. Therefore if a boy under fourteen, or a girl under twelve years of age, marries, this marriage is only inchoate and imperfect; and, when either of them comes to the age of conſent aforeſaid, they may diſagree and declare the marriage void, without any divorce or ſentence in the ſpiritual court. But it is ſo far a marriage, that, if at the age of conſent they agree to continue together, they need not be married again. If the huſband be of years of diſcretion, and the wife under twelve, when ſhe comes to years of diſcretion he may diſagree as well as ſhe may; for in contracts the obligation muſt be mutual; both muſt be bound, or neither: and ſo it is, *vice verſa*, when the wife is of years of diſcretion, and the huſband under.(*a*)

---

(*a*) But an agreement of marriage, though after the ages of twelve in females, and fourteen in males, would not be binding, on parties under twenty-one, unleſs had agreeably to the requiſitions of 26 Geo. II. c. 33. (after mentioned). See *Co. Lit.* 79.<sup>b</sup> n. 44. and it is further to be obſerved, that the rule of reciprocity where one of the parties is of years of diſcretion, and the other not, applies only to *actual* marriages, and not to mere *contracts of marriage* as ſtated in the text. See ibid. n. 45.

3. Another incapacity arises from want of consent of parents or guardians. By several statutes, penalties of 100l. are laid on every clergyman who marries a couple either without publication of banns (which may give notice to parents or guardians) or without a licence(*a*), to obtain which the consent of parents or guardians must be sworn to. And by the statute 4 & 5 Ph. and M. c. 8. whosoever marries any woman child under the age of sixteen years, without consent of parents or guardians, shall be subject to fine, or five years imprisonment: and her estate during the husband's life (*b*) shall go to, and be enjoyed by, the next heir. And by statute 26 Geo. II. c. 33. it is enacted, that all marriages celebrated by licence (for banns suppose notice) where either of the parties is under twenty-one, (not being a widow or widower, who are supposed emancipated) without the consent of the father, or, if he be not living, of the mother or guardians, shall be absolutely void.

4. A fourth incapacity is want of reason; without a competent share of which, as no other, so neither can the matrimonial contract, be valid. And the statute 15 Geo. II. c. 30. has provided, that the marriage of lunatics and persons under phrenzies (if found lunatics under a commission, or committed to the care of trustees by any act of parliament) before they are declared of sound mind by the lord chancellor or the majority of such trustees, shall be totally void.

Lastly, the parties must not only be willing and able to contract, but actually must contract themselves in due form

---

(*a*) And by 26 Geo. II. c. 33. this offence is made felony, and punished by transportation for seven years.

(*b*) And it seems to have been admitted in *Stephens, v. Bateman*, 1 *Brow. Ch. Ca.* 22, (grounded on the authority of 3 *Co.* 39 and 3 *Inst.* 62.) that the estate is forfeitable, not only during the *husband's* life but during the *wife's* also.

of law, to make it a good civil marriage. Neither is any marriage at prefent valid, that is not celebrated in fome parifh church or public chapel, unlefs by difpenfation from the archbifhop of Canterbury. It muft alfo be preceded by publication of banns, or by licence from the fpiritual judge. Many other formalities are likewife prefcribed by the act; the neglect of which, though penal, does not invalidate the marriage. It is held to be alfo effential to a marriage, that it be performed by a perfon in orders. As the law now ftands, therefore, we may upon the whole collect, that no marriage by the temporal law is *ipfo facto void,* that is celebrated by a perfon in orders,—in a parifh church or public chapel (or elfewhere, by fpecial difpenfation)—in purfuance of banns or a licence,—between fingle perfons,—confenting,—of found mind,—and of the age of twenty-one years;—or of the age of fourteen in males and twelve in females, with confent of parents or guardians, or without it, in cafe of widowhood. And no marriage is *voidable* by the ecclefiaftical law, after the death of either of the parties; nor during their lives, unlefs for the canonical impediments of pre-contract, (if that indeed ftill exifts); of confanguinity; and of affinity, or corporal imbecillity, fubfifting previous to the marriage.

II. I am next to confider the manner in which marriages may be diffolved; and this is either by death, or divorce. There are two kinds of divorce, the one total, the other partial; the one *a vinculo matrimonii,* the other merely *a menfa et thoro.* The total divorce, *a vinculo matrimonii,* muft be for fome of the canonical caufes of impediment before-mentioned; and thofe exifting *before* the marriage, as is always the cafe in confanguinity; not fupervenient, or arifing *afterwards,* as may be the cafe in affinity or corporal imbecillity. For in cafes of total divorce, the marriage is declared null, as having been abfolutely unlawful *ab initio;* and the parties are therefore feparated *pro falute animarum:* for which reafon, as was before obferved, no divorce can be obtained, but during the life of the parties. The issue of such marriage as is thus entirely dissolved, are bastards.

Divorce *a mensa et thoro* is when the marriage is just and lawful *ab initio,* and therefore the law is tender of dissolving it; but, for some supervenient cause, it becomes improper or impossible for the parties to live together: as in the case of intolerable ill temper, or adultery, in either of the parties.

In case of divorce *a mensa et thoro,* the law allows alimony to the wife: which is that allowance, which is made to a woman for her support out of the husband's estate; being settled at the discretion of the ecclesiastical judge, on consideration of all the circumstances in the case. It is generally proportioned to the rank and quality of the parties. But in case of elopement, and living with an adulterer, the law allows her no alimony.

III. Having thus shewn how marriages may be made, or dissolved, I come now, lastly, to speak of the legal consequences of such making, or dissolution.

By marriage, the husband and wife are one person in law: that is, the very being or legal existence of the woman is suspended during the marriage, or at least is incorporated and consolidated into that of the husband. For this reason, a man cannot grant any thing to his wife, or enter into covenant with her: for the grant would be to suppose her separate existence; and to covenant with her, would be only to covenant with himself: and therefore it is also generally true, that all compacts made between husband and wife, when single, are voided by the intermarriage. A woman indeed may be attorney for her husband; for that implies no separation from, but is rather a representation of, her lord. And a husband may also bequeath any thing to his wife by will; for that cannot take effect till the coverture is determined by his death. The husband is bound to provide his wife with necessaries by law, as much as himself: and if she contracts debts for them, he is obliged to pay them(a); but, for any thing besides necessaries, he is not chargeable. Also if a wife elopes, and lives with another man, the husband is not chargeable even for necessaries; at least if the person who furnishes them, is sufficiently apprized of her elopement. If the wife be indebted before marriage, the husband is bound afterwards to pay the debt (b); for he has adopted her and her circumstances together. If the wife be injured in her person or her property, she can bring no action for redress without her husband's concurrence, and in his name as well as her own: neither can she be sued, without making the husband a defendant. There is indeed one case where the wife shall sue and be sued as a feme sole, *viz.* where the husband has abjured the realm, or is banished (c): for then he is dead in law; and, the husband being thus disabled to sue for or defend the wife, it would be most unreasonable if she had no remedy, or could make no defence at all. In criminal prosecutions, it is true, the wife may be indicted and punished separately; for the union is only a civil union. But, in trials of any sort, they are not allowed to be evidence for, or

---

(a) If however the wife has a *separate maintainance*, she is held by the late decisions, not to be liable even for necessaries. See *Corbet, v. Poelnitz,* 1 *Term Rep.* 5.

(b) This is to be understood with some restriction; and extends to those debts only which remain unpaid during the coverture, for if the wife die, or there be a divorce *a vinculo matrimonii,* the husband is no longer chargeable for debts contracted before the intermarriage. See *E. of Thomond, v. E. of Suffolk,* 1 P. *Wms.* 461. *Heard & Ux. v. Stamford,* 3 ibid. 409. *and Ca Temp. Talb.* 173.

(c) This is not the only case in which a married woman is permitted to sue or be sued as a feme sole; for " where a woman has a separate maintainance and acts and receives credit as a *feme sole,* she shall be liable as such." *P. Mansfield, Ch. Just. Corbett, v. Poelnitz,* 1 *Term. Rep.* 5. See also *Gilchrist, v. Brown,* 4 *ibid* 766. and *Compton, v. Collison,* 2 *Brow. Ch. Ca.* 377. and 1 *H. Black. Rep.* 334.

against, each other: partly because it is impossible their testimony should be indifferent; but principally because of the union of person. But, where the offence is directly against the person of the wife, this rule has been usually dispensed with: and therefore, by statute 3 Hen. VII. c. 2. in case a woman be forcibly taken away, and married, she may be a witness against such her husband, in order to convict him of felony: for in this case she can with no propriety be reckoned his wife; because a main ingredient, her consent, was wanting to the contract: and also there is another maxim of law, that no man shall take advantage of his own wrong; which the ravisher here would do, if by forcibly marrying a woman, he could prevent her from being a witness, who is perhaps the only witness, to that very fact.

In the *civil* law the husband and the wife are considered as two distinct persons; and may have separate estates, contracts, debts, and injuries: and therefore, in our ecclesiastical courts, a woman may sue and be sued without her husband *(a)*.

But, though our law in general considers man and wife as one person, yet there are some instances in which she is separately considered; as inferior to him, and acting by his compulsion. And therefore all deeds executed, and acts done, by her, during her coverture, are void; except it be a fine, or the like matter of record, in which case she must be solely and secretly examined, to learn if her act be voluntarily. She cannot by will devise lands to her husband, unless under special circumstances; for at the time of making it she is supposed to be under his coercion. And in some felonies, and other inferior crimes, committed by her, through constraint

---

(a) As she may also in our courts of *equity*, where as far as regards her separate estate she is considered in all respects as a *feme sole*. See *Oxenden, v. Oxenden*, 2 *Vern.* 493, *Dubois, v. Hole, ibid* 613. *Brooks, v. Brooks, Prec. Chan.* 24. *Newsombe, v. Bowyer*, 3 *P. Wms.* 37.

of her husband, the law excuses her: but this extends not to treason or murder.

The husband also (by the old law) might give his wife moderate correction. But, with us, in the politer reign of Charles the second, this power of correction began to be doubted: and a wife may now have security of the peace against her husband; or, in return, a husband against his wife. Yet the courts of law will still permit a husband to restrain a wife of her liberty, in case of any gross misbehaviour.

These are the chief legal effects of marriage during the coverture; upon which we may observe, that even the disabilities, which the wife lies under, are, for the most part, intended for her protection and benefit. So great a favourite is the female sex of the laws of England.

## CHAPTER VIII.

### OF PARENT AND CHILD.

THE next, and the most universal relation in nature, is immediately derived from the preceding, being that between parent and child.

Children are of two sorts; legitimate, and spurious, or bastards.

I. A legitimate child is he that is born in lawful wedlock, or within a competent time afterwards. Let us inquire into, 1. The legal duties of parents to their legitimate children. 2. Their power over them. 3. The duties of such children to their parents.

1. And, first, the duties of parents, to legitimate children: which principally consist in three particulars; their maintenance, their protection, and their education.

## C. VIII. PARENT AND CHILD. 81

The duty of parents to provide for the *maintenance* of their children, is a principle of natural law.

Let us fee what provifion our own laws have made for this natural duty. It is a principle of law, that there is an obligation on every man to provide for thofe defcended from his loins; and the manner, in which this obligation fhall be performed, is thus pointed out, by various ftatutes. The father, and mother, grandfather, and grandmother of poor impotent perfons fhall maintain them at their own charge, if of fufficient ability, according as the quarter feffion fhall direct: and if a parent runs away, and leaves his children, the churchwardens and overfeers of the parifh fhall feife his rents, goods, and chattels, and difpofe of them toward their relief. By the interpretations which the courts of law have made upon thefe ftatutes, if a mother or grandmother marries again, and was before fuch fecond marriage of fufficient ability to keep the child, the hufband fhall be charged to maintain it: for this being a debt of hers, when fingle, fhall, like others, extend to charge the hufband (*a*). But at her death, the relation being diffolved, the hufband is under no farther obligation.

No perfon is bound to provide a maintenance for his iffue, unlefs where the children are impotent and unable to work, either through infancy, difeafe, or accident; and then is only obliged to find them with neceffaries, the penalty on refufal being no more than 20*s*. a month.

Our law has made no provifion to prevent the difinheriting

---

(*a*) The ftatute upon which the conftruction is here given, is 43 Eliz. c. 2. but it has fince been determined, that this ftatute extends to relations by blood only, and not thofe by affinity; and that therefore (contrary to the pofition in the text) a man is not bound to maintain the children of his wife by a former hufband. See *Rex*, v. *Munden*, 1 *Stra.* 190. *Tubb.* v. *Harrifon*, 4 *Term Rep.* 118.

G

of children by will: leaving every man's property in his own disposal, upon a principle of liberty in this, as well as every other, action. Heirs, however, and children, are favourites of our courts of justice, and cannot be disinherited by any dubious or ambiguous words; there being required the utmost certainty of the testator's intentions to take away the right of an heir.

From the duty of maintenance we may easily pass to that of *protection*; which is also a natural duty, but rather permitted than enjoined by any municipal laws: nature, in this respect, working so strongly as to need rather a check than a spur. A parent may, by our laws, maintain and uphold his children in their law-suits, without being guilty of the legal crime of maintaining quarrels. A parent may also justify an assault and battery in defence of the persons of his children.

The last duty of parents to their children is that of giving them an *education* suitable to their station in life: a duty pointed out by reason, and of far the greatest importance of any.

2. The *power* of parents over their children is derived from the former consideration, their duty: this authority being given them, partly to enable the parent more effectually to perform his duty, and partly as a recompence for his care and trouble in the faithful discharge of it. He may lawfully correct his child, being under age, in a reasonable manner; for this is for the benefit of his education. The consent or concurrence of the parent to the marriage of his child under age, was also *directed* by our antient law to be obtained: but now it is absolutely *necessary*; for without it the contract is void. A father has no other power over his son's *estate*, than as his trustee or guardian; for, though he may receive the profits during the child's minority, yet he must account for them when he comes of age. He may indeed have the benefit of his children's labour while they live with him, and are maintained by him: but this is no more than he is entitled to from his apprentices or servants. The legal power of a father (for

a mother, as such, is entitled to no power, but only to reverence and respect) the power of a father, I say, over the persons of his children ceases at the age of twenty-one: for they are then enfranchised by arriving at years of discretion, or that point which the law has established (as some must necessarily be established) when the empire of the father, or other guardian, gives place to the empire of reason. Yet, till that age arrives, this empire of the father continues even after his death; for he may, by his will, appoint a guardian to his children. He may also delegate part of his parental authority, during his life, to the tutor or schoolmaster, of his child; who is then *in loco parentis*, and has such a portion of the power of the parent committed to his charge, *viz.* that of restraint and correction, as may be necessary to answer the purposes for which he is employed.

3. The *duties* of children to their parents arise from a principle of natural justice and retribution. For to those, who gave us existence, we naturally owe subjection and obedience during our minority, and honour and reverence ever after: they, who protected the weakness of our infancy, are entitled to our protection in the infirmity of their age; they who, by sustenance and education, have enabled their offspring to prosper, ought in return to be supported by that offspring, in case they stand in need of assistance. Upon this principle proceeds all the duties of children to their parents, which are enjoined by positive laws.

The law does not hold the tie of nature to be dissolved by any misbehaviour of the parent; and therefore a child is equally justifiable in defending the person, or maintaining the cause or suit, of a bad parent, as a good one; and is equally compellable, if of sufficient ability, to maintain and provide for a wicked and unnatural progenitor, as for one who has shewn the greatest tenderness and parental piety.

II. We are next to confider the cafe of illegitimate children, or baftards; with regard to whom let us inquire, 1. Who are baftards. 2. The legal duties of the parents towards a baftard child. 3. The rights and incapacities attending fuch baftard children.

1. Who are baftards. A baftard, by our Englifh laws, is one that is not only begotten, but born, out of lawful matrimony. The civil and canon laws do not allow a child to remain a baftard, if the parents afterwards intermarry (a): and herein they differ moft materially from our law ; which, though not fo ftrict as to require that the child fhall be *begotten*, yet makes it an indifpenfable condition, to make it legitimate, that it fhall be *born*, after lawful wedlock. All children, therefore, born before matrimony are baftards by our law: and fo it is of all children born fo long after the death of the hufband, that, by the ufual courfe of geftation, they could not be begotten by him. But, this being a matter of fome uncertainty, the law is not exact as to a few days. And this gives occafion to a proceeding at common law, where a widow is fufpected to feign herfelf with child, in order to produce a fuppofititious heir to the eftate. In this cafe the heir prefumptive may have a writ *de ventre infpiciendo*, to examine whether fhe be with child or not; and, if fhe be, to keep her under proper reftraint, till delivered: but, if the widow be, upon due examination, found not pregnant, the prefumptive heir fhall be admitted to the inheritance, though liable to lofe it again, on the birth

---

(a) But whether they are to be confidered as legitimate from the time of the marriage of their parents only, or whether their legitimacy has relation back to the time of their birth, is a point varioufly difputed by the civilians and canonifts ; the prevailing opinion feems to be, that they are to be confidered as legitimate from the time of their birth, to all purpofes, but thofe, in which to confider them as fuch, would operate to the detriment of a third perfon. *Co. Lit.* 245ᵃ n. (1).

of a child within forty weeks from the death of the hufband. But if a man dies, and his widow foon after marries again, and a child is born within fuch a time, as that by the courfe of nature it might have been the child of either hufband; in this cafe he is faid to be more than ordinarily legitimate; for he may, when he arrives to years of difcretion, choofe which of the fathers he pleafes. .

As baftards may be born before the coverture or marriage ftate is begun, or after it is determined, fo alfo children born during wedlock may, in fome circumftances, be baftards. As if the hufband be out of the kingdom of England, (or, as the law fomewhat loofely phrafes it, *extra quatuor maria*) for above nine months, fo that no accefs, to his wife can be prefumed, her iffue during that period fhall be baftards. But, generally, during the coverture, accefs of the hufband fhall be prefumed, unlefs the contrary can be fhewn (*a*); which is fuch a negative as can only be proved by fhewing him to be elfewhere: for the general rule is, *præfumitur pro legitimatione*. In a divorce, *a menfa et thoro*, if the wife breeds children, they are baftards; for the law will prefume the hufband and wife conformable to the fentence of feparation, unlefs accefs be proved: but, in a voluntaray feparation by agreement, the law will fuppofe accefs, unlefs the negative be fhewn. So alfo, if there be an apparent impoffibility of procreation, on the part of the hufband, as if he be only eight years old, or the like, then the iffue of the wife fhall

---

(*a*) Subfequent determinations have relaxed this rule, and it is now held to be unneceffary that proof fhould be adduced of the non-accefs of the hufband; the modern practice (if not the more ancient, fee 1 *Salk.* 123. *Stra.* 925. 3 *P. Wms.* 276.) being to leave it to the jury to decide under all the circumftances of the cafe, whether accefs may reafonably be prefumed to have been had or not. See the *King,* v. *Inhabitants* of *Lubbenham,* 4 *Term Rep.* 251. *Thompfon,* v. *Saul. Ibid,* 356.

be baftard. Likewife, in cafe of divorce in the fpiritual court *a vinculo matrimonii*, all the iffue born during the coverture are baftards; becaufe fuch divorce is always upon fome caufe, that rendered the marriage unlawful and null from the beginning.

2. Let us next fee the duty of parents to their baftard children, by our law; which is principally that of maintenance.

The method in which the Englifh law provides maintenance for them is as follows. When a woman is delivered, or declares herfelf with child, of a baftard, and will, by oath before a juftice of peace, charge any perfon as having got her with child, the juftice fhall caufe fuch perfon to be apprehended, and commit him till he gives fecurity, either to maintain the child, or appear at the next quarter feffions to difpute and try the fact. But if the woman dies, or is married before delivery, or mifcarries, or proves not to have been with child, the perfon fhall be difcharged: otherwife the feffions, or two juftices out of feffions, upon original application to them, may take order for the keeping of the baftard, by charging the mother or the reputed father with the payment of money or other fuftentation for that purpofe. And if fuch putative father, or lewd mother, run away from the parifh, the overfeers, by direction of two juftices, may feize their rents, goods, and chattels, in order to bring up the faid baftard child. Yet fuch is the humanity of our laws, that no woman can be compulfively queftioned concerning the father of her child, till one month after her delivery: which indulgence is however very frequently a hardfhip upon parifhes, by giving the parents opportunity to efcape.

3. I next proceed to the rights and incapacities which appertain to a baftard. The rights are very few, being only fuch as he can *acquire*; for he can *inherit* nothing, being looked upon as the fon of nobody, and fometimes called

*filius nullius*, sometimes *filius populi*. Yet he may gain a firname by reputation, though he has none by inheritance. All other children have their primary settlement in their father's parish; but a bastard in the parish where born, for he hath no father. However, in case of fraud, as if a woman be sent either by order of justices, or comes to beg as a vagrant, to a parish which she does not belong to, and drops her bastard there; the bastard shall, in the first case, be settled in the parish from whence she was illegally removed; or, in the latter case, in the mother's own parish, if the mother be apprehended for her vagrancy. Bastards also, born in any licensed hospital for pregnant women, are settled in the parishes to which the mothers belong. The incapacity of a bastard consists principally in this, that he cannot be heir to any one, neither can he have heirs, but of his own body; for, being *nullius filius*, he is therefore of kin to nobody, and has no ancestor from whom any inheritable blood can be derived. In all other respects, there is no distinction between a bastard and another man *(a)*. A bastard may, lastly, be made legitimate, and capable of inheriting, by the transcendant power of an act of parliament, and not otherwise: as was done in the case of John of Gaunt's bastard children, by a statute of Richard the Second.

## CHAPTER IX.

### OF GUARDIAN AND WARD.

THE only general private relation, now remaining to be discussed, is that of guardian and ward; which bears a very near resemblance to the last, and is plainly de-

---

*(a)* See more particulaly as to this, Book II. c. 12.

rived out of it; the guardian being only a temporary parent; that is, for so long time as the ward is an infant, or under age. In examining this species of relationship, I shall first consider the different kinds of guardians, how they are appointed, and their power and duty: next, the different ages of persons, as defined by the law: and, lastly, the privileges and disabilities of an infant, or one under age and subject to guardianship.

Of the several species of guardians, the first are guardians *by nature*: viz. the father and (in some cases) the mother of the child. For if an estate be left to an infant, the father is, by common law, the guardian, and must account to his child for the profits (*a*). And, with regard to daughters, it seems, by construction of the statute 4 and 5 Ph. and Mar. c. 8. that the father might, by deed or will, assign a guardian to any woman child under the age of sixteen: and, if none be so assigned, the mother shall in this case be guardian. There are also guardians *for nurture*; which are, of course, the father or mother, till the infant attains the age of fourteen years: and in default of father or mother, the ordinary usually assigns some discreet person to take care of the infant's personal estate, and to provide for his maintenance and education. Next are guardians *in socage*, who are also called guardians *by the common law*. These take place only when the minor is entitled to some estate in lands, and then, by

---

(*a*) A father being, by nature, guardian to his children, it was formerly customary for executors, &c. to pay into his hands, legacies bequeathed for their benefit; and such payments were allowed to be good, 1 *Chan. Ca.* 245. But cases having arisen, where children were defrauded of their legacies by the insolvency of their father, it was determined in the case of *Digley*, v. *Tolferry*, reported, 1 *P. Wms.* 285. and 1 *Eq. Ca. Abr.* 300. that such payments were bad, and ought to be discouraged, as tending to the wrong of infant children. See also *Cooper*, v. *Thornton*, 3 *Brow. Ch. Ca.* 96. and *Cunningham*, v. *Harris*, cited, *ibid* 186.

the common law, the guardianſhip devolves upon his next of kin, to whom the inheritance cannot poſſibly deſcend (a); as, where the eſtate deſcended from his father, in this caſe his uncle, by the mother's ſide, cannot poſſibly inherit this eſtate, and therefore ſhall be the guardian. For the law judges it improper to truſt the perſon of an infant in his hands, who may, by poſſibility, become heir to him; that there may be no temptation, nor even ſuſpicion of temptation for him to abuſe his truſt. Theſe guardians in ſocage, like thoſe for nurture, continue only till the minor is fourteen years of age; for then, in both caſes, he is preſumed to have diſcretion, ſo far as to chooſe his own guardian. This he may do, unleſs one be appointed by the father, by virtue of the ſtatute 12 Car. II. c. 24. which, conſidering the imbecillity of judgment in children of the age of fourteen, and the abolition of guardianſhip *in chivalry* (which laſted till the age of twenty-one, and of which we ſhall ſpeak hereafter) enacts, that any father, under age or of full age, may, by deed or will, diſpoſe of the cuſtody of his child, either born or unborn, to any perſon, except a popiſh recuſant, either in poſſeſſion or reverſion, till ſuch child attains the age of one and twenty years. Theſe are called guardians *by ſtatute*, or *teſtamentary* guardians. There are alſo ſpecial guardians *by cuſtom* of London, and other places (b); but they are particular exceptions, and do not fall under the general law.

The power and reciprocal duty of a guardian and ward are the ſame, *pro tempore*, as that of a father and child; and therefore I ſhall not repeat them: but ſhall only add, that

---

(a) See obſervations on this rule of the common law, by *Macclesfield*, Ch. who, in *Dormer's* caſe, 2 *P.Wms.* 262. thought it " not grounded upon reaſon, but prevailed in barbarous times, before the nation was civilized."

(b) See theſe, as well as the other ſpecies of guardians, particularly noticed by Mr. *Hargrave, Co. Lit.* 88ᵇ and 89ᵃ. *notis.*

the guardian, when the ward comes of age, is bound to give him an account of all that he has transacted on his behalf, and must answer for all losses by his wilful default or negligence. In order, therefore, to prevent disagreeable contests with young gentlemen, it has become a practice for many guardians, of large estates especially, to indemnify themselves by applying to the court of chancery, acting under it's direction, and accounting annually before the officers of that court. For the lord chancellor is, by right derived from the crown, the general and supreme guardian of all infants, as well as idiots and lunatics; that is, of all such persons as have not discretion enough to manage their own concerns. In case therefore any guardian abuses his trust, the court will check and punish him; nay, sometimes will proceed to the removal of him, and appoint another in his stead.

2. Let us next consider the ward or person within age, for whose assistance and support these guardians are constituted by law; or who it is that is said to be within age. The ages of male and female are different for different purposes. A male at *twelve* years old may take the oath of allegiance; at *fourteen* is at years of discretion, and therefore may consent or disagree to marriage, may choose his guardian, and, if his discretion be actually proved, may make his testament of his personal estate; at *seventeen* may be an executor; and at *twenty-one* is at his own disposal, and may aliene his lands, goods, and chattels. A female also at *seven* years of age may be betrothed or given in marriage; at *nine* is entitled to dower; at *twelve* is at years of maturity, and therefore may consent or disagree to marriage, and, if proved to have sufficient discretion, may bequeath her personal estate; at *fourteen* is at years of legal discretion, and may choose a guardian; at *seventeen* may be executrix; and at *twenty-one* may dispose of herself and her lands. So that full age in male or female is twenty-one years, which age is completed on the day preceding the anniversary of a person's

birth; who till that time is an infant, and so stiled in law.

3. Infants have various privileges, and various disabilities: but their very disabilities are privileges; in order to secure them from hurting themselves by their own improvident acts. An infant cannot be sued but under the protection, and joining the name, of his guardian; for he is to defend him against all attacks as well by law as otherwise: but he may sue either by his guardian, or *prochein amy*, his next friend who is not his guardian (*a*). This *prochein amy* may be any person who will undertake the infant's cause; and it frequently happens, that an infant, by his *prochein amy*, institutes a suit in equity against a fraudulent guardian. In criminal cases, an infant of the age of *fourteen* years may be capitally punished for any capital offence: but under the age of *seven* he cannot. The period between *seven* and *fourteen* is subject to much uncertainty: for the infant shall, generally speaking, be judged *prima facie* innocent; yet if he was *doli capax*, and could discern between good and evil at the time of the offence committed, he may be convicted, and undergo judgment and execution of death, though he hath not attained to years of puberty or discretion.

With regard to estates and civil property, an infant hath many privileges, which will be better understood when we come to treat more particularly of those matters: but this may be said in general, that an infant shall lose nothing by non-claim, or neglect of demanding his right; nor shall any other *laches* or negligence be imputed to an infant, except in some very particular cases.

It is generally true, that an infant can neither aliene his lands, nor do any legal act, nor make a deed, nor indeed any manner of contract, that will bind him. But still to all

---

(*a*) This more particularly applies to the courts of common law. In courts of equity the practice is for infants to sue by *prochein amy*, and defend by guardian.

these rules there are some exceptions: part of which were just now mentioned in reckoning up the different capacities which they assume at different ages: and there are others, a few of which it may not be improper to recite, as a general specimen of the whole. And, first, it is true, that infants cannot aliene their estates: but infant trustees, or mortgagees, are enabled to convey, under the direction of the court of chancery or exchequer, or other court of equity, the estates they hold in trust or mortgage, to such person as the court shall appoint. Also it is generally true, that an infant can do no legal act: yet, an infant, who has an advowson, may present to the benefice when it becomes void (*a*). For the law, in this case, dispenses with one rule, in order to maintain others of far greater consequence: it permits an infant to present a clerk (who, if unfit, may be rejected by the bishop) rather than either suffer the church to be unserved till he comes of age, or permit the infant to be debarred of his right by lapse to the bishop. An infant may also purchase lands, but his purchase is incomplete: for, when he comes to age, he may either agree or disagree to it, as he thinks prudent or proper, without alledging any reason; and so may his heirs after him, if he dies without having completed his agreement. It is farther, generally true, that an infant, under twenty-one, can make no deed but what is afterwards voidable (*b*): yet, in some cases, he may bind

---

(*a*) Mr. *Hargrave* observes upon this, that though the *legal* right of an infant to present, is rendered indisputable by the case of *Arlington* and *Coverly*, 2 *Eq. Ca. Abr.* 520. it still remains to be seen, whether the want of discretion would induce a court of *equity* to controul the exercise, where a presentation is obtained from an infant without the concurrence of his guardian. See *Co. Lit.* 89 ª n. (1).

(*b*) The distinction taken by *Perkins*, (sec. 12.) as to the validity of deeds by infants, is, that those which do not take effect by delivery of his hand are absolutely *void*; and those which do are only *voidable*: and this distinction was recog-

himself apprentice by deed indented or indentures, for seven years; and he may, by deed or will, appoint a guardian to his children, if he has any. Lastly, it is generally true, that an infant can make no other contract that will bind him: yet he may bind himself to pay for his necessary meat, drink, apparel, physic, and such other necessaries; and likewise for his good teaching and instruction, whereby he may profit himself afterwards. And thus much, at present, for the privileges and disabilities of infants *(a)*.

---

## CHAPTER X.

### OF CORPORATIONS.

WE have hitherto considered persons in their natural capacities, and have treated of their rights and duties. But, as all personal rights die with the person; and, as the necessary forms of investing a series of individuals, one after another, with the same identical rights, would be very inconvenient, if not impracticable; it has been found necessary, when it is for the advantage of the public to have any particular rights kept on foot and continued, to constitute artificial persons, who may maintain a perpetual succession, and enjoy a kind of legal immortality. These artificial persons are called bodies politic, bodies corporate, *(corpora corporata)* or corporations.

Before we proceed to treat of the several incidents of corporations, as regarded by the laws of England, let us first

---

nized by the court of king's bench, in *Zouch,* v. *Parsons,* 4 *Bar.* 1806.

*(a)* See farther as to the privileges and disabilities of infants, *post.* Book II. Chap. XV. and *Co. Lit.* 8vo. *Ed. Index notis,* "Infant."

take a view of the feveral forts of them; and then we fhall be better enabled to apprehend their refpective qualities.

The firft divifion of corporation is into *aggregate* and *fole*. Corporations aggregate confift of many perfons united together into one fociety, and are kept up by a perpetual fucceffion of members, fo as to continue for ever: of which kind are the mayor and commonalty of a city, the head and fellows of a college, the dean and chapter of a cathedral church. Corporations fole confift of one perfon only and his fucceffors, in fome particular ftation, who are incorporated by law, in order to give them fome legal capacities and advantages, particularly that of perpetuity, which in their natural perfons they could not have had. In this fenfe the king is a fole corporation: fo is a bifhop: fo are fome deans, and prebendaries, diftinct from their feveral chapters: and fo is every parfon and vicar.

Another divifion of corporations, either fole or aggregate, is into *ecclefiaftical* and *lay*. Ecclefiaftical corporations are where the members that compofe it are entirely fpiritual perfons; fuch as bifhops; certain deans, and prebendaries; all archdeacons, parfons, and vicars; which are fole corporations: deans and chapters, and the like bodies aggregate. Lay corporations are of two forts, *civil* and *eleemofynary*. The civil are fuch as are erected for a variety of temporal purpofes. The king, for inftance, is made a corporation to prevent in general the poffibility of an *interregnum* or vacancy of the throne, and to preferve the poffeffions of the crown entire. Other lay corporations are erected for the good government of a town or particular diftrict, as a mayor and commonalty, bailiff and burgeffes, or the like. The eleemofynary fort are fuch as are conftituted for the perpetual diftribution of the free alms, or bounty, of the founder of them to fuch perfons as he has directed. Of this kind are all hofpitals for the maintenance of the poor, fick, and impotent: and all colleges, both *in* our univerfities and *out* of them *(a)*. And all these eleemosynary corporations are, strictly speaking, lay and not ecclesiastical, even though composed of ecclesiastical persons, and although they, in some things, partake of the nature, privileges, and restrictions of ecclesiastical bodies.

Having thus marshalled the several species of corporations, let us next proceed to consider, 1. How corporations, in general, may be created. 2. What are their powers, capacities, and incapacities. 3. How corporations are visited. And 4. How they may be dissolved.

I. The king's consent is absolutely necessary to the erection of any corporation, either impliedly or expresly given. The king's implied consent is to be found in corporations which exist by force of the *common law*, to which our former kings are supposed to have given their concurrence. Another method of implication, whereby the king's consent is presumed, is as to all corporations by *prescription*, such as the city of London, and many others, which have existed as corporations, time whereof the memory of man runneth not to the contrary; and therefore are looked upon in law to be well created. The methods, by which the king's consent is expresly given, are either by act of parliament or charter. By act of parliament, of which the royal assent is a necessary ingredient, corporations may undoubtedly be created. All the other methods, whereby corporations exist, by common law, by prescription, and by act of parliament, are for the most part reducible to this of the king's letters patent, or charter of incorporation.

When a corporation is erected, a name must be given to it; and by that name alone it must sue, and be sued, and do all legal acts.

II. After a corporation is so formed and named, it ac-

---

*(a)* Such as at Manchester, Eton, Winchester, &c. A.

quires many powers, rights, capacities, and incapacities, which we are next to confider. Some of thefe are neceffarily and infeparably incident to every corporation; which incidents, as foon as a corporation is duly erected, are tacitly annexed of courfe. As, 1. To have perpetual fucceffion. This is the very end of it's incorporation: for there cannot be a fucceffion for ever without an incorporation; and therefore all aggregate corporations have a power neceffarily implied of electing members in the room of fuch as go off. 2. To fue or be fued, implead or be impleaded, grant or receive, by it's corporate name, and do all other acts as natural perfons may. 3. To purchafe lands, and hold them, for the benefit of themfelves and their fucceffors: which two are confequential to the former. 4. To have a common feal. For a corporation, being an invifible body, cannot manifeft it's intentions by any perfonal act or oral difcourfe: it therefore acts and fpeaks only by it's common feal. 5. To make bye-laws or private ftatutes for the better government of the corporation; which are binding upon themfelves, unlefs contrary to the laws of the land, and then they are void. This is alfo included by law in the very act of incorporation: for, as natural reafon is given to the natural body for the governing it, fo bye-laws or ftatutes are a fort of political reafon to govern the body politic.

There are alfo certain privileges and difabilities that attend an aggregate corporation, and are not applicable to fuch as are fole; the reafon of them ceafing, and of courfe the law. It muft always appear by attorney; for it cannot appear in perfon, being, as fir Edward Coke fays, invifible, and exifting only in intendment and confideration of law. It cannot be executor or adminiftrator, or perform any perfonal duties; for it cannot take an oath for the due execution of the office. It cannot be feifed of lands to the ufe of another; for fuch kind of confidence is foreign to the end of it's inftitution: and it cannot be outlawed; for outlawry always fuppofes a precedent right of arrefting, which has been defeated by the parties abfconding: for which reafons the proceedings to compel a corporation to appear to any fuit by attorney are always by diftrefs on their lands and goods. Neither can a corporation be excommunicated; for it has no foul, as is gravely obferved by Sir Edward Coke: and therefore alfo it is not liable to be fummoned into the ecclefiaftical courts upon any account; for thofe courts act only *pro falute animæ*.

There are alfo other incidents and powers, which belong to fome fort of corporations, and not to others. An aggregate corporation may take goods and chattels for the benefit of themfelves and their fucceffors, but a fole corporation cannot *(a)*: for fuch moveable property is liable to be loft or embezzled, and would raife a multitude of difputes between the fucceffor and executor; which the law is careful to avoid. In ecclefiaftical and eleemofynary foundations, the king or the founder may give them rules, laws, ftatutes, and ordinances, which they are bound to obferve: but corporations merely lay, conftituted for civil purpofes, are fubject to no particular ftatutes; but to the common law, and to their own bye-laws, not contrary to the laws of the realm. Aggregate corporations alfo, that have by their conftitution a head, as a dean, warden, mafter, or the like, cannot do any acts during the vacancy of the headfhip, except only appointing another: neither are they then capable of receiving a grant; for fuch corporation is incomplete without a head. But there may be a corporation aggregate conftituted without

---

*(a)* Unlefs by fpecial cuftom, as, for inftance, in *London*, where the chamberlain though a fole corporation may take bonds, &c. concerning orphanage, which will defcend to his fucceffor. See *Furwood's Cafe*, 4 *Co.* 64. [b] and in fome inftances, particularly of chattels in action, the law is the fame, without a cuftom. *Co. Lit.* 9. [a] n. (1) (referring to 1 *Roll. Abr.* 575 *pl.* 3. 5.) and fee *ibid* 190. [a] n. (2).

a head: as the governors of the Charter-houſe, London, who have no preſident or ſuperior, but are all of equal authority. In aggregate corporations alſo, the act of the major part is eſteemed the act of the whole.

We before obſerved, that it was incident to every corporation, to have a capacity to purchaſe lands for themſelves and ſucceſſors: and this is regularly true at the common law. But they are excepted out of the ſtatute of wills: ſo that no deviſe of lands to a corporation by will is good: except for charitable uſes, by ſtatute 43 Eliz. c. 4. which exception is again greatly narrowed by the ſtatute 9 Geo. II. c. 36. And alſo, by a great variety of ſtatutes, their privilege even of purchaſing from any living grantor is much abridged: ſo that now a corporation, either eccleſiaſtical or lay, muſt have a licence from the king to purchaſe, before they can exert that capacity which is veſted in them by the common law: nor is even this in all caſes ſufficient.

The general *duties* of all bodies politic, conſidered in their corporate capacity, may, like thoſe of natural perſons, be reduced to this ſingle one; that of acting up to the end or deſign, whatever it be, for which they were created by their founder.

III. I proceed, therefore, next to inquire, how thoſe corporations may be *viſited*. With regard to all eccleſiaſtical corporations, the ordinary is their viſitor, ſo conſtituted by the canon law, and from thence derived to us. The king, as ſupreme ordinary, is the viſitor of the archbiſhop or metropolitan; the metropolitan has the charge and coercion of all his ſuffragan biſhops; and the biſhops in their ſeveral dioceſes are, in eccleſiaſtical matters, the viſitors of all deans and chapters, of all parſons and vicars, and of all other ſpiritual corporations. With reſpect to lay corporations, the founder, his heirs, or aſſigns, are the viſitors, whether the foundation be civil or eleemoſynary; for in a lay incorporation the ordinary neither can nor ought to viſit. In general, the king being the sole founder of all civil corporations, and the endower the perficient founder of all eleemosynary ones, the right of visitation of the former results, according to the rule laid down, to the king; and of the latter to the patron or endower.

The king being constituted by law visitor of all civil corporations, the law has also appointed the place, wherein he shall exercise this jurisdiction: which is the court of king's bench; where, and where only, all misbehaviours of this kind of corporations are inquired into and redressed, and all their controversies decided. And this is what I understand to be the meaning of our lawyers, when they say that these civil corporations are liable to no visitation; that is, that the law having, by immemorial usage, appointed them to be visited and inspected by the king their founder, in his majesty's court of king's bench, according to the rules of the common law, they ought not to be visited elsewhere, or by any other authority (*a*).

As to eleemosynary corporations, by the dotation the founder and his heirs are of common right the legal visitors, to see that such property is rightly employed, as might otherwise have descended to the visitor himself: but, if the founder has appointed and assigned any other person to be visitor, then his assignee, so appointed, is invested with all the founder's power, in exclusion of his heir. Eleemosynary corporations are chiefly hospitals, or colleges in the universities. And, with regard to hospitals, if the hospitals be spiritual,

---

(*a*) This notion is, perhaps, too refined. The court of king's bench (it may be said) from it's general superintendent authority, where other jurisdictions are deficient, has power to regulate all corporations where no special visitor is appointed. But not in the light of visitor: for, as it's judgments are liable to be reversed by writs of error, it may be thought to want one of the essential marks of visitatorial power. A.

the bishop shall visit; but if lay, the patron. And all the hospitals founded by virtue of the statute 39 Eliz. c. 5.' are to be visited by such persons as shall be nominated by the respective founders. But still, if the founder appoints nobody, the bishop of the diocese must visit.

IV. We come now, in the last place, to consider how corporations may be dissolved. Any particular member may be disfranchised, or lose his place in the corporation, by acting contrary to the laws of the society, or the laws of the land: or he may resign it by his own voluntary act. But the body politic may also itself be dissolved in several ways; which dissolution is the civil death of the corporation: and in this case their lands and tenements shall revert to the person, or his heirs, who granted them to the corporation: for the law doth annex a condition to every such grant, that if the corporation be dissolved, the grantor shall have the lands again, because the cause of the grant faileth (*a*). The debts of a corporation, either to or from it, are totally extinguished by it's dissolution; so that the members thereof cannot recover or be charged with them, in their natural capacities: agreeable to that maxim of the civil law, "*si quid univer-* "*sitati debetur, singulis non debetur*; *nec, quod debet universitas,* "*singuli debent.*"

A corporation may be dissolved, 1. By act of parliament, which is boundless in it's operations. 2. By the natural death of all it's members, in case of an aggregate corporation. 3. By surrender of it's franchises into the hands of the king, which is a kind of suicide. 4. By forfeiture of

---

(*a*) Thus *Coke*, " If land be given, in fee-simple, to a dean and chapter, or to a mayor and commonalty, and to their successors, and after such body politic, or incorporate, is dissolved, the donor shall have again the land, and *not the lord by escheat.*" *Co. Lit.* 13. ᵇ but see *ibid*, note (2) 8vo. *Ed.* where authorities are referred to, in which the contrary opinion was held; namely, that the *land shall escheat.*

it's charter, through negligence or abufe of it's franchifes; in which cafe the law judges that the body politic has broken the condition upon which it was incorporated, and thereupon the incorporation is void. And the regular courfe is to bring an information in nature of a writ of *quo warranto*, to inquire by what warrant the members now exercife their corporate power, having forfeited it by fuch and fuch proceedings (a).

---

(a) Such of our readers as are inclined to purfue the fubject of corporations to a greater extent, will find ample gratification from Mr. *Kyd*'s excellent ".*Treatife on the Law of Corporations*," where this peculiar branch of learning is ably inveftigated.

THE END OF THE FIRST BOOK.

# BOOK THE SECOND.

## OF THE RIGHTS OF THINGS.

### CHAPTER I.

#### OF REAL PROPERTY.

#### AND FIRST

#### OF CORPOREAL HEREDITAMENTS.

THE former book of these commentaries having treated at large of the *jura personarum*, or such rights and duties as are annexed to the persons of men, the objects of our inquiry in this second book will be the *jura rerum*, or, those rights which a man may acquire in and to such external things as are unconnected with his person.

The objects of dominion or property, are *things*, as contradistinguished from *persons*: and things are by the law of England distributed into two kinds; things *real*, and things *personal*. Things real are such as are permanent, fixed, and immoveable, which cannot be carried out of their place; as lands and tenements: things personal are goods, money, and all other moveables; which may attend the owner's person wherever he thinks proper to go.

In treating of things real, let us consider, first, their several sorts or kinds; secondly, the tenures by which they may be holden; thirdly, the estates which may be had in them; and, fourthly, the title to them, and the manner of acquiring and losing it.

First, with regard to their several sorts or kinds, things real are usually said to consist in lands, tenements, or hereditaments. *Land* comprehends all things of a permanent, substantial nature; being a word of a very extensive signification, as will presently appear more at large. *Tenement* is a word of still greater extent, and though in it's vulgar acceptation is only applied to houses and other buildings, yet in it's original, proper, and legal sense, it signifies every thing that may be *holden*, provided it be of a permanent nature; whether it be of a substantial and sensible, or of an unsubstantial ideal kind. Thus *liberum tenementum*, franktenement, or freehold, is applicable not only to lands and other solid objects, but also to offices, rents, commons, and the like: and, as lands and houses are tenements, so is an advowson a tenement; and a franchise, an office, a right of common, a peerage, or other property of the like unsubstantial kind, are, all of them, legally speaking, tenements. But an *hereditament*, says Sir Edward Coke, is by much the largest and most comprehensive expression: for it includes not only lands and tenements, but whatsoever may be *inherited*, be it corporeal, or incorporeal, real, personal, or mixed. Thus an heir loom, or implement of furniture which by custom descends to the heir together with an house, is neither land, nor tenement, but a mere moveable; yet, being inheritable, is comprized under the general word hereditament: and so a condition, the benefit of which may descend to a man from his ancestor, is also an hereditament.

Hereditaments then, to use the largest expression, are of two kinds, corporeal, and incorporeal. Corporeal consist of such as affect the senses; such as may be seen and handled by the body: incorporeal are not the object of sensation, can neither be seen nor handled, are creatures of the mind, and exist only in contemplation.

Corporeal hereditaments consist wholly of substantial and permanent objects; all which may be comprehended under the general denomination of land only. For *land*, says Sir Edward Coke, comprehendeth, in it's legal signification, any ground, soil, or earth whatsoever; as arable, meadows, pastures, woods, moors, waters, marshes, furzes, and heath. It legally includeth also all castles, houses, and other buildings: for they consist, saith he, of two things; *land*, which is the foundation, and *structure* thereupon: so that, if I convey the land or ground, the structure or building passeth therewith. It is observable that *water* is here mentioned as a species of land, which may seem a kind of solecism; but such is the language of the law: and therefore I cannot bring an action to recover possession of a pool or other piece of water, by the name of *water* only; either by calculating it's capacity, as, for so many cubical yards; or, by superficial measure, for twenty acres of water; or by general description, as for a pond, a watercourse, or a rivulet: but I must bring my action for the land that lies at the bottom, and must call it twenty acres of *land covered with water*. For water is a moveable wandering thing, and must of necessity continue common by the law of nature; so that I can only have a temporary, transient, usufructuary property therein: wherefore, if a body of water runs out of my pond into another man's, I have no right to reclaim it. But the land, which that water covers, is permanent, fixed, and immoveable: and therefore in this I may have a certain, substantial property; of which the law will take notice, and not of the other.

Land hath also, in it's legal signification, an indefinite

extent, upwards as well as downwards. *Cujus eſt ſolum, ejus eſt uſque ad cœlum*, is the maxim of the law, upwards; therefore no man may erect any building, or the like, to overhang another's land: and, downwards, whatever is in a direct line between the ſurface of any land and the center of the earth, belongs to the owner of the ſurface: as is every day's experience in the mining countries. So that the word " land " includes not only the face of the earth, but every thing under it, or over it. And therefore, if a man grants all his lands, he grants thereby all his mines of metal and other foſſils, his woods, his waters and his houſes, as well as his fields and meadows. Not but the particular names of the things are equally ſufficient to paſs them, except in the inſtance of water; by a grant of which, nothing paſſes but a right of fiſhing: but the capital diſtinction is this; that by the name of a caſtle, meſſuage, toft, croft, or the like, nothing elſe will paſs, except what falls with the utmoſt propriety under the term made uſe of *(a)*; but by the name of land, which is *nomen generaliſſimum*, every thing terreſtrial will paſs.

## CHAPTER II.

### OF INCORPOREAL HEREDITAMENTS.

AN incorporeal hereditament is a right iſſuing out of a thing corporate (whether real or perſonal) or concerning, or annexed to, or exerciſible within, the ſame. It is

---

(*a*) But, according to my *Lord Coke*, " By the name of a caſtle, one or more *manors* may be conveyed: *et è converſo*, by the name of a manor, &c. a caſtle may paſs." *Co. Lit.* 5*.

not the thing corporate itself, which may confift in lands, houfes, jewels, or the like; but fomething collateral thereto, as a rent iffuing out of thofe lands or houfes, or an office relating to thofe jewels. In fhort, as the logicians fpeak, corporeal hereditaments are the fubftance, which may be always feen, always handled: incorporeal hereditaments are but a fort of accidents, which inhere in and are fupported by that fubftance; and may belong, or not belong to it, without any vifible alteration therein. Their exiftence is merely in idea and abftracted contemplation; though their effects and profits may be frequently objects of our bodily fenfes. And, indeed, if we would fix a clear notion of an incorporeal hereditament, we muft be careful not to confound together the profits produced, and the thing, or hereditament, which produces them. An annuity, for inftance, is an incorporeal hereditament: for though the money, which is the fruit or product of this annuity, is, doubtlefs, of a corporeal nature, yet the annuity itfelf, which produces that money, is a thing invifible, has only a mental exiftence, and cannot be delivered over from hand to hand.

Incorporeal hereditaments are principally of ten forts; advowfons, tithes, commons, ways, offices, dignities, franchifes, corodies or penfions, annuities, and rents.

I. Advowfon is the right of prefentation to a church, or ecclefiaftical benefice. Advowfons are either advowfons *appendant*, or advowfons *in grofs*. Lords of manors being originally the only founders, and of courfe the only patrons, of churches, the right of patronage or prefentation, fo long as it continues annexed to the poffeffion of the manor, as fome have done from the foundation of the church to this day, is called an advowfon appendant: and it will pafs, or be conveyed, together with the manor, as incident and appendant thereto, by a grant of the manor only, without adding any other words. But where the property of the advowfon has been once feparated from the property of the manor, by legal conveyance, it is called an advowfon in grofs, or at large, and never can be appendant any more; but is, for the future, annexed to the perfon of it's owner, and not to his manor or lands.

Advowfons are alfo either *prefentative, collative,* or *donative.* An advowfon prefentative is where the patron hath a right of prefentation to the bifhop or ordinary, and moreover to demand of him to inftitute his clerk, if he finds him canonically qualified: and this is the moft ufual advowfon. An advowfon collative is where the bifhop and patron are one and the fame perfon: in which cafe the bifhop cannot prefent to himfelf; but he does, by the one act of collation, or conferring the benefice, the whole that is done in common cafes by both prefentation and inftitution. An advowfon donative is when the king, or any fubject by his licence, doth found a church or chapel, and ordains that it fhall be merely in the gift or difpofal of the patron; fubject to his vifitation only, and not to that of the ordinary; and vefted abfolutely in the clerk by the patron's deed of donation, without prefentation, inftitution, or induction.

And if, as the law now ftands, the true patron *once* waives this privilege of donation, and prefents to the bifhop, and his clerk is admitted and inftituted, the advowfon is become for ever prefentative, and fhall never be donative any more (a). For thefe exceptions to general rules, and common right, are ever looked upon by the law in an unfavourable view, and conftrued as ftrictly as poffible.

---

(a) Thefe are the words of *Lord Coke, (Com. Lit.* 344 *)* grounded on the authority *Furechild,* v. *Gayre, Cro. Jac.* 63. but, in a later cafe, *Ladd,* v. *Widdows,* 1 *Salk.* 541. it was held by *Holt,* C. J. and *Powell,* J. that "though a prefentation might deftroy an *impropriation*, yet it could not deftroy a *donative*; becaufe the creation thereof was by letters patent, whereby land is fettled to the parfon and his fucceffors, and he to come in by donation."

II. A second species of incorporeal hereditaments is that of tithes; which are defined to be the tenth part of the increase, yearly arising and renewing from the profits of lands, the stock upon lands, and the personal industry of the inhabitants: the first species being usually called *predial*, as of corn, grass, hops, and wood; the second *mixed*, as of wool, milk, pigs, &c. consisting of natural products, but nurtured and preserved in part by the care of man; and of these the tenth must be paid in gross; the third *personal*, as of manual occupations, trades, fisheries, and the like; and of these only the tenth part of the clear gains and profits is due (*a*).

It is not to be expected from the nature of these general commentaries, that I should particularly specify, what things are titheable, and what not. I shall only observe, that, in general, tithes are to be paid for every thing that yields an annual increase, as corn, hay, fruit, cattle, poultry, and the like; but not for any thing that is of the substance of the earth, or is not of annual increase, as stone, lime, chalk, and the like; nor for creatures that are of a wild nature, or *feræ naturæ*, as deer, hawks, &c. whose increase, so as to profit the owner, is not annual, but casual.

Upon the first introduction of tithes, though every man was obliged to pay tithes in general, yet he might give them to what priests he pleased: which were called *arbitrary* consecrations of tithes: or he might pay them into the hands of the bishop, who distributed among his diocesan clergy the revenues of the church, which were then in common. But, when dioceses were divided into parishes, the tithes of each parish were allotted to it's own particular minister; first, by

---

(*a*) Personal tithes are not due of common right, as those of the predial and mixed kind are, but only by special custom. See *Dodson,* v. *Oliver, Bunb.* 73. *Carleton,* v. *Brightwell.* 2 *P. Wms.* 462.

common confent, or the appointments of lords of manors, and afterwards by the written law of the land. And it is now univerfally held, that tithes are due, of common right, to the parfon of the parifh, unlefs there be a fpecial exemption. This parfon of the parifh, we have formerly feen (a), may be either the actual incumbent, or elfe the appropriator of the benefice: appropriations being a method of endowing monafteries, which feems to have been devifed by the regular clergy, by way of fubftitution to arbitrary confecrations of tithes.

We have obferved, that tithes are due to the parfon, of common right, unlefs by fpecial exemption; let us therefore fee, who may be exempted from the payment of tithes, and how lands, and their occupiers, may be exempted or difcharged from the payment of tithes, either in part or totally, firft, by a real *compofition*; or, fecondly, by *cuftom* or *prefcription*.

1. A real compofition is when an agreement is made between the owner of the lands, and the parfon or vicar, with the confent of the ordinary and the patron, that fuch lands fhall, for the future, be difcharged from payment of tithes, by reafon of fome land or other real recompenfe given to the parfon, in lieu and fatisfaction thereof: and hence have arifen all fuch compofitions as exift at this day by force of the common law. But, the poffeffions of the church being, by this and other means, every day diminifhed, the difabling ftatute 13 Eliz. c. 10. was made: which prevents, among other fpiritual perfons, all parfons and vicars from making any conveyances of the eftates of their churches, other than for three lives or twenty-one years. So that now, by virtue of this ftatute, no real compofition made fince the 13 Eliz. is good for any longer term than three lives, or twenty-one

---

(a) *Ante*, p. 57.

years, though made by consent of the patron and ordinary: which has indeed effectually demolished this kind of traffic; such compositions being now rarely heard of, unless by authority of parliament.

2. A discharge by custom or prescription, is where time out of mind such persons or such lands have been, either partially or totally, discharged from the payment of tithes. And this immemorial usage is binding upon all parties; as it is in it's nature an evidence of universal consent and acquiescence, and with reason supposes a real composition to have been formerly made. This custom or prescription is either *de modo decimandi*, or *de non decimando*.

A *modus decimandi*, commonly called by the simple name of a *modus* only, is where there is, by custom, a particular manner of tithing allowed, different from the general law of taking tithes in kind, which are the actual tenth part of the annual increase. This is sometimes a pecuniary compensation, as twopence an acre for the tithe land: sometimes it is a compensation in work and labour, as that the parson shall have only the twelfth cock of hay, and not the tenth, in consideration of the owner's making it for him: sometimes, in lieu of a large quantity of crude or imperfect tithe, the parson shall have a less quantity, when arrived to greater maturity, as a couple of fowls in lieu of tithe eggs; and the like. Any means, in short, whereby the general law of tithing is altered, and a new method of taking them is introduced, is called a *modus decimandi*, or special manner of tithing.

To make a good and sufficient *modus*, the following rules must be observed. 1. It must be *certain* and *invariable*, for payment of different sums will prove it to be no *modus*, that is, no original real composition; because that must have been one and the same, from it's first original to the present time. 2. The thing given, in lieu of tithes, must be beneficial to the *parson*, and not for the emolument of *third persons* only: thus a *modus* to repair the *church* in lieu of tithes, is not good, becaufe that is an advantage to the parifh only; but to repair the *chancel* is a good *modus*, for that is an advantage to the parfon. 3. It muft be fomething *different* from the thing compounded for: one load of hay, in lieu of *all* tithe hay, is no good *modus*: for no parfon would *bona fide* make a compofition to receive lefs than his due in the fame fpecies of tithe; and therefore the law will not fuppofe it poffible for fuch compofition to have exifted. 4. One cannot be difcharged from payment of one fpecies of tithe, by paying a *modus* for another. Thus a *modus* of 1$d$. for every *milch* cow will difcharge the tithe of *milch* kine, but not of *barren* cattle: for tithe is, of common right, due for both; and therefore a *modus* for one, fhall never be a difcharge for the other. 5. The recompenfe muft be in it's nature as durable as the tithes difcharged by it; that is, an inheritance certain: and therefore a *modus* that every *inhabitant* of a houfe fhall pay 4$d$. a year, in lieu of the owner's tithes, is no good *modus*; for poffibly the houfe may not be inhabited, and then the recompenfe will be loft. 6. The *modus* muft not be too large, which is called a *rank modus*: as if the real value of the tithes be 60$l$. *per annum*, and a *modus* is fuggefted of 40$l$. this *modus* will not be eftablifhed; though one of 40$s$. might have been valid. Indeed, properly fpeaking, the doctrine of *ranknefs* in a *modus*, is a mere rule of evidence, drawn from the improbability of the fact, and not a rule of law. For, in thefe cafes of prefcriptive or cuftomary *modus's*, it is fuppofed that an original real compofition was antiently made; which being loft by length of time, the immemorial ufage is admitted as an evidence to fhew that it once did exift, and that from thence fuch ufage was derived. Now time of memory hath been long ago afcertained by the law to commence from the beginning of the reign of Richard the firft; and any cuftom may be deftroyed by evidence of it's non-exiftence in any part of the long period from that time to the prefent; wherefore, as this real compofition is fuppofed to have been an equitable contract, or the full value of the tithes, at the time of making it, if the *modus* set up is so rank and large, as that it, beyond dispute, exceeds the value of the tithes in the time of Richard the first, this *modus* is (in point of evidence) *felo de se*, and destroys itself. For, as it would be destroyed by any direct evidence to prove it's non-existence at any time since that æra, so also it is destroyed by carrying in itself this internal evidence of a much later original.

A prescription *de non decimando* is a claim to be entirely discharged of tithes, and to pay no compensation in lieu of them. Thus the king by his prerogative is discharged from all tithes. So a vicar shall pay no tithes to the rector, nor the rector to the vicar, for *ecclesia decimas non solvit ecclesiæ*. But these *personal* privileges (not arising from or being annexed to the land) are personally confined to both the king and the clergy; for their tenant or lessee shall pay tithes (*a*), though in their own occupation their lands are not generally tithable. And, generally speaking, it is an established rule, that, in *lay* hands, *modus de non decimando non valet*. But spiritual persons or corporations, as monasteries, abbots, bishops, and the like, were always capable of having their lands totally discharged of tithes, by various ways, as, 1. By real composition: 2. By the pope's bull of exemption: 3. By unity of possession; as when the rectory of a parish, and lands in the same parish, both belonged to a religious house, those lands were discharged of tithes by this unity of possession: 4. By prescription; having never been liable to tithes, by being always in spiritual hands: 5. By virtue of their order; as the knights templars, cistercians, and others, whose lands

---

(*a*) But see 3 *Com. Dig.* 510. where it is said, on the authority of *Owen*, 46. 2 *Leo.* 71. *Mod.* 915. and *Hard.* 382. that lands shall be exempted in the hands of the king's tenants, if the freehold be in the king; who cannot, in regard to his dignity, occupy them himself.

were privileged by the pope with a difcharge of tithes. Though upon the diffolution of abbeys by Henry VIII. moft of thefe exemptions from tithes would have fallen with them, and the lands become tithable again; had they not been fupported and upheld by the ftatute 31 Hen. VIII. c. 13. which enacts, that all perfons who fhould come to the poffeffion of the lands of any abbey then (*a*) diffolved, fhould hold them free and difcharged of tithes, in as large and ample a manner as the abbey themfelves formerly held them. And from this original have fprung all the lands, which, being in lay hands, do at prefent claim to be tithe-free: for, if a man can fhew his lands to have been fuch abbey lands, and alfo immemorially difcharged of tithes by any of the means before-mentioned, this is now a good prefcription *de non decimando*. But he muft fhew both thefe requifites: for abbey lands, without a fpecial ground of difcharge, are not difcharged of courfe; neither will any prefcription *de non decimando* avail in total difcharge of tithes, unlefs it relates to fuch abbey lands.

III. Common, or right of common, appears, from it's very definition to be an incorporeal hereditament: being a profit which a man hath in the land of another; as to feed his beafts, to catch fifh, to dig turf, to cut wood, or the like. And hence common is chiefly of four forts; common of pafture, of pifcary, of turbary, and of eftovers.

1. Common of pafture is a right of feeding one's beafts on another's land: for in thofe wafte grounds, which are ufu-

---

(*a*) This adverb muft be underftood to refer to the abbeys diffolved by that *ftatute*, and not to thofe which might be at that *time* diffolved; for it has been determined, that the ftatute 31 Hen. VIII. does not extend to lands belonging to the abbeys diffolved by 27 Hen. VIII. c. 28. which, therefore, ftill remain liable to pay tithe. See *Sydowne*, v. *Holmes*, *Cro. Car.* 422.

ally called commons, the property of the soil is generally in the lord of the manor; as in common fields it is in the particular tenants. This kind of common is either appendant, appurtenant, because of vicinage, or in gross.

Common *appendant* is a right, belonging to the owners or occupiers of arable land, to put commonable beasts upon the lord's waste, and upon the lands of other persons within the same manor: commonable beasts are either beasts of the plough, or such as manure the ground. Common *appurtenant* ariseth from no connection of tenure, but may be annexed to lands in other lordships, or extend to other beasts, besides such as are generally commonable; as hogs, goats, or the like, which neither plough nor manure the ground. Common *because of vicinage*, or neighbourhood, is where the inhabitants of two townships, which lie contiguous to each other, have usually intercommoned with one another; the beasts of the one straying mutually into the other's fields, without any molestation from either. This is indeed only a permissive right, intended to excuse what in strictness is a trespass in both, and to prevent a multiplicity of suits: and therefore either township may enclose and bar out the other, though they have intercommoned time out of mind. Common *in gross*, or at large, is such as is neither appendant nor appurtenant to land, but is annexed to a man's person; being granted to him and his heirs by deed: or it may be claimed by prescriptive right, as by a parson of a church, or the like corporation sole. This is a separate inheritance, entirely distinct from any landed property, and may be vested in one who has not a foot of ground in the manor.

All these species, of pasturable common, may be and usually are limited as to number and time; but there are also commons without stint, and which last all the year. By the statute of Merton however, and other subsequent statutes, the lord of a manor may enclose so much of the waste as he pleases, for tillage or woodground, provided he leaves common sufficient for such as are entitled thereto. This enclosure, when justifiable, is called in law "approving:"(a) an ancient expression signifying the same as "improving." The lord hath the sole interest in the soil; but the interest of the lord and commoner, in the common, are looked upon in law as mutual. They may both bring actions for damage done, either against strangers, or each other; the lord for the public injury, and each commoner for his private damage.

2, 3. Common of *piscary* is a liberty of fishing in another man's water; as common of *turbary* is a liberty of digging turf upon another's ground. There is also a common of digging for coals, minerals, stones, and the like. All these bear a resemblance to common of pasture in many respects; though in one point they go much farther: common of pasture being only a right of feeding on the herbage and vesture of the soil, which renews annually; but common of turbary, and those aftermentioned, are a right of carrying away the very soil itself.

4. Common of estovers or *estouviers*, that is, *necessaries*, (from *estoffer*, to furnish) is a liberty of taking necessary wood, for the use or furniture of a house or farm, from off another's estate. The Saxon word, *bote*, is used by us as synonymous to the French *estovers*; and therefore house-bote is a sufficient allowance of wood, to repair, or to burn, in the house; which latter is sometimes called fire-bote: plough-bote and cart-bote are wood to be employed in making and repairing all instruments of husbandry: and hay-bote or hedge bote is wood for repairing of hays, hedges, or fences. These botes or estovers must be reasonable ones;

---

(a) This privilege is not confined to the lord of a manor, for any other person having the *fee* of waste ground, may *approve* it under the like restriction of leaving sufficient commonage. See *Glover, v. Lane*, 3 *Term Rep.* 445.

and such any tenant or lessee may take off the land let or demised to him, without waiting for any leave, assignment, or appointment of the lessor, unless he be restrained by special covenant to the contrary.

IV. A fourth species of incorporeal hereditaments is that of *ways*; or the right of going over another man's ground. This may be grounded on a special permission. A way may be also by prescription; as if all the inhabitants of such a hamlet, or all the owners and occupiers of such a farm, have immemorially used to cross such a ground, for such a particular purpose: for this immemorial usage supposes an original grant, whereby a right of way thus appurtenant to land or houses may clearly be created.

V. Offices, which are a right to exercise a public or private employment, and to take the fees and emoluments thereunto belonging, are also incorporeal hereditaments: whether public, as those of magistrates; or private, as of bailiffs, receivers, and the like.

By statute 5 and 6 Edw. VI. c. 16. no public office (a few only excepted) shall be sold, under pain of disability to dispose of or hold it. For the law presumes that he, who buys an office, will by bribery, extortion, or other unlawful means, make his purchase good, to the manifest detriment of the public.

VI. Dignities bear a near relation to offices, and are a species of incorporeal hereditaments, wherein a man may have a property or estate.

VII. Franchises are a seventh species. Franchise and liberty are used as synonymous terms: and their disinition is, a royal privilege, or branch of the king's prerogative, subsisting in the hands of a subject.

VIII. Corodies are a right of sustenance, or to receive certain allotments of victual and provision for one's maintenance. In lieu of which (especially when due from ecclesiastical persons) a pension or sum of money is sometimes substituted. And these may be reckoned another species of incorporeal hereditaments; though not chargeable on, or issuing from, any corporeal inheritance, but only charged on the person of the owner in respect of such his inheritance. To these may be added,

IX. Annuities, which are much of the same nature; only that these arise from temporal, as the former from spiritual, persons. An annuity is a thing very distinct from a rent-charge, with which it is frequently confounded: a rent-charge being a burthen imposed upon and issuing out of *lands*, whereas an annuity is a yearly sum chargeable only upon the *person* of the grantor. Therefore, if a man by deed grant to another the sum of 20l. *per annum*, without expressing out of what lands it shall issue, no land at all shall be charged with it; but it is a mere personal annuity: which is of so little account in the law, that, if granted to an eleemosynary corporation, it is not within the statutes of mortmain; and yet a man may have a real estate in it, though his security is merely personal.

X. Rents are the last species of incorporeal hereditaments. The word rent or render, *reditus*, signifies a compensation or return, it being in the nature of an acknowledgment given for the possession of some corporeal inheritance. It is defined to be a certain profit issuing yearly out of lands and tenements corporeal. It must be a *profit*; yet there is no occasion for it to be, as it usually is, a sum of money: for spurs, capons, horses, corn, and other matters may be rendered, and frequently are rendered by way of rent. It may also consist in services or manual operations; as, to plough so many acres of ground, to attend the king or the lord to the wars, and the like; which services in the eye of the law are profits. This profit must also be *certain*; or that which may be reduced to a certainty by either party. It must also issue *yearly*; though there is no occasion for it to issue every successive year; but it may be reserved every second, third, or fourth year: yet, as it is to be produced out of the profits of lands and tenements, as a recompense for being permitted to hold or enjoy them, it ought to be reserved yearly, because those profits do annually arise and are annually renewed. It must *issue out* of the thing granted, and not be part of the land or thing itself; wherein it differs from an exception in the grant, which is always of part of the thing granted. It must, lastly, issue out of *lands and tenements corporeal*; that is, from some inheritance whereunto the owner or grantee of the rent may have recourse to distrain. Therefore a rent cannot be reserved out of an advowson, a common, an office, a franchise, or the like. But a grant of such annuity or sum may operate as a personal contract, and oblige the grantor to pay the money reserved, or subject him to an action of debt: though it doth not affect the inheritance, and is no legal rent in contemplation of law. These are many sorts of rents, of which,

Rents of *assise* are the certain established rents of the freeholders and ancient copyholders of a manor, which cannot be departed from or varied. Those of the freeholders are frequently called *chief* rents, *reditus capitales;* and both sorts are indifferently denominated *quit* rents, *quieti reditus*; because thereby the tenant goes quit and free of all other services. A *fee-farm* rent is a rent-charge issuing out of an estate in fee; of at least one fourth of the value of the lands, at the time of it's reservation :(a) for a grant of lands, reserv-

---

(a) This definition of a *fee farm*, is taken from *Co. Lit.* 143.[a] but Mr. Hargrave thinks the quantum of the reservation immaterial; the name being founded on the *perpetuity* of the rent, or service, and not on the *quantum*; and its true meaning being a perpetual farm or rent, that is (as he afterwards defines it) "every rent or service reserved on a grant in *fee*."— See *ibid*, n. 5.

ing so considerable a rent, is indeed only letting lands to farm in fee simple instead of the usual methods for life or years.

Rent is regularly due and payable upon the land from whence it issues, if no particular place is mentioned in the reservation: but, in case of the king, the payment must be either to his officers at the exchequer, or to his receiver in the country. And, strictly, the rent is demandable and payable before the time of sun-set of the day whereon it is reserved; though perhaps not absolutely due till midnight. (*b*)

As to distresses and other remedies for their recovery, these belong to the third book of our commentaries, which will treat of civil injuries, and the means whereby they are redressed.

## CHAPTER III.

### OF THE MODERN ENGLISH TENURES.

I. OF burgage tenure. Tenure in *burgage* is where the king or other person is lord of an antient borough, in which the tenements are held by a rent certain. It is indeed only a kind of town socage; as common socage, by which other lands are holden, is usually of a rural nature.

---

(*b*) In consequence of this distinction, questions have arisen whether, when the lessor dies *after sun-set* and *before midnight*, on the day upon which the rent is reserved, such rent belongs to the *heir* or *executor* if unpaid at the time of his death: the better opinion as to which seems to be, that it belongs to the *executor*. See *Rockingham, v. Penrice*, 1 *P. Wms.* 177.

A borough, is usually distinguished from other towns by the right of sending members to parliament; and, where the right of election is by burgage tenure, that alone is proof of the antiquity of the borough. Tenure in burgage therefore, or burgage tenure, is where houses, or lands which were formerly the scite of houses, in an antient borough, are held of some lord in common socage, by a certain established rent.

II. Of tenure in gavelkind. It is universally known what struggles the Kentish men made to preserve their antient liberties, and it is principally in them that we meet with the custom of gavelkind, (though it was and is to be found in some other parts of the kingdom.) The distinguishing properties of this tenure are various: some of the principal are these; 1. The tenant is of age sufficient to alien his estate by feoffment at the age of fifteen. 2. The estate does not escheat in case of an attainder and execution for felony; their maxim being, "the father to the bough, the son to "the plough." 3. In most places he had a power of devising lands by will, before the statute for that purpose was made. 4. The lands descend, not to the eldest, youngest, or any one son only, but to all the sons together; which was indeed antiently the most usual course of descent all over England, though in particular places particular customs prevailed.

III. Of copyhold tenures. Copyhold tenures, as sir Edward Coke observes, although very meanly descended, yet come of an antient house; for, it appears, that copyholders are in truth no other but villeins, who, by a long series of immemorial encroachments on the lord, have at last established a customary right to those estates, which before were held absolutely at the lord's will. Which affords a very substantial reason for the great variety of customs that prevail in different manors, with regard both to the descent of the estates, and the privileges belonging to the tenants.

Thefe two main principles, are held to be the fupporters of the copyhold tenure, and without which it cannot exift; 1. That the lands be parcel of, and fituate within that manor, under which it is held. 2. That they have been demifed, or demifable, by copy of court roll immemorially: for immemorial cuftom is the life of all tenures by copy; fo that no new copyhold can, ftrictly fpeaking, be granted at this day.

In fome manors, where the cuftom hath been to permit the heir to fucceed the anceftor in his tenure, the eftates are ftiled copyholds of inheritance; in others, where the lords have been more vigilant to maintain their rights, they remain copyholds for life only; for the cuftom of the manor has in both cafes fo far fuperfeded the will of the lord, that, provided the fervices be performed or ftipulated for by fealty, he cannot, in the firft inftance, refufe to admit the heir of his tenant upon his death; nor, in the fecond, can he remove his prefent tenant fo long as he lives, though he holds nominally by the precarious tenure of his lord's will.

The fruits and appendages of a copyhold tenure, that it hath in common with free tenures, are fealty, fervices, (as well in rents as otherwife) reliefs, and efcheats. The two latter belong only to copyholds of inheritance; the former to thofe for life alfo. But, befides thefe, copyholds have alfo heriots, wardfhip, and fines. Heriots, which I think are agreed to be a Danifh cuftom, and of which we fhall fay more hereafter, are a render of the beft beaft or other good (as the cuftom may be) to the lord, on the death of the tenant. This is plainly a relic of villein tenure; there being originally lefs hardfhip in it, when all the goods and chattels belonged to the lord, and he might have feifed them even in the villein's lifetime. Thefe are incident to both fpecies of copyhold; but wardfhip and fines to thofe of inheritance only. Wardfhip, in copyhold eftates, partakes both of that in chivalry and that in focage. Like that in chivalry, the lord is the legal guardian; who ufually affigns fome relation of the infant tenant to act in his stead: and he, like guardian in socage, is accountable to his ward for the profits. Of fines, some are in the nature of primer seisins, due on the death of each tenant, others are mere fines for alienation of the lands; in some manors only one of these sorts can be demanded, in some both, and in others neither. They are sometimes arbitrary and at the will of the lord, sometimes fixed by custom: but, even when arbitrary, the courts of law, in favour of the liberty of copyholders, have tied them down to be *reasonable* in their extent; otherwise they might amount to a disherison of the estate. No fine therefore is allowed to be taken upon descents and alienations, (unless in particular circumstances) of more than two years improved value of the estate (*a*).

## CHAPTER IV.

### OF FREEHOLD ESTATES OF INHERITANCE.

THE next objects of our disquisitions are the nature and properties of *estates*. An estate in lands, tenements, and hereditaments, signifies such interest as the tenant hath therein. Estates may be considered in a threefold view: first, with regard to the *quantity of interest* which the tenant has in the tenement: secondly, with regard to the *time* at which that quantity of interest is to be enjoyed: and, thirdly, with regard to the *number* and *connexions* of the tenants.

First, with regard to the *quantity of interest* which the tenant has in the tenement, this is measured by it's duration

---

(*a*) Which valuation, it has been determined, is to be inclusive of *quit-rents*, but not of *land-tax*. See *Grant*, v. *Astle*, 2 *Dougl*. 697. (*Note*,—This was a case of *descent*).

and extent. Thus, either his right of poffeffion is to fubfift for an uncertain period, during his own life, or the life of another man; to determine at his own deceafe, or to remain to his defcendants after him: or it is circumfcribed within a certain number of years, months, or days: or, laftly, it is infinite and unlimited, being vefted in him and his reprefentatives for ever. And this occafions the primary divifion of eftates, into fuch as are *freehold*, and fuch as are *lefs than freehold*.

An eftate of freehold, *liberum tenementum*, or franktenement, is fuch an eftate in lands as is conveyed by livery of feifin, or, in tenements of an incorporeal nature, by what is equivalent thereto.

Eftates of freehold (thus underftood) are either eftates *of inheritance*, or eftates *not of inheritance*. The former are again divided into inheritances *abfolute* or fee-fimple; and inheritances *limited*, one fpecies of which we ufually call fee-tail.

I. Tenant in fee-fimple (or, as he is frequently ftiled, tenant in fee) is he that hath lands, tenements, or hereditaments, to hold to him and his heirs for ever; generally, abfolutely, and fimply; without mentioning *what* heirs, but referring that to his own pleafure, or to the difpofition of the law. A *fee* therefore, in general, fignifies an eftate of inheritance; being the higheft and moft extenfive intereft that a man can have in a feud: and when the term is ufed fimply, without any other adjunct, or has the adjunct of *fimple* annexed to it, (as a fee, or a fee fimple) it is ufed in contradiftinction to a fee conditional at the common law, or a fee-tail by the ftatute; importing an abfolute inheritance, clear of any condition, limitation, or reftrictions to particular heirs, but defcendible to the heirs general, whether male or female, lineal or collateral.

Taking, therefore, *fee* in this fenfe, as a ftate of inheritance, it is applicable to, and may be had in, **any kind of hereditaments either corporeal or incorporeal.**

But there is this distinction between the two species of hereditaments; that, of a corporeal inheritance a man shall be said to be seised *in his demesne, as of fee*; of an incorporeal one, he shall only be said to be seised *as of fee*, and not in his demesne.

The fee-simple or inheritance of lands and tenements is generally vested and resides in some person or other; though divers inferior estates may be carved out of it. As if one grants a lease for twenty-one years, or for one or two lives, the fee-simple remains vested in him and his heirs; and after the determination of those years or lives, the land reverts to the grantor or his heirs, who shall hold it again in fee-simple. Yet sometimes the fee may be in *abeyance*, that is (as the word signifies) in expectation, remembrance, and contemplation in law; there being no person in *esse*, in whom it can vest and abide (*a*): though the law considers it as always potentially existing, and ready to vest whenever a proper owner appears. This is always the case of a parson of a church, who hath only an estate therein for the term of his life; and the inheritance remains in abeyance. And not only the fee, but the freehold also, may be in abeyance; as, when a parson dies, the freehold of his glebe is in abeyance, until a successor be named, and then it vests in the successor (*b*).

---

(*a*) This doctrine of the fee being in abeyance, though supported by the opinion of *Lord Coke*, (*Com. Lit.* 342 ᵇ and acquiesced in by later authorities, see *Fick*, v. *Edwards*, 3 *P. Wms.* 372.) seems at length to be entirely exploded; and, in the cases where it was formerly considered as being in abeyance, it is now held to remain in the grantor and his heirs, until the contingency happens by which it becomes capable of vesting in the grantee. See *Fearne Cont. Rem.* 515. *Co. Lit.* 191 ᵃ note 78.

(*b*) In this latter case Mr. *Christian* considers the freehold as vesting and abiding in the successor, from the moment of the death of the parson, See 12 *Ed. Black.* p. 107. n. 3.

The word, heirs, is neceffary in the grant or donation in order to make a fee, or inheritance. For if land be given to a man for ever, or to him and his affigns for ever, this vefts in him but an eftate for life: but this rule is now foftened by many exceptions.

For, 1. It does not extend to devifes by will; in which as they were introduced at the time when the feodal rigor was apace wearing out, a more liberal conftruction is allowed: and therefore, by a devife to a man for ever, or to one and his affigns for ever, or to one in fee-fimple, the devifee hath an eftate of inheritance; for the intention of the devifor is fufficiently plain from the words of perpetuity annexed, though he hath omitted the legal words of inheritance (a). But if the devife be to a man and his affigns, without annexing words of perpetuity, there the devife fhall take only an eftate for life; for it does not appear that the devifor intended any more. 2. Neither does this rule extend to fines or recoveries, confidered as a fpecies of conveyance; for thereby an eftate in fee paffes by act and operation of law without the word "heirs:" as it does alfo for particular reafons, by certain other methods of conveyance, which have relation to a former grant or eftate, wherein the word "heirs" was expreffed. 3. In creations of nobility by writ, the peer fo created hath an inheritance in his title, without expreffing the word "heirs;" for heirfhip is implied in the creation, unlefs it be otherwife fpecially provided: but in creations by patent, which are *ftricti juris*, the word "heirs" muft be inferted, otherwife there is no inheritance. 4. In grants of lands to fole corporations and their fucceffors,

---

*(a)* And though there be no words of perpetuity annexed, yet, if it appear to have been the teftator's intention that the devifee fhould have the inheritance, the fee will pafs. See *Fletcher*, v. *Smith*, 2 Term Rep. 656. *Palmer*, v. *Richards*, 3 ibid, 356. *Doe*, v. *Woodhoufe*, 4 ibid, 89.

the word "succeffors" fupplies the place of "heirs;" for as heirs take from the anceftor, fo doth the fucceffor from the predeceffor Nay, in a grant to a bifhop, or other fole fpiritual corporation, in *frankalmoign*; the word "*frankalmoign*" fupplies the place of "succeffors" (as the word "succeffors" fupplies the place of "heirs") *ex vi termini*; and in all thefe cafes a fee-fimple vefts in fuch fole corporation. But, in a grant of lan's to a corporation aggregate, the word "succeffors is not neceffary, though ufually inferted: for, albeit fuch fimple grant be ftrictly only an eftate for life, yet, as that corporation never dies, fuch eftate for life is perpetual, or equivalent to a fee-fimple, and therefore the law allows it to be one *(a)*. 5. Laftly, in the cafe of the king, a fee-fimple will veft in him without the word "heirs" or "succeffors" in the grant; partly from the prerogative royal, and partly from a reafon fimilar to the laft, becaufe the king in judgment of law never dies. But the general rule is, that the word "heirs" is neceffary to create an eftate of inheritance.

II. We are next to confider limited fees, or fuch eftates of inheritance as are clogged and confined with conditions, or qualifications, of any fort. And thefe we may divide into two forts: 1. *Qualified*, or *bafe* fees: and 2. Fees *conditional*, fo called at the common law; and afterwards fees-*tail*, in confequence of the ftatute *de donis*.

1. A bafe, or qualified, fee, is fuch a one as has a qualification fubjoined thereto, and which muft be determined whenever the qualification annexed to it is at an end. As, in the cafe of a grant to A. and his heirs, *tenants of the manor of Dale*; in this inftance, whenever the heirs of A. ceafe to be tenants of that manor, the grant is entirely defeated.

2. A conditional fee, at the common law, was a fee reftrained to fome particular heirs, exclufive of others: "do-

---

(*a*) See *Ante*, B. I. Ch. 10.

"*natio stricta et coarctata; sicut certis hæredibus, quibusdam a successione exclusis:*" as to the heirs *of a man's body*, by which only his lineal defcendants were admitted, in exclufion of collateral heirs; or, to the heirs *male of his body*, in exclufion both of collaterals, and lineal females alfo. With regard to the condition annexed to thefe fees by the common law, our anceftors held, that fuch a gift (to a man and the heirs of his body) was a gift upon condition, that it fhould revert to the donor, if the donee had no heirs of his body; but, if he had, it fhould then remain to the donee. Now we muft obferve, that, when any condition is performed, it is thenceforth entirely gone; and the thing to which it was before annexed, becomes abfolute, and wholly unconditional. So that, as foon as the grantee had any iffue born, his eftate was fuppofed to become abfolute, by the performance of the condition; at leaft, for thefe three purpofes: 1. To enable the tenant to aliene the land, and thereby to bar not only his own iffue, but alfo the donor, of his intereft in the reverfion. 2. To fubject him to forfeit it for treafon. 3. To empower him to charge the land with rents, commons, and certain other incumbrances, fo as to bind his iffue.—And thus ftood the old law with regard to the conditional fees: which things, fays Sir Edward Coke, though they feem antient, are yet neceffary to be known; as well for the declaring how the common law ftood in fuch cafes, as for the fake of annuities, and fuch like inheritances, as are not within the ftatutes of entail, and therefore remain as at the common law.

The inconveniences, which attended thefe limited and fettered inheritances, were probably what induced the judges to give way to this fubtile fineffe of conftruction, in order to fhorten the duration of thefe conditional eftates. But, on the other hand, the nobility, who were willing to perpetuate their poffeffions in their own families, to put a ftop to this practice, procured the ftatute of Weftminfter the fecond, (commonly called the statute *de donis conditionalibus*) to be made. This statute revived, in some sort, the antient feodal restraints which were originally laid on alienations, by enacting, that from thenceforth the will of the donor should be observed; and that the tenements so given (to a man and the heirs of his body) should at all events go to the issue, if there were any; or, if none, should revert to the donor. Upon the construction of this act of parliament, the judges determined that the donee had no longer a conditional fee-simple, which became absolute and at his own disposal, the instant any issue was born; but they divided the estate into two parts, leaving in the donee a new kind of particular estate, which they denominated a *fee-tail*; and vesting in the donor the ultimate fee-simple of the land, expectant on the failure of issue; which expectant estate is what we now call a reversion.

I now proceed to consider, *what things* may, or may not, be entailed under the statute *de donis*. *Tenements* is the only word used in the statute: and this sir Edward Coke expounds to comprehend all corporeal hereditaments whatsoever; and also all incorporeal hereditaments which favour of the realty, that is, which issue out of corporeal ones, or which concern, or are annexed to, or may be exercised within the same; as, rents, estovers, commons, and the like. Also offices and dignities, which concern lands, or have relation to fixed and certain places, may be entailed. But mere personal chattels, which favour not at all of the realty, cannot be entailed. Neither can an office, which merely relates to such personal chattels; nor an annuity which charges only the person, and not the lands of the grantor. But in these last, if granted to a man and the heirs of his body, the grantee hath still a fee conditional at common law, as before the statute; and by his alienation (after issue born) may bar the heir or reversioner. An estate to a man and his heirs for another's life cannot be entailed; for this is strictly no estate of inheritance (as will appear hereafter), and therefore not within the statute *de donis*. Neither can a copyhold estate be entailed by virtue of the *statute*; for that would tend to encroach upon and restrain the will of the lord: but, by the *special custom* of the manor, a copyhold may be limited to the heirs of the body; for here the custom ascertains and interprets the lord's will.

Estates-tail are either *general*, or *special*. Tail-general is where lands and tenements are given to one, and the *heirs of his body begotten*: which is called tail-general, because, how often soever such donee in tail be married, his issue, in general by all and every such marriage is, in successive order, capable of inheriting the estate-tail, *per formam doni*. Tenant in tail-special is where the gift is restrained to certain heirs of the donee's body, and does not go to all of them in general. And this may happen several ways. I shall instance in only one; as where lands and tenements are given to a man and the *heirs of his body, on Mary his now wife to be begotten*: here no issue can inherit, but such special issue as is engendered between them two; not such as the husband may have by another wife: and therefore it is called special tail. And here we may observe, that the words of inheritance (to him and his *heirs*) give him an estate in fee; but they being heirs *to be by him begotten*, this makes it a fee-tail; and the person being also limited, on whom such heirs shall be begotten, (viz. *Mary his present wife*) this makes it a fee-tail special.

Estates, in general and special tail, are farther diversified by the distinction of sexes in such entails; for both of them may either be in tail *male* or tail *female*. As if lands be given to a man, and his *heirs male of his body begotten*, this is an estate in tail male general; but if to a man and the heirs *female of his body on his present wife begotten*, this is an estate in tail female special. And, in case of an entail male, the heirs female shall never inherit, nor any derived from them; nor *e converso*, the heirs male, in case of a gift in tail female.

K

As the word *heirs* is necessary to create a fee, so in farther imitation of the strictness of the feodal donation, the word *body*, or some other words of procreation, are necessary to make it a fee-tail, and ascertain to what heirs in particular the fee is limited. If therefore either the words of inheritance or words of procreation be omitted, albeit the others are inserted in the grant, this will not make an estate-tail. As, if the grant be to a man and the *issue of his body*, to a man and his *seed*, to a man and his *children*, or *offspring*; all these are only estates for life, there wanting the words of inheritance, his heirs. So, on the other hand, a gift to a man, and his *heirs male*, or *female*, is an estate in fee-simple, and not in fee-tail; for there are no words to ascertain the body out of which they shall issue. Indeed, in last wills and testaments, wherein greater indulgence is allowed, an estate-tail may be created by a devise to a man and his *seed*, or to a man and his *heirs male*; or by other irregular modes of expression.

The *incidents* to a tenancy in tail, under the statute Westm. 2. are chiefly these. 1. That a tenant in tail may commit *waste* on the estate tail, by felling timber, pulling down houses, or the like, without being impeached, or called to account, for the same. 2. That the wife of the tenant in tail shall have her *dower*, or thirds, of the estate-tail. 3. That the husband of a female tenant in tail may be tenant by the *curtesy* of the estate-tail. 4. That an estate-tail may be *barred*, or destroyed by a fine, by a common recovery, or by lineal warranty descending with assets to the heir. All which will hereafter be explained. Also by 26 Hen. VIII. c. 13. all estates of inheritance (under which general words estates-tail were covertly included) are declared to be forfeited to the king upon any conviction of high treason. (a)

---

(a) If tenant in tail be attaint of treason, the estate-tail is forfeited, and yet this attainder works no corruption of blood

By the statute 32 Hen. VIII. c. 28. certain leases made by tenants in tail, which do not tend to the prejudice of the issue, were allowed to be good in law, and to bind the issue in tail. The statute 32 Hen. VIII. c. 36. declares a fine duly levied by tenant in tail to be a complete bar to him and his heirs, and all other persons, claiming under such entail.

Lastly, by statute 33 Hen. VIII. c. 39. all estates-tail are rendered liable to be charged for payment of debts due to the king by record or special contract; as since, by the bankrupt laws, they are also subjected to be sold for the debts contracted by a bankrupt. And, by the construction put on the statute 43 Eliz. c. 4. an appointment by tenant in tail of the lands entailed, to a charitable use, is good without fine or recovery.

## CHAPTER V.

### OF FREEHOLDS, NOT OF INHERITANCE.

WE are next to discourse of such estates of freehold, as are not of inheritance, but *for life* only. And of these estates for life, some are *conventional*, or expressly created by the acts of the parties; others merely *legal*, or created by construction and operation of law.

I. Estates for life, expressly created by deed or grant, (which alone are properly conventional) are where a lease is made of lands or tenements to a man, to hold for the term

---

as in relation to the heir in tail : Vide Lord Lumley's case cited in Dowtie's case, 3 *Co. Rep.* 10. b. Grandfather, tenant in tail, father, and son, the father is attaint of treason and dies, the grandfather dies, the land shall descend to the grandchild, for the father could forfeit nothing, for he had nothing to forfeit ; and the stat. 26 Hen. VIII. that gives the forfeiture of tenant in tail, yet corrupts not the blood by the attainder of the father.

of his own life, or for that of any other person, or for more lives than one: in any of which cases he is stiled tenant for life; only, when he holds the estate by the life of another, he is usually called tenant *pur auter vie*.

Estates for life may be created, not only by the express words before-mentioned, but also by a general grant, without defining or limiting any specific estate. As, if one grants to A. B. the manor of Dale, this makes him tenant for life. For though, as there are no words of inheritance, or *heirs*, mentioned in the grant, it cannot be construed to be a fee, it shall however be construed to be as large an estate as the words of the donation will bear, and therefore an estate for life. Also such a grant at large, or a grant for term of life generally, shall be construed to be an estate for life *of the grantee*; in case the grantor hath authority to make such a grant: for an estate for a man's own life is more beneficial and of a higher nature than for any other life; and the rule of law is, that all grants are to be taken most strongly against the grantor, unless in the case of the king.

The *incidents* to an estate for life, are principally the following; which are applicable not only to that species of tenants for life, which are expressly created by deed; but also to those, which are created by act and operation of law.

1. Every tenant for life, unless restrained by covenant or agreement, may of common right take upon the land demised to him reasonable *estovers (a)* or *botes*. For he hath a right to the full enjoyment and use of the land, and all it's profits, during his estate therein. But he is not permitted to cut down timber or do other waste upon the premises: for the destruction of such things, as are not the temporary profits of the tenement, is not necessary for the tenant's complete enjoyment of his estate; but tends to the permanent and lasting loss of the person entitled to the inheritance.

---

(a) See *Ante*, p. 115.

2. Tenant for life, or his representatives, shall not be prejudiced by any sudden determination of his estate, because such a determination is contingent and uncertain. Therefore if a tenant for his own life sows the lands, and dies before harvest, his executors shall have the *emblements*, or profits of the crop: for the estate was determined by the *act of God*; and it is a maxim in the law, that *actus Dei nemini facit injuriam*. The representatives therefore of the tenant for life shall have the emblements, to compensate for the labour and expence of tilling, manuring, and sowing the lands; and also for the encouragement of husbandry; which being a public benefit, tending to the increase and plenty of provisions, ought to have the utmost security and privilege that the law can give it. So it is also, if a man be tenant for the life of another, and *cestuy que vie*, or he on whose life the land is held, dies after the corn sown, the tenant *pur auter vie* shall have the emblements. The same is also the rule, if a life-estate de determined by the *act of law*. Therefore, if a lease be made to husband and wife during coverture, (which gives them a determinable estate for life) and the husband sows the land, and afterwards they are divorced *a vinculo matrimonii*, the husband shall have the emblements in this case; for the sentence of divorce is the act of law. But if an estate for life be determined by the tenant's *own act*, (as, by forfeiture for waste committed; or, if a tenant during widowhood thinks proper to marry) in these, and similar cases, the tenants, having thus determined the estate by their own acts, shall not be entitled to take the emblements. The doctrine of emblements extends not only to corn sown, but to roots planted, or other annual artificial profit; but it is otherwise of fruit-trees, grass, and the like, which are not planted annually at the expense and labour of the tenant, but are either a permanent, or natural, profit of the earth. The advantages also of emblements are particularly extended to the parochial clergy by the statute 28 Hen. VIII. c. 11.

For all persons, who are presented to any ecclesiastical benefice, or to any civil office, are considered as tenants for their own lives, unless the contrary be expressed in the form of donation.

3. A third incident to estates for life relates to the under-tenants or lessees. For they have the same, nay greater indulgences than their lessors, the original tenants for life. The same; for the law of estovers and emblements, with regard to the tenant for life, is also law with regard to his under-tenant, who represents him and stands in his place: and greater; for in those cases where tenant for life shall not have the emblements, because the estate determines by his own act, the exception shall not reach his lessee who is a third person. As in the case of a woman who holds *durante viduitate*; her taking husband is her own act, and therefore deprives her of the emblements: but if she leases her estate to an under-tenant, who sows the land, and she then marries, this her act shall not deprive the tenant of his emblements, who is a stranger and could not prevent her. The lessees of tenant for life had also at the common law another most unreasonable advantage; for, at the death of their lessors the tenants for life, these under-tenants might if they pleased quit the premises, and pay no rent to any body for the occupation of the land since the last quarter day, or other day assigned for payment of rent. To remedy which it is now enacted (a), that the executors or administrators of tenant for life, on whose death any lease determined, shall recover of the lessee a ratable proportion of rent, from the last day of payment to the death of such lessor.

II. The next estate for life is of the legal kind, as contradistinguished from conventional; *viz.* that of tenant *in tail after possibility of issue extinct*. This happens, where one

---

(a) By 11 Geo. II. c. 19. Sec. 15.

is tenant in fpecial tail, and a perfon, from whofe body the iffue was to fpring, dies without iffue; or, having left iffue, that iffue becomes extinct: in either of thefe cafes the furviving tenant in fpecial tail becomes tenant in tail after poffibility of iffue extinct. As, where one has an eftate to him and his heirs on the body of his prefent wife to be begotten, and the wife dies without iffue.

This eftate muft be created by the act of God, that is, by the death of that perfon out of whofe body the iffue was to fpring; for no limitation, conveyance, or other human act can make it. For, if land be given to a man and his wife, and the heirs of their two bodies begotten, and they are divorced *a vinculo matrimonii*, they fhall neither of them have this eftate, but be barely tenants for life, notwithftanding the inheritance once vefted in them. A poffibility of iffue is always fuppofed to exift, in law, unlefs extinguifhed by the death of the parties; even though the donees be each of them an hundred years old.

This eftate is of an amphibious nature, partaking partly of an eftate-tail, and partly of an eftate for life. The tenant is, in truth, only tenant for life, but with many of the privileges of a tenant in tail; as, not to be punifhable for wafte, &c. or, he is tenant in tail, with many of the reftrictions of a tenant for life; as, to forfeit his eftate if he alienes it in fee-fimple: whereas fuch alienation by tenant in tail, though voidable by the iffue, is no forfeiture of the eftate to the reverfioner: who is not concerned in intereft, till all poffibility of iffue be extinct. But, in general, the law looks upon this eftate as equivalent to an eftate for life only; and, as fuch, will permit this tenant to exchange his eftate with a tenant for life; which exchange can only be made, as we fhall fee hereafter, of eftates that are equal in their nature.

III. Tenant *by the curtefy of England*, is where a man marries a woman feifed of an eftate of inheritance, that is, of lands and tenements in fee-simple or fee-tail; and has by her issue, born alive, which was capable of inheriting her estate. In this case, he shall, on the death of his wife, hold the lands for his life, as tenant by the curtesy of England.

There are four requisites necessary to make a tenancy by the curtesy; marriage, seisin of the wife, issue, and death of the wife. 1. The marriage must be canonical and legal. 2. The seisin of the wife must be an actual seisin, or possession of the lands; not a bare right to possess, which is a seisin in law, but an actual possession, which is a seisin in deed. And therefore a man shall not be tenant by the curtesy of a remainder or reversion. But of some incorporeal hereditaments a man may be tenant by the curtesy, though there have been no actual seisin of the wife: as in case of an advowson, where the church has not become void in the life time of the wife; which a man may hold by the curtesy, because it is impossible ever to have actual seisin of it, and *impotentia excusat legem.* If the wife be an idiot, the husband shall not be tenant by the curtesy of her lands; for the king by prerogative is entitled to them, the instant she herself has any title: and since she could never be rightfully seised of the lands, and the husband's title depends entirely upon her seisin, the husband can have no title as tenant by the curtesy (*a*). 3. The issue must be born alive. The issue also must be born during the life of the mother; for, if the mother dies in labour, and the Cæsarean operation is performed, the husband in this case shall not be tenant by the curtesy: because, at the instant of the mother's death, he was clearly not entitled, as having had no issue born, but the land descended to the child, while he was yet in his mother's womb;

---

(*a*) This rests on the authority of Coke (*Com. Lit.* 30. b) but Mr. Serjt. Hawkins doubted its correctness, " for the fee and freehold were in the wife, and the wife of an idiot shall have dower."—*Abrid.* 1 *Inst.* 43.—and see *Co. Lit.* 30 b. n. 2.

and the estate being once so vested, shall not afterwards be taken from him. In gavelkind lands, a husband may be tenant by the curtesy without having any issue. But in general there must be issue born; and such issue as is also capable of inheriting the mother's estate. Therefore if a woman be tenant in tail *male*, and hath only a *daughter* born, the husband is not thereby entitled to be tenant by the curtesy; because such issue female can never inherit the estate in tail male. The time when the issue was born is immaterial, provided it were during the coverture: for, whether it were born before or after the wife's seisin of the lands, whether it be living or dead at the time of the seisin, or at the time of the wife's decease, the husband shall be tenant by the curtesy. The husband by the birth of the child becomes (as was before observed) tenant by the curtesy *initiate*, and may do many acts to charge the lands: but his estate is not *consummate* till the death of the wife; which is the fourth and last requisite to make a complete tenant by the curtesy.

IV. Tenant in *dower* is where the husband of a woman is seised of an estate of inheritance, and dies; in this case, the wife shall have the third part of all the lands and tenements whereof he was seised at any time during the coverture, to hold to herself for the term of her natural life.

In treating of this estate, let us, first, consider, *who* may be endowed; secondly, of *what* she may be endowed; thirdly, the manner *how* she shall be endowed; and fourthly, how dower may be *barred* or prevented.

1. Who may be endowed. She must be the actual wife of the party at the time of his decease. If she be divorced *a vinculo matrimonii*, she shall not be endowed; for *ubi nullum matrimonium, ibi nulla dos*. But a divorce *a mensa et thoro* only, doth not destroy the dower; no, not even for adultery itself, by the common law. Yet now by the statute Westm. 2. (a)

---

(a) 13 Edw. I. c. 34.

if a woman voluntarily leaves (which the law calls eloping from) her husband, and lives with an adulterer, she shall lose her dower, unless her husband be voluntarily reconciled to her. Widows of traitors are barred of their dower, (except in the case of certain modern treasons relating to the coin) *(a)* but not the widows of felons. An alien also cannot be endowed, unless she be queen consort; for no alien is capable of holding lands. The wife must be above nine years old at her husband's death, otherwise she shall not be endowed.

2. We are next to inquire, of what a wife may be endowed. And she is now by law entitled to be endowed of all lands and tenements, of which her husband was seised in fee-simple or fee-tail at any time during the coverture; and of which any issue, which she might have had, might by possibility have been heir. Therefore if a man, seised in fee-simple, hath a son by his first wife, and after marries a second wife, she shall be endowed of his lands; for her issue might by possibility have been heir, on the death of the son by the former wife. But, if there be a donee in special tail, who holds lands to him and the heirs of his body begotten on Jane his wife; though Jane may be endowed of these lands, yet if Jane dies, and he marries a second wife, that second wife shall never be endowed of the lands entailed; for no issue, that she could have, could by any possibility inherit them. A seisin in law of the husband will be as effectual as a seisin in deed, in order to render the wife dowable; for it is not in the wife's power to bring the husband's title to an actual seisin, as it is in the husband's power to do with regard to the wife's lands: *(b)* which is one reason why he shall not

---

*(a)* Stat. 5 Eliz. c. 11. 18 Eliz. c. 1. 8 & 9 Wil. 3. c. 26. 15 & 16 Geo. II. c. 28. A.

*(b)* Thus where lands or tenements descend to the husband, before entry he hath but a seisin in law, and yet the wife shall be endowed, *Co. Litt.* 31.ᵃ

be tenant by the curtefy, but of fuch lands whereof the wife, or he himfelf in her right, was actually feifed in deed. The feifin of the hufband, for a tranfitory inftant only, when the fame act which gives him the eftate conveys it alfo out of him again, (as where by a fine land is granted to a man, and he immediately renders it back by the fame fine) fuch a feifin will not entitle the wife to dower: for the land was merely *in tranfitu*, and never refted in the hufband; the grant and render being one cont'nued act. But, if the land abides in him for the interval of but a fingle moment, it feems that the wife fhall be endowed thereof. And, in fhort, a widow may be endowed of all her hufband's lands, tenements, and hereditaments, corporeal or incorporeal, under the reftrictions before-mentioned; unlefs there be fome fpecial reafon to the contrary. Thus, a woman fhall not be endowed of a caftle, built for defence of the realm: nor of a common without ftint; for, as the heir would then have one portion of this common, and the widow another, and both without ftint, the common would be doubly ftocked. Copyhold eftates are alfo not liable to dower, being only eftates at the lord's will; unlefs by the fpecial cuftom of the manor, in which cafe it is ufually called the widow's free-bench. But, where dower is allowable, it matters not though the hufband aliene the lands during the coverture; for he alienes them liable to dower.

3. Next, as to the manner in which a woman is to be endowed. There are now fubfifting four fpecies of dower. 1. Dower by the *common law*; or that which is before defcribed. 2. Dower by particular *cuftom*; as that the wife fhould have half the hufband's lands, or in fome places the whole, and in fome only a quarter. 3. Dower *ad oftium ecclefiæ*: which is where tenant in fee-fimple of full age, openly at the church door, doth endow his wife with the whole, or fuch quantity as he fhall pleafe, of his lands; on which the wife, after her hufband's death, may enter without farther

ceremony.] 4. Dower *ex affensu patris*; which is only a species of dower *ad oftium ecclefiæ*, made when the hufband's father is alive, and the fon by his confent, exprefsly given, endows his wife with parcel of his father's lands. In either of thefe cafes, they muft (to prevent frauds) be made *in facie ecclefiæ et ad oftium ecclefiæ*. But thefe fpecific dowers, *ad oftium ecclefiæ* and *ex affenfu patris*, are now fallen into total difufe.

I proceed therefore to confider the method of endowment or affigning dower, by the common law, which is now the only ufual fpecies. By the charter of Henry I. and afterwards by *magna carta* (a), a woman fhall remain in her hufband's capital manfion-houfe for forty days after his death, during which time her dower fhall be affigned. Thefe forty days are called the widow's *quarentine*. The particular lands, to be held in dower, muft be affigned by the heir of the hufband, or his guardian. If the heir or his guardian do not affign her dower within the term of quarentine, or do affign it unfairly, fhe has her remedy at law, and the fheriff is appointed to affign it. Or if the heir (being under age) or his guardian affign more than fhe ought to have, it may be afterwards remedied by writ of *admeafurement* of dower (b). If the thing of which fhe be endowed be divifible, her dower muft be fet out by metes and bounds; but if it be indivifible, fhe muft be endowed fpecially; as, of the third prefentation to a church, the third toll-difh of a mill, the third part of the profits of an office, the third fheaf of tithe, and the like.

4. How dower may be *barred* or prevented. A widow may be barred of her dower not only by elopement, divorce, being an alien, the treafon of her hufband, and other difa-

---

(*a*) Chap. VII.
(*b*) Though the above are undoubtedly the ancient and *legal* modes of proving a due affignment of dower, they are now feldom reforted to in practice; the more eafy, and therefore more ufual, method being an application to the courts of equity.

bilities before-mentioned, but also by detaining the title deeds, or evidences of the estate from the heir, until she restores them: and, by the statute of Goucester (a), if a dowager alienes the land assigned her for dower she forfeits it *ipso facto*, and the heir may recover it by action. A woman also may be barred of her dower, by levying a fine or suffering a recovery of the lands, during her coverture. But the most usual method of barring dowers is by jointures, as regulated by the statute 27 Hen. VIII. c. 10.

A *jointure*, which, strictly speaking, signifies a joint estate, limited to both husband and wife, but in common acceptation extends also to a sole estate, limited to the wife only, is thus defined by Sir Edward Coke; " a competent " livelihood of freehold for the wife, of lands and tene- " ments; to take effect, in profit or possession, presently after " the death of the husband; for the life of the wife at least."
1. The jointure must take effect immediately on the death of the husband. 2. It must be for her own life at least, and not *per auter vie*, or for any term of years, or other smaller estate. 3. It must be made to herself, and no other in trust for her (b). 4. It must be made, and so in the deed particularly expressed to be (c), in satisfaction of her whole dower, and not of any particular part of it. If the jointure be made to her *after* marriage, she has her election after her husband's death, as in dower *ad ostium ecclesiæ*, and may either accept it, or refuse it and betake herself to her dower at common law; for she was not capable of consenting to it during coverture (d)

---

(a) 6 Edw. I. c. 7.
(b) Though this may be true at *law*, yet it is now settled, that a trust estate, or even an agreement to settle lands in jointure is a good *equitable* bar of dower. *Co. Lit.* 36 ᵇ n. 5.
(c) But it was resolved in *Vernon's* case, 4 *Co.* 3. (5th point) on the authority of many preceding cases, that this may be *averr.d*, though omitted to be expressed in the deed.
(d) And so it is also, and for the same reason, where the husband devises an estate to her by *will*, in lieu of dower. See *Co. Lit.* 36 ᵇ n. 6.

And if, by any fraud or accident, a jointure made before marriage proves to be on a bad title and the jointress is evicted, or turned out of poffeffion, she shall then (by the provisions of the same statute) have her dower *pro tanto* at the common law.

There are some advantages attending tenants in dower that do not extend to jointresses; and so *vice v. rsa*, jointresses are in some respects more privileged than tenants in dower. Tenant in dower, by the old common law, is subject to no tolls or taxes; and hers is almost the only estate on which, when derived from the king's debtor, the king cannot distrein for his debt, if contracted during the coverture. But, on the other hand, a widow may enter at once, without any formal process, on her jointure land; whereas no small trouble, and a very tedious method of proceeding, is necessary to compel a legal assignment of dower (a). And, what is more, though dower be forfeited by the treason of the husband, yet lands settled in jointure remain unimpeached to the widow (b).

## CHAPTER VI.

### OF ESTATES LESS THAN FREEHOLD.

OF estates that are less than freehold, there are three sorts: 1. Estates for years: 2. Estates at will: 3. Estates by sufferance.

I. An estate for *years* is a contract for the possession of lands or tenements, for some determinate period: and it

---

(a) See *Ante.* p. 140. n. (b).
(b) Nor is a jointure (as dower is) forfeited by *adultery* of the wife. See *Sidney,* v. *Sidney,* 3 *P. Wms.* 269.

takes place where a man letteth them to another for the term of a certain number of years, agreed upon between the leſſor and the leſſee, and the leſſee enters thereon. If the leaſe be but for half a year, or a quarter, or any leſs time, this leſſee is reſpected as a tenant for years, and is ſtiled ſo in ſome legal proceedings; a year being the ſhorteſt term which the law in this caſe takes notice of.

Every eſtate which muſt expire at a period certain and prefixed, by whatever words created, is an eſtate for years. And therefore this eſtate is frequently called a term, *terminus*, becauſe it's duration or continuance is bounded, limited, and determined: for every ſuch eſtate muſt have a certain beginning, and certain end. But *id certum eſt, quod certum reddi poteſt*: therefore if a man make a leaſe to another, for ſo many years as J. S. ſhall name, it is a good leaſe for years; for though it is at preſent uncertain, yet when J. S. hath named the years, it is then reduced to a certainty. If no day of commencement is named in the creation of this eſtate, it begins from the making, or delivery, of the leaſe.

An eſtate for life, even if it be *per auter vie*, we have ſeen, is a freehold; but an eſtate for a thouſand years is only a chattel, and reckoned part of the perſonal eſtate. Hence it follows, that a leaſe for years may be made to commence *in futuro*, though a leaſe for life cannot. As, if I grant lands to Titius to hold from Michaelmas next for twenty years, this is good; but to hold from Michaelmas next for the term of his natural life, is void. For no eſtate of freehold can commence *in futuro*; becauſe it cannot be created at common law without livery of ſeiſin, or corporal poſſeſſion of the land: and corporal poſſeſſion cannot be given of an eſtate now, which is not to commence now, but hereafter. And, becauſe no livery of ſeiſin is neceſſary to a leaſe for years, ſuch leſſee is not ſaid to be *ſeiſid* or to have true legal ſeiſin of the lands. Nor indeed does the bare leaſe veſt any eſtate in the leſſee; but only gives him a right of entry on the tenement, which right is called his *interest in the term*, or *interesse termini*: but when he has actually so entered, and thereby accepted the grant, the estate is then and not before vested in him, and he is *possessed*, not properly of the land, but of the term of years; the possession or seisin of the *land* remaining still in him who hath the freehold. Thus the word, *term*, does not merely signify the time specified in the lease, but the estate also and interest that passes by that lease; and therefore the *term* may expire, during the continuance of the *time*; as by surrender, forfeiture, and the like.

Tenant for term of years hath incident to and inseparable from his estate, unless by special agreement, the same estovers, which we formerly observed that tenant for life was entitled to; that is to say, house-bote, fire-bote, plough-bote, and hay-bote.

With regard to emblements, or the profits of lands sowed by the tenant for years, there is this difference between him and tenant for life: that where the term of tenant for years depends upon a certainty, as if he holds from midsummer for ten years, and in the last year he sows a crop of corn, and it is not ripe and cut before midsummer, the end of his term, the landlord shall have it; for the tenant knew the expiration of his term, and therefore it was his own folly to sow what he never could reap the profits of. But where the lease for years depends upon an uncertainty; as, upon the death of the lessor, being himself only tenant for life, or being a husband seised in right of his wife; or if the term of years be determinable upon a life or lives; in all these cases, the estate for years not being certainly to expire at a time foreknown, but merely by the act of God, the tenant or his executors, shall have the emblements in the same manner that a tenant for life or his executors shall be entitled thereto. Not so, if it determine by the act of the party himself; as if tenant for years does any thing that amounts to a forfeiture: in which case the emblements shall go to the lessor, and not to the leffee, who hath determined his eftate by his own default.

II. The fecond fpecies of eftates not freehold are eftates at *will.* An eftate at will is where lands and tenements are let by one man to another, to have and to hold at the will of the leffor; and the tenant by force of this leafe obtains poffeffion. Such tenant hath no certain indefeafible eftate, nothing that can be affigned by him to any other; becaufe the leffor may determine his will, and put him out whenever he pleafes. But every eftate at will is at the will of both parties, landlord and tenant; fo that either of them may determine his will, and quit his connexions with the other at his own pleafure. Yet this muft be underftood with fome reftriction. For, if the tenant at will fows his land, and the landlord before the corn is ripe, or before it is reaped, puts him out, yet the tenant fhall have the emblements, and free ingrefs, egrefs, and regrefs, to cut and carry away the profits. And this for the fame reafon, upon which all the cafes of emblements turn; *viz.* the point of uncertainty: fince the tenant could not poffibly know when his landlord would determine his will, and therefore could make no provifion againft it; and having fown the land, which is for the good of the public, upon a reafonable prefumption, the law will not fuffer him to be a lofer by it. But it is otherwife, and upon reafon equally good, where the tenant himfelf determines the will; for in this cafe the landlord fhall have the profits of the land.

What act does, or does not, amount to a determination of the will on either fide, has formerly been matter of great debate in our courts. But it is now, I think, fettled, that (befides the exprefs determination of the leffor's will, by declaring that the leffee fhall hold no longer; which muft either be made upon the land, or notice muft be given to the leffee) the exertion of any act of ownerfhip by the leffor, as entering upon the premifes and cutting timber, taking a distress for rent and impounding it thereon, or making a feoffment, or lease for years of the land to commence immediately; any act of desertion by the lessee, as assigning his estate to another *(a)*, or committing waste, which is an act inconsistent with such a tenure; or, which is *instar omnium*, the death or outlawry of either lessor or lessee: puts an end to or determines the estate at will.

The law is, however, careful that no sudden determination of the will by one party shall tend to the manifest and unforeseen prejudice of the other. This appears in the case of emblements before-mentioned; and, by a parity of reason, the lessee, after the determination of the lessor's will, shall have reasonable ingress and egress to fetch away his goods and utensils. And, if rent be payable quarterly or half-yearly, **and the lessee determines the will, the rent shall be paid to the end of the current quarter or half-year.** And, upon the same principle, courts of law have of late years leaned as much as possible against construing demises, where no certain term is mentioned, to be tenancies at will; but have rather held them to be tenancies from year to year so long as both parties please, especially where an annual rent is reserved: in which case they will not suffer either party to determine the tenancy even at the end of the year, without reasonable notice to the other, which is generally understood to be six months *(b)*.

---

*(a)* But this act of assigning the premises to another, seems not to be a *primâ facie* and absolute determination of the estate; but so only at the option of the lessor, who may construe it to be a disseisin or not at his election. See *Blanden,* v. *Baugh. Cro. Car.* 302. and *Co. Lit.* 57 ª n. 3.

*(b)* From the determinations which have occurred on this subject, the editor collects the rule to be, (though the cases seem, in some degree, contradictory) that where the tenancy commences at any *intermediate* period between the usual quarter days for payment of rent, the requisite notice is *six months* previous to the quittance, as stated in the text; but

## ESTATES LESS THAN FREEHOLD.

There is one species of estates at will, that deserve a more particular regard than any other; and that is, an estate held by copy of court roll; or, as we usually call it, a *copyhold* estate. This, as was before observed (a), was in it's original and foundation nothing better than a mere estate at will. But, the kindness and indulgence of successive lords of manors having permitted these estates to be enjoyed by the tenants and their heirs, according to particular customs established in their respective districts, therefore, though they still are held at the will of the lord, and so are in general expressed in the court rolls to be, yet that will is qualified, restrained, and limited, to be exerted according to the custom of the manor. This custom, being suffered to grow up by the lord, is looked upon as the evidence and interpreter of his will: his will is no longer arbitrary and precarious; but fixed and ascertained by the custom to be the same and no other, that has, time out of mind, been exercised and declared by his ancestors. A copyhold tenant is therefore now full as properly a tenant by the custom, as a tenant at will; the custom having arisen from a series of uniform wills.

Almost every copyhold tenant being therefore thus tenant at the will of the lord according to the custom of the manor; which customs differ as much as the humour and temper of the respective antient lords, (from whence we may account for their great variety) such tenant, I say, may have, so far

---

where it commences *on any of the quarter days,* then *half a year's* notice must be given; which notice, in the latter case, must expire at the end of *that* quarter upon which the tenancy began; but, in the former case, it seems sufficient if the notice be given at any time six months before the tenant is to leave the premises, without regard to the time when the tenancy commenced. See *Fowler,* v. *Derby,* 1 *Term Rep.* 159. and cases there referred to.

(a) *Ante,* p. 129.

as the cuſtom warrants, any other of the eſtates or quantities of intereſt, which we have hitherto confidered, or may hereafter confider, and hold them united with this cuſtomary eſtate at will. A copyholder may, in many manors, be tenant in fee-ſimple, in fee-tail, for life, by the curtefy, in dower, for years, at ſufferance, or on condition: ſubject however to be deprived of theſe eſtates upon the concurrence of thoſe circumſtances which the will of the lord, promulged by immemorial cuſtom, has declared to be a forfeiture or abſolute determination of thoſe intereſts; as in ſome manors the want of iſſue male, in others the cutting down timber, the nonpayment of a fine, and the like. Yet none of theſe intereſts amount to freehold; for the freehold of the whole manor abides always in the lord only, who hath granted out the uſe and occupation, but not the corporal ſeiſin or true legal poſſeſſion, of certain parcels thereof, to theſe his cuſtomary tenants at will.

But with regard to certain other copyholders, of free or privileged tenure, which are derived from the antient tenants in villein-ſocage, and are not ſaid to hold *at the will of the lord*, but only *according to the cuſtom of the manor*, there is no ſuch abſurdity in allowing them to be capable of enjoying a freehold intereſt: and therefore the law doth not ſuppoſe the freehold of ſuch lands to reſt in the lord of whom they are holden, but in the tenants themſelves; who are ſometimes called *cuſtomary freeholders*, being allowed to have a freehold *intereſt*, though not a freehold *tenure*.

III. An eſtate at *ſufferance*, is where one comes in poſſeſſion of land by lawful title, but keeps it afterwards without any title at all. As if a man takes a leaſe for a year, and, after the year is expired, continues to hold the premiſes without any freſh leave from the owner of the eſtate. Or, if a man maketh a leaſe at will, and dies, the eſtate at will is thereby determined: but if the tenant continueth poſſeſſion, he is a tenant at ſufferance. And landlords are obliged in thefe cafes to make formal entries upon their lands, and recover poffeffion by the legal procefs of ejectment: but by ftatute 4 Geo. II. c. 28. in cafe any tenant for life or years, or other perfon claiming under or by collufion with fuch tenant, fhall wilfully hold over after the determination of the term, and demand made and notice in writing given, by him to whom the remainder or reverfion of the premifes fhall belong, for delivering the poffeffion thereof; fuch perfon, fo holding over or keeping the other out of poffeffion, fhall pay for the time he detains the lands, at the rate of double their yearly *value.* And, by ftatute 11 Geo. II. c. 19. in cafe any tenant, having power to determine his leafe, fhall give notice of his intention to quit the premifes, (*a*) and fhall not deliver up the poffeffion at the time contained in fuch notice, he fhall thenceforth pay double the former *rent,* for fuch time as he continues in poffeffion. Thefe ftatutes have almoft put an end to the practice of tenancy by fufferance, unlefs with the tacit confent of the owner of the tenement.

## CHAPTER VII.

### OF ESTATES UPON CONDITION.

BESIDES the feveral divifions of eftates, in point of intereft, which we have confidered in the three preceding chapters, there is alfo another fpecies ftill remaining, which is called an eftate *upon condition*; being fuch whofe exiftence depends upon the happening or not happening of

---

(*a*) This ftatute not requiring (like 4 Geo. II. c. 28.) that the notice fhould be in *writing*, it has been held that a *parol* notice from the tenant is fufficient. See *Timmins, v. Robinfon,* 3 *Burr.* 1603.

some uncertain event, whereby the estate may be either originally created, or enlarged, or finally defeated. These conditional estates are indeed more properly qualifications of other estates, than a distinct species of themselves; seeing that any quantity of interest, a fee, a freehold, or a term of years, may depend upon these provisional restrictions. Estates then upon condition thus understood, are of two sorts: 1. Estates upon condition *implied*: 2. Estates upon condition *expressed*: under which last may be included, 3. Estates held in *vadio*, *gage*, or *pledge*. 4. Estates by *statute merchant* or *statute staple*: 5. Estates held by *elegit*.

I. Estates upon condition implied in law, are where a grant of an estate has a condition annexed to it inseparably from it's essence and constitution, although no condition be expressed in words. As if a grant be made to a man of an office, generally, without adding other words; the law tacitly annexes hereto a secret condition, that the grantee shall duly execute his office, on breach of which condition it is lawful for the grantor, or his heirs, to oust him, and grant it to another person. For an office, either public or private, may be forfeited by *mis-user* or *non-user*, (abuse or neglect) both of which are breaches of this implied condition.

Upon the same principle proceed all the forfeitures which are given by law of life estates and others; for any acts done by the tenant himself, that are incompatible with the estate which he holds.

II. An estate on condition expressed in the grant itself, is where an estate is granted, either in fee-simple or otherwise, with an express qualification annexed, whereby the estate granted shall either commence, be enlarged, or be defeated, upon performance or breach of such qualification or condition. These conditions are therefore either *precedent*, or *subsequent*. Precedent are such as must happen or be performed before the estate can vest or be enlarged: subsequent are such, by the failure or non-performance of which an estate already vested may be defeated.

A diftinction is however made between a *condition in deed* and a *limitation*, which Littleton denominates alfo a *condition in law*. For when an eftate is fo exprefsly confined and limited by the words of it's creation, that it cannot endure for any longer time than till the contingency happens upon which the eftate is to fail, this is denominated a *limitation*: as when land is granted to a man, *until* out of the rents and profits he fhall have made 500*l*. and the like. In fuch cafe the eftate determines as foon as the contingency happens, (when he has received the 500*l*.) and the next fubfequent eftate, which depends upon fuch determination, becomes immediately vefted, without any act to be done by him who is next in expectancy. But when an eftate is, ftrictly fpeaking, upon *condition in deed* (as if granted exprefsly *upon condition* to be void upon the payment of 40l. by the grantor, &c.) the law permits it to endure beyond the time when fuch contingency happens, unlefs the grantor, or his heirs or affigns, take advantage of the breach of the condition, and make either an entry or claim in order to avoid the eftate. Yet, though ftrict words of condition be ufed in the creation of the eftate, if on breach of the condition the eftate be limited over to a third perfon, and does not immediately revert to the grantor or his reprefentatives, as if a man by his will devifes land to his heir at law, on condition that he pays a fum of money, and for non-payment devifes it over, this fhall be confidered as a limitation; otherwife no advantage could be taken of the non-payment, for none but the heir himfelf could have entered for a breach of condition.

Thefe exprefs conditions, if they be *impoffible* at the time of their creation, or afterwards become impoffible by the act of God or the act of the feoffor himfelf, or if they be *contrary to law*, (*a*) or *repugnant* to the nature of the eftate, are void.

---

(*a*) See the queftion of conditions contrary to law, elabo-

In any of which cases, if they be conditions *subsequent*, that is, to be performed after the estate is vested, the estate shall become absolute in the tenant. But if the condition be *precedent*, or to be performed before the estate vests, the grantee shall take nothing by the grant: for he hath no estate until the condition be performed.

There are some estates defeasible upon condition subsequent, that require a more peculiar notice. Such are

III. Estates held *in vadio*, in *gage*, or pledge; which are of two kinds, *vivum vadium*, or living pledge; and *mortuum vadium*, dead pledge, or *mortgage*.

*Vivum vadium*, or living pledge, is when a man borrows a sum (suppose 200l.) of another; and grants him an estate, as, of 20l. *per annum*, to hold till the rents and profits shall repay the sum so borrowed. This is an estate conditioned to be void, as soon as such sum is raised. And in this case the land or pledge is said to be living: it subsists, and survives the debt; and, immediately on the discharge of that, reverts back to the borrower. But *mortuum vadium*, a dead pledge, or *mortgage*, (which is much more common than the other) is where a man borrows of another a specific sum (*e. g.* 200l.) and grants him an estate in fee, on condition that if he, the mortgagor, shall repay the sum of 200l. on a certain day mentioned in the deed, that then, the mortgagor may re-enter on the estate so granted in pledge; or, as is now the more usual way, that then the mortgagee shall reconvey the estate to the mortgagor: in this case the land, which is so put in

---

rately discussed by Parker, C. J. in delivering the opinion of the court in *Mitchel*, v. *Reynolds*, reported 1 *P. Wms.* 181, where the learned judge reduces the instances of conditions against law, under the heads of 1. To do what is either *malum in se*, or *malum prohibitum*. 2. To omit the doing something that is a duty, and 3. To encourage such crimes and omissions.

pledge, is by law, in case of non-payment at the time limited, for ever dead and gone from the mortgagor; and the mortgagee's estate in the lands is then no longer conditional, but absolute. But, so long as it continues conditional, that is, between the time of lending the money, and the time allotted for payment, the mortgagee is called tenant in mortgage. But, as it was formerly a doubt, whether, by taking such estate in fee, it did not become liable to the wife's dower, and other incumbrances, of the mortgagee (though that doubt has been long ago over-ruled by our courts of equity) it therefore became usual to grant only a long term of years, by way of mortgage; with condition to be void on re-payment of the mortgage-money: which course has been since pretty generally continued, principally because on the death of the mortgagee such term becomes vested in his personal representatives, who alone are entitled in equity to receive the money lent, of whatever nature the mortgage may happen to be.

As soon as the estate is created, the mortgagee may immediately enter on the lands; but is liable to be dispossessed, upon performance of the condition by payment of the mortgage-money at the day limited. And therefore the usual way is to agree that the mortgagor shall hold the land till the day assigned for payment; when, in case of failure, whereby the estate becomes absolute, the mortgagee may enter upon it and take possession, without any possibility *at law* of being afterwards evicted by the mortgagor, to whom the land is now for ever dead. But here again the courts of equity interpose; and, though a mortgage be thus forfeited, and the estate absolutely vested in the mortgagee at the common law, yet they will consider the real value of the tenements compared with the sum borrowed. And, if the estate be of greater value than the sum lent thereon, they will allow the mortgagor *(a)* at any reasonable time *(b)* to recall or redeem his estate; paying to the mortgagee his principal, interest, and expenses: for otherwise, in strictness of law, an estate worth 1000l. might be forfeited for non-payment of 100l. or a less sum. This reasonable advantage, allowed to mortgagors, is called the *equity of redemption;* and this enables a mortgagor to call on the mortgagee, who has possession of his estate, to deliver it back and account for the rents and profits received, on payment of his whole debt and interest; thereby turning the *mortuum* into a kind of *vivum vadium*. But, on the other hand, the mortgagee may either compel the sale of the estate, in order to get the whole of his money immediately; or else call upon the mortgagor to redeem his estate presently, or, in default thereof, to be for ever *foreclosed* from redeeming the same; that is, to lose his equity of redemption without possibility of recall. And also, in some cases of fraudulent mortgages; the fradulent mortgagor forfeits all equity of redemption whatsoever. *(c)* It is not however usual for mortgagees to take possession of the

---

*(a)* And all others having and estate or interest in the equity of redemption of the mortgagor.—See Mr. *Butler's* note to *Co. Lit.* 208.[a]

*(b)* Mortgages not being within the statute of limitations, there is no set time for their redemption in equity; but " Courts of equity have nevertheless judged that statute a reasonable guide for them to follow as to redemption, unless there are such particular circumstances as may vary the ordinary case, as infants, feme covert, &c. who are provided for by the same statute." *Ewre*, and *White*, 2 *Vent.* 340. *Knowles* and *Spence*, 1 *Eq. Ca. Abr.* 315. In general therefore, if the mortgagee has been 20 years in possession, courts of equity will not assist the mortgagor to recover his estate. See also 1 *Pow. Mortg.* 133. 1 *Fonb. Eq.* 323. n. *(s.)* 2 *Ib.* 268.

*(c)* See 4 and 5 *Will.* and *Mar.* c, 16. which provides, that where a person, for a valuable consideration, mortgages an estate which is already in mortgage, or otherwise encumbered,

mortgaged eftate, unlefs where the fecurity is precarious, or fmall; or where the mortgagor neglects even the payment of intereft: when the mortgagee is frequently obliged to bring an ejectment,(a) and take the land into his own hands. But, by ftatute 7 Geo. II. c. 20. after payment or tender by the mortgagor of principal, intereft, and cofts, the mortgagee can maintain no ejectment; but may be compelled to re-affign his fecurities.

IV. A fourth fpecies of eftates, defeafible on condition fubfequent, are thofe held by *ftatute merchant*, and *ftatute ftaple*; which are very nearly releated to the *vivum vadium* before-mentioned, or eftate held till the profits thereof fhall difcharge a debt liquidated or afcertained. For both the ftatute merchant and ftatute ftaple are fecurities for money; the one entered into before the chief magiftrate of fome trading town, purfuant to the ftatute 13 Edw. I. *de mercatoribus*, and thence called a ftatute-merchant; the other purfuant to ftatute 27 Edw. III. c. 9. before the mayor of the ftaple; whereby not only the body of the debtor may be imprifoned, and his goods feifed in fatisfaction of the debt, but alfo his lands may be delivered to the creditor, till out of the rents and profits of them the debt may be fatisfied: and, during fuch time as the creditor fo holds the lands, he is tenant by ftatute merchant or ftatute ftaple. (b)

V. Another fimilar conditional eftate, created by opera-

---

and fhall not apprife the mortgagee in writing of fuch incumbrance, he fhall be barred of all equity of redemption thereof. Sec. 2 and 3.

(a) But fee *Mofs* v. *Gallimore*, 1 *Dougl.* 266, where it was determined that if there be a tenant in poffeffion of the mortgaged eftate, under a leafe fubfifting prior to the mortgage, the mortgagee may give notice to fuch tenant to pay his rent to *him*, (the mortgagee) and on refufal may *diftrain* as well for the rent due at the time of the notice given as for fuch as may afterwards accrue.

(b) Eftates by ftatute merchant and ftatute ftaple, are

tion of law, for fecurity and fatisfaction of debts, is called an eftate by *elegit*. What an *elegit* is, and why fo called, will be explained in the third part of thefe commentaries. At prefent I need only mention, that it is the name of a writ, founded on the ftatute of Weftm. 2. (a) by which, after a plaintiff has obtained judgment for his debt at law, the fheriff gives him poffeffion of one half of the defendant's lands and tenements, to be occupied and enjoyed until his debt and damages are fully paid: and, during the time he fo holds them, he is called tenant by *elegit*.

## CHAPTER VIII.

### OF ESTATES IN POSSESSION, REMAINDER, AND REVERSION.

HITHERTO we have confidered eftates folely with regard to their duration, or the *quantity of intereft* which the owners have therein. We are now to confider them in another view; with regard to the *time of their enjoyment*, when the actual pernancy of the profits (that is, the taking, perception, or receipt, of the rents and other advantages arifing therefrom) begins. Eftates therefore, with refpect to this confideration, may either be in *poffeffion*, or in *expectancy*: and of expectancies there are two forts; one created by the act of the parties, called a *remainder*; the other by act of law, and called a *reverfion*.

I. Of eftates in *poffeffion*, (which are fometimes called eftates *executed*, whereby a prefent intereft paffes to and re-

---

however, as Mr. *Chriftian* has obferved, now unknown in practice, (p. 160, n. 5.)

(a) 13 Edw. I. c. 18.

fides in the tenant, not depending on any subsequent circumstance or contingency, as in the case of estates *executory*) there is little or nothing peculiar to be observed. All the estates we have hitherto spoken of are of this kind. But the doctrine of estates in expectancy contains some of the nicest and most abstruse learning in the English law. These will therefore require a minute discussion, and demand some degree of attention.

II. An estate then in remainder may be defined to be, an estate limited to take effect and be enjoyed after another estate is determined. As if a man seised in fee-simple granteth lands to A for twenty years, and, after the determination of the said term, then to B and his heirs for ever: here A is tenant for years, remainder to B in fee. But both these interests are in fact only one estate; the present term of years and the remainder afterwards, when added together, being equal only to one estate in fee; being nothing but parts or portions of one entire inheritance: and if there were a hundred remainders, it would still be the same thing; upon a principle grounded in mathematical truth, that all the parts are equal, and no more than equal, to the whole. And hence also it is easy to collect, that no remainder can be limited after the grant of an estate in fee-simple: because a fee-simple is the highest and largest estate, that a subject is capable of enjoying; and he that is tenant in fee hath in him the *whole* of the estate: a remainder therefore, which is only a portion, or residuary *part*, of the estate, cannot be reserved after the whole is disposed of.

Thus much being premised, we shall be the better enabled to comprehend the rules that are laid down by law to be observed in the creation of remainders, and the reasons upon which those rules are founded.

1. And, first, there must necessarily be some particular estate, precedent to the estate in remainder. As, an estate for years to A, remainder to B for life; or, an estate for life

to A, remainder to B in tail. This precedent eftate is called the *particular* eftate, as being only a fmall part, or *particula,* of the inheritance; the refidue or remainder of which is granted over to another. And as no remainder can be created, without fuch a precedent particular eftate, therefore the particular eftate is faid to *fupport* the remainder; hence it is generally true, that if the particular eftate is void in it's creation, or by any means is defeated afterwards, the remainder fupported thereby fhall be defeated alfo.

2. A fecond rule to be obferved is this; that the remainder muft commence or pafs out of the grantor at the time of the creation of the particular eftate. And it is this, which induces the neceffity at common law of livery of feifin being made on the particular eftate, whenever a *freehold* remainder is created. For, if it be limited even on an eftate for years, it is neceffary that the leffee for years fhould have livery of feifin, in order to convey the freehold from and out of the grantor; otherwife the remainder is void.

3. A third rule refpecting remainders is this; that the remainder muft veft in the grantee during the continuance of the particular eftate, or *eo inftanti* that it determines. Therefore, if an eftate be limited to A for life, remainder to the eldeft fon of B in tail, and A dies before B hath any fon: here the remainder will be void, for it did not veft in any one during the continuance, nor at the determination, of the particular eftate.

It is upon thefe rules, but principally the laft, that the doctrine of *contingent* remainders depends. For remainders are either *vefted* or *contingent*. *Vefted* remainders (or remainders *executed*, whereby a prefent intereft paffes to the party, though to be enjoyed *in futuro*) are where the eftate is invariably fixed, to remain to a determinate perfon, after the particular eftate is fpent. As if A be tenant for twenty years, remainder to B in fee; here B's is a vested remainder, which nothing can defeat, or set aside.

Contingent or *executory* remainders (whereby no present interest passes) are where the estate in remainder is limited to take effect, either to a dubious and uncertain *person*, or upon a dubious and uncertain *event*; so that the particular estate may chance to be determined, and the remainder never take effect.

First, they may be limited to a dubious and uncertain *person*. As if A be tenant for life, with remainder to B's eldest son (then unborn) in tail; this is a contingent remainder, for it is uncertain whether B will have a son or no: but the instant that a son is born, the remainder is no longer contingent, but vested. Though, if A had died before the contingency happened, that is, before B's son was born, the remainder would have been absolutely gone; for the particular estate was determined before the remainder could vest. But it is enacted, by statute 10 and 11 W. III. c. 16. that *posthumous* children shall be capable of taking in remainder, in the same manner as if they had been born in their father's lifetime: that is, the remainder is allowed to vest in them, while yet in their mother's womb.

This species of contingent remainders, to a person not in being, must, however, be limited to some one, that may, by common possibility, or *potentia propinqua*, be *in esse* at or before the particular estate determines. As if an estate be made to A for life, remainder to the heirs of B. This is a good contingent remainder, for the possibility of B's dying before A is *potentia propinqua*, and therefore allowed in law. But a remainder to the right heirs of B (if there be no such person as B *in esse*) is void. For here there must two contingencies happen; first, that such a person as B shall be born; and, secondly, that he shall also die during the continuance of the particular estate; which make it *potentia remotiſſima*, a moſt improbable poſſibility. And ſo a limitation of a remainder to a baſtard before it is born, is not good: for though the law allows the poſſibility of having baſtards, it preſumes it to be a very remote and improbable contingency— Thus may a remainder be contingent, on account of the uncertainty of the *perſon* who is to take it.

A remainder may alſo be contingent, where the perſon to whom it is limited is fixed and certain, but the *event* upon which it is to take effect is vague and uncertain. As, where land is given to A for life, and in caſe B ſurvives him, then with the remainder to B in fee: during the joint lives of A and B it is contingent; and if B dies firſt, it never can veſt in his heirs, but is for ever gone; but if A dies firſt, the remainder to B becomes veſted.

Contingent remainders of either kind, if they amount to a freehold, cannot be limited on an eſtate for years, or any other particular eſtate, leſs than a freehold. Thus if land be granted to A for ten years, with remainder in fee to the right heirs of B, this remainder is void: but if granted to A for life, with a like remainder, it is good. For, unleſs the freehold paſſes out of the grantor at the time when the remainder is created, ſuch freehold remainder is void: it cannot paſs out of him, without veſting ſomewhere; and in the caſe of a contingent remainder it muſt veſt in the particular tenant, elſe it can veſt no where: unleſs therefore the eſtate of ſuch particular tenant be of a freehold nature, the freehold cannot veſt in him, and conſequently the remainder is void.

Contingent remainders may be *defeated*, by deſtroying or determining the particular eſtate upon which they depend, before the contingency happens whereby they become veſted. Therefore when there is tenant for life, with divers remainders in contingency, he may, not only by his death, but by alienation, ſurrender, or other methods, deſtroy and determine his own life-eſtate, before any of thoſe remainders veſt;

C. VIII.   ESTATES IN POSSESSION, &c.

the confequence of which is that he utterly defeats them all. In thefe cafes, therefore, it is neceffary to have truftees appointed to preferve the contingent remainders; in whom there is vefted an eftate in remainder for the life of the tenant for life, to commence when his eftate determines. If therefore his eftate for life determines otherwife than by his death, the eftate of the truftees, for the refidue of his natural life, will then take effect, and become a particular eftate in poffeffion, fufficient to fupport the remainders depending in contingency. I muft not however omit, that, in devifes by laft will and teftament, (which, being often drawn up when the party is *inops confilii*, are always more favoured in conftruction than formal deeds, which are prefumed to be made with great caution, fore-thought, and advice) in thefe devifes, I fay, remainders may be created in fome meafure contrary to the rules before laid down: though our lawyers will not allow fuch difpofitions to be ftrictly remainders; but call them by another name, that of *executory devifes*, or devifes hereafter to be executed.

An executory devife of lands is fuch a difpofition of them by will, that thereby no eftate vefts at the death of the devifor, but only on fome future contingency. It differs from a remainder in three very material points: 1. That it needs not any particular eftate to fupport it. 2. That by it a fee-fimple or other lefs eftate, may be limited after a fee-fimple. 3. That by this means a remainder may be limited of a chattel intereft, after a particular eftate for life created in the fame.

1. The firft cafe happens when a man devifes a future eftate to arife upon a contingency; and, till that contingency happens, does not difpofe of the fee-fimple, but leaves it to defcend to his heir at law. This limitation, though it would be void in a deed, yet is good in a will, by way of executory devife. For, fince by a devife a freehold may pafs without corporal tradition or livery of feifin, (as it muft

M

do, if it passes at all) therefore it may commence *in futuro*; because the principal reason why it cannot commence *in futuro* in other cases, is the necessity of actual seisin, which always operates *in præsenti*. And, since it may thus commence *in futuro*, there is no need of a particular estate to support it; the only use of which is to make the remainder, by it's unity with the particular estate, a present interest. And hence also it follows, that such an executory devise, not being a present interest, cannot be barred by a recovery, suffered before it commences.

2. By executory devise a fee, or other less estate, may be limited after a fee. And this happens where a devisor devises his whole estate in fee, but limits a remainder thereon to commence on a future contingency. As if a man devises land to A and his heirs; but, if he dies before the age of twenty-one, then to B and his heirs: this remainder, though void in a deed, is good by way of executory devise. But, in both these species of executory devises, the contingencies ought to be such as may happen within a reasonable time; for courts of justice will not indulge even wills, so as to create a perpetuity, which the law abhors.—The utmost length that has been hitherto allowed for the contingency of an executory devise of either kind to happen in, is that of a life or lives in being, and one and twenty years afterwards.

3. By executory devise a term of years may be given to one man for his life, and afterwards limited over in remainder to another, which could not be done by deed: for by law the first grant of it, to a man for life, was a total disposition of the whole term; a life estate being esteemed of a higher and larger nature than any term of years: yet, in order to prevent the danger of perpetuities, though such remainders may be limited to as many persons successively as the devisor thinks proper, yet they must all be *in esse* during the life of the first devisee; for then all the candles are lighted and are consuming together, and the ultimate remainder is in reality

only to that remainder-man who happens to survive the rest: and that such remainder may not be limited to take effect, unless upon such contingency as must happen (if at all) during the life of the first devisee *(a)*.

Thus much for such estates in expectancy, as are created by the express words of the parties themselves; the most intricate title in the law. There is yet another species, which is created by the act and operation of the law itself, and this is called a reversion.

III. An estate in *reversion* is the residue of an estate left in the grantor, to commence in possession after the determination of some particular estate granted out by him. As, if there be a gift in tail, the reversion of the fee is, without any special reservation, vested in the donor by act of law: and so also the reversion, after an estate for life, years, or at will, continues in the lessor. A reversion is never therefore created by deed or writing, but arises from construction of law; a remainder can never be limited, unless by either deed or devise. But both are equally transferable, when actually vested, being both estates *in præsenti*, though taking effect *in futuro*.

In order to assist such persons as have any estate in remainder, reversion, or expectancy, after the death of others, against fraudulent concealments of their deaths, it is enacted by the statute 6 Ann. c. 18. that all persons on whose lives any lands or tenements are holden, shall (upon application to the court of chancery and order made thereupon) once in

---

*(a)* The editor cannot pass by the author's observations upon contingent remainders and executory devises, without earnestly referring the reader to the late Mr. *Fearne*'s Essays on those subjects; where he will find them treated of in a manner so elegant and masterly, as to have deservedly conferred the most eminent renown upon their author whilst living, and will, no doubt, insure to his memory the highest veneration and gratitude of the profession.

every year, if required, be produced to the court, or it's commiſſioners; or, upon neglect or refuſal, they ſhall be taken to be actually dead, and the perſon entitled to ſuch expectant eſtate may enter upon and hold the lands and tenements, till the party ſhall appear to be living.

Before we conclude the doctrine of remainders and reverſions, it may be proper to obſerve, that whenever a greater eſtate and a leſs coincide and meet in one and the ſame perſon, without any intermediate eſtate, the leſs is immediately annihilated; or, in the law-phraſe, is ſaid to be *merged*, that is, ſunk or drowned, in the greater. Thus, if there be tenant for years, and the reverſion in fee-ſimple deſcends to or is purchaſed by him, the term of years is merged in the inheritance, and ſhall never exiſt any more. But they muſt come to one and the ſame perſon in one and the ſame right; elſe, if the freehold be in his own right, and he has a term in right of another, there is no merger. An eſtate-tail is an exception to this rule: for a man may have in his own right both an eſtate-tail and a reverſion in fee; and the eſtate-tail, though a leſs eſtate, ſhall not merge in the fee. For eſtates-tail are protected and preſerved from merger by the operation and conſtruction, though not by the expreſs words, of the ſtatute *de donis*.

## CHAPTER IX.
### OF ESTATES IN SEVERALTY, JOINT-TENANCY, COPARCENARY, AND COMMON.

WE come now to treat of eſtates, with reſpect to the number and connexions of their owners, the tenants who occupy and hold them. And, conſidered in this view, eſtates of any quantity or length of duration, and whether they be in actual poſſeſſion or expectancy, may be held in four different ways; in feveralty, in joint-tenancy, in coparcenary, and in common.

I. He that holds lands or tenements in *feveralty*, or is fole tenant thereof, is he that holds them in his own right only, without any other perfon being joined or connected with him in point of intereft, during his eftate therein. This is the moft common and ufual way of holding an eftate; and there is little or nothing peculiar to be remarked concerning it, fince all eftates are fuppofed to be of this fort, unlefs where they are exprefsly declared to be otherwife.

II. An eftate in *joint-tenancy* is where lands or tenements are granted to two or more perfons, to hold in fee-fimple, fee-tail, for life, for years, or at will. In confequence of fuch grants an eftate is called an eftate in joint-tenancy.

In unfolding this title, and the two remaining ones in the prefent chapter, we will firft inquire, how thefe eftates may be *created;* next, their *properties* and refpective *incidents;* and laftly, how they may be *fevered* or *deftroyed.*

1. The *creation* of an eftate in joint-tenancy depends on the wording of the deed or devife, by which the tenants claim title; for this eftate can only arife by purchafe or grant, that is, by the act of the parties, and never by the mere act of law. Now, if an eftate be given to a plurality of perfons, without adding any reftrictive, exclufive, or explanatory words, as if an eftate be granted to A and B and their heirs, this makes them immediately joint-tenants in fee of the lands.

2. The *properties* of a joint eftate are derived from it's unity, which is fourfold; the unity of *intereft,* the unity of *title,* the unity of *time,* and the unity of *poffeffion:* or, in other words, joint-tenants have one and the fame intereft, accruing by one and the fame conveyance, commencing at one and the fame time, and held by one and the fame undivided poffeffion.

Joint-tenants are faid to be feifed *per my et per tout,* by the *half* or *moiety,* and by *all*; that is, they each of them have the entire poffeffion, as well of every *parcel,* as of the *whole.* They have not one of them a feifin of one half or moiety, and the other of the other moiety; neither can one be exclusively seised of one acre, and his companion of another; but each has an undivided moiety of the whole, and not the whole of an undivided moiety. And therefore, if an estate in fee be given to a man and his wife, they are neither properly joint-tenants, nor tenants in common: for husband and wife being considered as one person in law, they cannot take the estate by moieties, but both are seised of the entirety, *per tout, et non per my;* the consequence of which is, that neither the husband nor the wife can dispose of any part without the assent of the other, but the whole must remain to the survivor.

Upon these principles, of a thorough and intimate union of interest and possession, depend many other consequences and incidents to the joint-tenant's estate. If two joint-tenants let a verbal lease of their land, reserving rent to be paid to one of them, it shall enure to both, in respect of the joint reversion. If their lessee surrenders his lease to one of them, it shall also enure to both, because of the privity, or relation of their estate. On the same reason, livery of seisin, made to one joint-tenant, shall enure to both of them: and the entry or re-entry, of one joint-tenant is as effectual in law as if it were the act of both. In all actions also relating to their joint estate, one joint-tenant cannot sue or be sued without joining the other. But if two or more joint-tenants be seised of an advowson, and they present different clerks, the bishop may refuse to admit either: because neither joint-tenant hath a several right of patronage, but each is seised of the whole: and, if they do not both agree within six months, the right of presentation shall lapse. Upon the same ground it is held, that one joint-tenant cannot have an action against another for trespass, in respect of his land; for each has an equal right to enter on any part of it. But one joint-tenant is not capable by himself to do any act, which may tend to defeat or injure the estate of the other; as to let leases, or to grant copyholds: and, if any waste be done, which tends to the destruction of the inheritance, one joint-tenant may have an action of waste against the other, by construction of the statute Westm. 2. c. 22. So too, by the statute 4 Ann.

c. 16. joint-tenants may have actions of account against each other, for receiving more than their due share of the profits of the tenements held in joint-tenancy (a).

From the same principle also arises the remaining grand incident of joint estates; *viz.* the doctrine of *survivorship*: by which, when two or more persons are seised of a joint estate of inheritance, for their own lives, or *pur auter vie*, or are jointly possessed of any chattel interest, the entire tenancy upon the decease of any of them remains to the survivors, and at length to the last survivor; and he shall be entitled to the whole estate, whatever it be, whether an inheritance or common freehold only, or even a less estate.

3. We are, lastly, to inquire, how an estate in joint-tenancy may be *severed* and *destroyed*. And this may be done by destroying any of it's constituent unities. 1. That of *time*, which respects only the original commencement of the joint-estate, cannot, indeed, (being now past) be affected by any subsequent transactions. But, 2. The joint-tenants' estate may be destroyed, without any alienation, by merely disuniting their *possession*. By common law one of them could not compel the other so to do. But now, by the statutes 31 Hen. VIII. c. 1. and 32 Hen. VIII. c. 32, joint-tenants, either of inheritances or other less estates, are compellable by writ of partition to divide their lands. 3. The jointure may be destroyed by destroying the unity of *title*. As if one joint-tenant alienes and conveys his estate to a third person: here the joint-tenancy is severed, and turned into tenancy in common; for the grantee and the remaining joint-tenant hold by different titles, (one derived from the original, the other from the subsequent, grantor) though, till partition made, the unity of possession continues. But a devise of one's share by will is no severance of the jointure: for no

---

(a) This action, however, I apprehend is now seldom or ever resorted to; a more effectual method of obtaining relief, in these cases, being by bill in equity.

testament takes effect till after the death of the testator, and by such death the right of the survivor (which accrued at the original creation of the estate, and has therefore a priority to the other) is already vested. 4. It may also be destroyed, by destroying the unity of *interest*. And, therefore, if there be two joint-tenants for life, and the inheritance is purchased by or descends upon either, it is a severance of the jointure: though, if an estate is originally limited to two for life, and after to the heirs of one of them, the freehold shall remain in jointure, without merging in the inheritance; because, being created by one and the same conveyance, they are not separate estates, (which is requisite in order to a merger) but branches of one entire estate. And, by whatever means the jointure ceases or is severed, the right of survivorship or *jus accrescendi* the same instant ceases with it.

III. An estate held in *coparcenary* is where lands of inheritance descend from the ancestor to two or more persons. It *arises* either by common law, or particular custom. By common law: as where a person seised in fee-simple or in fee-tail dies, and his next heirs are two or more females, his daughters, sisters, aunts, cousins, or their representatives; in this case they shall all inherit, as will be more fully shewn, when we treat of descents hereafter: and these co-heirs are then called *coparceners*; or, for brevity, *parceners* only. Parceners by particular custom are where lands descend, as in gavelkind, to all the males in equal degree, as sons, brothers, uncles, &c. And, in either of these cases, all the parceners put together make but one heir; and have but one estate among them.

The *properties* of parceners are, in some respects, like those of joint-tenants; they having the same unities of *interest, title,* and *possession*. They may sue and be sued jointly for matters relating to their own lands: and the entry of one of them shall, in some cases (a), enure as the entry of them all.

---

(a) See the principal of these cases collected in *Co. Lit.* 188ᵃ, 243ᵇ. and the notes there.

They cannot have an action of trespass against each other: but herein they differ from joint-tenants, that they are also excluded from maintaining an action of waste. Parceners also differ materially from joint-tenants in four other points : 1. They always claim by descent, whereas joint-tenants always claim by purchase. Therefore if two sisters purchase lands, to hold to them and their heirs, they are not parceners, but joint-tenants. 2. There is no unity of *time* necessary to an estate in coparcenary. For if a man hath two daughters, to whom his estate descends in coparcenary, and one dies before the other; the surviving daughter and the heir of the other, or, when both are dead, their two heirs, are still parceners. 3. Parceners, though they have an *unity*, have not an *entirety*, of interest. They are properly entitled each to the whole of a distinct moiety; and of course there is no *jus accrescendi*, or survivorship between them : for each part descends severally to their respective heirs, though the unity of possession continues to parceners, as so called because they may be constrained to make partition.

But there are some things which are in their nature impartible. The mansion-house, common of estovers, common of piscary uncertain, or any other common without stint, shall not be divided; but the eldest sister, if she pleases, shall have them, and make the others a reasonable satisfaction in other parts of the inheritance: or, if that cannot be, then they shall have the profits of the thing by turns, in the same manner as they take the advowson (*a*).

The estate in coparcenary may be *dissolved*, either by partition, which disunites the possession; by alienation of one parcener, which disunites the title, and may disunite the interest; or by the whole at last descending to and vesting in one single person, which brings it to an estate in severalty.

---

(*a*) The learned judge here proceeds to enumerate the various modes of making partition between coparceners at common law; but as the usual mode of effecting this, as well in respect to coparceners, as also joint-tenants and tenants in common, is by application to a court of equity, I have omitted to retain them in the present extracts.

IV. Tenants in *common* are such as hold by several and distinct titles, but by unity of possession. Tenancy in common may be created, either by the destruction of the two other estates in joint-tenancy and coparcenary, or by special limitation in a deed. By the destruction of the two other estates, I mean such destruction as does not sever the unity of possession, but only the unity of title or interest: as, if one of two joint-tenants in fee, alienes his estate for the life of the alienee, the alienee and the other joint-tenant are tenants in common: for they now have several titles, the other joint-tenant by the original grant, the alienee by the new alienation; and they also have several interests, the former joint-tenant in fee-simple, the alienee for his own life only. If one of two parceners alienes, the alienee and the remaining parcener are tenants in common; because they hold by different titles, the parcener by descent, the alienee by purchase. In short, whenever an estate in joint-tenancy or coparcenary is dissolved, so that there be no partition made, but the unity of possession continues, it is turned into a tenancy in common.

A tenancy in common may also be created by express limitation in a deed: but here care must be taken not to insert words which imply a joint estate; and then if the lands be given to two or more, and it be not joint-tenancy, it must be a tenancy in common. And the nicety in wording of grants makes it the most usual as well the safest way, when a tenancy in common is meant to be created, to add express words of exclusion as well as description, and limit the estate to A and B, to hold *as tenants in common, and not as joint-tenants.*

As to the *incidents* attending a tenancy in common: tenants in common (like joint-tenants) are compellable by the statutes of Henry VIII. and William III. before-mentioned; to make partition of their lands; which they were not at common law. They properly take by distinct moieties, and have no entirety of interest; and therefore there is no survivorship between tenants in common. Their other incidents are such as merely arise from the unity of possesfion; and are therefore the same as appertain to joint-tenants merely upon that account: such as being liable to reciprocal actions of waste, and of account, by the statutes of Westm. 2. c. 22. and 4 Ann. c. 16.

Estates in common can only be *dissolved* two ways: 1. By uniting all the titles and interests in one tenant by purchase or otherwise; which brings the whole to one severalty: 2. By making partition between the several tenants in common, which gives them all respective severalties. For, indeed, tenancies in common differ in nothing from sole estates, but merely in the blending and unity of possession. And this finishes our inquiries with respect to the nature of *estates*.

---

## CHAPTER X.

### OF THE TITLE TO THINGS REAL, IN GENERAL.

THE foregoing chapters having been principally employed in defining the *nature* of things real, in describing the *tenures* by which they may be holden, and in distinguishing the several kinds of *estate* or interest that may be had therein; I come now to consider, lastly, the *title* to things real, with the manner of acquiring and losing it.

A title is thus defined by Sir Edward Coke, *titulus est justa causa possidendi id quod nostrum est*; or, it is the means whereby the owner of lands hath the just possession of his property.

There are several stages or degrees requisite to form a complete title to lands and tenements. We will consider them in a progressive order.

I. The lowest and most imperfect degree of title consists in the mere *naked possession*, or actual occupation of the estate; without any apparent right, or any shadow or pretence of right, to hold and continue such possession.

II. The next step to a good and perfect title is the *right of possession*, which may reside in one man, while the actual possession is not in himself but in another. For if a man be diffeifed, or otherwife kept out of poffeffion, though the *actual* poffeffion be loft, yet he has ftill remaining in him the *right* of poffeffion. This right of poffeffion is of two forts: an *apparent* right of poffeffion, which may be defeated by proving a better; and an *actual* right of poffeffion, which will ftand the teft againft all opponents. Thus if the diffeifor, or other wrongdoer, dies poffeffed of the land whereof he fo became feifed by his own unlawful act, and the fame defcends to his heir; now, by the common law, the heir hath obtained an *apparent* right, though the *actual* right of poffeffion refides in the perfon diffeifed; and it fhall not be lawful for the perfon diffeifed to diveft this apparent right by mere entry or other act of his own, but only by an action at law. Yet, if he omits to bring his poffeffory action within a competent time, his adverfary may imperceptibly gain an actual right of poffeffion, in confequence of the other's negligence. And by this means, the party kept out of poffeffion may have nothing left in him, but what we are next to fpeak of; *viz.*

III. The mere *right of property*, the *jus proprietatis*, without either poffeffion or even the right of poffeffion.

Thus, if a diffeifor turns me out of poffeffion of my lands, he thereby gains a *mere naked poffeffion*, and I ftill retain the *right of poffeffion*, and *right of property*. If the diffeifor dies, and the lands defcend to his fon, the fon gains an *apparent* right of *poffeffion*; but I ftill retain the *actual* right both of *poffeffion* and *property*. If I acquiefce for thirty years, without bringing any action to recover poffeffion of the lands, the fon gains the *actual right of poffeffion*, and I retain nothing but the *mere right of property*. And even this right of property will fail, or at leaft it will be without a remedy, unlefs I purfue it within the fpace of fixty years. Hence it will follow, that one man may have the *poffeffion*, another the *right of poffeffion*, and a third the *right of property*. For if tenant in tail enfeoffs A in fee-fimple, and dies, and B diffeifes A; now B will have the *poffeffion*, A the *right of poffeffion*, and the iffue in tail the *right of property*: A may recover the poffeffion againft B; and afterwards the iffue in tail may evict A, and unite in himself the possession, the right of possession, and also the right of property. In which union consists,

IV. A complete title to lands, tenements, and hereditaments. For when there is, according to the expression of Fleta, *juris et seisinæ conjunctio*, then, and then only, is the title completely legal.

## CHAPTER XI.

### OF TITLE BY DESCENT.

THE several gradations and stages, requisite to form a complete title to lands, tenements, and hereditaments, having been briefly stated in the preceding chapter, we are next to consider the several manners, in which this complete title (and therein principally the right of *propriety*) may be reciprocally lost and acquired: whereby the dominion of things real is either continued, or transferred from one man to another. The methods of acquiring on the one hand, and of losing on the other, a title to estates in things real, are reduced by our law to two: *descent*, where title is vested in a man by the single operation of law; and *purchase*, where the title is vested in him by his own act or agreement.

Descent, or hereditary succession, is the title whereby a man on the death of his ancestor acquires his estate by right of representation, as his heir at law. An heir therefore is he upon whom the law casts the estate immediately on the death of the ancestor: and an estate, so descending to the heir, is in law called the inheritance.

The doctrine of descents, or law of inheritances in fee-simple, is a point of the highest importance; and is indeed the principal object of the laws of real property in England. And, as it depends not a little on the nature of kindred, and the several degrees of consanguinity, it will be previously neceffary to ftate, as briefly as poffible, the true notion of this kindred or alliance in blood (a).

Confanguinity, or kindred, is defined by the writers on thefe fubjects to be " *vinculum perfonarum ab eodem ftipite de-* " *fcendentium;*" the connexion or relation of perfons defcended from the fame ftock or common anceftor. This confanguinity is either lineal, or collateral.

Lineal confanguinity is that which fubfifts between perfons, of whom one is defcended in a direct line from the other, as between John Stiles and his father, grandfather, great-grandfather, and fo upwards in the direct afcending line; or between John Stiles and his fon, grandfon, great-grandfon, and fo downwards in the direct defcending line. Every generation, in this lineal direct confanguinity, conftitutes a different degree, reckoning either upwards or downwards: the father of John Stiles is related to him in the firft degree, and fo likewife is his fon; his grandfire and grandfon in the fecond; his great-grandfire, and great-grandfon in the third.

This lineal confanguinity, we may obferve, falls ftrictly within the definition of *vinculum perfonarum ab eodem ftipite defcendentium*; fince lineal relations are fuch as defcend one from the other, and both of courfe from the fame common anceftor.

Collateral kindred anfwers to the fame defcription: collateral relations agreeing with the lineal in this, that they defcend from the fame ftock or anceftor; but differing in this, that they do not defcend one from the other. Collateral kinfmen are fuch then as lineally fpring from one and the fame anceftor, who is the *ftirps*, or root, the *ftipes*, trunk, or common ftock, from whence thefe relations are branched out. As if John Stiles hath two fons, who have each a numerous iffue; both thefe iffues are lineally defcended from

---

*(a)* For a fuller explanation of the doctrine of confanguinity, and the confequences refulting from a right apprehenfion of it's nature, fee *An Effay on collateral Confanguinity.* (Law Tracts, *Oxon.* 1762. 8vo. or 1771. 4to.) A.

John Stiles as their common anceſtor; and they are collateral kinſmen to each other, becauſe they are all deſcended from this common anceſtor, and all have a portion of his blood in their veins, which denominates them *conſanguineos*.

The method of computing theſe degrees in the canon law, which our law has adopted, is as follows. We begin at the common anceſtor, and reckon downwards; and in whatſoever degree the two perſons, or the moſt remote of them, is diſtant from the common anceſtor, that is the degree in which they are related to each other. Thus *Titius* and his brother are related in the firſt degree; for from the father to each of them is counted only one; *Titius* and his nephew are related in the ſecond degree; for the nephew is two degrees removed from the common anceſtor; *viz.* his own grandfather, the father of *Titius*.

The nature and degrees of kindred being thus in ſome meaſure explained, I ſhall next proceed to lay down a ſeries of rules, or canons of inheritance, according to which eſtates are tranſmitted from the anceſtor to the heir.

I. The firſt rule is, that inheritances ſhall lineally deſcend to the iſſue of the perſon who laſt died actually ſeiſed, *in infinitum*; but ſhall never lineally aſcend.

To explain the more clearly both this and the ſubſequent rules, it muſt firſt be obſerved, that by law no inheritance can veſt, nor can any perſon be the actual complete heir of another, till the anceſtor is previouſly dead. *Nemo eſt hæres viventis*. Before that time the perſon who is next in the line of ſucceſſion is called an heir apparent, or heir preſumptive. Heirs apparent are ſuch, whoſe right of inheritance is indefeaſible, provided they outlive the anceſtor; as the eldeſt ſon or his iſſue, who muſt, by the courſe of the common law, be heir to the father whenever he happens to die. Heirs preſumptive are ſuch who, if the anceſtor ſhould die immediately, would, in the preſent circumſtances of things, be his heirs; but whoſe right of inheritance may be defeated by the contingency of ſome nearer heir being born: as a brother, or nephew, whoſe preſumptive ſucceſſion may be deſtroyed by the birth of a child; or a daughter, whoſe present hopes may be hereafter cut off by the birth of a son. Nay, even if the estate hath descended, by the death of the owner, to such brother, or nephew, or daughter; in the former cases, the estate shall be devested and taken away by the birth of a posthumous child; and, in the latter, it shall also be totally devested by the birth of a posthumous son.

We must also remember, that no person can be properly such an ancestor, as that an inheritance of lands or tenements can be derived from him, unless he hath had actual seisin of such lands, either by his own entry, or by the possession of his own or his ancestor's lessee for years, or by receiving rent from a lessee of the freehold: or unless he hath had what is equivalent to corporal seisin in hereditaments that are incorporeal; such as the receipt of rent, a presentation to the church in case of an advowson, and the like. But he shall not be accounted an ancestor, who hath had only a bare right or title to enter or be otherwise seised. And therefore all the cases, which will be mentioned in the present chapter, are upon the supposition that the deceased (whose inheritance is now claimed) was the last person actually seised thereof. For the law requires this notoriety of possession, as evidence that the ancestor had that property in himself, which is now to be transmitted to his heir. The seisin therefore of any person, thus understood, makes him the root or stock, from which all future inheritance by right of blood must be derived: which is very briefly expressed in this maxim, *seisina facit stipitem*.

When, therefore, a person dies so seised, the inheritance first goes to his issue: as if there be Geoffrey, John, and Matthew, grandfather, father, and son; and John purchases lands, and dies; his son Matthew shall succeed him as heir, and not the grandfather Geoffrey; to whom the land shall never ascend, but shall rather escheat to the lord.

II. A second general rule or canon is, that the male issue shall be admitted before the female.

Thus sons shall be admitted before daughters; or, as our male lawgivers have somewhat uncomplaisantly expressed it, the worthiest of blood shall be preferred. As if John Stiles hath two fons, Matthew and Gilbert, and two daughters, Margaret and Charlotte, and dies; firft Matthew, and (in cafe of his death without iffue) then Gilbert, fhall be admitted to the fucceffion in preference to both the daughters. But our law does not extend to a total exclufion of females, it only poftpones them to males; for, though daughters are excluded by fons, yet they fucceed before any collateral relations.

III. A third rule, or canon of defcent, is this; that where there are two or more males in equal degree, the eldeft only fhall inherit; but the females all together.

As if a man hath two fons, Matthew and Gilbert, and two daughters, Margaret and Charlotte, and dies; Matthew his eldeft fon fhall alone fucceed to his eftate, in exclufion of Gilbert the fecond fon and both the daughters; but, if both the fons die without iffue before the father, the daughters Margaret and Charlotte fhall both inherit the eftate as coparceners. However, the fucceffion by primogeniture, even among females, takes place as to the inheritance of the crown; wherein the neceffity of a fole and determinate fucceffion is as great in the one fex as the other. And the right of fole fucceffion, though not of primogeniture, is alfo eftablifhed with refpect to female dignities and titles of honour. For if a man holds an earldom to him and the heirs of his body, and dies, leaving only daughters; the eldeft fhall not, of courfe, be countefs, but the dignity is in fufpence or abeyance, till the king fhall declare his pleafure; for he, being the fountain of honour, may confer it on which of them he pleafes.

IV. A fourth rule, or canon of defcents, is this; that the lineal defcendants, *in infinitum*, of any perfon deceafed, fhall reprefent their anceftor; that is, fhall ftand in the fame place as the perfon himfelf would have done, had he been living.

Thus the child, grandchild, or great-grandchild (either male or female) of the eldeft fon fucceeds before the younger fon, and fo *in infinitum*. And thefe reprefentatives fhall take neither more nor lefs, but juft fo much as their principals would have done. As if there be two fifters, Margaret and Charlotte; and Margaret dies, leaving fix daughters; and then John Stiles the father of the two fifters dies, without other iffue: thefe fix daughters fhall take among them exactly the fame as their mother Margaret would have done, had fhe been living; that is, a moiety of the lands of John Stiles in coparcenary: fo that, upon partition made, if the land be divided into twelve parts, thereof Charlotte the furviving fifter fhall have fix, and her fix nieces, the daughters of Margaret, one apiece.

This taking by reprefentation is called fucceffion *in ftirpes*, according to the roots; fince all the branches inherit the fame fhare that their root, whom they reprefent, would have done. And among thefe feveral iffues, or reprefentatives of the refpective roots, the fame preference to males and the fame right of primogeniture obtain, as would have obtained at the firft among the roots themfelves, the fons or daughters of the deceafed. As if a man hath two fons, A and B, and A dies, leaving two fons, and then the grandfather dies; now the eldeft fon of A fhall fucceed to the whole of his grandfather's eftate: and if A had left only two daughters, they fhould have fucceeded alfo to equal moieties of the whole, in exclufion of B and his iffue. But if a man hath only three daughters, C, D, and E; and C dies leaving two fons, D leaving two daughters, and E leaving a daughter and a fon who is younger than his fifter: here, when the grandfather dies, the eldeft fon of C fhall fucceed to one third, in exclufion of the younger; the two daughters of D to another third in partnerfhip; and the fon of E to the remaining third, in exclufion of his elder fifter. And the fame right of reprefentation, guided and reftrained by the fame rules of defcent, prevails downwards *in infinitum*.

V. A fifth rule is, that on failure of lineal defcendants, or iffue, of the perfon laft feifed, the inheritance fhall defcend to his collateral relations, being of the blood of the firft purchafor; fubject to the three preceding rules.

Thus, if Geoffrey Stiles purchafes land, and it defcends

to John Stiles his son, and John dies seised thereof without issue; whoever succeeds to this inheritance must be of the blood of Geoffrey, the first purchasor of this family. Therefore, if lands come to John Stiles by descent from his mother Lucy Baker, no relation of his father (as such) shall ever be his heir of these lands; and, *vice versa*, if they descended from his father Geoffrey Stiles, no relation of his mother (as such) shall ever be admitted thereto; for his father's kindred have none of his mother's blood, nor have his mother's relations any share of his father's blood.

This then is the great and general principle, upon which the law of collateral inheritances depends; that, upon failure of issue in the last proprietor, the estate shall descend to the blood of the first purchasor; or, that it shall result back to the heirs of the body of that ancestor, from whom it either really has, or is supposed by fiction of law to have originally descended: according to the rule laid down in the year books, Fitzherbert, Brook, and Hale, "that he who would "have been heir to the father of the deceased" (and, of course, to the mother, or any other real or supposed purchasing ancestor) "shall also be heir to the son;" a maxim, that will hold universally, except in the case of a brother or sister of the half blood, which exception depends upon very special grounds.

The rules of inheritance that remain are only rules of evidence, calculated to investigate who the purchasing ancestor was.

VI. A sixth rule or canon therefore is, that the collateral heir of the person last seised must be his next collateral kinsman, of the whole blood.

First, he must be his next collateral kinsman, either personally or *jure repraesentationis*; which proximity is reckoned according to the canonical degrees of consanguinity beforementioned. Therefore, the brother being in the first degree, he and his descendants shall exclude the uncle and his issue, who is only in the second.

The right of representation being thus established, the former part of the present rule amounts to this; that, on failure of issue of the person last seised, the inheritance shall descend to the other subsisting issue of his next immediate ancestor. Thus, if John Stiles dies without issue, his estate shall descend to Francis his brother, or his representatives; he being lineally descended from Geoffrey Stiles, John's next immediate ancestor, or father. On failure of brethren, or sisters, and their issue, it shall descend to the uncle of John Stiles, the lineal descendant of his grandfather George, and so on *in infinitum*. And therefore, in order to ascertain the collateral heir of John Stiles, it is first necessary to recur to his ancestors in the first degree; and if they have left any other issue besides John, that issue will be his heir. On default of such, we must ascend one step higher, to the ancestors in the second degree, and then to those in the third, and fourth, and so upwards *in infinitum*; till some couple of ancestors be found, who have other issue descending from them besides the deceased, in a parallel or collateral line. From these ancestors the heir of John Stiles must derive his descent; and in such derivation the same rules must be observed, with regard to sex, primogeniture, and representation, that have before been laid down with regard to lineal descents from the person of the last proprietor.

But, secondly, the heir need not be the nearest kinsman absolutely, but only *sub modo*; that is, he must be the nearest kinsman of the *whole* blood; for, if there be a much nearer kinsman of the *half* blood, a distant kinsman of the whole blood shall be admitted, and the other entirely excluded: nay, the estate shall escheat to the lord, sooner than the half blood shall inherit.

A kinsman of the whole blood is he that is derived, not only from the same ancestor, but from the same couple of ancestors. For, as every man's own blood is compounded of the bloods of his respective ancestors, he only is properly of the whole or entire blood with another, who hath (so far as the distance of degrees will permit) all the same ingredients in the composition of his blood that the other hath. Thus, the blood of John Stiles being composed of those of **Geoffrey** Stiles his father and **Lucy Baker** his mother, therefore his brother Francis, being descended from both the same parents, hath entirely the same blood with John Stiles; or he is his brother of the whole blood. But if, after the death of Geoffrey, Lucy Baker the mother marries a second husband, Lewis Gay, and hath issue by him; the blood of this issue, being compounded of the blood of Lucy Baker (it is true) on the one part, but that of Lewis Gay (instead of Geoffrey Stiles) on the other part, it hath therefore only half the same ingredients with that of John Stiles, so that he is only his brother of the half blood, and for that reason they shall never inherit to each other. So also, if the father has two sons, A and B, by different venters or wives; now these two brethren are not brethren of the whole blood, and therefore shall never inherit to each other, but the estate shall rather escheat to the lord.

The doctrine of the whole blood was calculated to supply the frequent impossibility of proving a descent from the first purchasor, without some proof of which (according to our fundamental maxim) there can be no inheritance allowed of. And this purpose it answers, for the most part, effectually enough. For he who is my kinsman of the whole blood can have no ancestors beyond or higher than the common stock, but what are equally my ancestors also; and mine are *vice versa* his: he therefore is very likely to be derived from that unknown ancestor of mine, from whom the inheritance descended. But a kinsman of the half blood has but one half of his ancestors above the common stock the same as mine; and therefore there is not the same probability of that standing requisite in the law, that he be derived from the blood of the first purchasor. Therefore the much less probability of the half blood's descent from the first purchasor, compared with that of the whole blood, in the several degrees, has occasioned a general exclusion of the half blood in all. But the crown (which is the highest inheritance in the nation) may descend to the half blood of the preceding sovereign, so that it be the blood of the first monarch, purchasor, or (in the feodal language) conqueror of the reigning family. Thus it actually did descend from king Edward the sixth to queen Mary, and from her to queen Elizabeth, who were respectively of the half blood to each other. For the royal pedigree being always a matter of sufficient notoriety, there is no occasion to call in the aid of this presumptive rule of evidence, to render probable the descent from the royal stock, which was formerly king William the Norman, and is now (by act of parliament) *(a)* the princess Sophia of Hanover. Hence also it is, that in estates-tail, where the pedigree from the first donee must be strictly proved, half blood is no impediment to the descent: because, when the lineage is clearly made out, there is no need of this auxiliary proof.

VII. The seventh and last rule or canon is, that in collateral inheritances the male stocks shall be preferred to the female; (that is, kindred derived from the blood of the male ancestors, however remote, shall be admitted before those from the blood of the female, however near,) unless where the lands have, in fact, descended from a female.

Thus the relations on the father's side are admitted *in infinitum,* before those on the mother's side are admitted at all; and the relations of the father's father, before those of the father's mother; and so on. But whenever the lands have notoriously descended to a man from his mother's side, this rule is totally reversed; and no relation of his by the father's side, as such, can ever be admitted to them: because he cannot possibly be of the blood of the first purchasor. And so, *e converso,* if the lands descended from the father's side, no relation of the mother, as such, shall ever inherit. Whereas, when the side from which they descended is forgotten, or never known, (as in the case of an estate newly purchased to be holden *ut feudum antiquum*) here the right of inheritance first runs up all the father's side, with a preference to the male stocks in every instance; and, if it finds no heirs there, it then, and then only, resorts to the mother's side; leaving no place untried, in order to find heirs that may by possibility be derived from the original purchasor. The greatest probability of finding such was among those descended from the

---

*(a)* 12 Wil. III. c. 2.

male anceftors; but, upon failure of iffue there, they may poffibly be found among thofe derived from the females (a).

## CHAPTER XII.

#### OF TITLE BY PURCHASE; AND FIRST BY ESCHEAT.

PURCHASE, taken in it's largeft and moft extenfive fenfe, is thus defined by Littleton; the poffeffion of lands and tenements, which a man hath by his own act or agreement, and not by defcent from any of his anceftors or kindred. In this fenfe it is contradiftinguifhed from acquifition by right of blood, and includes every other method of coming to an eftate, but merely that by inheritance: wherein the title is vefted in a perfon, not by his own act or agreement, but by the fingle operation of law.

The difference in effect, between the acquifition of an eftate by defcent and by purchafe, confifts principally in thefe two points: 1. That by purchafe the eftate acquires a new inheritable quality, and is defcendible to the owner's blood in general, and not the blood only of fome particular anceftor; whereby it becomes inheritable to his heirs general, firft of the paternal, and then of the maternal line. 2. An eftate taken by purchafe will not make the heir anfwerable for the acts of the anceftor, as an eftate by defcent will. For, if the anceftor by any deed, obligation, covenant, or the like, bindeth himfelf and his heirs, and dieth; this deed, obligation, or covenant, fhall be binding upon the heir, fo far forth only as he (or any other in truft for him) had any eftate of inheritance vefted in him by defcent from (or any eftate

---

*(a)* Thofe who wifh to inveftigate this fubject more minutely than is done by the learned judge, may find it confidered with great perfpicuoufnefs and ability by Mr. *Watkins*, in his *Treatife on the Law of Defcents*; which I beg leave to recommend to the ftudent's perufal, as a fenfible and judicious work.

*pur auter vie* coming to him by special occupancy, as heir to) that ancestor, sufficient to answer the charge; whether he remains in possession, or hath aliened it before action brought.

This legal signification of the word *perquisitio*, or purchase, includes the five following methods of acquiring a title to estates: 1. Escheat. 2. Occupancy. 3. Prescription. 4. Forfeiture. 5. Alienation. Of all these in their order.

I. Escheat, was one of the fruits and consequences of feodal tenure. The word itself denotes an obstruction of the course of descent, and a consequent determination of the nure, by some unforeseen contingency: in which case the and naturally results back, by a kind of reversion, to the original grantor or lord of the fee *(a)*.

The law of escheats is founded upon this single principle, that the blood of the person last seised in fee-simple is, by some means or other, utterly extinct and gone: and, since none can inherit his estate but such as are of his blood and consanguinity, it follows as a regular consequence, that when such blood is extinct, the inheritance itself must fail; the land must become what the feodal writers denominate *feudum apertum*; and must result back again to the lord of the fee, by whom, or by those whose estate he hath, it was given.

The first three cases, wherein inheritable blood is wanting, may be collected from the rules of descent laid down and explained in the preceding chapter, and therefore will need very little illustration or comment. First, when the tenant dies without any relations on the part of any of his ancestors: secondly, when he dies without any relations on the part of those ancestors from whom his estate descended: thirdly, when he dies without any relations of the whole blood.

4. A monster, which hath not the shape of mankind, but

---

*(a)* "An escheat doth happen two manner of ways, *aut per defectum sanguinis*, i.e. for default of heir; *aut per delictum tenentis*, i.e. for felony: and that is by judgment three manner of ways, *aut quia suspensus per collum, aut quia abjuravit regnum, aut quia utlegatus est*," *Co. Lit.* 13 ª.

in any part evidently bears the resemblance of the brute creation, hath no inheritable blood, and cannot be heir to any land, albeit it be brought forth in marriage: but, although it hath deformity in any part of its body, yet if it hath a human shape it may be heir. And therefore, if there appears no other heir than such a prodigious birth, the land shall escheat to the lord.

5. Bastards are incapable of being heirs. Bastards, by our law, are such children as are not born either in lawful wedlock, or within a competent time after its determination. Such are held to be *nullius filii*, the sons of nobody; for the maxim of law is, *qui ex damnato coitu nascuntur, inter liberos non computantur*. Being thus the sons of nobody, they have no blood in them, at least no heritable blood; consequently, none of the blood of the first purchasor: and therefore, if there be no other claimant than such illegitimate children, the land shall escheat to the lord.

As bastards cannot be heirs themselves, so neither can they have any heirs but those of their own bodies. For, as all collateral kindred consists in being derived from the same common ancestor, and as a bastard has no legal ancestors, he can have no collateral kindred; and consequently, can have no legal heirs, but such as claim by a lineal descent from himself. And therefore if a bastard purchases land, and dies seised thereof without issue, and intestate, the land shall escheat to the lord of the fee.

6. Aliens also are incapable of taking by descent, or inheriting, for they are not allowed to have any inheritable blood in them; wherefore if a man leaves no other relations but aliens, his land shall escheat to the lord.

And farther, if an alien be made a denizen by the king's letters patent, and then purchases lands, (which the law allows such a one to do) his son, born before his denization, shall not (by the common law) inherit those lands; but a son born afterwards may, even though his elder brother be living; for the father, before denization, had no inheritable blood to communicate to his eldest son; but by denization it acquires an hereditary quality, which will be transmitted to his subsequent posterity. Yet, if he had been naturalized by act of parliament, such eldest son might then have inherited; for that cancels all defects, and is allowed to have a retrospective energy, which simple denization has not. And it is now held for law, that the sons of an alien, born here, may inherit to each other; the descent from one to another being an *immediate* descent. It is also enacted, by the statute 11 and 12 W. III. c. 6. that all persons, being natural-born subjects of the king, may inherit and make their titles by descent from any of their ancestors lineal or collateral; although their father, or mother, or other ancestor, by, from, through, or under whom they derive their pedigrees, were born out of the king's allegiance. And it is provided by the statute 25 Geo. II. c. 39, that no right of inheritance shall accrue by virtue of the former statute to any persons whatsoever, unless they are in being and capable to take as heirs at the death of the person last seised:—with an exception however to the case where lands shall descend to the daughter of an alien; which descent shall be divested in favour of an after-born brother, or the inheritance shall be divided with an after-born sister or sisters, according to the usual rule of descents by the common law.

7. By attainder also, for treason or other felony, the blood of the person attainted is so corrupted, as to be rendered no longer inheritable.

The doctrine of escheat upon attainder, taken singly, is this: that the blood of the tenant, by the commission of any felony, (under which denomination all treasons were formerly comprised) is corrupted and stained, and the original dominion of the feud is thereby determined, it being always granted to the vassal on the implied condition of *dum bene se gesserit*. Upon the thorough demonstration of which guilt, by legal attainder, the feodal covenant and mutual bond of fealty are held to be broken, the estate instantly falls back from the offender to the lord of the fee, and the inheritable quality of his blood is extinguished and blotted out for ever In consequence of which corruption and extinction of hereditary blood, the land of all felons would immediately revest in the lord, but that the superior law of forfeiture intervenes, and intercepts it in its passage: in case of treason, for ever; in case of other felony, for only a year and a day; after which time it goes to the lord in a regular course of escheat. And a person attainted is neither allowed to retain his former estate nor to inherit any future one, nor to transmit any inheritance to his issue, either immediately from himself, or mediately through himself from any remoter ancestor; for his inheritable blood, which is necessary either to hold, to take, or to transmit any feodal property, is blotted out, corrupted, and extinguished for ever: the consequence of which is, that estates, thus impeded in their descent, result back and escheat to the lord.

This corruption of blood, thus arising from feodal principles, but perhaps extended farther than even those principles will warrant, has been long looked upon as a peculiar hardship: and by the statute 7 Ann. c. 21. (the operation of which is postponed by the statute 17 Geo. II. c. 39.) it is enacted, that, after the death of the late pretender, and his sons, no attainder for treason shall extend to the disinheriting any heir, nor the prejudice of any person, other than the offender himself.

Before I conclude this head, of escheat, I must mention one singular instance in which lands held in fee-simple are not liable to escheat to the lord, even when their owner is no more, and hath left no heirs to inherit them. And this is the case of a corporation; for if that comes by any accident to be dissolved, the donor or his heirs shall have the land again in reversion, and not the lord by escheat; which is perhaps the only instance where a reversion can be expectant on a grant in fee-simple absolute. But the law, we are told, 'doth tacitly annex a condition to every such gift or grant, that if the corporation be dissolved, the donor or grantor shall re-enter; for the cause of the gift or grant faileth.

## CHAPTER XIII.

### OF TITLE BY OCCUPANCY; AND BY PRESCRIPTION. FIRST BY OCCUPANCY.

OCCUPANCY is the taking poffeffion of thofe things which before belonged to nobody. This right of occupancy, fo far as it concerns real property, (for of perfonal chattels I am not in this place to fpeak) hath been confined by the laws of England within a very narrow compafs; and was extended only to a fingle inftance: namely, where a man was tenant *pur auter vie*, or had an eftate granted to himfelf only (without mentioning his heirs) for the life of another man, and died during the life of *ceftuy que vie*, or him by whofe life it was holden: in this cafe he, that could firft enter on the land, might lawfully retain the poffeffion fo long as *ceftuy que vie* lived, by right of occupancy. And, had the eftate *pur auter vie* been granted to a man *and his heirs* during the life of *ceftuy que vie*, there the heir might, and ftill may, enter and hold poffeffion, and is called in law a *fpecial occupant*; as having a fpecial exclufive right, by the terms of the original grant, to enter upon and occupy this *hæreditas jacens*, during the refidue of the eftate granted: though fome have thought him fo called with no very great propriety; and that fuch eftate is rather a defcendible freehold. But the title of common occupancy is now reduced almoft to nothing by two ftatutes: the one, 29 Car. II. c. 3. which enacts (according to the ancient rule of law) that where there is no fpecial occupant, in whom the eftate may veft, the tenant *pur auter vie* may devife it by will, or it fhall go to the executors or adminiftrators and be affets in their hands for payment of debts: the other that of 14 Geo. II. c. 20. which enacts, that the furplus of fuch eftate *pur auter vie*, after payment of debts, fhall go in a courfe of diftribution like a chattel intereft.

By thefe two ftatutes the title of *common* occupancy is utterly extinct and abolished: though that of *special* occupancy, by the heir at law, continues to this day; such heir being held to succeed to the ancestor's estate, not by descent, for then he must take an estate of inheritance, but as an occupant, specially marked out and appointed by the original grant.

### Secondly, by Prescription.

Another method of acquiring real property by purchase is that by *prescription*; as when a man can shew no other title to what he claims, than that he, and those under whom he claims, have immemorially used to enjoy it. Concerning customs, or immemorial usages, in general, with the several requisites and rules to be observed, in order to prove their existence and validity, we inquired at large in the preceding part of these commentaries. At present therefore I shall only, first, distinguish between *custom*, strictly taken, and *prescription*; and then shew, what sort of things may be prescribed for.

And, first, the distinction between custom and prescription is this; that custom is properly a local usage, and not annexed to any *person:* such as a custom in the manor of Dale that lands shall descend to the youngest son: prescription is merely a *personal* usage; as, that Sempronius, and his ancestors, or those whose estate he hath, have used time out of mind to have such an advantage or privilege. All prescription must be either in a man and his ancestors, or in a man and those whose estate he hath: which last is called prescribing in a *que estate.* But by the statute of limitations 32 Hen. VIII. c. 2. it is enacted, that no person shall make any prescription by the seisin or possession of his ancestor or predecessor, unless such seisin or possession hath been within threescore years next before such prescription made.

Secondly, as to the several species of things which may, or may not, be prescribed for: we may, in the first place, observe, that nothing but incorporeal hereditaments can be claimed by prescription; as a right of way, a common, &c. but that no prescription can give a title to lands, and other corporeal substances, of which more certain evidence may be had. 2. A prescription must always be laid in him that is tenant of the fee. And therefore a copyholder must prescribe under cover of his lord's estate, and a tenant for life under cover of the tenant in fee-simple. 3. A prescription cannot be for a thing which cannot be raised by grant. For the law allows prescription only in supply of the loss of a grant, and therefore every prescription presupposes a grant to have existed. A fourth rule is, that what is to arise by matter of record cannot be prescribed for, but must be claimed by grant, entered on record; such as, for instance, the royal franchises of deodands, felons' goods, and the like. But the franchises of treasure-trove, waifs, estrays, and the like, may be claimed by prescription; for they arise from private contingencies, and not from any matter of record. 5. Among things incorporeal, which may be claimed by prescription, a distinction must be made with regard to the manner of prescribing; that is, whether a man shall prescribe in a *que estate*, or in himself and his ancestors. For, if a man prescribes in a *que estate*, (that is, in himself and those whose estate he holds) nothing is claimable by this prescription, but such things as are incident, appendant, or appurtenant to lands; but, if he prescribes in himself and his ancestors, he may prescribe for any thing whatsoever that lies in grant; not only things that are appurtenant, but also such as may be in gross. 6. Lastly, we may observe, that estates gained by prescription are not, of course, descendible to the heirs general, like other purchased estates, but are an exception to the rule: and therefore, if a man prescribes for a right of way in himself and his ancestors, it will descend only to the blood of that line of ancestors in whom he so prescribes. But, if he prescribes for it in a *que estate*, it will follow the nature of that estate in which the prescription is laid: for every accessory followeth the nature of it's principal.

## CHAPTER XIV.

### OF TITLE BY FORFEITURE.

FORFEITURE is a punishment annexed by law to some illegal act, or negligence, in the owner of lands, tenements, or hereditaments: whereby he loses all his interest therein, and they go to the party injured, as a recompense for the wrong which either he alone, or the public together with himself, hath sustained.

Lands, tenements, and hereditaments, may be forfeited in various degrees and by various means: 1. By crimes and misdemesnors. 2. By alienation contrary to law. 3. By non-presentation to a benefice, when the forfeiture is denominated a *lapse*. 4. By simony. 5. By non-performance of conditions. 6. By waste. 7. By breach of copyhold customs. 8. By bankruptcy.

I. The offences which induce a forfeiture of lands and tenements to the crown, are principally the following six: 1. Treason. 2. Felony. 3. Misprision of treason. 4. *Præmunire*. 5. Drawing a weapon on a judge, or striking any one in the presence of the king's principal courts of justice. 6. Popish recusancy, or non-observance of certain laws enacted in restraint of papists.

II. Lands and tenements may be forfeited by *alienation*, or conveying them to another, contrary to law. This is either alienation in *mortmain*, alienation to an *alien*, or alienation by *particular tenants*; in the two former of which cases the forfeiture arises from the incapacity of the alienee to take, in the latter from the incapacity of the alienor to grant.

1. Alienation in *mortmain*, *in mortua manu*, is an alienation of lands or tenements to any corporation, sole or aggregate, ecclesiastical or temporal. But these purchases having been chiefly made by religious houses, in consequence whereof the lands became perpetually inherent in one dead hand, this hath occasioned the general appellation of mortmain to be applied to such alienations, and the religious houses them-

selves to be principally considered in forming the statutes of mortmain.

By the common law any man might dispose of his lands to any other private man at his own discretion, especially when the feodal restraints of alienation were worn away. Yet, in consequence of these, it was always, and is still, necessary, for corporations to have a licence in mortmain from the crown, to enable them to purchase lands. And, as during the times of popery lands were frequently given to superstitious uses, though not to any corporate bodies; or were made liable in the hands of heirs and devisees to the charge of obits, chaunteries, and the like, which were equally pernicious in a well-governed state as actual alienations in mortmain; therefore, at the dawn of the reformation, the statute 23 Hen. VIII. c. 10. declares, that all future grants of lands for any of the purposes aforesaid, if granted for any longer term than twenty years, shall be void.

But for the augmentation of poor livings, it was enacted, by the statute 17 Car. II. c. 3. that appropriators may annex the great tithes to the vicarages; and that all benefices under 100*l. per annum* may be augmented by the purchase of lands, without licence of mortmain in either case: and the like provision hath been since made, in favour of the governors of queen Anne's bounty (*a*). It hath also been held, that the statute 23 Hen. VIII. did not tend to any thing but *superstitious* uses; and that therefore a man may give lands for the maintenance of a school, an hospital, or any other *charitable* uses. But it is enacted, by the statute 9 Geo. II. c. 36. that no lands or tenements, or money to be laid out thereon, shall be given for or charged with any *charitable* uses whatsoever, unless by deed indented, executed in the presence of two witnesses twelve calendar months before the death of the donor, and enrolled in the court of chancery within six months after it's execution, (except stocks in the public funds, which may be transferred within six months previous to the donor's

---

(*a*) Statute 2 and 3 Anne, c. 11.

death) and unless such gift be made to take effect immediately, and be without power of revocation: and that all other gifts shall be void. The two universities, their colleges, and the scholars upon the foundation of the colleges of Eton, Winchester, and Westminster, are excepted out of this act: but such exemption was granted with this proviso, that no college shall be at liberty to purchase more advowsons, than are equal in number to one moiety of the fellows or students, upon the respective foundations.

2. Secondly, alienation *to an alien* is also a cause of forfeiture to the crown of the lands so alienated; not only on account of his incapacity to hold, which occasions him to be passed by in the descents of land, but likewise on account of his presumption in attempting, by an act of his own, to acquire any real property.

3. Lastly, alienations *by particular tenants*, when they are greater than the law entitles them to make, and divest the remainder or reversion, are also forfeitures to him whose right is attacked thereby. The same law, which is thus laid down with regard to tenants for life, holds also with respect to all tenants of the mere freehold or of chattel interests; but if the tenant in tail alienes in fee, this is no immediate forfeiture to the remainder-man, but a mere *discontinuance* (as it is called) of the estate-tail (a). But, in case of such forfeitures by particular tenants, all legal estates by them before created (as if tenant for twenty years grants a lease for fifteen) and all charges by him lawfully made on the lands, shall be good and available in law.

III. Lapse is a species of forfeiture, whereby the right of presentation to a church accrues to the ordinary by neglect of the patron to present; to the metropolitan by neglect of the ordinary; and to the king by neglect of the metropolitan.

---

(a) See a learned and perspicuous note on the law of discontinuance by Mr. *Butler, Co. Lit.* 235 ª. where all the material distinctions on that subject are adverted to, and their reasons explained.

This right of lapſe was firſt eſtabliſhed when the biſhops began to exerciſe, univerſally, the right of inſtitution to churches. And therefore, where there is no right of inſtitution, there is no right of lapſe: ſo that no donative can lapſe to the ordinary, unleſs it hath been augmented by the queen's bounty. But no right of lapſe can accrue, when the original preſentation is in the crown.

The term, in which the title to preſent by lapſe accrues from the one to the other, ſucceſſively, is ſix *calendar* months; and this excluſive of the day of the avoidance. But if the biſhop be both patron and ordinary, he ſhall not have a double time allowed him to collate in; for the forfeiture accrues by law, whenever the negligence has continued ſix months in the ſame perſon. And alſo if the biſhop doth not collate his own clerk immediately to the living, and the patron preſents, though after the ſix months are lapſed, yet his preſentation is good, and the biſhop is bound to inſtitute the patron's clerk. For as the law only gives the biſhop this title by lapſe, to puniſh the patron's negligence, there is no reaſon that, if the biſhop himſelf be guilty of equal or greater negligence, the patron ſhould be deprived of his turn. If the biſhop ſuffer the preſentation to lapſe to the metropolitan, the patron alſo has the ſame advantage if he preſents before the arch-biſhop has filled up the benefice; and that for the ſame reaſon. Yet the ordinary cannot, after lapſe to the metropolitan, collate his own clerk to the prejudice of the arch-biſhop. For he had no permanent right and intereſt in the advowſon, as the patron hath, but merely a temporary one; which having neglected to make uſe of during the time, he cannot afterwards receive it. But if the preſentation lapſes to the king, prerogative here intervenes and makes a difference; and the patron ſhall never recover his right, till the king has ſatisfied his turn by preſentation: for *nullum tempus occurrit regi.* And therefore it may ſeem, as if the church might continue void for ever, unleſs the king ſhall be pleaſed to preſent; and a patron thereby be abſolutely defeated of his advowſon. But to prevent this inconvenience, the law has lodged a power in the patron's hands, of as it were compelling the king to present. For if, during the delay of the crown, the patron himself presents, and his clerk is instituted, the king, indeed, by presenting another may turn out the patron's clerk, or, after induction, may remove him by *quare impedit*, but if he does not, and the patron's clerk dies incumbent, or is canonically deprived, the king hath lost his right, which was only to the next or first presentation.

In case the benefice becomes void by death, or cession through plurality of benefices, there the patron is bound to take notice of the vacancy at his own peril; for these are matters of equal notoriety to the patron and ordinary: but in case of a vacancy by resignation, or canonical deprivation, or if a clerk presented be refused for insufficiency, these being matters of which the bishop alone is presumed to be cognizant, here the law requires him to give notice thereof to the patron, otherwise he can take no advantage by way of lapse. Neither shall any lapse thereby accrue to the metropolitan or to the king; for it is universally true, that neither the archbishop or the king shall ever present by lapse, but where the immediate ordinary might have collated by lapse, within the six months, and hath exceeded his time; for the first step or beginning faileth, *et quod non habet principium, non habet finem.* If the bishop refuse or neglect to examine and admit the patron's clerk, without good reason assigned, or notice given, he is stiled a disturber by the law, and shall not have any title to present by lapse; for no man shall take advantage of his own wrong. Also if the right of presentation be litigious or contested, and an action be brought against the bishop to try the title, no lapse shall incur till the question of right be decided.

IV. By *simony*, the right of presentation to a living is forfeited and vested *pro hac vice* in the crown. Simony is the corrupt presentation of any one to an ecclesiastical benefice for money, gift, or reward.

By the statute 31 Eliz. c. 6. it is, for avoiding of simony, enacted, that if any patron for any corrupt consideration, by gift or promise, directly or indirectly, shall present or collate any person to an ecclesiastical benefice or dignity; such presentation shall be void, and the presentee be rendered incapable of ever enjoying the same benefice: and the crown shall pref. it to it for that turn only. But if the presentee dies, without being convicted of such simony in his life-time, it is enacted, by stat. 1 W. & M. c. 16. that the simoniacal contract shall not prejudice any other innocent patron, on pretence of lapse to the crown or otherwise (*a*). Also by the statute 12 Ann. stat. 2. c. 12. if any person for money or profit shall procure, in his own name or the name of any other, the next presentation to any living ecclesiastical, and shall be presented thereupon, this is declared to be a simoniacal contract; and the party is subjected to all the ecclesiastical penalties of simony, is disabled from holding the benefice, and the presentation devolves to the crown.

Upon these statutes many questions have arisen, with regard to what is, and what is not simony. And, among others, these points seem to be clearly settled: 1. That to purchase a presentation, the living being actually vacant, is open and notorious simony; this being expressly in the face of the statute. 2. That for a clerk to bargain for the next presentation, the incumbent being sick and about to die, was simony, even before the statute of queen Anne: and now, by that statute, to purchase, either in his own name or another's, the next presentation, and be thereupon presented at any future time to the living, is direct and palpable simony. But, 3. It is held that for a father to purchase such a presentation, in order to provide for his son, is not simony: for the son is not concerned in the bargain, and the father is by nature bound to make a provision for him. 4. That if a simoniacal contract be made with the patron, the clerk not being privy thereto, the presentation for that turn shall, indeed, devolve to the crown, as a punishment of the guilty

---

(*a*) By the same statute it is also enacted, that no lease *bona fide* to be made by any person simoniacally promoted, for valuable consideration, to any person not having notice of such simony, shall be avoided by reason thereof.

patron; but the clerk, who is innocent, does not incur any disability or forfeiture. 5. That bonds given to pay money to charitable uses, on receiving a presentation to a living, are not simoniacal, provided the patron or his relations be not benefited thereby; for this is no corrupt consideration, moving to the patron. 6. That bonds of resignation, in case of non-residence or taking any other living, are not simoniacal; there being no corrupt consideration herein, but such only as is for the good of the public. So also bonds to resign, when the patron's son comes to canonical age, are legal; upon the reason before given, that the father is bound to provide for his son. 7. Lastly, general bonds to resign at the patron's request are held to be legal (*a*): for they may possibly be given for one of the legal considerations beforementioned; and where there is a possibility that a transaction may be fair, the law will not suppose it iniquitous without proof.

V. The next kind of forfeitures are those by *breach* or non-performance of a *condition* annexed to the estate, either expressly by deed at it's original creation, or impliedly by law from a principle of natural reason. Both which we considered in a former chapter (*b*).

VI. I therefore now proceed to another species of forfeiture, *viz.* by *waste*. Waste is a spoil or destruction in houses, gardens, trees, or other corporeal hereditaments, to the disherison of him that hath the remainder or reversion in fee-simple or fee-tail.

Waste is either *voluntary*, which is a crime of commission, as by pulling down a house; or it is *permissive*, which is a matter of omission only, as by suffering it to fall for

---

(*a*) It was so determined in *Babington*, v. *Ward*, *Cro. Car.* 180. (which is the authority referred to by the learned judge,) and this determination was afterwards sanctioned by a series of judicial decisions; until the house of lords, in the great case of *Ffytche* and the *Bp. of London*, (May, 1783) adjudged, that general bonds of resignation were simoniacal and therefore illegal. See *Cuningh. Sim.* 52.

(*b*) B. II. Ch. vii.

want of necessary reparations. Whatever does a lasting damage to the freehold or inheritance is waste. Therefore removing wainscot, floors, or other things once affixed to the freehold of a house, is waste (a). If a house be destroyed by tempest, lightning, or the like, which is the act of providence, it is no waste: but otherwise, if the house be burnt by the carelessness or negligence of the lessee; though now, by the statute 6 Ann. c. 31. no action will lie against a tenant for an accident of this kind. Waste may also be committed in ponds, dove-houses, warrens, and the like, by so reducing the number of the creatures therein, that there will not be sufficient for the reversioner when he comes to the inheritance. Timber also is part of the inheritance. Such are oak, ash, and elm in all places: and in some particular countries, by local custom, where other trees are generally used for building, they are for that reason considered as timber; and to cut down such trees, or top them, or do any other act whereby the timber may decay, is waste. But underwood the tenant may cut down at any seasonable time that he pleases; and may take sufficient estovers of common right for house-bote and cart-bote; unless restrained (which is usual) by particular covenants or exceptions. The conversion of land from one species to another is waste. To convert wood, meadow, or pasture, into arable; to turn arable, meadow, or pasture, into woodland; or to turn arable or woodland into meadow or pasture; are all of them waste. For, as Sir Edward Coke observes, it not only changes the course of husbandry, but the evidence of the estate; when such a close, which is conveyed and described

---

(a) " All the old cases agree, that whatever is connected with the freehold, although put up by the the tenant, belongs to the heir; but there has been a relaxation of the *strict rule* (for the benefit of trade) between landlord and tenant; and many things may now be taken away, which could not formerly, such as erections for carrying on trade, marble chimney-pieces, and the like, when put up by the tenant." Per *Lord Mansfield*, in *Lawton*, v. *Salmon*, 1 *H. Blac. Rep.* 259. n. (a) where the cases in respect to the removal of fixtures are collected, and their principles considered and applied.

as pasture, is found to be arable, and *e converso*. And the same rule is observed, for the same reason, with regard to converting one species of edifice into another, even though it is improved in it's value. To open the land to search for mines of metal, coal, &c. is waste; for that is a detriment to the inheritance: but, if the pits or mines were open before, it is no waste for the tenant to continue digging them for his own use; for it is now become the mere annual profit of the land. These three are the general heads of waste, *viz.* in houses, in timber, and in land. Though, as was before said, whatever else tends to the destruction, or depreciating the value of the inheritance, is considered by the law as waste.

Let us next see who are liable to be punished for committing waste. In favour of the owner of the inheritance, the statutes of Marlbridge 52 Hen. III. c. 23. and of Gloucester 6 Edw. I. c. 5. provided that the writ of waste shall not only lie against tenants by the law of England, (or curtesy) and those in dower, but against any farmer or other that holds in any manner for life or years. But tenant in tail after possibility of issue extinct is not impeachable for waste; because his estate was at it's creation an estate of inheritance, and so not within the statutes. Neither does an action of waste lie *for the debtor* against tenant by statute, recognizance, or *elegit*; because against them the debtor may set off the damages in account: but it seems reasonable that it should lie *for the reversioner*, expectant on the determination of the debtor's own estate, or of these estates derived from the debtor. And, by the statute of Gloucester, the tenants shall lose and forfeit the place wherein the waste is committed, and also treble damages, to him that hath the inheritance. If waste be done *sparsim*, or here and there, all over a wood, the whole wood shall be recovered; or if in several rooms of a house, the whole house shall be forfeited. But if waste be done only in one end of a wood (or perhaps in one room of a house, if that can be conveniently separated from the rest) that part only is the *locus vastatus*, or thing wasted, and that only shall be forfeited to the reversioner.

VII. A seventh species of forfeiture is that of *copyhold* estates, by *breach* of the *customs* of the manor. Copyhold estates are not only liable to the same forfeitures as those which are held in socage, for treason, felony, alienation, and waste; whereupon the lord may seize them without any presentment by the homage; but also to peculiar forfeitures, annexed to this species of tenure, which are incurred by the breach of either the general customs of all copyholds, or the peculiar local customs of certain particular manors. As, by subtraction of suit and service; by disclaiming to hold of the lord, or swearing himself not his copyholder; by neglect to be admitted tenant within a year and a day; by contumacy in not appearing in court after three proclamations; or by refusing, when sworn of the homage, to present the truth according to his oath. In these, and a variety of other cases, which it is impossible here to enumerate, the forfeiture does not accrue to the lord till after the offences are presented by the homage, or jury of the lord's court baron.

VIII. The eighth and last method, whereby lands and tenements may become forfeited, is that of *bankruptcy*, or the act of becoming a bankrupt.

By the statute 13 Eliz. c. 7. the commissioners for that purpose, when a man is declared a bankrupt, shall have full power to dispose of all his lands and tenements, which he had in his own right at the time when he became a bankrupt, or which shall descend or come to him at any time afterwards, before his debts are satisfied or agreed for; and all lands and tenements which were purchased by him jointly with his wife or children to his own use, (or such interest therein as he may lawfully part with) or purchased with any other person upon secret trust for his own use; and to cause them to be appraised to their full value, and to sell the same by deed indented and inrolled, or divide them proportionably among the creditors. This statute expressly included not only free, but customary and copyhold, lands: but did not extend to estates-tail, farther than for the bankrupt's life; nor to equities of redemption on a mortgaged estate, wherein the bankrupt has no legal interest, but only an equitable reversion.

Whereupon the statute 21 Jac. I. c. 19. enacts, that the commissioners shall be empowered to sell or convey, by deed indented and inrolled, any lands or tenements of the bankrupt, wherein he shall be seised of an estate-tail in possession, remainder, or reversion, unless the remainder or reversion thereof shall be in the crown; and that such sale shall be good against all such issues in tail, remainder-men, and reversioners, whom the bankrupt himself might have barred by a common recovery, or other means: and that all equities of redemption upon mortgaged estates, shall be at the disposal of the commissioners; for they shall have power to redeem the same, as the bankrupt himself might have done, and after redemption to sell them. And also, by this and a former act (*a*), all fraudulent conveyances to defeat the intent of these statutes are declared void; but that no purchaser *bona fide*, for a good or valuable consideration, shall be affected by the bankrupt laws, unless the commission be sued forth within five years after the act of bankruptcy committed.

By virtue of these statutes a bankrupt may lose all his real estates; which may at once be transferred by his commissioners to their assignees, without his participation or consent.

## CHAPTER XV.

### OF TITLE BY ALIENATION.

THE most usual and universal method of acquiring a title to real estates is that of alienation, conveyance, or purchase in its limited sense: under which may be comprised any method wherein estates are voluntarily resigned by one man, and accepted by another; whether that be effected by sale, gift, marriage settlement, devise, or other transmission of property by the mutual consent of the parties.

In examining the nature of alienation, let us first inquire, briefly, *who* may aliene and to *whom*; and then, more largely, *how* a man may aliene, or the several modes of conveyance.

---

(*a*) 1 Jac. I. c. 15.

I. Who may aliene, and to whom: or, in other words, who is capable of conveying and who of purchasing. And herein we must consider rather the incapacity, than capacity, of the several parties: for all persons in *possession* are *prima facie* capable both of conveying and purchasing, unless the law has laid them under any particular disabilities. But if a man has only in him the *right* of either possession or property, he cannot convey it to any other, lest pretended titles might be granted to great men, whereby justice might be trodden down, and the weak oppressed. Yet reversions and vested remainders may be granted; because the possession of the particular tenant is the possession of him in reversion or remainder: but *contingencies*, and mere *possibilities*, though they may be released, or devised by will, or may pass to the heir or executor, yet cannot (it hath been said) *(a)* be assigned to a stranger, unless coupled with some present interest.

Persons attainted of treason, felony, and *præmunire*, are incapable of conveying, from the time of the offence committed, provided attainder follows: for such conveyance by them may tend to defeat the king of his forfeiture, or the lord of his escheat. But they may *purchase* for the benefit of the crown, or the lord of the fee, though they are disabled to *hold*: the lands so purchased, if after attainder, being subject to immediate forfeiture; if before, to escheat as well as forfeiture, according to the nature of the crime. So also corporations, religious or others, may purchase lands; yet, unless they have a licence to hold in mortmain, they cannot retain such purchase; but it shall be forfeited to the lord of the fee.

Idiots and persons of nonsane memory, infants, and persons under duress, are not totally disabled either to convey or purchase, but *sub modo* only. For their conveyances and purchases are voidable, but not actually void. The king indeed, on behalf of an idiot, may avoid his grants or other

---

*(a)* Per Ld. Coke, *Lampet's case*, 10 *Rep.* 48 ᵃ but though *mere* possibilities are disregarded at *law*, they are, under particular circumstances, assignable in *equity*. See the authorities referred to in 1 *Fonbl. Eq.* 203. *marg.* (5) and *ibid* 202. n.*(g)*

acts. But it hath been faid, that a *non compos* himfelf, though he be afterwards brought to a right mind, fhall not be permitted to alledge his own infanity in order to avoid fuch grant: for that no man fhall be allowed to ftultify himfelf, or plead his own difabilty. Though later opinions, feeling the inconvenience of the rule, have in many points endeavoured to reftrain it (*a*). And, clearly, the next heir, or other perfon interefted, may, after the death of the idiot or *non compos*, take advantage of his incapacity and avoid the grant. And fo too, if he purchafes under this difability, and does not afterwards upon recovering his fenfes agree to the purchafe, his heir may either waive or accept the eftate at his option. In like manner, an infant may waive fuch purchafe or conveyance, when he comes to full age; or, if he does not then actually agree to it, his heirs may waive it after him. Perfons alfo, who purchafe or convey under durefs, may affirm or avoid fuch tranfaction, whenever the durefs is ceafed. For all thefe are under the protection of the law; which will not fuffer them to be impofed upon, through the imbecillity of their prefent condition; fo that their acts are only binding, in cafe they be afterwards agreed to, when fuch imbecillity ceafes. Yet the guardians or committees of a lunatic, by the ftatute of 11 Geo. III. c. 20. are impowered to renew in his right, under the directions of the court of chancery, any leafe for lives or years, and apply the profits of fuch renewal for the benefit of fuch lunatic, his heirs, or executors.

The cafe of a feme-covert is fomewhat different. She may *purchafe* an eftate without the confent of her hufband, and the conveyance is good during the coverture, till he avoids it by fome act declaring his diffent. And, though he does nothing to avoid it, or even if he actually confents, the feme-covert herfelf may, after the death of her hufband, waive or difagree to the fame: nay, even her heirs may waive it after her, if fhe dies before her hufband, or if in her widowhood fhe does nothing to exprefs her confent or agreement. But the *conveyance* or other contract of a feme-

---

(*a*) See 1 *Eq. Ca. ab.* 279, and 1 *Fonbl. Eq.* 42. n. (*d*)

covert (except by some matter of record) is absolutely void, and not merely voidable; and therefore cannot be affirmed or made good by any subsequent agreement.

The case of an alien born is also peculiar. For he may purchase any thing; but after purchase he can *hold* nothing, except a lease for years of a house for convenience of merchandize *(a)*, in case he be an alien-friend: all other purchases (when found by an inquest of office) being immediately forfeited to the king.

Papists, lastly, and persons professing the popish religion, and neglecting to take the oath prescribed by statute 18 Geo. III. c. 60, within the time limited for that purpose, are by statute 11 & 12 W. III. c. 4. disabled to purchase any lands, rents, or heriditaments: and all estates made to their use, or in trust for them, are void *(b)*.

II. We are next, but principally, to enquire, *how* a man may aliene or convey; which will lead us to consider the several modes of conveyance.

These are of four kinds: 1. By matter *in pais*, or deed; which is an assurance transacted between two or more private persons *in pais*, in the country; that is (according to the old common law) upon the very spot to be transferred. 2. By matter of *record*, or an assurance transacted only in the king's public courts of record. 3. By special *custom*, obtaining in some particular places, and

---

*(a)* It is noticed by Mr. *Hargrave, Co. Lit.* 2<sup>b</sup>, n. 7, that even *leases for years* to an alien being an *artificer* or *handicraftsman* are void by 32 Hen. VIII. c. 16, but that in favor of aliens the statute has been very strictly construed.

*(b)* This statute of 11 & 12 Will. c. 4. declares, that in case of estates coming to papists, the next of kin, being protestants, shall enter and enjoy during the life, or till the conformity of the papist. But on the construction of this statute it was observed by *Cowp. Chan.* to be remarkable that it extends " only to papists under the age of 18 at the time the lands come to him; but where the papist is above 18 when the lands come to him, or in trust for him, such papist is utterly disabled to take, and the estate void." See *Vane* v. *Fletcher.* 1 *F. Williams.* 352.

relating only to some particular species of property. Which three are such as take effect during the life of the party conveying or assuring. 4. The fourth takes no effect till after his death; and that is by *devise*, contained in his last will and testament. We shall treat of each in its order.

## CHAPTER XVI.

### OF ALIENATION BY DEED.

IN treating of deeds I shall consider, first, their general nature; and, next, the several sorts or kinds of deeds, with their respective incidents. And in explaining the former, I shall examine, first, what a deed is; secondly, its requisites; and, thirdly, how it may be avoided.

I. First then, a deed is a writing sealed and delivered by the parties. If a deed be made by more parties than one, there ought to be regularly as many copies of it as there are parties, and each should be cut or indented on the top or side, to tally or correspond with the other; which deed, so made, is called an indenture (*a*). When the several parts of an indenture are interchangeably executed by the several parties, that part or copy which is executed by the grantor is usually called the *original*, and the rest are *counterparts*: though of late it is most frequent for all the parties to execute every part; which renders them all originals. A deed made by one party only is not indented, but *polled* or shaved quite even; and therefore called a *deed poll*, or a single deed.

II. We are in the next place to consider the *requisites* of a deed. The first of which is, that there be persons able to contract and be contracted with, for the purposes intended by the deed; and also a thing, or subject matter to be contracted for; all which must be expressed by sufficient names. So as in every grant there must be a grantor, a grantee, and

---

(*a*) A short history of the introduction and progress of *indenting* deeds is given by Mr. *Butler*, *Co. Lit.* 229. \*. n. (1).

a thing granted; in every leafe a leffor, a leffee, and a thing demifed.

Secondly; the deed muft be founded upon good and fufficient *confideration.* Not upon an ufurious contract; nor upon fraud or collufion, either to deceive purchafors *bona fide*, or juft and lawful creditors; any of which bad confiderations will vacate the deed, and fubject fuch perfons, as put the fame in ufe, to forfeitures, and often to imprifonment. A deed alfo, or other grant, made without any confideration, is, as it were, of no effect; for it is conftrued to enure, or to be effectual, only to the ufe of the grantor himfelf *(a)*. The confideration may be either a *good*, or a *valuable* one. A good confideration is fuch as that of blood, or of natural love and affection, when a man grants an eftate to a near relation; being founded on motives of generofity, prudence, and natural duty: a valuable confideration is fuch as money, marriage, or the like, which the law efteems an equivalent given for the grant; and is therefore founded in motives of juftice. Deeds made upon good confideration only, are confidered as merely voluntary, and are frequently fet afide in favour of creditors, and *bona fide* purchafors.

Thirdly; the deed muft be *written*, or I prefume *printed*, for it may be in any character or any language; but it muft be upon paper or parchment. For if it be written on ftone, board, linen, leather, or the like, it is no deed. It muft alfo have the regular ftamps, impofed on it by the feveral ftatutes for the increafe of the public revenue; elfe it cannot be given in evidence. Formerly many conveyances were made by parol, or word of mouth only, without writing; but this giving a handle to a variety of frauds, the ftatute 29

---

(a) This, Mr. *Chriftian* conceives, (on the authority of *Shep. Touch.* 221, where it is faid that a *bargain and fale* cannot be without a confideration, though a *gift* may) to be true only of a bargain and fale.—See the defects of confideration in deeds, and the legal and equitable confequences of fuch defects diftinctly confidered in 1 *Fonb. Eq.* 326.

Car. II. c. 3. enacts, that no leafe eftate, or intereft in lands, tenements, or hereditaments, made by livery of feifin, or by parol only, (except leafes, not exceeding three years from the making, and whereon the referved rent is at leaft two-thirds of the value) fhall be looked upon as of greater force than a leafe or eftate at will; nor fhall any affignment, grant, or furrender of any intereft in any freehold hereditaments be valid; unlefs in both cafes the fame be put in writing, and figned by the party granting, or his agent lawfully authorized in writing.

Fourthly; the matter written muft be *legally* and *orderly* fet forth: that is, there muft be words fufficient to fpecify the agreement and bind the parties: which fufficiency muft be left to the courts of law to determine. For it is not abfolutely neceffary in law to have all the formal parts that are ufually drawn out in deeds, fo as there be fufficient words to declare clearly and legally the party's meaning. But, as thefe formal and orderly parts are calculated to convey that meaning in the cleareft, diftincteft, and moft effectual manner, and have been well confidered and fettled by the wifdom of fucceffive ages, it is prudent not to depart from them without good reafon or urgent neceffity; and therefore I will here mention them in their ufual order.

1. The *premifes* may be ufed to fet forth the number and names of the parties with their additions or titles. They alfo contain the recital, if any, of fuch deeds, agreements, or matters of fact, as are neceffary to explain the reafons upon which the prefent tranfaction is founded: and herein alfo is fet down the confideration upon which the deed is made. And then follows the certainty of the grantor, grantee, and thing granted.

2, 3. Next come the *habendum* and *tenendum*. The office of the *habendum* is properly to determine what eftate or intereft is granted by the deed: though this may be performed, and fometimes is performed, in the premifes. In which cafe the *habendum* may leffen, enlarge, explain, or qualify, but not totally contradict or be repugnant to, the eftate granted in the premises. The *tenendum*, "and to hold," is now of very little use, and is only kept in by custom.

4. Next follow the terms of stipulation, if any, upon which the grant is made: the first of which is the *reddendum* or reservation, whereby the grantor doth create or reserve some new thing to himself out of what he had before granted. To make a *reddendum* good, if it be of any thing newly created by the deed, the reservation must be to the grantors, or some, or one of them, and not to any stranger to the deed. But if it be of ancient services or the like, annexed to the land, then the reservation may be to the lord of the fee.

5. Another of the terms upon which a grant may be made is a *condition*; which is a clause of contingency, on the happening of which the estate granted may be defeated; as "provided always, that if the mortgagor shall pay the mort-"gagee 500*l*. upon such a day, the whole estate granted shall "determine;" and the like.

6. Next may follow the clause of *warranty*; whereby the grantor doth, for himself and his heirs, warrant and secure to the grantee the estate so granted; which is a kind of covenant real, and can only be created by the verb *warrantizo* or *warrant*.

But by statute 4 & 5 Ann. c. 16. all warranties by any tenant for life shall be void against those in remainder or reversion; and all collateral warranties by any ancestor, who has no estate of inheritance in possession shall be void against his heir. But collateral warranty (though without assets,) was at common law, a sufficient bar of the estate tail and all remainders and reversions expectant thereon. And so it still continues to be, notwithstanding the statute of queen Anne, if made by tenant in tail in possession: which, if accompanied with assets, bars his own issue and without them bars such of his heirs as may be in remainder or reversion.

7. After warranty usually follow *covenants*, or conventions, which are clauses of agreement contained in a deed, whereby either party may stipulate for the truth of certain facts, or

may bind himself to perform, or give, something to the other. Thus the grantor may covenant that he hath a right to convey; for the grantee's quiet enjoyment; or the like: the grantee may covenant to pay his rent, or keep the premises in repair, &c. If the covenantor covenants for himself and his *heirs*, it is then a covenant real, and descends upon the heirs; who are bound to perform it, provided they have assets by descent, but not otherwise: if he covenants also for his *executors* and *administrators*, his personal assets, as well as his real, are likewise pledged for the performance of the covenant (a); which makes such covenant a better security than any warranty. It is also in some respects a less security, and therefore more beneficial to the grantor; who usually *covenants* only for the acts of himself and his ancestors, whereas a general *warranty* extends to all mankind. For which reasons the covenant has in modern practice totally superseded the other.

8. Lastly, comes the *conclusion*, which mentions the execution and date of the deed, or time of its being given or executed, either expressly, or by reference to some day and year before-mentioned.

I proceed now to the *fifth* requisite for making a good deed; the *reading* of it. This is necessary, wherever any of the parties desire it; and, if it be not done on his request, the deed is void as to him. If he can, he should read it himself: if he be blind or illiterate, another must read it to him. If it be read falsely, it will be void; at least for so much as is miscredited: unless it be agreed by collusion that the deed shall be read false, on purpose to make it void; for in such case it shall bind the fraudulent party.

---

(a) But " a covenant lies against an executor " (and consequently an administrator) " in every case, *although he be not named*, unless it be such a covenant as is to be performed by the person of the testator, which they cannot perform." Hyde v. *Dean of Windsor*, Cro. Eliz. 552.

Sixthly, it is requisite that the party, whose deed it is, should *seal*, and now in most cases, I apprehend, should *sign* it also.

A seventh requisite to a good deed is, that it be *delivered* by the party himself or his certain attorney: which therefore is also expressed in the attestation; " sealed and *delivered.*". A deed takes effect only from this tradition or delivery; for if the date be false or impossible, the delivery ascertains the time of it. And if another person seals the deed, yet if the party delivers it himself, he thereby adopts the sealing, and by a parity of reason the signing also, and makes them both his own. A delivery may be either absolute, that is, to the party or grantee himself; or to a third person, to hold till some conditions be performed on the part of the grantee: in which last case it is not delivered as a *deed*, but as an *escrow*; that is, as a scrowl or writing, which is not to take effect as a deed till the conditions be performed; and then it is a deed to all intents and purposes.

The *last* requisite to the validity of a deed is the *attestation*, or execution of it *in the presence of witnesses:* though this is necessary, rather for preserving the evidence, than for constituting the essence of the deed.

III. We are next to consider, how a deed may be *avoided*, or rendered of no effect. And from what has been before laid down it will follow, that if a deed wants any of the essential requisites before-mentioned; either, 1. Proper parties, and a proper subject matter; 2. A good and sufficient consideration: 3. Writing, on paper or parchment, duly stamped: 4. Sufficient and legal words, properly disposed: 5. Reading, if desired, before the execution: 6. Sealing; and, by the statute, in most cases signing also: or, 7. Delivery; it is a void deed *ab initio*. It may also be avoided by matter *ex post facto*: as, 1. By rasure, interlining, or other alteration in any material part; unless a memorandum be made thereof at the time of the execution and attestation. 2. By breaking off, or defacing the seal. 3. By delivering it up to be cancelled; that is, to have lines drawn over it in form of lattice work or *cancelli;* though the phrase is now used figuratively for any manner of obliteration or defacing it. 4. By the disagreement of such, whose concurrence is necessary, in order for the deed to stand: as, the husband, where a feme-covert is concerned; an infant, or person under duress, when those disabilities are removed; and the like. 5. By the judgment or decree of a court of judicature. This is now the province of the court of chancery: when it appears that the deed was obtained by fraud, force, or other foul practice; or is proved to be an absolute forgery. In any of these cases the deed may be voided, either in part or totally, according as the cause of avoidance is more or less extensive.

And, having thus explained the general nature of deeds, we are next to consider their several species, together with their respective incidents: deeds or conveyances are either those at *common law*, or such as receive their force and efficacy by virtue of the *statute of uses*.

I. Of conveyances by the common law, some may be called *original*, or *primary* conveyances; which are those by means whereof the benefit or estate is created or first arises: others are *derivative*, or *secondary*; whereby the benefit or estate, originally created, is enlarged, restrained, transferred, or extinguished.

Original conveyances are the following: 1. Feoffment; 2. Gift; 3. Grant; 4. Lease; 5. Exchange; 6. Partition: Derivative are, 7. Release; 8. Confirmation; 9. Surrender; 10. Assignment; 11. Defeazance.

1. A feoffment, *feoffamentum*, is a substantive derived from the verb, to enfeoff, *feoffare* or *infeudare*, to give one a feud; and therefore feoffment is properly *donatio feudi*. It is the most antient method of conveyance, the most solemn and public, and therefore the most easily remembered and proved. And it may properly be defined, the gift of any corporeal hereditament to another. He that so gives, or enfeoffs, is called the *feoffor*; and the person enfeoffed is denominated the *feoffee*.

But by the mere words of the deed, the feoffment is by no

means perfected, there remains a very material ceremony to be performed, called *livery of feifin*; without which the feoffee has but a mere eftate at will. This livery of feifin is no other than the pure feodal inveftiture, or delivery of corporal poffeffion of the land or tenement; which was held abfolutely neceffary to complete the donation. "*Nam feudum fine inveftitura nullo modo conftitui potuit:*" and an eftate was then only perfect, when, as the author of Fleta expreffes it in our law, "*fit juris et feifinæ conjunctio.*

Livery of feifin, by the common law, is neceffary to be made upon every grant of an eftate of freehold, in hereditaments corporeal, whether of inheritance or for life only. In hereditaments incorporeal it is impoffible to be made; for they are not the object of the fenfes: and in leafes for years, or other chattel interefts, it is not neceffary.

On the creation of a *freehold* remainder, at one and the fame time with a particular eftate for years, we have before feen that at the common law livery muft be made to the particular tenant. But if fuch a remainder be created afterwards, expectant on a leafe for years now in being, the livery muft not be made to the leffee for years, for then it operates nothing; "*nam quod femel meum eft, amplius meum effe non poteft*; but it muft be made to the remainder-man himfelf, by confent of the leffee for years: for without his confent no livery of the poffeffion can be given; becaufe fuch forcible livery would be an ejectment of the tenant for his term (*a*).

2. The conveyance by *gift*, *donatio*, is properly applied to the creation of an eftate-tail, as feoffment is to that of an

---

(*a*) Since the introduction of ufes and trufts, and the ftatute of 27 Hen. VIII. for transferring ufes into poffeffion, the neceffity of livery of feifin, for paffing a freehold in corporeal hereditaments, has been almoft wholly fuperfeded and, in confequence, the conveyance by feoffment now very little ufed. *Co. Lit.* 48 ª. n. (3). The above fhort extracts are then fufficient on this fubject.

eſtate in fee, and leaſe to that of an eſtate for life or years. It differs in nothing from a feoffment, but in the nature of the eſtate paſſing by it: for the operative words of conveyance in this caſe are *do* or *dedi*; and gifts in tail are equally imperfect without livery of ſeiſin, as feoffments in fee ſimple. In common acceptation gifts are frequently confounded with the next ſpecies of deeds: which are,

3. Grants, *conceſſiones*; the regular method by the common law of transferring the property of *incorporeal* hereditaments, or ſuch things whereof no livery can be had. For which reaſon all corporeal hereditaments, as lands and houſes, are ſaid to lie in *livery;* and the others, as advowſons, commons, rents, reverſions, *&c.* to lie in *grant*. Theſe, therefore, paſs merely by the delivery of the deed: for the operative words therein commonly uſed are *dedi et conceſſi*, " have " given and granted."

4. A leaſe is properly a conveyance of any lands or tenements, (uſually in conſideration of rent or other annual recompenſe) made for life, for years, or at will, but always for a *leſs* time than the leſſor hath in the premiſes: for if it be for the *whole* intereſt, it is more properly an aſſignment than a leaſe. The uſual words of operation in it are, " de- " miſe, grant, and to farm let." By this conveyance an eſtate for life, for years, or at will, may be created, either in corporeal or incorporeal hereditaments; though livery of ſeiſin is indeed incident and neceſſary to one ſpecies of leaſes, *viz.* leaſes for life of corporeal hereditaments; but to no other.

By the common law, as it ſtood for many centuries, all perſons ſeiſed of any eſtate, might let leaſes to endure ſo long as their own intereſt laſted, but no longer. Whereas now, by ſeveral ſtatutes, this power, where it was unreaſonable, and might be made an ill uſe of, is reſtrained; and, where in the other caſes the reſtraint by the common law ſeemed too hard, it is in ſome meaſure removed. The former ſtatutes are called the *reſtraining*, the latter the *enabling* ſtatute.

And firſt, of *enabling* ſtatutes: the *enabling* ſtatute, 32 Hen. VIII. c. 28. empowers three manner of perſons to make leafes, to endure for three lives or one and twenty years, which they could not do before. As, firſt, tenant in tail may, by ſuch leaſes, bind his iſſue in tail, but not thoſe in remainder or reverſion. Secondly, a huſband feifed in right of his wife, in fee-ſimple or fee-tail, provided the wife joins in ſuch leaſe, may bind her and her heirs thereby. Laſtly, all perſons ſeifed of an eſtate of fee-ſimple in right of their churches, which extends not to parſons and vicars, may (without the concurrence of any other perſon) bind their ſucceſſors. But then there muſt many requiſites be obſerved, which the ſtatute ſpecifies, otherwiſe ſuch leaſes are not binding. 1. The leaſe muſt be by indenture; and not by deed poll, or by parol. 2. It muſt begin from the making, or day of the making, and not at any greater diſtance of time. 3. If there be any old leaſe in being, it muſt be firſt abſolutely ſurrendered, or be within a year of expiring. 4. It muſt be either for twenty-one years, or three lives; and not for both. 5. It muſt not exceed the term of three lives, or twenty-one years, but may be for a ſhorter term. 6. It muſt be of corporeal hereditaments, and not of ſuch things as lie merely in grant; for no rent can be reſerved thereout by the common law, as the leſſor cannot reſort to them to diſtrein (a). 7. It muſt be of lands and tenements moſt commonly letten for twenty years paſt; ſo that if they had been let for above half the time (or eleven years out of the twenty) either for life, for years, at will, or by copy of court roll, it is ſufficient. 8. The moſt uſual and cuſtomary feorm or rent, for twenty years paſt, muſt be reſerved yearly on ſuch leaſe. 9. Such leaſes muſt not be made without impeachment of waſte. Theſe are the guards, impoſed by the ſtatute (which was avowedly made for the ſecurity of farmers and the conſequent improve-

---

(a) But now, by the ſtatute 5 Geo. III. c. 17. a leaſe of tithes or other incorporeal hereditaments, alone, may be granted by any biſhop or any ſuch eccleſiaſtical or eleemoſynary corporation, and the ſucceſſor ſhall be entitled to recover the rent by an action of debt, which (in caſe of a free-hold leaſe) he could not have brought at the common law. A.

ment of tillage) to prevent unreasonable abuses, in prejudice of the issue, the wife, or the successor, of the reasonable indulgence here given.

Next follow the *disabling* or *restraining* statutes, (made entirely for the benefit of the successor) from all which together we may collect, that all colleges, cathedrals, and other ecclesiastical, or eleemosynary corporations, and all parsons and vicars, are restrained from making any leases of their lands, unless under the following regulations: 1. They must not exceed twenty-one years, or three lives, from the making. 2. The accustomed rent, or more, must be yearly reserved thereon. 3. Houses in corporations, or market towns, may be let for forty years; provided they be not the mansion-houses of the lessors, nor have above ten acres of ground belonging to them; and provided the lessee be bound to keep them in repair: and they may also be aliened in fee-simple for lands of equal value in recompense. 4. Where there is an old lease in being, no concurrent lease shall be made, unless where the old one will expire within three years. 5. No lease (by the equity of the statute) shall be made without impeachment of waste. 6. All bonds and covenants tending to frustrate the provisions of the statutes of 13 & 18 Eliz. shall be void.

Concerning these restrictive statutes there are two observations to be made. First, that they do not, by any construction, enable any persons to make such leases as they were by common law disabled to make. Therefore a parson, or vicar, though he is restrained from making longer leases than for twenty-one years or three lives, even *with* the consent of patron and ordinary, yet is not enabled to make any lease at all, so as to bind his successor, *without* obtaining such consent. Secondly, that though leases contrary to these acts are declared void, yet they are good against the *lessor* during his life, if he be a sole corporation; and are also good against an aggregate corporation so long as the head of it lives, who is presumed to be the most concerned in interest. For the act was intended for the benefit of the successor only; and no man shall make an advantage of his own wrong.

There is yet another reftriction with regard to college leafes, by ftatute 18 Eliz. c. 6. which directs, that one third of the old rent, then paid, fhould for the future be referved in wheat or malt, referving a quarter of wheat for each 6s. 8d. or a quarter of malt for every 5s. or that the leffees fhould pay for the fame according to the price that wheat and malt fhould be fold for, in the market next adjoining to the refpective colleges, on the market-day before the rent becomes due.

The leafes of beneficed clergymen are farther reftrained, in cafe of their non-refidence, by ftatutes 13 Eliz. c. 20. 14 Eliz. c. 11. 18 Eliz. c. 11. and 43 Eliz. c. 9. which direct, that if any beneficed clergyman be abfent from his cure above fourfcore days in any one year, he fhall not only forfeit one year's profit of his benefice, to be diftributed among the poor of the parifh; but that all leafes made by him, of the profits of fuch benefice, and all covenants and agreements of like nature, fhall ceafe and be void: except in the cafe of licenfed pluralifts, who are allowed to demife the living, on which they are non-refident, to their curates only; provided fuch curates do not abfent themfelves above forty days in any one year. And thus much for leafes, with their feveral enlargements and reftrictions (a).

5. An *exchange* is a mutual grant of equal interefts, the one in confideration of the other (b). The word "exchange"

---

(a) For the other learning relating to leafes, which is very curious and diffufive, I muft refer the reader to 3 *Bac. Abridg.* 295. (title *Leafe and Terms for Years*) where the fubject is treated in a perfpicuous and mafterly manner; being fuppofed to be extracted from a manufcript of Sir Geoffrey Gilbert. A.

(b) The author leaves it undefinite as to the number of parties between whom an exchange may be made; it may be proper, therefore, to remark, that it has lately been held, that it cannot be made between any greater number than *two. Eton Col.* v. *Bp. Winch.* 3 *Wils.* 483. "The principles of it not being applicable to more than two *diftinct* contracting parties, for want of the mutuality and reciprocity on which is so individually requisite and appropriated by law to this case, that it cannot be supplied by any other word, or expressed by any circumlocution. The estates exchanged must be equal in quantity; not of *value*, for that is immaterial, but of *interest;* as fee-simple for fee-simple, a lease for twenty years for a lease for twenty years, and the like. And the exchange may be of things that lie either in grant or in livery. But no livery of seisin, even in exchanges of freehold, is necessary to perfect the conveyance: for each party stands in the place of the other and occupies his right, and each of them hath already had corporeal possession of his own land. But entry must be made on both sides: for, if either party die before entry, the exchange is void, for want of sufficient notoriety. And so also, if two parsons, by consent of patron and ordinary, exchange their preferments; and the one is presented, instituted, and inducted, and the other is presented, and instituted, but dies before induction; the former shall not keep his new benefice, because the exchange was not completed, and therefore he shall return back to his own. For if, after an exchange of lands or other hereditaments, either party be evicted of those which were taken by him in exchange, through defect of the other's title; he shall return back to the possession of his own, by virtue of the implied warranty contained in all exchanges.

6. A partition, is when two or more joint-tenants, coparceners, or tenants in common, agree to divide the lands so held among them in severalty, each taking a distinct part. Here, as in some instances there is a unity of interest, and in all a unity of possession, it is necessary that they all mutually convey and assure to each other the several estates, which they are to take and enjoy separately.

These are the several species of *primary*, or *original* conveyances. Those which remain are of the *secondary*, or *derivative* sort; which presuppose some other conveyance

---

its operation so entirely depends." *Co. Lit.* 50 $^b$. n. (1). and see *ibid* 51 $^a$. n. (1).

precedent, and only serve to enlarge, confirm, alter, restrain, restore, or transfer the interest granted by such original conveyance. As,

7. Releases; which are a discharge or conveyance of a man's right in lands or tenements, to another that hath some former estate in possession. The words generally used therein are "remised, released, and for ever quit-claimed:" And these releases may enure either, 1. By way of *enlarging an estate*, or *enlarger l'estate*: as if there be tenant for life or years, remainder to another in fee, and he in remainder releases all his right to the particular tenant and his heirs, this gives him the estate in fee. But in this case the relessee must be in *possession* of some estate, for the release to work upon; for if there be lessee for years, and before he enters and is in possession, the lessor releases to him all his right in the reversion, such release is void for want of possession in the relessee. 2. By way of *passing an estate*, or *mitter l'estate*: as when one of two coparceners releaseth all her right to the other, this passeth the fee-simple of the whole. And in both these cases there must be a privity of estate between the relessor and relessee; that is, one of their estates must be so related to the other, as to make but one and the same estate in law *(a)*.

8. A confirmation is of a nature nearly allied to a release. Sir Edward Coke defines it to be a conveyance of an estate or right *in esse*, whereby a voidable estate is made sure and unavoidable, or whereby a particular estate is increased: and the words of making it are these, " have given, granted, " ratified, approved, and confirmed." An instance of the first branch of the definition is, if tenant for life leaseth for forty years, and dieth during that term; here the lease for years is voidable by him in reversion: yet, if he hath confirmed the estate of the lessee for years, before the death

---

*(a)* Other ways to which a release may enure, are mentioned by the author; but those we have preferred are the only ones which are now material. Of these more may be seen, *Co. Lit.* 273 ª. n. (1). 273 ᵇ. n. (2). and *Gil. Ten.* 53.

of tenant for life, it is no longer voidable but fure. The latter branch, or that which tends to the increafe of a particular eftate, is the fame in all refpects with that fpecies of releafe, which operates by way of enlargement (*a*).

9. A furrender, *furfumredditio*, or rendering up, is of a nature directly oppofite to a releafe; for, as that operates by the greater eftate's defcending upon the lefs, a furrender is the falling of a lefs eftate into a greater. It is defined, a yielding up of an eftate for life or years to him that hath the immediate reverfion or remainder, wherein the particular eftate may merge or drown, by mutual agreement between them. It is done by thefe words, " hath furrendered, gran- " ted, and yielded up." The furrenderor muft be in poffeffion; and the furrenderee muft have a higher eftate, in which the eftate furrendered may merge: therefore tenant for life cannot furrender to him in remainder for years. In a furrender there is no occafion for livery of feifin; for there is a privity of eftate between the furrenderor, and the furrenderee; the one's particular eftate, and the other's remainder are one and the fame eftate; and livery having been once made at the creation of it, there is no neceffity for having it afterwards. And, for the fame reafon, no livery is required on a releafe or confirmation in fee to tenant for years or at will, though a freehold thereby paffes: fince the reverfion of the releffor, or confirmor, and the particular eftate of the releffee, or confirmee, are one and the fame eftate; and where there is already a poffeffion, derived from fuch a privity of eftate, any farther delivery of poffeffion would be vain and nugatory (*b*).

10. An *affignment* is properly a transfer, or making over to another, of the right one has in *any* eftate; but it is ufually applied to an eftate for life or years. And it differs from a

---

(*a*) See further illuftrations of this fpecies of affurance, *Gil. Ten.* 75. *Co. Lit.* 295 b. 297 a. *in notis.*

(*b*) Many valuable obfervations upon the nature and effect of furrenders, may be found in *Co. Lit.* 8vo. 337 b. *notis.*

leafe only in this: that by a leafe one grants an intereft lefs than his own, referving to himfelf a reverfion; in affignments he parts with the whole property, and the affignee, ftands to all intents and purpofes in the place of the affignor *(a)*.

11. A defeazance is a collateral deed, made at the fame time with a feoffment or other conveyance, containing certain conditions, upon the performance of which the eftate then created may be *defeated* or totally undone.

II. There yet remain to be fpoken of fome few conveyances, which have their force and operation by virtue of the *ftatute of ufes.*

This ftatute (27 Hen. VIII. c. 10) enacts, that, " when any
" perfon fhall be *feifed* of lands, &c. to the ufe, confidence,
" or truft, of any other perfon or body politic, the perfon
" or corporation entitled to the ufe in fee-fimple, fee-tail,
" for life, or years, or otherwife, fhall from thenceforth
" ftand and be feifed or poffeffed of the land, &c. of and in
" the like eftates as they have in the ufe, truft, or confi-
" dence; and that the eftate of the perfon fo feifed to ufes
" fhall be deemed to be in him or them that have the ufe,
" in fuch quality, manner, form, and condition, as they
" had before in the ufe." The ftatute thus *executes* the ufe,

---

*(a)* This muft be underftood with fome qualification, and is true only in refpect of fuch acts of the affignor as in the legal phrafe *run with the land.* Thefe are, principally, covenants to repair, or to do any other matter *upon* the land demifed; and covenants for the title, as, that the grantor is feifed in fee, has a right to convey, for quiet enjoyment, and further affurance. But no acts or covenants of the affignor, which are in their nature merely *collateral* to the thing demifed, are binding upon the affignee. See *Spencer's* cafe, 5 *Co.* 16 *a* nor is the affignee liable for fuch covenants of the affignor as were broken previous to the affignment. *Church- w. St. Saviour's* v. *Smith.* 3 *Bur.* 1271. The cafes on this fubject have lately been collected, and arranged, in a ufeful little treatife on the laws refpecting landlords and tenants, to which we refer the reader, as a book well adapted for common ufe.

as our lawyers term it; that is, conveys the poffeffion to the ufe, and transfers the ufe into poffeffion: thereby making *ceftuy que ufe* complete owner of the lands and tenements, as well in law as equity. This has given way to

12. A twelfth fpecies of conveyance, called a *covenant to ftand feifed to ufes*: by which a man feized of lands, covenants, in confideration of blood or marriage, that he will ftand feifed of the fame to the ufe of his child, wife, or kinfman; for life, in tail, or in fee. Here the ftatute executes at once the eftate; for the party intended to be benefited, having thus acquired the ufe, is thereby put at once into corporal poffeffion of the land, without ever feeing it, by a kind of parliamentary magic. But this conveyance can only operate, when made upon fuch weighty and interefting confiderations as thofe of blood or marriage.

13. A thirteenth fpecies of conveyance, introduced by this ftatute, is that of a *bargain and fale* of lands; which is a kind of real contract, whereby the bargainor for fome pecuniary confideration bargains and fells, that is, contracts to convey, the land to the bargainee; and becomes by fuch bargain, a truftee for, or feized to the ufe of, the bargainee; and then the ftatute of ufes completes the purchafe: or, as it hath been well expreffed, the bargain firft vefts the ufe, and then the ftatute vefts the poffeffion. But as it was forefeen that conveyances, thus made, would want all thofe benefits of notoriety, which the old common law affurances were calculated to give; to prevent therefore clandeftine conveyances of freeholds, it was enacted in the fame feffion of parliament, by ftatute 27 Hen. VIII. c. 16. that fuch bargains and fales fhould not enure to pafs a freehold, unlefs the fame be made by indenture, and *enrolled* within fix months in one of the courts of Weftminfter-hall, or with the *cuftos rotulorum* of the county. Clandeftine bargains and fales of chattel interefts, or leafes for years, were thought not worth regarding, as fuch interefts were very precarious till about fix years before; which alfo occafioned them to be overlooked in framing the ftatute of ufes: and therefore fuch bargains and fales are not directed to be enrolled. But how impoffi-

ble it is to forefee and provide againft *all* the confequences of innovations! This omiffion has given rife to

14. A fourteenth fpecies of conveyance, viz. by *leafe and releafe*. It is thus contrived: a leafe, or rather bargain and fale, upon fome pecuniary confideration, for one year, is made by the tenant of the freehold to the leffee or bargainee. Now this, without any enrollment, makes the bargainor ftand feifed to the ufe of the bargainee, and vefts in the bargainee the *ufe* of the term for a year; and then the ftatute immediately annexes the *poffeffion*. He therefore being thus in poffeffion, is capable of receiving a releafe of the freehold and reverfion; which we have feen before (*a*), muft be made to a tenant in poffeffion: and, accordingly, the next day, a releafe is granted to him. This is held to fupply the place of livery of feifin; and fo a conveyance by leafe and releafe is faid to amount to a feoffment (*b*).

15. To thefe may be added deeds to *lead* or *declare the ufes* of other more direct conveyances, as feoffments, fines, and recoveries; of which we fhall fpeak in the next chapter: and,

16. Deeds of *revocation of ufes*; founded in a previous power, referved at the raifing of the ufes, to revoke fuch as were then declared; and to appoint others in their ftead, which is incident to the power of revocation (*c*). And this

---

(*a*) *Ante*, p. 218.

(*b*) The conveyance by leafe and releafe having of late fuperfeded the ufe of the ancient feoffment at common law, and having from its great convenience and effectivenefs, become one of the moft common modes of affurance, it were to be wifhed that the learned commentator had been more particular in explaining its nature and properties. This deficiency however (if it be fuch) is amply fupplied by the ingenious annotator on the latter part of Coke's commentaries, where, p. 271.[b]. *n*. (1) the feveral fpecies of affurances, founded on the doctrine of ufes, are learnedly and perfpicuoufly difcuffed.

(*c*) Of the principles and extent of powers of revocation, fee *Powell on Powers*, where all the learning on this fubject is fet forth with the ufual abilities of that gentleman.

may suffice for a specimen of conveyances founded upon the statute of uses; and will finish our observations upon such deeds as serve to *transfer* real property.

Before we conclude, it will not be improper to subjoin a few remarks upon such deeds as are used not to *convey*, but to *charge* or incumber lands, and to *discharge* them again: of which nature are *obligations* or bonds, *recognizances*, and *defeazances* upon them both.

1. An *obligation*, or bond, is a deed whereby the obligor obliges himself, his heirs, executors, and administrators, to pay a certain sum of money to another at a day appointed. If this be all, the bond is called a single one, *simplex obligatio*; but there is generally a condition added, that if the obligor does some particular act, the obligation shall be void, or else shall remain in full force: as, payment of rent; performance of covenants in a deed; or repayment of a principal sum of money borrowed of the obligee, with interest, which principal sum is usually one half of the penal sum specified in the bond. In case this condition is not performed, the bond becomes forfeited, or absolute at law, and charges the obligor while living; and after his death the obligation descends upon his heir, who (on defect of personal assets) is bound to discharge it, provided he has real assets by descent as a recompense. So that it may be called, though not a *direct*, yet a *collateral* charge upon the lands. How it affects the personal property of the obligor, will be more properly considered hereafter.

If the condition of a bond be impossible at the time of making it, or be to do a thing contrary to some rule of law that is merely positive, or be uncertain, or insensible, the condition alone is void, and the bond shall stand single, and unconditional: for it is the folly of the obligor to enter into such an obligation, from which he can never be released. If it be to do a thing that is *malum in se*, the obligation itself is void: for the whole is an unlawful contract, and the obligee shall take no advantage from such a transaction. And if the condition be possible at the time of making it, and afterwards becomes impossible by the act of God, the act of law, or the act of the obligee himself, there the penalty of the obligation is saved: for no prudence or foresight of the obligor could guard against such contingency. On the forfeiture of a bond, or its becoming single, the whole penalty was formerly recoverable at law: but here the courts of equity interposed, and would not permit a man to take more than in conscience he ought; viz. his principal, interest, and expences, in case the forfeiture accrued by non-payment of money borrowed; the damages sustained, upon non-performance of covenants, and the like. And the like practice having gained some footing in the courts of law, the statute 4 & 5 Ann. c. 16. at length enacted, in the same spirit of equity, that, in case of a bond conditioned for the payment of money, the payment or tender of the principal sum due, with interest and costs, even though the bond be forfeited and a suit commenced thereon, shall be a full satisfaction and discharge.

2. A *recognizance* is an obligation of record, which a man enters into before some court of record or magistrate duly authorized, with condition to do some particular act; as to appear at the assises, to keep the peace, to pay a debt, or the like. It is in most respects like another bond: the difference being chiefly this: that the bond is the creation of a fresh debt or obligation *de novo*, the recognizance is an acknowledgment of a former debt upon record; which being either certified to, or taken by the officer of some court, is witnessed only by the record of that court, and not by the party's seal: so that it is not in strict propriety a deed, though the effects of it are greater than a common obligation; being allowed a priority in point of payment, and binding the lands of the cognizor, from the time of enrollment on record.

3. A defeazance, on a bond, or recognizance, or judgment recovered, is a condition which, when performed, defeats or undoes it, in the same manner as a defeazance of an estate before-mentioned. It differs only from the common condition of a bond, in that the one is always inserted in the deed or bond itself, the other is made between the same parties by a separate, and frequently a subsequent deed.

This, like the condition of a bond, when performed, difcharges and difincumbers the eftate of the obligor.

## CHAPTER XVII.

### OF ALIENATION BY MATTER OF RECORD.

ASSURANCES by *matter of record* are fuch as do not entirely depend on the act or confent of the parties themfelves; but the fanction of a court of record is called in to fubftantiate, preferve, and be a perpetual teftimony of the transfer of property from one man to another; or of its eftablifhment, when already transferred. Of this nature are, 1. Private acts of parliament. 2. The king's grants. 3. Fines. 4. Common recoveries.

I. Private *acts of parliament* are, efpecially of late years, become a very common mode of affurance. For it may fometimes happen, that by the ingenuity of fome, and the blunders of other practitioners, an eftate is moft grievoufly entangled by a multitude of contingent remainders, refulting trufts, fpringing ufes, executory devifes, and the like artificial contrivances; fo that it is out of the power of either the courts of law or equity to relieve the owner. In thefe, or other cafes of the like kind, the tranfcendent power of parliament is called in, to cut the Gordian knot; and by a particular law, enacted for this very purpofe, to unfetter an eftate; to give its tenant reafonable powers; or to affure it to a purchafor, againft the remote or latent claims of infants or difabled perfons, by fettling a proper equivalent in proportion to the intereft fo barred.

II. The *king's grants* are alfo matter of public record. Thefe grants, whether of lands, honours, liberties, franchifes, or aught befides, are contained in charters, or letters *patent*, that is, open letters, *literæ patentes*. Grants or letters patent muft firft pafs by *bill*: which is prepared by the attorney and folicitor general, in confequence of a warrant from the crown.

The *manner* of granting by the king does not more differ from that by a subject, than the *construction* of his grants when made. 1. A grant made by the king, *at the suit of the grantee*, shall be taken most beneficially *for* the king, and *against* the party: whereas the grant of a subject is construed most strongly *against the grantor*. 2. A subject's grant shall be construed to include many things besides what are expressed, if necessary for the operation of the grant: therefore, in a private grant of the profits of land for one year, free ingress, egress, and regress, to cut and carry away those profits, are also inclusively granted: but the king's grant shall not enure to any other intent, than that which is precisely expressed in the grant. 3. When it appears, from the face of the grant, that the king is mistaken, or deceived, either in matter of fact, or matter of law, as in case of false suggestion, misinformation, or mis-recital of former grants; or if his own title to the thing granted be different from what he supposes; or if the grant be informal; or if he grants an estate contrary to law; in any of these cases the grant is absolutely void. And, to prevent deceits of the king, with regard to the value of the estate granted, it is particularly provided by the statute 1 Hen. IV. c. 6. that no grant of his shall be good, unless, in the grantee's petition for them, express mention be made of the real value of the lands.

III. We are next to a consider a very usual species of assurance, which is also of record; viz. a *fine* of lands and tenements. In which it will be necessary to explain, 1. The *nature* of a fine; 2. Its several *kinds*; and 3. Its *force* and *effect*.

1. A fine is sometimes said to be a feoffment on record: though it might with more accuracy be called, an acknowledgment of a feoffment on record. It is one of those methods of transferring estates of freehold by the common law, in which livery of seisin is not necessary to be actually given; the supposition and acknowledgment thereof in a court of record, however fictitious, inducing an equal notoriety. But, more particularly, a fine may be described to be an amicable composition or agreement of a suit, either ac-

tual or fictitious, by leave of the king or his justices; whereby the lands in question become, or are acknowledged to be, the right of one of the parties. In its original it was founded on an actual suit, commenced at law for recovery of the possession of land or other hereditaments; and the possession thus gained by such composition was found to be so sure and effectual, that fictitious actions were, and continue to be, every day commenced, for the sake of obtaining the same security.

A fine is so called because it puts an *end*, not only to the suit thus commenced, but also to all other suits and controversies concerning the same matter. Fines indeed are of equal antiquity with the first rudiments of the law itself; so that the statute 18 Edw. I. called *modus levandi fines*, did not give them original, but only declared and regulated the manner in which they should be levied, or carried on. And that is as follows:

1. The party, to whom the land is to be conveyed or assured, commences an action or suit at law against the other, generally an action of covenant, by suing out a writ or *præcipe*, called a writ of covenant: the foundation of which is a supposed agreement or covenant, that the one shall convey the lands to the other; on the breach of which agreement the action is brought. The suit being thus commenced, then follows,

2. The *licentia concordandi*, or leave to agree the suit. For, as soon as the action is brought, the defendant, knowing himself to be in the wrong, is supposed to make overtures of peace and accommodation to the plaintiff. Who, accepting them, but having, upon suing out the writ, given pledges to prosecute his suit, which he endangers if he now deserts it without licence, he therefore applies to the court for leave to make the matter up.

3. Next comes the *concord*, or agreement itself, after leave obtained from the court; which is usually an acknowledgment from the deforciants (or those who keep the other out of possession) that the lands in question are the right of the complainant. And from this acknowledgment, or recog-

nition of right, the party levying the fine is called the *cognizor*, and he to whom it is levied the *cognizee*. This acknowledgment muſt be made either openly in the court of common pleas, or before the lord chief juſtice of that court; or elſe before one of the judges of that court, or two or more commiſſioners in the country, empowered by a ſpecial authority called a writ of *dedimus poteſtatem*; which judges and commiſſioners are bound by ſtatute 18 Edw. I. ſt. 4. to take care that the cognizors be of full age, ſound memory, and out of priſon. If there be any feme-covert among the cognizors, ſhe is privately examined whether ſhe does it willingly and freely, or by compulſion of her huſband.

By theſe acts all the eſſential parts of a fine are completed: and, if the cognizor dies the next moment after the fine is acknowledged, provided it be ſubſequent to the day on which the writ is made returnable, ſtill the fine ſhall be carried on in all it's remaining parts: of which the next is

4. The *note* of the fine: which is only an abſtract of the writ of covenant, and the concord; naming the parties, the parcels of land, and the agreement. This muſt be enrolled of record in the proper office, by direction of the ſtatute 5 Hen. IV. c. 14.

5. The fifth part is the *foot* of the fine, or concluſion of it: which includes the whole matter, reciting the parties, day, year, and place, and before whom it was acknowledged or levied. Of this there are indentures made, or engroſſed, at the chirographer's office, and delivered to the cognizor and the cognizee; uſually beginning thus, "*hæc eſt finalis concordia*, this is the final agreement," and then reciting the whole proceeding at length. And thus the fine is completely levied at common law.

2. Fines, thus levied, are of four kinds. 1. What in our law French is called a fine "*ſur cognizance de droit, come ceo que il a de ſon done;*" or, a fine upon acknowledgment of the right of the cognizee, as that which he hath of the gift of the cognizor. This is the beſt and ſureſt kind of fine; for thereby the deforciant, in order to keep his covenant with the plaintiff, of conveying to him the lands in

question, and at the same time to avoid the formality of an actual feoffment and livery, acknowledges in court a former feoffment, or gift in poſſeſſion, to have been made by him to the plaintiff. This fine is therefore ſaid to be a feoffment of record; the livery, thus acknowledged in court, being equivalent to an actual livery: ſo that this aſſurance is rather a confeſſion of a former conveyance, than a conveyance now originally made; for the deforciant, or cognizor, acknowledges, *cognoſcit*, the right to be in the plaintiff, or cognizee, as that which he hath *de ſon done*, of the proper gift of himſelf, the cognizor. 2. A fine "*ſur cognizance de droit tantum*," or, upon acknowledgment of the right merely; not with the circumſtance of a preceding gift from the cognizor. This is commonly uſed to paſs a *reverſionary* intereſt, which is in the cognizor: for of ſuch reverſions there can be no feoffment, or donation with livery, ſuppoſed; as the poſſeſſion during the particular eſtate belongs to a third perſon. It is worded in this manner; "that the cognizor ac-
"knowledges the right to be in the cognizee; and grants
"for himſelf and his heirs, that the reverſion, after the par-
"ticular eſtate determines, ſhall go to the cognizee." 3. A fine "*ſur conceſſit*" is where the the cognizor, in order to make an end of diſputes, though he acknowledges no precedent right, yet grants to the cognizee an eſtate *de novo*, uſually for life or years, by way of ſuppoſed compoſition. And this may be done reſerving a rent, or the like: for it operates as a new grant. 4. A fine "*ſur done, grant, et render*," is a double fine, comprehending the fine *ſur cognizance de droit come ceo*, &c. and the fine *ſur conceſſit*: and may be uſed to create particular limitations of eſtate: whereas the fine *ſur cognizance de droit come ceo*, &c. conveys nothing but an abſolute eſtate, either of inheritance or at leaſt of freehold. In this laſt ſpecies of fine, the cognizee, after the right is acknowledged to be in him, grants back again, or renders to the cognizor, or perhaps to a ſtranger, ſome other eſtate in the premiſes. But, in general, the firſt ſpecies of fine, "*ſur cognizance de droit come ceo*, &c." is the moſt uſed, as it conveys a clean and abſolute freehold, and gives the cogni-

zee a seisin in law, without any actual livery; and is therefore called a fine executed, whereas the others are but executory.

3. We are next to consider the *force* and *effect* of a fine. These principally depend on the common law, and the two statutes, 4 Hen. VII. c. 24. and 32 Hen. VIII. c. 36. from which it appears, that a fine is a solemn conveyance on record from the cognizor to the cognizee, and that the persons bound by a fine are *parties, privies,* and *strangers.*

The *parties* are either the cognizors, or cognizees; and these are immediately concluded by the fine, and barred of any latent right they might have, even though under the legal impediment of coverture. And indeed, as this is almost the only act that a *feme-covert,* or married woman, is permitted by law to do, (and that because she is privately examined as to her voluntary consent, which removes the general suspicion of compulsion by her husband) it is therefore the usual and almost the only safe method, whereby she can join in the sale, settlement, or incumbrance, of any estate.

Privies to a fine are such as are any way related to the parties who levy the fine, and claim under them by any right of blood, or other right of representation. Such as are the heirs general of the cognizor, the issue in tail since the statute of Henry the eighth, the vendee, the devisee, and all others who must make title by the persons who levied the fine. For the act of the ancestor shall bind the heir, and the act of the principal his substitute, or such as claim under any conveyance made by him subsequent to the fine so levied.

Strangers to a fine are all other persons in the world except only parties and privies. And these are also bound by a fine, unless, within five years after proclamations made, they interpose their claim; provided they are under no legal impediments, and have then a present interest in the estate. The impediments are coverture, infancy, imprisonment, insanity, and absence beyond sea: and persons who are thus incapacitated to prosecute their rights, have five years allowed them to put in their claims after such impediments are removed. Persons also that have not a present, but a future interest only, as those in remainder or reversion, have five years allowed them to claim in, from the time that such right accrues. And if within that time they neglect to claim, or (by statute 4 Ann. c. 16.) if they do not bring an action to try the right, within one year after making such claim, and prosecute the same with effect, all persons whatsoever are barred of whatever right they may have, by force of the statute of non-claim.

But, in order to make a fine of any avail at all, it is necessary that the parties should have some interest or estate in the lands to be affected by it. Else it were possible that two strangers, by a mere confederacy, might without any risque defraud the owners, by levying fines of their lands.

IV. The fourth species of assurance, by matter of record, is a *common recovery*. I shall consider, first, the *nature* of a common recovery; and, secondly, it's *force* and *effect*.

1. And, first, the *nature* of it; or what a common recovery is. A common recovery is so far like a fine, that it is a suit or action, either actual or fictitious: and in it the lands are *recovered* against the tenant of the freehold; which recovery, being a supposed adjudication of the right, binds all persons, and vests a free and absolute fee-simple in the recoveror. A recovery therefore being in the nature of an action at law, not immediately compromised like a fine, but carried on through every regular stage of proceeding, I am greatly apprehensive that it's form and method will not be easily understood by the student, who is not yet acquainted with the course of judicial proceedings. However I shall endeavour to state it's nature and progress, as clearly and concisely as I can.

Let us, in the first place, suppose David Edwards to be tenant of the freehold, and desirous to suffer a common recovery, in order to bar all entails, remainders, and reversions, and to convey the same in fee-simple to Francis Golding. To effect this, Golding is to bring an action against him for the lands; and he accordingly sues out a writ, called a *praecipe quod reddat.* In this writ the demandant Golding alleges, that the defendant Edward (here called the tenant) has no legal title to the land; but that he came into poffeffion of it after one Hugh Hunt had turned the demandant out of it. The fubfequent proceedings are made up into a record or recovery roll, in which the writ and complaint of the demandant are firft recited: whereupon the tenant appears, and calls upon one Jacob Morland, who is fuppofed, at the original purchafe, to have warranted the title to the tenant; and thereupon he prays, that the faid Jacob Morland may be called in to defend the title which he fo warranted. This is called the *voucher*, *vocatio*, or calling of Jacob Morland to warranty: and Morland is called the *vouchee*. Upon this, Jacob Morland, the vouchee, appears, is impleaded, and defends the title. Whereupon Golding, the demandant, defires leave of the court to *imparl*, or confer with the vouchee in private; which is (as ufual) allowed him. And foon afterwards the demandant, Golding, returns to court, but Morland the vouchee difappears, or makes default. Whereupon judgment is given for the demandant Golding, now called the recoveror, to recover the lands in queftion againft the tenant Edwards, who is now the recoveree: and Edwards has judgment to recover of Jacob Morland lands of equal value, in recompenfe for the lands fo warranted by him, and now loft by his default. This is called the recompenfe, or *recovery in value*. But Jacob Morland having no lands of his own, being ufually the cryer of the court (who, from being frequently thus vouched, is called the *common vouchee*) it is plain that Edwards has only a nominal recompenfe for the lands fo recovered againft him by Golding; which lands are now abfolutely vefted in the faid recoveror by judgment of law, and feifin thereof is delivered by the fheriff of the county. So that this collufive recovery operates merely in the nature of a conveyance in fee-fimple from Edwards the tenant in tail to Golding the purchafor.

The recovery, here defcribed, is with a *fingle* voucher only; but fometimes it is with *double*, *treble*, or farther voucher, as the exigency of the cafe may require. And in-

## C. XVII. ALIENATION BY MATTER OF RECORD. 233

deed it is now ufual always to have a recovery with double voucher at the leaft: by firft conveying an eftate of freehold to any indifferent perfon, againft whom the *præcipe* is brought; and then he vouches the tenant in tail, who vouches over the common vouchee. For, if a recovery be had immediately againft tenant in tail, it bars only fuch eftate in the premifes of which he is then actually feifed; whereas if the recovery be had againft another perfon, and the tenant in tail be vouched, it bars every latent right and intereft which he may have in the lands recovered. If Edwards therefore be tenant of the freehold in poffeffion, and John Barker be tenant in tail in remainder, here Edwards doth firft vouch Barker, and then Barker vouches Jacob Morland, the common vouchee; who is always the laft perfon vouched, and always makes default: whereby the demandant Golding recovers the land againft the tenant Edwards, and Edwards recovers a recompenfe of equal value againft Barker the firft vouchee; who recovers the like againft Morland the common vouchee, againft whom fuch ideal recovery in value is always ultimately awarded.

2. The *force* and *effect* of common recoveries may appear, from what has been faid, to be an abfolute bar not only of all eftates tail, but of remainders and reverfions expectant on the determination of fuch eftates. So that a tenant in tail may, by this method of affurance, convey the lands held in tail to the recoveror, his heirs and affigns, abfolutely free and difcharged of all conditions and limitations in tail, and of all remainders and reverfions. But by the ftatute 11 Hen. VII. c. 20. no woman, after her hufband's death, fhall fuffer a recovery of lands fettled on her by her hufband, or fettled on her hufband and her by any of his anceftors. And by ftatute 14 Eliz. c. 8. no tenant for life, of any fort, can fuffer a recovery, fo as to bind them in remainder or reverfion. For which reafon, if there be tenant for life, with remainder in tail, and other remainders over, and the tenant for life is defirous to fuffer a valid recovery, either he, or the tenant to the *præcipe* by him made, muft *vouch* the remainder-man in tail, otherwife the recovery is void.

In all recoveries it is neceſſary that the recoveree, or tenant to the *præcipe*, as he is uſually called, be actually ſeiſed of the freehold, elſe the recovery is void. For all actions to recover the ſeiſin of lands, muſt be brought againſt the actual tenant of the freehold, elſe the ſuit will loſe it's effect; ſince the freehold cannot be recovered of him who has it not. But by 14 Geo. II. c. 20. though the legal freehold be veſted in leſſees, yet thoſe who are entitled to the next freehold eſtate in remainder or reverſion may make a good tenant to the *præcipe*;—that, though the deed or fine which creates ſuch tenant be ſubſequent to the judgment of recovery, yet, if it be in the ſame term, the recovery ſhall be valid in law;— and that, though the recovery itſelf do not appear to be entered, or be not regularly entered, on record, yet the deed to make a tenant to the *præcipe*, and declare the uſes of the recovery, ſhall, after a poſſeſſion of twenty years, be ſufficient evidence, on behalf of a purchaſor for valuable conſideration, that ſuch recovery was duly ſuffered.

Before I conclude this head, I muſt add a word concerning deeds to *lead*, or to *declare*, the *uſes* of fines, and of recoveries. For if they be levied or ſuffered without any good conſideration, and without any uſes declared, they, like other conveyances, enure only to the uſe of him who levies or ſuffers them. And if a conſideration appears, yet as the moſt uſual fine, "*ſur cognizance de droit come ceo, &c.*" conveys an abſolute eſtate, without any limitations, to the cognizee; and as common recoveries do the ſame to the recoveror; theſe aſſurances could not be made to anſwer the purpoſe of family ſettlements, (wherein a variety of uſes and deſignations is very often expedient) unleſs their force and effect were ſubjected to the direction of other more complicated deeds, wherein particular uſes can be more particularly expreſſed. If theſe deeds are made previous to the fine or recovery, they are called deeds to *lead* the uſes; if ſubſequent, deeds to *declare* them.

## CHAPTER XVIII.

### OF ALIENATION BY SPECIAL CUSTOM.

WE are next to confider affurances by fpecial cuftom, obtaining only in particular places, and relative only to a particular fpecies of real property. This therefore is a very narrow title; being confined to copyhold lands, and fuch cuftomary eftates, as are holden in antient demefne, or in manors of a fimilar nature: which being of a very peculiar kind, and originally no more than tenancies in pure or privileged villenage, were never alienable by deed; for, as that might tend to defeat the lord of his figniory, it is therefore a forfeiture of a copyhold. Nor are they transferrable by matter of record, even in the king's courts, but only in the court baron of the lord. The method of doing this is generally by *furrender*; though in fome manors, by fpecial cuftom, recoveries may be fuffered of copyholds.

Surrender, *furfumredditio*, is the yielding up of the eftate by the tenant into the hands of the lord, for fuch purpofes as in the furrender are expreffed. As, it may be, to the ufe and behoof of A and his heirs: to the ufe of his own will; and the like. The procefs, in moft manors, is, that the tenant comes to the fteward, either in court, (or, if the cuftom permits, out of court) or elfe to two cuftomary tenants of the fame manor, provided there be alfo a cuftom to warrant it; and there by delivering up a rod, a glove, or other fymbol, as the cuftom directs, refigns into the hands of the lord, by the hands and acceptance of his faid fteward, or of the faid two tenants, all his intereft and title to the eftate; in truft to be again granted out by the lord, to fuch perfons and for fuch ufes as are named in the furrender, and the cuftom of the manor will warrant. If the furrender be made out of court, then, at the next or fome fubfequent court, the jury or homage muft prefent and find it upon their oaths; which prefentment is an information to the lord or his fteward, of what has been tranfacted out of court. Immediately upon fuch furrender in court, or upon prefentment of a furrender made out of court, the lord, by his fteward, grants the fame land again to *ceſtuy que uſe*, (who is fometimes, though rather improperly, called the furrenderee) to hold by the antient rents and cuftomary fervices; and thereupon admits him tenant to the copyhold, according to the form and effect of the furrender; which muft be exactly purfued. And this is done by delivering up to the new tenant the rod, or glove, or the like, in the name, and as the fymbol, of coporal feifin of the lands and tenements. Upon which admiffion he pays a fine to the lord according to the cuftom of the manor, and takes the oath of fealty.

This method of conveyance is fo effential to the nature of a copyhold eftate, that it cannot properly be transferred by any other affurance. No feoffment or grant has any operation thereupon.

In order the more clearly to apprehend the nature of this peculiar affurance, let us take a feparate view of it's feveral parts; the furrender, the prefentment, and the admittance.

1. A furrender, by an admittance fubfequent whereto the conveyance is to receive it's perfection and confirmation, is rather a manifeftation of the alienor's intention, than a transfer of any intereft in poffeffion. For, till admittance of *ceſtuy que uſe*, the lord taketh notice of the furrenderor as his tenant; and he fhall receive the profits of the land to his own ufe, and fhall difcharge all fervices due to the lord. Yet the intereft remains in him not abfolutely, but *fub modo*; for he cannot pafs away the land to any other, or make it fubject to any other incumbrance than it was fubject to at the time of the furrender. Yet, though upon the original furrender the nominee hath but a poffibility, it is, however, fuch a poffibility, as may, whenever he pleafes, be reduced to a certainty: for he cannot, either by force or fraud, be deprived or deluded of the effect and fruits of the furrender; but if the lord refufe to admit him, he is compellable to do it by a bill in chancery, or a *mandamus*: and the furrenderor can in no wife defeat his grant.

2. As to the *presentment:* that, by the *general* custom of manors, is to be made at the next court baron immediately after the surrender; but by *special* custom in some places it will be good, though made at the second or other subsequent court. And it is to be brought into court by the *same* persons that took the surrender, and then to be presented by the homage; and in all points material must correspond with the true tenor of the surrender itself. If a man surrenders out of court, and dies before presentment, and presentment be made after his death, according to the custom, this is sufficient. So too, if *cestuy, que use* dies before presentment, yet, upon presentment made after his death, his heir, according to the custom, shall be admitted. The same law is, if those into whose hands the surrender is made, die before presentment; for, upon sufficient proof in court that such a surrender was made, the lord shall be compelled to admit accordingly.

3. Admittance is the last stage, or perfection, of copyhold assurances. And this is of three sorts: first, an admittance upon a voluntary grant from the lord; secondly, an admittance upon surrender by the former tenant; and thirdly, an admittance upon a descent from the ancestor.

In admittances, even upon a *voluntary grant* from the lord, when copyhold lands have escheated or reverted to him, the lord is considered as an instrument. For, though it is in his power to keep the lands in his own hands, or to dispose of them at his pleasure, by granting an absolute fee-simple, a freehold, or a chattel interest therein; and quite to change their nature from copyhold to socage tenure, so that he may well be reputed their absolute owner and lord; yet if he will still continue to dispose of them as copyhold, he is bound to observe the antient custom precisely in every point, and can neither in tenure nor estate introduce any kind of alteration; for that were to create a new copyhold: wherefore in this respect the law accounts him custom's instrument. For if a copyhold for life falls into the lord's hands, by the tenant's death, though the lord may destroy the tenure and enfranchise the land, yet if he grants it out again by copy, he can neither add nor diminish the antient rent, nor make any the minutest variation in other respects; nor is the tenant's estate, so granted, subject to any charges or incumbrances by the lord.

In admittances upon *surrender* of another, the lord is to no intent reputed as owner, but wholly as an instrument: and the tenant admitted shall likewise be subject to no charges or incumbrances of the lord; for his claim to the estate is solely under him that made the surrender.

And, as in admittances upon surrenders, so in admittances *upon descents* by the death of the ancestor, the lord is used as a mere instrument; and, as no manner of interest passes into him by the surrender or the death of his tenant, so no interest passes out of him by the act of admittance. And therefore, neither in the one case, nor the other, is any respect had to the quantity or quality of the lord's estate in the manor. For whether he be tenant in fee or for years, whether he be in possession by right or by wrong, it is not material; since the admittances made by him shall not be impeached on account of his title, because they are judicial, or rather ministerial, acts, which every lord in possession is bound to perform.

Admittances, however, upon surrender, differ from admittances upon descent in this: that by surrender nothing is vested in *cestuy que use* before admittance, no more than in voluntary admittances; but upon descent the heir is tenant by copy immediately upon the death of his ancestor: not indeed to all intents and purposes, for he cannot be sworn on the homage, nor maintain an action in the lord's court as tenant; but to most intents the law taketh notice of him as of a perfect tenant of the land instantly upon the death of his ancestor, especially where he is concerned with any stranger. He may enter into the land before admittance; may take the profits; may punish any trespass done upon the ground; nay, upon satisfying the lord for his fine due upon the descent, may surrender into the hands of the lord to whatever use he pleases. For which reasons we may conclude, that the admittance of an heir is principally for the benefit of the lord, to intitle him to his fine, and not so much necessary for the strengthening and compleating the heir's title. Hence indeed an observation might arise, that if the benefit, which the heir is to receive by the admittance, is not equal to the charges of the fine, he will never come in and be admitted to his copyhold in court; and so the lord may be defrauded of his fine. But to this we may reply in the words of Sir Edward Coke, " I assure myself, if it " were in the election of the heir to be admitted or not " to be admitted, he would be best contented without " admittance; but the custom in every manor is in this " point compulsory. For, either upon pain of forfeiture " of their copyhold, or of incurring some great penalty, " the heirs of copyholders are inforced, in every manor, to " come into court and be admitted according to the custom, " within a short time after notice given of their ancestor's " decease."

## CHAPTER XIX.

### OF ALIENATION BY DEVISE.

THE last method of conveying real property, is by *devise*, or disposition contained in a man's last will and testament. We find that, by the common law of England since the conquest, no estate greater than for term of years, could be disposed of by testament; except only in Kent, and in some antient burghs, and a few particular manors, where their Saxon immunities by special indulgence subsisted. But, by statute 32 Hen. VIII. c. 1. explained by 34 Hen. VIII. c. 5. it was enacted, that all persons being seised in fee-simple (except feme-coverts, infants, ideots, and persons of nonsane memory) might by will and testament in writing devise to any other *person*, except to bodies corporate, two-thirds of their lands, tenements and hereditaments, held in chivalry, and the whole of those held in socage:

which now, through the alteration of tenures by the ftatute of Charles the fecond, amounts to the whole of their landed property, except their copyhold tenements.

Corporations were excepted in thefe ftatutes, to prevent the extenfion of gifts in mortmain; but now, by conftruction of the ftatute 43 Eliz. c. 4. it is held, that a devife to a corporation for a charitable ufe is valid, as operating in the nature of an *appointment*, rather than of a *bequeft*; and it is held that the ftatute of Elizabeth, which favours appointments to charities, fuperfedes and repeals all former ftatutes, and fupplies all defects of affurances: and therefore not only a devife to a corporation, but a devife by a copyhold tenant without furrendering to the ufe of his will, and a devife (nay even a fettlement) by tenant in tail without either fine or recovery, if made to a charitable ufe, are good by way of appointment.

With regard to devifes in general, the ftatute of frauds and perjuries, 29 Car. II. c. 3. directs that all devifes of lands and tenements *(a)* fhall not only be in writing, but figned by

---

(a) It may be proper to obferve to the ftudent, that though the words ufed in the act feem to be fufficiently comprehenfive to include every defcription of eftate, yet the ftatute is held not to extend to *copyholds*, which will pafs therefore (if previoufly furrendered to the ufe of the will) without any of the formalities required for the devifing real eftates of inheritance " the claufe in the ftatute of frauds and perjuries, which requires the teftator's figning in the prefence of three witneffes, and their atteftation in his prefence being confined only to fuch eftates as pafs by the ftatute of wills 34 & 35 Hen. 8. c. 5. which is an act made to explain one made in the 31ft of the fame king, and at the clofe of the third fection enacts, that the words *eftate of inheritance* in the former ftatute fhall be declared, expounded, taken, and judged, of eftates of fee-fimple only; which fhews plainly that it does not extend to cuftomary eftates, and has been fo fettled ever fince the cafe of the *Attorney General* v. *Barnes*, reported 2 *Vern.* 598." Per *Hardw. Chan.* in *Tuffnell* v. *Page*, 2 *Atk.* 37.

the teſtator, or ſome other perſon in his preſence, and by his expreſs direction; and be ſubſcribed, in his preſence, by three or four credible witneſſes. And a ſolemnity nearly ſimilar *(a)* is requiſite for revoking a deviſe by writing; though the ſame may be alſo revoked by burning, cancelling, tearing, or obliterating thereof by the deviſor, or in his preſence and with his conſent: as likewiſe *impliedly*, by ſuch a great and intire alteration in the circumſtances and ſituation of the deviſor, as ariſes from marriage and the birth of a child.

In the conſtruction of this laſt ſtatute, it has been adjudged that the teſtator's name, written with his own hand, at the beginning of his will, as "I John Mills do make this my "laſt will and teſtament," is a ſufficient ſigning, without any name at the bottom; though the other is the ſafer way. It has alſo been determined, that though the witneſſes muſt all ſee the teſtator ſign, or at leaſt acknowledge the ſigning, yet they may do it at different times. But they muſt all ſubſcribe their names as witneſſes *in his preſence*, left by any poſſibility they ſhould miſtake the inſtrument. The judges were formerly extremely ſtrict in regard to the credibility, or rather the competency of the witneſſes: for they would not allow any legatee, nor by conſequence a creditor, where the legacies and debts were charged on the real eſtate, to be a competent witneſs to the deviſe, as being too deeply concerned in intereſt not to wiſh the eſtabliſhment of the will. This occaſioned the ſtatute 25 Geo. II. c. 6. which reſtored both the competency and the credit of ſuch *legatees*, by declaring void all legacies given to witneſſes, and thereby removing all poſſibility of their intereſt affecting their teſtimony. The ſame ſtatute likewiſe eſtabliſhed the competency of *creditors*, by

---

*(a)* The difference is this; that a revocation muſt be ſigned by the teſtator *in the preſence of three witneſſes*, whilſt the publication of a *will*, though it muſt be atteſted by three or more witneſſes, who muſt ſubſcribe in the *preſence of the teſtator*, yet the witneſſes need not be preſent together at the time of publication. See 29 Car. c. 3. and *Paw. Deviſ.* 646.

directing the testimony of all such creditors to be admitted, but leaving their credit (like that of all other witnesses) to be considered, on a view of all the circumstances, by the court and jury before whom such will shall be contested.

A will of lands, made by the permission and under the control of these statutes, is considered by the courts of law not so much in the nature of a testament, as of a conveyance declaring the uses to which the land shall be subject: with this difference, that in other conveyances the actual *subscription* of the witnesses is not required by law, though is is prudent for them so to do in order to assist their memory when living and to supply their evidence when dead; but in devises of lands such subscription is now absolutely necessary by statute, in order to identify a conveyance, which in its nature can never be set up till after the death of the devisor. And upon this notion, that a devise affecting lands is merely a species of conveyance is founded this distinction between such devises and testaments of personal chattels; that the latter will operate upon whatever the testator dies possessed of, the former only upon such real estates as were his at the time of executing and publishing his will. Wherefore no after-purchased lands will pass under such devise, unless, subsequent to the purchase or contract, the devisor re-publishes his will *(a)*.

We have now considered the several species of common assurances, whereby a title to lands and tenements may be transferred and conveyed from one man to another. Before we conclude this head, it may not be improper to take notice of a few general rules and maxims, which have been laid down by courts of justice, for the construction and exposition of them all. These are,

1. That the construction be *favourable*, and as near the minds and apparent intents of the parties, as the rules of law

---

*(a)* See more relating to devises, revocations, and other incidents to wills. *Pow. Devises,* where much learning is adduced on those heads.

will admit. And therefore the conſtruction muſt alſo be *reaſonable*, and agreeable to common underſtanding.

2. That *quoties in verbis nulla eſt ambiguitas, ibi nulla expoſitio contra verba fienda eſt:* but that, where the *intention* is clear, too minute a ſtreſs be not laid on the ſtrict and preciſe ſignification of *words; num qui hæret in litera, hæret in cortice.*

3. That the conſtruction be made upon the entire deed, and not merely upon disjointed parts of it. " *Nam ex antecedentibus et conſequentibus fit optima interpretatio.*

4. That the deed be taken moſt ſtrongly againſt him that is the agent or contractor, and in favour of the other party. But here a diſtinction muſt be taken between an indenture and a deed-poll: for the words of an indenture, executed by both parties, are to be conſidered as the words of them both; but in a deed-poll, executed only by the grantor, they are the words of the grantor only, and ſhall be taken moſt ſtrongly againſt him.

5. That, if the words will bear two ſenſes, one agreeable to, and another againſt, law; that ſenſe be preferred, which is moſt agreeable thereto.

6. That, in a deed, if there be two clauſes ſo totally repugnant to each other, that they cannot ſtand together, the firſt ſhall be received and the latter rejected: wherein it differs from a will; for there, of two ſuch repugnant clauſes the latter ſhall ſtand.

7. That a deviſe be moſt favourably expounded, to purſue if poſſible the will of the deviſor, who for want of advice or learning may have omitted the legal or proper phraſes. Thus in a will a fee may be conveyed without words of inheritance; and an eſtate-tail without words of procreation. By a will alſo an eſtate may paſs by mere implication, without any expreſs words to direct its courſe. But, in general, where any implications are allowed, they muſt be ſuch as are *neceſſary* (or at leaſt highly *probable*) and not merely *poſſible* implications.

## CHAPTER XX.

### OF THINGS PERSONAL;
### AND FIRST
### OF PROPERTY IN THINGS PERSONAL.

UNDER the name of things *perfonal* are included all forts of things *moveable*, which may attend a man's perfon wherever he goes.

Property, in things perfonal, may be either in *poffeffion;* which is where a man hath not only the right to enjoy, but hath the actual enjoyment of the thing: or elfe it is in *action;* where a man hath only a bare right, without any occupation or enjoyment. And of thefe the former, or property in *poffeffion*, is divided into two forts, an *abfolute* and a *qualified* property.

I. Firft then of property in *poffeffion abfolute;* which is where a man hath, folely and exclufively, the right, and alfo the occupation, of any moveable chattels; fo that they cannot be transferred from him, or ceafe to be his, without his own act or default. Such may be all *inanimate* things, as goods, plate, money, jewels, implements of war, garments, and the like: fuch alfo may be all *vegetable* productions, as the fruit or other parts of a plant, when fevered from the body of it; or the whole plant itfelf, when fevered from the ground. But with regard to *animals*, which have in themfelves a principle and power of motion, and (unlefs particularly confined) can convey themfelves from one part of the world to another, there is a great difference made with refpect to their feveral claffes, not only in our law, but in the law of nature and of all civilized nations. They are diftinguifhed into fuch as are *domitæ*, and fuch as are *feræ naturæ*: fome being of a *tame* and others of a *wild* difpofition. In fuch as are of a nature tame and domeftic, (as horfes, kine, fheep, poultry, and the like) a man may have as abfolute a property as in any inanimate beings; for thefe are things of intrinfic value, ferving for the food of man, or elfe for the ufes of hufbandry. But in animals *feræ naturæ* a man can have no abfolute property.

Of all tame and domeftic animals, the brood belongs to the owner of the dam or mother ; the Englifh law agreeing with the civil, that " *partus fequitur ventrem*" in the brute creation, though for the moft part in the human fpecies it difallows that maxim. And, for this, Puffendorf gives a fenfible reafon : not only becaufe the male is frequently unknown; but alfo becaufe the dam, during the time of her pregnancy, is almoft ufelefs to the proprietor, and muft be maintained with great expence and care: wherefore as her owner is the lofer by her pregnancy, he ought to be the gainer by her brood. An exception to this rule is in the cafe of young cygnets; which belong equally to the owner of the cock and hen, and fhall be divided between them. But here the reafons of the general rule ceafe and " *ceffante* " *ratione ceffat et ipfa lex* :" for the male is well known, by his conftant affociation with the female ; and for the fame reafon the owner of the one doth not fuffer more difadvantage during the time of pregnancy and nurture, than the owner of the other.

II. Other animals, that are not of a tame and domeftic nature, are either not the objects of property at all, or elfe fall under our other divifion, namely, that of *qualified, limited,* or *fpecial* property: which is fuch as is not in it's nature permanent, but may fometimes fubfift, and at other times not fubfift.

Firft, then, a man may be invefted with a qualified, but not an abfolute, property in all creatures that are *feræ naturæ,* either *per induftriam, propter impotentiam,* or *propter privilegium.*

1. A qualified property may fubfift in animals *feræ naturæ, per induftriam hominis :* by a man's reclaiming and making them tame by art, induftry, and education ; or by fo confining them within his own immediate power, that they cannot efcape and ufe their natural liberty. Such as are deer in a park, hares or rabbets in an inclofed warren, doves

in a dovehouſe, pheaſants or partridges in a mew, hawks that are fed and commanded by their owner, and fiſh in a private pond or in trunks. Theſe are no longer the property of a man, than while they continue in his keeping or actual poſſeſſion: but if at any time they regain their natural liberty, his property inſtantly ceaſes; unleſs they have *animum revertendi*, which is only to be known by their uſual cuſtom of returning. But if they ſtray without my knowledge, and do not return in the uſual manner, it is then lawful for any ſtranger to take them. Bees alſo are *feræ naturæ*; but, when hived and reclaimed, a man may have a qualified property in them; and a ſwarm, which fly from and out of my hive, are mine ſo long as I can keep them in ſight, and have power to purſue them; and in theſe circumſtances no one elſe is entitled to take them.

In all theſe creatures, reclaimed from the wildneſs of their nature, the property is not abſolute, but defeaſible: a property, that may be deſtroyed if they reſume their antient wildneſs, and are found at large. But while they thus continue my qualified or defeaſible property, they are as much under the protection of the law, as if they were abſolutely and indefeaſibly mine: and an action will lie againſt any man that detains them from me, or unlawfully deſtroys them. It is alſo as much felony by common law to ſteal ſuch of them as are fit for food, as it is to ſteal tame animals: but not ſo, if they are only kept for pleaſure, curioſity, or whim, as dogs, bears, cats, apes, parrots, and ſinging birds; becauſe their value is not intrinſic, but depending only on the caprice of the owner: though it is ſuch an invaſion of property as may amount to a civil injury, and be redreſſed by a civil action. And thus much of qualified property in wild animals, reclaimed *per induſtriam*.

2. A qualified property may alſo ſubſiſt with relation to animals *feræ naturæ*, *ratione impotentiæ*, on account of their own inability. As when hawks, herons, or other birds build in my trees, or coneys or other creatures make their neſts or burrows in my land, and have young ones there; I have a qualified property in thoſe young ones till ſuch time

as they can fly or run away, and then my property expires.

3. A man may, laftly, have a qualified property in animals *feræ naturæ, propter privilegium:* that is, he may have the privilege of hunting, taking, and killing them, in exclufion of other perfons. The manner in which this privilege is acquired, will be fhewn in a fubfequent chapter.

Property may alfo be of a qualified or fpecial nature, on account of the peculiar circumftances of the owner. As in cafe of *bailment*, or delivery of goods to another perfon for a particular ufe; as to a carrier to convey to London, to an innkeeper to fecure in his inn, or the like. Here there is no abfolute property in either the bailor or the bailee, the perfon delivering, or him to whom it is delivered. But it is a qualified property in them both; and each of them is entitled to an action, in cafe the goods be damaged or taken away. So alfo in cafe of goods pledged or pawned upon condition, either to repay money or otherwife; both the pledgor and pledgee have a qualified, but neither of them an abfolute, property in them. But a fervant, who hath the care of his mafter's goods or chattels, as a butler of plate, a fhepherd of fheep, and the like, hath not any property or poffeffion either abfolute or qualified, but only a mere charge or overfight.

We have thus confidered the feveral divifions of property in *poffeffion*, which fubfifts there only, where a man hath both the right and alfo the occupation of the thing; but there is alfo property in *action*, or fuch where a man hath not the occupation, but merely a bare right to occupy the thing in queftion; the poffeffion whereof may however be recovered by a fuit or action at law: from whence the thing fo recoverable is called a thing, or *chofe, in action.* Thus money due on a bond is a *chofe* in action; for a property in the debt vefts at the t me of forfeiture mentioned in the obligation, but there is no poffeffion till recovered by courfe of law. All property in action depends entirely upon contracts, either exprefs or implied; which are the only regular means of acquiring a *chofe* in action, and of the nature of which we shall discourse more at large in a subsequent chapter.

And, having thus distinguished the different *degree* or *quantity* of *dominion* or *property* to which things personal are subject, we may add a word or two concerning the *time* of their *enjoyment*, and the *number* of their *owners*.

First, as to the *time* of *enjoyment*. By the rules of the antient common law, there could be no future property, to take place in expectancy, created in personal goods and chattels; but now that distinction is disregarded: and therefore if a man, either by deed or will, limits his books or furniture to A for life, with remainder over to B, this remainder is good. But, where an estate-tail in things personal is given to the first or any subsequent possessor, it vests in him the total property, and no remainder over shall be permitted on such a limitation. For this, if allowed, would tend to a perpetuity, as the devisee or grantee in tail of a chattel has no method of barring the entail.

Next, as to the *number* of *owners*. Things personal may belong to the owners, not only in severalty, but also in joint-tenancy, and in common, as well as real estates. They cannot indeed be vested in coparcenary; because they do not descend from the ancestor to the heir, which is necessary to constitute coparceners. But if a horse, or other personal chattel, be given to two or more, absolutely, they are joint-tenants thereof; and, unless the jointure be severed, the same doctrine of survivorship shall take place as in estates of lands and tenements *(a)*. But, for the encouragement of husbandry and trade, it is held that a stock on a farm, though

---

*(a)* And upon the same principle, it is held, that executors and residuary legatees hold the property, which devolves upon them in right of those capacities, as joint-tenants; and, consequently, if either of them dies before severance, so much as remains undivided will accrue to the survivor. See *Willing* v. *Baine*, 3 *P. Wms.* 113. *Frewen* and *Berry*, 2 *Brow. Ch. Ca.* 220. *Balwyn*, v. *Johnson*, 3 *ibid*, 455.

occupied jointly, and alfo a ftock ufed in a joint undertaking, by way of partnerfhip in trade, fhall always be confidered as common and not as joint property; and there fhall be no furvivorfhip therein.

## CHAPTER XXI.

### OF TITLE TO THINGS PERSONAL, BY OCCUPANCY, PREROGATIVE, AND FORFEITURE;

#### FIRST BY OCCUPANCY.

WE are next to confider the *title* to things perfonal, or the various means of *acquiring*, and of *lofing*, fuch property as may be had therein. And thefe methods of acquifition or lofs are principally twelve: 1. By occupancy. 2. By prerogative. 3. By forfeiture. 4. By cuftom. 5. By fucceffion. 6. By marriage. 7. By judgment. 8. By gift, or grant. 9. By contract. 10. By bankruptcy. 11. By teftament. 12. By adminiftration.

And, firft, a property in goods and chattels may be acquired by *occupancy*.

Thus, whatever moveables are found upon the furface of the earth, or in the fea, and are unclaimed by any owner, are fuppofed to be abandoned by the laft proprietor; and therefore belong, as in a ftate of nature, to the firft occupant or fortunate finder, unlefs they fall within the defcription of waifs, or eftrays, or wreck, or hidden treafure; for thefe, we have formerly feen, are vefted by law in the king.

Thus too the benefit of the elements, the light, the air, and the water, can only be appropriated by occupancy. If I have an antient window overlooking my neighbour's ground, he may not erect any blind to obftruct the light: if my neighbour makes a tan-yard, fo as to annoy and render lefs falubrious the air of my houfe or gardens, the law will furnifh me with a remedy. If a ftream be unoccupied, I may erect a mill thereon, and detain the water; yet not so as to injure my neighbour's prior mill, or his meadow: for he hath by the first occupancy acquired a property in the current.

There is still another species of property, which being grounded on labour and invention, is more reducible to the head of occupancy than any other. And this is the right, which an author may be supposed to have in his own original literary compositions: so that no other person without his leave may publish or make profit of the copies. And the statute 8 Ann, c. 19. (amended by statute 15 Geo. III. c. 53.) hath declared that the author and his assigns shall have the sole liberty of printing and reprinting his works for the term of fourteen years, *and no longer(a);* and hath also protected that property by additional penalties and forfeitures: directing farther, that if, at the end of that term, the author himself be living, the right shall then return to him for another term of the same duration:—and a similar privilege is extended to the inventors of prints and engravings, for the term of eight and twenty years, by the statutes 8 Geo. II. c. 13. and 7 Geo. III. c. 38. besides an action for damages, with double costs, by statute 17 Geo. III. c. 57. All which parliamentary protections appear to have been suggested by the exception in the statute of monopolies, 21 Jac. I. c. 3. which allows a royal patent of privilege to be granted for fourteen years to any inventor of a new manufacture, for the sole working or making of the same; by virtue whereof it is held, that a temporary property therein becomes vested in the king's patentee.

### SECONDLY, BY PREROGATIVE.

A second method of acquiring property in personal chattels is by the *king's prerogative:* whereby a right may accrue

---

(a) But (by the last-mentioned act) this limitation is declared not to extend to the universities of England or Scotland, or the colleges of Eton, Westminster or Winchester, who have therefore a *perpetual* exclusive right of printing their own books.

either to the crown itself, or to such as claim under the title of the crown, as by the king's grant, or by prescription, which supposes an ancient grant.

Such in the first place are all *tributes*, *taxes*, and *customs*; whether constitutionally inherent in the crown, and branches of the *census regalis* or antient royal revenue, or whether they be occasionally created by authority of parliament.

There is also a kind of prerogative *copyright* subsisting in certain books, which is held to be vested in the crown upon different reasons. Thus, 1. The king, as the executive magistrate, has the right of promulging to the people all acts of state and government. This gives him the exclusive privilege of printing, at his own press, or that of his grantees, all *acts of parliament*, *proclamations*, and *orders of council*. 2. As supreme head of the church, he hath a right to the publication of all *liturgies* and books of *divine service*. 3. He is also said to have a right, by purchase, to the copies of such *lawbooks*, *grammars*, and other compositions, as were compiled or translated at the expence of the crown. And upon these two last principles, combined, the exclusive right of printing the translation of the *bible* is founded.

There still remains another species of prerogative property, founded upon a very different principle from any that have been mentioned before; the property of such animals *feræ naturæ*, as are known by the denomination of *game*, with the right of pursuing, taking, and destroying them: which is vested in the king alone, and from him derived to such of his subjects as have received the grants of a chase, a park, a free warren, or free fishery *(a)*. And, we find that

---

*(a)* This doctrine so frequently inculcated by the learned author, of the right of killing game being vested in the king alone, is sedulously attempted to be refuted by Mr. *Christian*, who, with great adroitness, maintains, that the land-owner is, by the original common law of England, invested with an absolute right of traversing his own demesnes in pursuit of game, without any such grant as is contended for in the subsequent pages. See 12 *Ed. Com.* 419. n. (10).

the municipal laws of many nations have extended their protection to such particular animals as are usually the objects of pursuit; and have invested the prerogative of hunting and taking such animals in the sovereign of the state only, and such as he shall authorise. Many reasons have concurred for making these constitutions: as, 1. For the encouragement of agriculture and improvement of lands, by giving every man an exclusive dominion over his own soil. 2. For preservation of the several species of these animals, which would soon be extirpated by a general liberty. 3. For prevention of idleness and dissipation in husbandmen, artificers, and others of lower rank; which would be the unavoidable consequence of universal licence. 4. For prevention of popular insurrections and resistance to the government, by disarming the bulk of the people: which last is a reason oftener meant than avowed by the makers of forest or game laws.

The principal intention of granting to any one the sefranchises or liberties was in order to protect the game, by giving the grantee a sole and exclusive power of killing it himself, provided he prevented other persons. And no man, but he who has a chase or free warren, by grant from the crown, or prescription which supposes one, can justify hunting or sporting upon another man's soil; nor indeed, in thorough strictness of common law, either hunting or sporting at all.

It is true, that, by the acquiescence of the crown, the frequent grants of free warren in antient times, and the introduction of new penalties of late by certain statutes for preserving the game, this exclusive prerogative of the king is little known or considered; every man that is exempted from these modern penalties, looking upon himself as at liberty to do what he pleases with the game: whereas, the truth of the matter is that the game laws do indeed *qualify* nobody, except in the instance of a gamekeeper, to kill game: but only to save the trouble and formal process of an action by the person injured, who perhaps too might remit the offence, these statutes inflict *additional* penalties, to be recovered either in a regular or summary way, by any of the king's subjects, from certain persons of inferior rank who may be found offending in this particular. But it does not follow that perfons, excufed from thefe additional penalties, are therefore *authorifed* to kill game. The circumftance of having 100l. *per annum*, and the reft, are not properly qualifications, but exemptions. And thefe perfons, fo exempted from the penalties of the game ftatutes, are not only liable to actions of trefpafs by the owners of the land; but alfo, if they kill game within the limits of any royal franchife, they are liable to the actions of fuch who may have the right of chafe or free warren therein. And it muft alfo be remembered, that fuch perfons as may thus lawfully hunt, fifh, or fowl, *ratione privilegii*, have (as has been faid) only a qualified property in thefe animals: it not being abfolute or permanent, but lafting only fo long as the creatures remain within the limits of fuch refpective franchife or liberty, and ceafing the inftant they voluntarily pafs out of it. It is held indeed, that if a man ftarts any game within his own grounds, and follows it into another's, and kills it there, the property remains in himfelf. And this is grounded on reafon and natural juftice: for the property confifts in the poffeffion; which poffeffion commences by the finding it in his own liberty, and is continued by the immediate purfuit. And fo, if a ftranger ftarts game in one man's chafe or free warren, and hunts it into another liberty, the property continues in the owner of the chafe or free warren; this property arifing from privilege, and not being changed by the act of a mere ftranger. Or if a man ftarts game on another's private grounds and kills it there, the property belongs to him in whofe ground it was killed, becaufe it was alfo ftarted there; this property arifing *ratione foli*. Whereas if, after being ftarted there, it is killed in the grounds of a third perfon, the property belongs not to the owner of the firft ground, becaufe the property is local; nor yet to the owner of the fecond, becaufe it was not ftarted in his foil; but it vefts in the perfon who ftarted and killed it, though guilty of a trefpafs againft both the owners.

### Thirdly by Forfeiture.

I proceed now to a third method, whereby a title to goods and chattels may be acquired and loft, viz. by *forfeiture;* as a punishment for some crime or misdemesnor in the party forfeiting, and as a compensation for the offence and injury committed against him to whom they are forfeited. Of forfeitures, considered as the means whereby *real* property might be loft and acquired, we treated in a former chapter. It remains, therefore, in this place only to mention by what means, or for what offences, goods and chattels become liable to forfeiture.

In the variety of penal laws with which the subject is at present encumbered, it were a tedious and impracticable task to reckon up the various forfeitures, inflicted by special statutes, for particular crimes and misdemesnors: I shall therefore confine myself to those offences, only, by which *all* the goods and chattels of the offender are forfeited.

Goods and chattels then are totally forfeited by conviction of *high treason* or *misprision* of treason; of *petit treason*; of *felony* in general, and particularly of *felony de se*, and of *manslaughter*; nay even by conviction of *excusable homicide*; by *outlawry* for treason or felony; by conviction of *petit larceny*; by *flight* in treason or felony, even though the party be acquitted of the fact; by *standing mute*, when arraigned of felony; by *drawing a weapon on a judge*, or *striking* any one *in the presence of the king's courts*; by *præmunire*; by *pretended prophecies*, upon a second conviction; by *owling*; by the *residing abroad* of artificers: and by *challenging to fight* on account of money won at gaming. All these offences, as will more fully appear in the fourth book of these commentaries, induce a total forfeiture of goods and chattels.

And this forfeiture commences from the time of *conviction*, not the time of committing the fact, as in forfeitures of real property. Yet a fraudulent conveyance of them, to defeat the interest of the crown, is made void by statute 13 Eliz. c. 5.

## CHAPTER XXII.

### OF TITLE BY CUSTOM.

A FOURTH method of acquiring property in things perſonal, or chattels, is by *cuſtom:* whereby a right veſts in ſome particular perſons, either by the local uſage of ſome particular place, or by the almoſt general and univerſal uſage of the kingdom. It were endleſs, ſhould I attempt to enumerate all the ſeveral kinds of ſpecial cuſtoms, which may entitle a man to a chattel intereſt in different parts of the kingdom: I ſhall therefore content myſelf with making ſome obſervations on three ſorts of cuſtomary intereſts, which obtain pretty generally throughout moſt parts of the nation, and are therefore of more univerſal concern, viz. *heriots, mortuaries,* and *heir-looms.*

1. Heriots, which were ſlightly touched upon in a former chapter, are uſually divided into two ſorts, heriot-*ſervice,* and heriot-*cuſtom.* The former are ſuch as are due upon a ſpecial reſervation in a grant or leaſe of lands, and therefore amount to little more than a mere rent: the latter ariſe upon no ſpecial reſervation whatſoever, but depend merely upon immemorial uſage and cuſtom; and are defined to be a cuſtomary tribute of goods and chattels, payable to the lord of the fee on the deceaſe of the owner of the land.

Theſe are now for the moſt part confined to copyhold tenures, and are due by cuſtom only, which is the life of all eſtates by copy; and perhaps are the only inſtance where cuſtom has favoured the lord. For this payment was originally a voluntary donation, or gratuitous legacy of the tenant; perhaps in acknowledgment of his having been raiſed a degree above villenage, when all his goods and chattels were quite at the mercy of the lord: and cuſtom, which has on the one hand confirmed the tenant's intereſt in excluſion of the lord's will, has on the other hand eſtabliſhed this diſcretional piece of gratitude into a permanent duty. An heriot may alſo appertain to free land, that is held by ſervice and suit of court; in which cafe it is moſt commonly a copyhold enfranchiſed, whereupon the heriot is ſtill due by cuſtom.

This heriot is ſometimes the beſt live beaſt, or *averium*, which the tenant dies poſſeſſed of, (which is particularly denominated the villein's relief in the twenty-ninth law of king William the conqueror) ſometimes the beſt inanimate good, under which a jewel or piece of plate may be included: but it is always a *perſonal* chattel, which, immediately on the death of the tenant who was the owner of it, being aſcertained by the option of the lord, becomes veſted in him as his property; and is no charge upon the lands, but merely on the goods and chattels. The tenant muſt be the owner of it, elſe it cannot be due; and therefore on the death of a feme-covert no heriot can be taken; for ſhe can have no ownerſhip in things perſonal. In ſome places there is a cuſtomary compoſition in money, as ten or twenty ſhillings in lieu of a heriot, by which the lord and tenant are both bound, if it be an indiſputably antient cuſtom: but a new compoſition of this ſort will not bind the repreſentatives of either party; for that amounts to the creation of a new cuſtom, which is now impoſſible.

2. Mortuaries are a ſort of eccleſiaſtical heriots, being a cuſtomary gift claimed by and due to the miniſter in very many pariſhes on the death of his pariſhioners. This cuſtom varies in different places, not only as the mortuary to be paid, but the perſon to whom it is payable: which variety of cuſtoms, with regard to mortuaries, giving frequently a handle to exactions on the one ſide, and frauds or expenſive litigations on the other; it was thought proper by ſtatute 21 Hen. VIII. c. 6. to reduce them to ſome kind of certainty. For this purpoſe it is enacted, that all mortuaries, or corſe-preſents to parſons of any pariſh, ſhall be taken in the following manner; (unleſs where by cuſtom leſs or none at all is due:) *viz.* for every perſon who does not leave goods to the value of ten marks, nothing: for every perſon who leaves goods to the value of ten marks and under thirty pounds, 3*s.* 4*d.* if above thirty pounds, and under forty pounds, 6*s.* 8*d.* if above forty pounds, of what value ſoever

they may be, 10s. and no more. And no mortuary shall throughout the kingdom be paid for the death of any feme-covert; nor for any child; nor for any one of full age, that is not a housekeeper; nor for any wayfaring man; but such wayfaring man's mortuary shall be paid in the parish to which he belongs. And upon this statute stands the law of mortuaries to this day.

3. Heir-looms are such goods and personal chattels, as, contrary to the nature of chattels, shall go by special custom to the heir along with the inheritance, and not to the executor of the last proprietor. They are generally such things as cannot be taken away without damaging or dismembering the freehold: otherwise the general rule is, that no chattel interest whatsoever shall go to the heir, notwithstanding it be expressly limited to a man and his heirs, but shall vest in the executor. But deer in a real authorised park, fishes in a pond, doves in a dove-house, &c. though in themselves personal chattels, yet they are so annexed to and so necessary to the well-being of the inheritance, that they shall accompany the land wherever it vests, by either descent or purchase. For this reason also I apprehend it is, that the antient jewels of the crown are held to be heir-looms; for they are necessary to maintain the state, and support the dignity of the sovereign for the time being. Charters likewise, and deeds, court-rolls, and other evidences of the land, together with the chests in which they are contained, shall pass together with the land to the heir, in the nature of heir-looms, and shall not go to the executor. By special custom also, in some places, carriages, utensils, and other household implements, may be heir-looms; but such custom must be strictly proved. On the other hand, by almost general custom, whatever is strongly affixed to the freehold or inheritance, and cannot be severed from thence without violence or damage, "*quod ab aedibus non facile revellitur,*" is become a member of the inheritance, and shall thereupon pass to the heir; as chimney-pieces, pumps, old fixed or dormant tables, benches, and the like.

Other personal chattels there are, which also descend to the heir in the nature of heir-looms, as a monument or tombstone in a church, or the coat-armor of his ancestor there hung up, with the penons and other ensigns of honor, suited to his degree. In this case, albeit the freehold of the church is in the parson, and these are annexed to that freehold, yet cannot the parson or any other take them away or deface them, but is liable to an action from the heir. Pews in the church are somewhat of the same nature, which may descend by custom immemorial (without any ecclesiastical concurrence) from the ancestor to the heir. But though the heir has a property in the monuments and escutcheons of his ancestors, yet he has none in their bodies or ashes; nor can he bring any civil action against such as indecently at least, if not impiously, violate and disturb their remains, when dead and buried. The parson indeed, who has the freehold of the soil, may bring an action of trespass against such as dig and disturb it: and, if any one in taking up a dead body steals the shroud or other apparel, it will be felony (a); for the property thereof remains in the executor, or whoever was at the charge of the funeral.

But to return to heir-looms: these, though they be mere chattels, yet cannot be devised away from the heir by will; but such a devise is void, even by a tenant in fee-simple. For, they being, at his death, instantly vested in the heir, the devise (which is subsequent, and not to take effect till *after* his death) shall be postponed to the custom, whereby they have already descended.

---

(a) And to steal the body alone, *without the apparel accompanying it*, is, by the common law, an indictable offence as a misdemesnor; "being highly indecent, and *contra bonos mores:*" and it makes no difference whether the offence be committed from motives of wantonness and impiety, or for the purpose of dissection. See *The King*, v. *Lynn*, 2 *Term. Rep.* 733.

## CHAPTER XXIII.

OF TITLE BY SUCCESSION, MARRIAGE, AND JUDGMENT.

THE fifth method of gaining a property in chattels, either perfonal or real, is by *fucceffion:* which is, in ftrictnefs of law, only applicable to corporations aggregate of many, as dean and chapter, mayor and commonalty, mafter and fellows, and the like ; in which one fet of men may, by fucceeding another fet, acquire a property in all the goods, moveables, and other chattels of the corporation. The true reafon whereof is, becaufe in judgment of law a corporation never dies ; and therefore the predeceffors, who lived a century ago, and their fucceffors now in being, are one and the fame body corporate. Which identity is a property fo inherent in the nature of a body politic, that, even when it is meant to give any thing to be taken in fucceffion by fuch a body, that fucceffion need not be expreffed: but the law will of itfelf imply it. So that a gift to fuch a corporation, either of lands or of chattels, without naming their fucceffors, vefts an abfolute property in them fo long as the corporation fubfifts. And thus a leafe for years, an obligation, a jewel, a flock of fheep, or other chattel intereft, will veft in the fucceffors, by fucceffion, as well as in the identical members, to whom it was originally given.

But, with regard to fole corporations, a confiderable diftinction muft be made. For if fuch fole corporation be the reprefentative of a number of perfons; as the mafter of an hofpital, who is a corporation for the benefit of the poor brethren ; or the dean of fome antient cathedral, who ftands in the place of, and reprefents in his corporate capacity, the chapter ; fuch fole corporations as thefe have in this refpect the fame powers, as corporations aggregate have, to take perfonal property or chattels in fucceffion. And therefore a bond to fuch a mafter or dean, and his fucceffors, is good in law ; and the fucceffor fhall have the advantage of it, for the benefit of the aggregate fociety, of which he is in law the reprefentative. Whereas, in the cafe of fole corporations, which reprefent no others but themfelves, as bifhops, parfons, and the like, no chattel intereft can regularly go in fucceffion: and therefore, if a leafe for years be made to the bifhop of Oxford and his fucceffors, in fuch cafe his executors or adminiftrators, and not his fucceffors, fhall have it. For the word *fucceffors*, when applied to a perfon in his political capacity, is equivalent to the word *heirs* in his natural; and fuch a leafe for years, if made to John and his heirs, would not veft in his heirs, but his executors.

Yet to this rule there are two exceptions. One in the cafe of the king, in whom a chattel may veft by a grant of it formerly made to a preceding king and his fucceffors. The other exception is, where, by a *particular* cuftom, fome *particular* corporations fole have acquired a power of taking *particular* chattel interefts in fucceffion. And this cuftom, being againft the general tenor of the common law, muft be ftrictly interpreted, and not extended to any other chattel interefts than fuch immemorial ufage will ftrictly warrant. Thus the chamberlain of London, who is a corporation fole, may, by the cuftom of London, take *bonds* and *recognizances* to himfelf and his fucceffors, for the benefit of the orphan's fund: but it will not follow from thence, that he may take a *bond* to himfelf and his fucceffors, for any other purpofe than the benefit of the orphan's fund; for that is not warranted by the cuftom. Wherefore, upon the whole, we may clofe this head with laying down this general rule; that fuch right of fucceffion to chattels is univerfally inherent by the common law in all aggregate corporations, in the king, and in fuch fingle corporations as reprefent a number of perfons; and may, by fpecial cuftom, belong to certain other fole corporations for fome particular purpofes: although, generally, in fole corporations no fuch right can exift.

A fixth method of acquiring property in goods and chattels is by *marriage;* whereby thofe chattels, which belonged formerly to the wife, are by act of law vefted in the hufband, with the fame degree of property and with the fame powers, as the wife, when fole, had over them.

In a real estate, he only gains a title to the rents and profits during coverture: for that, depending upon feodal principles, remains entire to the wife after the death of her husband, or to her heirs, if she dies before him; unless, by the birth of a child, he becomes tenant for life by the curtesy. But, in chattel interests, the sole and absolute property vests in the husband, to be disposed of at his pleasure, if he chuses to take possession of them: for, unless he reduces them to possession, by exercising some act of ownership upon them, no property vests in him, but they shall remain to the wife, or to her representatives, after the coverture is determined.

There is therefore a very considerable difference in the acquisition of this species of property by the husband, according to the subject-matter; *viz.* whether it be a chattel *real*, or a chattel *personal;* and, of chattels personal, whether it be in *possession*, or in *action* only. A *chattel real* vests in the husband, not absolutely, but *sub modo*. As in case of a lease for years, the husband shall receive all the rents and profits of it, and may, if he pleases, sell, surrender, or dispose of it during the coverture: if he be outlawed or attainted, it shall be forfeited to the king; it is liable to execution for his debts: and, if he survives his wife, it is to all intents and purposes his own. Yet, if he has made no disposition thereof in his lifetime, and dies before his wife, he cannot dispose of it by will: for, the husband having made no alteration in the property during his life, it never was transferred from the wife; but after his death she shall remain in her antient possession, and it shall not go to his executors. So it is also of chattels personal (or *choses*) in *action;* as debts upon bond, contracts, and the like: these the husband may have if he pleases; that is, if he reduces them into possession by receiving or recovering them at law. And, upon such receipt or recovery, they are absolutely and entirely his own; and shall go to his executors or administrators, or as he shall bequeath them by will, and shall not revest in the wife. But, if he dies before he has recovered or reduced them into possession, so that at his death they still continue *choses in action*, they shall survive to the wife (*a*): for the husband never exerted the power he had of obtaining an exclusive property in them. And so, if an estray comes into the wife's franchise, and the husband seises it, it is absolutely his property: but, if he dies without seising it, his executors are not now at liberty to seise it, but the wife or her heirs; for the husband never exerted the right he had, which right determined with the coverture. Thus in both these species of property the law is the same, in case the wife survives the husband; but, in case the husband survives the wife, the law is very different with respect to *chattels real*, and *choses in action*: for he shall have the *chattel real* by survivorship, but not the *chose in action*; except in the case of arrears of rent, due to the wife before her coverture, which in case of her death are given to the husband by statute 32 Hen. VIII. c. 37. But he still will be entitled to be her administrator; and may, in that capacity, recover such things in action as became due to her before or during the coverture (*b*).

Thus, and upon these reasons, stands the law between husband and wife, with regard to *chattels real*, and *choses in action*: but, as to *chattels personal* (or *choses*) *in possession*, which the wife hath in her own right, as ready money, jewels, household goods, and the like, the husband hath therein an immediate and absolute property, devolved to him by the

---

(*a*) *Note*,—An assignment of choses in action, by the husband, does not seem to be such a reducing to possession, as to take away the interest of the wife; for it appears by the case of *Squibb* v. *Wyn*, 1. P. *Wms*. 378. and the authorities referred to in Mr. *Cox*'s note, *ibid*, 381. that she will be bound only to the amount of the consideration for which such assignment was made. And see further as to the husband's interest in the *real chattels* and *choses in action* of his wife, *Co. Lit.* 351 ª. n. (1.)

(*b*) And (subject to the payment of her debts) is entitled to retain the same to his own use. See 29 Car II. c. 3. sec. 25. and the construction thereof in favour of the husband, *Squibb* v. *Wyn*, 1 P. *Wms*. 378. *Co. Lit.* 351 ª. n. (1).

marriage, not only potentially but in fact, which never can again re-vest in the wife or her reprefentatives.

And, as the hufband may thus generally acquire a property in all the perfonal fubftance of the wife, fo in one particular inftance the wife may acquire a property in fome of her hufbands goods; which fhall remain to her after his death, and not go to his executors. Thefe are called her *paraphernalia*. Our law ufes it to fignify the apparel and ornaments of the wife, fuitable to her rank and degree; and therefore, even the jewels of a peerefs, ufually worn by her, have been held to be *paraphernalia*. Thefe fhe becomes entitled to at the death of her hufband, over and above her jointure or dower, and preferably to all other reprefentatives. Neither can the hufband devife by his will fuch ornaments and jewels of his wife; though during his life perhaps he hath power (if unkindly inclined to exert it) to fell them or give them away. But if fhe continues in the ufe of them till his death, fhe fhall afterwards retain them againft his executors and adminiftrators, and all other perfons except creditors, where there is a deficiency of affets (*a*). And her neceffary apparel is protected even againft the claim of creditors.

A judgment, in confequence of fome fuit or action in a court of juftice, is frequently the means of vefting the right and property of chattel interefts in the prevailing party. And here we muft be careful to diftinguifh between property, the *right* of which is before vefted in the party, and of which only *poffeffion* is recovered by fuit or action; and property, to which a man before had no determinate title or certain claim, but he gains as well the right as the poffeffion by

---

(*a*) And in this cafe fhe may recover againft the *heir at law*, to the value of fuch *paraphernalia* as have been applied for the payment of her hufband's creditors, *Tipping* v. *Tipping*, 1 *P. Wms.* 729. *Tynt* v. *Tynt*, 2 *ibid*, 542. as fhe may alfo againft *truftees* of the real eftate, devifed for the payment of debts, *Incledon* v. *Northcote* 3 *Atk.* 438. but not, it feems, againft a *fimple devifee* of fuch eftates, *Robert* v. *Clifford*, *Amb.* 6. (2 *P. Wms.* 544. n. (1.) *fame cafe*).

the procefs and judgment of the law. Of the former fort are all debts and *chofes in action*; as if a man gives bond for 20*l*. or agrees to buy a horfe at a ftated fum, or takes up goods of a tradefman upon an implied contract to pay as much as they are reafonably worth: in all thefe cafes the right accrues to the creditor, and is completely vefted in him, at the time of the bond being fealed, or the contract or agreement made; and the law only gives him a remedy to recover the poffeffion of that right, which already in juftice belongs to him. But there is alfo a fpecies of property to which a man has not any claim or title whatfoever, till after fuit commenced and judgment obtained in a court of law. Of this nature are,

1. Such penalties as are given by particular ftatutes, to be recovered on an action *popular*; or, in other words, to be recovered by him or them that will fue for the fame.

2. Another fpecies of property, that is acquired and loft by fuit and judgment at law, is that of *damages* given to a man by a jury, as a compenfation and fatisfaction for fome injury fuftained; as for a battery, for imprifonment, for flander, or for trefpafs.

3. Hither alfo may be referred, upon the fame principle, all title to cofts and expences of fuit; which are often arbitrary, and reft entirely on the determination of the court, upon weighing all circumftances, both as to the *quantum*, and alfo (in the courts of equity efpecially, and upon motions in the courts of law) whether there fhall be any cofts at all. Thefe cofts therefore, when given by the court to either party, may be looked upon as an acquifition made by the judgment of law.

## CHAPTER XXIV.

### OF TITLE BY GIFT, GRANT, AND CONTRACT.

WE are now to proceed to the difcuffion of two of the remaining methods of acquiring a title to property in things perfonal, which are much connected together, and answer in some measure to the conveyances of real estates; being those by *gift* or *grant*, and by *contract:* whereof the former vests a property in *possession*, the latter a property in *action*.

Gifts then, or *grants*, which are the eighth method of transferring personal property, are thus to be distinguished from each other, that *gifts* are always gratuitous, *grants* are upon some consideration or equivalent: and they may be divided, with regard to their subject-matter, into gifts or grants of chattels *real*, and gifts or grants of chattels *personal*. Under the head of gifts or grants of chattels *real*, may be included all leases for years of land, assignments, and surrenders of those leases; and all the other methods of conveying an estate less than freehold.

Grants or gifts of chattels *personal*, are the act of transferring the right and the possession of them; whereby one man renounces, and another man immediately acquires, all title and interest therein: which may be done either in writing, or by word of mouth attested by sufficient evidence, of which the delivery of possession is the strongest and most essential. But this conveyance, when merely voluntary, is somewhat suspicious; and is usually construed to be fraudulent, if creditors or others become sufferers thereby. And, particularly, by statute 3 Hen. VII. c. 4. all deeds of gift of goods, made in trust to the use of the donor, shall be void: because otherwise persons might be tempted to commit treason or felony, without danger of forfeiture; and the creditors of the donor might also be defrauded of their rights. And by statute 13 Eliz. c. 5. every grant or gift of chattels, as well as lands, with an intent to defraud creditors or others, shall be void as against such persons to whom such fraud would be prejudicial; but, as against the grantor himself, shall stand good and effectual: and all persons partakers in, or privy to, such fraudulent grants, shall forfeit the whole value of the goods, one moiety to the king, and another moiety to the party grieved; and also on conviction shall suffer imprisonment for half a year.

A true and proper gift or grant is always accompanied with delivery of possession, and takes effect immediately. And if the gift does not take effect, by delivery of immediate possession, it is then not properly a gift, but a contract: and this a man cannot be compelled to perform, but upon good and sufficient consideration.

A contract, which usually conveys an interest merely in action, is thus defined: " an agreement upon sufficient " consideration, to do or not to do a particular thing." From which definition there arises three points to be contemplated in all contracts; 1. The *agreement*: 2. The *consideration*: and 3. The *thing* to be done or omitted, or the different species of contracts.

This contract or agreement may be either express or implied. *Express* contracts are where the terms of the agreement are openly uttered and avowed at the time of the making, as to deliver an ox, or ten load of timber, or to pay a stated price for certain goods. *Implied* are such as reason and justice dictate, and which therefore the law presumes that every man undertakes to perform. As, if I employ a person to do any business for me, or perform any work: the law implies that I undertook, or contracted, to pay him as much as his labour deserves.

A contract may also be either *executed*, as, if A agrees to change horses with B, and they do it immediately; in which case the possession and the right are transferred together: or it may be *executory*, as, if they agree to change next week; here the right only vests, and their reciprocal property in each other's horse is not in possession but in action; for a contract *executed* (which differs nothing from a grant) conveys a *chose in possession*; a contract *executory* conveys only a *chose in action*.

Having thus shewn the general nature of a contract, We are, secondly, to proceed to the *consideration* upon which it is founded; or the reason which moves the contracting party to enter into the contract. And it must be a thing lawful in itself, or else the contract is void. A *good* consideration, we have before seen, is that of blood or natural affection between near relations; this consideration may sometimes however be set aside, and the contract become void, when it tends in its confequences to defraud creditors or other third perfons of their juft rights. But a contract for any *valuable* confideration, as for marriage, for money, for work done, or for other reciprocal contracts, can never be impeached at law; and if it be of a fufficient adequate value, is never fet afide in equity: for the perfon contracted with has then given an equivalent in recompenfe, and is therefore as much an owner, or a creditor, as any other perfon.

A confideration of fome fort or other is fo abfolutely neceffary to the forming of a contract, that a *nudum pactum*, or agreement to do or pay any thing on one fide, without any compenfation on the other, is totally void in law: and a man cannot be compelled to perform it (*a*). But any degree of reciprocity will prevent the pact from being nude: nay, even if the thing be founded on a prior moral obligation, (as a promife to pay a juft debt, though barred by the ftatute of limitations) it is no longer *nudum pactum*. And as this rule was principally eftablifhed to avoid the inconvenience that would arife from fetting up mere verbal promifes, for which no good reafon could be affigned, it therefore does not hold in fome cafes, where fuch promife is authentically proved by written documents. For if a man enters into a voluntary bond, or gives a promiffory note, he fhall not be allowed to aver the want of a confideration in order to evade the payment (*b*): for every bond from the folemnity of the inftru-

---

(*a*) This is indifputably the cafe of *verbal* contracts, but it has been doubted by eminent authorities whether (as the rule was adopted from the civil law in order to guard againft fraud) it extends to contracts deliberately reduced into writing. See the argument of *Wilmot*, Juft. in *Fillans* v. *Van Mierop*, 3 *Bur.* 1670. This queftion is alfo minutely confidered by Mr. *Fonblanque*, *Treat. Eq.* 326. n. (*a*), who concludes, on the fanction of authorities, that, agreeably to the general pofition in the text, "A confideration is by our law neceffary to an agreement, though evidenced by writing, unlefs the writing, being of the higheft folemnity, imports a confideration, or unlefs it be negotiable at law, and the interefts of third perfons are involved in its efficacy."

(*b*) This is correct in refpect to a promiffory *note*, only

ment, and every note from the subscription of the drawer, carries with it an internal evidence of a good consideration. Courts of justice will therefore support them both, as against the contractor himself; but not to the prejudice of creditors, or strangers to the contract.

We are next to consider, *thirdly*, the thing agreed to be done or omitted. The most usual contracts, whereby the right of chattels personal may be acquired in the laws of England, are, 1. That of *sale* or *exchange*. 2. That of *bailment*. 3. That of *hiring* and *borrowing*. 4. That of *debt*.

1. Sale or *exchange* is a transmutation of property from one man to another, in consideration of some price or recompense in value: for there is no sale without a recompense; there must be a *quid pro quo*. If it be a commutation of goods, it is more properly an *exchange*; but, if it be a transferring of goods for money, it is called a *sale*. But with regard to the *law* of sales and exchanges there is no difference. I shall therefore treat of them both under the denomination of sales only; and shall consider their force and effect, in the first place where the vendor *hath* in himself, and secondly where he *hath not*, the property of the thing sold.

Where the vendor *hath* in himself the property of the goods sold, he hath the liberty of disposing of them to whom ever he pleases, at any time, and in any manner: unless judgment has been obtained against him for a debt or damages,

---

when the action is brought by an *indorsee* of the note, for if it be brought by the *payee*, the want of consideration may be averred, and, if proved, will be a bar to the recovery, *Guichard* v. *Roberts*, 1 *Black. Rep.* 445. *Jefferies* v. *Austin*, 1 *Stra.* 674, and so too if the note be not made agreeable to the custom of merchants under 3 and 4 Anne, c. 9. See *Pearson* v. *Garrett*, 4 *Mod.* 242. " and from this distinction," it is observed by Mr. *Fonblanque* (1 *Treat. Eq.* 326. n. (*u*) " it appears that the law does not give to promisory notes and bills of exchange the above effect in respect of the undertaking being in *writing*, but in order to strengthen and facilitate that commercial intercourse which is carried on through the medium of such securities."

and the writ of execution is actually delivered to the sheriff. For then, by the statute of frauds, the sale shall be looked upon as fraudulent, and the property of the goods shall be bound to answer the debt, from the time of delivering the writ. Formerly it was bound from the *teste*, or issuing, of the writ, and any subsequent sale was fraudulent; but the law was thus altered in favour of *purchasors*, though it still remains the same between the *parties*: and therefore, if a defendant dies after the awarding and before the delivery of the writ, his goods are bound by it in the hands of his executors.

If a man agrees with another for goods at a certain price, he may not carry them away before he hath paid for them; for it is no sale without payment, unless the contrary be expressly agreed. And therefore, if the vendor says, the price of a beast is four pounds, and the vendee says he will give four pounds, the bargain is struck; and they neither of them are at liberty to be off, provided immediate possession be tendered by the other side. But if neither the money be paid, nor the goods delivered, nor tender made, nor any subsequent agreement be entered into, it is no contract, and the owner may dispose of the goods as he pleases. But if any part of the price is paid down, if it be but a penny, or any portion of the goods delivered by way of *earnest*; the property of the goods is absolutely bound by it *(a)*: and the vendee may recover the goods by action, as well as the vendor may the price of them. And such regard does the law pay to earnest as an evidence of a contract, that, by the same statute 29 Car. II. c. 3. no contract for the sale of goods, to the value of 10*l*. or more, shall be valid, unless the buyer actually re-

---

*(a)* Viz. So far bound, as that, after earnest given, the vendor cannot sell the goods to another, without a default in the vendee; but if (after request by the vendor) the vendee does not pay for the goods, and fetch them away in a convenient time, the agreement is dissolved, and he is at liberty to sell them to any other person. Ruled per *Holt, Ch. J. Lanfert* v. *Administ.* of *Tiler*, 1 *Salk*, 113.

ceives part of the goods fold, by way of earneft on his part; or unlefs he gives part of the price to the vendor by way of earneft to bind the bargain, or in part of payment; or unlefs some note in writing be made and signed by the party, or his agent, who is to be charged with the contract *(a)*. And, with regard to goods under the value of 10*l*. no contract or agreement for the fale of them fhall be valid, unlefs the goods are to be delivered within one year, or unlefs the contract be made in writing, and signed by the party, or his agent, who is to be charged therewith.

As foon as the bargain is ftruck, the property of the goods is transferred to the vendee, and that of the price to the vendor; but the vendee cannot take the goods, until he tenders the price agreed on. And by a regular fale, without delivery, the property is fo abfolutely vefted in the vendee, that if A fells a horfe to B for 10*l*. and B pay him earneft, or figns a note in writing of the bargain; and afterwards, before the delivery of the horfe or money paid, the horfe dies in the vendor's cuftody; ftill he is entitled to the money, becaufe by the contract, the property was in the vendee.

But property may alfo in fome cafes be transferred by fale, though the vendor *hath none at all* in the goods: for it is expedient that the buyer, by taking proper precautions, may at all events be fecure of his purchafe; otherwife all commerce between man and man muft foon be at an end. And therefore the general rule of law is, that all fales and contracts of any thing vendible, in fairs or markets *overt*, (that is, open) fhall not only be good between the parties, but alfo be binding on all thofe that have any right or property therein. Market overt in the country is only held on the fpecial days,

---

*(a)* It has been determined, however, that the ftatute extends only to goods in being at the time of the contract, and to be delivered immediately, and not to fuch as are agreed to be manufactured and delivered at a future period; a contract of this nature, therefore, is binding though not in writing and though no earneft be given. See *Clayton* v. *Andrews*, 4 *Bur.* 2101. and *Towers* v. *Robinfon*, 1 *Stra.* 506.

provided for particular towns by charter or prescription; but in London every day, except Sunday, is market day. The market place, or spot of ground set apart by custom for the sale of particular goods, is also in the country the only market overt; but in London every shop in which goods are exposed publickly to sale, is market overt, for such things only as the owner professes to trade in. But if my goods are stolen from me, and sold, out of market overt, my property is not altered, and I may take them wherever I find them. And it is expressly provided by statute 1 Jac. I. c. 21. that the sale of any goods wrongfully taken, to any pawnbroker in London, or within two miles thereof, shall not alter the property: for this, being usually a clandestine trade, is therefore made an exception to the general rule: or if the goods be stolen from a common person, and then taken by the king's officer from the felon, and sold in open market; still, if the owner has used due diligence in prosecuting the thief to conviction, he loses not his property in the goods. So likewise, if the buyer knoweth the property not to be in the seller; or there be any other fraud in the transaction; if he knoweth the seller to be an infant, or feme covert not usually trading for herself; if the sale be not originally and wholly made in the fair or market, or not at the usual hours; the owner's property is not bound thereby. If a man buys his own goods in a fair or market, the contract of sale shall not bind him, so that he shall render the price; unless the property had been previously altered by a former sale. And, notwithstanding any number of intervening sales, if the original vendor, who sold without having the property, comes again into possession of the goods, the original owner may take them, when found in his hands who was guilty of the first breach of justice.

But there is one species of personal chattels, in which the property is not easily altered by sale, without the express consent of the owner, and those are horses. For a purchaser gains no property in a horse that has been stolen, unless it be bought in a fair or market overt, according to the directions of the statutes 2 P. & M. c. 7. and 31 Eliz. c. 12.

By which it is enacted, that the horſe ſhall be openly expoſed, in the time of ſuch fair or market, for one whole hour together, between ten in the morning and ſunſet, in the public place uſed for ſuch ſales, and not in any private yard or ſtable; and afterwards brought by both the vendor and the vendee to the book keeper of ſuch fair or market: that toll be paid, if any be due; and if not, one penny to the bookkeeper, who ſhall enter down the price, colour, and marks of the horſe, with the names, additions, and abode of the vendee and vendor; the latter being properly atteſted. Nor ſhall ſuch ſale take away the property of the owner, if within ſix months after the horſe is ſtolen he puts in his claim before ſome magiſtrate, where the horſe ſhall be found; and, within forty days more, proves ſuch his property by the oath of two witneſſes, and tenders to the perſon in poſſeſſion ſuch price as he *bona fide* paid for him in market overt. But in caſe any one of the points before-mentioned be not obſerved, ſuch ſale is utterly void; and the owner ſhall not loſe his property, but at any diſtance of time may ſeize or bring an action for his horſe, wherever he happens to find him.

A purchaſer of goods and chattels may have a ſatisfaction from the ſeller, if he ſells them as his own and the title proves deficient, without any expreſs warranty for that purpoſe. But, with regard to the goodneſs of the wares ſo purchaſed, the vendor is not bound to anſwer; unleſs he expreſsly warrants them to be ſound and good, or unleſs he knew them to be otherwiſe and hath uſed any art to diſguiſe them, or unleſs they turn out to be different from what he repreſented to the buyer.

2. Bailment is a delivery of goods in truſt, upon a contract expreſſed or implied, that the truſt ſhall be faithfully executed on the part of the bailee. As if cloth be delivered to a taylor to make a ſuit of cloaths, he has it upon an implied contract to render it again when made, and that in a workmanly manner. If money or goods be delivered to a common carrier, to convey from Oxford to London, he is under a contract in law to pay, or carry, them to the perſon appointed. If a friend delivers any thing to his friend to

## C. XXIV. TITLE BY GIFT, GRANT, AND CONTRACT. 273

keep for him, the receiver is bound to restore it on demand: but such a general bailment will not charge the bailee with any loss, unless it happens by gross neglect, which is an evidence of fraud: but, if he undertakes specially to keep the goods safely and securely, he is bound to take the same care of them, as a prudent man would take of his own.

In all these instances there is a special qualified property transferred from the bailor to the bailee, together with the possession. And, on account of this qualified property of the bailee, he may (as well as the bailor) maintain an action against such as injure or take away these chattels *(a)*.

3. Hiring and *borrowing* are also contracts by which a qualified property may be transferred to the hirer or borrower: in which there is only this difference, that hiring is always for a price, a stipend, or additional recompence; borrowing is merely gratuitous. But the law in both cases is the same *(b)*. They are both contracts, whereby the possession and a transient property is transferred for a particular time or use, on condition to restore the goods so hired or borrowed, as soon as the time is expired or use performed; together with the price or stipend (in case of hiring) either expressly agreed on by the parties, or left to be implied by law according to the value of the service.

There is one species of this price or reward, the most usual of any, but concerning which many good and learned men have in former times very much perplexed themselves and other people, by raising doubts about it's legality *in foro conscientiæ*. That is, when money is lent on a contract to receive not only the principal sum again, but also an increase

---

*(a)* See much learning, in respect to the law of bailment, collected by *Holt, Ch. J.* in *Cogs* v. *Bernard*, 2 *Ld. Raym.* 909. but more particularly *Jones's Essay on the Law of Bailments*, where the various distinctions which govern the important subject of bailment, are treated with uncommon discrimination and ability.

*(b) Quere* this; and see *Jon. Bail.* 85.

by way of compensation for the use. The necessity of individuals will always make borrowing unavoidable. Without some profit allowed by law, there will be but few lenders: and those principally bad men, who will break through the law, and take a profit; and then will endeavour to indemnify themselves from the danger of the penalty, by making that profit exorbitant. A capital distinction must therefore be made between a moderate and exorbitant profit; to the former of which we usually give the name of interest, to the latter the truly odious appellation of usury: the former is necessary in every civil state, if it were but to exclude the latter, which ought never to be tolerated in any well-regulated society. For, as the whole of this matter is well summed up by Grotius, " if the compensation allowed by law " does not exceed the proportion of the hazard run, or the " want felt, by the loan, it's allowance is neither repugnant " to the revealed nor the natural law: but if it exceeds those " bounds, it is then oppressive usury; and though the muni- " cipal laws may give it impunity, they never can make it " just."

But sometimes the hazard may be greater than the rate of interest allowed by law will compensate. And this gives rise to the practice of, 1. Bottomry, or *respondentia*. 2. Policies of insurance. 3. Annuities upon lives.

And first, *bottomry* is in the nature of a mortgage of a ship; when the owner takes up money to enable him to carry on his voyage, and pledges the keel or *bottom* of the ship *(partem pro toto)* as a security for the repayment. In which case it is understood, that if the ship be lost, the lender loses also his whole money; but, if it returns in safety, then he shall receive back his principal, and also the premium or interest agreed upon, however it may exceed the legal rate of interest. And in this case the ship and tackle, if brought home, are answerable (as well as the person of the borrower) for the money lent. But if the loan is not upon the vessel, but upon the goods and merchandize, which must necessarily be sold or exchanged in the course of the voyage, then only the borrower, personally, is bound to answer the contract; who therefore in this case is said to take up money at *respondentia*.

Secondly, a policy of *insurance* is a contract between A and B, that, upon A's paying a premium equivalent to the hazard run, B will indemnify or insure him against a particular event. But, in order to prevent these insurances from being turned into a mischievous kind of gaming, it is enacted by statute 14 Geo. III. c. 48. that no insurance shall be made on lives, or any other event, wherein the party insured hath no interest; that in all policies the name of such interested party shall be inserted; and nothing more shall be recovered thereon than the amount of the interest of the insured.

This doth not, however, extend to marine insurances. But, as a practice had obtained of insuring large sums without having any property on board, which were called insurances, *interest or no interest*; and also of insuring the same goods several times over, both of which were a species of gaming, without any advantage to commerce, and were denominated *wagering* policies: it is therefore enacted by the statute 19 Geo. II. c. 37, that all insurances, interest or no interest, or without farther proof of interest than the policy itself, or by way of gaming or wagering, or without benefit of salvage to the insurer, (all which had the same pernicious tendency) shall be totally null and void, except upon privateers, or upon ships or merchandize from the Spanish and Portuguese dominions, for reasons sufficiently obvious; and that no re-assurance shall be lawful, except the former insurer shall be insolvent, a bankrupt, or dead; and lastly, that in the East India trade the lender of money on bottomry, or at *respondentia*, shall alone have a right to be insured for the money lent, and the borrower shall (in case of a loss) recover no more upon any insurance than the surplus of his bottomry or *respondentia* bond.

Thirdly, the practice of purchasing *annuities for lives* at a certain price or premium, instead of advancing the same sum on an ordinary loan, arises usually from the inability of the borrower to give the lender a permanent security for the return of the money borrowed, at any one period of time. He therefore stipulates (in effect) to repay annually, during his life, some part of the money borrowed; together with legal interest for so much of the principal as annually remains unpaid, and an additional compensation for the extraordinary hazard run, of losing that principal intirely by the contingency of the borrower's death: all which considerations, being calculated and blended together, will constitute the just proportion or *quantum* of the annuity which ought to be granted. The real value of that contingency must depend on the age, constitution, situation, and conduct of the borrower; and therefore the price of such annuities cannot without the utmost difficulty be reduced to any general rules. So that if, by the terms of the contract, the lender's principal is *bona fide* (and not colourably) put in jeopardy, no inequality of price will make it an usurious bargain; though, under some circumstances of imposition, it may be relieved against in equity. To throw, however, some check upon improvident transactions of this kind, which are usually carried on with great privacy, the statute 17 Geo. III. c. 26. has directed, that upon the sale of any life annuity of more than the value of ten pounds *per annum* (unless on a sufficient pledge of lands in fee-simple or stock in the public funds) (*a*) the true consideration, which shall be in money only (*b*), shall be set forth and described in the security itself; and a memorial of the date of the security, of the names of the parties, *cestui que trusts*, *cestui que vies*, and witnesses, and of the consideration money, shall within twenty days after its execution be inrolled in the court of chancery; else the security shall be null and void: and, in case of collusive practices respecting the consideration, the court, in which any action is brought

---

(*a*) " Or fee-tail in possession," by the same statute.

(*b*) But on this part of the act it has been determined that *Bank notes*, if not objected to at the time of payment, shall be considered as a pecuniary consideration within the *spirit* of the act. *Wright* v. *Reid*, 3 *Term Rep.* 554.

C. XXIV. TITLE BY GIFT, GRANT, AND CONTRACT. 277

or judgment obtained upon such collusive security, may order the same to be cancelled, and the judgment (if any) to be vacated: and also all contracts *(a)* for the purchase of annuities from infants shall remain utterly void, and be incapable of confirmation after such infants arrive to the age of maturity *(b)*.

But as to the rate of legal interest, it has varied and decreased for two hundred years past, according as the quantity of specie in the kingdom has increased by accessions of trade, the introduction of paper credit, and other circumstances. And by the statute 12 Ann. stat. 2. c. 16. it was brought down to five *per cent* yearly, which is now the extremity of legal interest that can be taken. But yet, if a contract which carries interest be made in a foreign country, our courts will direct the payment of interest according to the law of that country in which the contract was made. And, by statute 14 Geo. III. c. 79. all mortgages and other securities upon estates or other property in Ireland or the plantations, bearing interest not exceeding six *per cent*, shall be legal; though executed in the kingdom of Great Britain: unless the money lent shall be known at the time to exceed the value of the thing in pledge; in which case also, to prevent usurious contracts at home under colour of such foreign

---

*(a)* The student will observe, that the act, when speaking of *infants*, vacates the *contract*, but when speaking of *other persons* makes void only the *securities*. Upon this difference in the wording of the act, Mr. *Powell*, in his treatise on the law of contracts, attempts to substantiate an important distinction in respect to the validity of the annuity in the one case though it be void in the other; but *quære.* See 1 *ibid*, 209, 281.

*(b)* This act, however, is declared not to extend to annuities given by will, or by marriage settlement, or for the advancement of a child; nor to any voluntary annuity granted without pecuniary consideration: nor to annuities granted by any body corporate, or under any authority, or trust enacted by act of parliament.

securities, the borrower shall forfeit treble the sum so borrowed.

4. The last general species of contracts, which I have to mention, is that of *debt*; whereby a *chose* in action, or right to a certain sum of money, is mutually acquired and lost. This may be a counterpart of, and arise from, any of the other species of contracts. Any contract, in short, whereby a determinate sum of money becomes due to any person, and is not paid, but remains in action merely, is a contract of debt. And, taken in this light, it comprehends a great variety of acquisition; being usually divided into debts of *record*, debts by *special*, and debts by *simple* contract.

A debt of *record* is a sum of money, which appears to be due by the evidence of a court of record. As when any specific sum is adjudged to be due from the defendant to the plaintiff, on an action or suit at law; debts upon recognizance, statutes merchant, and statutes staple, are also ranked among this first and principal class of debts.

Debts by *specialty*, or special contract, are such whereby a sum of money becomes, or is acknowledged to be due by deed of sale, by lease reserving rent, or by bond or obligation. These are looked upon as the next class of debts after those of record.

Debts by *simple contract* are such, where the contract upon which the obligation arises is neither ascertained by matter of record, nor yet by deed or special instrument, but by mere oral evidence, the most simple of any; or by notes unsealed, which are capable of a more easy proof, and (therefore only) better, than a verbal promise. And by the statute 29 Car. II. c. 3. no executor or administrator shall be charged upon any promise to answer damages out of his own estate, and no person shall be charged upon any promise to answer for the debt or default of another, or upon any agreement in consideration of marriage, or upon any contract or sale of any real estate, or upon any agreement that is not to be performed within one year from the making; unless the agreement or some memorandum thereof, be in writing, and signed by the party himself or by his authority.

C. XXIV. TITLE BY GIFT, GRANT, AND CONTRACT. 279

But there is one species of debts upon simple contract, which is a transaction now introduced into all sorts of civil life, under the name of *paper credit*. These are debts by *bills of exchange*, and *promissory notes*.

A bill *of exchange* is an open letter of request from one man to another, desiring him to pay a sum named therein to a third person on his account. These bills are either *foreign*, or *inland*; *foreign*, when drawn by a merchant residing abroad upon his correspondent in England, or *vice versa;* and *inland*, when both the drawer and the drawee reside within the kingdom. But there is not in law any manner of difference between them *(a)*.

Promissory notes, or notes of hand, are a plain and direct engagement in writing, to pay a sum specified at the time therein limited to a person therein named, or sometimes to his order, or often to the bearer at large. These, by statute 3 & 4 Ann. c. 9. are made assignable and indorsable in like manner as bills of exchange. But, by statute 15 Geo. III. c. 51. all promissory or other notes, bills of exchange, drafts, and undertakings in writing, being negotiable or transferrable, for the payment of less than twenty shillings, are declared to be null and void: and it is made penal to utter or publish any such; they being deemed prejudicial to trade and public credit. And by 17 Geo. III. c. 30. all such notes, bills, drafts, and undertakings, to the amount of twenty shillings and less than five pounds, are subjected to

---

*(a)* This seems to be too generally expressed, for there is a very material distinction (as has been noticed by Mr. *Christian*) between foreign and inland bills, which is not altered by the provisions of 9 & 10 Wm. and 3 & 4 Anne; upon which the learned judge founds his observations. In foreign bills it is necessary, in order to recover against the drawers or indorsers, that they should be protested for non-acceptance or non-payment. *Rogers* v. *Stephens*, 2 *Term Rep.* 713. *Gale* v. *Walsh*, 5 *ibid*, 239. But this is no farther requisite in an inland bill, only that it enables the holder to recover *interest* and *costs* to the time of payment, *Harris* v. *Benson*, 1 *Stra.* 910. *Borough* v. *Perkins*, 1 *Salk.* 131.

many other regulations and formalities *(a)*; the omiſſion of any one of which vacates the ſecurity, and is penal to him that utters it.

The payee, either of a bill of exchange or promiſſory note, has clearly a property veſted in him (not indeed in poſſeſſion but in action) by the *expreſs* contract of the drawer in the caſe of a promiſſory note, and, in the caſe of a bill of exchange, by his *implied* contract, *viz.* that, provided the drawee will not pay the bill, the drawer will. And this property, ſo veſted, may be transferred and aſſigned from the payee to any other man, by indorſement, or writing his name in *dorſo* or on the back of it; and he may aſſign the ſame to another, and ſo on *in infinitum*. And a promiſſory note, payable to A or *bearer*, is negotiable without any indorſement, and payment thereof may be demanded by any bearer of it. But, in caſe of a bill of exchange, the payee, or the indorſee, (whether it be a general or particular indorſement) is to go to the drawee, and offer his bill for acceptance; which acceptance (ſo as to charge the drawer with coſts) muſt be in writing, under or on the back of the bill. If the drawee accepts the bill, either verbally or in

---

*(a)* An editor ſhould be cautious in adding to what his author has deemed ſufficient; but the general importance, and uſe of this medium of commerce, will, I truſt, be conſidered, in ſome meaſure, as an apology, ſhould I be thought to exceed my province, by ſubjoining the purport of the regulations alluded to in the text. Theſe are, that ſuch notes, &c. ſhall ſpecify the names and places of abode of the perſon to whom, or to whoſe order, they ſhall be payable; bear date at or before the time when they ſhall be iſſued; made payable within twenty-one days after date; and not be transferrable after the time limited for payment; and further that every indorſement thereon ſhall be made before the expiration of the ſame time, and bear date at or before the time of making; ſhall ſpecify the name and place of abode of the perſon to whom, or to whoſe order, the ſum contained in the note, &c. is to be paid; and that the ſigning of every ſuch note, &c. and alſo of every ſuch indorſement ſhall be atteſted by at leaſt one ſubſcribing witneſs.

writing, he then makes himself liable to pay it. If the drawee refuses to accept the bill, and it be of the value of 20*l.* or upwards, and expressed to be for value received, the payee or indorsee may protest it for *non-acceptance*: and notice of such protest must, within fourteen days after, be given to the drawer.

But, in case such bill be accepted by the drawee, and after acceptance he fails or refuses to pay it within three days after it becomes due, (which three days are called days of grace) the payee or indorsee is then to get it protested for *non-payment*, and such protest must also be notified, within fourteen days after, to the drawer (*a*). And he, on producing such protest, either of non-acceptance or non-payment, is bound to make good to the payee, or indorsee, not only the amount of the said bills, but also interest and all charges, to be computed from the time of making such protest. But if no protest be made or notified to the drawer, and any damage accrues by such neglect, it shall fall on the holder of the bill. The bill, when refused, must be demanded of the drawer as soon as conveniently may be: for otherwise the law will imply it paid: since it would be prejudicial to commerce, if a bill might rise up to charge the drawer at any distance of time; when, in the mean time, all reckonings and accounts may be adjusted between the drawer and the drawee.

If the bill be an indorsed bill, and the indorsee cannot get the drawee to discharge it, he may call upon either the

---

(*a*) This is the time required by 9 and 10 Will. III. c. 17. but in order to entitle the holder to a remedy against the drawer or indorser, *immediate* notice must be given of the non-acceptance or non-payment. By immediate notice is meant the earliest possible, as by the next post after the bill is dishonoured, &c. *Goostrey* v. *Mead, Bul. N. P.* 271. *Doug.* 497. *Tindal* v. *Brown,* 1 *Term Rep.* 167.

But *note*, that as the statute mentions so many days after *date*, it is held not to extend to bills payable after *sight*; inland bills at sight, therefore, need not be protested, *Leftly* v. *Mills,* 4 *Term Rep.* 171.

drawer or the indorser, or if the bill has been negotiated through many hands, upon any of the indorsers; for each indorser is a warrantor for the payment of the bill, which is frequently taken in payment as much (or more) upon the credit of the indorser, as of the drawer. And if such indorser, so called upon, has the names of one or more indorsers prior to his own, to each of whom he is properly an indorsee, he is also at liberty to call upon any of them to make him satisfaction; and so upwards. But the first indorser has nobody to resort to, but the drawer only.

What has been said of bills of exchange is applicable also to promissory notes, that are indorsed over, and negotiated from one hand to another: only that, in this case, as there is no drawee, there can be no protest for non-acceptance; or rather, the law considers a promissory note in the light of a bill drawn by a man upon himself, and accepted at the time of drawing. And, in case of non-payment by the drawer, the several indorsees of a promissory note have the same remedy, as upon bills of exchange, against the prior indorsers.

## CHAPTER XXV.

### OF TITLE BY BANKRUPTCY.

THE preceding chapter having treated of the acquisition of personal property by several commercial methods, we from thence shall be easily led to take into our present consideration a tenth method of transferring property, which is that of

Bankruptcy; a title which we before lightly touched upon; so far as it related to the transfer of the real estate of the bankrupt. At present we are to treat of it more minutely, as it principally relates to the disposition of chattels, in which the property of persons concerned in trade more usually consists, than in lands or tenements. Let us therefore first of all consider, 1. *Who* may become a bankrupt:

2. What *acts* make a bankrupt: 3. The *proceedings* on a commiffion of bankrupt: and, 4. In what manner an eftate in goods and chattels may be *transferred* by bankruptcy.

1. Who may become a bankrupt. A bankrupt was before defined to be " a trader, who fecretes himfelf, or does " certain other acts, tending to defraud his creditors." The laws of bankruptcy are confidered as laws calculated for the benefit of trade, and founded on the principles of humanity as well as juftice; and to that end they confer fome privileges, not only on the creditors, but alfo on the bankrupt or debtor himfelf. On the creditors; by compelling the bankrupt to give up all his effects to their ufe, without any fraudulent concealment: on the debtor; by exempting him from the rigor of the general law, whereby his perfon might be confined at the difcretion of his creditor, though in reality he has nothing to fatisfy the debt.

By ftatute 13 Eliz. c. 7. bankruptcy is confined to fuch perfons only as have *ufed the trade of merchandize*, in grofs or by retail, by way of bargaining, exchange, rechange, bartering, chevifance, or otherwife; or have *fought their living by buying and felling*. And, by ftatute 21 Jac. I. c. 19. perfons ufing the trade or profeffion of a *fcrivener*, receiving other men's monies and eftates into their truft and cuftody, are alfo made liable to the ftatutes of bankruptcy: and the benefits, as well as the penal parts of the law, are extended as well to *aliens* and *denizens* as to natural-born fubjects. Laftly, by ftatute 5 Geo. II. c. 30. *bankers, brokers*, and *factors*, are declared liable to the ftatutes of bankruptcy. But, by the fame act, no *farmer, grazier*, or *drover*, fhall (as fuch) be liable to be deemed a bankrupt; alfo, a *receiver of the king's taxes* is not capable, as fuch, of being a bankrupt. By the fame ftatute, no perfon fhall have a commiffion of bankrupt awarded againft him, unlefs at the petition of fome *one* creditor, to whom he owes 100*l*; or of *two*, to whom he is indebted 150*l*; or of *more*, to whom altogether he is indebted 200*l*.

In the interpretation of thefe feveral ftatutes, it hath been held, that buying only, or felling only, will not qualify a man to be a bankrupt; but it muſt be both buying and ſelling, and alſo getting a livelihood by it. As, by exerciſing the calling of a merchant, a grocer, a mercer, or, in one general word, a *chapman*, who is one that buys and ſells any thing. But no handicraft occupation (where nothing is bought and ſold, and where therefore an extenſive credit, for the ſtock in trade, is not neceſſary to be had) will make a man a regular bankrupt; as that of a huſbandman, a gardener, and the like. Alſo an inn-keeper cannot, as ſuch, be a bankrupt. But where perſons buy goods, and make them up into ſaleable commodities, as ſhoe-makers, ſmiths, and the like; here, though part of the gain is by bodily labour, and not by buying and ſelling, yet they are within the ſtatutes of bankrupts: for the labour is only in melioration of the commodity, and rendering it more fit for ſale.

One ſingle act of buying and ſelling will not make a man a trader; but a repeated practice, and profit by it. Buying and ſelling bank-ſtock, or other government ſecurities, will not make a man a bankrupt, they not being goods, wares, or merchandize, within the intent of the ſtatute, by which a profit may be fairly made. Neither will buying and ſelling under particular reſtraints, or for particular purpoſes; as, if a commiſſioner of the navy uſes to buy victuals for the fleet, and diſpoſe of the ſurplus and refuſe, he is not thereby made a trader within the ſtatutes. No perſon can be made a bankrupt for debts which he is not liable at law to pay. But a feme covert in London, being a ſole trader according to the cuſtom, is liable to a commiſſion of bankrupt.

2. Having thus conſidered, who may, and who may not be made a bankrupt, we are to inquire, ſecondly, by what *acts* a man may become a bankrupt. And, in general, whenever ſuch a trader as is before deſcribed, hath endeavoured to avoid his creditors, or evade their juſt demands, this hath been declared by the legiſlature to be an act of bankruptcy, upon which a commiſſion may be ſued out.

Among theſe may therefore be reckoned, 1. Departing

from the realm with intent to defraud his creditors (*a*). 2. Departing from his own houfe, with intent to fecrete himfelf, and avoid his creditors. 3. Keeping in his own houfe, privately, fo as not to be feen or fpoken with by his creditors, except for juft and neceffary caufe. 4. Procuring or fuffering himfelf willingly to be arrefted, or outlawed, or imprifoned, without juft and lawful caufe. 5. Procuring his money, goods, chattels, and effects to be attached or fequeftered by any legal procefs (*b*). 6. Making any fraudulent conveyance to a friend, or fecret truftee, of his lands, tenements, goods, or chattels (*c*). 7. Procuring any protection, not being himfelf privileged by parliament, in order to fcreen his perfon from arrefts. 8. Endeavouring or defiring, by any petition to the king, or bill exhibited in any of the king's courts' againft any creditors, to compel them to take lefs than their juft debts; or to procraftinate the time of payment, originally contracted for. 9. Lying in prifon for two months, or

---

(*a*) And though it were not with an exprefs *intent* to defraud his creditors, yet, if in *fact* they were defrauded or delayed by fuch abfence, it will be confidered to be a departure for that purpofe. *Woodier's cafe*, Bul. Ni. Pri. 39. *Raikes* v. *Porceau*, 1 Cooke's Bank. L. 92. Upon which Mr. *J. Buller*, in his obfervations upon the latter cafe remarked, that, " if he were then laying down the law for the firft time, he did not know that he fhould do it in that manner, but that he was bound by decided authority."

(*b*) Hence one might conclude that a fraudulent judgment and execution would conftitute an act of bankruptcy, but it is faid, that the attachment the legiflature had in view, is that by which fuits are commenced in London, and other places where that procefs is ufed; and it has been held, therefore, that execution on judgment is not within the ftatute. *Clavey* v. *Haley*, Cowp. 427. *Harman* v. *Spottifwood*, 1 Cooke's B. L. 122.

(*c*) This feems to be fomewhat too indefinitely expreffed, for it has been held, that a fraudulent conveyance, to come within the meaning of the ftatute, muft be by *deed*; therefore a fale of goods without deed, though fraudulent, is no act of bankruptcy. *Martin* v. *Pewtrefs*, 4 Bur. 2478.

more, upon arreſt or other detention for debt, without finding bail, in order to obtain his liberty. 10. Eſcaping from priſon after an arreſt for a juſt debt of 100l. or upwards. 11. Neglecting to make ſatisfaction for any juſt debt to the amount of 100l. within two months after ſervice of legal proceſs for ſuch debt, upon any trader having privilege of parliament. Let us next conſider,

3. The *proceedings* on a commiſſion of bankrupt, ſo far as they affect the bankrupt himſelf.

And, firſt, there muſt be a *petition* to the lord chancellor by one creditor to the amount of 100l. or by two to the amount of 150l. or by three or more to the amount of 200l; which debts muſt be proved by *affidavit*: upon which he grants a *commiſſion* to ſuch diſcreet perſons as to him ſhall ſeem good, who are then ſtiled commiſſioners of bankrupt. The petitioners, to prevent malicious applications, muſt be bound in a ſecurity of 200l. to make the party amends in caſe they do not prove him a bankrupt. And if on the other hand they receive any money or effects from the bankrupt, as a recompenſe for ſuing out the commiſſion, ſo as to receive more than their rateable dividends of the bankrupt's eſtate, they forfeit not only what they ſhall have ſo received, but the whole debt.

When the commiſſioners have received their commiſſion, they are firſt to receive proof of the perſon's being a trader, and having committed ſome act of bankruptcy; and then to declare him a bankrupt, if proved ſo; and to give notice thereof in the Gazette, and at the ſame time to appoint three meetings. At one of theſe meetings an election muſt be made of aſſignees, or perſons to whom the bankrupt's eſtate ſhall be aſſigned, and in whom it ſhall be veſted for the benefit of the creditors; which aſſignees are to be choſen by the major part, in value, of the creditors, who ſhall then have proved their debt; but may be originally appointed by the commiſſioners, and afterwards approved or rejected by the creditors: but no creditor ſhall be admitted to vote in the choice of aſſignees, whoſe debt on the ballance of accounts does not amount to 10l. And at the third meeting, at far-theft, which muſt be on the forty-ſecond day after the advertiſement in the gazette, (unleſs the time be enlarged by the lord chancellor) the bankrupt, upon notice alſo perſonally ſerved upon him or left as his uſual place of abode, muſt ſurrender himſelf perſonally to the commiſſioners; which ſurrender (if voluntary) protects him from all arreſts till his final examination is paſt: and he muſt thenceforth in all reſpects conform to the directions of the ſtatutes of bankruptcy; or, in default of either ſurrender or conformity, ſhall be guilty of felony without benefit of clergy, and ſhall ſuffer death, and his goods and eſtate ſhall be diſtributed among his creditors.

When the bankrupt appears, the commiſſioners are to examine him touching all matters relating to his trade and effects. The bankrupt, upon this examination, is bound upon pain of death to make a full diſcovery of all his eſtate and effects, as well in expectancy as poſſeſſion, and how he has diſpoſed of the ſame; together with all books and writings relating thereto: and is to deliver up all in his own power to the commiſſioners; (except the neceſſary apparel of himſelf, his wife, and his children) or, in caſe he conceals or embezzles any effects to the amount of 20l. or withholds any books or writings, with intent to defraud his creditors, he ſhall be guilty of felony without benefit of clergy; and his goods and eſtate ſhall be divided among his creditors.

After the time allowed to the bankrupt for ſuch diſcovery is expired, any other perſon voluntarily diſcovering any part of his eſtate, before unknown to the aſſignees, ſhall be entitled to *five per cent.* out of the effects ſo diſcovered, and ſuch farther reward as the aſſignees and commiſſioners ſhall think proper. And any truſtee wilfully concealing the eſtate of any bankrupt, after the expiration of the two and forty days, ſhall forfeit 100l. and double the value of the eſtate concealed to the creditors (*a*).

---

(*a*) But by 28 Geo. III. c. 24. ſ. 21, in order to make a truſtee ſo liable, notice muſt be given in the *London Gazette* of the party's being bankrupt.

If the bankrupt hath conformed in all points to the directions of the law, and the creditors, or four parts in five of them in number and value, (but none of them creditors for lefs than 20l.) will sign a certificate to that purport; the commiſſioners are then to authenticate ſuch certificate under their hands and ſeals, and to tranſmit it to the lord chancellor: and he, or two of the judges whom he ſhall appoint, on oath made by the bankrupt that ſuch certificate was obtained without fraud, may allow the ſame; or diſallow it upon cauſe ſhewn by any of the creditors of the bankrupt.

If no cauſe be ſhewn to the contrary, the certificate is allowed of courſe; and then the bankrupt is entitled to a decent and reaſonable allowance out of his effects. If his effects will not pay one half of his debts, or ten ſhillings in the pound, he is left to the diſcretion of the commiſſioners and aſſignees, to have a competent ſum allowed him, not exceeding *three per cent.* but if they pay ten ſhillings in the pound, he is to be allowed *five per cent.*; if twelve ſhillings and ſixpence, then *ſeven and a half per cent.*; and if fifteen ſhillings in the pound, then the bankrupt ſhall be allowed *ten per cent.* provided that ſuch allowance do not in the firſt caſe exceed 200l. in the ſecond, 250l. and in the third, 300l.

Beſides this allowance, he has alſo an indemnity granted him, of being free and diſcharged for ever from all debts owing by him at the time he became a bankrupt.

But if any creditor produces a fictitious debt, and the bankrupt does not make diſcovery of it, but ſuffers the fair creditors to be impoſed upon, he loſes all title to theſe advantages. Neither can he claim them if he has given with any of his children above 100l. for a marriage portion, unleſs he had at that time ſufficient left to pay all his debts; or if he has loſt at any one time 5l. or in the whole 100l. within a twelvemonth before he became bankrupt, by any manner of gaming or wagering whatſoever; or within the ſame time has loſt to the value of 100l. by ſtock-jobbing. Alſo, ſuch as have been once cleared by a commiſſion of bankrupt, or have been delivered by an act of inſolvency, and afterwards become bankrupts again, unleſs they pay full fifteen shillings in the pound, are only thereby indemnified as to the confinement of their bodies ; but any future estate they shall acquire remains liable to their creditors, excepting their necessary apparel, household goods, and the tools and implements of their trades.

Let us next consider,

4. How such proceedings affect or transfer the *estate* and *property* of the bankrupt. The method whereby a *real* estate, in lands, tenements, and hereditaments, may be transferred by bankruptcy, was shewn under its proper head in a former chapter. At present we are only to consider the transfer of things *personal* by this operation of law.

All the personal estate and effects of the bankrupt are considered as vested, by the act of bankruptcy, in the future assignees of his commissioners, whether they be goods in actual *possession*, or debts, contracts, and other choses in *action* ; and the commissioners by their warrant may cause any house or tenement of the bankrupt to be broke open, in order to enter upon and seize the same. And when the assignees are chosen or approved by the creditors, the commissioners are to assign every thing over to them ; and the property of every part of the estate is thereby as fully vested in them, as it was in the bankrupt himself, and they have the same remedies to recover it.

The property vested in the assignees is the whole that the bankrupt had in himself, at the time he committed the first act of bankruptcy, or that has been vested in him since, before his debts are satisfied or agreed for. Insomuch that all transactions of the bankrupt are from that time absolutely null and void, either with regard to the alienation of his property, or the receipt of his debts from such as are privy to his bankruptcy ; for they are no longer his property, or his debts, but those of the future assignees. And, if an execution be sued out, but not served and executed on the bankrupt's effects till after the act of bankruptcy, it is void as against the assignees. But the king is not bound by this fictitious relation, nor is within the statutes of bankrupts ; for if, after the act of bankruptcy committed, and before the assignment of his effects, an extent issues for the debt of the crown, the goods are bound thereby. But as acts of bankruptcy may sometimes be secret to all but a few, it is provided by statute 19 Geo. II. c. 32. that no money paid by a bankrupt to a *bona fide* or real creditor, in a course of trade, even after an act of bankruptcy done, shall be liable to be refunded. Nor, by statute 1 Jac. I. c. 15. shall any debtor of a bankrupt, that pays him his debt, without knowing of his bankruptcy, be liable to account for it again.

The assignees may pursue any *legal* method of recovering this property so vested in them, by their own authority; but cannot commence a suit in *equity*, nor compound any debts owing to the bankrupt, nor refer any matters to arbitration, without the consent of the creditors, or the major part of them in value, at a meeting to be held in pursuance of notice in the Gazette.

When they have got in all the effects they can reasonably hope for, and reduced them to ready money, the assignees must, after four and within twelve months after the commission issued, give one and twenty days notice to the creditors of a meeting for a dividend or distribution; at which time they must produce their accounts, and verify them upon oath, if required. And then the commissioners shall direct a dividend to be made, at so much in the pound, to all creditors who have before proved, or shall then prove, their debts. This dividend must be made equally, and in a rateable proportion, to all the creditors, according to the *quantity* of their debts; no regard being had to the *quality* of them. Mortgages indeed, for which the creditor has a real security in his own hands, are entirely safe; for the commission of bankrupt reaches only the equity of redemption. So are also personal debts, where the creditor has a chattel in his hands, as a pledge or pawn for the payment, or has taken the debtor's lands or goods in execution. And, upon the equity of the statute 8 Ann. c. 14. (which directs, that, upon all executions of goods being on any premises demised to a tenant, one year's rent and no more, shall, if due, be paid to the landlord) it hath alfo been held, that under a commiffion of bankrupt, which is in the nature of a ftatute-execution, the landlord fhall be allowed his arrears of rent to the fame amount, in preference to other creditors, even though he hath neglected to diftrein, while the goods remained on the premifes (a): which he is otherwife entitled to do for his intire rent, be the *quantum* what it may. But, otherwife, judgments and recognizances, (both which are debts of record, and therefore at other times have a priority) and alfo bonds and obligations by deed or fpecial inftrument (which are called debts by fpecialty, and are ufually the next in order) are put on a level with debts by mere fimple contract, and all paid *pari paffu*. Nay, fo far is this matter carried, that, by the exprefs provifion of the ftatutes, debts not due at the time of the dividend made, as bonds or notes of hand payable at a future day certain, fhall be proved and paid equally with the reft, allowing a difcount or drawback in proportion. And infurances, and obligations upon bottomry or *refpondentia*, *bona fide* made by the bankrupt, though forfeited after the commiffion is awarded, fhall be looked upon in the fame light as debts contracted before any act of bankruptcy.

Within eighteen months after the commiffion iffued, a fecond and final dividend fhall be made, unlefs all the effects were exhaufted by the firft. And if any furplus remains, after felling his eftates and paying every creditor his full debt, it fhall be reftored to the bankrupt.

---

(a) This is not correct: the landlord has a lien on the goods of a bankrupt, notwithftanding the commiffion and affignment, *whilft the goods remain upon the premifes*, Ex parte, *Plummer*, 1 *Atk.* 103. but *not afterwards.* Ex parte *Devine* reported, 1 *Cooke's B. L.* 221, and *Bradyll* v. *Ball*, 1 *Brow. Ch. Ca.* 427.

## CHAPTER XXVI.

### OF TITLE BY TESTAMENT, AND ADMINISTRATION.

THERE yet remain to be examined, in the present chapter, two other methods of acquiring personal estates, viz. by *testament* and *administration*. Regularly, every person hath full power and liberty to make a will, that is not under some special prohibition by law or custom: which prohibitions are principally upon three accounts; for want of sufficient discretion; for want of sufficient liberty and free will; and on account of their criminal conduct.

1. In the first species are to be reckoned infants, under the age of fourteen if males, and twelve if females; so that no objection can be admitted to the will of an infant of fourteen, merely for want of age: but, if the testator was not of sufficient discretion, whether at the age of fourteen or four and twenty, that will overthrow his testament. Madmen, or otherwise *non compotes*, ideots or natural fools, persons grown childish by reason of old age or distemper, such as have their senses besotted with drunkenness,—all these are incapable, by reason of mental disability, to make any will so long as such disability lasts.

2. Such persons as are intestable for want of liberty or freedom of will, are, by the civil law, of various kinds; as prisoners, captives, and the like. But the law of England leaves it to the discretion of the court to judge, upon the consideration of their particular circumstances of duress, whether or no such persons could be supposed to have *liberum animum testandi*. And, with regard to feme-coverts, a married woman is not only utterly incapable of devising *lands*, being excepted out of the statute of wills, 34 & 35 Hen. VIII. c. 5. but also she is incapable of making a testament of *chattels* without the licence of her husband. For all her personal chattels are absolutely his. Yet by her husband's licence she may make a testament; and the husband, upon marriage, frequently covenants with her friends to allow her that li-

cence: but such licence is more properly his assent; for, unless it be given to the particular will in question, it will not be a complete testament, even though the husband beforehand hath given her permission to make a will. Yet it shall be sufficient to repel the husband from his general right of administering his wife's effects; and administration shall be granted to her appointee, with such testamentary paper annexed. And any feme-covert may make her will of goods, which are in her possession *in auter droit*, as executrix or administratrix; for these can never be the property of the husband: and, if she has any pinmoney or separate maintenance, it is said she may dispose of her saving thereout by testament, without the controul of her husband. But, if a feme-sole makes her will, and afterwards marries, such subsequent marriage is esteemed a revocation in law, and entirely vacates the will.

3. Persons incapable of making testaments, on account of their criminal conduct, are in the first place all traitors and felons, from the time of conviction; for then their goods and chattels are no longer at their own disposal, but forfeited to the king. Neither can a *felo de se* make a will of goods and chattels, for they are forfeited by the act and manner of his death; but he may make a devise of his lands, for they are not subjected to any forfeiture. Outlaws also, though it be but for debt, are incapable of making a will, so long as the outlawry subsists, for their goods and chattels are forfeited during that time.

Let us next, *thirdly*, consider what this last will and testament is, which almost every one is thus at liberty to make; or, what are the nature and incidents of a testament.

Testaments are divided into two sorts; *written*, and *verbal* or *nuncupative*; of which the former is committed to writing, the latter depends merely upon oral evidence, being declared by the testator *in extremis* before a sufficient number of witnesses, and afterwards reduced to writing. A *codicil*, is a supplement to a will; or an addition made by the testator, and annexed to, and to be taken as part of, a testament: being for it's explanation, or alteration, or to make some addition to, or elſe ſome ſubtraction from, the former diſpoſitions of the teſtator. This may alſo be either written or nuncupative.

But, as *nuncupative* wills and codicils are liable to great impoſitions, and may occaſion many perjuries, the ſtatute of frauds, 29 Car. II. c. 3. hath laid them under many reſtrictions; except when made by mariners at ſea, and ſoldiers in actual ſervice. As to all other perſons, it enacts;
1. That no written will ſhall be revoked or altered by a ſubſequent nuncupative one, except the ſame be in the lifetime of the teſtator reduced to writing, and read over to him, and approved; and unleſs the ſame be proved to have been ſo done by the oaths of three witneſſes at the leaſt; who, by ſtatute 4 & 5 Ann. c. 16. muſt be ſuch as are admiſſible upon trials at common law. 2. That no nuncupative will ſhall in any wiſe be good, where the eſtate bequeathed exceeds 30*l.* unleſs proved by three ſuch witneſſes, preſent at the making thereof, and unleſs they or ſome of them were ſpecially required to bear witneſs thereto by the teſtator himſelf; and unleſs it was made in his laſt ſickneſs, in his own habitation or dwelling-houſe, or where he had been previouſly reſident ten days at the leaſt, except he be ſurprized with ſickneſs on a journey, or from home, and dies without returning to his dwelling. 3. That no nuncupative will ſhall be proved by the witneſſes after ſix months from the making, unleſs it were put in writing within ſix days. Nor ſhall it be proved till fourteen days after the death of the teſtator, nor till proceſs hath firſt iſſued to call in the widow, or next of kin, to conteſt it if they think proper.

As to *written* wills, they need not any witneſs of their publication. I ſpeak not here of deviſes of lands, which are quite of a different nature; but a teſtament of chattels, written in the teſtator's own hand, though it has neither his name nor ſeal to it, nor witneſſes preſent at it's publication, is good; provided ſufficient proof can be had that it is his hand-writing. And though written in another man's hand, and never ſigned by the teſtator, yet if proved to be according to his inſtructions and approved by him, it hath been held a good teftament of the perfonal eftate. Yet it is the fafer and more prudent way, and leaves lefs in the breaft of the ecclefiaftical judge, if it be figned or fealed by the teftator, and publifhed in the prefence of witneffes.

No teftament is of any effect till after the death of the teftator. " *Nam omne teftamentum morte confummatum eft: et voluntas teftatoris eft ambulatoria ufque ad mortem.*" And therefore, if there be many teftaments, the laft overthrows all the former: but the republication of a former will revokes one of a later date, and eftablifhes the firft again.

Hence it follows, that teftaments may be avoided three ways: 1. If made by a perfon labouring under any of the incapacities before-mentioned: 2. By making another teftament of a later date: and, 3, By cancelling or revoking it. It hath alfo been held, that, without an exprefs revocation, if a man, who hath made his will, afterwards marries and hath a child, this is a prefumptive or implied revocation of his former will, which he made in his ftate of celibacy.

We are next to confider, *fourthly*, what is an executor, and what an adminiftrator; and how they are both to be appointed.

An executor is he to whom another man commits by will the execution of that his laft will and teftament. And all perfons are capable of being executors, that are capable of making wills, and many others befides; as feme-coverts, and infants: nay, even infants unborn, or *in ventre fa mere*, may be made executors. But no infant can act as fuch till the age of feventeen years; till which time adminiftration muft be granted to fome other, *durante minore ætate*. In like manner as it may be granted *durante abfentia*, or *pendente lite*; when the executor is out of the realm, or when a fuit is commenced in the ecclefiaftical court touching the validity of the will. This appointment of an executor is effential to the making of a will: and it may be performed either by exprefs words, or fuch as ftrongly imply the fame. But if the teftator makes an incomplete will, without naming any executors, or if he names incapable perfons, or if the executors named refufe to act; in any of thefe cafes, the ordinary muft grant administration *cum testamento annexo* to some other person; and then the duty of the administrator, as also when he is constituted only *durante minore ætate, &c.* of another, is very little different from that of an executor.

But if the deceased died wholly intestate, without making either will or executors, then general letters of administration must be granted by the ordinary to such administrator as the statutes of Edward the third and Henry the eighth direct. In consequence of which we may observe; 1. That the ordinary is compellable to grant administration of the goods and chattels of the wife, to the husband or his representatives: and of the husband's effects, to the widow, or next of kin; but he may grant it to either, or both, at his discretion 2. That, among the kindred, those are to be preferred that are the nearest in degree to the intestate; but, of persons in equal degree, the ordinary may take which he pleases. 3. That this *nearness* or propinquity of degree shall be reckoned according to the computation of the civilians; and not of the canonists, which the law of England adopts in the descent of real estates. And therefore in the first place the children, or, (on failure of children) the parents of the deceased, are entitled to the administration: both which are indeed in the first degree; but with us the children are allowed the preference. Then follow brothers, grandfathers, uncles or nephews, (and the females of each class respectively) and lastly cousins. 4. The half blood is admitted to the administration as well as the whole: for they are of the kindred of the intestate, and only excluded from inheritances of land upon feodal reasons. Therefore the brother of the half blood shall exclude the uncle of the whole blood; and the ordinary may grant administration to the sister of the half, or the brother of the whole blood, at his own discretion. 5. If none of the kindred will take out administration, a creditor may, by custom, do it. 6. If the executor refuses, or dies intestate, the administration may be granted to the residuary legatee, in exclusion of the next of kin. 7. And, lastly, the ordinary may, in defect of all these, commit administration to such discreet person as he approves of:

or may grant him letters *ad colligendum bona defuncti*, which neither makes him executor nor adminiftrator; his only bufinefs being to keep the goods in his fafe cuftody, and to do other acts for the benefit of fuch as are entitled to the property of the deceafed. If a baftard, who has no kindred, being *nullius filius*, or any one elfe that has no kindred, dies inteftate and without wife or child, the ufual courfe is for fome one to procure letters patent, or other authority from the king; and then the ordinary of courfe grants adminiftration to fuch appointee of the crown.

The intereft, vefted in the executor, by the will of the deceafed, may be continued and kept alive by the will of the fame executor: fo that the executor of A's executor is to all intents and purpofes the executor and reprefentative of A himfelf; but the executor of A's adminiftrator, or the adminiftrator of A's executor, is not the reprefentative of A. Wherefore in both thefe cafes, and whenever the courfe of reprefentation from executor to executor is interrupted by any one adminiftration, it is neceffary for the ordinary to commit adminiftration afrefh, *of the goods* of the deceafed *not* adminiftered by the former executor or adminiftrator. And this adminiftrator, *de bonis non*, is the only legal reprefentative of the deceafed in matters of perfonal property. But he may, as well as an original adminiftrator, have only a *limited* or *fpecial* adminiftration committed to his care, *viz.* of certain fpecific effects, fuch as a term of years and the like; the reft being committed to others.

Having thus fhewn what is, and who may be, an executor or adminiftrator, I proceed now, *fifthly* and laftly, to inquire into fome few of the principal points of their office and duty. Thefe in general are very much the fame in both executors and adminiftrators; excepting, firft, that the executor is bound to perform a will, which an adminiftrator is not, unlefs where a teftament is annexed to his adminiftration, and then he differs ftill lefs from an executor: and, fecondly, that an executor may do many acts before he proves the will, but an adminiftrator may do nothing till letters of adminiftration are iffued; for the former derives his power from the will and not from the probate, the latter owes his entirely to the appointment of the ordinary. If a stranger takes upon him to act as executor, without any just authority, (as by intermeddling with the goods of the deceased, and many other transactions) he is called in law an executor of his own wrong, *de son tort*, and is liable to all the trouble of an executorship, without any of the profits or advantages: but merely doing acts of necessity or humanity, as locking up the goods, or burying the corpse of the deceased, will not amount to such an intermeddling, as will charge a man as executor of his own wrong. Such a one cannot bring an action himself in right of the deceased, but actions may be brought against him. And, in all actions by creditors, against such an officious intruder, he shall be named an executor, generally; for the most obvious conclusion, which strangers can form from his conduct, is that he hath a will of the deceased, wherein he is named executor, but hath not yet taken probate thereof. He is chargeable with the debts of the deceased, so far as assets come to his hands: and, as against creditors in general, shall be allowed all payments made to any other creditor in the same or a superior degree, himself only excepted. And though, as against the rightful executor or administrator, he cannot plead such payment, yet it shall be allowed him in mitigation of damages; unless perhaps upon a deficiency of assets, whereby the rightful executor may be prevented from satisfying his own debt. But let us now see what are the power and duty of a rightful executor or administrator.

1. He must *bury* the deceased in a manner suitable to the estate which he leaves behind him. Necessary funeral expences are allowed, previous to all other debts and charges; but if the executor or administrator be extravagant, it is a species of *devastation* or waste of the substance of the deceased, and shall only be prejudicial to himself, and not to the creditors or legatees of the deceased.

2. The executor, or the administrator *durante minore ætate*, or *durante absentia*, or *cum testamento annexo*, must *prove the will* of the deceased: which is done either in *common form*,

which is only upon his own oath before the ordinary, or his furrogate; or *per testes*, in more folemn form of law, in cafe the validity of the will be difputed. When the will is fo proved, the original muft be depofited in the regiftry of the ordinary; and a copy thereof in parchment is made out under the feal of the ordinary, and delivered to the executor or adminiftrator, together with a certificate of it's having been proved before him: all which together is ufually ftiled the *probate*. In defect of any will, the perfon entitled to be adminiftrator muft alfo at this period take out letters of adminiftration under the feal of the ordinary; whereby an executorial power to collect and adminifter, that is, difpofe of the goods of the deceafed, is vefted in him: and he muft, by ftatute 22 & 23 Car. II. c. 10. enter into a bond with fureties, faithfully to execute his truft. If all the goods of the deceafed lie within the fame jurifdiction, a probate before the ordinary, or an adminiftration granted by him, are the only proper ones: but if the deceafed had *bona notabilia*, or chattels to the value of a *hundred fhillings*, in two diftinct diocefes or jurifdictions, then the will muft be proved, or adminiftration taken out, before the metropolitan of the province, by way of fpecial prerogative; whence the courts where the validity of fuch wills is tried, and the offices where they are regiftered, are called the prerogative courts, and the prerogative offices, of the provinces of Canterbury and York.

3. The executor or adminiftrator is to make an *inventory* of all the goods and chattels, whether in poffeffion or action, of the deceafed; which he is to deliver in to the ordinary upon oath, if thereunto lawfully required.

4. He is to *collect* all the goods and chattels fo inventoried; and to that end he has very large powers and interefts conferred on him by law; being the reprefentative of the deceafed, and having the fame property in his goods as the principal had when living, and the fame remedies to recover them. And if there be two or more executors, a fale or releafe by one of them fhall be good againft all the reft; but in cafe of adminiftrators it is otherwife. Whatever is fo recovered, that is of a faleable nature and may be con-

verted into ready money, is called *affets* in the hands of the executor or adminiſtrator; that is ſufficient or enough (from the French *affez*) to make him chargeable to a creditor or legatee, ſo far as ſuch goods and chattels extend. Whatever affets ſo come to his hands he may convert into ready money, to anſwer the demands that may be made upon him: which is the next thing to be conſidered; for,

5. The executor or adminiſtrator muſt *pay* the *debts* of the deceaſed. In payment of debts he muſt obſerve the rules of priority; otherwiſe, on deficiency of aſſets, if he pays thoſe of a lower degree firſt, he muſt anſwer thoſe of a higher out of his own eſtate. And, firſt, he may pay all funeral charges, and the expence of proving the will, and the like. Secondly, debts due to the king on record or ſpecialty. Thirdly, ſuch debts as are by particular ſtatutes to be preferred to all others; as the forfeitures for not burying in woollen, money due upon poors rates, for letters to the poſt-office, and ſome others. Fourthly, debts of record; as judgments (docquetted according to the ſtatute 4 & 5 W. & M. c. 20.) ſtatutes, and recognizances *(a)*. Fifthly, debts due on ſpecial contracts; as for rent, (for which the leſſor has often a better remedy in his own hands, by diſtreining) or upon bonds, covenants and the like, under ſeal *(b)*. Laſtly, debts on ſimple contracts, *viz.* upon notes unſealed, and verbal promiſes. Among theſe ſimple contracts, ſervants wages are by ſome with reaſon preferred to any other. Among debts of equal degree, the executor or adminiſtrator is allowed to pay himſelf firſt; by retaining in his hands ſo much as his debt amounts to. But an executor of his own wrong is not allowed to retain. If a creditor conſtitutes his debtor his executor, this is a releaſe or diſcharge of the debt, whether

---

*(a)* And decrees of courts of equity, *Morrice* v. *Bank of England,* Ca. Temp. Talb. 217. ‡ 1 P. Wms. 401. n. [F.]

*(b) Viz.* If founded on valuable conſideration, otherwiſe they will, in equity, be poſtponed to ſimple contract debts, per *Jekyll,* M. R. in *Lechmere* v. *E. of Carliſle,* 3 P. Wms. 222.

the executor acts or no; provided there be affets fufficient to pay the teftator's debts. Alfo, if no fuit is commenced againft him, the executor may pay one creditor in equal degree his whole debt, though he has nothing left for the reft: for, without a fuit commenced, the executor has no legal notice of the debt.

6. When the debts are all difcharged, the *legacies* claim the next regard; which are to be paid by the executor fo far as his affets will extend; but he may not give himfelf the preference herein, as in the cafe of debts.

A legacy is a bequeft, or gift, of goods and chattels by teftament; and the perfon to whom it was given is ftiled the legatee: which every perfon is capable of being, unlefs particularly difabled by the common law or ftatutes, as traitors, papifts, and fome others. This bequeft transfers an inchoate property to the legatee; but the legacy is not perfect without the affent of the executor: for if I have a *general* or *pecuniary* legacy of 100*l*. or a *fpecific* one of a piece of plate, I cannot, in either cafe, take it without the confent of the executor. For in him all the chattels are vefted; and it is his bufinefs firft of all to fee whether there is a fufficient fund left to pay the debts of the teftator. And in cafe of a deficiency of affets, all the *general* legacies muft abate proportionably, in order to pay the debts; but a *fpecific* legacy (of a piece of plate, a horfe, or the like) is not to abate at all, or allow any thing by way of abatement, unlefs there be not fufficient without it. Upon the fame principle, if the legatees have been paid their legacies, they are afterwards bound to refund a rateable part, in cafe debts come in, more than fufficient to exhauft the *refiduum* after the legacies paid.

If the legatee dies before the teftator, the legacy is a loft or *lapfed* legacy, and fhall fink into the *refiduum*. And if a *contingent* legacy be left to any one; as *when* he attains, or *if* he attains, the age of twenty-one; and he dies before that time; it is a lapfed legacy. But a legacy to one, *to be paid* when he attains the age of twenty-one years, is a *vefted* legacy; an intereft which commences *in præfenti*, although it be *solvendum in futuro (a)*: and, if the legatee dies before that age, his representatives shall receive it out of the testator's personal estate, at the same time that it would have become payable, in case the legatee had lived. And, in case of a vested legacy, due immediately, and charged on lands or money in the funds, which yield an immediate profit, interest shall be payable thereon from the testator's death; but if charged only on the personal estate, which cannot be immediately got in, it shall carry interest only from the end of the year after the death of the testator.

Besides these formal legacies, contained in a man's will and testament, there is also permitted another death-bed disposition of property; which is called a donation *causa mortis*. And that is, when a person in his last sickness (b), apprehending his dissolution near, delivers or causes to be delivered to another the possession of any personal goods, (under which have been included bonds, and bills drawn by the deceased upon his banker) (c) to keep in case of his deceafe. This gift, if the donor dies, needs not the assent of his executor: yet it shall not prevail against creditors; and is accompanied with this implied trust, that, if the donor lives,

---

(a) This distinction in the construction of wills, was adopted because it was imagined to be consonant with the *intention* of the testator, which the courts are, in all cases, anxious to preserve; if, therefore, there are any circumstances in the will to controul this construction, the intention shall prevail, however inexplicitly the testator may have expressed himself. See *D. of Chandos* v. *Talbot*, 2 P. Wms. 601. and the authorities referred to by Mr. *Cox, ibid,* 612. n. (1). also *Co. Lit.* 237 ª. n. (1).

(b) That it should be in his last sickness was held to be material by *Sir J. Jekyl, M. R.* in *Miller* v. *Miller*, 3 P. Wms. 356. but in *Jones* v. *Selby, Prec. Ch.* 300. and *Hill* v. *Chapman*, 2 Brow. Ch. Ca. 612. this circumstance seems to have been disregarded.

(c) *Sed vid, Tate* v. *Tate*, 4 Brow. Ch. Ca. 286. 2 F. *Vez.* 111. where a draft on the deceased's banker was considered not to be the subject of a *donatio causa mortis.*

the property thereof shall revert to himself, being only given in contemplation of death, or *mortis caufa*.

7. When all the debts and particular legacies are difcharged, the furplus or *refiduum* muft be paid to the refiduary legatee, if any be appointed by the will; and if there be none, it was long a fettled notion that it devolved to the executor's own ufe, by virtue of his executorfhip. But whatever ground there might have been formerly for this opinion, it feems now to be underftood with this reftriction; that, although where the executor has no legacy at all the *refiduum* fhall in general be his own, yet wherever there is fufficient on the face of a will, (by means of a competent legacy or otherwife) to imply that the teftator intended his executor fhould *not* have the refidue, the undevifed furplus of the eftate fhall go to the next of kin, the executor then ftanding upon exactly the fame footing as an adminiftrator: concerning whom indeed there formerly was much debate, whether or no he could be compelled to make any diftribution of the inteftate's eftate. But now, by ftatute 22 & 23 Car. II. c. 10. explained by 29 Car. II. c. 30. it is enacted, that the furplufage of inteftates' eftates, (except of femes covert, which are left as at common law) fhall, after the expiration of one full year from the death of the inteftate, be diftributed in the following manner. One third fhall go to the widow of the inteftate, and the refidue in equal proportions to his children, or if dead, to their reprefentatives; that is, their lineal defcendants: if there are no children or legal reprefentatives fubfifting, then a moiety fhall go to the widow, and a moiety to the next of kindred in equal degree and their reprefentatives: if no widow, the whole fhall go to the children: if neither widow nor children, the whole fhall be diftributed among the next of kin in equal degree and their reprefentatives: but no reprefentatives are admitted, among collaterals, farther than the children of the inteftate's brothers and fifters. The next of kindred, here referred to, are to be inveftigated by the fame rules of confanguinity, as thofe who are entitled to letters of adminiftration.

And therefore, by this statute, the mother, as well as the father, succeeded to all the personal effects of their children, who died intestate and without wife or issue: in exclusion of the other sons and daughters, the brothers and sisters of the deceased. And so the law still remains with respect to the father; but, by statute 1 Jac. II. c. 17. if the father be dead, and any of the children die intestate without wife or issue, in the lifetime of the mother, she and each of the remaining children, or their representatives, shall divide his effects in equal portions.

There is another part of the statute of distributions, where directions are given that no child of the intestate, (except his heir at law) on whom he settled in his lifetime any estate in lands, or any pecuniary portion equal to the distributive shares of the other children, shall have any part of the surplusage with their brothers and sisters; but if the estates so given them, by way of advancement, are not quite equivalent to the other shares, the children so advanced shall now have so much as will make them equal.

The statute of distributions expressly excepts and reserves the customs of the city of London, of the province of York, and of all other places having peculiar customs of distributing intestates' effects. I shall therefore conclude this chapter, and with it the present book, with a few remarks on those customs.

In the first place we may observe, that in the city of London, and province of York, as well as in the kingdom of Scotland, and probably also in Wales, (concerning which there is little to be gathered, but from the statute 7 & 8 W. III. c. 38.) the effects of the intestate, after payment of his debts, are in general divided according to the antient universal doctrine of the *pars rationabilis*. If the deceased leaves a widow and children, his substance (deducting for the widow's her apparel and the furniture of her bed-chamber, which in London is called the *widow's chamber*) is divided into three parts; one of which belongs to the widow, another to the children, and the third to the administrator: if only a widow, or only children, they shall respectively, in either case, take one moiety, and the administrator the other; if neither widow nor child, the administrator shall have the whole. And this portion, or *dead man*'s part, the administrator was wont to apply to his own use, till the statute 1 Jac. II. c. 17. declared that the same should be subject to the statute of distribution. So that if a man dies worth 1800*l*. personal estate, leaving a widow and two children, this estate shall be divided into eighteen parts; whereof the widow shall have eight, six by the custom and two by the statute; and each of the children five, three by the custom and two by the statute: if he leaves a widow and one child, she shall still have eight parts, as before; and the child shall have ten, six by the custom and four by the statute: if he leaves a widow and no child, the widow shall have three fourths of the whole, two by the custom and one by the statute; and the remaining fourth shall go by the statute to the next of kin. It is also to be observed, that if the wife be provided for by a jointure before marriage, in bar of her customary part, it puts her in a state of non-entity, with regard to the custom only; but she shall be entitled to her share of the dead man's part under the statute of distributions, unless barred by special agreement. And if any of the children are advanced by the father in his lifetime with any sum of money (not amounting to their full proportionable part) they shall bring that portion into hotchpot with the rest of the brothers and sisters, but not with the widow, before they are entitled to any benefit under the custom: but, if they are fully advanced, the custom entitles them to no farther dividend.

Thus far in the main the customs of London and of York agree: but, besides certain other less material variations, there are two principal points in which they considerably differ. One is, that in London the share of the children (or orphanage part) is not fully vested in them till the age of twenty-one, before which they cannot dispose of it by testament: and if they die under that age, whether sole or married, their share shall survive to the other children; but after the age of twenty-one, it is free from any orphanage custom, and in case of intestacy, shall fall under the statute of distributions. The other, that in the province of York, the heir at common law, who inherits any land either in fee or in tail, is excluded from any filial portion or reasonable part.

THE END OF THE SECOND BOOK.

# BOOK THE THIRD.

## OF PRIVATE WRONGS.

### CHAPTER I.
#### OF THE REDRESS OF PRIVATE WRONGS BY THE MERE ACT OF THE PARTIES.

WRONGS are divisible into two sorts or species; *private wrongs*, and *public wrongs*. The former are an infringement or privation of the private or civil rights belonging to individuals, considered as individuals; and are thereupon frequently termed *civil injuries:* the latter are a breach and violation of public rights and duties, which affect the whole community, considered as a community; and are distinguished by the harsher appellation of *crimes* and *misdemesnors*.

The more effectually to accomplish the redress of private injuries, courts of justice are instituted in every civilized society. This remedy is therefore principally sought by application to these courts of justice; that is, by civil suit or action. But as there are certain injuries of such a nature, that some of them furnish and others require a more speedy remedy than can be had in the ordinary forms of justice, there is allowed in those cases an extra-judicial or eccentrical kind of remedy; of which I shall first of all treat, before I consider the several remedies by suit: and, to that end, shall distribute the redress of private wrongs into three several species; first, that which is obtained by the *mere act of the parties* themselves; secondly, that which is effected by the *mere act* and operation of law; and, thirdly, that which arises from *suit* or *action* in courts, which consists in a conjunction of the other two, the act of the parties co-operating with the act of law.

And, first, of that redress of private injuries, which is obtained by the mere act of the parties. This is of two sorts; first, that which arises from the act of the injured party only; and, secondly, that which arises from the joint act of all the parties together: both which I shall consider in their order.

Of the first sort, or that which arises from the sole act of the injured party, is,

I. The *defence* of one's self, or the mutual and reciprocal defence of such as stand in the relations of husband and wife, parent and child, master and servant. In these cases, if the party himself, or any of these his relations, be forcibly attacked in his person or property, it is lawful for him to repel force by force (*a*) and the breach of the peace, which happens, is chargeable upon him only who began the affray. But care must be taken that the resistance does not exceed the bounds of mere defence and prevention; for then the defender would himself become the aggressor.

II. Recaption or *reprisal* is another species of remedy by the mere act of the party injured. This happens, when any one hath deprived another of his property in goods or chattels personal, or wrongfully detains one's wife, child, or servant: in which case the owner of the goods, and the husband, parent, or master, may lawfully claim and retake them, wherever he happens to find them; so it be not in a riotous manner, or attended with a breach of the peace. If, for instance, my horse is taken away, and I find him in a common, a fair, or a public inn, I may lawfully seize him to my own use: but I cannot justify breaking open a private stable, or enter-

---

(*a*) But in *Leeward* v. *Basilec*, 1 *Salk.* 407. there was said to be this difference, that though the wife might justify an assault in defence of her husband; and a servant of his master, yet a master could not in defence of his servant, because he might have an action *per quod servitium amisit.*

ing on the grounds of a third person, to take him, except he be feloniously stolen; but must have recourse to an action at law.

III. As recaption is a remedy given to the party himself, for an injury to his *personal* property, so, thirdly, a remedy of the same kind for injuries to *real* property, is by *entry* on lands and tenements, when another person without any right has taken possession thereof. There is some nicety required to define and distinguish the cases, in which such entry is lawful or otherwise: it will therefore be more fully considered in a subsequent chapter; being only mentioned in this place for the sake of regularity and order.

IV. A fourth species of remedy by the mere act of the party injured, is the *abatement*, or removal, of *nusances*. What nusances are, and their several species, we shall find a more proper place to inquire under some of the subsequent divisions. At present I shall only observe, that whatsoever unlawfully annoys or doth damage to another is a nusance; and such nusance may be abated, that is, taken away or removed, by the party aggrieved thereby, so as he commits no riot in the doing of it. If a house or wall is erected so near to mine that it stops my antient lights, which is a *private* nusance, I may enter my neighbour's land, and peaceably pull it down. Or if a new gate be erected across the public highway, which is a *common* nusance, any of the king's subjects passing that way may cut it down, and destroy it.

V. A fifth case, in which the law allows a man to be his own avenger, or to minister redress to himself, is that of *distreining* cattle or goods for non-payment of rent, or other duties; or distreining another's cattle *damage-feasant*, that is, doing damage, or trespassing upon his land.

As the law of distresses is a point of great use and consequence, I shall consider it with some minuteness: by inquiring, first, for what injuries a distress may be taken; secondly, what things may be distreined; and thirdly, the manner of taking, disposing of, and avoiding distresses.

1. And, first, it is necessary to premise, that a distress, *districtio*, is the taking of a personal chattel out of the posses-

sion of the wrong-doer into the custody of the party injured, to procure a satisfaction for the wrong committed. 1. The most usual injury, for which a distress may be taken, is that of non-payment of rent. A distress may be taken for any kind of rent in arrear; the detaining whereof beyond the day of payment is an injury to him that is entitled to receive it. 2. For neglecting to do suit to the lord's court, or other personal service, the lord may distrein of common right. 3. For amercements in a court-leet a distress may be had of common right; but not for amercement in a court-baron, without a special prescription to warrant it. 4. Another injury, for which distresses may be taken, is where a man finds beasts of a stranger wandering in his grounds, *damage-feasant*; that is, doing him hurt or damage, by treading down his grass, or the like; in which case the owner of the soil may distrein them, till satisfaction be made him for the injury he has thereby sustained. 5. Lastly, for several duties and penalties inflicted by special acts of parliament, (as for assessments made by commissioners of sewers, or for the relief of the poor) remedy by distress and sale is given; for the particulars of which we must have recourse to the statutes themselves: remarking only, that such distresses are partly analogous to the antient distress at common law, as being repleviable and the like; but more resembling the common law process of execution, by seising and selling the goods of the debtor under a writ of *fieri facias*.

2. Secondly; as to the things which may be distressed, or taken in distress, we may lay it down as a general rule, that all chattels personal are liable to be distreined, unless particularly protected or exempted. Instead therefore of mentioning what things are distreinable, it will be easier to recount those which are not so, with the reason of their particular exemptions. And, 1. As every thing which is distreined is presumed to be the property of the wrong-doer, it will follow that such things, wherein no man can have an absolute and valuable property (as dogs, cats, rabbets, and all animals *feræ naturæ*) cannot be distreined. Yet if deer (which are *feræ naturæ*) are kept in a private inclosure for the purpose

of fale or profit, this fo far changes their nature, by reducing them to a kind of ftock or merchandize, that they may be diftreined for rent. 2. Whatever is in the perfonal ufe or occupation of any man, is for the time privileged and protected from any diftrefs; as an ax with which a man is cutting wood, or a horfe while a man is riding him. But horfes, drawing a cart, may (cart and all) be diftreined for rent-arrear; and alfo if a horfe, though a man be riding him, be taken *damage feafant*, or trefpaffing in another's grounds, the horfe (notwithftanding his rider) may be diftreined and led away to the pound (*a*). 3. Valuable things in the way of trade fhall not be liable to diftrefs. As a horfe ftanding in a fmith's fhop to be fhoed, or in a common inn; or cloth at a taylor's houfe; or corn fent to a mill, or a market. For all thefe are protected and privileged for the benefit of trade; and are fuppofed in common prefumption not to belong to the owner of the houfe, but to his cuftomers (*b*). But, generally fpeaking, whatever goods and chattels the landlord finds upon the premifes, whether they in fact belong to the tenant or a ftranger, are diftreinable by him for rent: for otherwife a door would be open to infinite frauds upon the landlord; and the ftranger has *his* remedy over by action on the cafe againft the tenant, if by the tenant's default the chattels are diftreined, fo that he cannot render them when called upon. With regard to a ftranger's beafts which are found on the tenant's land, the following diftinctions are however taken. If they are put in by confent of the owner of the beafts, they are diftreinable immediately afterwards for rent-arrear by the landlord. So alfo, if the ftranger's cattle break the fences, and commit a trefpafs by coming on the land, they

---

(*a*) This is faid on the authority of 1 *Sid.* 440. but per *Hargrave* " the opinion was extrajudicial, and may be queftioned." See *Co. Lit.* 47$^a$. n. 12.

(*b*) This privilege, however, does not extend to horfes or carriages at livery, or cattle agifting. *Francis* v. *Wyatt*, 3 *Bur.* 1498.

are diftreinable immediately by the leffor for his tenant's rent, as a punifhment to the owner of the beafts for the wrong committed through his negligence. But if the lands were not fufficiently fenced fo as to keep out cattle, the landlord cannot diftrein them, till they have been *levant* and *couchant (levantes et cubantes)* on the land; that is, have been long enough there to have laid down and rofe up to feed; which in general is held to be one night at leaft: and then the law prefumes, that the owner may have notice whither his cattle have ftrayed, and it is his own negligence not to have taken them away. Yet, if the leffor or his tenant were bound to repair the fences and did not, and thereby the cattle efcaped into their grounds without the negligence or default of the owner; in this cafe, though the cattle may have been *levant* and *couchant*, yet they are not diftreinable for rent, till actual notice is given to the owner that they are there, and he neglects to remove them: for the law will not fuffer the landlord to take advantage of his own or his tenant's wrong. 4. There are alfo other things privileged by the antient common law; as a man's tools and utenfils of his trade, the ax of a carpenter, the books of a fcholar, and the like. So, beafts of the plough, *averia carucæ*, and fheep, are privileged from diftreffes at common law; while dead goods, or other fort of beafts, which Bracton calls *catalla otiofa*, may be diftreined. But, as beafts of the plough may be taken in execution for debt, fo they may be for diftreffes by ftatute, which partake of the nature of executions. And perhaps the true reafon why thefe and the tools of a man's trade were privileged at the common law, was becaufe the diftrefs was then merely intended to compel the payment of the rent, and not as a fatisfaction for its non-payment: and therefore, to deprive the party of the inftruments and means of paying it, would counteract the very end of the diftrefs (*a*). 5. Nothing

---

(*a*) But by the modern decifions, thefe are held to be diftreinable for rent, *provided no other fufficient diftrefs is to be had.* See *Gorton* v. *Faulkner*, 4 *Term Rep.* 565. and in *all cafes* are they diftreinable for poor's rates. 43 Eliz. c. 2.

shall be diſtreined for rent, which may not be rendered again in as good plight as when it was diſtreined: for which reaſon milk, fruit, and the like, cannot be diſtreined; a diſtreſs at common law being only in the nature of a pledge or ſecurity, to be reſtored in the ſame plight when the debt is paid. So antiently, ſheaves or ſhocks of corn could not be diſtreined, becauſe ſome damage muſt needs accrue in their removal: but a cart loaded with corn might; as that could be ſafely reſtored. But now by ſtatute 2 W. & M. c. 5. corn in ſheaves or cocks, or looſe in the ſtraw, or hay in barns or ricks, or otherwiſe, may be diſtreined as well as other chattels. 6. Laſtly, things fixed to the freehold may not be diſtreined; as caldrons, windows, doors, and chimney-pieces: for they favour of the realty. For this reaſon alſo corn growing could not be diſtreined; till the ſtatute 11 Geo. II. c. 19. empowered landlords to diſtrein corn, graſs, or other products of the earth, and to cut and gather them when ripe.

Let us next conſider, thirdly, how diſtreſſes may be taken, diſpoſed of, or avoided. And, firſt, I muſt premiſe, that the law of diſtreſſes is greatly altered within a few years laſt paſt. Formerly they were looked upon in no other light than as a mere pledge or ſecurity, for payment of rent or other duties, or ſatisfaction for damage done. And ſo the law ſtill continues with regard to diſtreſſes of beaſts taken *damage-feaſant*, and for other cauſes, not altered by act of parliament; over which the diſtreiner has no other power than to retain them till ſatisfaction is made. But diſtreſſes for rent-arrear being found by the legiſlature to be the ſhorteſt and moſt effectual method of compelling the payment of ſuch rent, many beneficial laws for this purpoſe have been made in the preſent century; which have much altered the common law, as laid down in our antient writers.

In pointing out therefore the methods of diſtreining, I ſhall in general ſuppoſe the diſtreſs to be made for rent; and remark, where neceſſary, the differences between ſuch diſtreſs, and one taken for other cauſes.

In the firſt place then, all diſtreſſes muſt be made *by day*, unless in the case of *damage-feasant*; an exception being there allowed, lest the beasts should escape before they are taken. And, when a person intends to make a distress, he must, by himself or his bailiff, enter on the demised premises; formerly during the continuance of the lease, but now, if the tenant holds over, the landlord may distrein within six months after the determination of the lease; provided his own title or interest, as well as the tenant's possession, continue at the time of distress. If the lessor does not find sufficient distress on the premises, formerly he could resort no where else. But now the landlord may distrein any goods of his tenant, carried off the premises clandestinely, wherever he finds them within thirty days after, unless they have been *bona fide* sold for a valuable consideration: and all persons privy to, or assisting in, such fraudulent conveyance, forfeit double the value to the landlord. The landlord may also distrein the beasts of his tenant, feeding upon any commons or wastes, appendant or appurtenant to the demised premises. And he may, by the assistance of the peace officer of the parish, break open in the day-time any place, whither the goods have been fraudulently removed and locked up to prevent a distress; oath being first made, in case it be a dwelling-house, of a reasonable ground to suspect that such goods are concealed therein.

Where a man is entitled to distrein for an entire duty, he ought to distrein for the whole at once; and not for part at one time, and part at another. But if he distreins for the whole, and there is not sufficient on the premises, or he happens to mistake in the value of the thing distreined, and so takes an insufficient distress, he may take a second distress to complete his remedy.

Distresses must be proportioned to the thing distreined for. By the statute of Marlbridge, 52 Hen. III. c. 4. if any man takes a great or unreasonable distress, for rent-arrear, he shall be heavily amerced for the same. As, if the landlord distreins two oxen for twelvepence rent; the taking of *both* is an unreasonable distress; but, if there were no other distress nearer the value to be found, he might reasonably have diftreined *one* of them; but for homage, fealty, or fuit and fervice, as alfo for parliamentary wages, it is faid that no diftrefs can be exceffive. For as thefe diftreffes cannot be fold, the owner, upon making fatisfaction, may have his chattels again. The remedy for exceffive diftreffes is by a fpecial action on the ftatute of Marlbridge; for an action of trefpafs is not maintainable upon this account, it being no injury at the common law.

When the diftrefs is thus taken, the next confideration is the difpofal of it. For which purpofe the things diftreined muft in the firft place be carried to fome pound, and there impounded by the taker. But, in their way thither, they may be *refcued* by the owner, in cafe the diftrefs was taken without caufe, or contrary to law: as if no rent be due; if they were taken upon the highway, or the like; in thefe cafes the tenant may lawfully make refcue. But if they be once impounded, even though taken without any caufe, the owner may not break the pound and take them out; for they are then in the cuftody of the law.

A pound *(parcus,* which fignifies any inclofure) is either pound-*overt,* that is, open overhead; or pound-*covert,* that is, clofe. By the ftatute 1 & 2 P. & M. c. 12. no diftrefs of cattle can be driven out of the hundred where it is taken, unlefs to a pound-overt within the fame fhire; and within three miles of the place where it was taken. This is for the benefit of the tenants, that they may know where to find and replevy the diftrefs. And by ftatute 11 Geo. II. c. 19. which was made for the benefit of landlords, any perfon diftreining for rent may turn any part of the premifes, upon which a diftrefs is taken, into a pound, *pro hac vice,* for fecuring of fuch diftrefs. If a live diftrefs, of animals, be impounded in a *common* pound overt, the owner muft take notice of it at his peril; but if in any *fpecial* pound-overt, fo conftituted for this particular purpofe, the diftreinor muft give notice to the owner: and in both thefe cafes, the owner, and not the diftreinor, is bound to provide the beafts with food and neceffaries. But if they are put in a pound-covert, as in a ftable or the like, the landlord or diftreinor muft feed and fuftain them. A diftrefs of houfehold goods, or other dead chattels, which are liable to be ſtolen or damaged by weather, ought to be impounded in a pound-covert, elſe the diſtreinor muſt anſwer for the conſequences.

When impounded, the goods were formerly. as was before obſerved, only in the nature of a pledge or ſecurity to compel the performance of ſatisfaction; and upon this account it hath been held, that the diſtreinor is not at liberty to work or uſe a diſtreined beaſt. And thus the law ſtill continues with regard to beaſts taken damage-feaſant, and diſtreſſes for ſuit or ſervices; which muſt remain impounded till the owner makes ſatisfaction; or conteſts the right of diſtreining, by replevying the chattels. To *replevy*, (*replegiare*, that is, to take back the pledge) is, when a perſon diſtreined upon applies to the ſheriff or his officers, and has the diſtreſs returned into his own poſſeſſion, upon giving good ſecurity to try the right of taking it in a ſuit at law, and, if that be determined againſt him, to return the cattle or goods once more into the hands of the diſtreinor. This is called a replevin, of which more will be ſaid hereafter. At preſent I ſhall only obſerve, that, as a diſtreſs is at common law only in nature of a ſecurity for the rent or damages done, a replevin anſwers the ſame end to the diſtreinor as the diſtreſs itſelf; ſince the party replevying gives ſecurity to return the diſtreſs, if the right be determined againſt him.

This kind of diſtreſs, though it puts the owner to inconvenience, and is therefore a puniſhment to *him*, yet, if he continues obſtinate and will make no ſatisfaction or payment, it is no remedy at all to the diſtreinor. But for a debt due to the crown, unleſs paid within forty days, the diſtreſs was always ſaleable at the common law. And for an amercement impoſed at a court-leet, the lord may alſo ſell the diſtreſs: partly, becauſe being the king's court of record, its proceſs partakes of the royal prerogative; but principally becauſe it is in the nature of an execution to levy a legal debt. And, ſo in the ſeveral ſtatute-diſtreſſes, before mentioned, which are alſo in the nature of executions, the power of ſale is likewiſe uſually given, to effectuate and complete the remedy. And, in like manner, by ſeveral acts of parliament, in all cafes of diftrefs for rent, if the tenant or owner do not, within five days after the diftrefs is taken, and notice of the caufe thereof given him, replevy the fame with fufficient fecurity; the diftreinor, with the fheriff or conftable, fhall caufe the fame to be appraifed by two fworn appraifers, and fell the fame towards fatisfaction of the rent and charges; rendering the overplus, if any, to the owner himfelf. And, by this means, a full and entire fatisfaction may now be had for rent in arrear, by the mere act of the party himfelf, viz. by diftrefs, the remedy given at common law; and fale confequent thereon, which is added by act of parliament.

Before I quit this article, I muft obferve, that the many particulars which attend the taking of a diftrefs, ufed formerly to make it a hazardous kind of proceeding: for, if any one irregularity was committed, it vitiated the whole, and made the diftreinors trefpaffors *ab initio*. But now by the ftatute 11 Geo. II. c. 19. it is provided, that, for any unlawful act done, the whole fhall not be unlawful, or the parties trefpaffors *ab initio*: but that the party grieved fhall only have an action for the real damage fuftained; and not even that, if tender of amends is made before any action is brought.

VI. The feifing of heriots, when due on the death of a tenant, is alfo another fpecies of felf-remedy; not much unlike that of taking cattle or goods in diftrefs. As for that divifion of heriots, which is called heriot-fervice, and is only a fpecies of rent, the lord may diftrein for this, as well as feife: but for heriot-cuftom (which Sir Edward Coke fays lies only in *prender*, and not in *render*) the lord may feife the identical thing itfelf, but cannot diftrein any other chattel for it. The like fpeedy and effectual remedy, of feifing, is given with regard to many things that are faid to lie in franchife; as waifs, wrecks, eftrays, deodands, and the like; all which the perfon entitled thereto may feife, without the formal procefs of a fuit or action.

Thefe are the feveral fpecies of remedies, which may be had by the mere act of the party injured. I fhall, next, briefly mention fuch as arife from the joint act of all the parties together. And these are only two, *accord*, and *arbitration*.

I. Accord is a satisfaction agreed upon between the party injuring and the party injured; which, when performed, is a bar of all actions upon this account. As if a man contract to build a house or deliver a horse, and fail in it; this is an injury, for which the sufferer may have his remedy by action; but if the party injured accepts a sum of money, or other thing, as a satisfaction, this is a redress of that injury, and entirely takes away the action. By several late statutes, (particularly 11 Geo. II. c. 19. in case of irregularity in the method of distreining; and 24 Geo. II. c. 24. in case of mistakes committed by justices of the peace) even *tender* of sufficient amends to the party injured is a bar of all actions, whether he thinks proper to accept such amends or no.

II. Arbitration is where the parties, injuring and injured, submit all matters in dispute, concerning any personal chattels or personal wrong, to the judgment of two or more *arbitrators*; who are to decide the controversy: and if they do not agree, it is usual to add, that another person is called in as *umpire*, (*imperator* or *impar*) to whose sole judgment it is then referred: or frequently there is only one arbitrator originally appointed (a). This decision, in any of these cases, is called an *award*. And thereby the question is as fully determined, and the right transferred or settled, as it could have been by the agreement of the parties or the judgment of a court of justice. But the right of real property cannot thus pass by a mere award: which subtilty in point of form (for it is now reduced to nothing else) had it's rise from feodal principles; for, if this had been permitted, the land

---

(a) As there is no way that can be found out, while men are in a state of nature, more equitable for putting an end to strife and contention, than a reference of the matter to some person unconcerned; it follows that for peace, and quietness sake, men acting in that state, ought to take that course; and by consequence that it is a law of nature, that two contending parties refer the question of right to the arbitrament of some third. Vide *Dawson's Origo Legum*, p. 32.

might have been aliened collufively without the confent of the fuperior. Yet doubtlefs an arbitrator may now award a conveyance or a releafe of land; and it will be a breach of the arbitration-bond to refufe compliance. For, though originally the fubmiffion to arbitration ufed to be by word, or by deed, yet both of thefe being revocable in their nature, it is now become the practice to enter into mutual bonds, with condition to ftand to the award or arbitration of the arbitrators or umpire therein named. And experience having fhewn the great ufe of thefe peaceable and domeftic tribunals, efpecially in fettling matters of account, and other mercantile tranfactions, which are difficult and almoft impoffible to be adjufted on a trial at law; the legiflature has now eftablifhed the ufe of them, as well in controverfies where caufes are depending, as in thofe where no action is brought: enacting, by ftatute 9 & 10 W. III. c. 15. that all merchants and others, who defire to end any controverfy, fuit, or quarrel, (for which there is no other remedy but by perfonal action or fuit in equity) may agree, that their fubmiffion of the fuit to arbitration or umpirage fhall be made a rule of any of the king's courts of record, and may infert fuch agreement in their fubmiffion, or promife, or condition of the arbitration bond: which agreement being proved upon oath by one of the witneffes thereto, the court fhall make a rule that fuch fubmiffion and award fhall be conclufive: and, after fuch rule made, the parties difobeying the award fhall be liable to be punifhed, as for a contempt of the court; unlefs fuch award fhall be fet afide, for corruption or other mifbehaviour in the arbitrators or umpire, proved on oath to the court, within one term after the award is made. And, in confequence of this ftatute, it is now become a confiderable part of the bufinefs of the fuperior courts, to fet afide fuch awards when partially or illegally made; or to enforce their execution, when legal, by the fame procefs of contempt, as is awarded for difobedience to thofe rules and orders which are iffued by the courts themfelves.

## CHAPTER II.

### OF REDRESS BY THE MERE OPERATION OF LAW.

THE remedies for private wrongs, which are effected by the mere operation of the law, will fall within a very narrow compass: there being only two instances of this sort that at present occur to my recollection; the one that of *retainer*, where a creditor is made executor or administrator to his debtor; the other, in the case of what the law calls a *remitter*.

I. If a person indebted to another makes his creditor or debtee his executor, or if such creditor obtain letters of administration to his debtor; in these case the law gives him a remedy for his debt, by allowing him to retain so much as will pay himself, before any other creditors whose debts are of equal degree. But the executor shall not retain his own debt, in prejudice to those of a higher degree; for the law only puts him in the same situation, as if he had sued himself as executor, and recovered his debt; which he never could be supposed to have done, while debts of a higher nature subsisted. Neither shall one executor be allowed to retain his own debt, in prejudice to that of his co-executor in equal degree; but both shall be discharged in proportion. Nor shall an executor of his own wrong be in any case permitted to retain.

II. Remitter is where he, who hath the true property or *jus proprietatis* in lands, but is out of possession thereof and hath no right to enter without recovering possession in an action, hath afterwards the freehold cast upon him by some subsequent, and of course defective title *(a)*. As if A dissei-

---

*(a) Quod prius est, verius est; et quod prius est tempore, potius est jure:* therefore many books, instead of remitter, say, that he is *En son primer estate*, or, *en son melior droit*, or *en son melior estate*, or the like. *Co. Lit. lib.* 3. p. 347.

ſes B, that is, turns him out of poſſeſſion, and dies leaving a
ſon C; hereby the eſtate deſcends to C the ſon of A, and B
is barred from entering thereon till he proves his right in an
action: now, if afterwards C the heir of the diſſeiſor makes
a leaſe for life to D, with remainder to B the diſſeiſee for
life, and D dies; hereby the remainder accrues to B the
diſſeiſee: who thus gaining a new freehold by virtue of the
remainder, which is a bad title, is by act of law *remitted*, or
in of his former and ſurer eſtate.

If the ſubſequent eſtate, or right of poſſeſſion, be gained
by a man's own act or conſent, as by immediate purchaſe
being of full age, he ſhall not be remitted. For the taking
ſuch ſubſequent eſtate was his own folly, and ſhall be looked
upon as a waiver of his prior right. Therefore it is to be
obſerved, that to every remitter there are regularly theſe incidents; an antient right, and a new defeaſible eſtate of freehold, uniting in one and the ſame perſon; which defeaſible
eſtate muſt be *caſt upon* the tenant, not gained by his own
act or folly. But there ſhall be no remitter to a right, for
which the party has no remedy by action: as if the iſſue in
tail be barred by the fine or warranty of his anceſtor, and the
freehold is afterwards caſt upon him; he ſhall not be remitted to his eſtate tail: for the operation of the remitter is exactly the ſame, after the union of the two rights, as that of
a real action would have been before it. As therefore the
iſſue in tail could not by any action have recovered his antient eſtate, he ſhall not recover it by remitter.

## CHAPTER III.

### OF WRONGS, AND THEIR REMEDIES RESPECTING THE RIGHTS OF PERSONS.

THE former chapters of this part of our commentaries
having been employed in deſcribing the ſeveral methods of redreſſing private wrongs, either by the mere act of

the parties, or the mere operation of the law; I come now to confider at large, and in a more particular manner, the refpective remedies in the public and general courts of common law, for injuries or private wrongs. And, in treating of thefe, I fhall at prefent confine myfelf to fuch wrongs as may be committed in the mutual intercourfe between fubject and fubject; which the king as the fountain of juftice is officially bound to redrefs in the ordinary forms of law; referving fuch injuries or encroachments as may occur between the crown and the fubject, to be diftinctly confidered hereafter, as the remedy in fuch cafes is originally of a peculiar and eccentrical nature.

I proceed therefore now to enumerate the feveral kinds, and to inquire into the refpective natures, of all private wrongs or civil injuries, which may be offered to the rights of either a man's perfon or his property; recounting at the fame time the refpective remedies, which are furnifhed by the law for every infraction of right. But I muft firft beg leave to premife, that all civil injuries are of two kinds, the one *without force* or violence, as flander or breach of contract; the other coupled *with force* and violence, as batteries, or falfe imprifonment. And this diftinction of private wrongs, into injuries *with* and *without* force, we fhall find to run through all the variety of which we are now to treat. In confidering of which, I fhall follow the fame method that was purfued with regard to the diftribution of rights. As therefore we divided all rights into thofe of *perfons*, and thofe of *things*, fo we muft make the general diftribution of injuries into fuch as affect the *right of perfons*, and fuch as affect the *rights of property*.

The rights of perfons, we may remember, were diftributed into *abfolute* and *relative*: *abfolute*, which were fuch as appertained and belonged to private men, confidered merely as individuals, or fingle perfons; and *relative*, which were incident to them as members of fociety, and connected to each other by various ties and relations. And the abfolute rights of each individual were defined to be the right of perfonal fecurity, the right of perfonal liberty, and the right of private property, so that the wrongs or injuries affecting them must consequently be of a correspondent nature.

I. As to injuries which affect the personal security of individuals, they are either injuries against their lives, their bodies, their health, or their reputations.

1. With regard to the first subdivision, or injuries affecting the life of man, they do not fall under our present contemplation; being one of the most atrocious species of crimes, the subject of the next book of our commentaries.

2, 3. The two next species of injuries, affecting the limbs or bodies of individuals, I shall consider in one and the same view. And these may be committed, 1. By *threats* and menaces of bodily hurt, through fear of which a man's business is interrupted. A menace alone, without a consequent inconvenience, makes not the injury; but, to complete the wrong, there must be both of them together. The remedy for this is in pecuniary damages, to be recovered by action of *trespass vi et armis;* this being an inchoate, though not an absolute, violence. 2. By *assault*; which is an attempt or offer to beat another, without touching him: as if one lifts up his cane, or his fist, in a threatening manner at another; or strikes at him, but misses him; this is an assault, *insultus*, which Finch describes to be " an unlawful setting upon " one's person." This also is an inchoate violence, amounting considerably higher than bare threats; and therefore, though no actual suffering is proved, yet the party injured may have redress by action of *trespass vi et armis;* wherein he shall recover damages as a compensation for the injury. 3. By *battery:* which is the unlawful beating of another. The least touching of another's person wilfully, or in anger, is a battery; for the law cannot draw the line between different degrees of violence, and therefore totally prohibits the first and lowest stage of it: every man's person being sacred, and no other having a right to meddle with it, in any the slightest manner. But battery is, in some cases, justifiable or lawful; as where one who hath authority, a parent or master, gives moderate correction to his child, his scholar, or his apprentice. So also on the principle of self-defence: for if one strikes me first, or even only assaults me, I may strike in my own defence; and, if sued for it, may plead *son assault demesne*, or that it was the plaintiff's own original assault that occasioned it. So likewise in defence of my goods, or possession, if a man endeavours to deprive me of them, I may justify laying hands upon him to prevent him; and, in case he persists with violence, I may proceed to beat him away. Thus too in the exercise of an office, as that of church-warden or beadle, a man may lay hands upon another to turn him out of his church, and prevent his disturbing the congregation. And, if sued for this or the like battery, he may set forth the whole case, and plead that he laid hands upon him gently, *molliter manus imposuit*, for this purpose. On account of these causes of justification, battery is defined to be the *unlawful* beating of another; for which the remedy is, as for assault, by action of *trespass vi et armis*: wherein the jury will give adequate damages. 4. By *wounding*; which consists in giving another some dangerous hurt, and is only an aggravated species of battery. 5. By *mayhem*: which is an injury still more atrocious, and consists in violently depriving another of the use of a member proper for his defence in fight. This is a battery, attended with this aggravating circumstance, that thereby the party injured is for ever disabled from making so good a defence against future external injuries, as he otherwise might have done. Among these defensive members are reckoned not only arms and legs, but a finger, an eye, and a foretooth, and also some others. But the loss of one of the jaw-teeth, the ear, or the nose, is no mayhem at common law; as they can be of no use in fighting. The same remedial action of *trespass vi et armis* lies also to recover damages for this injury, an injury, which (when wilful) no motive can justify, but necessary self-preservation. If the ear be cut off, treble damages are given by 37 Hen. VIII. c. 6. though this is not mayhem at common law. And here I must observe that for these four last injuries, assault, battery, wounding and mayhem, an indictment may be brought as well as an action; and frequently both are accordingly prosecuted; the one at the suit of the crown for the crime against the public; the other at the suit of the party injured, to make him a reparation in damages.

4. Injuries, affecting a man's *health*, are where by any unwholesome practices of another, a man sustains any apparent damage in his vigour or constitution. As by selling him bad provisions or wine; by the exercise of a noisome trade, which infects the air in the neighbourhood; or by the neglect or unskilful management of his physician, surgeon, or apothecary. For it hath been solemnly resolved, that *mala praxis* is a great misdemesnor and offence at common law, whether it be for curiosity and experiment, or by neglect; because it breaks the trust which the party had placed in his physician, and tends to the patient's destruction. These are wrongs unaccompanied by force, for which there is a remedy in damages by a special action of *trespass, upon the case*. This action, of *trespass*, or transgression, *on the case*, is an universal remedy, given for all personal wrongs and injuries without force; so called because the plaintiff's whole case or cause of complaint is set forth at length in the original writ. And it is a settled distinction, that where an act is done which is in itself an *immediate* injury to another's person or property, there the remedy is usually by an action of trespass *vi et armis*: but where there is no act done, but only a culpable omission; or where the act is not immediately injurious, but only by *consequence* and collaterally; there no action of trespass *vi et armis* will lie, but an action on the special case, for the damages consequent on such omission or act.

5. Lastly; injuries affecting a man's *reputation* or good name, are, first, by malicious, scandalous, and slanderous *words*, tending to his damage and derogation. As if a man, maliciously and falsely, utter any slander or false tale of another; which may either endanger him in law, by impeaching him of some heinous crime, as to say that a man hath poisoned another, or is perjured; or which may exclude him from society, as charging him with having an infectious disease; or which may impair or hurt his trade or livelihood, as

to call a tradesman a bankrupt, a physician a quack, or a lawyer a knave. Words spoken in derogation of a peer, a judge, or other great officer of the realm, which are called *scandalum magnatum*, are held to be still more heinous; and, though they be such as would not be actionable in the case of a common person, yet when spoken in disgrace of such high and respectable characters, they amount to an atrocious injury: which is redressed by an action on the case founded on many antient statutes; as well on behalf of the crown, to inflict the punishment of imprisonment on the slanderer, as on behalf of the party, to recover damages for the injury sustained. Words also tending to scandalize a magistrate, or person in a public trust, are reputed more highly injurious than when spoken of a private man: and it is now held, that for scandalous words of the several species before-mentioned, (that may endanger a man by subjecting him to the penalties of the law, may exclude him from society, may impair his trade, or may affect a peer of this realm, a magistrate, or one in public trust) an action on the case may be had, without proving any particular damage to have happened, but merely upon the probability that it might happen. But with regard to words that do not thus apparently, and upon the face of them, import such defamation as will of course be injurious, it is necessary that the plaintiff should aver some particular damage to have happened; which is called laying his action with a *per quod*. As if I say that such a clergyman is a bastard, he cannot for this bring any action against me, unless he can shew some special loss by it; in which case he may bring his action against me, for saying he was a bastard, *per quod* he lost the presentation to such a living. In like manner to slander another man's title, by spreading such injurious reports, as, if true, would deprive him of his estate (as to call the issue in tail, or one who hath land by descent, a bastard) is actionable, provided any special damage accrues to the proprietor thereby; as if he loses an opportunity of selling the land. But mere scurrility, or opprobrious words, which neither in themselves import, nor are in fact attended with, any injurious effects, will not support an action. So scandals, which concern matters merely spiritual, as to call a man heretic or adulterer, are cognizable only in the ecclefiaftical court; unlefs any temporal damage enfues, which may be a foundation for a *per quod*. Words of heat and paffion, as to call a man rogue and rafcal, if productive of no ill confequence, and not of any of the dangerous fpecies before-mentioned, are not actionable: neither are words fpoken in a friendly manner, as by way of advice, admonition, or concern, without any tincture or circumftance of ill will: for, in both thefe cafes, they are not *malicioufly* fpoken, which is part of the definition of flander. Neither (as was formerly hinted) are any reflecting words made ufe of in legal proceedings, and pertinent to the caufe in hand, a fufficient caufe of action for flander. Alfo if the defendant be able to juftify, and prove the words to be true, no action will lie, even though fpecial damage hath enfued: for then it is no flander or falfe tale. As if I can prove the tradefman a bankrupt, the phyfician a quack, the lawyer a knave, and the divine a heretic, this will deftroy their refpective actions: for though there may be damage fufficient accruing from it, yet, if the fact be true, it is *damnum abfque injuria;* and where there is no injury, the law gives no remedy.

A fecond way of affecting a man's reputation is by printed or written libels, pictures, figns, and the like; which fet him in an odious or ridiculous light, and thereby diminifh his reputation. What was faid with regard to words fpoken, will alfo hold in every particular (a) with regard to libels by writing or printing, and the civil actions confequent thereupon: but as to figns or pictures, it feems neceffary always to fhew, by proper *innuendo's* and averments of the defendant's meaning, the import and application of the fcandal, and that fome fpecial damage has followed; otherwife it

---

(a) But in *Villers* v. *Monfley*, 2 *Wilf.* 403. cafes are put as being infufficient to fupport an action for *defamation* though evidently *libellous*. This diftinction, however, does not appear to the editor, to be warranted by any exprefs authority. See the cafes collected in *Efp. Ni. Pri.* ch. x.

cannot appear, that such libel by picture was understood to be levelled at the plaintiff, or that it was attended with any actionable consequences.

A third way of destroying or injuring a man's reputation is by preferring malicious indictments or prosecutions against him; which, under the mask of justice and public spirit, are sometimes made the engines of private spite and enmity. For this however the law has given a very adequate remedy in damages, either by an action of *conspiracy*, which cannot be brought but against two at the least; or, which is the more usual way, by a special action on the case for a false and malicious prosecution.

II. We are next to consider the violation of the right of personal liberty. This is effected by the injury of false imprisonment, for which the law has not only decreed a punishment, as a heinous public crime, but also given a private reparation to the party; as well by removing the actual confinement for the present, as, after it is over, by subjecting the wrongdoer to a civil action, on account of the damage sustained by the loss of time and liberty.

To constitute the injury of false imprisonment there are two points requisite: 1. The detention of the person: and, 2. The unlawfulness of such detention. Every confinement of the person is an imprisonment, whether it be in a common prison, or in a private house, or in the stocks, or even by forcibly detaining one in the public streets. Unlawful, or false, imprisonment consists in such confinement or detention without sufficient authority: which authority may arise either from some process from the courts of justice, or from some warrant from a legal officer having power to commit, under his hand and seal, and expressing the cause of such commitment; or from some other special cause warranted, for the necessity of the thing, either by common law, or act of parliament; such as the arresting of a felon by a private person without warrant, the impressing of mariners for the public service, or the apprehending of waggoners for misbehaviour in the public highways. False imprisonment also may arise by executing a lawful warrant or process at an unlawful time, as on a funday; for the ftatute hath declared, that fuch fervice of procefs fhall be void. This is the injury. Let us next fee the remedy: which is of two forts; the one *removing* the injury, the other *making fatisfaction* for it.

The means of *removing* the injury of falfe imprifonment, are four-fold. 1. By writ of *mainprize*. 2. By writ *de odio et atia*. 3. By writ *de homine replegiando*. 4. By writ of *habeas corpus*.

But the incapacity of the three firft of thefe remedies to give complete relief in every cafe, hath almoft entirely antiquated them, and hath caufed a general recourfe to be had, in behalf of perfons aggrieved by illegal imprifonment, to

The writ of *habeas corpus*, the moft celebrated writ in the Englifh law. Of this there are various kinds made ufe of by the courts at Weftminfter, for removing prifoners from one court into another for the more eafy adminiftration of juftice. Such is the *habeas corpus ad refpondendum*, when a man hath a caufe of action againft one who is confined by the procefs of fome inferior court; in order to remove the prifoner, and charge him with this new action in the court above. Such is that *ad fatisfaciendum*, when a prifoner hath had judgment againft him in an action, and the plaintiff is defirous to bring him up to fome fuperior court to charge him with procefs of execution. Such alfo are thofe *ad profequendum, teftificandum, deliberandum, &c.* which iffue when it is neceffary to remove a prifoner, in order to profecute or bear teftimony in any court, or to be tried in the proper jurifdiction wherein the fact was committed. Such is, laftly, the common writ *ad faciendum et recipiendum*, which iffues out of any of the courts of Weftminfter-hall, when a perfon is fued in fome inferior jurifdiction, and is defirous to remove the action into the fuperior court; commanding the inferior judges to produce the body of the defendant, together with the day and caufe of his caption and detainer (whence the writ is frequently denominated an *habeas corpus cum caufa*) to do and receive whatfoever the king's court fhall confider in that behalf. This is a writ grantable of common right, without any motion in court ; and it inftantly fuperfedes all proceedings in the court below. But, in order to prevent the furreptitious difcharge of prifoners, it is ordered by ftatute 1 & 2 P. & M. c. 13. that no *habeas corpus* fhall iffue to remove any prifoner out of any gaol, unlefs figned by fome judge of the court out of which it is awarded. And by ftatute 19 Geo. III. c. 70. no caufe, under the value of ten pounds, fhall be removed by *habeas corpus*, or otherwife, into any fuperior court, unlefs the defendant, fo removing the fame, fhall give fpecial bail for payment of the debt and cofts.

But the great and efficacious writ, in all manner of illegal confinement, is that of *habeas corpus ad fubjiciendum;* directed to the perfon detaining another, and commanding him to produce the body of the prifoner, with the day and caufe of his caption and detention, *ad faciendum*, *fubjiciendum*, *et recipiendum*, to do, fubmit to, and receive whatfoever the judge or court awarding fuch writ fhall confider in that behalf. This is a high prerogative writ, and therefore by the common law iffuing out of the court of king's bench not only in term-time, but alfo during the vacation, by a *fiat* from the chief juftice or any other of the judges, and running into all parts of the king's dominions: but fince the mention of the king's bench and common pleas, as co-ordinate in this jurifdiction by ftatute 16 Car. I. c. 10. it hath been holden, that every fubject of the kingdom is equally entitled to the benefit of the common law writ, in either of thofe courts, at his option.

In the king's bench and common pleas it is neceffary to apply for it by motion to this court, as in the cafe of all other prerogative writs (*certiorari*, prohibition, *mandamus*, &c.) which do not iffue as of mere courfe, without fhewing fome probable caufe why the extraordinary power of the crown is called in to the party's affiftance. On the other hand, if a probable ground be fhewn, that the party is imprifoned without juft caufe, and therefore hath a right to be delivered, the writ of *habeas corpus* is then a writ of right, which " may " not be denied, but ought to be granted to every man that " is committed, or detained in prifon, or otherwife reftrain-

"ed, though it be by the command of the king, the privy "council, or any other."

The oppression of an obscure individual gave birth to this famous *habeas corpus* act, 31 Car. II. c. 2. which is frequently considered as another *magna charta* of the kingdom. The statute enacts, 1. That on complaint and request in writing by or on behalf of any person committed and charged with any *crime* (unless committed for treason or felony expressed in the warrant; or as accessory, or on suspicion of being accessory, before the fact, to any petit-treason or felony, plainly expressed in the warrant; or unless he is convicted or charged in execution by legal process) the lord chancellor or any of the twelve judges, in vacation, upon viewing a copy of the warrant, or affidavit that a copy is denied, shall (unless the party has neglected for two terms to apply to any court for his enlargement) award a *habeas corpus* for such prisoner, returnable immediately before himself or any other of the judges; and upon the return made shall discharge the party, if bailable, upon giving security to appear and answer to the accusation in the proper court of judicature. 2. That such writs shall be indorsed, as granted in pursuance of this act, and signed by the person awarding them. 3. That the writ shall be returned and the prisoner brought up, within a limited time according to the distance, not exceeding in any case twenty days. 4. That officers and keepers neglecting to make due returns, or not delivering to the prisoner or his agent within six hours after demand a copy of the warrant of commitment, or shifting the custody of a prisoner from one to another, without sufficient reason or authority (specified in the act) shall for the first offence forfeit 100l. and for the second offence 200l. to the party grieved, and be disabled to hold his office. 5. That no person, once delivered by *habeas corpus*, shall be re-committed for the same offence, on penalty of 500l. 6. That every person committed for treason or felony shall, if he requires it the first week of the next term or the first day of the next session of *oyer* and *terminer*, be indicted in that term or session, or else admitted to bail: unless the king's witnesses cannot be produced at that time: and if acquitted, or if not indicted and tried in the second term or session, he shall be discharged from his imprisonment for such imputed offence: but that no person, after the assises shall be opened for the county in which he is detained, shall be removed by *habeas corpus*, till after the assises are ended; but shall be left to the justice of the judges of assise. 7. That any such prisoner may move for and obtain his *habeas corpus*, as well out of the chancery or exchequer, as out of the king's bench or common pleas; and the lord chancellor or judges denying the same, on sight of the warrant or oath that the same is refused, forfeit severally to the party grieved the sum of 500l. 8. That this writ of *habeas corpus* shall run into the counties palatine, cinque ports, and other privileged places, and the islands of Jersey and Guernsey. 9. That no inhabitant of England (except persons contracting, or convicts praying, to be transported; or having committed some capital offence in the place to which they are sent) shall be sent prisoner to Scotland, Ireland, Jersey, Guernsey, or any places beyond the seas, within or without the king's dominions: on pain that the party committing, his advisers, aiders, and assistants, shall forfeit to the party grieved a sum not less than 500l. to be recovered with treble costs; shall be disabled to bear any office of trust or profit; shall incur the penalties of *præmunire*; and shall be incapable of the king's pardon. By which admirable regulations, judicial as well as parliamentary, the remedy is now complete for *removing* the injury of unjust and illegal confinement.

The *satisfactory* remedy for this injury of false imprisonment, is by an action of trespass, *vi et armis*, usually called an action of false imprisonment; which is generally, and almost unavoidably, accompanied with a charge of assault and battery also: and therein the party shall recover damages for the injury he has received; and also the defendant is, as for all other injuries committed with force, or *vi et armis*, liable to pay a fine to the king for the violation of the public peace.

I shall here conclude the head of injuries affecting the *absolute* rights of individuals.

We are next to contemplate those which affect their *relative* rights; or such as are incident to persons considered as members of society, and connected to each other by various ties and relations: and, in particular, such injuries as may be done to persons under the four following relations; husband and wife, parent and child, guardian and ward, master and servant.

I. Injuries that may be offered to a person, considered as a *husband*, are principally three: *abduction*, or taking away a man's wife; *adultery*, or criminal conversation with her; and *beating* or otherwise abusing her. 1. As to the first sort, *abduction* or taking her away, this may either be by fraud and persuasion, or open violence: though the law in both cases supposes force and constraint, the wife having no power to consent; and therefore gives a remedy by writ of *ravish*, or action of *trespass vi et armis, de uxore rapta et abducta*. This action lay at the common law; and thereby the husband shall recover, not the possession of his wife, but damages for taking her away: and by statute Westm. 1. 3 Edw. I. c. 13. the offender shall also be imprisoned two years, and be fined at the pleasure of the king. Both the king and the husband may have this action; and the husband is also entitled to recover damages in an action on the case against such as persuade and entice the wife to live separate from him without a sufficient cause. 2. *Adultery*, or criminal conversation with a man's wife, though it is, as a public crime, left by our laws to the coercion of the spiritual courts; yet, considered as a civil injury, (and surely there can be no greater) the law gives a satisfaction to the husband for it by action of trespass *vi et armis* against the adulterer, wherein the damages recovered are usually very large and exemplary. But these are properly increased and diminished by circumstances; as the rank and fortune of the plaintiff and defendant; the relation or connection between them; the seduction or otherwise of the wife, founded on her previous behaviour and character; and the husband's obligation by settlement or otherwife to provide for those children, which he cannot but suspect to be spurious. In this case, and upon indictments for polygamy, a marriage *in fact* must be proved; though generally, in other cases, reputation and cohabitation are sufficient evidence of marriage. 3. The third injury is that of *beating* a man's wife or otherwise ill using her; for which, if it be a common assault, battery, or imprisonment, the law gives the usual remedy to recover damages, by action of trespass *vi et armis,* which must be brought in the names of the husband and wife *jointly:* but if the beating or other maltreatment be very enormous, so that thereby the husband is deprived for any time of the company and assistance of his wife, the law then gives him a *separate* remedy by an action of trespass, in nature of an action upon the case, for this ill-usage, *per quod consortium amisit*; in which he shall recover a satisfaction in damages.

II. An injury may be offered to a person considered in the relation of a *parent,* by *abduction,* or taking his children away; and this is remediable by a writ of *ravishment,* or, action of *trespass vi et armis, de filio, vel filia, rapto vel abducto*; in the same manner as the husband may have it, on account of the abduction of his wife.

III. Of a similar nature to the last is the relation of *guardian* and *ward*; and the like actions *mutatis mutandis,* as are given to fathers, the guardian also has for recovery of damages, when his ward is stolen or ravished away from him. But a more speedy and summary method of redressing all complaints relative to wards and guardians hath of late obtained by an application to the court of chancery; which is the supreme guardian, and has the superintendent jurisdiction, of all the infants in the kingdom. And it is expresly provided by statute 12 Car. II. c. 24. that testamentary guardians may maintain an action of ravishment or trespass, for recovery of any of their wards, and also for damages to be applied to the use and benefit of the infants.

IV. To the relation between *master* and *servant,* and the rights accruing therefrom, there are two species of injuries incident. The one is, retaining a man's hired servant before his time is expired; the other is beating or confining him in such a manner that he is not able to perform his work. As to the first, the retaining another person's servant during the time he has agreed to serve his present master; this, as it is an ungentlemanlike, so it is also an illegal act; and for that injury the law has given a remedy by special action on the case: and also an action against the servant for the non-performance of his agreement. But, if the new master was not apprized of the former contract, no action lies against *him*, unless he refuses to restore the servant upon demand. The other point of injury, is that of beating, confining, or disabling a man's servant, which depends upon the same principle as the last; viz. the property which the master has by his contract acquired in the labour of the servant. In this case, besides the remedy of an action of battery or imprisonment, which the servant himself as an individual may have against the aggressor, the master also, as a recompense for *his* immediate loss, may maintain an action of trespass, *vi et armis*; in which he must allege and prove the special damage he has sustained by the beating of his servant, *per quod servitium amisit*: and then the jury will make him a proportionable pecuniary satisfaction.

---

## CHAPTER IV.

### OF INJURIES TO PERSONAL PROPERTY.

IN the preceding chapter we considered the wrongs or injuries that affected the rights of persons, either considered as individuals, or as related to each other; and are at present to enter upon the discussion of such injuries as affect the rights of property, together with the remedies which the law has given to repair or redress them.

And here again we must follow our former division of property into personal and real: *personal*, which consists in goods, money, and all other moveable chattels, and things thereunto incident; a property, which may attend a man's person wherever he goes, and from thence receives its denomination: and *real* property, which confifts of fuch things as are permanent, fixed, and immoveable; as lands, tenements, and hereditaments of all kinds, which are not annexed to the perfon, nor can be moved from the place in which they fubfift.

Firft then we are to confider the injuries that may be offered to the rights of perfonal property; and, of thefe, firft the rights of perfonal property in *poffeffion*, and then thofe that are in *action* only.

I. The rights of perfonal property in *poffeffion* are liable to two fpecies of injuries: the amotion or deprivation of that poffeffion; and the abufe or damage of the chattels, while the poffeffion continues in the legal owner. The former, or deprivation of poffeffion, is alfo divifible into two branches; the unjuft and unlawful *taking* them away; and the unjuft *detaining* them, though the original taking might be lawful.

1. And firft of an unlawful *taking*. When I once have gained a rightful poffeffion of any goods or chattels, either by a juft occupancy or by a legal transfer, whoever either by fraud or force difpoffeffes me of them is guilty of a tranfgreffion againft the law of fociety, which is a kind of fecondary law of nature.

The wrongful taking of goods being thus moft clearly an injury, the next confideration is, what remedy the law of England has given for it. And this is, in the firft place, the reftitution of the goods themfelves fo wrongfully taken, with damages for the lofs fuftained by fuch unjuft invafion; which is effected by action of *replevin*. This obtains only in one inftance of an unlawful taking, that of a wrongful diftrefs: In the cafe of a *diftrefs*, the goods are from the firft taking in the cuftody of the law, and not merely in that of the diftreinor; and therefore they may not only be identified, but alfo reftored to their firft poffeffor, without any material change in their condition. And, being thus in the cuftody of the law, the taking them back by force is looked upon as an atrocious injury, and denominated a *refcous*, for which the diftreinor has a remedy for damages, either by writ of *refcous*, in cafe they were going to the pound, or by writ *de parca fracto*, or *pound breach*, in cafe they were actually impounded. He may alfo at his option bring an action on the cafe for this injury: and fhall therein, if the diftrefs were taken for rent, recover treble damages.

An action of replevin, the regular way of contefting the validity of the tranfaction, is founded upon a diftrefs taken wrongfully and without fufficient caufe: being a re-delivery of the pledge, or thing taken in diftrefs, to the owner, upon his giving fecurity to try the right of the diftrefs, and to reftore it if the right be adjudged againft him: after which the diftreinor may keep it, 'till tender made of fufficient amends: but muft then re-deliver it to the owner. And, for the greater eafe of the parties, it is provided by ftatute 1 P. & M. c. 12. that the fheriff fhall make at leaft four deputies in each county, for the fole purpofe of making replevins. Upon application, therefore, either to the fheriff, or one of his faid deputies, fecurity is to be given, in purfuance of the ftatute of Weftm. 2. 13 Edw. I. c. 2. 1. That the party replevying will purfue his action againft the diftreinor, for which purpofe he puts in *plegios de profequendo*, or pledges to profecute; and, 2. That if the right be determined againft him, he will return the diftrefs again; for which purpofe he is alfo bound to find *plegios de retorno habendo*. Befides thefe pledges, the fufficiency of which is difcretionary and at the peril of the fheriff, the ftatute 11 Geo. II. c. 19. requires that the officer, granting a replevin on a diftrefs for rent, fhall take a bond with two fureties in a fum of double the value of the goods diftreined, conditioned to profecute the fuit with effect and without delay, and for return of the goods; which bond fhall be affigned to the avowant or perfon making cognizance, on requeft made to the officer; and, if forfeited, may be fued in the name of the affignee. The fheriff, on receiving fuch fecurity, is immediately, by his officers, to caufe the chattels taken in diftrefs to be reftored into the poffeffion of the party diftreined upon; unlefs the diftreinor claims a property in goods fo taken. For if, by this method of distress, the distreinor happens to come again into possession of his own property in goods which before he had lost, the law allows him to keep them, without any reference to the manner by which he thus has regained possession; being a kind of personal *remitter*. If, therefore, the distreinor claims any such property, the party replevying must sue out a writ *de proprietate probanda*, in which the sheriff is to try, by an inquest, in whom the property previous to the distress subsisted. And if it be found to be in the distreinor, the sheriff can proceed no farther; but must return the claim of property to the court of king's bench or common pleas, to be there farther prosecuted, if thought advisable, and there finally determined.

But, in common cases, the goods are delivered back to the party replevying, who is then bound to bring his action of replevin; which may be prosecuted in the county court, be the distress of what value it may. But either party may remove it to the superior courts of king's bench or common pleas, by writ of *recordari* or *pone;* the plaintiff at pleasure, the defendant upon reasonable cause: and also, if in the course of proceeding any right of freehold comes in question, the sheriff can proceed no farther; so that it is usual to carry it up in the first instance to the courts of Westminster-hall.

In like manner, other remedies for other unlawful takings of a man's goods consist only in recovering a satisfaction in damages. As if a man takes the goods of another out of his actual or virtual possession, without having a lawful title so to do, it is an injury; which, though it doth not amount to felony unless it be done *animo furandi*, is nevertheless a transgression, for which an action of *trespass vi et armis* will lie; wherein the plaintiff shall not recover the thing itself, but only damages for the loss of it. Or, if committed without force, the party may, at his choice, have another remedy in damages by action of *trover* and *conversion*, of which I shall presently say more.

2. Deprivation of possession may also be by an unjust *detainer* of another's goods, though the original *taking* was lawful. As if I distrein another's cattle damage-feasant, and

## C. IV. INJURIES TO PERSONAL PROPERTY. 339

before they are impounded he tenders me sufficient amends; now, though the original taking was lawful, my subsequent detainment of them after tender of amends is wrongful, and he shall have an action of *replevin* against me to recover them: in which he shall recover damages only for the *detention* and not for the *caption*, because the original taking was lawful. Or, if I lend a man a horse, and he afterwards refuses to restore it, this injury consists in the detaining, and not in the original taking, and the regular method for me to recover possession is by action of *detinue*. In this action, of *detinue*, it is necessary to ascertain the thing detained, in such a manner as that it may be specifically known and recovered. In order therefore to ground an action of detinue, which is only for the detaining, these points are necessary: 1. That the defendant came lawfully into possession of the goods, as either by delivery to him, or finding them; 2. That the plaintiff have a property; 3. That the goods themselves be of some value; and 4. That they be ascertained in point of identity. Upon this the jury, if they find for the plaintiff, assess the respective values of the several parcels detained, and also damages for the detention. And the judgment is conditional; that the plaintiff recover the said goods, or (if they cannot be had) their respective values, and also the damages for detaining them. But this action is of late much disused, and has given place to the action of *trover*.

This action of *trover* and *conversion*, was in it's original an action of trespass upon the case, for recovery of damages against such person as had *found* another's goods, and refused to deliver them on demand, but *converted* them to his own use; from which finding and converting it is called an action of *trover* and *conversion*. The injury lies in the conversion: for any man may take the goods of another into possession, if he finds them; but no finder is allowed to acquire a property therein, unless the owner be for ever unknown: and therefore he must not convert them to his own use, which the law presumes him to do, if he refuses to restore them to the owner: for which reason such refusal alone is, *prima facie*, sufficient evidence of a conversion. The fact of the finding, or *trover*, is therefore now totally immaterial: for the plaintiff needs only to suggest (as words of form) that he lost such goods, and that the defendant found them: and, if he proves that the goods are *his* property, and that the defendant had them in his possession, it is sufficient. But a conversion must be fully proved: and then in this action the plaintiff shall recover damages, equal to the value of the thing converted, but not the thing itself; which nothing will recover but an action of *detinue* or *replevin*.

As to the damage that may be offered to things personal, while in the possession of the owner, as hunting a man's deer, shooting his dogs, poisoning his cattle, or in any wise taking from the value of any of his chattels, or making them in a worse condition than before, these are injuries too obvious to need explication. I have only therefore to mention the remedies given by the law to redress them, which are in two shapes; by action of *trespass vi et armis*, where the act is in itself *immediately* injurious to another's property, and therefore necessarily accompanied with some degree of force; and by special action *on the case*, where the act is in itself indifferent, and the injury only *consequential*, and therefore arising without any breach of the peace. In both of which suits the plaintiff shall recover damages, in proportion to the injury which he proves that his property has sustained.

II. Hitherto of injuries affecting the right of things personal, in *possession*. We are next to consider those which regard things in *action* only; or such rights as are founded on, and arise from *contracts*. Contracts are either *express* or *implied*.

Express contracts include three distinct species; debts, covenants, and promises.

1. The legal acceptation of *debt* is, a sum of money due by certain and express agreement: as, by a bond for a determinate sum; a bill or note; a special bargain; or a rent reserved on a lease; where the quantity is fixed and specific, and does not depend upon any subsequent valuation to settle it. The non-payment of these is an injury, for which the

## C. IV. INJURIES TO PERSONAL PROPERTY.

proper remedy is by action of *debt*, to compel the performance of the contract and recover the specifical sum due. This is the shortest and surest remedy; particularly where the debt arises upon a specialty, that is, upon a deed or instrument under seal. So also, if I verbally agree to pay a man a certain price for a certain parcel of goods, and fail in the performance, an action of debt lies against me; for this is also a *determinate* contract: but if I agree for no settled price, I am not liable to an action of debt, but a special action on the case, according to the nature of my contract.

2. A covenant also, contained in a deed, to do a direct act or to omit one, is another species of express contracts, the violation or breach of which is a civil injury. The remedy for this is by a writ of *covenant*: which directs the sheriff to command the defendant generally to keep his covenant with the plaintiff (without specifying the nature of the covenant) or shew good cause to the contrary: and if he continues refractory, or the covenant is already so broken that it cannot now be specifically performed, then the subsequent proceedings set forth with precision the covenant, the breach, and the loss which has happened thereby; whereupon the jury will give damages, in proportion to the injury sustained by the plaintiff, and occasioned by such breach of the defendant's contract.

There is one species of covenant, of a different nature from the rest; and that is a covenant *real*, to convey or dispose of lands, which seems to be partly of a personal and partly of a real nature. For this the remedy is by a special writ of covenant, for a specific performance of the contract, concerning certain lands particularly described in the writ. It therefore directs the sheriff to command the defendant, here called the deforciant, to keep the covenant made between the plaintiff and him concerning the identical lands in question: and upon this process it is that fines of land are usually levied at common law; the plaintiff, or person to whom the fine is levied, bringing a writ of covenant, in which he suggests some agreement to have been made between him and the deforciant, touching those particular lands, for the completion of which he brings this action. And, for the end of this fuppofed difference, the fine or *finalis concordia* is made, whereby the deforciant (now called the cognizor) acknowleges the tenements to be the right of the plaintiff, now called the cognizee.

3. A promife is in the nature of a verbal covenant, and wants nothing but the folemnity of writing and fealing to make it abfolutely the fame. If therefore it be to do any explicit act, it is an exprefs contract, as much as any covenant; and the breach of it is an equal injury. The remedy indeed is not exactly the fame: fince, inftead of an action of covenant, there only lies an action upon the cafe, for what is called the *affumpfit* or undertaking of the defendant; the failure of performing which is the wrong or injury done to the plaintiff, the damages whereof a jury are to eftimate and fettle. As if a builder promifes, undertakes, or affumes to Caius, that he will build and cover his houfe within a time limited, and fails to do it; Caius has an action on the cafe againft the builder, for this breach of his exprefs promife, undertaking, or *affumpfit*; and fhall recover a pecuniary fatisfaction for the injury fuftained by fuch delay. So alfo in the cafe before-mentioned, of a debt by fimple contract, if the debtor promifes to pay it and does not, this breach of promife entitles the creditor to his action on the cafe, inftead of being driven to action of debt. Thus likewife, a promiffory note, or note of hand not under feal, to pay money at a day certain, is an exprefs *affumpfit*; and the payee at common law, or by cuftom and act of parliament the indorfee, may recover the value of the note in damages, if it remains unpaid. Some agreements, indeed, though never fo exprefsly made, are deemed of fo important a nature, that they ought not to reft in verbal promife only, which cannot be proved but by the memory (which fometimes will induce the perjury) of witneffes. To prevent which, the ftatute of frauds, and perjuries, 29 Car. II. c. 3. enacts, that in the five following cafes no verbal promife fhall be fufficient to ground an action upon, but at the leaft fome note or *memorandum* of it fhall be made in writing, and figned by the party to be

charged therewith: 1. Where an executor or administrator promises to answer damages out of his own estate. 2. Where a man undertakes to answer for the debt, default, or miscarriage of another. 3. Where any agreement is made, upon consideration of marriage. 4. Where any contract or sale is made of lands, tenements, or hereditaments, or any interest therein. 5. And, lastly, where there is any agreement that is not to be performed within a year from the making thereof. In all these cases a mere verbal *assumpsit* is void (*a*).

From these *express* contracts the transition is easy to those that are only *implied* by law. Which are such as reason and justice dictate, and which therefore the law presumes that every man has contracted to perform ; and, upon this presumption, makes him answerable to such persons as suffer by his non-performance.

Of this nature are, first, such as are necessarily implied by the fundamental constitution of government, to which every man is a contracting party. And thus it is that every person is bound, and hath virtually agreed to pay such particular sums of money as are charged on him by the sentence, or assessed by the interpretation of the law. For it is a part of the original contract, entered into by all mankind who partake the benefits of society, to submit in all points to the municipal constitutions and local ordinances of that state, of which each individual is a member. Whatever, therefore, the laws order any one to pay, that becomes instantly a debt, which he hath beforehand contracted to discharge. And this implied agreement it is that gives the plaintiff a right to institute a second action, founded merely on the general contract, in order to recover such damages, or sum of money, as are assessed by the jury and adjudged by the court to be due from the defendant to the plaintiff in any former action.

---

(*a*) It should be observed, however, that though verbal contracts are void at law, they will, under particular circumstances, be enforced in equity. See the cases on this subject collected, and their principles ably investigated, by Mr. *Fonblanque*, in 1 *Treat. Eq.* c. 3. sec. 8 & 9 *notis*.

So that if he hath once obtained a judgment againſt another for a certain ſum, and neglects to take out execution thereupon, he may afterwards bring an action of debt upon this judgment, and ſhall not be put upon the proof of the original cauſe of action; but upon ſhewing the judgment once obtained, ſtill in full force, and yet unſatisfied, the law immediately implies, that by the original contract of ſociety the defendent hath contracted a debt, and is bound to pay it.

On the ſame principle it is, (of an implied original contract to ſubmit to the rules of the community, whereof we are members) that a forfeiture impoſed by the bye-laws and private ordinances of a corporation upon any that belong to the body, or an amercement ſet in a court-leet or court-baron upon any of the ſuitors to the court (for otherwiſe it will not be binding) immediately create a debt in the eye of the law: and ſuch forfeiture or amercement, if unpaid, work an injury to the party or parties entitled to receive it; for which the remedy is by action of debt.

The ſame reaſon may with equal juſtice be applied to all penal ſtatutes, that is, ſuch acts of parliament whereby a forfeiture is inflicted for tranſgreſſing the proviſions therein enacted. The party offending is here bound by the fundamental contract of ſociety to obey the directions of the legiſlature, and pay the forfeiture incurred to ſuch perſons as the law requires. The uſual application of this forfeiture is either to the party grieved, or elſe to any of the king's ſubjects in general. Of the former ſort is the forfeiture inflicted by the ſtatute of Wincheſter (explained and enforced by ſeveral ſubſequent ſtatutes) upon the hundred wherein a man is robbed, which is meant to oblige the hundredors to make hue and cry after the felon; for if they take him, they ſtand excuſed. But otherwiſe the party robbed is entitled to proſecute them, by a ſpecial action on the caſe, for damages equivalent to his loſs. And of the ſame nature is the action given by ſtatute 9 Geo. I. c. 22. commonly called the black act, againſt the inhabitants of any hundred, in order to make ſatisfaction in damages to all perſons who have ſuffered by the offences enumerated and made felony by that act. But, more ufually, thefe forfeitures created by ftatute are given at large, to any common informer ; or, in other words, to any fuch perfon or perfons as will fue for the fame: and hence fuch actions are called *popular* actions, becaufe they are given to the people in general. Sometimes one part is given to the king, to the poor, or to fome public ufe; and the other part to the informer or profecutor ; and then the fuit is called a *qui tam* action, becaufe it is brought by a perfon " *qui tam* " *pro domino rege, &c. quam pro fe ipfo in hac parte fequitur.*" If the king, therefore, himfelf commences this fuit, he fhall have the whole forfeiture. But if any one hath begun a *qui tam*, or *popular* action, no other perfon can purfue it ; and the verdict paffed upon the defendant in the firft fuit is a bar to all others, and conclufive even to the king himfelf.

A fecond clafs of implied contracts are fuch as do not arife from the exprefs determination of any court, or the pofitive direction of any ftatute ; but from natural reafon, and the juft conftruction of law. Which clafs extends to all prefumptive undertakings or *affumpfits* ; which, though never perhaps actually made, yet conftantly arife from this general implication and intendment of the courts of judicature, that every man hath engaged to perform what his duty or juftice requires. Thus,

1. If I employ a perfon to tranfact any bufinefs for me, or perform any work, the law implies that I undertook or affumed to pay him fo much as his labour deferved. And if I neglect to make him amends, he has a remedy for this injury by bringing his action on the cafe upon this implied *affumpfit* ; wherein he is at liberty to fuggeft that I promifed to pay him fo much as he reafonably deferved, and then to aver that his trouble was really worth fuch a particular fum, which the defendant has omitted to pay. But this valuation of his trouble is fubmitted to the determination of a jury ; who will affefs fuch a fum in damages as they think he really merited. This is called an *affumpfit* on a *quantum meruit*.

2. There is alfo an implied *affumpfit* on a *quantum valebat*, which is very fimilar to the former, being only where one takes up goods or wares of a tradefman, without exprefsly

agreeing for the price. There the law concludes, that both parties did intentionally agree that the real value of the goods should be paid, and an action on the case may be brought accordingly, if the vendee refuses to pay that value.

3. A third species of implied *assumpsits* is when one has had and received money belonging to another, with any valuable consideration given on the receiver's part: for the law construes this to be money had and received for the use of the owner only; and implies that the person so receiving promised and undertook to account for it to the true proprietor. And, if he unjustly detains it, an action on the case lies against him for the breach of such implied promise and undertaking; and he will be made to repair the owner in damages, equivalent to what he has detained in violation of such his promise. This is a very extensive and beneficial remedy, applicable to almost every case where the defendant has received money which *ex æquo et bono* he ought to refund. It lies for money paid by mistake, or on a consideration which happens to fail, or through imposition, extortion, or oppression, or where any undue advantage is taken of the plaintiff's situation.

4. Where a person has laid out and expended his own money for the use of another, at his request, the law implies a promise of re-payment, and an action will lie on this *assumpsit*.

5. Likewise fifthly, upon a stated account between two merchants, or other persons, the law implies that he against whom the balance appears has engaged to pay it to the other; though there be not any actual promise. And from this implication it is frequent for actions on the case to be brought, declaring that the plaintiff and defendant had settled their accounts together, *insimul computassent*, (which gives name to this species of *assumpsit*) and that the defendant engaged to pay the plaintiff the balance, but has since neglected to do it. But if no account has been made up, then the legal remedy is by bringing a writ of *account*, *de computo*, commanding the defendant to render a just account to the contrary. But, however, it is found by experience, that the most ready and effectual way to settle these matters of account is by bill

in a court of equity, where a difcovery may be had on the defendant's oath, without relying merely on the evidence which the plaintiff may be able to produce. Wherefore actions of account, to compel a man to bring in and fettle his accounts, are now very feldom ufed; though, when an account is once ftated, nothing is more common than an action upon the implied *affumpfit* to pay the balance.

6. The laft clafs of contracts, implied by reafon and conftruction of law, arifes upon this fuppofition, that every one who undertakes any office, employment, truft, or duty, contracts with thofe who employ or entruft him, to perform it with integrity, diligence, and fkill. And, if by his want of either of thofe qualities any injury accrues to individuals, they have therefore their remedy in damages by a fpecial action on the cafe. A few inftances will fully illuftrate this matter. If an officer of the public is guilty of neglect of duty, or a palpable breach of it, of non-feafance or of miffeafance; as, if the fheriff does not execute a writ fent to him, or if he wilfully makes a falfe return thereof; in both thefe cafes the party aggrieved fhall have an action *on the cafe*, for damages to be affeffed by a jury. If a fheriff or goaler fuffers a prifoner, who is taken upon mefne procefs (that is, during the pendency of a fuit) to efcape, he is liable to an action *on the cafe*. But if, after judgment, a gaoler or a fheriff permits a debtor to efcape, who is charged in execution for a certain fum, the debt immediately becomes his own, and he is compellable by action of *debt*, being for a fum liquidated and afcertained, to fatisfy the creditor his whole demand: which doctrine is grounded on the equity of the ftatutes of Weftm. 2. 13 Edw. I. c. 11. and 1 Ric. II. c. 12. An advocate or attorney that betrays the caufe of their client, or, being retained, neglect to appear at the trial, by which the caufe mifcarries, are liable to an action on the cafe, for a reparation to their injured client. There is alfo, in law, always an implied contract with a common inn-keeper, to fecure his gueft's goods in his inn; with a common carrier or bargemafter, to be anfwerable for the goods he carries: with a common farrier, that he fhoes a horfe well, without laming him; with a common taylor, or other workman, that

he performs his bufinefs in a workmanlike manner : in which if they fail, an action on the cafe lies to recover damages for fuch breach of their general undertaking. But if I employ a perfon to tranfact any of thefe concerns, whofe common profeffion and bufinefs it is not, the law implies no fuch *general* undertaking ; but, in order to charge him with damages, a *special* agreement is required. Alfo, if an inn-keeper, or other victualler, hangs out a fign and opens his houfe for travellers, it is an implied engagement to entertain all perfons who travel that way ; and upon this univerfal *affumpfit* an action on the cafe will lie againft him for damages, if he without good reafon refufes to admit a traveller. If any one cheats me with falfe cards or dice, or by falfe weights and meafures, or by felling me one commodity for another, an action on the cafe alfo lies againft him for damages, upon the contract which the law always implies, that every tranfaction is fair and honeft. In contracts likewife for fales, it is conftantly underftood that the feller undertakes that the commodity he fells is his own ; and if it proves otherwife, an action on the cafe lies againft him, to exact damages for this deceit. In contracts for provifions it is always implied that they are wholefome ; and, if they be not, the fame remedy may be had. Alfo, if he that felleth any thing doth upon the fale warrant it to be good, the law annexes a tacit contract to this warranty, that if it be not fo he fhall make compenfation to the buyer ; elfe it is an injury to good faith, for which an action on the cafe will lie to recover damages. The warranty muft be *upon the fale* ; for if it be made *after*, and not *at* the time of the fale, it is a void warranty. But if the vendor knew the goods to be unfound, and hath ufed any art to difguife them, or if they are in any fhape different from what he reprefents them to be to the buyer, this artifice fhall be equivalent to an exprefs warranty, and the vendor is anfwerable for their goodnefs. A general warranty will not extend to guard againft defects that are plainly and obvioufly the object of one's fenfes, as, if a horfe be warranted perfect, and wants either a tail or an ear, unlefs the buyer in this cafe be blind. But if cloth is warranted to be of fuch a length, when it is not, there an action on the case lies for damages; for that cannot be discerned by sight, but only by a collateral proof, the measuring it.

Besides the special action on the case, there is also a peculiar remedy, entitled an action of *deceit*, to give damages in some particular cases of fraud; and principally where one man does any thing in the name of another, by which he is deceived or injured; as if one brings an action in another's name, and then suffers a non-suit, whereby the plaintiff becomes liable to costs; or where one obtains or suffers a fraudulent recovery of lands, tenements, or chattels, to the prejudice of him that hath right. As, when by collusion the attorney of the tenant makes default in real action, or where the sheriff returns that the tenant was summoned when he was not so, and in either case he loses the land, the writ of *deceit* lies against the demandant, and also the attorney or the sheriff and his officers; to annul the former proceedings and recover back the land. It also lies in the cases of warranty beforementioned, and other personal injuries committed contrary to good faith and honesty. But an action *on the case*, for damages, in nature of a writ of *deceit*, is more usually brought upon these occasions. And indeed it is the only remedy for a lord of a manor, in or out of antient demesne, to reverse a fine or recovery had in the king's courts of lands lying within his jurisdiction; which would otherwise be thereby turned into frank fee. And this may be brought by the lord against the parties and *cestuy que use* of such fine or recovery; and thereby he shall obtain judgment not only for damages (which are usually remitted) but also to recover his court, and jurisdiction over the lands, and to annul the former proceedings.

Thus much for the non-performance of contracts express or implied, which includes every possible injury to what is by far the most considerable species of personal property, viz. that which consists in action merely, and not in possession. Which finishes our inquiries into such wrongs as may be offered to *personal* property, with their several remedies by suit or action.

## CHAPTER V.

### OF INJURIES TO REAL PROPERTY;

AND FIRST,

OF DISPOSSESSION, OR OUSTER OF THE FREEHOLD.

I COME now to confider fuch injuries as affect that fpecies of property which the laws of England have denominated *real*; as being of a more fubftantial and permanent nature, than thofe tranfitory rights of which perfonal chattels are the object.

Real injuries then, or injuries affecting real rights, are principally fix; 1. Oufter; 2. Trefpafs; 3. Nufance; 4. Wafte; 5. Subtraction; 6. Difturbance.

Oufter, or difpoffeffion, is a wrong or injury that carries with it the amotion of poffeffion: for thereby the wrongdoer gets into the actual occupation of the land or hereditament, and obliges him that hath a right to feek his legal remedy; in order to gain poffeffion, and damages for the injury fuftained. And fuch oufter, or difpoffeffion, may either be of the *freehold*, or of *chattels real*. Oufter of the *freehold* is effected by one of the following methods, 1. Abatement; 2. Intrufion; 3. Diffeifin; 4. Difcontinuance; 5. Deforcement.

1. And, firft, an *abatement* is where a perfon dies feifed of an inheritance, and before the heir or devifee enters, a ftranger who has no right makes entry, and gets poffeffion of the freehold: this entry of him is called an abatement, and he himfelf is denominated an abator.

2. The fecond fpecies of injury by oufter, or amotion of poffeffion from the freehold, is by *intrufion*: which is the entry of a ftranger, after a particular eftate of freehold is determined, before him in remainder or reverfion. And it happens where a tenant for term of life dieth feifed of certain lands and tenements, and a ftranger entereth thereon, after fuch death of the tenant, and before any entry of him in remainder or reverfion.

3. The third species of injury by ouster, or privation of the freehold, is by *disseisin*. Disseisin is a wrongful putting out of him that is seised of the freehold. The two former species of injury were by a wrongful entry where the possession was vacant; but this an attack upon him who is in actual possession, and turning him out of it.

These three species of injury, *abatement, intrusion,* and *disseisin,* are such wherein the entry of the tenant *ab initio,* as well as the continuance of his possession afterwards, is unlawful. But the two remaining species are where the entry of the tenant was at first lawful, but the wrong consists in the detaining of possession afterwards.

4. Such is, fourthly, the injury of *discontinuance;* which happens when he who hath an estate-tail, maketh a larger estate of the land than by law he is entitled to do: in which case the estate is good, so far as his power extends who made it, but no farther. As if tenant in tail makes a feoffment in fee-simple, or for the life of the feoffee, or in tail; all which are beyond his power to make, for that by the common law extends no farther than to make a lease for his own life: in such case the entry of the feoffee is lawful during the life of the feoffor; but if he retains the possession after the death of the feoffor, it is an injury, which is termed a discontinuance; the antient legal estate, which ought to have survived to the heir in tail, being gone, or at least suspended, and for a while discontinued.

5. The fifth and last species of injuries by ouster or privation of the freehold, where the entry of the present tenant or possessor was originally lawful, but his detainer is now become unlawful, is that by *deforcement.* This, in it's most extensive sense, is *nomen generalissimum;* a much larger and more comprehensive expression than any of the former: it then signifying the holding of any lands or tenements to which another person hath a right. So that this includes as well an abatement, an intrusion, a disseisin, a discontinuance, as any other species of wrong whatsoever, whereby he that hath right to the freehold is kept out of possession. But, as contra-distinguished from the former, it is only such a detainer of the

freehold, from him that hath the right of property, but never had any poffeffion under that right, as falls within none of the injuries which we have before explained.

The feveral fpecies and degrees of injury by *oufter* being thus afcertained and defined, the next confideration is the remedy: which is, univerfally, the *reftitution* or *delivery of poffeffion* to the right owner; and, in fome cafes, *damages* alfo for the unjuft amotion. The methods, whereby thefe remedies, or either of them, may be obtained, are various.

I. The firft is that extrajudicial and fummary one, of *entry* by the legal owner, when another perfon, who hath no right, hath previoufly taken poffeffion of lands or tenements. In this cafe the party entitled may make a formal, but peaceable, entry thereon, declaring that thereby he takes poffeffion. Such an entry gives a man feifin, or puts into immediate poffeffion him that hath right of entry on the eftate, and thereby makes him complete owner, and capable of conveying it from himfelf by either defcent or purchafe.

This remedy by entry takes place in three only of the five fpecies of oufter, *viz.* abatement, intrufion, and diffeifin: for, as in thefe the original entry of the wrongdoer was unlawful, they may therefore be remedied by the mere entry of him who hath right. But, upon a difcontinuance or deforcement, the owner of the eftate cannot enter, but is driven to his action. Yet a man may enter on his tenant by fufferance: for fuch tenant hath no freehold, but only a bare poffeffion; which may be defeated, like a tenancy at will, by the mere entry of the owner.

On the other hand, in cafe of abatement, intrufion, or diffeifin, where entries are generally lawful, this right of entry may be *tolled*, that is, taken away, by defcent. Defcents, which take away entries, are when any one, feifed by any means whatfoever of the inheritance of a corporeal hereditament, dies, whereby the fame defcends to his heir: in this cafe, however feeble the right of the anceftor might be, the entry of any other perfon who claims title to the freehold is taken away; and he cannot recover poffeffion againft the heir by this fummary method, but is driven to his action to gain a legal feifin of the eftate.

So that in general it appears, that no man can recover poffeffion by mere entry on lands, which another hath by defcent. Yet this rule hath fome exceptions, wherein thofe reafons ceafe upon which the general doctrine is grounded; efpecially if the claimant were under any legal difabilities, during the life of the anceftor, either of infancy, coverture, imprifonment, infanity, or being out of the realm: in all which cafes there is no neglect or *laches* in the claimant, and therefore no defcent fhall bar, or take away his entry. And this title of taking away entries by defcent, is ftill farther narrowed by the ftatute 32 Hen. VIII. c. 33. which enacts, that if any perfon diffeifes or turns another out of poffeffion, no defcent to the heir of the diffeifor fhall take away the entry of him that has right to the land, unlefs the diffeifor had peaceable poffeffion five years next after the diffeifin. But the ftatute extendeth not to any feoffee or donee of the diffeifor, mediate or immediate (*a*). On the other hand, it is enacted, by the ftatute of limitations, 21 Jac. I. c. 16. that no entry fhall be made by any man upon lands, unlefs within twenty years after his right fhall accrue. And by ftatute 4 & 5 Ann. c. 16. no entry fhall be of force to fatisfy the faid ftatute of limitations, or to avoid a fine levied of lands, unlefs an action be thereupon commenced within one year after, and profecuted with effect.

II. Thus far of remedies, where the tenant or occupier of the land hath gained only a *mere poffeffion*, and no apparent fhadow of right. Next follow another clafs, which are in ufe where the title of the tenant or occupier is advanced one ftep nearer to perfection; fo that he hath in him not only a bare poffeffion, which may be deftroyed by a bare entry, but

---

(*a*) See the particular cafes mentioned by *Littleton*, b. 3. ch. 6. the principles of which are well explained in *Gilbert's Law of Tenures*. A.

also an *apparent right of possession*, which cannot be removed but by orderly course of law: in the process of which it must be shewn, that though he hath at present possession and therefore hath the presumptive right, yet there is a right of possession, superior to his, residing in him who brings the action.

These remedies are either by a *writ of entry*, or an *assise:* which are actions merely *possessory;* serving only to regain that possession, whereof the demandant (that is, he who sues for the land) or his ancestors have been unjustly deprived by the tenant or possessor of the freehold, or those under whom he claims. They decide nothing with respect to the *right of property:* only restoring the demandant to that state or situation, in which he was (or by law ought to have been) before the dispossession committed. But this without any prejudice to the right of ownership: for, if the dispossessor has any legal claim, he may afterwards exert it, notwithstanding a recovery against him in these possessory actions.

I have now gone through the several species of injury by ouster and dispossession of the freehold, with the remedies applicable to each: there are, however, but very few instances for more than a century past of prosecuting any real action for land by writ of *entry, assise, formedon,* writ of *right,* or otherwise; the title of lands being now usually tried in actions of *ejectment* or *trespass;* of which in the following chapters.

## CHAPTER VI.

### OF DISPOSSESSION, OR OUSTER OF CHATTELS REAL.

HAVING, in the preceding chapter, considered the several species of injury by dispossession or ouster of the *freehold*, the method which I there marked out leads me next to consider injuries by ouster of *chattels real*; that is, by amoving the possession of the tenant from an estate by statute-merchant, statute-staple, recognizance in the nature of it, or *elegit;* or from an estate for years.

1. Ouster, or amotion of possession, from estates held by statute, recognizance, or *elegit*, is only liable to happen by a species of disseisin, or turning out of the legal proprietor, before his estate is determined by raising the sum for which it is given him in pledge.

II. As for ouster, or amotion of possession, from an estate for years; this happens only by a like kind of disseisin, ejection, or turning out, of the tenant from the occupation of the land during the continuance of his term. For this injury the law has provided him with two remedies, according to the circumstances and situation of the wrongdoer: the writ of *ejectione firmæ*; which lies against any one, the lessor, reversioner, remainder-man, or any stranger, who is himself the wrongdoer and has committed the injury complained of: and the writ of *quare ejecit infra terminum;* which lies not against the wrongdoer or ejector himself, but his feoffee or other person claiming under him. These are mixed actions, somewhat between real and personal; for therein are two things recovered, as well restitution of the term of years, as damages for the ouster or wrong.

1. A writ then of *ejectione firmæ*, or action of trespass in *ejectment*, lieth where lands or tenements are let for a term of years; and afterwards the lessor, reversioner, remainder-man, or any stranger, doth eject or oust the lessee of his term.

Since the disuse of real actions, this mixed proceeding is become the common method of trying the title to lands or tenements. And, to prevent fraudulent recoveries of the possession, by collusion with the tenant of the land, all tenants are obliged, by statute 11 Geo. II. c. 19. on pain of forfeiting three years rent, to give notice to their landlords, when served with any declaration in ejectment: and any landlord may, by leave of the court, be made a co-defendant to the action, in case the tenant himself appears to it.

The damages recovered in these actions, though formerly their only intent, are now usually (since the title has been considered as the principal question) very small and inadequate; amounting commonly to one shilling or some other trivial sum. In order therefore to complete the remedy, when the possession has been long detained from him that had the right to it, an action of trespass also lies, after a recovery in ejectment, to recover the mesne profits which the tenant in possession has wrongfully received. Which action may be brought in the name of either the nominal plaintiff in the ejectment, or his lessor, against the tenant in possession: whether he be made party to the ejectment, or suffers judgment to go by default. In this case the judgment in ejectment is conclusive evidence against the defendant, for all profits which have accrued since the date of the demise stated in the former declaration of the plaintiff; but if the plaintiff sues for any antecedent profits, the defendant may make a new defence.

Such is the modern way, of obliquely bringing in question the title to lands and tenements, in order to try it in this collateral manner; a method which is now universally adopted in almost every case: because the form of the proceeding being entirely fictitious, it is wholly in the power of the court to direct the application of that fiction, so as to prevent fraud and chicane, and eviscerate the very truth of the title.

But a writ of ejectment is not an adequate means to try the title of all estates; for on those things, whereon an entry cannot in fact be made, no entry shall be supposed by any fiction of the parties. Therefore an ejectment will not lie of an advowson, a rent, a common or other incorporeal hereditament: except for tithes in the hands of lay appropriators, by the express purview of statute 32 Hen. VIII. c. 7. which doctrine hath since been extended by analogy to tithes in the hands of the clergy: nor will it lie in such cases, where the entry of him that hath right is taken away by descent, discontinuance, twenty years dispossession, or otherwise.

This action of ejectment is however rendered a very easy and expeditious remedy to landlords whose tenants are in arrear, by statute 4 Geo. II. c. 28. which enacts, that every landlord, who hath by his lease a right of re-entry in case of non-payment of rent, when half a year's rent is due, and no sufficient distress is to be had, may serve a declaration in ejectment on his tenant, or fix the same upon some notorious part of the premises, which shall be valid, without any formal re-entry or previous demand of rent. And a recovery in such ejectment shall be final and conclusive, both in law and equity, unless the rent and all costs be paid or tendered within six calendar months afterwards.

2. The writ of *quare ejecit infra terminum* lieth, by the antient law, where the wrongdoer or ejector is not himself in possession of the lands, but another who claims under him. But since the introduction of fictitious ousters, whereby the title may be tried against any tenant in possession (by what means soever he acquired it) and the subsequent recovery of damages by action of trespass for mesne profits, this action is fallen into disuse.

## CHAPTER VII.

### OF TRESPASS.

IN the two preceding chapters we have considered such injuries to real property, as consisted in an ouster, or amotion of the possession. Those which remain to be discussed are such as may be offered to a man's real property without any amotion from it.

The second species therefore of real injuries, or wrongs that affect a man's lands, tenements, or hereditaments, is that of *trespass*. Trespass, in it's largest, and most extensive sense, signifies any transgression or offence against the law of nature, of society, or of the country in which we live; whether it relates to a man's person, or his property. But in the limited and confined sense, in which we are at present to consider it, it signifies no more than an entry on another man's ground without a lawful authority, and doing some damage, however inconsiderable, to his real property.

Every unwarrantable entry on another's soil the law entitles a trespass by *breaking his close*; the words of the writ of trespass commanding the defendant to shew cause, *quare clausum querentis fregit*. For every man's land is in the eye of the law inclosed and set apart from his neighbours: and that either by a visible and material fence, as one field is divided from another by a hedge; or, by an ideal invisible boundary, existing only in the contemplation of law, as when one man's land adjoins to another's in the same field. And every such entry or breach of a man's close carries necessarily along with it some damage or other: for, if no other special loss can be assigned, yet still the words of the writ itself specify one general damage, viz. the treading down and bruising his herbage.

One must have a property (either absolute or temporary) in the soil, and actual possession by entry, to be able to maintain an action of trespass: or at least, it is requisite that the party have a lease and possession of the vesture and herbage of the land. Thus, if a meadow be divided annually among the parishioners by lot, then, after each person's several portion is allotted, they may be respectively capable of maintaining an action for the breach of their several closes: for they have an exclusive interest and freehold therein for the time. But before entry and actual possession, one cannot maintain an action of trespass, though he hath the freehold in law. And, therefore, an heir before entry cannot have this action against an abator; though a disseisee might have it against the disseisor, for the injury done by the disseisin itself, at which time the plaintiff was seised of the land; but he cannot have it for any act done after the disseisin, until he hath gained possession by re-entry, and then he may well maintain it for the immediate damage done; for after his re-entry, the law, by a kind of *jus postliminii*, supposes the freehold to have all along continued in him. Neither, by the common law, in case of an intrusion or deforcement, could the party kept out of possession sue the wrong-doer by a mode of redress, which was calculated merely for injuries committed against the land while *in the possession* of the owner. But now by the statute 6 Ann. c. 18. if a guardian or trustee for any infant, a husband seised *jure uxoris*, or a person having any estate or in-

## C. VII. TRESPASS.

tereſt determinable upon a life or lives, ſhall after the determination of their reſpective intereſts, hold over and continue in poſſeſſion of the lands or tenements, without the conſent of the perſon intitled thereto, they are adjudged to be treſpaſſers; and any reverſioner or remainder-man, expectant on any life-eſtate, may once in every year, by motion to the court of chancery, procure the *ceſtui que vie* to be produced by the tenant of the land, or may enter thereon in caſe of his refuſal or wilful neglect. And, by the ſtatutes of 4 Geo. II. c. 28. and 11 Geo. II. c. 19. in caſe after the determination of any term of life, lives, or years, any perſon ſhall wilfully hold over the ſame, the leſſor or reverſioner is entitled to recover by action of debt, either at the rate of double the annual value of the premiſes, in caſe he himſelf hath demanded and given notice in writing to the tenant to deliver the poſſeſſion; or elſe double the uſual rent, in caſe the notice of quitting proceeds from the tenant himſelf, having power to determine his leaſe, and he afterwards neglects to carry that notice into due execution.

A man is anſwerable for not only his own treſpaſs, but that of his cattle alſo: for if, by his negligent keeping they ſtray upon the land of another (and much more if he permits, or drives them on) and they there tread down his neighbour's herbage, and ſpoil his corn or his trees, this is a treſpaſs for which the owner muſt anſwer in damages. And the law gives the party injured a double remedy in this caſe, by permitting him to diſtrein the cattle thus *damage-feaſant*, or doing damage, till the owner ſhall make him ſatisfaction; or elſe by leaving him to the common remedy *in foro contentioſo*, by action. And the action that lies in either of theſe caſes, of treſpaſs committed upon another's land, either by a man himſelf or his cattle, is the action of treſpaſs *vi et armis*; whereby a man is called upon to anſwer, *quare vi et armis clauſum ipſius A. apud B. fregit, et blada ipſius A. ad valentiam centum ſolidorum ibidem nuper creſcentia cum quibuſdam averiis depaſtus fuit, conculcavit, et conſumpſit, &c.* for the law always couples the idea of force with that of intruſion upon the property of another. And herein, if any unwarrantable act of the defendant or his beasts in coming upon the land be proved, it is an act of trespass for which the plaintiff must recover some damages; such however as the jury shall think proper to assess.

In some cases trespass is justifiable; or, rather, entry on another's land or house shall not in those cases be accounted trespass: as, if a man comes thither to demand or pay money, there payable: or to execute, in a legal manner, the process of the law. Also a man may justify entering into an inn or public house, without the leave of the owner first specially asked; because, when a man professes the keeping of such inn or public house, he thereby gives a general licence to any person to enter his doors. So a landlord may justify entering to distrein for rent; a commoner to attend his cattle, commoning on another's land; and a reversioner, to see if any waste be committed on the estate, for the apparent necessity of the thing. Also, it hath been said, that by the common law and custom of England, the poor are allowed to enter and glean upon another's ground after the harvest, without being guilty of trespass (a): which humane provision seems borrowed from the mosaical law. In like manner the common law warrants the hunting of ravenous beasts of prey, as badgers and foxes in another man's land; because the destroy-

---

(a) The dicta referred to by the learned judge are those of *Hale, C. J. (Tryal per pais,* 8th *edit.* 534) and *Gilbert, Ch. B. (Law of Evidence,* 4th *edit.* 250) and these have since been recognized, and their consonance with the common law strenuously asserted by *Gould, J.* in *Steel* v. *Houghton,* 1 *H. Blac. Rep.* 51. but his opinion was over-ruled by the other judges who concurred in declaring the practice of *gleaning* to be endured on mere *indulgence,* unsupported by any legal right whatever, because " 1. *(per Loughborough, C. J.)* Inconsistent with the nature of property, which implies exclusive enjoyment. 2. Destructive of the peace and good order of society, and amounting to a general vagrancy, and, 3. Incapable of enjoyment, since nothing which is not inexhaustible, like a perennial stream, can be capable of universal promiscuous enjoyment." *Supra,* where the question is *seriatim* and learnedly discussed.

ing such creatures is said to be profitable to the public. But in cases where a man misdemeans himself, or makes an ill use of the authority with which the law entrusts him, he shall be accounted a trespassor *ab initio*: as if one comes into a tavern and will not go out in a reasonable time, but tarries there all night contrary to the inclinations of the owner; this wrongful act shall affect and have relation back even to his first entry, and make the whole a trespass. But a bare non-feasance, as not paying for the wine he calls for, will not make him a trespasser; for this is only a breach of contract, for which the taverner shall have an action of debt or *assumpsit* against him. So if a landlord distreined for rent, and wilfully killed the distress, this by the common law made him a trespasser *ab initio*: and so indeed would any other irregularity have done, till the statute 11 Geo. II. c. 19. which enacts, that no subsequent irregularity of the landlord shall have a special action of trespass; but the party injured shall have a special action of trespass or on the case for the real specific injury sustained, unless tender of amends hath been made. But still, if a reversioner, who enters on pretence of seeing waste, breaks the house, or stays there all night, or if the commoner who comes to tend his cattle, cuts down a tree; in these and similar cases the law judges that he entered for this unlawful purpose, and therefore, as the act which demonstrates such his purpose is a trespass, he shall be esteemed a trespassor *ab initio*. So, also, in the case of hunting the fox or the badger, a man cannot justify breaking the soil, and digging him out of his earth: for though the law warrants the hunting of such noxious animals for the public good, yet it is held that such things must be done in an ordinary and usual manner; therefore, as there is an ordinary course to kill them, *viz.* by hunting, the court held that the digging for them was unlawful.

A man may also justify in an action of trespass, on account of the freehold and right of entry being in himself; and this defence brings the title of the estate in question. This is therefore one of the ways devised, since the disuse of real actions, to try the property of estates; though it is not so usual as that by ejectment, because that, being now a mixed action, not only gives damages for the ejection, but also possession of the land: whereas in trespass, which is merely a personal suit, the right can be only ascertained, but no possession delivered; nothing being recovered but damages for the wrong committed.

In order to prevent trifling and vexatious actions of trespass, as well as other personal actions, it is *(inter alia)* enacted by statutes 43 Eliz. c. 6. and 22 & 23 Car. II. c. 9. § 136. that where the jury, who try an action of trespass, give less damages than forty shillings, the plaintiff shall be allowed no more costs than damages; unless the judge shall certify under his hand that the freehold or title of the land came chiefly in question. But this rule now admits of two exceptions more, which have been made by subsequent statutes. One is by statute 8 & 9 W. III. c. 11. which enacts, that in all actions of trespass, wherein it shall appear that the trespass was wilful and malicious, and it be so certified by the judge, the plaintiff shall recover full costs. Every trespass is *wilful*, where the defendant has notice, and is specially forewarned not to come on the land; as every trespass is *malicious*, though the damage may not amount to forty shillings, where the intent of the defendant plainly appears to be to harass and distress the plaintiff. The other exception is by statute 4 and 5 W. & M. c. 23. which gives full costs against any inferior tradesman, apprentice, or other dissolute person, who is convicted of a trespass in hawking, hunting, fishing, or fowling upon another's land. Upon this statute it has been adjudged, that if a person be an inferior tradesman, as clothier for instance, it matters not what qualification he may have in point of estate; but, if he be guilty of such trespass, he shall be liable to pay full costs.

## CHAPTER VIII.

### OF NUSANCE.

A THIRD fpecies of real injuries to a man's lands and tenements, is by *nufance*. Nufance, *nocumentum*, or annoyance, fignifies any thing that worketh hurt, inconvenience, or damage. And nufances are of two kinds; *public* or *common* nufances, which affect the public, and are an annoyance to *all* the king's fubjects; for which reafon we muft refer them to the clafs of public wrongs, or crimes and mifdemefnors: and *private* nufances, which are the objects of our prefent confideration, and may be defined, any thing done to the hurt or annoyance of the lands, tenements, or hereditaments of another. We will therefore, firft, mark out the feveral kinds of nufances, and then their refpective remedies.

I. In difcuffing the feveral kinds of nufances, we will confider, firft, fuch nuifances as may affect a man's corporeal hereditaments, and then thofe that may damage fuch as are incorporeal.

1. Firft, as to *corporeal* inheritances. If a man builds a houfe fo clofe to mine that his roof overhangs my roof, and throws the water off his roof upon mine, this is a nufance, for which an action will lie. Likewife to erect a houfe or other building fo near to mine that it obftructs my antient lights and windows, is a nufance of a fimilar nature. But, in this latter cafe it is neceffary that the windows be *antient*, (*a*), have fubfifted there a long time without interruption, otherwife there is no injury done. For he hath as much right to build a new edifice upon his ground, as I have upon mine; fince every man may erect what he pleafes upon the upright or perpendicular of his own foil, fo as not to preju-

---

(*a*) The time held to be fufficiently *antient* to entitle the owner to a perpetuity of enjoyment, feems to be 20 years, in conformity to the time limited for bringing an ejectment. See *Lewis* v. *Price*, 2 *Efp. Ni. Pri.* 636.

dice what has long been enjoyed by another; and it was my folly to build so near another's ground. Also, if a person keeps his hogs, or other noisome animals, so near the house of another, that the stench of them incommodes him, and makes the air unwholesome, this is an injurious nusance, as it tends to deprive him of the use and benefit of his house. A like injury is, if one's neighbour sets up and exercises any offensive trade; as a tanner's, a tallowchandler's, or the like; for though these are lawful and necessary trades, yet they should be exercised in remote places; for the rule is, "*sic utere tuo, ut alienum non lædas:*" this therefore is an actionable nusance. So that the nusances which affect a man's *dwelling* may be reduced to these three: 1. Overhanging it; which is also a species of trespass, for *cujus est solum ejus est usque ad cœlum*: 2. Stopping antient lights: and, 3. Corrupting the air with noisome smells: for light and air are two indispensable requisites to every dwelling. But depriving one of a mere matter of pleasure, as of a fine prospect, by building a wall, or the like; this, as it abridges nothing really convenient or necessary, is no injury to the sufferer, and is therefore not an actionable nusance.

As to nusance to one's *lands*: if one erects a smelting house for lead so near the land of another, that the vapour and smoke kills his corn and grass, and damages his cattle therein, this is held to be a nusance. And by consequence it follows, that if one does any other act, in itself lawful, which yet being done in that place necessarily tends to the damage of another's property, it is a nusance: for it is incumbent on him to find some other place to do that act, where it will be less offensive. So also, if my neighbour ought to scour a ditch, and does not, whereby my land is overflowed, this is an actionable nusance.

With regard to *other* corporeal hereditaments: it is a nusance to stop or divert water that uses to run to another's meadow or mill; to corrupt or poison a water-course, by erecting a dye-house or a lime-pit for the use of trade, in the upper part of the stream; or in short to do any act therein, that in it's consequences must necessarily tend to the prejudice of one's neighbour. So closely does the law of England enforce that excellent rule of gospel-morality, of "doing to others, as we would they should do unto ourselves."

2. As to *incorporeal* hereditaments, the law carries itself with the same equity. If I have a way, annexed to my estate, across another's land, and he obstructs me in the use of it, either by totally stopping it, or putting logs across it, or ploughing over it, it is a nusance: for in the first case I cannot enjoy my right at all, and in the latter I cannot enjoy it so commodiously as I ought. Also, if I am entitled to hold a fair or market, and another person sets up a fair or market so near mine that he does me a prejudice, it is a nusance to the freehold which I have in my market or fair. But in order to make this out to be a nusance, it is necessary, 1. That my market or fair be the elder, otherwise the nusance lies at my own door. 2. That the market be erected within the third part of twenty miles from mine. For Sir Matthew Hale construes the *dieta*, or reasonable day's journey, mentioned by Bracton, to be twenty miles: as indeed it is usually understood not only in our own laws, but also in the civil, from which we probably borrowed it. So that if the new market be not within seven miles of the old one, it is no nusance: for it is held reasonable that every man should have a market within one third of a day's journey from his own home; that, the day being divided into three parts, he may spend one part in going, another in returning, and the third in transacting his necessary business there. If such market or fair be on the same day with mine, it is *prima facie* a nusance to mine, and there needs no proof of it, but the law will intend it to be so: but if it be on any other day, it *may* be a nusance; though whether it *is* so or not, cannot be intended or presumed, but I must make proof of it to the jury. If a ferry is erected on a river, so near another antient ferry as to draw away it's custom, it is a nusance to the owner of the old one. For where there is a ferry by prescription, the owner is bound to keep it always in repair and readiness, for the ease of all the king's subjects; otherwise he may be grievously amerced: it would be therefore

extremely hard, if a new ferry were fuffered to fhare his profits, which does not alfo fhare his burthen. But where the reafon ceafes, the law alfo ceafes with it: therefore it is no nufance to erect a mill fo near mine, as to draw away the cuftom, unlefs the miller alfo intercepts the water. Neither is it a nufance to fet up any trade, or a fchool, in neighbourhood or rivalfhip with another: for by fuch emulation the public are like to be gainers; and, if the new mill or fchool occafion a damage to the old one, it is *damnum abfque injuria*.

II. Let us next attend to the remedies, which the law has given for this injury of nufance. And here I muft premife that the law gives no *private* remedy for any thing but a *private* wrong. Therefore no *action* lies for a public or common nufance, but an *indictment* only: becaufe the damage being common to *all* the king's fubjects, no *one* can affign his particular proportion of it; or if he could, it would be extremely hard if every fubject in the kingdom were allowed to harafs the offender with feparate actions. For this reafon, no perfon, natural or corporate, can have an action for a public nufance, or punifh it; but only the king in his public capacity of fupreme governor, and *pater-familias* of the kingdom. Yet this rule admits of one exception; where a private perfon fuffers fome extraordinary damage, beyond the reft of the king's fubjects, by a public nufance; in which cafe he fhall have a private fatisfaction by action. As if, by means of a ditch dug acrofs a public way, which is a common nufance, a man or his horfe fuffer any injury by falling therein; there, for this particular damage, which is not common to others, the party fhall have his action. Alfo if a man hath abated, or removed, a nufance which offended him (as we may remember it was ftarted in the firft chapter of this book, that the party injured hath a right to do) in this cafe he is entitled to no action. For he had choice of two remedies; either without fuit, by abating it himfelf, by his own mere act and authority; or by fuit, in which he may both recover damages, and remove it by the aid of the law: but, having made his election of one remedy, he is totally precluded from the other.

The remedies by suit are, 1. By action *on the case* for damages; in which the party injured shall only recover a satisfaction for the injury sustained; but cannot thereby remove the nusance. Indeed every continuance of a nusance is held to be a fresh one; and therefore a fresh action will lie, and very exemplary damages will probably be given, if, after one verdict against him, the defendant has the hardiness to continue it. Yet the founders of the law of England did not rely upon probabilities merely, in order to give relief to the injured. They have therefore provided two other actions; the *assise of nusance*, and the writ of *quod permittat prosternere*: which not only give the plaintiff satisfaction for his injury past, but also strike at the root and remove the cause itself, the nusance that occasioned the injury. These two actions, however, can only be brought by the tenant of the freehold; so that a lessee for years is confined to his action upon the case. And both these actions, of *assise of nusance*, and of *quod permittat prosternere*, are now out of use, and have given way to the action on the case.

## CHAPTER IX.

### OF WASTE.

THE fourth species of injury that may be offered to one's real property, is by *waste*, or destruction in lands and tenements. What shall be called waste was considered in a former volume, as it was a means of forfeiture, and thereby of transferring the property of real estates. I shall therefore here only beg leave to remind the student, that waste is a spoil and destruction of the estate, either in houses, woods, or lands; by demolishing not the temporary profits only, but the very substance of the thing; thereby rendering it wild and desolate; which the common law expresses very significantly by the word *vastum*: and that this *vastum*, or waste, is either voluntary, or permissive; the one by an actual and designed demolition of the lands, woods, and houses; the other arising from mere negligence, and want of sufficient care in reparations, fences, and the like. So that my only business is, at present, to shew, to whom this waste is an injury; and, of course, who is entitled to any, and what, remedy by action.

I. The persons who may be injured by waste, are such as have some *interest* in the estate wasted; for if a man be the absolute tenant in fee-simple, without any incumbrance or charge on the premisses, he may commit whatever waste his own indiscretion may prompt him to, without being impeachable or accountable for it to any one. And, though his heir is sure to be the sufferer, yet *nemo est hæres viventis*: no man is certain of succeeding him, as well on account of the uncertainty which shall die first, as also because he has it in his own power to constitute what heir he pleases, according to the civil law notion of an *hæres natus* and an *hæres factus*: or, in the more accurate phraseology of our English law, he may aliene or devise his estate to whomever he think proper, and by such alienation or devise may disinherit his heir at law. Into whose hands soever, therefore, the estate wasted comes, after a tenant in fee-simple, though the waste is undoubtedly *damnum*, it is *damnum absque injuria*.

One species of interest, which is injured by waste, is that of a person who has a right of common in the place wasted; especially if it be common of *estovers*, or a right of cutting and carrying away wood for house-bote, plough-bote, &c. Here, if the owner of the wood demolishes the whole wood, and thereby destroys all possibility of taking estovers, this is an injury to the commoner, amounting to no less than a disseisin of his common of estovers, if he chooses so to consider it; for which he has his remedy to recover possession and damages by assise, if entitled to a freehold in such common: but if he has only a chattel interest, then he can only recover damages by an action on the case for this waste and destruction of the woods, out of which his estovers were to issue.

But the most usual and important interest, that is hurt by

this commiffion of wafte, is that of him who hath the remainder or reverfion of the inheritance, after a particular eftate for life or years in being. Here, if the particular tenant, (be it the tenant in dower or by curtefy, who was anfwerable for wafte at the common law, or the leffee for life or years, who was firft made liable by the ftatutes of Marlbridge and of Glocefter) if the particular tenant, I fay, commits or fuffers any wafte, it is a manifeft injury to him that has the inheritance, as it tends to mangle and difmember it of it's moft defirable incidents and ornaments, among which timber and houfes may juftly be reckoned the principal. To him therefore in remainder or reverfion, to whom the *inheritance* appertains in expectancy, the law hath given an adequate remedy. For he, who hath the remainder *for life* only, is not entitled to fue for wafte; fince his intereft may never perhaps come into poffeffion, and then he hath fuffered no injury. Yet a parfon, vicar, arch-deacon, prebendary, and the like, who are feifed in right of their churches of any remainder or reverfion, may have an action of wafte; for they, in many cafes, have for the benefit of the church and of the fucceffor a fee-fimple qualified: and yet, as they are not feifed in their own right, the writ of wafte fhall not fay, *ad exhæredationem ipfius*, as for other tenants in fee-fimple; but *ad exhæredationem ecclefiæ*, in whofe right the fee-fimple is holden.

II. The redrefs for this injury of wafte is of two kinds, preventive, and corrective: the former of which is by writ of *eftrepement*, the latter by that of *wafte*. But, befides this preventive redrefs at common law, the courts of equity, upon bill exhibited therein, complaining of wafte and deftruction, will grant an injunction in order to ftay wafte, until the defendant fhall have put in his anfwer, and the court fhall thereupon make farther order. Which is now become the moft ufual way of preventing wafte.

When the wafte and damages are afcertained, either by confeffion, verdict, or inquiry of the fheriff, judgment is given, in purfuance of the ftatute of Glocefter, c. 5. that the plaintiff shall recover the place wasted; for which he has immediately a writ of *seisin*, provided the particular estate be still subsisting, (for, if it be expired, there can be no forfeiture of the land) and also that the plaintiff shall recover treble the damages assessed by the jury; which he must obtain in the same manner as all other damages, in actions personal and mixed, are obtained, whether the particular estate be expired, or still in being.

## CHAPTER X.

### OF SUBTRACTION.

SUBTRACTION, which is the fifth species of injuries affecting a man's real property, happens, when any person who owes any suit, duty, custom, or service to another, withdraws or neglects to perform it. But the remedy differs according to the nature of the services; whether they be due by virtue of any tenure, or by custom only.

I. Fealty, suit of court, and rent, are duties and services usually issuing and arising *ratione tenuræ*, being the conditions upon which the antient lords granted out their lands to their feudatories: whereby it was stipulated, that they and their heirs should take the oath of fealty or fidelity to their lord, which was the feodal bond or *commune vinculum* between lord and tenant; that they should do suit, or duly attend and follow the lord's courts, and there, from time to time, give their assistance, by serving on juries, either to decide the property of their neighbours in the court-baron, or correct their misdemesnors in the court-leet; and, lastly, that they should yield to the lord certain annual stated returns, in military attendance, in provisions, in arms, in matters of ornament or pleasure, in rustic employments or prædial labours, or (which is *instar omnium*) in money, which will provide all the rest; all which are comprized under the one general name of *reditus*, return, or rent. And the subtraction or non-observance of any of these conditions, by neglecting to swear fealty, to do suit of court, or to render the rent or service reserved, is an injury to the freehold of the lord, by diminishing and depreciating the value of his seignory.

The general remedy for all these is by *distress;* and it is the only remedy at the common law for the two first of them. The nature of distresses, their incidents and consequences we have before more than once explained: it may here suffice to remember, that they are a taking of beasts, or other personal property, by way of pledge to enforce the performance of something due from the party distreined upon. And for the most part it is provided that distresses be reasonable and moderate; but, in case of distress for fealty or suit of court, no distress can be unreasonable, immoderate, or too large: for this is the only remedy to which the party aggrieved is entitled, and therefore it ought to be such as is sufficiently compulsory; and, be it of what value it will, there is no harm done, especially as it cannot be sold or made away with, but must be restored immediately on satisfaction made. A distress of this nature, that has no bounds with regard to it's quantity, and may be repeated from time to time, until the stubbornness of the party is conquered, is called a *distress infinite;* which is also used for some other purposes, as in summoning jurors, and the like.

Other remedies for subtraction of rents or services are, 1. By action of *debt*, for the breach of this express contract, of which enough has been formerly said. This is the most usual remedy, when recourse is had to any action at all for the recovery of pecuniary rents, to which species of render almost all free services are now reduced, since the abolition of the military tenures. But for a freehold rent, reserved on a lease for life, &c. no action of *debt* lay by the common law, during the continuance of the freehold out of which it issued; for the law would not suffer a *real* injury to be remedied by an action that was merely *personal*. However, by the statutes 8 Ann. c. 14. and 5 Geo. III. c. 17. actions of debt may now be brought at any time to recover such freehold rents.

And, by statute, 11 Geo. II. c. 19. §. 16. which enacts, that where any tenant at rack-rent shall be one year's rent in arrear, and shall desert the demised premises, leaving the same uncultivated or unoccupied, so that no sufficient distress can be had; two justices of the peace (after notice affixed on the premises for fourteen days without effect) may give the landlord possession thereof, and thenceforth the lease shall be void.

II. Thus far of the remedies for subtraction of rents or other services due by *tenure*. There are also other services, due by antient *custom* and *prescription* only. Such is that of doing suit to another's mill: where the persons, resident in a particular place, by usage time out of mind have been accustomed to grind their corn at a certain mill; and afterwards any of them go to another mill, and withdraw their suit from the antient mill. But besides these special remedies for subtractions, to compel the specific performance of the service due by custom; an action *on the case* will also lie for all of them, to repair the party injured in damages. And thus much for the injury of subtraction.

## CHAPTER XI.

### OF DISTURBANCE.

THE sixth and last species of real injuries is that of *disturbance*; which is usually a wrong done to some incorporeal hereditament, by hindering or disquieting the owners in their regular and lawful enjoyment of it. I shall consider five sorts of this injury; viz. 1. Disturbance of *franchises*. 2. Disturbance of *common*. 3. Disturbance of *ways*. 4. Disturbance of *tenure*. 5. Disturbance of *patronage*.

I. Disturbance of *franchises* happens, when a man has the franchise of holding a court-leet, of keeping a fair or market, of free-warren, of taking toll, of seising waifs or estrays, or (in short) any other species of franchise whatsoever; and he is disturbed or incommoded in the lawful exercise thereof. As, if another by distress, menaces, or persuasions, prevails upon the suitors not to appear at my court; or obstructs the passage to my fair or market; or hunts in my free-warren; or refuses to pay me the accustomed toll; or hinders me from seising the waif or estray, whereby it escapes or is carried out of my liberty: in every case of this kind, all which it is impossible here to recite or suggest, there is an injury done to the legal owner; his property is damnified, and the profits arising from such his franchise are diminished. To remedy which, as the law has given no other writ, he is therefore entitled to sue for damages by a special action *on the case:* or, in case of toll, may take a distress if he pleases.

II. The disturbance of *common* comes next to be considered; where any act is done, by which the right of another to his common is incommoded or diminished. This may happen, in the first place, where one who hath no right of common puts his cattle into the land, and thereby robs the cattle of the commoners of their respective shares of the pasture. Or if one, who hath a right of common, puts in cattle which are not commonable, as hogs and goats, which amounts to the same inconvenience. But the lord of the soil may (by custom or prescription, but not without) put a stranger's cattle into the common; and also, by a like prescription for common appurtenant, cattle that are not commonable may be put into the common. The lord also of the soil may justify making burrows therein, and putting in rabbits, so as they do not increase to so large a number as totally to destroy the common. But in general, in case the beasts of a stranger, or the uncommonable cattle of a commoner, be found upon the land, the lord or any of the commoners may distrein them damage-feasant: or the commoner may bring an action on the case to recover damages, provided the injury done be any thing considerable: so that he may lay his action with a *per quod*, or allege that *thereby* he was deprived of his common. But for a trivial trespass the commoner has no action; but the lord of the soil only, for the entry and trespass committed.

Another disturbance of common is by *surcharging* it; or putting more cattle therein than the pasture and herbage will sustain, or the party hath a right to do. In this case, he that surcharges does an injury to the rest of the owners, by depriving them of their respective portions, or at least contracting them into a smaller compass. This injury by surcharging can properly speaking only happen, where the common is *appendant* or *appurtenant*, and of course limitable by law; or where, when *in grofs*, it is exprefly limited and certain: for where a man hath common *in grofs, fans nombre* or *without stint*, he cannot be a surcharger. However, even where a man is said to have common without stint, still there must be left sufficient for the lord's own beasts: for the law will not suppose that, at the original grant of the common, the lord meant to exclude himself.

The usual remedies for surcharging the common, are either by distreining so many of the beasts as are above the number allowed, or else by an action of trespass; both which may be had by the lord: or lastly, by a special action on the case for damages; in which any commoner may be plaintiff. The antient and most effectual method of proceeding is by writ of *admeafurement* of *pafture*. This lies, either where a common appurtenant or in grofs is certain as to number, or where a man has common appendant or appurtenant to his land, the quantity of which common has never yet been ascertained. In either of these cases, as well the lord, as any of the commoners, is entitled to this writ of admeafurement. The rule for this admeafurement is generally understood to be, that the commoner shall not turn more cattle upon the common, than are sufficient to manure and stock the land to which his right of common is annexed; which being a thing uncertain before admeafurement, has frequently, though erroneously occasioned this unmeafured right of common to be called a common *without stint* or *fans nombre*; a thing which, though possible in law, does in fact very rarely exist.

There is yet another disturbance of common, when the owner of the land, or other person, so enclofes or otherwise obstructs it, that the commoner is precluded from enjoying the benefit, to which he is by law entitled. This may be done, either by erecting fences, or by driving the cattle off the land, or by ploughing up the foil of the common. Or it may be done by erecting a warren therein, and stocking it with rabbits in such quantities, that they devour the whole herbage, and thereby destroy the common. For in such case, though the commoner may not destroy the rabbits, yet the law looks upon this as an injurious disturbance of his right, and has given him his remedy action against the owner.

These are cases indeed, in which the lord may enclose and abridge the common, for which, as they are no injury to any one, so no one is entitled to any remedy. For it is provided by the statute of Merton, 20 Hen. III. c. 4. that the lord may *approve*, that is, enclose and convert to the uses of husbandry, (which is a melioration or approvement) any waste grounds, woods, or pastures, in which his tenants have common *appendant* to their estates, provided he leaves sufficient common to his tenants, according to the proportion of their land. The statute Westm. 2. 13 Edw. I. c. 46. extends this liberty of approving, in like manner, against *all others* that have common *appurtenant*, or *in gross*, as well as against the tenants of the lord, who have their common *appendant*. And lastly, by statute 29 Geo. II. c. 36. and 31 Geo. II. c. 41. it is particularly enacted, that any lords of wastes and commons, with the consent of the major part, in number and value, of the commoners, may enclose any part thereof, for the growth of timber and underwood.

III. The third species of disturbance, that of *ways*, is very similar in its nature to the last: it principally happening when a person, who hath a right to way over another's grounds, by grant or prescription, is obstructed by inclosures, or other obstacles, or by ploughing across it; by which means he cannot enjoy his right of way, or at least not in so commodious a manner as he might have done. If this be a way annexed to his estate, and the obstruction is made by the tenant of the land, this brings it to another species of injury; for it is then a *nusance*, for which an assise will lie. But if the right of way thus obstructed by the tenant, be only *in gross*, (that is, annexed to a man's person and unconnected with any lands or tenements) or if the obstruction of a way belonging to an houfe or land is made by a ſtranger, it is then in either caſe merely a diſturbance: for the obſtruction of a way in groſs is no detriment to any lands or tenements, and therefore does not fall under the legal notion of a nuſance, which muſt be laid, *ad nocumentum liberi tenementi*; and the obſtruction of it by a ſtranger can never tend to put the *right of way* in diſpute: the remedy therefore for theſe diſturbances is not by aſſiſe or any real action, but by the univerſal remedy of action on the caſe to recover damages.

IV. The fourth ſpecies of diſturbance is that of diſturbance of *tenure*, or breaking that connection which ſubſiſts between the lord and his tenant, and to which the law pays ſo high a regard, that it will not ſuffer it to be wantonly diſſolved by the act of a third perſon. To have an eſtate well tenanted is an advantage that every landlord muſt be very ſenſible of; and therefore the driving away of a tenant from off his eſtate is an injury of no ſmall conſequence. So that if there be a tenant at will of any lands or tenements, and a ſtranger either by menaces and threats, or by unlawful diſtreſſes, or by fraud and circumvention, or other means, contrives to drive him away, or inveigle him to leave his tenancy, this the law very juſtly conſtrues to be a wrong and injury to the lord, and gives him a reparation in damages againſt the offender by a ſpecial action on the caſe.

V. The fifth and laſt ſpecies of diſturbance, but by far the moſt conſiderable, is that of diſturbance of *patronage*; which is an hindrance or obſtruction of a patron to preſent his clerk to a benefice.

Diſturbers of a right of advowſon may be theſe three perſons; the pſeudo-patron, his clerk, and the ordinary: the pretended patron, by preſenting to a church to which he has no right, and thereby making it litigious or diſputable; the clerk, by demanding or obtaining inſtitution, which tends to and promotes the ſame inconvenience; and the ordinary, by refuſing to admit the real patron's clerk, or admitting the clerk of the pretender. Theſe diſturbances are vexatious and injurious to him who hath the right: and therefore, if he be not wanting to himſelf, the law (beſides the *right of advowſon*, which is a final and concluſive remedy) hath given him two inferior poffeffory actions for his relief; an affife of *darrein prefentment*, and a writ of *quare impedit*; in which the patron is always the plaintiff, and not the clerk. For the law fuppofes the injury to be offered to him only, by obftructing or refufing the admiffion of his nominee; and not to the clerk, who hath no right in him till inftitution, and of courfe can fuffer no injury.

Affifes of *darrein prefentment*, now not being in any wife conclufive, have been totally difufed, as indeed they began to be before; a *quare impedit* being a more general, and therefore a more ufual action. For the affife of *darrein prefentment* lies only where a man has an advowfon by defcent from his anceftors; but the writ of *quare impedit* is equally remedial whether a man claims title by defcent or by purchafe.

I proceed, therefore, to inquire into the nature of a writ of *quare impedit*, now the only action ufed in cafe of the difturbance of patronage: and fhall firft premife the ufual proceedings previous to the bringing of the writ.

Upon the vacancy of a living, the patron, we know, is bound to prefent within fix calendar months, otherwife it will lapfe to the bifhop. But if the prefentation be made within that time, the bifhop is bound to admit and inftitute the clerk, if found fufficient, unlefs the church be full, or there be notice of any litigation. For if any oppofition be intended, it is ufual for each party to enter a *caveat* with the bifhop, to prevent his inftitution of his antagonift's clerk. An inftitution after a *caveat* entered is void by the ecclefiaftical law; but this the temporal courts pay no regard to, and look upon a *caveat* as a mere nullity. But if two prefentations be offered to the bifhop upon the fame avoidance, the church is then faid to become *litigious*; and, if nothing farther be done, the bifhop may fufpend the admiffion of either, and fuffer a lapfe to incur. Yet if the patron or clerk on either fide requeft him to award a *jus patronatus*, he is bound to do it. A *jus patronatus* is a commiffion from the bifhop, directed ufually to his chancellor and others of competent learning; who are to fummon a jury of fix clergymen and fix laymen, to inquire into and examine who is the rightful patron; and if, upon such inquiry made and certificate thereof returned by the commissioners, he admits and institutes the clerk of that patron whom they return as the true one, the bishop secures himself at all events from being a disturber, whatever proceedings may be had afterwards in the temporal courts.

The clerk refused by the bishop may also have a remedy against him in the spiritual court, denominated a *duplex querela*: which is a complaint in the nature of an appeal from the ordinary to his next immediate superior; as from a bishop to the archbishop, or from an archbishop to the delegates: and if the superior court adjudges the cause of refusal to be insufficient, it will grant institution to the appellant.

Thus far matters *may* go on in the mere ecclesiastical course; but in contested presentations they seldom go so far: for, upon the first delay or refusal of the bishop to admit his clerk, the patron usually brings his writ of *quare impedit* against the bishop, for the temporal injury done to his property, in disturbing him in his presentation. And, if the delay arises from the bishop alone, as upon pretence of incapacity, or the like, then he only is named in the writ; but if there be another presentation set up, then the pretended patron and his clerk are also joined in the action; or it may be brought against the patron and clerk, leaving out the bishop; or against the patron only. But it is most adviseable to bring it against all three: for if the bishop be left out, and the suit be not determined till the six months are past, the bishop is entitled to present by lapse; for he is not party to the suit: but, if he be named, no lapse can possibly accrue till the right is determined. If the patron be left out, and the writ be brought only against the bishop and the clerk, the suit is of no effect, and the writ shall abate; for the right of the patron is the principal question in the cause. If the clerk be left out, and has received institution before the action brought (as is sometimes the case) the patron by this suit may recover his right of patronage, but not the present turn; for he cannot have judgment to remove the clerk, unless he be made a defendant and party to the suit, to hear what he can allege againſt it. For which reaſon it is the ſafer way to inſert all three in the writ.

The writ of *quare impedit* commands the diſturbers, the biſhop, the pſeudo-patron, and his clerk, to permit the plaintiff to preſent a proper perſon (without ſpecifying the particular clerk) to ſuch a vacant church, which pertains to his patronage, and which the defendants, as he alleges, do obſtruct; and unleſs they ſo do, then that they appear in court to ſhew the reaſon why they hinder him.

Beſides theſe poſſeſſory actions, there may be alſo had a writ of *right of advowſon*, which reſembles other writs of right: the only diſtinguiſhing advantage now attending it, being, that it is more concluſive than a *quare impedit*; ſince to an action of *quare impedit* a recovery had in a writ of right may be pleaded in bar.

There is no limitation with regard to the time within which any actions touching advowſons are to be brought; at leaſt none later than the times of Richard I and Henry III: for by ſtatute 1 Mar. ſt. 2. c. 5. the ſtatute of limitations, 32 Hen. VIII. c. 2. is declared not to extend to any writ of right of advowſon, *quare impedit*, or aſſiſe of *darrein preſentment*, or *jus patronatus*. And this upon very good reaſon: becauſe it may very eaſily happen that the title to an advowſon may not come in queſtion, nor the right have opportunity to be tried, within ſixty years; which is the longeſt period of limitation aſſigned by the ſtatute of Henry VIII.

In a writ of *quare impedit*, which is almoſt the only real action that remains in common uſe, and alſo in the aſſiſe of *darrein preſentment*, and a writ of right, the patron only, and not the clerk, is allowed to ſue the diſturber. But, by virtue of ſeveral acts of parliament, there is one ſpecies of preſentations, in which a remedy, to be ſued in the temporal courts, is put into the hands of the clerks preſented, as well as of the owners of the advowſon. I mean the preſentation to ſuch beneﬁces, as belong to Roman Catholic patrons; which, according to their ſeveral counties, are veſted in and ſecured to the two univerſities of this kingdom. And particularly by the ſtatute of 12 Ann. ſt. 2. c. 14. §. 4. a new method of proceeding is provided, viz. that, beſides the writs of *quare impedit,* which the universities as patrons are entitled to bring, they, or their clerks, may be at liberty to file a bill in equity against any person presenting to such livings, and disturbing their right of patronage, or his *cestuy que trust,* or any other person whom they have cause to suspect, in order to compel a discovery of any secret trusts, for the benefit of papists, in evasion of those laws whereby this right of advowson is vested in those learned bodies: and also (by the statute 11 Geo. II. c. 17.) to compel a discovery whether any grant or conveyance, said to be made of such advowson, were made *bona fide* to a protestant purchasor, for the benefit of protestants, and for a full consideration; without which requisites every such grant and conveyance of any advowson or avoidance is absolutely null and void.

## CHAPTER XII.

### OF INJURIES PROCEEDING FROM, OR AFFECTING THE CROWN.

HAVING in the nine preceding chapters considered the injuries, or private wrongs, that may be offered by one subject to another, all of which are redressed by the command and authority of the king, signified by his original writs returnable in his several courts of justice, which thence derive a jurisdiction of examining and determining the complaint; I proceed now to inquire into the mode of redressing those injuries to which the crown itself is a party; which injuries are either where the crown is the aggressor, and which therefore cannot, without a solecism admit of the same kind of remedy; or else is the sufferer, and which then are usually remedied by peculiar forms of process, appropriated to the royal prerogative. In treating therefore of these, we will consider first, the manner of redressing those wrongs or injuries which a subject may suffer from the crown, and then of redressing those which the crown may receive from a subject.

1. That the king can do no wrong, is a neceſſary and fundamental principal of the Engliſh conſtitution: meaning only, as has formerly been obſerved, that, in the firſt place, whatever may be amiſs in the conduct of public affairs is not chargeable perſonally on the king; nor is he, but his miniſters, accountable for it to the people: and, ſecondly, that the prerogative of the crown extends not to do any injury; for, being created for the benefit of the people, it cannot be exerted to their prejudice. Whenever therefore it happens that, by miſinformation or inadvertence, the crown hath been induced to invade the private rights of any of its ſubjects, though no action will lie againſt the ſovereign, (for who ſhall command the king?) yet the law hath furniſhed the ſubject with a decent and reſpectful mode of removing that invaſion, by informing the king of the true ſtate of the matter in diſpute: and, as it preſumes that to *know of* any injury and to *redreſs* it are inſeparable in the royal breaſt, it then iſſues as of courſe, in the king's own name, his orders to his judges to do juſtice to the party aggrieved.

The diſtance between the ſovereign and his ſubjects is ſuch, that it rarely can happen that any *perſonal* injury can immediately and directly proceed from the prince to any private man: and, as it can ſo ſeldom happen, the law in decency ſuppoſes that it never will or can happen at all; becauſe it feels itſelf incapable of furniſhing any adequate remedy, without infringing the dignity and deſtroying the ſovereignty of the royal perſon, by ſetting up ſome ſuperior power with authority to call him to account. The inconveniency therefore of a miſchief that is barely poſſible, is (as Mr. Locke has obſerved) well recompenſed by the peace of the public and ſecurity of the government, in the perſon of the chief magiſtrate being ſet out of the reach of coercion. But injuries to the rights of *property* can ſcarcely be committed by the crown without the intervention of it's officers; for whom the law in matters of right entertains no reſpect or delicacy, but furniſhes various methods of detecting the errors or miſconduct of thoſe agents, by whom the king has been deceived, and induced to do a temporary injuſtice.

The common law methods of obtaining poffeffion or reftitution from the crown, of either real or perfonal property, are, 1. By *petition de droit*, or petition of right, which is faid to owe it's original to king Edward the firft. 2. By *monſtrans de droit*, manifeftation or plea of right: both of which may be preferred or profecuted either in the chancery or exchequer. But as the remedy by *petition* was extremely tedious and expenfive, that by *monſtrans* was much enlarged and rendered almoft univerfal by feveral ftatutes, particularly 36 Edw. III. c. 13. and 2 & 3. Edw. VI. c. 8. which alfo allow inquifitions of office to be traverfed or denied, wherever the right of a fubject is concerned, except in a very few cafes. Thefe proceedings are had in the petty bag office in the court of chancery: and, if upon either of them the right be determined againft the crown, the judgment is, *quod manus domini regis amoveantur et poſſeſſio reſtituatur petenti, falvo jure domini regis;* which laft caufe is always added to judgments againft the king, to whom no *laches* is ever imputed, and whofe right (till fome late ftatutes) was never defeated by any limitation or length of time. And by fuch judgment the crown is inftantly out of poffeffion; fo that there needs not the indecent interpofition of his own officers to transfer the feifin from the king to the party aggrieved.

II. The methods of redreffing fuch injuries as the crown may receive from a fubject, are,

1. By fuch ufual common law actions, as are confiftent with the royal prerogative and dignity. As therefore the king, by reafon of his legal ubiquity, cannot be diffeifed or difpoffeffed of any real property which is once vefted in him, he can maintain no action which fuppofes a difpoffeffion of the plaintiff; fuch as an affife or an ejectment: but he may bring a *quare impedit*, which always fuppofes the complainant to be feifed or poffeffed of the advowfon: and he may profecute this writ, like every other by him brought, as well in the king's bench as the common pleas, or in whatever court he pleafes. So too, he may bring an action of trefpafs for taking away his goods; but fuch actions are not ufual (though in ftrictnefs maintainable) for breaking his clofe, or other

C. XII.   INJURIES AFFECTING THE CROWN.   383

injury done upon his foil or poffeffion. It would be equally tedious and difficult, to run through every minute diftinction that might be gleaned from our antient books with regard to this matter; nor is it in any degree neceffary, as much eafier and more effectual remedies are ufually obtained by fuch prerogative modes of procefs, as are peculiarly confined to the crown.

2. Such is that of *inquifition* or *inqueft of office*: which is an inquiry made by the king's officer, his fheriff, coroner (a), or efcheator, *virtute officii*, or by writ to them fent for that purpofe, or by commiffioners fpecially appointed, concerning any matter that entitles the king to the poffeffion of lands or tenements, goods or chattels. This is done by a jury of no determinate number; being either twelve, or lefs, or more.

With regard to other matters, the inquefts of office ftill remain in force, and are taken upon proper occafions; being extended not only to lands, but alfo to goods and chattels perfonal, as in the cafe of wreck, treafure-trove, and the like; and efpecially as to forfeitures for offences. For every jury which tries a man for treafon or felony, every coroner's inqueft that fits upon a *felo de fe*, or one killed by chance-medley, is, not only with regard to chattels, but alfo to real interefts, in all refpects an inqueft of office: and if they find the treafon or felony, or even the flight of the party accufed, (though innocent) the king is thereupon, by virtue of this *office found*, entitled to have his forfeitures (b); and alfo, in

---

(a) Before the ftatute of magna charta, (cap. 17.) the coroner held pleas of the crown, by that ftatute *nullus vice-comes, conftabularius, coronator vel alii ballavi noftri teneant placita coronæ,* fo that thereby their power in proceeding to trial or judgment in pleas of the crown is taken away. But yet they retained a juridiction ftill as to matters of inquiry, taking of appeals, &c. all which is fet down at large in the ftatute 4 Edw. I. ftiled *De officio coronatorum,—Hale's Hif. Pla. Co.* v. 2. p. 56.

(b) If there be a prefentment before the coroner of a *fugam fecit*, the ftatute of 1 Rich. III. takes no place as to that,

the case of chance-medley, he or his grantees are entitled to such things by way of deodand, as have moved to the death of the party.

3. Where the crown hath unadvisedly granted any thing by letters patent, which ought not to be granted, or where the patentee hath done an act that amounts to a forfeiture of the grant, the remedy to repeal the patent is by writ of *scire facias* in chancery.

4. An *information* on behalf of the crown, filed in the exchequer by the king's attorney general, is a method of suit for recovering money or other chattels, or for obtaining satisfaction in damages for any personal wrong committed in the lands or other possessions of the crown. The most usual informations are those of *intrusion* and *debt*: *intrusion*, for any trespass committed on the lands of the crown, as by entering thereon without title, holding over after a lease is determined, taking the profits, cutting down timber, or the like; and *debt*, upon any contract for monies due to the king, or for any forfeiture due to the crown upon the breach of a penal statute. This is most commonly used to recover forfeitures occasioned by transgressing those laws, which are enacted for the establishment and support of the revenue: others, which regard mere matters of police and public convenience, being usually left to be inforced by the common informers, in the *qui tam* informations or actions, of which we have formerly spoken. But after the attorney-general has informed upon the breach of a penal law, no other information can be received. There is also an information *in rem*, when any goods are supposed to become the property of the crown, and no man appears to claim them, or to dispute the title of the king. As antiently in the case of treasure-trove, wrecks, waifs, and estrays, seised by the king's officer for his use.

---

because, whether convict or acquit, the *fugam fecit* stands as an unavoidable forfeiture, and therefore the coroner may, without question, seise the goods so found by inquisition upon a *fugam fecit*, and commit them to the township. *Hist. P. C. v.* 2, *p.* 63.

Upon such seisure an information was usually filed in the king's exchequer, and thereupon a proclamation was made for the owner (if any) to come in and claim the effects; and at the same time there issued a commission of *appraisement* to value the goods in the officer's hands: after the return of which, and a second proclamation had, if no claimant appeared, the goods were supposed derelict, and condemned to the use of the crown. And when, in later times, forfeitures of the goods themselves, as well as personal penalties on the parties, were inflicted by act of parliament for transgressions against the laws of the customs and excise, the same process was adopted in order to secure such forfeited goods for the public use, though the offender himself had escaped the reach of justice.

5. A writ of *quo warranto* is in the nature of a writ of right for the king, against him who claims or usurps any office, franchise, or liberty, to inquire by what authority he supports his claim, in order to determine the right. It lies also in case of non-user or long neglect of a franchise, or misuser or abuse of it; being a writ commanding the defendant to shew by what warrant he exercises such a franchise, having never had any grant of it, or having forfeited it by neglect or abuse.

The judgment on a writ of *quo warranto* (being in the nature of a writ of right) is final and conclusive even against the crown. Which, together with the length of it's process, probably occasioned that disuse into which it is now fallen, and introduced a more modern method of prosecution, by *information* filed in the court of king's bench by the attorney-general, in the nature of a writ of *quo warranto*; wherein the process is speedier, and the judgment not quite so decisive. This is properly a criminal method of prosecution, as well to punish the usurper by a fine for the usurpation of the franchise, as to oust him, or seise for the crown: but hath long been applied to the mere purposes of trying the civil right, seising the fanchise, or ousting the wrongful possessor; the fine being nominal only. And this proceeding is now applied to the decision of corporation disputes between party and party, by virtue of the statute 9 Ann. c. 20. which permits an information in nature of *quo warranto* to be brought with leave of the court, at the relation of any person desiring to prosecute the same, (who is then stiled the *relator)* against any person usurping, intruding into, or unlawfully holding any franchise or office in any city, borough, or town corporate; provides for it's speedy determination; and directs that, if the defendant be convicted, judgment of ouster (as well as a fine) may be given against him, and that the relator shall pay or receive costs according to the event of the suit.

6. The writ of *mandamus* is also made by the same statute 9 Ann. c. 20. a most full and effectual remedy, in the first place, for refusal of admission where a person is entitled to an office or place in any such corporation: and, secondly, for wrongful removal, when a person is legally possessed. These are injuries, for which though redress for the party interested may be had by assise, or other means, yet as the franchises concern the public, and may affect the administration of justice, this prerogative writ also issues from the court of king's bench; commanding, upon good cause shewn to the court, the party complaining to be admitted or restored to his office. And the statute requires, that a return be immediately made to the first writ of *mandamus*; which return may be pleaded to or traversed by the prosecutor, and his antagonist may reply, take issue, or demur, and the same proceedings may be had, as if an action on the case had been brought, for making a false return: and, after judgment obtained for the prosecutor, he shall have a peremptory writ of *mandamus* to compel his admission or restitution; which latter (in case of an action) is effected by a writ of restitution. So that now the writ of *mandamus*, in cases within this statute, is in the nature of an action: whereupon the party applying and succeeding may be entitled to costs, in case it be the franchise of a citizen, burgess, or freeman; and also, in general, a writ of error may be had thereupon.

This writ of *mandamus* may also be issued, in pursuance of

the ftatute 11 Geo. I. c. 4. in cafe within the regular time no election fhall be made of the mayor or other chief officer of any city, borough, or town corporate, or (being made) it fhall afterwards become void; requiring the electors to proceed to election, and proper courts to be held for admitting and fwearing in the magiftrates fo refpectively chofen.

We have now gone through the whole circle of civil injuries, and the redrefs which the laws of England have anxioufly provided for each. And I may venture to affirm, that there is hardly a poffible injury, that can be offered either to the perfon or property of another, for which the party injured may not find a remedial writ, conceived in fuch terms as are properly and fingularly adapted to his own particular grievance.

## CHAPTER XIII.

### OF THE TRIAL BY JURY.

THE fubject of our next inquiries will be the nature and method of the trial *by jury*; called alfo the trial *per pais*, or *by the country*: a trial that hath been ufed time out of mind in this nation, and feems to have been co-eval with the firft civil government thereof. And it was ever efteemed, in all countries, a privilege of the higheft and moft beneficial nature.

But I will not mifpend the reader's time in fruitlefs encomiums on this method of trial: but fhall proceed to the diffection and examination of it in all it's parts, from whence indeed it's higheft encomium will arife; fince, the more it is fearched into and underftood, the more it is fure to be valued. And this is a fpecies of knowledge moft abfolutely neceffary for every gentleman in the kingdom: as well becaufe he may be frequently called upon to determine in this capacity the rights of others, his fellow-fubjects; as becaufe his own property, his liberty, and his life, depend upon maintaining, in it's legal force, the conftitutional trial by jury.

Trials by jury, in civil caufes, are of two kinds; *extraordinary*, and *ordinary*. I fhall confine the main of my obfervations to that which is more ufual and ordinary.

Jurors returned by the fheriff are either *fpecial* or *common* jurors. Special juries were originally introduced in trials at bar, when the caufes were of too great nicety for the difcuffion of ordinary freeholders; or where the fheriff was fufpected of partiality, though not upon fuch apparent caufe as to warrant an exception to him. He is in fuch cafes, upon motion in court, and a rule granted thereupon, to attend the prothonotary or other proper officer with his freeholder's book; and the officer is to take, indifferently, fortyeight of the principal freeholders, in the prefence of the attornies on both fides; who are each of them to ftrike off twelve, and the remaining twenty-four are returned upon the panel. By the ftatute 3 Geo. II. c. 25. either party is entitled, upon motion, to have a fpecial jury ftruck upon the trial of any iffue, as well at the affifes as at bar; he paying the extraordinary expence, unlefs the judge will certify (in purfuance of the ftatute 24 Geo. II. c. 18.) that the caufe required fuch fpecial jury.

A common jury is one returned by the fheriff according to the directions of the ftatute 3 Geo. II. c. 25. which appoints, that the fheriff or officer fhall not return a feparate panel for every feparate caufe, as formerly; but one and the fame panel for every caufe to be tried at the fame affifes, containing not lefs than forty-eight, nor more than feventy-two, jurors: and that their names being written on tickets, fhall be put into a box or glafs; and when each caufe is called, twelve of thefe perfons, whofe names fhall be firft drawn out of the box, fhall be fworn upon the jury, unlefs abfent, challenged, or excufed; or unlefs a previous view of the meffuages, lands, or place in queftion, fhall have been thought neceffary by the court: in which cafe fix or more of the jurors, returned, to be agreed on by the parties, or named by a judge or other proper officer of the court, fhall be appointed by fpecial writ of *habeas corpora* or *diftringas*, to have the matter in queftion fhewn to them by two perfons named in the writ; and then such of the jury as have had the view, or so many of them as appear, shall be sworn on the inquest previous to any other jurors. These acts are well calculated to restrain any suspicion of partiality in the sheriff, or any tampering with the jurors when returned.

As the jurors appear, when called, they shall be sworn, unless *challenged* by either party. Challenges are of two sorts; challenges to the *array*, and challenges to the *polls*.

Challenges to the array are at once an exception to the whole panel, in which the jury are arrayed or set in order by the sheriff in his return; and they may be made upon account of partiality or some default in the sheriff, or his under-officer who arrayed the panel. And, generally speaking, the same reasons that before the awarding the *venire* were sufficient to have directed it to the coroners or elisors, will be also sufficient to quash the array, when made by a person or officer of whose partiality there is any tolerable ground of suspicion. Also, though there be no personal objection against the sheriff, yet if he arrays the panel at the nomination, or under the direction of either party, this is good cause of challenge to the array. The array by the antient law may also be challenged, if an alien be party to the suit, and, upon a rule obtained by his motion to the court for a jury *de medietate linguæ*, such a one be not returned by the sheriff, pursuant to the statute 28 Edward III. c. 13. enforced by 8 Hen. VI. c. 29. which enact, that where either party is an alien born, the jury shall be one half denizens, and the other aliens (if so many be forthcoming in the place) for the more impartial trial. But where both parties are aliens, no partiality is to be presumed to one more than another; and therefore it was resolved, soon after the statute 8 Hen. VI. that where the issue is joined between two aliens (unless the plea be had before the mayor of the staple, and thereby subject to the restrictions of statute 27 Edw. III. st. 2. c. 8.) the jury shall all be denizens.

Challenges to the polls, *in capita*, are exceptions to particular jurors. Challenges to the polls of the jury (who are judges of fact) are reduced to four heads by Sir Edward

Coke: *propter honoris respectum*; *propter defectum*; *propter affectum*; and *propter delictum*.

1. *Propter honoris respectum*; as if a lord of parliament be impanelled on a jury, he may be challenged by either party, or he may challenge himself.

2. *Propter defectum*; as if a juryman be an alien born, this is defect of birth; if he be a slave or bondman, this is defect of liberty, and he cannot be *liber et legalis homo*. But the principal deficiency is defect of estate, sufficient to qualify him to be a juror. This depends upon a variety of statutes. By the statute 4 and 5 W. & M. c. 24. it was raised to 10*l. per annum* in England and 6*l.* in Wales, of freehold lands *or copyhold*; which is the first time that copyholders (as such) were admitted to serve upon juries in any of the king's courts, though they had before been admitted to serve in some of the sheriff's courts, by statutes 1 Ric. III. c. 4. and 9 Hen. VII. c. 13. And, lastly, by statute 3 Geo. II. c. 25. any leaseholder for the term of five hundred years absolute, or for any term determinable upon life or lives, of the clear yearly value of 20*l. per annum* over and above the rent reserved *(a)*, is qualified to serve upon juries. When the jury is *de medietate linguæ*, that is, one moiety of the English tongue or nation, and the other of any foreign one, no want of lands shall be cause of challenge to the alien; for, as he is incapable to hold any, this would totally defeat the privilege.

3. Jurors may be challenged *propter affectum*, for suspicion of bias or partiality. This may be either a *principal* challenge, or *to the favour*. A *principal* challenge is such, where the cause assigned carries with it *prima facie* evident marks of suspicion, either of malice or favour: as, that a juror is of kin to either party within the ninth degree; that he has

---

(*a*) But (by 4 Geo. II. c. 7.) the act of 3 Geo. II. c. 25. is declared not to extend to the county of *Middlesex*; and, by the same act, leaseholders, for any number of years, whose improved rent shall amount to 50*l. per annum*, over and above ground-rents and other reservations, shall be liable to serve on juries.

been arbitrator on either fide; that he has an intereft in the caufe; that there is an action depending betwen him and the party; that he has taken money for his verdict; that he has formerly been a juror in the fame caufe; that he is the party's mafter, fervant, counfellor, fteward or attorney, or of the fame fociety or corporation with him: all thefe are principal caufes of challenge; which, if true, cannot be over-ruled, for jurors muft be *omni exceptione majores*. Challenges *to the favour*, are where the party hath no principal challenge; but objects only fome probable circumftances of fufpicion, as acquaintance and the like; the validity of which muft be left to the determination of *triors*, whofe office it is to decide whether the juror be favourable or unfavourable. The triors, in cafe the firft man called be challenged, are two indifferent perfons named by the court; and, if they try one man and find him indifferent, he fhall be fworn; and then he and the two triors fhall try the next; and, when another is found indifferent and fworn, the two triors fhall be fuperfeded; and the two firft fworn on the jury fhall try the reft.

4. Challenges *propter delictum* are for fome crime or mifdemefnor, that affects the juror's credit and renders him infamous. As for a conviction of treafon, felony, perjury, or confpiracy; or if for fome infamous offence he hath received judgment of the pillory, tumbrel, or the like; or to be branded, whipt, or ftigmatized; or if he be outlawed or excommunicated, or hath been attainted of falfe verdict, *præmunire*, or forgery; or laftly, if he hath proved recreant when champion in the trial by battle, and thereby hath loft his *liberam legem*. A juror may himfelf be examined on oath of *voir dire*, *veritatem dicere*, with regard to fuch caufes of challenge, as are not to his difhonour or difcredit; but not with regard to any crime, or any thing which tends to his difgrace or difadvantage.

Befides thefe challenges which are exceptions againft the fitnefs of jurors, and whereby they may be *excluded* from ferving, there are alfo other caufes to be made ufe of by the jurors themfelves, which are matter of exemption; whereby their fervice is *excufed*, and not *excluded*. As by ftatute

Weft. 2. 13 Edw. I. c. 38. fick and decrepit perfons, perfons not commorant in the county, and men above feventy years old; and by the ftatute of 7 and 8 W. III. c. 32. infants under twenty-one. This exemption is alfo extended to divers ftatutes, cuftoms, and charters, to phyficians and other medical perfons, counfel, attorneys, officers of the courts, and the like; all of whom, if impanelled, muft fhew their fpecial exemption. Clergymen are alfo ufually excufed, out of favour and refpect to their function: but, if they are feifed of lands and tenements, they are in ftrictnefs liable to be impanelled in refpect of their lay-fees, unlefs they be in the fervice of the king or of fome bifhop: " *in obfequio domini* " *regis, vel alicujus epifcopi.*"

If by means of challenges, or other caufe, a fufficient number of unexceptionable jurors doth not appear at the trial, either party may pray a *tales*. A *tales* is a fupply of *fuch* men as are fummoned upon the firft panel, in order to make up the deficiency. For this purpofe a writ of *decem tales, octo tales,* and the like, was ufed to be iffued to the fheriff at common law, and muft be ftill fo done at a trial at bar, if the jurors make default. But at the affifes or *nifi prius*, by virtue of the ftatute 35 Hen. VIII. c. 6. and other fubfequent ftatutes, the judge is impowered at the prayer of either party to award a *tales de circumftantibus*, of perfons prefent in court, to be joined to the other jurors to try the caufe; who are liable however to the fame challenges as the principal jurors.

When a fufficient number of perfons impannelled, or *tales*men, appear, they are then feparately fworn, well and truly to try the iffue between the parties, and a true verdict to give according to the evidence; and hence they are denominated the jury, *jurata,* and jurors, *fc. juratores.*

The jury are now ready to hear the merits; and, to fix their attention the clofer to the facts which they are impanelled and fworn to try, the pleadings are opened to them by counfel on that fide which holds the affirmative of the queftion in iffue. For the iffue is faid to lie, and proof is always firft required, upon that fide which affirms the matter in queftion; in which our law agrees with the civil:

" *ei incumbit probatio, qui dicit, non qui negat: cum per rerum naturam factum-negantis probatio nulla sit.*" The opening counsel briefly informs them what has been transacted in the court above; the parties, the nature of the action, the declaration, the plea, replication, and other proceedings, and lastly, upon what point the issue is joined, which is there sent down to be determined. Instead of which, formerly, the whole record and process of the pleadings was read to them in English by the court, and the matter in issue clearly explained to their capacities. The nature of the case, and the evidence intended to be produced, are next laid before them by counsel also on the same side: and, when their evidence is gone through, the advocate on the other side opens the adverse case, and supports it by evidence; and then the party which began is heard by way of reply.

The nature of my present design will not permit me to enter into the numberless niceties and distinctions of what is, or is not, legal *evidence* to a jury (*a*). I shall only, therefore, select a few of the general heads and leading maxims, relative to this point, together with some observations on the manner of giving evidence.

And, first, evidence signifies that which demonstrates, makes clear, or ascertains the truth of the very fact or point in issue, either on the one side or on the other; and no evidence ought to be admitted to any other point. Therefore upon an action of debt, when the defendant denies his bond by the plea of *non est factum*, and the issue is, whether it be the defendant's deed or no; he cannot give a release of this

---

(*a*) This is admirably well performed in lord chief baron *Gilbert*'s excellent treatise of evidence: a work, which it is impossible to abstract or abridge, without losing some beauty and destroying the chain of the whole; and which hath lately been engrafted into a very useful work, the *introduction to the law of nisi prius*, 4to. 1767. A.——This was afterwards printed in 8vo. with the name of the author, *Francis Buller*, Esq. (now *Sir Francis Buller*, Bart.) late one of the justices of the court of King's Bench, and now of the court of Common pleas; and who is generally deemed the *Coke* of the present day.

bond in evidence: for that does not deſtroy the bond, and therefore does not prove the iſſue which he has choſen to rely upon, viz. that the bond has no exiſtence.

Again; evidence in the trial by jury is of two kinds, either that which is given in proof, or that which the jury may receive by their own private knowlege. The former, or *proofs,* (to which in common ſpeech the name of evidence is uſually confined) are either written, or *parol,* that is, by word of mouth. Written proofs, or evidence, are, 1. Records, and 2. Antient deeds of thirty years ſtanding, which prove themſelves; but 3. Modern deeds, and 4. Other writings, muſt be atteſted and verified by *parol* evidence of witneſſes. And the one general rule that runs through all the doctrine of trials is this, that the beſt evidence the nature of the caſe will admit of ſhall always be required, if poſſible to be had; but, if not poſſible, then the beſt evidence that can be had ſhall be allowed. For if it be found that there is any better evidence exiſting than is produced, the very not producing it is a preſumption that it would have detected ſome falſehood that at preſent is concealed. Thus, in order to prove a leaſe for years, nothing elſe ſhall be admitted but the very deed of leaſe itſelf, if in being; but if that be poſitively proved to be burnt or deſtroyed (not relying on any looſe negative, as that it cannot be found, or the like) then an atteſted copy may be produced; or *parol* evidence be given of its contents. So, no evidence of a diſcourſe with another will be admitted, but the man himſelf muſt be produced; yet in ſome caſes (as in proof of any general cuſtoms, or matters of common tradition or repute) the courts admit of *hearſay* evidence, or an account of what perſons deceaſed have declared in their life-time: but ſuch evidence will not be received of any particular facts. So too, books of account, or ſhop-books, are not allowed of themſelves to be given in evidence for the owner; but a ſervant who made the entry may have recourſe to them to refreſh his memory: and, if ſuch ſervant (who was accuſtomed to make thoſe entries) be dead, and his hand be proved, the book may be read in evidence: for as tradeſmen are often under a neceffity of giving credit without any note or writing, this is therefore, when accompanied with such other collateral proofs of fairness and regularity, the best evidence that can then be produced. However this dangerous species of evidence is not carried so far in England as abroad; where a man's own books of accounts, by a distortion of the civil law (which seems to have meant the same thing as is practised with us) with the suppletory oath of the merchant, amount at all times to full proof. But as this kind of evidence, even thus regulated, would be much too hard upon the buyer at any long distance of time, the statute 7 Jac. I. c. 12. (the penners of which seem to have imagined that the books of themselves were evidence at common law) confines this species of proof to such transactions as have happened within one year before the action brought; unless between merchant and merchant in the usual intercourse of trade. For accounts of so recent a date, if erroneous, may more easily be unraveiled and adjusted.

With regard to *parol* evidence, or *witnesses*, it must first be remembered, that there is a process to bring them in by writ of *subpœna ad testificandum:* which commands them, laying aside all pretences and excuses, to appear at the trial on pain of 100l. to be forfeited to the king; to which the statute 5 Eliz. c. 9. has added a penalty of 10l. to the party aggrieved, and damages equivalent to the loss sustained by want of his evidence. But no witness, unless his reasonable expences be tendered him, is bound to appear at all; nor, if he appears, is he bound to give evidence till such charges are actually paid him; except he resides within the bills of mortality, and is summoned to give evidence within the same. This compulsory process, to bring in unwilling witnesses, and the additional terrors of an attachment in case of disobedience, are of excellent use in the thorough investigation of truth: and, upon the same principle, in the Athenian courts, the witnesses who were summoned to attend the trial had their choice of three things: either to swear to the truth of the fact in question, to deny or abjure it, or else to pay a fine of a thousand drachmas.

All witnesses, of whatever religion or country, that have the use of their reason, are to be received and examined, except such as are *infamous*, or such as are *interested* in the event of the cause. All others are *competent* witnesses: though the jury from other circumstances will judge of their *credibility* (a). Infamous persons are such as may be challenged as jurors, *propter delictum*; and therefore never shall be admitted to give evidence to inform that jury, with whom they were too scandalous to associate. Interested witnesses may be examined upon a *voir dire*, if suspected to be secretly concerned in the event; or their interest may be proved in court. Which last is the only method of supporting an objection to the former class; for no man is to be examined to prove his own infamy. And no counsel, attorney, or other person, intrusted with the secrets of the cause by the party himself, shall be compelled, or perhaps allowed, to give evidence of such conversation or matters of privacy, as came to his knowlege by virtue of such trust and confidence: but he may be examined as to mere matters of fact, as the execution of a deed or the like, which might have come to his knowlege without being intrusted in the cause.

One witness (if credible) is *sufficient* evidence to a jury of any single fact; though undoubtedly the concurrence of two or more corroborates the proof. Yet our law considers that there are many transactions to which only one person is privy; and therefore does not *always* demand the testimony of two, as the civil law universally requires. " *Unius responsio testis* " *omnino non audiatur.*" To extricate itself out of which absurdity, the modern practice of the civil law courts has plunged itself into another. For, as they do not allow a less number than two witnesses to be *plena probatio*, they call the testimony of one, though never so clear and positive, *semiplena probatio* only, on whom no sentence can be founded. To make up therefore the necessary complement of witnesses,

---

(a) A person of non sane memory, however, cannot be a witness, while he is under that infirmity; but if he have *lucida intervalla*, then during the time he hath understanding he may be a witness. *Co. Lit.* 6.

when they have one only to a single fact, they admit the party himself (plaintiff or defendant) to be examined in his own behalf; and administer to him what is called the *suppletory* oath: and, if his evidence happens to be in his own favour, this immediately converts the half proof into a whole one. By this ingenious device satisfying at once the forms of the Roman law, and acknowleging the superior reasonableness of the law of England which permits one witness to be sufficient where no more are to be had; and, to avoid all temptations of perjury, lays it down as an invariable rule, that *nemo testis esse debet in propria causa.*

Positive proof is always required, where from the nature of the case it appears it might possibly have been had. But, next to *positive* proof, *circumstantial* evidence or the doctrine of *presumptions* must take place: for when the fact itself cannot be demonstratively evinced, that which comes nearest to the proof of the fact is the proof of such circumstances which either *necessarily* or *usually* attend such facts; and these are called presumptions, which are only to be relied upon till the contrary be actually proved. *Stabitur præsumptioni donec probetur in contrarium.* *Violent* presumption is many times equal to full proof; for there those circumstances appear, which *necessarily* attend the fact. As, if a landlord sues for rent due at Michaelmas 1754, and the tenant cannot prove the payment, but produces an acquittance for rent due at a subsequent time, in full of all demands, this is a violent presumption of his having paid the former rent, and is equivalent to full proof; for though the actual payment is not proved, yet the acquittance in full of all demands is proved, which could not be without such payment; and it therefore induces so forcible a presumption, that no proof shall be admitted to the contrary (a). *Probable* presumption arising

---

(a) The authority on which the learned commentator relies (and to which he refers) is the *Tenures of Ch. J. Gilbert*, (p. 161.) But the passage is there incorrect, and should be understood of such acquittances only as are under the *hand and seal* of the party, " for if it be not under seal the law *will* admit of proof to the contrary." *Co. Lit.* 8vo. 373. ª n. (3.)

from such circumstances as *usually* attend the fact, hath also its due weight: as if in a suit for rent due in 1754, the tenant proves the payment of the rent due in 1755; this will prevail to exonerate the tenant, unless it be clearly shewn that the rent of 1754 was retained for some special reason, or that there was some fraud or mistake; for otherwise it will be presumed to have been paid before that in 1755, as it is most usual to receive first the rents of longest standing. *Light*, or rash presumptions have no weight or validity at all.

The oath administered to the witness is not only that what he deposes shall be true, but that he shall also depose the *whole* truth: so that he is not to conceal any part of what he knows, whether interrogated particularly to that point or not. And all this evidence is to be given in open court, in the presence of the parties, their attorneys, the counsel, and all by-standers; and before the judge and jury: each party having liberty to except to its competency, which exceptions are publicly stated, and by the judge are openly and publicly allowed or disallowed, in the face of the country (*a*): which must curb any secret bias or partiality, that might arise in his own breast. And if, either in his directions or decisions, he mis-states the law by ignorance, inadvertence, or design, the counsel on either side may require him publicly to seal a *bill of exceptions*, stating the point wherein he is supposed to err; and this he is obliged to seal by statute Westm. 2. 13 Edw. I. c. 31. or, if he refuses so to do, the party may have a compulsory writ against him, commanding him to seal it, if the fact alleged be truly stated: and if he returns, that the fact is untruly stated, when the case is otherwise, an action will lie against him for making a false return. This bill of exceptions is in the nature of an appeal; examinable, not in the court out of which the record issues for the trial,

---

(*a*). It is, however, now become a common practice, at the request of either party, to prevent the witnesses being present in court during the examination of evidences; and this rule certainly facilitates the acquirement of truth, as it thereby proves some sort of check to that combination of evidence too often adduced in courts of justice to support a particular cause, or to maintain an unjust prosecution.

at *nisi prius*, but in the next immediate superior court, upon a writ of error, after judgment given in the court below. But a *demurrer* to evidence shall be determined by the court, out of which the record is sent. This happens, where a record or other matter is produced in evidence, concerning the legal consequences of which there arises a doubt in law: in which case the adverse party may if he pleases demur to the whole evidence; which admits the truth of every fact that has been alleged, but denies the sufficiency of them all in point of law to maintain or overthrow the issue: which draws the question of law from the cognizance of the jury, to be decided (as it ought) by the court. But neither these demurrers to evidence, nor the bills of exceptions, are at present so much in use as formerly; since the more frequent extension of the discretionary powers of the court in granting a new trial, which is now very commonly had for the mis-direction of the judge at *nisi prius*. As to such evidence as the jury may have in their own consciences, by their private knowlege of facts, it was an antient doctrine, that this had as much right to sway their judgment as the written or parol evidence which is delivered in court. But now if a juror knows any thing of the matter in issue, he may be sworn as a witness, and give his evidence publicly in court.

When the evidence is gone through on both sides, the judge in the presence of the parties, the counsel, and all others, sums up the whole to the jury; with such remarks as he thinks necessary for their direction, and giving them his opinion in matters of law arising upon that evidence.

The jury, after the proofs are summed up, unless the case be very clear, withdraw from the bar to consider of their verdict: and, in order to avoid intemperance and causeless delay, are to be kept without meat, drink, fire, or candle, unless by permission of the judge, till they are all unanimously agreed. If the jury eat or drink at all, or have any eatables about them, without consent of the court, and before verdict, it is fineable; and if they do so at his charge for whom they afterwards find, it will set aside the verdict. Also if they speak with either of the parties or their agents, after they are gone from the bar; or if they receive any freſh evidence in private; or if to prevent diſputes they caſt lots for whom they ſhall find; any of theſe circumſtances will entirely vitiate the verdict.

A verdict, *vere dictum*, is either *privy* or *public;* but the only effectual and legal verdict is the *public* verdict: in which they openly declare to have found the iſſue for the plaintiff, or for the defendant; and if for the plaintiff, they aſſeſs the damages alſo ſuſtained by the plaintiff, in conſequence of the injury upon which the action is brought.

Sometimes, if there ariſes in the caſe any difficult matter of law, the jury for the ſake of better information, and to avoid the danger of having their verdict attainted, will find a *ſpecial* verdict; which is grounded on the ſtatute Weſtm. 2. 13 Edw. I. c. 30. §. 2. And herein they ſtate the naked facts, as they find them to be proved, and pray the advice of the court thereon; concluding, conditionally, that if upon the whole matter the court ſhall be of opinion that the plaintiff had cauſe of action, they then find for the plaintiff; if otherwiſe, then for the defendant. This is entered at length on the record, and afterwards argued and determined in the court at Weſtminſter, from whence the iſſue came to be tried.

Another method of finding a ſpecies of ſpecial verdict, is when the jury find a verdict generally for the plaintiff, but ſubject neverthelefs to the opinion of the judge or the court above, on a *ſpecial caſe* ſtated by the counſel on both ſides with regard to a matter of law: but the jury may, if they think proper, take upon themſelves to determine, at their own hazard, the complicated queſtion of fact and law; and, without either ſpecial verdict or ſpecial caſe, may find a verdict abſolutely either for the plaintiff or defendant.

When the jury have delivered in their verdict, and it is recorded in court, they are then diſcharged. And ſo ends the trial by jury: a trial, which beſides the other vaſt advantages which we have occaſionally obſerved in it's progreſs, is alſo as expeditious and cheap, as it is convenient, equitable and certain; for a commiſſion out of chancery, or the civil law courts, for examining witneſſes in one cauſe will frequently laſt as long, and of courſe be full as expenſive, as the trial of a hundred iſſues at *niſi prius:* and yet the fact cannot be determined by ſuch commiſſioners at all; no, not till the depoſitions are publiſhed, and read at the hearing of the cauſe in court.

## CHAPTER XIV.

### OF JUDGMENT, AND IT'S INCIDENTS.

NEXT follows, ſixthly, the judgment of the court upon what has previouſly paſſed; both the matter of law and matter of fact being now fully weighed and adjuſted. Judgment may however, for certain cauſes, be *ſuſpended,* or finally *arreſted:* for it cannot be entered till the next term after trial had, and that upon notice to the other party. So that if any defect of juſtice happened at the trial, by ſurprize, inadvertence, or miſconduct, the party may have relief in the court above, by obtaining a new trial; or, if, notwithſtanding the iſſue of fact be regularly decided, it appears that the complaint was either not actionable in itſelf, or not made with ſufficient preciſion and accuracy, the party may ſuperſede it, by arreſting or ſtaying the judgment.

1. Cauſes of *ſuſpending* the judgment by granting a *new trial,* are at preſent wholly *extrinſic,* ariſing from matter foreign to or *dehors* the record. Of this ſort are want of notice of trial; or any flagrant miſbehaviour of the party prevailing towards the jury, which may have influenced their verdict; or any groſs miſbehaviour of the jury among themſelves: alſo if it appears by the judge's report, certified to the court, that the jury have brought in a verdict without or contrary to evidence, ſo that he is reaſonably diſſatisfied therewith; or if they have given exorbitant damages; or if the judge himſelf has miſ-directed the jury, ſo that they found an unjuſtifiable verdict; for theſe, and other reaſons of the like kind, it is the practice of the court to award a *new,* or ſecond *trial.* But if two juries agree in the ſame or a ſimilar verdict, a third trial is ſeldom awarded: for the law will not readily ſuppoſe, that the verdict of any one ſubſequent jury can countervail the oaths of the two preceding ones.

A sufficient ground must, however, be laid before the court, to satisfy them that it is necessary to justice that the cause should be farther considered. If the matter be such as did not or could not appear to the judge who presided at *nisi prius*, it is disclosed to the court by *affidavit*: if it arises from what passed at the trial, it is taken from the judge's information; who usually makes a special and minute report of the evidence. Counsel are heard on both sides to impeach or establish the verdict, and the court give their reasons at large why a new examination ought or ought not to be allowed. The true import of the evidence is duly weighed, false colours are taken off, and all points of law which arose at the trial are, upon full deliberation, clearly explained and settled.

Nor do the courts lend too easy an ear to every application for a review of the former verdict. They must be satisfied, that there are strong probable grounds to suppose that the merits have not been fairly and fully discussed, and that the decision is not agreeable to the justice and truth of the case. A new trial is not granted, where the value is too inconsiderable to merit a second examination. It is not granted upon nice and formal objections, which do not go to the real merits. It is not granted in cases of strict right or *summum jus*, where the rigorous exaction of extreme legal justice is hardly reconcileable to conscience. Nor is it granted where the scales of evidence hang nearly equal: that, which leans against the former verdict, ought always very strongly to preponderate.

In granting such farther trial (which is matter of sound discretion) the court has also an opportunity, which it seldom fails to improve, of supplying those defects in this mode of trial which were stated in the preceding chapter; by laying the party applying under all such equitable terms, as his antagonist shall desire and mutually offer to comply with: such as the discovery of some facts upon oath; the admission of others, not intended to be litigated; the production of deeds, books, and papers; the examination of witnesses, infirm or going beyond sea; and the like. And the delay and expence of this proceeding are so small and trifling, that it seldom can be moved for to gain time or to gratify humour. The motion muſt be made within the firſt four days of the next ſucceeding term, within which term it is uſually heard and decided.

2. Arreſts of judgment ariſe from *intrinſic* cauſes, appearing upon the face of the record. Of this kind are, firſt, where the declaration varies totally from the original writ: alſo, ſecondly, where the verdict materially differs from the pleadings and iſſue thereon: or, thirdly, if the caſe laid in the declaration is not ſufficient in point of law to found an action. And this is an invariable rule with regard to arreſts of judgment upon matter of law, "that whatever is alledged "in arreſt of judgment muſt be ſuch matter, as would upon "demurrer have been ſufficient to overturn the action or "plea." But the rule will not hold *e converſo*, "that every "thing that may be alledged as cauſe of demurrer will be "good in arreſt of judgment:" for if a declaration or plea omits to ſtate ſome particular circumſtance, without proving of which, at the trial, it is impoſſible to ſupport the action or defence, this omiſſion ſhall be added by a verdict. For the verdict aſcertains thoſe facts, which before from the inaccuracy of the pleadings might be dubious. Exceptions, therefore, that are moved in arreſt of judgment, muſt be much more material and glaring than ſuch as will maintain a demurrer: or, in other words, many inaccuracies and omiſſions, which would be fatal, if early obſerved, are cured by a ſubſequent verdict; and not ſuffered, in the laſt ſtage of a cauſe, to unravel the whole proceedings. But if the thing omitted be eſſential to the action or defence, as if the plaintiff does not merely ſtate his title in a defective manner, but ſets forth a title that is totally defective in itſelf, or if to an action of debt the defendant pleads *not guilty* inſtead of *nil debet*, theſe cannot be cured by a verdict for the plaintiff in the firſt caſe, or for the defendant in the ſecond.

If judgment is not by ſome of theſe means arreſted within the firſt four days of the next term after the trial, it is then to be entered on the roll or record. Judgments are the ſentence of the law, pronounced by the court upon the matter contained in the record; and are of four ſorts. Firſt, where the facts are confessed by the parties, and the law determined by the court; as in case of judgment upon *demurrer*: secondly, where the law is admitted by the parties, and the facts disputed; as in case of judgment on a *verdict*: thirdly, where both the fact and the law arising thereon are admitted by the defendant; which is the case of judgments by *confession* or *default*: or, lastly, where the plaintiff is convinced that either fact, or law, or both, are insufficient to support his action, and therefore abandons or withdraws his prosecution; which is the case in judgments upon a *nonsuit* or *retraxit*.

All these species of judgments are either *interlocutory* or *final*. *Interlocutory* judgments are such as are given in the middle of a cause, upon some plea proceeding, or default, which is only intermediate, and does not finally determine or complete the suit.

But the interlocutory judgments, most usually spoken of, are those incomplete judgments, whereby the *right* of the plaintiff is indeed established, but the *quantum* of damages sustained by him is not ascertained: which is a matter that cannot be done without the intervention of a jury. This can only happen where the plaintiff recovers; for, when judgment is given for the defendant, it is always complete as well as final. And this happens, in the first place, where the defendant suffers judgment to go against him by default, or *nihil dicit;* as if he puts in no plea at all to the plaintiff's declaration: by confession or *cognovit actionem*, where he acknowledges the plaintiff's demand to be just: or by *non sum informatus*, when the defendant's attorney declares he has no instructions to say any thing in answer to the plaintiff, or in defence of his client; which is a species of judgment by default. If these, or any of them, happen in actions where the specific thing sued for is recovered, as in actions of debt for a sum certain, the judgment is absolutely complete. And therefore it is very usual, in order to strengthen a creditor's security, for the debtor to execute a warrant of attorney to some attorney named by the creditor, empowering him to confess a judgment by either of the ways just now mentioned *(by nihil dicit, cognovit actionem, or non sum informatus)* in an action of debt to be brought by the creditor against the debtor for the specific sum due: which judgment, when confessed, is absolutely complete and binding; provided the same (as is also required in all other judgments) be regularly *docquetted*, that is, abstracted and entered in a book, according to the directions of statute 4 & 5 W. & M. c. 20. But, where damages are to be recovered, a jury must be called in to assess them; unless the defendant, to save charges, will confess the whole damages laid in the declaration: otherwise the entry of the judgment is, "that the plaintiff ought to recover "his damages, (indefinitely) but because the court know "not what damages the said plaintiff hath sustained, there- "fore the sheriff is commanded, that by the oaths of twelve "honest and lawful men he inquire into the said damages, "and return such inquisition into court." This process is called a *writ of inquiry*: in the execution of which the sheriff sits as judge, and tries by a jury, subject to nearly the same law and conditions as the trial by jury at *nisi prius*, what damages the plaintiff hath really sustained; and when their verdict is given, which must assess *some* damages, the sheriff returns the inquisition, which is entered upon the roll in manner of a *postea*; and thereupon it is considered that the plaintiff do recover the exact sum of the damages so assessed. In like manner, when a demurrer is determined for the plaintiff upon an action wherein damages are recovered, the judgment is also incomplete, without the aid of a writ of inquiry.

Final judgments are such as at once put an end to the action, by declaring that the plaintiff has either entitled himself, or has not, to recover the remedy he sues for. In which case, if the judgment be for the plaintiff, it is also considered that the defendant be either amerced, for his wilful delay of justice in not immediately obeying the king's writ by rendering the plaintiff his due; or be taken up, *capiatur*, till he pays a fine to the king for the public misdemeinor which is coupled with the private injury, in all cases of force, of falshood in denying his own deed or unjustly claiming property in replevin, or of contempt by disobeying the command of the king's writ or the exprefs prohibition of any ftatute. But now in cafe of trefpafs, ejectment, affault, and falfe imprifonment, it is provided, by the ftatute 5 & 6 W. & M. c. 12. that no writ of *capias* fhall iffue for this fine, nor any fine be paid; but the plaintiff fhall pay 6*s*. 8*d*. to the proper officer, and be allowed it againft the defendant among his other cofts. And therefore upon fuch judgments in the common pleas they ufed to enter that the fine was remitted, and now in both courts they take no notice of any fine or *capias* at all. But if judgment be for the defendant, then in cafe of fraud or deceit to the court, or malicious or vexatious fuits, the plaintiff may alfo be fined; but in moft cafes it is only confidered, that he and his pledges of profecuting be (nominally) amerced for his falfe claim, *pro falfo clamore fuo*, and that the defendant may go thereof without a day, *eat inde fine die*, that is, without any farther continuance or adjournment; the king's writ, commanding his attendance, being now fully fatisfied, and his innocence publickly cleared.

Thus much for judgments; to which cofts are a neceffary appendage; it being now as well the maxim of ours as of the civil law, that "*victus victori in expenfis condemnandus eft:*" Thefe cofts on both fides are taxed and moderated by the prothonotary, or other proper officer of the court.

The king (and any perfon fuing to his ufe) fhall neither pay, nor receive cofts. And it feems reafonable to fuppofe, that the queen-confort participates of the fame privilege. In two other cafes an exemption alfo lies from paying cofts. Executors and adminiftrators, when fuing in the right of the deceafed, fhall pay none (*a*): for the ftatute 23 Hen. VIII. c. 15. doth not give cofts to defendants, unlefs where the action fuppofeth the contract to be made with, or the wrong to be done to, the plaintiff himfelf. And paupers, that is fuch as will fwear themfelves not worth five pounds, are, by ftatute 11 Hen. VII. c. 12. to have original writs and *fubpoenas gratis*, and counfel and attorney affigned them without fee; and are excufed from paying cofts, when plaintiffs, by

---

(*a*) *Quare*; and fee 5 *Term Rep.* 234. 2 *Cromp. Prac.* 476.

the statute 23 Hen. VIII. c. 15. but shall suffer other punishment at the discretion of the judges. It seems, however, agreed, that a pauper may recover costs, though he pays none; for the counsel and clerks are bound to give their labour to *him*, but not to his antagonists. To prevent also trifling and malicious actions, for words, for assault and battery, and for trespass, it is enacted by statutes 43 Eliz. c. 6. 21 Jac. I. c. 16. and 22 & 23 Car. II. c. 9. §. 136. that, where the jury who try any of these actions shall give less damages than 40*s*. (a) the plaintiff shall be allowed no more costs than damages, unless the judge before whom the cause is tried shall certify under his hand on the back of the record, that an actual battery (and not an assault only) was proved, or that in trespass the freehold or title of the land came chiefly in question. Also, by statute 4 & 5 W. & M. c. 23. and 8 & 9 W. III. c. 11. if the trespass were committed in hunting or sporting by an inferior tradesman, or if it appear to be wilfully and maliciously committed, the plaintiff shall have full costs, though his damages as assessed by the jury amount to less than 40*s*.

After *judgment* is entered, *execution* will immediately follow, unless the party condemned thinks himself unjustly aggrieved by any of these proceedings; and then he has his remedy to reverse them by several writs in the nature of appeals, which we shall consider in the succeeding chapter.

## CHAPTER XV.

### OF PROCEEDINGS IN THE NATURE OF APPEALS.

PROCEEDINGS, in the nature of *appeals* from the proceedings of the king's courts of law, are of various kinds: according to the subject matter in which they are concerned. They are principally four.

---

*(a)* And by the same statute of 43 Eliz. " the justice before whom the action was tried, shall certify that the debt or damages did not amount to that sum."

I. A writ of *attaint*: which lieth to inquire whether a jury of *twelve* men gave a false verdict; that so the judgment following thereupon may be reversed: and this must be brought in the life-time of him for whom the verdict was given, and of two at least of the jurors who gave it. But the practice of setting aside verdicts upon motion, and granting *new trials*, has superseded the use of attaints.

II. The writ of *deceit*, or action on the case in nature of it, may be brought in the court of common pleas, to reverse a judgment there had by fraud or collusion in a real action, whereby lands and tenements have been recovered to the prejudice of him that hath right; but of this enough hath been observed in a former chapter.

III. An *audita querela* is where a defendant, against whom judgment is recovered, and who is therefore in danger of execution, or perhaps actually in execution, may be relieved upon good matter of discharge, which has happened since the judgment. But the indulgence now shewn by the courts in granting a summary relief upon motion, in cases of such evident oppression, has almost rendered useless the writ of *audita querela*, and driven it quite out of practice.

IV. But, fourthly; the principal method of redress for erroneous judgments in the king's courts of record, is by *writ of error* to some superior court of appeal.

A writ of error lies for some supposed mistake in the proceedings of a court of record; for, to amend errors in a base court, not of record, a writ of *false judgment* lies. The writ of error only lies upon matter of *law* arising upon the face of the proceedings; so that no evidence is required to substantiate or support it: there being no method of reversing an error in the determination of *facts*, but by an attaint, or a new trial, to correct the mistakes of the former verdict.

Formerly the suitors were much perplexed by writs of error brought upon very slight and trivial grounds, as misspellings and other mistakes of the clerks. But now the courts are become more liberal; and where justice requires it, will allow of amendments at any time while the suit is depending, notwithstanding the record be made up, and the term be past: but when judgment is once given and enrolled, no amendment is permitted in any subsequent term. Mistakes are also effectually helped by the statutes of amendment and *jeofails;* so called, because when a pleader perceives any slip in the form of his proceedings, and acknowleges such error *(jeo faile)* he is at liberty, by those statutes, to amend it; which amendment is seldom actually made, but the benefit of the acts is attained by the court's overlooking the exception. These statutes are many in number, and the provisions in them too minute to be here taken notice of, otherwise than by referring to the statutes themselves; by which all trifling exceptions are so thoroughly guarded against, that writs of error cannot now be maintained, but for some material mistake assigned.

If a writ of error be brought to reverse any judgment of an inferior court of record, where the damages are less than ten pounds; or, if it is brought to reverse the judgment of any superior court after verdict, he that brings the writ, or that is plaintiff in error, must (except in some peculiar cases) find substantial pledges of prosecution, or bail: to prevent delays by frivolous pretences to appeal; and for securing payment of costs and damages.

A writ of error lies from the inferior courts of record in England into the king's bench, and not into the common pleas. Also from the king's bench in Ireland to the king's bench in England (*a*). It likewise may be brought from the common pleas at Westminster to the king's bench; and then from the king's bench the cause is removeable to the house of lords. From proceedings on the law side of the exchequer a writ of error lies into the court of exchequer chamber before the lord chancellor, lord treasurer, and the judges of the court of king's bench and common pleas: and from thence

---

(*a*) So it formerly was, (*viz.* from the time of Hen. VIII. to the 6 Geo. I.) but by 23 Geo. III. c. 28. this appeal was taken away; and it is enacted, that no writ of error or appeal, from any court in Ireland, shall, from thenceforth, be brought into any of the courts in England.

it lies to the houfe of peers. From proceedings in the king's bench, in debt, detinue, covenant, account, cafe, ejectment, or trefpafs, originally begun therein by bill, (except where the king is party) it lies to the exchequer chamber, before the juftices of the common pleas, and barons of the exchequer; and from thence alfo to the houfe of lords; but where the proceedings in the king's bench do not firft commence therein by bill, but by original writ fued out of chancery, this takes the cafe out of the general rule laid down by the ftatute; fo that the writ of error then lies, without any intermediate ftage of appeal, directly to the houfe of lords, the dernier refort for the ultimate decifion of every civil action. Each court of appeal, in their refpective ftages, may, upon hearing the matter of law in which the error is affigned, reverfe or affirm the judgment of the inferior courts; but none of them are final, fave only the houfe of peers, to whofe judicial decifions all other tribunals muft therefore fubmit, and conform their own. And thus much for the reverfal or affirmance of judgments at law, by writs in the nature of appeals.

## CHAPTER XVI.

### OF EXECUTION.

IF the regular judgment of the court, after the decifion of the fuit, be not fufpended, fuperfeded, or reverfed, by one or other of the methods mentioned in the two preceding chapters, the next and laft ftep is the *execution* of that judgment, or, putting the fentence of the law in force. This is performed in different manners, according to the nature of the action upon which it is founded, and of the judgment which is had or recovered.

If the plaintiff recovers in an action real or mixed, whereby the feifin or poffeffion of land is awarded to him, the writ of execution fhall be an *habere facias feifinam,* or writ of feifin, of a freehold; or an *habere facias poffeffionem,* or writ of pof-

*feffion*, of a chattel intereft. Thefe are writs directed to the fheriff of the county, commanding him to give actual poffeffion to the plaintiff of the land fo recovered: in the execution of which the fheriff may take with him the *poffe comitatus*, or power of the county; and may juftify breaking open doors, if the poffeffion be not quietly delivered. But, if it be peaceably yielded up, the delivery of a twig, a turf, or the ring of the door, in the name of feifin, is fufficient execution of the writ. Upon a prefentation to a benefice recovered in a *quare impedit*, or affife of *darrein prefentment*, the execution is by a writ *de clerico admittendo*, directed, not to the fheriff, but to the bifhop or archbifhop, and requiring him to admit and inftitute the clerk of the plaintiff.

In other actions, where the judgment is that fomething in fpecial be done or rendered by the defendant, then, in order to compel him fo to do, and to fee the judgment executed, a fpecial writ of execution iffues to the fheriff according to the nature of the cafe. As, upon an affife of nufance, or *quod permittat profternere*, where one part of the judgment is *quod nocumentum amoveatur*, a writ goes to the fheriff to abate it at the charge of the party, which likewife iffues even in cafe of an indictment. Upon a replevin, the writ of execution is the writ *de retorno habendo*; and, if the diftrefs be eloigned, the defendant fhall have a *capias in withernam*, but, on the plaintiff's tendering the damages and fubmitting to a fine, the procefs *in withernam* fhall be ftayed. In detinue, after judgment, the plaintiff fhall have a *diftringas*, to compel the defendant to deliver the goods, by repeated diftreffes of his chattels; or elfe a *fcire facias* againft any third perfon in whofe hands they may happen to be, to fhew caufe why they fhould not be delivered: and if the defendant ftill continues obftinate, then (if the judgment hath been by default or on demurrer) the fheriff fhall fummon an inqueft to afcertain the value of the goods, and the plaintiff's damages; which (being either fo affeffed, or by the verdict in cafe of an iffue) fhall be levied on the perfon or goods of the defendant. So that, after all, in replevin and detinue, (the only actions for recovering the fpecific poffeffion of perfonal chattels) if the wrong-doer be very perverfe, he cannot be compelled to a reftitution of the identical thing taken or detained; but he ftill has his election, to deliver the goods or their value; an imperfection in the law, that refults from the nature of perfonal property, which is eafily concealed or conveyed out of the reach of juftice, and not always amenable to the magiftrate.

Executions in actions where money only is recovered, as a debt or damages, (and not any fpecific chattel) are of five forts; either againft the body of the defendant; or againft his goods and chattels, or againft his goods and the *profits* of his lands; or againft his goods and the *poffeffion* of his lands: or againft all three, his body, lands, and goods.

1. The firft of thefe fpecies of execution, is by writ of *capias ad fatisfaciendum*; which addition diftinguifhes it from the former *capias, ad refpondendum,* which lies to compel an appearance at the beginning of a fuit. And, properly fpeaking, this cannot be fued out againft any but fuch as were liable to be taken upon the former *capias*. The intent of it is, to imprifon the body of the debtor till fatisfaction be made for the debt, cofts, and damages: it therefore doth not lie againft any privileged perfons, peers or members of parliament, nor againft executors or adminiftrators, nor againft fuch other perfons as could not be originally held to bail. And fir Edward Coke alfo gives us a fingular inftance, where a defendant in 14 Edw. III. was difcharged from a *capias* becaufe he was of fo advanced an age, *quod pœnam imprifonamenti fubire non poteft.* If an action be brought againft an hufband and wife for the debt of the wife, when fole, and the plaintiff recovers judgment, the *capias* fhall iffue to take both the hufband and wife in execution: but, if the action was orignally brought againft herfelf, when fole, and pending the fuit fhe marries, the *capias* fhall be awarded againft her only, and not againft her hufband. Yet, if judgment be recovered againft an hufband and wife for the contract, nay even for the perfonal mifbehaviour of the wife during her coverture, the *capias* fhall iffue againft the hufband

only: which is one of the many great privilges of English wives.

The writ of *capias ad satisfaciendum* is an execution of the highest nature, inasmuch as it deprives a man of his liberty, till he makes the satisfaction awarded; and therefore, when a man is once taken in execution upon this writ, no other process can be sued out against his lands or goods. Only by statute 21 Jac. I. c. 24. if the defendant dies, while charged in execution upon this writ, the plaintiff may, after his death, sue out a new execution against his lands, goods, or chattels. The writ is directed to the sheriff, commanding him to take the body of the defendant and have him at Westminster, on a day therein named, to make the plaintiff satisfaction for his demand. And, if he does not then make satisfaction, he must remain in custody till he does. This writ may be sued out, as may all other executory process, for costs, against a plaintiff as well as a defendant, when judgment is had against him.

When a defendant is once in custody upon this process, he is to be kept in *arɛta et salva custodia*: and, if he be afterwards seen at large, it is an *escape*: and the plaintiff may have an action thereupon against the sheriff for his whole debt. For though, upon arrests 'and what is called *mesne* process, being such as intervenes between the commencement and end of a suit, the sheriff, till the statute 8 & 9 W. III. c. 27. might have indulged the defendant as he pleased, so as he produced him in court to answer the plaintiff at the return of the writ: yet, upon a taking in execution, he could never give any indulgence; for, in that case, confinement is the whole of the debtor's punishment, and of the satisfaction made to the creditor. Escapes are either voluntary, or negligent. Voluntary are such as are by the express consent of the keeper; of which he never can retake his prisoner again, (though the plaintiff may retake him at any time) but the sheriff must answer for the debt. Negligent escapes are where the prisoner escapes without his keeper's knowlege or consent; and then upon fresh pursuit the defendant may be retaken, and the sheriff shall be excused, if he has him again before any action brought against himself for the escape. A rescue of a prisoner *in execution*, either going to the gaol or in gaol, or a breach of prison, will not excuse the sheriff from being guilty of and answering for the escape; for he ought to have sufficient force to keep him, since he may command the power of the county. But by statute 32 Geo. II. c. 28. if a defendant, charged in execution for any debt less than 100l. (a) will surrender all his effects to his creditors, (except his apparel, bedding, and tools of his trade, not amounting in the whole to the value of 10l) and will make oath of his punctual compliance with the statute, the prisoner may be discharged, unless the creditor insists on detaining him; in which case he shall allow him 2s. 4d. *per* week, to be paid on the first day of every week, and on failure of regular payment the prisoner shall be discharged. Yet the creditor may at any future time have execution against the lands and goods of such defendant, though never more against his person. And, on the other hand, the creditors may, as in case of bankruptcy, compel (under pain of transportation for seven years) such debtor charged in execution for any debt under 100l. to make a discovery and surrender of all his effects for their benefit; whereupon he is also entitled to the like discharge of his person.

If a *capias ad satisfaciendum* is sued out, and a *non est inventus* is returned thereon, the plaintiff may sue out a process against the bail, if any were given: who, we may remember, stipulated in this triple alternative, that the defendant should, if condemned in the suit, satisfy the plaintiff his debt and costs; or, that he should surrender himself a prisoner; or, that they would pay it for him: as therefore the two former branches of the alternative are neither of them complied with, the latter must immediately take place. In order to which a writ of *scire facias* may be sued out against the bail, commanding them to shew cause why the plaintiff should not have execution against them for his debt and damages:

---

(a) Since extended to 300l. by 33 Geo. III. c. 5.

and on such writ, if they shew no sufficient cause, or the defendant does not surrender himself on the day of the return, or of shewing cause (for afterwards is not sufficient) the plaintiff may have judgment against the bail, and take out a writ of *capias ad satisfaciendum*, or other process of execution against them.

2. The next species of execution is against the goods and chattels of the defendant; and is called a writ of *fieri facias*, from the words in it where the sheriff is commanded, *quod fieri faciat de bonis*, that he cause to be made of the goods and chattels of the defendant the sum or debt recovered. This lies as well against privileged persons, peers, &c. as other commons persons; and against executors or administrators with regard to the goods of the deceased. The sheriff may not break open any outer doors to execute either this, or the former writ, but must enter peaceably, and may then break open any inner door belonging to the defendant, in order to take the goods. And he may sell the goods and chattels (even an estate for years, which is a chattel real) of the defendant, till he has raised enough to satisfy the judgment and costs: first paying the landlord of the premises upon which the goods are found, the arrears of rent then due, not exceeding one year's rent in the whole. If part only of the debt be levied on a *fieri facias*, the plaintiff may have a *capias ad satisfaciendum* for the residue.

3. A third species of execution is by writ of *levari facias*; which affects a man's goods and the *profits* of his lands, by commanding the sheriff to levy the plaintiff's debt on the lands and goods of the defendant; whereby the sheriff may seize all his goods, and receive the rents and profits of his lands, till satisfaction be made to the plaintiff. Little use is now made of this writ; the remedy by *elegit*, which takes possession of the lands themselves, being much more effectual. But of this species is a writ of execution proper only to ecclesiastics; which is given when the sheriff, upon a common writ of execution sued, returns that the defendant is a beneficed clerk, not having any lay fee. In this case a writ goes to the bishop of the diocese, in the nature of a *levari* or *fieri*

*facias*, to levy the debt and damage *de bonis ecclesiasticis*, which are not to be touched by lay hands: and thereupon the bishop sends out a *sequestration* of the profits of the clerk's benefice, directed to the churchwardens, to collect the same and pay them to the plaintiff till the full sum be raised.

4. The fourth species of execution is by the writ of *elegit*; which is a judicial writ given by the statute Westm. 2. 13 Edw. I. c. 18. either upon a judgment for debt, or damages; or upon the forfeiture of a recognizance taken in the king's court. By the common law a man could only have satisfaction of goods, chattels, and the present profits of lands, by the two last-mentioned writs of *fieri facias*, or *levari facias*: but not the possession of the lands themselves; which was a natural consequence of the feodal principles, which prohibited the alienation, and of course the incumbering of the fief with the debts, of the owner. And, when the restriction of alienation began to wear away, the consequence still continued; and no creditor could take the possession of lands, but only levy the growing profits: so that, if the defendant aliened his lands, the plaintiff was ousted of his remedy. The statute therefore granted this writ, (called an *elegit*, because it is in the choice or election of the plaintiff whether he will sue out this writ or one of the former) by which the defendant's goods and chattels are not sold, but only appraised; and all of them (except oxen and beasts of the plough) are delivered to the plaintiff, at such reasonable appraisement and price, in part of satisfaction of his debt. If the goods are not sufficient, then the moiety or one half of his freehold lands, which he had at the time of the judgment given, whether held in his own name, or by any other in trust for him; are also to be delivered to the plaintiff; to hold, till out of the rents and profits thereof the debt be levied, or till the defendant's interest be expired; as, till the death of the defendant, if he be tenant for life or in tail. During this period the plaintiff is called tenant by *elegit*, of whom we spoke in a former part of these commentaries. We there observed that till this statute, by the antient common law, lands were not liable to be charged with,

or seised for, debts; because by these means the connection between lord and tenant might be destroyed, fraudulent alienations might be made, and the services be transferred to be performed by a stranger; provided the tenant incurred a large debt, sufficient to cover the land. And therefore, even by this statute, only one half was, and now is, subject to execution; that out of the remainder sufficient might be left for the lord to distrein upon for his services. And, upon the same feodal principle, copyhold lands are at this day not liable to be taken in execution upon a judgment. But, in case of a debt to the king, it appears by *magna carta*, c. 8. that it was allowed by the common law for him to take possession of the lands till the debt was paid. For he, being the grand superior and ultimate proprietor of landed estates, might seise the lands into his own hands, if any thing was owing from the vassal; and could not be said to be defrauded of his services, when the ouster of the vassal proceeded from his own command. This execution, or seising of lands by *elegit*, is of so high a nature, that after it the body of the defendant cannot be taken: but if execution can only be had of the goods, because there are no lands, and such goods are not sufficient to pay the debt, a *capias ad satisfaciendum* may then be had after the *elegit*; for such *elegit* is in this case no more in effect than a *fieri facias*. So that body and goods may be taken in execution, or land and goods; but not body and land too, upon any judgment between subject and subject in the course of the common law. But

5. Upon some prosecutions given by statute; as in the case of recognizances or debts acknowleged on statutes merchant, or statutes staple; (pursuant to the statutes 13 Edw. I. *de mercatoribus*, and 27 Edw. III. c. 9.) upon forfeiture of these, the body, lands, and goods, may all be taken at once in execution, to compel the payment of the debt. The process hereon is usually called an *extent* or *extendi facias*, because the sheriff is to cause the lands, &c. to be appraised to their full extended value, before he delivers them to the plaintiff, that it may be certainly known how soon the debt

will be satisfied. And by statute 33 Hen. VIII. c. 39. all obligations made to the king shall have the same force, and of consequence the same remedy to recover them, as a statute staple: though indeed, before this statute, the king was intitled to sue out execution against the body, lands, and goods of his accountant or debtor. And his debt shall, in suing out execution, he preferred to that of every other creditor, who hath not obtained judgment before the king commenced his suit. The king's judgment also affects all lands, which the king's debtor hath at or after the time of contracting his debt, or which any of his officers mentioned in the statute 13 Eliz. c. 4. hath at or after the time of his entering on the office: so that, if such office of the crown alienes for a valuable consideration, the land shall be liable to the king's debt, even in the hands of a *bona fide* purchasor; though the debt due to the king was contracted by the vendor many years after the alienation. Whereas judgments between subject and subject related, even at common law, no farther back than the first day of the term in which they were recovered, in respect of the lands of the debtor; and did not bind his goods and chattels, but from the date of the writ of execution: and now, by the statute of frauds, 29 Car. II. c. 3. the judgment shall not bind the land in the hands of a *bona fide* purchasor, but only from the day of actually signing the same; which is directed by the statute to be punctually entered on the record: nor shall the writ of execution bind the goods in the hands of a stranger, or a purchasor, but only from the actual delivery of the writ to the sheriff or other officer, who is therefore ordered to endorse on the back of it the day of his receiving the same.

These are the methods which the law of England has pointed out for the execution of judgments: and when the plaintiff's demand is satisfied, either by the voluntary payment of the defendant, or by this compulsory process, or otherwise, satisfaction ought to be entered on the record, that the defendant may not be liable to be hereafter harrassed a second time on the same account. But all these writs of execution must be sued out within a year and a day after the judgment is entered; otherwife the court concludes *prima facie* that the judgment is fatisfied and extinct: yet however it will grant a writ of *fcire facias* in purfuance of ftatute Weftm. 2. 13 Edw. I. c. 45. for the defendant to fhew caufe why the judgment fhould not be revived, and execution had againft him; to which the defendant may plead fuch matter as he has to allege, in order to fhew why procefs of execution fhould not be iffued: or the plaintiff may ftill bring an action of debt, founded on this dormant judgment, which was the only method of revival allowed by the common law.

THE END OF THE THIRD BOOK.

# BOOK THE FOURTH.

## OF PUBLIC WRONGS.

### CHAPTER I.

#### OF THE NATURE OF CRIMES, AND THEIR PUNISHMENT.

WE are now arrived at the fourth and laſt branch of theſe commentaries, which treats of *public wrongs*, or *crimes* and *miſdemeſnors*. In the purſuit of which ſubject I ſhall conſider in the firſt place, the general nature of crimes and puniſhments; ſecondly, the perſons capable of committing crimes; thirdly, their ſeveral degrees of guilt, as principals or acceſſories; fourthly, the ſeveral ſpecies of crimes, with the puniſhment annexed to each by the laws of England; fifthly, the means of inflicting thoſe puniſhments, which the law has annexed to each ſeveral crime and miſdemeſnor.

Firſt, as to the general nature of crimes and their puniſhment: the diſcuſſion and admeaſurement of which forms in every country the code of criminal law; or, as it is more uſually denominated with us in England, the doctrine of the *pleas of the crown*; ſo called, becauſe the king, in whom centers the majeſty of the whole community, is ſuppoſed by the law to be the perſon injured by every infraction of the public rights belonging to that community, and is therefore in all caſes the proper proſecutor for every public offence.

I. A crime, or miſdemeſnor, is an act committed, or omitted, in violation of a public law, either forbidding or commanding it. This general definition comprehends both crimes and miſdemeſnors; which, properly ſpeaking, are mere fynonymous terms: though, in common ufage, he word "crimes" is made to denote fuch offences as are of a deeper and more attrocious dye; while fmaller faults, and omiffions of lefs confequence, are comprifed under the gentler name of " mifdemefnors " only.

The diftinction of public wrongs from private, of crimes and mifdemefnors from civil injuries, feems principally to confift in this: that private wrongs, or civil injuries, are an infringement or privation of the civil rights which belong to individuals, confidered merely as individuals; public wrongs, or crimes and mifdemefnors, are a breach and violation of the public rights and duties, due to the whole community, confidered as a community, in its focial aggregate capacity. As, if I detain a field from another man, to which the law has given him a right, this is a civil injury, and not a crime; for here only the right of an individual is concerned, and it is immaterial to the public, which of us is in poffeffion of the land: but treafon, murder, and robbery are properly ranked among crimes; fince, befides the injury done to individuals, they ftrike at the very being of fociety; which cannot poffibly fubfift, where actions of this fort are fuffered to efcape with impunity.

In taking cognizance of all wrongs, or unlawful acts, the law has a double view, viz. not only to redrefs the party injured, by either reftoring to him his right if poffible, or by giving him an equivalent; the manner of doing which was the object of our inquiries in the preceding book of thefe commentaries: but alfo to fecure to the public the benefit of fociety, by preventing or punifhing every breach and violation of thofe laws, which the fovereign power has thought proper to eftablifh for the government and tranquillity of the whole. What thofe breaches are, and how prevented or punifhed, are to be confidered in the prefent book.

II. The nature of *crimes and mifdemefnors* in general being thus afcertained and diftinguifhed, I proceed in the next place to confider the general nature of *punifhments:* which are evils or inconveniencies confequent upon crimes and mifdemefnors; being devifed, denounced, and inflicted by human laws, in confequence of difobedience or mifbehaviour in thofe, to regulate whofe conduct fuch laws were refpectively made. And herein we will briefly confider the *power*, the *end*, and the *meafure* of human punifhment.

1. As to the *power* of human punifhment, or the right of the temporal legiflator to inflict difcretionary penalties for crimes and mifdemefnors. It is clear, that the right of punifhing crimes againft the law of nature, as murder and the like, is in a ftate of mere nature vefted in every individual. But in a ftate of fociety this right is tranferred from individuals to the fovereign power; whereby men are prevented being judges in their own caufes, which is one of the evils that civil government was intended to remedy.

As to offences merely againft the laws of fociety, which are only *mala prohibita*, and not *mala in fe*; the temporal magiftrate is alfo empowered to inflict coercive penalties for fuch tranfgreffions: and this by the confent of individuals; who, in forming focieties, did, either tacitly or exprefsly, inveft the fovereign power with a right of making laws, and of enforcing obedience to them when made, by exercifing, upon their non-obfervance, feverities adequate to the evil. The lawfulnefs, therefore, of punifhing fuch criminals is founded upon this principle, that the law by which they fuffer was made by their own confent; it is a part of the original contract into which they entered, when firft they engaged in fociety; it was calculated for, and has long contributed to, their own fecurity.

2. As to the *end*, or final caufe of human punifhments. This is not by way of atonement or expiation for the crime committed; for that muft be left to the juft determination of the Supreme Being; but as a precaution againft future offences of the fame kind. This is effected three ways: either by the amendment of the offender himfelf; for which purpofe all corporal punifhments, fines, and temporary exile or imprifonment are inflicted: or, by deterring others by the dread of his example from offending in the like way, " *ut pœna* (as Tully expreffes it) *ad paucos, metus ad omnes perveniat;*" which gives rife to all ignominious punifhments,

and to such executions of justice as are open and public: or, lastly, by depriving the party injuring of the power to do future mischief; which is effected by either putting him to death, or condemning him to perpetual confinement, slavery, or exile. The same one end, of preventing future crimes, is endeavoured to be answered by each of these three species of punishment. The public gains equal security, whether the offender himself be amended by wholesome correction, or whether he be disabled from doing any farther harm: and if the penalty fails of both these effects, as it may do, still the terror of his example remains as a warning to other citizens.

3. As to the *measure* of human punishments. From what has been observed we may collect, that the quantity of punishment can never be absolutely determined by any standing invariable rule; but it must be left to the arbitration of the legislature to inflict such penalties as are warranted by the laws of nature and society, and such as appear to be the best calculated to answer the end of precaution against future offences.

## CHAPTER II.

OF THE PERSONS CAPABLE OF COMMITTING CRIMES.

HAVING, in the preceding chapter, considered in general the nature of crimes, and punishments, we are next led, in the order of our distribution, to inquire what persons are, or are not, *capable* of committing crimes; or which is all one, who are exempted from the censures of the law upon the commission of those acts, which in other persons would be severely punished. In the process of which inquiry, we must have recourse to particular and special exceptions: for the general rule is, that no person shall be excused from punishment for disobedience to the laws of his country, excepting such as are expressly defined and exempted by the laws themselves.

All the several pleas and excuses, which protect the committer of a forbidden act from the punishment which is otherwise annexed thereto, may be reduced to this single consideration, the want or defect of *will*. An involuntary act, as it has no claim to merit, so neither can it induce any guilt: the concurrence of the will, when it has it's choice either to do or to avoid the fact in question, being the only thing that renders human actions either praiseworthy or culpable.

Now there are three cases, in which the will does not join with the act: 1. Where there is a defect of understanding. For where there is no discernment, there is no choice; and where there is no choice, there can be no act of the will, which is nothing else but a determination of one's choice to do or to abstain from a particular action: he therefore, that has no understanding, can have no will to guide his conduct. 2. Where there is understanding and will sufficient, residing in the party; but not called forth and exerted at the time of the action done; which is the case of all offences committed by chance or ignorance. Here the will sits neuter; and neither concurs with the act, nor disagrees to it. 3. Where the action is constrained by some outward force and violence. Here the will counteracts the deed: and is so far from concurring with, that it loaths and disagrees to, what the man is obliged to perform. It will be the business of the present chapter briefly to consider all the several species of defect in will, as they fall under some one or other of these general heads: as infancy, idiocy, lunacy, and intoxication, which fall under the first class; misfortune, and ignorance, which may be referred to the second; and compulsion or necessity, which may properly rank in the third.

I. First, we will consider the case of *infancy*, or nonage; which is a defect of the understanding.

The law of England does, in some cases, privilege an infant, under the age of twenty-one, as to common misdemesnors; so as to escape fine, imprisonment, and the like: and particularly in cases of omission, as not repairing a bridge, or a highway, and other similar offences; for, not having the command of his fortune till twenty-one, he wants the capacity to do thofe things, which the law requires. But where there is any notorious breach of the peace, a riot, battery, or the like, (which infants, when full grown, are at leaft as liable as others to commit) for thefe an infant, above the age of fourteen, is equally liable to fuffer, as a perfon of the full age of twenty-one.

With regard to capital crimes, the law is ftill more minute and circumfpect; diftinguifhing with greater nicety the feveral degrees of age and difcretion. But the capacity of doing ill, or contracting guilt, is not fo much meafured by years and days, as by the ftrength of the delinquent's underftanding and judgment. For one lad of eleven years old may have as much cunning as another of fourteen; and in thefe cafes our maxim is, that "*malitia fupplet ætatem.*" Under feven years of age, indeed, an infant cannot be guilty of felony; for then a felonious difcretion is almoft an impoffibility in nature: but at eight years old he may be guilty of felony. Alfo, under fourteen, though an infant fhall be *prima facie* adjudged to be *doli incapax*; yet if it appear to the court and jury, that he was *doli capax*, and could difcern between good and evil, he may be convicted and fuffer death.

II. The fecond cafe of a deficiency in will, which excufes from the guilt of crimes, arifes alfo from a defective or vitiated underftanding, viz. in an *idiot* or a *lunatic*. For the rule of law as to the latter, which may eafily be adapted alfo to the former, is, that "*furiofus furore folum punitur.*" But as to artificial, voluntarily contracted madnefs, by *drunkennefs* or intoxication, which, depriving men of their reafon, puts them in a temporary phrenzy; our law looks upon this as an aggravation of the offence, rather than as an excufe for any criminal mifbehaviour.

III. A third deficiency of will, is where a man commits an unlawful act by *misfortune* or *chance*, and not by defign. Here the will obferves a total neutrality, and does not cooperate with the deed; which therefore wants one main ingredient of a crime. Of this when it affects the life of another, we shall find more occasion to speak hereafter; at present only observing, that if any accidental mischief happens to follow from the performance of a *lawful* act, the party stands excused from all guilt: but if a man be doing any thing *unlawful*, and a consequence ensues which he did not foresee or intend, as the death of a man or the like, his want of foresight shall be no excuse; for, being guilty of one offence, in doing antecedently what is in itself unlawful, he is criminally guity of whatever consequence may follow the first misbehaviour.

IV. Fourthly, *ignorance* or *mistake* is another defect of will; when a man, intending to do a lawful act, does that which is unlawful. For here the deed and the will acting separately, there is not that conjunction between them which is necessary to form a criminal act. But this must be an ignorance or mistake of fact, and not an error in point of law. For a mistake in point of law, which every person of discretion not only may, but is bound and presumed to know, is in criminal cases no sort of defence. *Ignorantia juris, quod quisque tenetur scire, neminem excusat*, is as well the maxim of our own law, as it was of the Roman.

V. A fifth species of defect of will is that arising from *compulsion* and inevitable *necessity*.

Of this nature, in the first place, is the obligation of *civil subjection*, whereby the inferior is constrained by the superior to act contrary to what his own reason and inclination would suggest. The principal case, where constraint of a superior is allowed as an excuse for criminal misconduct, is with regard to the matrimonial subjection of the wife to her husband: for neither a son or a servant are excused for the commission of any crime, whether capital or otherwise, by the command or coercion of the parent or master; though in some cases the command or authority of the husband, either express or implied, will privilege the wife from punishment, even for capital offences. And, therefore, if a woman commit theft, burglary, or other civil offences against the laws of society, by the coercion of her husband; or even in his company, which the law construes a coercion; she is not guilty of any crime: being confidered as acting by compulfion and not of her own will. But this rule admits of an exception in crimes that are *mala in fe*, and prohibited by the law of nature, as murder and the like. In treafon alfo, (the higheft crime which a member of fociety can, as fuch, be guilty of) no plea of coverture fhall excufe the wife. In inferior mifdemefnors alfo, we may remark another exception; that a wife may be indicted and fet in the pillory *with* her hufband, for keeping a brothel; for this is an offence touching the domeftic œconomy or government of the houfe, in which the wife has a principal fhare; and is alfo fuch an offence as the law prefumes to be generally conducted by the intrigues of the female fex. And in all cafes, where the wife offends alone, without the company or coercion of her hufband, fhe is refponfible for her offence, as much as any feme-fole.

## CHAPTER III.

### OF OFFENCES AGAINST GOD AND RELIGION.

I SHALL next proceed to diftribute the feveral offences, which are either directly or by confequence injurious to civil fociety, and therefore punifhable by the laws of England, under the following general heads: firft, thofe which are more immediately injurious to God and his holy religion; fecondly, fuch as violate and tranfgrefs the law of nations; thirdly, fuch as more efpecially affect the fovereign executive power of the ftate, or the king and his government; fourthly, fuch as more directly infringe the rights of the public or commonwealth; and, laftly, fuch as derogate from thofe rights and duties, which are owing to particular individuals, and in the prefervation and vindication of which the community is deeply interefted.

Firft then, of fuch crimes and mifdemefnors, as more immediately offend Almighty God, by openly tranfgreffing the precepts of religion either natural or revealed; and mediately, by their bad example and confequence, the law of fociety alfo; which conftitutes that guilt in the action, which human tribunals are to cenfure.

I. Of this fpecies, the principal are thofe which affect the *eftablifhed church*. And thefe are either pofitive, or negative: pofitive, by reviling it's ordinances; or negative, by non-conformity to it's worfhip. Of both of thefe in their order.

1. And, firft, of the offence of *reviling the ordinances* of the church. This is a crime of a much groffer nature than the other of mere non-conformity: and it is provided, by ftatutes 1 Edw. VI. c. 1. and 1 Eliz. c. 1. that whoever reviles the facrament of the lord's fupper fhall be punifhed by fine and imprifonment: and, by the ftatute 1 Eliz. c. 2. if any minifter fhall fpeak any thing in derogation of the book of common prayer, he fhall, if not beneficed, be imprifoned one year for the firft offence, and for life for the fecond: and, if he be beneficed, he fhall for the firft offence be imprifoned fix months, and forfeit a year's value of his benefice; for the fecond offence he fhall be deprived, and fuffer one year's imprifonment; and, for the third, fhall in like manner be deprived, and fuffer imprifonment for life. And if *any perfon* whatfoever fhall, in plays, fongs, or other open words, fpeak any thing in derogation, depraving, or defpifing of the faid book, or fhall forcibly prevent the reading of it, or caufe any other fervice to be ufed in it's ftead, he fhall forfeit for the firft offence an hundred marks; for the fecond, four hundred; and for the third fhall forfeit all his goods and chattels, and fuffer imprifonment for life.

II. Non-conformity to the worfhip of the church is the other, or negative branch of this offence. And for this there is much more to be pleaded than for the former; being a matter of private confcience, to the fcruples of which our prefent laws have fhewn a very juft and chriftian indulgence. But care muft be taken not to carry this indulgence into fuch extremes, as may endanger the national church: there is always a difference to be made between toleration and eftablifhment.

Non-conformists are of two sorts: first, such as absent themselves from divine worship in the established church, through total irreligion, and attend the service of no other persuasion. These, by the statutes of 1 Eliz. c. 2. 23 Eliz. c. 1. and 3 Jac. I. c. 4. forfeit one shilling to the poor every lord's day they so absent themselves, and 20*l.* to the king if they continue such default for a month together. And if they keep any inmate, thus irreligiously disposed, in their houses, they forfeit 10*l. per* month.

The second species of non-conformists, are those who offend through a mistaken or perverse zeal. Such were esteemed by our laws, enacted since the time of the reformation, to be papists and protestant dissenters: both of which were supposed to be equally schismatics in not communicating with the national church. But, by the statute 1 W. & M. st. 1. c. 18. commonly called the toleration act; no penal laws made against popish recusants (except the test acts) shall extend to any dissenters, other than papists and such as deny the trinity: provided, 1. that they take the oaths of allegiance and supremacy (or make a similar affirmation, being quakers) and subscribe the declaration against popery; 2. that they repair to some congregation certified to and registered in the court of the bishop or archdeacon, or at the county sessions; 3. that the doors of such meeting-house shall be unlocked, unbarred, and unbolted; in default of which the persons meeting there are still liable to all the penalties of the former acts. Dissenting teachers, in order to be exempted from the penalties of the statutes 13 & 14 Car. II. c. 4. 15 Car. II. c. 6. 17 Car. II. c. 2. and 22 Car. II. c. 1. are also to subscribe the articles of religion mentioned in the statute 13 Eliz. c. 12. (which only concern the confession of the true christian faith and the doctrine of the sacraments) with an express exception of those relating to the government and powers of the church, and to infant baptism; or if they scruple subscribing the same, shall make and subscribe the declaration prescribed by statute 19 Geo. III. c. 44. professing themselves to be christians and protestants, and that they believe the scriptures to contain the revealed will of God, and to be the rule of doctrine and practice. Thus, though the crime of non-conformity is by no means univerfally abrogated, it is fufpended and ceafes to exift with regard to thefe proteftant diffenters, during their compliance with the conditions impofed by thefe acts: and, under thefe conditions, all perfons, who will approve themfelves no papifts or oppugners of the trinity, are at full liberty to act as their confciences fhall direct them, in the matter of religious worfhip. And, if any perfon fhall wilfully, malicioufly, or contemptuoufly difturb any congregation, affembled in any church or permitted meeting-houfe, or fhall mifufe any preacher or teacher there, he fhall (by virtue of the fame ftatute 1 W. & M.) be bound over to the feffions of the peace, and forfeit twenty pounds. But, by ftatute 5 Geo. I. c. 4. no mayor or principal magiftrate, muft appear at any diffenting meeting with the enfigns of his office, on pain of difability to hold that or any other office: the legiflature judging it a matter of propriety, that a mode of worfhip, fet up in oppofition to the national, when allowed to be exercifed in peace, fhould be exercifed alfo with decency, gratitude, and humility. Diffenters alfo, who fubfcribe the declaration of the act 19 Geo. III. are exempted (unlefs in the cafe of endowed fchools and colleges) from the penalties of the ftatutes 13 & 14 Car. II. c. 4. & 17 Car. II. c. 2. which prohibit (upon pain of fine and imprifonment) all perfons from teaching fchool unlefs they be licenced by the ordinary, and fubfcribe a declaration of conformity to the liturgy of the church, and reverently frequent divine fervice *eftablifhed* by the laws of this kingdom.

Let us now take a view of the laws in force againft papifts; who may be divided into three claffes, perfons profeffing popery, popifh recufants convict, and popifh priefts. 1. Perfons profeffing the popifh religion, befides the former penalties for not frequenting their parifh church, are difabled from taking their lands either by defcent or purchafe, after eighteen years of age, until they renounce their errors; they muft at the age of twenty-one regifter their eftates before acquired, and all future conveyances and wills relating to them; they are incapable of prefenting to any advowfon, or granting to any other perfon any avoidance of the fame; they may not teach or keep any fchool under pain of perpetual imprifonment; and, if they willingly fay or hear mafs, they forfeit the one two hundred, the other one hundred marks, and each fhall fuffer a year's imprifonment *(a)*. 2. Popifh recufants, convicted in a court of law of not attending the fervice of the church of England, are fubject to the following difabilities, penalties, and forfeitures, over and above thofe before-mentioned. They are confidered as perfons excommunicated; they can hold no office or employment; they muft not keep arms in their houfes, but the fame may be feized by the juftices of the peace; they may not come within ten miles of London, on pain of 100*l*; they can bring no action at law, or fuit in equity; they are not permitted to travel above five miles from home, unlefs by licence, upon pain of forfeiting all their goods; and they may not come to court under pain of 100*l*. No marriage or burial of fuch recufant, or baptifm of his child, fhall be had otherwife than by the minifters of the church of England, under other fevere penalties. A married woman, when recufant, fhall forfeit two thirds of her dower or jointure, may not be executrix or adminiftratrix to her hufband, nor have any part of his goods; and during the coverture may be kept in prifon, unlefs her hufband redeems her at the rate of 10*l*. a month, or the third part of all his lands. And, laftly, as a feme-covert recufant may be imprifoned, fo all others muft, within three months after conviction, either fubmit and renounce their errors, or, if required fo to do by four juftices, muft abjure and renounce the realm; and if they do not depart, or if they return without the king's licence, they fhall be guilty of felony, and fuffer death as felons, without benefit of clergy. There is alfo an inferior fpecies of recufancy, (refufing to make the declaration againft popery enjoined by ftatute 30 Car. II. ft. 2. when tendered by

---

*(a)* But fee 31 Geo. III. c. 32. *poft.* p. 432. n. *(a)*.

the proper magistrate) which, if the party resides within ten miles of London, makes him an absolute recusant convict; or, if at a greater distance, suspends him from having any seat in parliament, keeping arms in his house, or any horse above the value of five pounds. This is the state, by the laws now in being, of a lay papist. But, 3. The remaining species or degree, *viz.* popish priests, are in a still more dangerous condition. For, by statute 11 & 12 W. III. c. 4. popish priests or bishops, celebrating mass or exercising any part of their functions in England, except in the houses of embassadors, are liable to perpetual imprisonment. And, by statute 27 Eliz. c. 2. any popish priest, born in the dominions of the crown of England, who shall come over hither from beyond sea, (unless driven by stress of weather and tarrying only a reasonable time) or shall be in England three days without conforming and taking the oaths, is guilty of high treason: and all persons harbouring him are guilty of felony without the benefit of clergy.

But, by statute 18 Geo. III. c. 60. with regard to such papists as duly take the oath therein prescribed, of allegiance to his majesty, abjuration of the pretender, renunciation of the pope's civil power, and abhorrence of the doctrines of destroying and not keeping faith with heretics, and deposing or murdering princes excommunicated by authority of the see of Rome: the statute of 11 & 12 W. III. is repealed, so far as it disables them from purchasing or inheriting, or authorizes the apprehending or prosecuting the popish clergy, or subjects to perpetual imprisonment either them or any teachers of youth (*a*).

---

(*a*) And, further, (to the honour of a nation possessing the liberal sentiments of Englishmen) it is enacted, by 31 Geo. III. c. 32. (the provisions of which are extended to Scotland, by 33 Geo. III. c. 44.) that no roman catholic, who shall take the oath of allegiance, abjuration, and supremacy, thereby required, shall be prosecuted for not resorting to his parish church or chapel, according to the rights of the church of England; nor be prosecuted for being a papist, or belonging to, or attending any community of the church of Rome.

## OFFENCES AGAINST GOD AND RELIGION.

In order the better to secure the established church against perils from non-conformists of all denominations, infidels, turks, jews, heretics, papists, and sectaries, there are however two bulwarks erected; called the *corporation* and *test* acts: by the former of which no person can be legally elected to any office relating to the government of any city or corporation, unless, within a twelvemonth before, he has received the sacrament of the lord's supper according to the rites of the church of England; and he is also enjoined to take the oaths of allegiance and supremacy at the same time that he takes the oath of office: or, in default of either of these requisites, such election shall be void. The other, called the test act, directs all officers civil and military to take the oaths and make the declaration against transubstantiation, in any of the king's courts at Westminster, or at the quarter sessions, within six calendar months after their admission; and also within the same time to receive the sacrament of the lord's supper, according to the usage of the church of England, in some public church immediately after divine service and sermon, and to deliver into court a certificate thereof, signed by the minister and church-warden, and also to prove the same by two credible witnesses; upon forfeiture of 500*l.* and disability to hold the said office. And of much the same nature with these is the statute 7 Jac. I. c. 2. which permits no persons to be naturalized or restored in blood, but such as undergo a like test: which test having been removed in 1753, in favour of the Jews, was the next session of parliament restored again with some precipitation.

Thus much for offences, which strike at our national religion, or the doctrine and discipline of the church of England in particular. I proceed now to consider some gross impieties

---

Also, the acts of 1 Geo. I. c. 55. and 9 *ibid.* c. 18. requiring papists to register their names and real estates, are repealed; and all deeds and wills thereof declared to be good both at law and in equity.

and general immoralities, which are taken notice of and punished by our municipal law.

IV. The fourth species of offences therefore, more immediately against God and religion, is that of *blasphemy* against the Almighty, by denying his being or providence; or by contumelious reproaches of our saviour Christ. Whither also may be referred all profane scoffing at the holy scripture, or exposing it to contempt and ridicule. These are offences punishable at common law by fine and imprisonment, or other infamous corporal punishment: for christianity is part of the laws of England.

V. Somewhat allied to this, though in an inferior degree, is the offence of profane and common *swearing* and *cursing*. By the last statute against which, 19 Geo. II. c. 21. which repeals all former ones, every labourer, sailor, or soldier profanely cursing or swearing shall forfeit 1s. every other person under the degree of a gentleman 2s. and every gentleman or person of superior rank 5s. to the poor of the parish; and, on a second conviction, double; and, for every subsequent offence, treble the sum first forfeited; with all charges of conviction: and in default of payment shall be sent to the house of correction for ten days. Any justice of the peace may convict upon his own hearing, or the testimony of one witness: and any constable or peace officer, upon his own hearing, may secure any offender and carry him before a justice, and there convict him. If the justice omits his duty, he forfeits 5l. and the constable 40s. And the act is to be read in all parish churches, and public chapels, the sunday after every quarter day, on pain of 5l. to be levied by warrant from any justice. Besides this punishment for taking God's name in vain in common discourse, it is enacted by statute 3 Jac. I. c. 21. that if in any stage play, interlude, or shew, the name of the holy trinity, or any of the persons therein, be jestingly or profanely used, the offender shall forfeit 10l; one moiety to the king, and the other to the informer.

VI. A sixth species of offences against God and religion, of which our antient books are full, is the offence of *witchcraft, conjuration, inchantment,* or *sorcery*. As to which it is enacted

## C. III. OFFENCES AGAINST GOD AND RELIGION. 435

by 9 Geo. II. c. 5. that perſons pretending to uſe witchcraft, tell fortunes, or diſcover ſtolen goods by ſkill in the occult ſciences, ſhall be puniſhed with a year's impriſonment, and ſtanding four times in the pillory.

VII. A ſeventh ſpecies of offenders in this claſs are all *religious impoſtors;* ſuch as falſely pretend an extraordinary commiſſion from heaven; or terrify and abuſe the people with falſe denunciations of judgments. Theſe, as tending to ſubvert all religion, by bringing it into ridicule and contempt, are puniſhable by the temporal courts with fine, impriſonment, and infamous corporal puniſhment.

VIII. Simony, or the corrupt preſentation of any one to an eccleſiaſtical benefice for gift or reward, is alſo to be conſidered as an offence againſt religion; as well by reaſon of the ſacredneſs of the charge which is thus profanely bought and ſold, as becauſe it is always attended with perjury in the perſon preſented. The ſtatute 31 Eliz. c. 6. enacts, that if any patron, for money or any other corrupt conſideration or promiſe, directly or indirectly given, ſhall preſent, admit, inſtitute, induct, inſtall, or collate any perſon to an eccleſiaſtical benefice or dignity, both the giver and the taker ſhall forfeit two years value of the benefice or dignity; one moiety to the king, and the other to any one who ſhall ſue for the ſame. If perſons alſo corruptly reſign or exchange their benefices, both the giver and taker ſhall, in like manner, forfeit double the value of the money or other corrupt conſideration. And perſons who ſhall corruptly ordain or licence any miniſter, or procure him to be ordained or licenced (which is the true idea of ſimony) ſhall incur a like forfeiture of forty pounds; and the miniſter himſelf of ten pounds, beſides an incapacity to hold any eccleſiaſtical preferment for ſeven years afterwards. Corrupt elections and reſignations in colleges, hoſpitals, and other eleemoſynary corporations, are alſo puniſhed by the ſame ſtatute with forfeiture of the double value, vacating the place or office, and a devolution of the right of election for that turn to the crown.

IX. Profanation of the lord's day, vulgarly (but improperly) called *sabbath-breaking*, is a ninth offence against God and religion, punished by the municipal law of England. And by the statute 27 Hen. VI. c. 5. no fair or market shall be held on the principal festivals, good friday, or any sunday, (except the four sundays in harvest) on pain of forfeiting the goods exposed to sale. And, since by the statute 1 Car. I. c. 1. no person shall assemble, out of their own parishes, for any sport whatsoever upon this day; nor, in their parishes, shall use any bull or bear baiting, interludes, plays, or other *unlawful* exercises or pastimes; on pain that every offender shall pay 3*s*. 4*d*. to the poor. This statute does not prohibit, but rather impliedly allows, any innocent recreation or amusement, within their respective parishes, even on the lord's day, after divine service is over. But by statute 29 Car. II. c. 7. no person is allowed to *work* on the lord's day, or use any boat or barge, or expose any goods to sale; except meat in public houses, milk at certain hours, and works of necessity (*a*) or charity, on forfeiture of 5*s*. Nor shall any drover, carrier, or the like, travel upon that day, under pain of twenty shillings.

X. Drunkenness is also punished by statute 4 Jac. I. c. 5. with the forfeiture of 5*s*. or the sitting six hours in the stocks: by which time the statute presumes the offender will have regained his senses, and not be liable to do mischief to his neighbours. And there are many wholesome statutes, by way of prevention, chiefly passed in the same reign of king James I. which regulate the licencing of ale-houses, and punish persons found tippling therein; or the masters of such houses permitting them.

---

(*a*) Under the head of necessity (as analogously applied to the selling of milk, meat, and mackrel) *baking* would seem to be included; and formerly this was permitted, but now, by 34 Geo. III. c. 61. bakers are prohibited from exercising their occupation on a sunday, unless between the hours of *nine* o'clock in the morning and *one* in the afternoon.

XI. The last offence which I shall mention, more immediately against religion and morality, and cognizable by the temporal courts, is that of open and notorious *lewdness:* either by frequenting houses of ill fame, which is an indictable offence; or by some grossly scandalous and public indecency, for which the punishment is by fine and imprisonment.

But, before we quit this subject, we must take notice of the temporal punishment for having *bastard children,* considered in a criminal light; for with regard to the maintenance of such illegitimate offspring, which is a civil concern, we have formerly spoken at large. By the statute 18 Eliz. c. 3. two justices may take order for the punishment of the mother and reputed father; but what that punishment shall be is not therein ascertained; though the contemporary exposition was, that a corporal punishment was intended. By statute 7 Jac. I. c. 4. a specific punishment *(viz.* commitment to the house of correction) is inflicted on the woman only. But in both cases, it seems that the penalty can only be inflicted, if the bastard becomes chargeable to the parish; for otherwise the very maintenence of the child is considered as a degree of punishment (a). By the last-mentioned statute the justices may commit the mother to the house of correction, there to be punished and set on work for one year; and, in case of a second offence, till she find sureties never to offend again.

## CHAPTER IV.

### OF OFFENCES AGAINST THE LAW OF NATIONS.

ACCORDING to the method marked out in the preceding chapter, we are next to consider the offences more immediately repugnant to that universal law of society,

---

(a) But Lord Coke maintains, that, by the statute 18 Eliz. the mother may be punished, although she discharges the parish from keeping the bastard. 2 *Inst.* 733.

which regulates the mutual intercourse between one state and another; those, I mean, which are particularly animadverted on, as such, by the English law.

The principal offences against the law of nations (a) animadverted on as such by the municipal law of England, are of three kinds; 1. Violation of safe-conducts; 2. Infringements of the rights of embassadors; and, 3. Piracy.

I. As to the first, *violation* of *safe-conducts* or *passports*, expressly granted by the king or his embassadors to the subjects of a foreign power in time of mutual war; or committing acts of hostilities against such as are in amity, league, or truce with us, who are here under a general implied safe-conduct: these are breaches of the public faith, without the preservation of which there can be no intercourse or commerce between one nation and another. And it is, therefore, enacted by the statute 31 Hen. VI. c. 4. that if any of the king's subjects attempt or offend upon the sea, or in any port within the king's obeysance, against any stranger in amity, league, or truce, or under safe conduct; and especially by attaching his person, or spoiling him or robbing him of his goods; the lord chancellor with any of the justices of either the king's-bench, or common pleas, may cause full restitution and amends to be made to the party injured.

II. As to the rights of *embassadors*, which are also established by the law of nations, and are therefore matter of universal concern. It may be sufficient to remark, that the common law of England recognizes them in their full extent, by immediately stopping all legal process, sued out through the ignorance or rashness of individuals, which may intrench upon the immunities of a foreign minister or any of his train. And the more effectually to enforce the law of nations in this respect, when violated through wantonness or insolence, it is declared, by the statute 7 Ann. c. 12. that all process whereby the person of any embassador, or of his

---

(a) *Justinian* saith "*Usu exigente, et humanis necessitatibus, gentes humanae jura quaedam sibi constituerunt.*"

## C. IV. OFFENCES AGAINST THE LAW OF NATIONS. 439

domeſtic or domeſtic ſervant, may be arreſted, or his goods diſtreined or ſeiſed, ſhall be utterly null and void; and that all perſons proſecuting, ſoliciting, or executing ſuch proceſs, being convicted by confeſſion or the oath of one witneſs, before the lord chancellor and the chief juſtices, or any two of them, ſhall be deemed violators of the laws of nations, and diſturbers of the public repoſe; and ſhall ſuffer ſuch penalties and corporal puniſhment as the ſaid judges, or any two of them, ſhall think fit. Thus, in caſes of extraordinary outrage, for which the law hath provided no ſpecial penalty, the legiſlature hath intruſted to the three principal judges of the kingdom an unlimited power of proportioning the puniſhment to the crime.

III. Laſtly, the crime of *piracy*, or robbery and depredation upon the high ſeas, is an offence againſt the univerſal law of ſociety. The offence of piracy, by common law, conſiſts in committing thoſe acts of robbery and depredation upon the high ſeas, which, if committed upon land, would have amounted to felony there. But, by ſtatute, ſome other offences are made piracy alſo: as, by ſtatute 11 & 12 W. III. c. 7. if any natural born ſubject commits any act of hoſtility upon the high ſeas, againſt others of his majeſty's ſubjects, under colour of a commiſſion from any foreign power; this, though it would only be an act of war in an alien, ſhall be conſtrued piracy in a ſubject. And farther, any commander, or other ſeafaring perſon, betraying his truſt, and running away with any ſhip, boat, ordnance, ammunition, or goods; or yielding them up voluntarily to a pirate; or conſpiring to do theſe acts; or any perſon aſſaulting the commander of a veſſel to hinder him from fighting in defence of his ſhip, or confining him, or making or endeavouring to make a revolt on board, ſhall, for each of theſe offences, be adjudged a pirate, felon, and robber, and ſhall ſuffer death, whether he be principal, or merely acceſſory by ſetting forth ſuch pirates or abetting them before the fact, or receiving or concealing them or their goods after it. And the ſtatute 4 Geo. I. c. 11. expreſsly excludes the principals from the benefit of clergy. By the ſtatute 8 Geo. I. c. 24. the trading with known pirates, or furnishing them with stores or ammunition, or fitting out any vessel for that purpose, or in any wise consulting, combining, confederating, or corresponding with them; or the forcibly boarding any merchant vessel, though without seising or carrying her off, and destroying or throwing any of the goods overboard, shall be deemed piracy: and such accessories to piracy as are described by the statute of king William, are declared to be principal pirates, and all pirates convicted by virtue of this act are made felons without benefit of clergy. By the same statutes also, (to encourage the defence of merchant vessels against pirates) the commanders or seamen wounded, and the widows of such seamen as are slain, in any piratical engagement, shall be entitled to a bounty, to be divided among them, not exceeding one fiftieth part of the value of the cargo on board: and such wounded seamen shall be entitled to the pension of Greenwich hospital; which no other seamen are, except only such as have served in a ship of war. And if the commander shall behave cowardly, by not defending the ship, if she carries guns or arms, or shall discharge the mariners from fighting, so that the ship falls into the hands of pirates, such commander shall forfeit all his wages, and suffer six months imprisonment. Lastly, by statute 18 Geo. II. c. 30. any natural born subject, or denizen, who in time of war shall commit hostilities at sea against any of his fellow subjects, or shall assist an enemy on that element, is liable to be tried and convicted as a pirate.

These are the principal cases, in which the statute law of England interposes, to aid and enforce the law of nations.

## CHAPTER V.

### OF HIGH TREASON.

THE third general division of crimes consists of such as more especially affect the supreme executive power, or the king and his government, which amount either to a total renunciation of that allegiance, or at least to a criminal neglect of that duty which is due from every fubject to his fovereign. Every offence more immediately affecting the royal perfon, his crown, or dignity, is in fome degree a breach of this duty of allegiance, whether natural and innate, or local and acquired by refidence: and thefe may be diftinguifh- ed into four kinds; 1. Treafon. 2. Felonies injurious to the king's prerogative. 3. *Præmunire.* 4. Other mifprifions and contempts. Of which crimes the firft and principal is that of treafon.

Treafon, *proditio,* in its very name imports a betraying, treachery, or breach of faith. As this is the higheft civil crime which (confidered as a member of the community) any man can poffibly commit, it ought therefore to be the moft precifely afcertained. For if the crime of high treafon be in- determinate, this alone (fays the prefident Montefquieu) is fufficient to make any government degenerate into arbitrary power. And yet, by the antient common law, there was a great latitude left in the breaft of the judges, to determine what was treafon, or not fo: whereby the creatures of tyran- nical princes had opportunity to create abundance of con- ftructive treafons; that is, to raife, by forced and arbitrary conftructions, offences into the crime and punifhment of treafon, which never were fufpected to be fuch. But, how- ever, to prevent the inconveniences which began to arife in England from this multitude of conftructive treafons, the ftatute 25 Edw. III. c. 2. mas made; which defines what offences only for the future fhould be held to be treafon. This ftatute muft therefore be our text and guide, in order to examine into the feveral fpecies of high treafon. And we fhall find that it comprehends all kinds of high treafon under feven diftinct branches.

1. " When a man doth compafs or imagine the death of " our lord the king, of our queen, or of their eldeft fon and " heir." Let us fee, what is a *compaffing* or *imagining* the death of the king, &c. Thefe are fynonymous terms: the word *compafs* fignifying the purpofe or defign of the mind or will, and not, as in common fpeech, the carrying fuch defign to effect. But, as this compaffing or imagination is an act

of the mind, it cannot poffibly fall under judicial cognizance, unlefs it be demonftrated by fome open, or *overt*, act. And therefore in this, and the three next fpecies of treafon, it is neceffary that there appear an open or *overt* act to convict the traitor upon. Thus, to provide weapons or ammunition for the purpofe of killing the king, is held to be a palpable overt act of treafon in imagining his death. To confpire to imprifon the king by force, and move towards it by affembling company, is an overt act of compaffing the king's death. There is no queftion alfo, but that taking any meafures to render fuch treafonable purpofes effectual, as affembling and confulting of the means to kill the king, is a fufficient overt act of high-treafon (*a*).

How far mere *words*, fpoken by an individual, and not relative to any treafonable act or defign then in agitation, fhall amount to treafon, has been formerly matter of doubt. But now it feems clearly to be agreed, that, by the common law and the ftatute of Edward III. words fpoken amount only to a high mifdemefnor, and no treafon.

2. The fecond fpecies of treafon is, " that if a man do " violate the king's companion, or the king's eldeft daughter " unmarried, or the wife of the king's eldeft fon and heir." By the king's companion is meant his wife; and by violation

---

(*a*) And now by 36 Geo. III. c. 7. If any perfon during the life of his majefty and until the end of the next feffion of parliament after a demife of the crown, fhall compafs, imagine, invent, devife, or intend death or deftruction, or any bodily harm tending to deftruction, maim, or wounding, imprifonment, or reftraint of the king, his heirs, and fucceffors; or to depofe him or them, or to levy war in order to compel a change of meafures, or counfels, or in order to put any force or conftraint upon, or to intimidate or overawe either houfe of parliament; or to move or ftir any foreigner, or ftranger, with force to invade this realm, or any other his majefty's dominions, and fuch compaffing, &c. fhall exprefs by publifhing any printing or writing, or by any overt act or deed; fuch perfon fhall be adjudged to be a traitor, and fhall fuffer death.

is underſtood carnal knowledge, as well without force, as with it: and this is high treaſon in both parties, if both be conſenting; as ſome of the wives of Henry the eighth by fatal experience evinced. The plain intention of this law is to guard the blood royal from any ſuſpicion of baſtardy, whereby the ſucceſſion to the crown might be rendered dubious: and therefore, when this reaſon ceaſes, the law ceaſes with it; for to violate a queen or princeſs dowager is held to be no treaſon.

3. The third ſpecies of treaſon is, " if a man do levy " war againſt our lord the king in his realm." And this may be done by taking arms, not only to dethrone the king, but under pretence to reform religion, or the laws, or to remove evil counſellors, or other grievances whether real or pretended (a). To reſiſt the king's forces by defending a caſtle againſt them, is a levying of war: and ſo is an inſurrection with an avowed deſign to pull down *all* incloſures, *all* brothels, and the like; the univerſality of the deſign making it a rebellion againſt the ſtate, an uſurpation of the powers of government, and an inſolent invaſion of the king's authority. But a tumult with a view to pull down a particular incloſure, amounts at moſt to a riot; this being no general defiance of public government. A bare conſpiracy to levy war does not amount to this ſpecies of treaſon; but (if particularly pointed at the perſon of the king or his government) it falls within the firſt, of compaſſing or imagining the king's death.

---

(a) But a bare conſpiracy, or conſultations of perſons to levy war, and to provide weapons for that purpoſe; this though it may in ſome caſes amount to an overt-act of compaſſing the king's death, yet it is not a levying of war within the clauſe of the ſtatute; and therefore there have been many temporary acts of parliament to make ſuch a conſpiracy to levy war treaſon, during the life of the prince, as 13 Eliz. c. 1. 13 Car. II. c. 1. (*Hale's P. C.* v. 1. 131.) and 36 Geo. III. c. 7. *ante* 442.

4. "If a man be adherent to the king's enemies in his "realm, giving to them aid and comfort in the realm, or "elfewhere," he is alfo declared guilty of high treafon. This muft likewife be proved by fome overt act, as by giving them intelligence, by fending them provifions, by felling them arms, by treacheroufly furrendering a fortrefs (*a*), or the like. By enemies are here underftood the fubjects of foreign powers with whom we are at open war. As to foreign pirates or robbers, who may happen to invade our coafts, without any open hoftilities between their nation and our own, and without any commiffion from any prince or ftate at enmity with the crown of Great Britain, the giving them any affiftance is alfo clearly treafon; either in the light of adhering to the public enemies of the king and kingdom, or elfe in that of levying war againft his majefty. And, moft indifputably, the fame acts of adherence or aid, which (when applied to foreign enemies) will conftitute treafon under this branch of the ftatute, will (when afforded to our own fellow-fubjects in actual rebellion at home) amount to high treafon under the defcription of levying war againft the king. But to relieve a rebel, fled out of the kingdom, is no treafon; for the ftatute is taken ftrictly, and a rebel is not an *enemy;* an enemy being always the fubject of fome foreign prince, and one who owes no allegiance to the crown of England. And if a perfon be under circumftances of actual force and conftraint, through a well-grounded apprehenfion of injury to his life or perfon, this fear or compulfion will excufe

---

(*a*) If a captain or other officer, that hath the cuftody of the king's caftles or garrifons fhall treacheroufly by combination with the king's enemies, or by bribery or for reward, deliver them up, this is adherence to the king's enemies: but if delivered up upon cowardice, or imprudence, without any treachery, though it is an offence againft the laws of war, fubjecting the party to the fentence of death by the martial law, yet it is not treafon by the common law. (Vide the cafes of William Wefton for delivering up the caftle of Oughtrewicke, and John de Gomeneys for delivering up the caftle of Ardres, in France. *Rot. Par.* 1 R. 2. n. 40.)

his even joining with either rebels or enemies *in* the kingdom, provided he leaves them whenever he hath a safe opportunity.

5. "If a man counterfeit the king's great or privy seal," this is also high treason (a).

6. The sixth species of treason under this statute, is "if "a man counterfeit the king's money; and if a man bring "false money into the realm counterfeit to the money of "England, knowing the money to be false, to merchan- "dize and make payment withal." As to the first branch, counterfeiting the king's money; this is treason, whether the false money be uttered in payment or not. Also if the king's own minters alter the standard or alloy established by law, it is treason. But gold and silver money only are held to be within this statute. With regard likewise to the second branch, importing foreign counterfeit money, in order to utter it here; it is held that uttering it, without importing it, is not within the statute. But of this we shall presently say more.

7. The last species of treason ascertained by this statute, is "if a man slay the chancellor, treasurer, or the king's "justices of the one bench or the other, justices in eyre, or "justices of assise, and all other justices assigned to hear and "determine, being in their places doing their offices." These high magistrates, as they represent the king's majesty during the execution of their offices, are therefore for the time equally regarded by the law. But this statute extends only to the actual killing of them, and not to wounding, or a bare attempt to kill them. It extends also only to the officers therin specified; and therefore the barons of the exchequer, as such, are not within the protection of this act: but the lord keeper or commissioners of the great seal now seem to be within it, by virtue of the statute 5 Eliz. c. 18. and 1 W. & M. c. 21.

---

(a) The great seal of England being the great instrument, whereby the king dispenseth the great acts of his government, and the administration of justice.

Other treasons, not comprehended under the description of statute 25 Edw. III. I shall comprize under three heads. 1. Such as relate to papists. 2. Such as relate to falsifying the coin or other royal signatures. 3. Such as are created for the security of the protestant succession in the house of Hanover.

1. The first species, relating to *papists*, was considered in a preceding chapter, among the penalties incurred by that branch of non-conformists to the national church.

2. With regard to treasons relative to the *coin* or other *royal signatures*, we may recollect that the only two offences respecting the coinage, which are made treason by the statute 25 Edw. III. are the actual counterfeiting the gold and silver coin of this kingdom; or the importing such counterfeit money with intent to utter it, knowing it to be false. But these not being found sufficient to restrain the evil practices of coiners and false moneyers, other statutes have been since made for that purpose. As, by statute 1 Mar. st. 2. c. 6. it is provided, 1. That if any person falsly forge or counterfeit any such kind of coin of gold or silver, as is not the proper coin of this realm, but shall be current within this realm by consent of the crown; or, 2. shall falsly forge or counterfeit the sign manual, privy signet, or privy seal; such offences shall be deemed high treason. And, by statute 1 & 2 P. & M. c. 11. if any persons do bring into this realm such false or counterfeit foreign money, being current here, knowing the same to be false, with intent to utter the same in payment, they shall be deemed offenders in high treason. And now, by statute 5 Eliz. c. 11. clipping, washing, rounding, or filing, for wicked gain's sake, any of the money of this realm, or other money suffered to be current here, shall be adjudged high treason; and, by statute 18 Eliz. c. 1. the same species of offence is described in other more general words ; *viz.* impairing, diminishing, falsifying, scaling, and lightening ; and made liable to the same penalties. By statute 8 & 9 W. III. c. 26. made perpetual by 7 Ann. c. 25. whoever, without proper authority, shall knowingly make or mend, or assist in so doing, or shall buy, sell, conceal,

hide, or knowingly have in his poffeffion, any implements of coinage fpecified in the act, or other tools or inftruments proper only for the coinage of money; or fhall convey the fame out of the king's mint; he, together with his counfellors, procurers, aiders, and abettors, fhall be guilty of high treafon: which is by much the fevereft branch of the coinage law. The ftatute goes on farther, and enacts, that to mark any coin on the edges with letters, or otherwife, in imitation of thofe ufed in the mint; or to colour, gild, or cafe over any coin refembling the current coin, or even round blanks of bafe metal; fhall be conftrued high treafon. But all profecutions on this act are to be commenced within *three* months after the commiffion of the offence: except thofe for making or mending any coining tool or inftrument, or for marking money round the edges; which are directed to be commenced within *fix* months after the offence committed. And, laftly, by ftatute 15 & 16 Geo. II. c. 28. if any perfon colours or alters any fhilling or fixpence, either lawful or counterfeit, to make them refpectively refemble a guinea or a half guinea; or any halfpenny or farthing to make them refpectively refemble a fhilling or fixpence; this is alfo high treafon: but the offender fhall be pardoned, in cafe (being out of prifon) he difcovers and convicts two other offenders of the fame kind.

3. The other new fpecies of high treafon is fuch as is created for the fecurity of the *proteftant fucceffion*, over and above fuch treafons againft the king and government as were comprized under the ftatute 25 Edw. III. By the ftatute 1 Ann. ft. 2. c. 17. if any perfon fhall endeavour to deprive or hinder any perfon, being the next in fucceffion to the crown according to the limitations of the act of fettlement, from fucceeding to the crown, and fhall malicioufly and directly attempt the fame by any overt act, fuch offence fhall be high treafon. And, by ftatute 6 Ann. c. 7. if any perfon fhall malicioufly, advifedly, and directly, by writing or printing, maintain and affirm, that any perfon hath any right or title to the crown of this realm, otherwife than according to the act of fettlement; or that the kings of this

realm with the authority of parliament are not able to make laws and statutes, to bind the crown and the descent thereof; such person shall be guilty of high treason.

The punishment of high treason in general is very solemn and terrible. 1. That the offender be drawn to the gallows, and not be carried or walk; though usually (by connivance at length ripened by humanity into law) a sledge or hurdle is allowed, to preserve the offender from the extreme torment of being dragged on the ground or pavement. 2. That he be hanged by the neck, and then cut down alive. 3. That his entrails be taken out, and burned, while he is yet alive. 4. That his head be cut off. 5. That his body be divided into four parts. 6. That his head and quarters be at the king's disposal.

In the case of coining, which is a treason of a different complexion from the rest, the punishment is milder for male offenders; being only to be drawn, and hanged by the neck till dead. But in treasons of every kind the punishment of women is the same, and different from that of men. For, as the decency due to the sex forbids the exposing and publickly mangling their bodies, their sentence (which is to the full as terrible to the sensation as the other) is to be drawn to the gallows, and there to be burned alive (a).

The consequences of this judgment, (attainder, forfeiture, and corruption of blood) must be referred to the latter end of this book, when we shall treat of them all together, as well in treason as other offences.

---

(a) This punishment, so terrible in itself, and so repugnant to the sensations of humanity, particularly when considered as applicable solely to the female sex, has since been abrogated by 30 Geo. III. c. 48. which provides, that the judgment of women convicted of treason, shall only be that they be "drawn to the place of execution, and be there hanged by the neck until they be dead."

## CHAPTER VI.

OF FELONIES INJURIOUS TO THE KING'S PREROGATIVE.

ACCORDING to the method I have adopted, we are next to confider fuch felonies as are more immediately injurious to the king's prerogative. Thefe are, 1. Offences relating to the coin, not amounting to treafon. 2. Offences againft the king's council. 3. The offence of imbezzling or deftroying the king's armour or ftores of war. To which may be added a fifth, 5. Defertion from the king's armies in time of war.

1. Offences relating to the *coin*, under which may be ranked fome inferior mifdemefnors not amounting to felony, are thus declared by a feries of ftatutes, which I fhall recite in the order of time. And, firft, by ftatute 27 Edw. I. c. 3. none fhall bring pollards and crockards, which were foreign coins of bafe metal, into the realm, on pain of forfeiture of life and goods. By ftatute 9 Edw. III. ft. 2. no fterling money fhall be melted down, upon pain of forfeiture thereof. By ftatute 17 Edw. III. none fhall be fo hardy to bring falfe and ill money into the realm, on pain of forfeiture of life and member by the perfons importing, and the fearchers permitting fuch importation. By ftatute 3 Hen. V. ft. 1. to make, coin, buy, or bring into the realm any gally-halfpence, fufkins, or dotkins, in order to utter them, is felony; and knowingly to receive or pay either them or *blanks* is forfeiture of an hundred fhillings. By ftatute 14 Eliz. c. 3. fuch as forge any foreign coin, although it be not made current here by proclamation, fhall (with their aiders and abettors) be guilty of mifprifion of treafon: a crime which we fhall hereafter confider. By ftatute 13 & 14 Car. II. c. 31. the offence of melting down any current filver money fhall be punifhed with forfeiture of the fame, and alfo the double value: and the offender, if a freeman of any town, fhall be disfranchifed; if not, fhall fuffer fix months imprifonment. By ftatute 6

& 7 W. III. c. 17. if any perſon buys or ſells, or knowingly has in his cuſtody, any clippings or filings of the coin, he ſhall forfeit the ſame and 500*l.* one moiety to the king, and the other to the informer; and be branded in the cheek with the letter R. By ſtatute 8 & 9 W. III. c. 26. if any perſon ſhall blanch, or whiten, copper for ſale; (which makes it reſemble ſilver) or buy or ſell or offer to ſale any malleable compoſition, which ſhall be heavier than ſilver, and look, touch, and wear like gold, but be beneath the ſtandard: or if any perſon ſhall receive or pay at a leſs rate than it imports to be of (which demonſtrates a conſciouſneſs of it's baſeneſs, and a fraudulent deſign) any counterfeit or diminiſhed milled money of this kingdom, not being cut in pieces; an operation which is expreſsly directed to be performed when any ſuch money ſhall be produced in evidence, and which any perſon, to whom any gold or ſilver money is tendered, is empowered by ſtatutes 9 & 10 W. III. c. 21. 13 Geo. III. c. 71. and 14 Geo. III. c. 70. to perform at his own hazard, and the officers of the exchequer and receivers general of the taxes are particularly required to perform: all ſuch perſons ſhall be guilty of felony; and may be proſecuted for the ſame at any time within three months after the offence committed. But theſe precautions not being found ſufficient to prevent the uttering of falſe or diminiſhed money, which was only a miſdemeſnor at common law, it is enacted, by ſtatute 15 & 16 Geo. II. c. 28. that if any perſon ſhall utter or tender in payment any counterfeit coin, knowing it ſo to be, he ſhall for the firſt offence be impriſoned ſix months; and find ſureties for his good behaviour for ſix months more: for the ſecond offence, ſhall be impriſoned two years, and find ſureties for two years longer: and, for the third offence, ſhall be guilty of felony without benefit of clergy. Alſo if a perſon knowingly tenders in payment any counterfeit money, and at the ſame time has more in his cuſtody; or ſhall, within ten days after, knowingly tender other falſe money; he ſhall be deemed a common utterer of counterfeit money, and ſhall for the firſt offence be impriſoned one year, and find ſureties for his good behaviour for two years longer; and for the ſecond, be guilty of felony without benefit of clergy. By the fame ftatute it is alfo enacted, that, if any perfon counterfeits the copper coin, he fhall fuffer two years imprifonment, and find fureties for two years more. By ftatute 11 Geo. III. c. 40. perfons counterfeiting copper halfpence or farthings, with their abettors; or buying, felling, receiving, or putting off any counterfeit copper money (not being cut in pieces or melted down) at a lefs value than it imports to be of; fhall be guilty of fingle felony. And by a temporary ftatute (14 Geo. III. c. 42.) if any quantity of money, exceeding the fum of five pounds, being or purporting to be the filver coin of this realm, but below the ftandard of the mint in weight or finenefs, fhall be imported into Great Britain or Ireland, the fame fhall be forfeited in equal moieties to the crown and profecutor. Thus much for offences relating to the coin, as well mifdemefnors as felonies, which I thought it moft convenient to confider in one and the fame view.

2. Felonies, againft the king's *council*, are thefe. Firft, by ftatute 3 Hen. VII. c. 14. if any fworn fervant of the king's houfhold confpires or confederates to kill any lord of this realm, or other perfon, fworn of the king's council, he fhall be guilty of felony. Secondly, by ftatute 9 Ann. c. 16. to affault, ftrike, wound, or attempt to kill, any privy counfellor in the execution of his office, is made felony without benefit of clergy.

3. Felonies in *ferving foreign ftates*, which fervice is generally inconfiftent with allegiance to one's natural prince, are reftrained and punifhed by ftatute 3 Jac. I. c. 4. And, by ftatute 9 Geo. II. c. 30. enforced by ftatute 29 Geo. II. c. 17. if any fubject of Great Britain fhall enlift himfelf, or if any perfon fhall procure him to be enlifted, in any foreign fervice, or detain or embark him for that purpofe, without licence under the king's fign manual, he fhall be guilty of felony without benefit of clergy: but if the perfon fo enlifted or enticed, fhall difcover his feducer within fifteen days, fo as he may be apprehended and convicted of the fame, he fhall be indemnified.

4. Felony, by *imbezzling* or *deſtroying* the king's *armour* or warlike *ſtores*, is, in the firſt place, ſo declared to be by ſtatute 31 Eliz. c. 4. Other inferior imbezzlements and miſdemeſnors, that fall under this denomination, are puniſhed by ſtatutes 9 & 10 W. III. c. 41. 1 Geo. I. c. 25. 9 Geo. I. c. 8. and 17 Geo. II. c. 40. with fine, corporal puniſhment, and impriſonment. And, by ſtatute 12 Geo. III. c. 24. to ſet on fire, burn, or deſtroy any of his majeſty's ſhips of war, whether built, building, or repairing; or any of the king's arſenals, magazines, dock-yards, rope-yards, or victualling-offices, or materials thereunto belonging; or military, naval, or victualling ſtores or ammunition; or cauſing, aiding, procuring, abetting, or aſſiſting in, ſuch offence; ſhall be felony without benefit of clergy.

5. Deſertion from the king's armies in time of war, whether by land or ſea, in England or in parts beyond the ſeas, is, by the ſtanding laws of the land (excluſive of the annual acts of parliament to puniſh mutiny and deſertion) and particularly by ſtatute 18 Hen. VI. c. 19. and 5 Eliz. c. 5. made felony, but not without benefit of clergy. But by the ſtatute 2 & 3 Edw. VI. c. 2. clergy is taken away from ſuch deſerters, and the offence is made triable by the juſtices of every ſhire. The ſame ſtatutes puniſh other inferior military offences with fines, impriſonment, and other penalties.

## CHAPTER VII.

### OF MISPRISIONS AND CONTEMPTS AFFECTING THE KING AND GOVERNMENT.

THE fourth ſpecies of offences, more immediately againſt the king and government, are entitled miſpriſions and contempts.

Miſpriſions (a term derived from the old French, *meſpris*, a neglect or contempt) are, in the acceptation of our law, generally underſtood to be all ſuch high offences as are under the degree of capital, but nearly bordering thereon. Mifprifions are generally divided into two forts; negative, which confift in the concealment of fomething which ought to be revealed; and pofitive, which confift in the commiffion of fomething which ought not to be done.

I. Of the firft, or negative kind, is what is called *mifprifion of treafon;* confifting in the bare knowledge and concealment of treafon, without any degree of affent thereto: for any affent makes the party a principal traitor; as indeed the concealment, which was conftrued aiding and abetting, did at the common law: in like manner, as the knowledge of a plot againft the ftate, and not revealing it, was a capital crime at Florence, and other ftates of Italy. But it is now enacted, by the ftatute 1 & 2 Ph. & Mar. c. 10. that a bare concealment of treafon fhall be only held a mifprifion.

There is alfo one pofitive mifprifion of treafon, created fo by act of parliament. The ftatute 13 Eliz. c. 2. enacts, that thofe who forge foreign coin, not current in this kingdom, their aiders, abettors, and procurers, fhall all be guilty of mifprifion of treafon. For, though the law would not put foreign coin upon quite the fame footing as our own; yet, if the circumftances of trade concur, the falfifying it may be attended with confequences almoft equally pernicious to the public; as the counterfeiting of Portugal money would be at prefent: and therefore the law made it an offence juft below capital, and that is all. For the punifhment of mifprifion of treafon is lofs of the profits of lands during life, forfeiture of goods, and imprifonment during life (*a*). Which total forfeiture of the goods was originally inflicted while the offence amounted to principal treafon, and of courfe included in it a felony, by the common law; and therefore is no exception to the general rule laid down in a former chapter, that wherever an offence is punifhed by fuch total forfeiture it is felony at the common law.

Mifprifion *of felony* is alfo the concealment of a felony which a man knows, but never affented to; for, if he affented, this makes him either principal or acceffory. And the punifhment of this, in a public officer, by the ftatute Weft. 1. 3 Edw. I. c. 9. is imprifonment for a year and a day; in a common perſon, impriſonment for a leſs diſcretionary time; and, in both, fine and ranſom at the king's pleaſure: which pleaſure of the king muſt be obſerved, once for all, not to mention any extrajudicial will of the ſovereign, but ſuch as is declared by his repreſentatives, the judges in his courts of juſtice; "*voluntas regis in curia, non in camera.*"

There is another ſpecies of negative miſpriſions, namely, the *concealing of treaſure-trove*, which belongs to the king or his grantees by prerogative royal: the concealment of which was formerly puniſhable by death, but now only by fine and impriſonment.

II. Miſpriſions, which are merely poſitive, are generally denominated *contempts* or *high miſdemeſnors;* of which

1. The firſt and principal is the *mal-adminiſtration* of ſuch high officers, as are in public truſt and employment. This is uſually puniſhed by the method of parliamentary impeachment: wherein ſuch penalties, ſhort of death, are inflicted, as to the wiſdom of the houſe of peers ſhall ſeem proper; conſiſting uſually of baniſhment, impriſonment, fines, or perpetual diſability. Hitherto alſo may be referred the offence of *imbezzling the public money*, called among the Romans *peculatus*, which the Julian law puniſhed with death in a magiſtrate, and with deportation or baniſhment, in a private perſon. With us it is not a capital crime, but ſubjects the committer of it to a diſcretionary fine and impriſonment. Other miſpriſions are, in general, ſuch contempts of the executive magiſtrate, as demonſtrate themſelves by ſome arrogant and undutiful behaviour towards the king and government. Theſe are

2. Contempts againſt the king's *prerogative*, as, by refuſing to aſſiſt him for the good of the public, either in his councils, by advice if called upon; or in his wars, by perſonal ſervice for the defence of the realm, againſt a rebellion or invaſion. Under which claſs may be ranked the neglecting to join the *poſſe comitatus*, or power of the county, being thereunto required by the ſheriff or juſtices, according to the ſtatute 2 Hen. V. c. 8. which is a duty incumbent upon all that

are fifteen years of age, under the degree of nobility, and able to travel. Or, by difobeying the king's lawful commands; whether by writs iffuing out of his courts of juftice, or by a fummons to attend his privy council, or by letters from the king to a fubject commanding him to return from beyond the feas, (for difobedience to which his lands fhall be feifed till he does return, and himfelf afterwards punifhed) or by his writ of *ne exeat regnum,* or proclamation, commanding the fubject to ftay at home. Difobedience to any of thefe commands is a high mifprifion and contempt: and fo, laftly, is difobedience to any act of parliament, where no particular penalty is affigned; for then it is punifhable, like the reft of thefe contempts, by fine and imprifonment, at the difcretion of the king's courts of juftice.

3. Contempts and mifprifions againft the king's *perfon* and *government*, may be by fpeaking or writing againft them, curfing or wifhing him ill, giving out fcandalous ftories concerning him, or doing any thing that may tend to leffen him in the efteem of his fubjects, may weaken his government, or may raife jealoufies between him and his people.

4. Contempts againft the king's *title,* not amounting to treafon or *præmunire,* are the denial of his right to the crown in common and unadvifed difcourfe; for, if it be by advifedly fpeaking, we have feen that it amounts to a *præmunire.* This heedlefs fpecies of contempt is however punifhed by our law with fine and imprifonment. Likewife if any perfon fhall in any wife hold, affirm, or maintain, that the common laws of this realm, not altered by parliament, ought not to direct the right of the crown of England; this is a mifdemefnor, by ftatute 13 Eliz. c. 1. and punifhable with forfeiture of goods and chattels. A contempt may alfo arife from refufing or neglecting to take the oaths, appointed by ftatute for the better fecuring the government; and yet acting in a public office, place of truft, or other capacity, for which the faid oaths are required to be taken; viz. thofe of allegiance, fupremacy, and abjuration: which muft be taken within fix calendar months after admiffion. The penalties for this contempt, inflicted by ftatute 1 Geo. I. ft. 2, c. 13.

are very little, if any thing, short of those of a *præmunire*: being an incapacity to hold the said offices, or any other; to prosecute any suit; to be guardian or executor; to take any legacy or deed of gift; and to vote at any election for members of parliament: and after conviction the offender shall also forfeit 500l. to him or them that will sue for the same. Members on the foundation of any college in the two universities, who by this statute are bound to take the oaths, must also register a certificate thereof in the college register, within one month after; otherwise, if the electors do not remove him, and elect another within twelve months, or after, the king may nominate a person to succeed him by his great seal or sign manual (a).

5. Contempts against the king's *palaces* or *courts of justice* have always been looked upon as high misprisions: and by the statute 33 Hen. VIII. c. 12. malicious striking in the king's palace, wherein his royal person resides, whereby blood is drawn, is punishable by perpetual imprisonment, and fine at the king's pleasure; and also with loss of the offender's right hand, the solemn execution of which sentence is prescribed in the statute at length.

But *striking* in the king's superior courts of justice, in Westminster-hall, or at the assises, is made still more penal than even in the king's palace. The reason seems to be, that those courts being anciently held in the king's palace, and before the king himself, striking there included the former contempt against the king's palace, and something more; viz. the disturbance of public justice. For this reason, by the antient common law before the conquest, striking in the king's courts of justice, or drawing a sword therein, was a capital felony: and our modern law retains so much of the

---

*(a)* The severity, combined with the supposed expediency, of these laws, has induced the legislature, *annually*, to pass an act indemnifying persons against the penalties of the statute of 1 Geo. I. provided they comply with its requisitions within a limited time, therein specified; and provided no judgment has actually been obtained for the offence.

antient feverity as only to exchange the lofs of life for the lofs of the offending limb. Therefore a ftroke or blow in fuch a court of juftice, whether blood be drawn or not, or even affaulting a judge fitting in the court, by drawing a weapon, without any blow ftruck, is punifhable with the lofs of the right hand, imprifonment for life, and forfeiture of goods and chattels, and of the profits of his lands during life. A *refcue* alfo of a prifoner from any of the faid courts, without ftriking a blow, is punifhed with perpetual imprifonment, and forfeiture of goods, and of the profits of lands during life: being looked upon as an offence of the fame nature with the laft; but only, as no blow is actually given, the amputation of the hand is excufed. For the like reafon an affray, or riot, near the faid courts; but out of their actual view, is punifhed only with fine and imprifonment.

Not only fuch as are guilty of an actual violence, but of threatening or reproachful words to any judge fitting in the courts, are guilty of a high mifprifion, and have been punifhed with large fines, imprifonment, and corporal punifhment. And, even in the inferior courts of the king, an affray, or contemptuous behaviour, is punifhable with a fine by the judges there fitting; as by the fteward in a court-leet, or the like.

Likewife, all fuch as are guilty of any injurious treatment to thofe who are immediately under the protection of a court of juftice, are punifhable by fine and imprifonment: as if a man affaults or threatens his adverfary for fuing him, a counfellor or attorney for being employed againft him, a juror for his verdict, or a gaoler or other minifterial officer for keeping him in cuftody, and properly executing his duty.

Laftly, to endeavour to diffuade a witnefs from giving evidence; to difclofe an examination before the privy council; or, to advife a prifoner to ftand mute; (all of which are impediments of juftice) are high mifprifions, and contempts of the king's courts, and punifhable by fine and imprifonment.

## CHAPTER VIII.

### OF OFFENCES AGAINST PUBLIC JUSTICE.

THE order of our distribution will next lead us to take into consideration such crimes and misdemesnors as more especially affect the *commonwealth*, or public polity of the kingdom. The crimes and misdemesnors that more especially affect the commonwealth may be divided into five species; viz. offences against public *justice*, against the public *peace*, against public *trade*, against the public *health*, and against the public *police* or *œconomy*: of each of which we will take a cursory view in their order.

First then, of offences against public *justice*: some of which are felonious, whose punishment may extend to death; others only misdemesnors. I shall begin with those that are most penal, and descend gradually to such as are of less malignity.

1. Imbezzling or vacating *records*, or falsifying certain other proceedings in a court of judicature, is a felonious offence against public justice. It is enacted by statute 8 Hen. VI. c. 12. that if any clerk, or other person, shall wilfully take away, withdraw, or avoid any record, or process in the superior courts of justice in Westminster-hall, by reason whereof the judgment shall be reversed or not take effect; it shall be felony not only in the principal actors, but also in their procurers, and abettors. Likewise by statute 21 Jac. I. c. 26. to acknowledge any fine, recovery, deed enrolled, statute, recognizance, bail, or judgment, in the name of another person not privy to the same, is felony without benefit of clergy. Which law extends only to proceedings in the courts themselves: but by statute 4 W. & M. c. 4. to personate any other commissioner authorised to take bail in the country, is also felony.

2. To prevent abuses by the extensive power, which the law is obliged to repose in gaolers, it is enacted by statute 14 Edw. III. c. 10. that if any *gaoler* by too great duress of imprisonment makes any prisoner, that he hath in ward,

C. VIII.   OFFENCES AGAINST PUBLIC JUSTICE.   459

become an *approver* or an *appellor* againſt his will; that is, as we ſhall ſee hereafter, to accuſe and turn evidence againſt ſome other perſon: it is felony in the gaoler.

3. A third offence againſt public juſtice is *obſtructing* the execution of lawful *proceſs*. And it hath been holden, that the party oppoſing ſuch arreſt becomes thereby *particeps criminis;* that is, an acceſſory in felony, and a principal in high treaſon. And by the ſtatutes 8 & 9 Will. III. c. 27. 9 Geo. I. c. 28. and 11 Geo. I. c. 22. perſons oppoſing the execution of any proceſs in pretended *privileged* places within the bills of mortality, or abuſing any officer in his endeavours to execute his duty therein, ſo that he receives bodily hurt, ſhall be guilty of felony, and tranſported for ſeven years: and perſons in diſguiſe, joining in or abetting any riot or tumult on ſuch account, or oppoſing any proceſs, or aſſaulting and abuſing any officer executing, or for having executed the ſame, ſhall be felons without benefit of clergy.

4. An *eſcape* of a perſon arreſted upon criminal proceſs, by eluding the vigilance of his keepers before he is put in hold, is alſo an offence againſt public juſtice, and the party himſelf is alſo puniſhable by fine or impriſonment; for he ought to ſubmit himſelf quietly to cuſtody, till cleared by due courſe of juſtice. Officers who, after arreſt, *negligently* permit a felon to eſcape, are alſo puniſhable by fine; but *voluntary* eſcapes, by conſent and connivance of the officer, are a much more ſerious offence: for it is generally agreed that ſuch eſcapes amount to the ſame kind of offence, and are puniſhable in the ſame degree, as the offence of which the priſoner is guilty, and for which he is in cuſtody, whether he were actually committed to gaol, or only under a bare arreſt. But the officer cannot be thus puniſhed till the original delinquent hath actually received judgment or been attainted, upon verdict, confeſſion, or outlawry, of the crime for which he was ſo committed or arreſted. But, before the conviction of the principal party, the officer thus neglecting his duty may be fined and impriſoned for a miſdemeſnor.

5. Breach of priſon by the offender himſelf, when committed for *any* cauſe, was felony at the common law: or

even conspiring to break it. But this severity is mitigated by the statute *de frangentibus prisonam*, 1 Edw. II. which enacts, that no person shall have judgment of life or member for breaking prison, unless committed for some capital offence. So that to break prison and escape, when lawfully committed for any treason or felony, remains still felony as at the common law; and to break prison (whether it be the county gaol, the stocks, or other usual place of security) when lawfully confined upon any other inferior charge, is still punishable as a high misdemesnor by fine and imprisonment. For the statute, which ordains that such offence shall be no longer capital, never meant to exempt it entirely from every degree of punishment.

6. Rescue is the forcibly and knowingly freeing another from an arrest or imprisonment; and it is generally the same offence in the stranger so rescuing, as it would have been in a gaoler to have *voluntarily* permitted an escape. A rescue therefore of one apprehended for felony, is felony; for treason, treason; and for a misdemesnor, a misdemesnor also. But here likewise, as upon voluntary escapes, the principal must first be attainted or receive judgment before the rescuer can be punished: and for the same reason; because perhaps in fact it may turn out that there has been no offence committed. By statute 11 Geo. II. c. 26. and 24 Geo. II. c. 40. if five or more persons assemble to rescue any retailers of spirituous liquors, or to assault the informers against them, it is felony, and subject to transportaion for seven years. By the statute 16 Geo. II. c. 31. to convey to any prisoner in custody for treason, or felony, any arms, instruments of escape, or disguise, without the knowlege of the gaoler, though no escape be attempted, or any way to assist such prisoner to attempt an escape, though no escape be actually made, is felony, and subjects the offender to transportation for seven years: or if the prisoner be in custody for petit larceny or other inferior offence, or charged with a debt of 100l. it is then a misdemesnor, punishable with fine and imprisonment. And by several special statutes, to rescue, or attempt a rescue, any person committed for the offences enumerated in those acts, is felony without benefit of clergy; and to rescue, or

C. VIII.   OFFENCES AGAINST PUBLIC JUSTICE.   461

attempt to refcue, the body of a felon executed for murder, is single felony, and fubject to a tranfportation for feven years. Nay, even if any perfon be charged with any of the offences againft the black-act, 9 Geo. I. c. 22. and, being required by order of the privy council to furrender himfelf, neglects fo to do for forty days, both he and all that knowingly conceal, aid, abet, or fuccour him, are felons without benefit of clergy.

7. Another capital offence againft public juftice is the *returning from tranfportation*, or being feen at large in Great Britain, before the expiration of the term for which the offender was ordered to be tranfported, or had agreed to tranfport himfelf. This is made felony without benefit of clergy in all cafes, by ftatutes 4 Geo. I. c. 11. 6 Geo. I. c. 23. 16 Geo. II. c. 15. and 8 Geo. III. c. 15. as is alfo the affifting them to efcape from fuch as are conveying them to the port of tranfportation.

8. An eighth is that of *taking a reward*, under pretence of *helping* the owner to his *ftolen goods*. This was a contrivance carried to a great length of villany in the beginning of the reign of George the firft: the confederates of the felons thus difpofing of ftolen goods, at a cheap rate, to the owners themfelves, and thereby ftifling all farther inquiry. The famous Jonathan Wild had under him a well-difciplined corps of thieves who brought in all their fpoils to him; and he kept a fort of public office for reftoring them to the owners at half price. To prevent which audacious practice, to the ruin and in defiance of public juftice, it was enacted by ftatute 4 Geo. I. c. 11. that whoever fhall take a reward under the pretence of helping any one to ftolen goods, fhall fuffer as the felon who ftole them; unlefs he caufes fuch principal felon to be apprehended and brought to trial, and alfo gives evidence againft them. Wild, ftill continuing in his old practice, was upon this ftatute at laft convicted and executed.

9. Receiving of ftolen goods, *knowing them to be ftolen*, is alfo a high mifdemefnor and affront to public juftice. And it is enacted by ftatute 1 Ann. c. 9. and 5 Ann. c. 31. that fuch receivers may be profecuted for a mifdemefnor, and punifhed by fine and imprifonment, though the principal felon

be not before taken fo as to be profecuted and convicted. And, in cafe of receiving ftolen lead, iron, and certain other metals, fuch offence is by ftatute 29 Geo. II. c. 30. punifhable by tranfportation for fourteen years (a). So that now the profecutor has two methods in his choice. either to punifh the receivers for the mifdemefnor immediately, before the thief is taken; or to wait till the felon is convicted, and then punifh them as acceffories to the felony. But it is provided by the fame ftatutes, that he fhall only make ufe of one, and not both of thefe methods of punifhment. By the fame ftatute alfo 29 Geo. II. c. 30. perfons having lead, iron, and other metals in their cuftody, and not giving a fatisfactory account how they came by the fame, are guilty of a mifdemefnor, and punifhable by fine or imprifonment. And by ftatute 10 Geo. III. c. 48. all knowing receivers of ftolen plate or jewels, taken by robbery on the highway, or when a burglary accompanies the ftealing, may be tried as well before as after the conviction of the principal, and whether he be in or out of cuftody; and, if convicted, fhall be adjudged guilty of felony, and tranfported for fourteen years (b).

10. Of a nature fomewhat fimilar to the two laft is the offence of *theft-bote,* which is where the party robbed not only knows the felon, but alfo takes his goods again, or other amends, upon agreement not to profecute. This is fre-

---

(a) See alfo ftatute 2 Geo. III. c. 28. §. 12. for the punifhment of receivers of goods ftolen by bum-boats, &c. on the Thames. A.

(b) And further by ftatute Geo. III. c. 68. the receiving any ftolen copper, brafs, bell-metal, or utenfil fixed to any building, or any iron rails or fencing fet up in any court or other place, is made tranfportation for feven years, or three years imprifonment to be kept to hard labour. Alfo, by the fame ftatute, c. 69. the receiving ftolen pewter of any kind is fubjected to the like penalty, although the principal has not been convicted. And by 22 Geo. III. c. 58. the receiving any ftolen goods (except lead, iron, copper, brafs, bell-metal, and folder) is made a mifdemefnor, punifhable by fine and imprifonment, or whipping, as the court fhall appoint.

quently called compounding felony, and formerly was held to make a man an acceſſory; but is now puniſhed only with fine and impriſonment. By ſtatute 25 Geo. II. c. 36. even to advertiſe a reward for the return of things ſtolen, with no queſtions aſked, or words to the ſame purport, ſubjects the advertiſer and the printer to a forfeiture of 50l. each.

11. Common *barretry* is the offence of frequently exciting and ſtirring up ſuits and quarrels between his majeſty's ſubjects, either at law or otherwiſe. The puniſhment for this offence, in a common perſon, is by fine and impriſonment: but if the offender (as is too frequently the caſe) belongs to the profeſſion of the law, a barretor, who is thus able as well as willing to do miſchief, ought alſo to be diſabled from practiſing for the future. This offence, if committed in any of the king's ſuperior courts, is left, as a high contempt, to be puniſhed at their diſcretion. But in courts of a lower degree, where the crime is equally pernicious, but the authority of the judges not equally extenſive, it is directed by ſtatute 8 Eliz. c. 2. to be puniſhed by ſix months impriſonment, and treble damages to the party injured.

12. Maintenance is an offence that bears a near relation to the former; being an officious intermeddling in a ſuit that no way belongs to one, by maintaining or aſſiſting either party with money or otherwiſe, to proſecute or defend it. A man may however maintain the ſuit of his near kinſman, ſervant, or poor neighbour, out of charity and compaſſion, with impunity. Otherwiſe the puniſhment by common law is fine and impriſonment; and by the ſtatute 32 Hen. VIII. c. 9. a forfeiture of ten pounds.

13. Champerty, *campi-partitio*, is a ſpecies of maintenance, and puniſhed in the ſame manner: being a bargain with a plaintiff or defendant *campum partire*, to divide the land or other matter ſued for between them, if they prevail at law, and ſignifies the purchaſing of a ſuit, or right of ſuing. Hitherto alſo muſt be referred the proviſion of the ſtatute 32 Hen. VIII. c. 9. that no one ſhall ſell or purchaſe any pretended right or title to land, unleſs the vendor hath received the profits thereof for one whole year before ſuch

grant, or hath been in actual poffeffion of the land, or of the reverfion or remainder; on pain that both purchafor and vendor fhall each forfeit the value of fuch land to the king and the profecutor. Thefe offences relate chiefly to the commencement of *civil* fuits: but

14. The *compounding of informations* upon penal ftatutes are an offence of an equivalent nature in *criminal* caufes; and are, befides, an additional mifdemefnor againft public juftice, by contributing to make the laws odious to the people. At once therefore to difcourage malicious informers, and to provide that offences, when once difcovered, fhall be duly profecuted, it is enacted, by ftatute 18 Eliz. c. 5. that if any perfon informing under pretence of any penal law, makes any compofition without leave of the court, or takes any money or promife from the defendant to excufe him, (which demonftrates his intent in commencing the profecution to be merely to ferve his own ends, and not for the public good) he fhall forfeit 10*l*. fhall ftand two hours on the pillory, and fhall be for ever difabled to fue on any popular or penal ftatute.

15. A confpiracy alfo to indict an innocent man of felony falfely and malicioufly, who is accordingly indicted and acquitted, is a farther abufe and perverfion of public juftice; for which the party injured may either have a civil action by writ of confpiracy, or the confpirators (for there muft be at leaft two to form a confpiracy) may be indicted at the fuit of the king; and the delinquents are ufually fentenced to imprifonment, fine, and pillory. To this head may be referred the offence of fending letters, threatening to accufe any perfon of a crime punifhable with death, tranfportation, pillory, or other infamous punifhment, with a view to extort from him any money or other valuable chattels. This is punifhable by ftatute 30 Geo. II. c. 24. at the difcretion of the court, with fine, imprifoment, pillory, whipping, or tranfportation for feven years.

16. The next offence againft public juftice is when the fuit is paft it's commencement, and come to trial. And that is the crime of wilful and corrupt *perjury*; which is defined

by Sir Edward Coke, to be a crime committed when a *lawful* oath is administered, in some *judicial* proceeding, to a person who swears *wilfully, absolutely,* and *falsly,* in a matter *material* to the issue or point in question. The law takes no notice of any perjury but such as is committed in some court of justice, having power to administer an oath; or before some magistrate or proper officer, invested with a similar authority, in some proceedings relative to a civil suit or a criminal prosecution: for it esteems all other oaths unnecessary at least, and therefore will not punish the breach of them. For which reason it is much to be questioned, how far any magistrate is justifiable in taking a voluntary *affidavit* in any extrajudicial matter, as is now too frequent upon every petty occasion: since it is more than possible, that by such idle oaths a man may frequently *in foro conscientiæ* incur the guilt, and at the same time evade the temporal penalties, of perjury. The perjury must also be corrupt, (that is, committed *malo animo*) wilful, positive, and absolute; not upon surprize, or the like: it also must be in some point material to the question in dispute; for if it only be in some trifling collateral circumstance, to which no regard is paid, it is no more penal than in the voluntary extrajudicial oaths before-mentioned. *Subornation* of perjury is the offence of procuring another to take such a false oath, as constitutes perjury in the principal. The punishment of perjury and subornation, at common law, has been various. It was antiently death; afterwards banishment, or cutting out the tongue; then forfeiture of goods; and now it is fine and imprisonment, and never more to be capable of bearing testimony. But the statute 5 Eliz. c. 9. (if the offender be prosecuted thereon) inflicts the penalty of perpetual infamy, and a fine of 40*l.* on the suborner; and in default of payment, imprisonment for six months, and to stand with both ears nailed to the pillory. Perjury itself is thereby punished with six months imprisonment, perpetual infamy, and a fine of 20*l.* or to have both ears nailed to the pillory. But the prosecution is usually carried on for the offence at common law; especially as, to the penalties before inflicted, the ftatute 2 Geo. II. c. 25. fuperadds a power, for the court to order the offender to be fent to the houfe of correction for a term not exceeding feven years, or to be tranfported for the fame period; and makes it felony without benefit of clergy to return or efcape within the time.

17. Bribery is the next fpecies of offence againft public juftice; which is, when a judge, or other perfon concerned in the adminiftration of juftice, takes any undue reward to influence his behaviour in his office.

This offence of taking bribes is punifhed, in inferior officers, with fine and imprifonment; and in thofe who offer a bribe, though not taken, the fame. But in judges, efpecially the fuperior ones, it hath been always looked upon as fo heinous an offence, that the chief juftice Thorp was hanged for it in the reign of Edward III. By a ftatute 11 Hen. IV. all judges and officers of the king, convicted of bribery, fhall forfeit treble the bribe, be punifhed at the king's will, and be difcharged from the king's fervice for ever.

18. Embracery is an attempt to influence a jury corruptly to one fide by promifes, perfuafions, entreaties, money, entertainments, and the like. The punifhment for the perfon embracing is by fine and imprifonment; and for the juror fo embraced, if it be by taking money, the punifhment is (by divers ftatutes of the reign of Edward III.) perpetual infamy, imprifonment for a year, and forfeiture of the tenfold value.

19. Another offence of the fame fpecies is the *negligence of public officers*, entrufted with the adminiftration of juftice, as fheriffs, coroners, conftables, and the like: which makes the offender liable to be fined; and in very notorious cafes will amount to a forfeiture of his office, if it be a beneficial one. Alfo the omitting to apprehend perfons offering ftolen iron, lead, and other metals to fale, is a mifdemefnor, and punifhable by a ftated fine, or imprifonment, in purfuance of the ftatute 29 Geo. II. c. 30.

20. There is yet another offence against public justice, which is a crime of deep malignity; and so much the deeper as there are many opportunities of putting it in practice, and the power and wealth of the offenders may often deter the injured from a legal prosecution. This is the *oppression* and tyrannical partiality of judges, justices, and other *magistrates*, in the administration and under the colour of their office. However, when prosecuted, either by impeachment in parliament, or by information in the court of king's bench, (according to the rank of the offenders) it is sure to be severely punished with forfeiture of their offices, (either consequential or immediate) fines, imprisonment, or other discretionary censure, regulated by the nature and aggravations of the offence committed.

21. Lastly, *extortion* is an abuse of public justice, which consists in any officer's unlawfully taking, by colour of his office, from any man, any money or thing of value, that is not due to him, or more than is due, or before it is due. The punishment is fine and imprisonment, and sometimes a forfeiture of the office.

## CHAPTER X.

### OF OFFENCES AGAINST THE PUBLIC PEACE.

WE are next to consider offences against the public *peace*; the conservation of which is intrusted to the king and his officers. These offences are either such as are an actual breach of the peace; or constructively so, by tending to make others break it. Both of these species are also either felonious, or not felonious. The felonious breaches of the peace are strained up to that degree of malignity by virtue of several modern statutes: and, particularly,

1. The *riotous assembling* of *twelve* persons, or more, and not dispersing upon proclamation. The statute 1 Geo. I.

c. 5. enacts, that if any twelve perſons are unlawfully aſſembled to the diſturbance of the peace, and any one juſtice of the peace, ſheriff, under-ſheriff, or mayor of a town ſhall think proper to command them by proclamation to diſperſe, if they contemn his orders and continue together for one hour afterwards, ſuch contempt ſhall be felony without benefit of clergy. And farther, if the reading of the proclamation be by force oppoſed, or the reader be in any manner wilfully hindered from the reading of it, ſuch oppoſers and hinderers are felons, without benefit of clergy: and all perſons to whom ſuch proclamation *ought to have been made*, and knowing of ſuch hindrance, and not diſperſing, are felons, without benefit of clergy (a). There is an indemnifying

---

*(a)* The ſpirit of this act has ſince been followed up, and greatly extended by 36 Geo. III. c. 8. which having been the ſubject of much converſation, and being extremely important to the intereſts of the community, it may be proper to notice at ſome length. After ſtating that aſſemblies of divers perſons, collected for the purpoſe or under the pretext of deliberating on public grievances, and of agreeing on petitions, remonſtrances, or other addreſſes, to the king, or to parliament, have of late been made uſe of to ſerve the ends of factious and ſeditious perſons, to the great danger of the public peace, and that the ſame may become the means of producing confuſion and calamities in the nation: it proceeds to enact,

Sec. 1. That no meeting exceeding 50 perſons, (except county meetings, called by the lord lieutenant or ſheriff, or meetings called by the convener of any county or ſtewartry in Scotland; or meetings called by two or more juſtices, or by the major part of the grand jury of the county, or of the diviſion of the county where ſuch meetings ſhall be held, at their general aſſizes or general quarter ſeſſions; or meetings of any city or town, called by the mayor or other head officer; or meetings of any ward, called by the alderman or other head officer; or meetings of any corporate body), ſhall be held for the purpoſe or on the pretext of conſidering of or preparing any petition, remonſtrance, or other addreſs to the king, or parliament, for alteration of matters eſtabliſhed in church or ſtate, or for deliberating on any grievance therein, unleſs notice of the intention to hold ſuch meeting, and of the time and place thereof ſhall be given in the

clause, in case any of the mob be unfortunately killed in endeavour to disperse them. And, by a subsequent clause, if any person so riotously assembled, begin even before proclamation to pull down any church, chapel, meeting-house, dwelling-house, or out-houses, they shall be felons without benefit of clergy.

names of seven householders resident in the place where such meeting shall be proposed to be held, by advertisement in some public newspaper usually circulated in the county and division where such meeting shall be held, five days previous; and such notice shall not be inserted in any newspaper unless the authority shall be signed by seven householders, and written at the foot of a true copy of such notice, and delivered to the person required to insert the same; which notice and authority shall be carefully preserved, and, within fourteen days after the meeting, shall be produced (if required) to any justice; and if any person shall insert such notice in any newspaper, without such authority, or shall refuse to produce it within three days after being required, he shall forfeit 50*l.* to the prosecutor.

Sec. 2. Notice signed as aforesaid may be given five days before the day on which such meeting shall be held, to the clerk of the peace, who shall forthwith send a true copy thereof to three justices of the county, &c. or if the justices of the place where such meeting shall be proposed to be held shall have exclusive jurisdiction, then to three of such justices, if so many shall then be resident within such jurisdiction, and if not, then to so many as shall be there resident; and notice so given shall be as effectual as if the same had been given by public advertisement.

Sec. 3. All meetings, exceeding 50 persons (except as aforesaid) held without such previous notice for the purpose of preparing any petition, remonstrance, or other address, to the king, or parliament, for alteration of matters established in church or state, or for the purpose of deliberating on any grievance therein, shall be deemed unlawful assemblies.

Sec. 4. If any persons, exceeding 50, assembled contrary to the above provisions, and being required by any justice, or sheriff of the county, or by the mayor or other head officer or justice of any place where such assembly shall be, by proclamation in the form herein-after directed, to disperse themselves, and peaceably to depart to their habitations, or to their lawful business, shall, to the number of 12, not-

2. By the statute 9 Geo. I. c. 22. to appear armed in any inclosed forest or place where deer are usually kept, or in any warren for hares or conies, or in any high road, open heath, common, or down, by day, or night, with faces

---

withstanding such proclamation made, continue together by the space of one hour, the offenders shall suffer death.

Sec. 5. The form of the proclamation shall be as hereafter followeth; *viz.* the justice shall, among the said persons assembled, or as near to them as he can safely come, command silence, and after that shall make proclamation in these words, or like in effect:

' OUR sovereign lord the king chargeth and command-
' eth all persons being assembled immediately to disperse
' themselves, and peaceably to depart to their habitations or
' to their lawful business, upon the pains contained in the
' act made in the thirty-sixth year of King *George* the Third,
' *for the more effectually preventing seditious meetings and assem-*
' *blies.*

GOD save the KING.'

Sec. 6. In case any meeting shall be held in pursuance of any such notice, and the matter propounded or deliberated upon shall purport that any thing by law established may be altered otherwise than by the authority of the king, lords, and commons, or shall tend to incite or stir up the people to hatred or contempt of the person of His Majesty, his heirs or successors, or of the government and constitution of this realm, as by law established, any magistrate may, by proclamation, require the persons assembled to disperse themselves; and if any persons, to the number of 12, shall thereafter continue together for one hour, the offender shall suffer death.

Sec. 7. Justices present at such meetings may order persons who shall propound or maintain propositions for altering any thing by law established, otherwise than by the authority of the king, lords, and commons, or shall wilfully make any proposition, or hold any discourse, for the purpose of inciting and stirring up the people to hatred or contempt of the person of His Majesty, his heirs or successors, or the government and constitution of this realm, as by law established, to be taken into custody; and in case of resistance, the justice may make proclamation as aforesaid; and if 12 or

blacked or otherwife *difguifed*, or (being fo difguifed) to hunt, wound, kill, or fteal any deer, to rob a warren, or to fteal fifh, or to procure by gift or promife of reward any perfon to join them in fuch unlawful act, is felony without benefit of clergy.

more fhall thereafter continue together for one hour, the offenders fhall fuffer death.

Sec. 8. Magiftrates may refort to affemblies and act, and may require the affiftance of peace officers.

Sec. 9. If 12 or more perfons, after proclamation made, fhall not difperfe themfelves within one hour, any magiftrate or peace officer may command all His Majefty's fubjects to affift in apprehending them; and if any of the perfons fo affembled fhall happen to be killed, or hurt in the difperfing or apprehending them, the magiftrate, &c. fhall be indemnified.

Sec. 10. If any perfon fhall obftruct any juftice or other perfon authorized as aforefaid, attending or going to attend any fuch meeting, or obftruct any perfon making proclamation, he fhall fuffer death; and perfons affembled as aforefaid, to the number of 50, to whom any fuch proclamation ought to have been made, if the fame had not been hindered, fhall likewife, in cafe they continue together to the number of 12, for one hour after fuch hindrance, fhall fuffer death; as fhall alfo perfons at fuch affemblies oppofing the taking offenders into cuftody.

Sec. 11. The fheriffs, juftices, magiftrates, and peace officers in Scotland, fhall have the fame powers and authorities, for putting this act in execution, as the juftices in England; and perfons convicted of any of the felonies afore-mentioned within Scotland, fhall fuffer death, and confifcation of moveables.

Sec. 12. And as certain houfes or places in *London* and *Weftminfter*, and in the neighbourhood thereof, and in other places, have of late been frequently ufed for the purpofe of delivering lectures and difcourfes concerning fuppofed public grievances, tending to ftir up hatred and contempt of his majefty's perfon, and of the government and conftitution as by law eftablifhed: it is enacted, that every houfe or other place where lectures or difcourfes fhall be delivered, concerning any money, or any grievance, or any matters relating to the laws or government of thefe kingdoms, for the purpofe of raifing money, or any other valuable thing, from the perfons admitted, unlefs the

3. Also, by the same statute 9 Geo. I. c. 22. amended by statute 27 Geo. II. c. 15. knowingly to send any *letter* without a name, or with a fictitious name, *demanding* money, venison, or any other valuable thing, or *threatening* (without

opening or using thereof shall have been previously licenced in manner herein-after mentioned, shall be deemed a disorderly house or place, and the person by whom such house or place shall be opened or used, shall forfeit 100l. for every day or time that such house or place shall be opened or used, to the prosecutor, and be otherwise punished as the law directs; and every person managing the proceedings, or acting as president or chairman at such house or place, or delivering any discourse or lecture for the purpose aforesaid, and also every person paying or receiving money for admission, or delivering out or receiving tickets of admission, shall forfeit 100l. to the prosecutor.

Sec. 13. Any person who shall act as master or mistress, or shall have the management of any such house or place as aforesaid, shall be deemed the person by whom the same is opened or used, and shall be liable to be prosecuted and punished as such.

Sec. 14. Magistrates who, by information on oath, have reason to suspect that any place is opened for delivering lectures or discourses, may demand to be admitted; and in case of refusal, the place to be deemed disorderly, and the person refusing admittance shall forfeit 100l.

Sec. 15. Magistrates may demand admittance to any licenced place at the time of delivering lectures or discourses, and if refused it shall be deemed disorderly, and the person refusing admittance shall forfeit 100l.

Sec. 16. Two justices of the place where any house or other building shall be, which any person shall be desirous to open for any of the purposes aforesaid, by writing under their hands and seals, at the general quarter session, or at any special session, may grant a licence to any person desiring the same, to open such house or other building, for the purpose of delivering for money any such lectures or discourses as aforesaid, the same being expressed in such licence, for which a fee of 1s. shall be paid, and the same shall be in force for one year, or for any less space of time therein to be specified; and which licence the justices in session may revoke and declare void.

C. X.   OFFENCES AGAINST THE PUBLIC PEACE.   473

any demand) to kill any of the king's subjects, or to fire their houses, out-houses, barns, or ricks, is made felony, without benefit of clergy.

4. By the statute 4 Geo. III. c. 12. maliciously to damage or destroy any banks, sluices, or other works on such navigable river, to open the floodgates, or otherwise obstruct the navigation, is made felony, punishable with transportation for seven years. And by the statute 7 Geo. III. c. 40. (which repeals all former acts relating to turnpikes) maliciously to pull down or otherwise destroy any *turnpike-gate*, or fence, toll-house, or weighing-engine thereunto belonging, erected by authority of parliament, or to rescue any person in custody for the same, is made felony without benefit of clergy; and the indictment may be inquired of and tried in any adjacent county (*a*). The remaining offences against the public peace are merely misdemesnors, and no felonies; as,

---

Sec. 17. This act shall not extend to any lectures or discourses to be delivered in any of the universities.

Sec. 18. Nor shall any payment made to any schoolmaster or other person by law allowed to teach youth, in respect of any lectures or discourse delivered by him for the instruction of youth, be deemed a payment for admission to lectures or discourses within the intent of this act.

Sec. 19. Nothing herein shall be deemed to abridge any provision already made by law for the suppression or punishment of any offence described in this act.

Sec. 20. This act shall be openly read at every *Epiphany* quarter sessions, and at every leet or law day.

Sec. 21. No person shall be prosecuted by virtue of this act, unless such prosecution shall be commenced within six months after the offence committed; and no action shall be brought for any of the penalties by this act imposed, unless the same shall be brought within three months after the offence is committed.

Sec. 22. This act shall continue in force for three years, and until the end of the next session.

(*a*) But now by the statute 13 Geo. 3. c. 84. which repealed the stat. 7 Geo. III. c. 40. the offender shall be transported for seven years, or imprisoned for any time not exceeding three years.

5. Affrays (from *affraier*, to terrify) are the fighting of two or more perſons in ſome public place, to the terror of his majeſty's ſubjects: for, if the fighting be in private, it is no *affray* but an *aſſault*. Affrays may be ſuppreſſed by any private perſon preſent, who is juſtifiable in endeavouring to part the combatants, whatever conſequence may enſue. But more eſpecially the conſtable, or other ſimilar officer, however denominated, is bound to keep the peace; and to that purpoſe may break open doors to ſuppreſs an affray, or apprehend the affrayers; and may either carry them before a juſtice, or impriſon them by his own authority for a convenient ſpace till the heat is over; and may then perhaps alſo make them find ſureties for the peace. The puniſhment of common affrays is by fine and impriſonment; the meaſure of which muſt be regulated by the circumſtances of the caſe; for where there is any material aggravation, the puniſhment proportionably increaſes. As, where two perſons coolly and deliberately engage in a duel: this being attended with an apparent intention and danger of murder, and being a high contempt of the juſtice of the nation, is a ſtrong aggravation of the affray, though no miſchief has actually enſued. Another aggravation is, when thereby the officers of juſtice are diſturbed in the due execution of their office: or where a reſpect to the particular place ought to reſtrain and regulate men's behaviour, more than common ones; as in the king's court, and the like. And upon the ſame account alſo, all affrays in a church or church-yard are deemed very heinous offences, as being indignities to him to whoſe ſervice thoſe places are conſecrated. Therefore mere quarrelſome words, which are neither an affray nor an offence in any other place, are penal here. *Two* perſons may be guilty of an affray, but,

6. Riots, *routs*, and *unlawful aſſemblies*, muſt have *three* perſons at leaſt to conſtitute them. An *unlawful aſſembly* is when three, or more, do aſſemble themſelves together to do an unlawful act, as to pull down incloſures, to deſtroy a warren or the game therein; and part without doing it, or

making any motion towards it. A *rout* is where three or more meet to do an unlawful act upon a common quarrel, as forcibly breaking down fences upon a right claimed of common, or of way; and make some advances towards it. A *riot* is where three or more actually do an unlawful act of violence, either with or without a common cause or quarrel: as if they beat a man; or hunt and kill game in another's park, chafe, warren, or liberty; or do any other unlawful act with force and violence; or even do a lawful act, as removing a nusance, in a violent and tumultuous manner. The punishment of unlawful assemblies, if to the number of twelve, we have just now seen, may be capital, according to the circumstances that attend it; but, from the number of three to eleven, is by fine and imprisonment only. The same is the case in riots and routs by the common law; to which the pillory in very enormous cases has been sometimes superadded. And by the statute 13 Hen. IV. c. 9. any two justices, together with the sheriff or under-sheriff of the county, may come with the *posse comitatus*, if need be, and suppress any such riot, assembly, or rout, arrest the rioters, and record upon the spot the nature and circumstances of the whole transaction; which record alone shall be a sufficient conviction of the offenders. In the interpretation of which statute it hath been holden, that all persons, noblemen and others, except women, clergymen, persons decrepit, and infants under fifteen, are bound to attend the justices in suppressing a riot, upon pain of fine and imprisonment; and that any battery, wounding, or killing the rioters, that may happen in suppressing the riot is justifiable.

7. Nearly related to this head of riots is the offence of *tumultuous petitioning;* which was carried to an enormous height in the times preceding the grand rebellion. Wherefore by statute 13 Car. II. st. 1. c. 5. it is enacted, that not more than twenty names shall be signed to any petition to the king or either house of parliament, for any alteration of matters established by law in church or state; unless the contents thereof be previously approved, in the country, by three justices, or the majority of the grand jury at the assises

or quarter-sessions; and, in London, by the lord mayor, aldermen, and common council: and that no petition shall be delivered by a company of more than ten persons: on pain in either case of incurring a penalty not exceeding 100l. and three months imprisonment.

8. An eighth offence against the public peace is that of a *forcible entry* or *detainer*, which is committed by violently taking or keeping possession of lands and tenements, with menaces, force, and arms, and without the authority of law. But this does not extend to such as endeavour to maintain possession by force, where they themselves, or their ancestors, have been in the peaceable enjoyment of the lands and tenements for three years immediately preceding.

9. The offence of *riding* or *going armed*, with dangerous or unusual weapons, is a crime against the public peace, by terrifying the good people of the land, and is particularly prohibited by the statute of Northampton, 2 Edw. III. c. 3. upon pain of forfeiture of the arms, and imprisonment during the king's pleasure.

10. Spreading *false news*, to make discord between the king and nobility, or concerning any great man of the realm, is punishable by common law with fine and imprisonment.

11. False and *pretended prophecies*, with intent to disturb the peace, are equally unlawful, and more penal, as they raise enthusiastic jealousies in the people, and terrify them with imaginary fears, And by the statute 5 Eliz. c. 15. the penalty for the first offence is a fine of ten pounds and one year's imprisonment; for the second, forfeiture of all goods and chattels, and imprisonment during life.

12. Besides actual breaches of the peace, any thing that tends to provoke or excite others to break it, is an offence of the same denomination. Therefore *challenges to fight*, either by word or letter, or to be the bearer of such challenge, are punishable by fine and imprisonment, according to the circumstances of the offence. If this challenge arises on account of any money won at gaming, or if any assault or affray happen upon such account, the offender, by statute 9 Ann. c. 14. shall forfeit all his goods to the crown, and suffer two years imprisonment.

13. Of a nature very similar to challenges are *libels, libelli famosi,* which, taken in their largest and most extensive sense, signify any writings, pictures, or the like, of an immoral or illegal tendency; but, in the sense under which we are now to consider them, are malicious defamations of any person, and especially a magistrate, made public by either printing, writing, signs or pictures, in order to provoke him to wrath, or expose him to public hatred, contempt, and ridicule. The direct tendency of these libels is the breach of the public peace, by stirring up the objects of them to revenge, and perhaps to bloodshed. The communication of a libel to any one person is a publication in the eye of the law, and therefore the sending an abusive private letter to a man is as much a libel as if it were openly printed, for it equally tends to a breach of the peace. For the same reason it is immaterial with respect to the essence of a libel, whether the matter of it be true or false, since the provocation, and not the falsity, is the thing to be punished criminally: though, doubtless, the falsehood of it may aggravate its guilt, and enhance its punishment. In a civil action, we may remember, a libel must appear to be false, as well as scandalous; for, if the charge be true, the plaintiff has received no private injury, and has no ground to demand a compensation for himself, whatever offence it may be against the public peace: and therefore, upon a civil action, the truth of the accusation may be pleaded in bar of the suit. But, in a criminal prosecution, the tendency which all libels have to create animosities, and to disturb the public peace, is the whole that the law considers. And therefore, in such prosecutions, the only points to be inquired into, are, first, the making or publishing of the book or writing; and, secondly, whether the matter be criminal: and, if both these points are against the defendant, the offence against the public is complete (*a*). The punishment of such

---

(*a*) But doubts having arisen in respect to the functions of juries in cases of libels, it is now provided by 32 Geo. III. c. 60. that on the trial of an indictment or information for a libel the jury may give a *general* verdict of guilty or not guilty,

libellers, for either making, repeating, printing, or publishing the libel, is fine, and such corporal punishment as the court in its discretion shall inflict; regarding the quantity of the offence, and the quality of the offender (a).

## CHAPTER XI.

### OF OFFENCES AGAINST PUBLIC TRADE.

OFFENCES against public *trade*, like those of the preceding classes, are either felonious, or not felonious. Of the first sort are,

1. Owling, so called from its being usually carried on in the night, which is the offence of transporting wool or sheep out of this kingdom, to the detriment of its staple manufacture (b).

---

upon the *whole matter* put in issue, and shall not be required by the court to find the defendant guilty, merely on proof of the publication, and of the sense ascribed to the same in the indictment or information.

(a) Under this head, and in addition to the several offences against the public peace, enumerated by the learned judge, may be subjoined the act of 36 Geo. III. c. 7. whereby it is provided that, if any person in England during three years, and until the end of the next session of parliament, shall maliciously and advisedly, by writing, printing, preaching, or other speaking, express, publish, utter, or declare any words, or sentences to invite or stir up the people to hatred or contempt of the person of his majesty, his heirs, or successors, or the government and constitution of this realm, as by law established, he shall be liable to such punishment as may by law be inflicted on high misdemesnors, and for a second offence, shall be liable (at the discretion of the court) either to such punishment as aforesaid, or be transported for a term not exceeding seven years.

(b) Various penalties have at different periods been inflicted for the exportation of sheep and wool, but by the 8

2. Smuggling, or the offence of importing goods without paying the duties impofed thereon by the laws of the cuftoms and excife, is an offence generally connected and carried on hand in hand with the former. This is reftrained by a great variety of ftatutes, which inflict pecuniary penalties and feifure of the goods for clandeftine fmuggling; and affix the guilt of felony, with tranfportation for feven years, upon more open, daring, and avowed practices.

3. Another offence againft public trade is fraudulent *bankruptcy*, which was fufficiently fpoken of in a former book; I fhall therefore here barely mention the feveral fpecies of fraud, taken notice of by the ftatute law; *viz.* the bankrupt's neglect of furrendering himfelf to his creditors; his non-conformity to the directions of the feveral ftatutes; his concealing or imbezzling his effects to the value of 20*l.* and his withholding any books or writings with intent to defraud his creditors: all which the policy of our commercial country has made felony without benefit of clergy. And, even without actual fraud, if the bankrupt cannot make it appear that he is difabled from paying his debts by fome cafual lofs, he fhall, by the ftatute 21 Jac. I. c. 19. be fet on the pillory for two hours, with one of his ears nailed to the fame, and cut off. To this head we may alfo fubjoin, that, by ftatute 32 Geo. II. c. 28. it is felony punifhable by tranfportation for feven years, if a prifoner, charged in execution for any debt under 100*l.* neglects or refufes, on demand, to difcover and deliver up his effects for the benefit of his creditors. And thefe are the only felonious offences againft public trade; the refidue being mere mifdemefnors: as,

4. Ufury, which is an unlawful contract upon the loan of money, to receive the fame again with exorbitant increafe.

---

Eliz. c. 3. only was it made *felony*, and that not till the *fecond* offence. This act, however, as well as all fubfequent *acts*, relative to this offence, was repealed by 28 Geo. III. c. 38. which has reduced the offence to a common *mifdemefnor*, punifhable at the moft by heavy forfeitures, and three months folitary imprifonment.

Of this also, we had occasion to discourse at large in a former book. Wherefore not only all contracts for taking more are in themselves totally void, but also the lender shall forfeit treble the money borrowed. Also if any scrivener or broker takes more than five shillings *per cent* procuration money, or more than twelve-pence for making a bond, he shall forfeit 20*l*. with costs, and shall suffer imprisonment for half a year. And, by statute 17 Geo. III. c. 26. to take more than ten shillings *per cent* for procuring any money to be advanced on any life-annuity, is made an indictable misdemesnor, and punishable with fine and imprisonment: as is also the offence of procuring or soliciting any infant to grant any life-annuity; or to promise, or otherwise engage to ratify it when he comes of age.

5. Cheating is another offence, more immediately against public trade; as that cannot be carried on without a punctilious regard to common honesty, and faith between man and man. Hither therefore may be referred that prodigious multitude of statutes, which are made to restrain and punish deceits in particular trades, and which are enumerated by Hawkins and Burn, but are chiefly of use among the traders themselves. The general punishment for all frauds of this kind, if indicted (as they may be) at common law, is by fine and imprisonment: though the easier and more usual way is by levying on a summary conviction, by distress and sale, the forfeitures imposed by the several acts of parliament. Lastly, any deceitful practice, in cozening another by artful means, whether in matters of trade or otherwise, as by playing with false dice, or the like, is punishable with fine, imprisonment, and pillory. And, by the statutes 33 Hen. VIII. c. 1. and 30 Geo. II. c. 24. if any man defrauds another of any valuable chattels by colour of any false token, counterfeit letter, or false pretence, or pawns or disposes of another's goods without the consent of the owner, he shall suffer such punishment by imprisonment, fine, pillory, transportation, whipping, or other corporal pain, as the court shall direct.

6. The offence of *foreſtalling* the market is alſo an offence againſt public trade. This, which (as well as the two following) is alſo an offence at common law, was deſcribed by ſtatute 5 & 6 Edw. VI. c. 14. to be the buying or contracting for any merchandize or victual coming in the way to market; or diſſuading perſons from bringing their goods or proviſions there; or perſuading them to enhance the price, when there: any of which practices make the market dearer to the fair trader.

7. Regrating was deſcribed by the ſame ſtatute to be the buying of corn, or other dead victual, in any market, and ſelling it again in the ſame market, or within four miles of the place. For this alſo enhances the price of the proviſions, as every ſucceſſive ſeller muſt have a ſucceſſive profit.

8. Engroſſing was alſo deſcribed to be the getting into one's poſſeſſion, or buying up, large quantities of corn or other dead victuals, with intent to ſell them again. This muſt of courſe be injurious to the public, by putting it in the power of one or two rich men to raiſe the price of proviſions at their own diſcretion. And ſo the total engroſſing of any other commodity, with intent to ſell it at an unreaſonable price, is an offence indictable and finable at the common law. And the general penalty for theſe three offences by the common law (for all the ſtatutes concerning them were repealed by 12 Geo. III. c. 71.) is, as in other minute miſdemeſnors, diſcretionary fine and impriſonment.

9. Monopolies are much the ſame offence in other branches of trade, that engroſſing is in proviſions: being a licence or privilege allowed by the king for the ſole buying and ſelling, making, working, or uſing of any thing whatſoever; whereby the ſubject in general is reſtrained from that liberty of manufacturing or trading which he had before; but theſe were in a great meaſure remedied by ſtatute 21 Jac. I. c. 3. which declares ſuch monopolies to be contrary to law and void; (except as to patents, not exceeding the grant of fourteen years, to the authors of new inventions, and except alſo patents concerning printing, ſalt-petre, gunpowder,

great ordnance, and shot) and monopolists are punished with the forfeiture of treble damages and double costs, to those whom they attempt to disturb. Combinations also among victuallers or artificers, to raise the price of provisions, or any commodities, or the rate of labour, are in many cases severely punished by particular statutes; and in general, by statute 2 & 3 Edw. VI. c. 15. with the forfeiture of 10*l.* or twenty days imprisonment, with an allowance of only bread and water, for the first offence; 20*l.* or the pillory, for the second; and 40*l.* for the third, or else the pillory, loss of one ear, and perpetual infamy.

10. To exercise a *trade* in any town, without having previously served as an *apprentice* for seven years, is looked upon to be detrimental to public trade, upon the supposed want of sufficient skill in the trader; and therefore is punished by statute 5 Eliz. c. 4. with the forfeiture of forty shillings by the month.

11. Lastly, to prevent the destruction of our home manufactures, by *transporting and seducing our artists* to settle abroad, it is provided, by statute 5 Geo. I. c. 27. that such as so entice or seduce them shall be fined 100*l.* and be imprisoned three months; and for the second offence shall be fined at discretion, and be imprisoned a year: and the artificers, so going into foreign countries, and not returning within six months after warning given them by the British embassador where they reside, shall be deemed aliens, and forfeit all their lands and goods, and shall be incapable of any legacy or gift. By statute 23 Geo. II. c. 13. the seducers incur, for the first offence, a forfeiture of 500*l.* for each artificer contracted with to be sent abroad, and imprisonment for twelve months; and for the second 1000*l.* and are liable to two years imprisonment: and by the same statute, connected with 14 Geo. III. c. 71. if any person exports any tools or utensils used in the silk, linen, cotton, or woollen manufactures, (excepting woolcards to North America) he forfeits the same and 200*l.* and the captain of the ship (having knowlege thereof) 100*l.* and if any captain of a king's ship, or officer of the customs, knowingly suffers such ex-

portation, he forfeits 100*l.* (*a*) and his employment; and is for ever made incapable of bearing any public office: and every perſon collecting ſuch tools or utenſils, in order to export the ſame, ſhall on conviction at the aſſiſes forfeit ſuch tools and alſo 200*l* (*b*).

## CHAPTER XII.

### OF OFFENCES AGAINST THE PUBLIC HEALTH, AND THE PUBLIC POLICE OR OECONOMY.

THE fourth ſpecies of offences, more eſpecially affecting the commonwealth, are ſuch as are againſt the public *health* of the nation.

1. The firſt of theſe offences is a felony. For, by ſtatute 1 Jac. I. c. 31. it is enacted, that if any perſon infected with the plague, or dwelling in any infected houſe, be commanded by the mayor or conſtable, or other head officer of his town or vill, to keep his houſe, and ſhall venture to diſobey it, and goes abroad, and converſes in company, if he has no plague ſore upon him, he ſhall be puniſhed as a vagabond by whipping, and be bound to his good behaviour: but, if he has any infectious ſore upon him uncured, he then ſhall be guilty of felony. By the ſtatute 26 Geo. II. c. 6. (explained and amended by 29 Geo. II. c. 8. *and* 28 *Geo.* III. *c.* 34.) the method of performing *quarantine*, or forty days probation, by ſhips coming from infected countries, is put in a much more regular and effectual order than formerly; and maſters of ſhips, coming from infected places, and diſobeying the directions there given, or having the plague on

---

(*a*) Augmented by 21 Geo. III. c. 37. to 200*l*.

(*b*) And by 25 Geo. III. c. 67. and 26 *ibid.* c. 89. ſtill further regulations and penalties are impoſed in relation to the above offences.

board and concealing it, are guilty of felony without benefit of clergy. The fame penalty alfo attends perfons efcaping from the *lazarets*, or places wherein quarantine is to be performed; and officers and watchmen neglecting their duty; and perfons conveying goods or letters from fhips performing quarantine.

2. A fecond, but much inferior fpecies of offence againft public health is the felling of *unwholefome provifions*. To prevent which the ftatute 51 Hen. III. ft. 6. and the ordinance for bakers, c. 7. prohibit the fale of corrupted wine, contagious or unwholefome flefh, or flefh that is bought of a Jew; under pain of amercement for the firft offence, pillory for the fecond, fine and imprifonment for the third, and abjuration of the town for the fourth. And, by the ftatute 12 Car. II. c. 25. §. 11. any brewing or adulteration of wine is punifhed with the forfeiture of 100*l*. if done by the wholefale merchant; and 40*l*. if done by the vintner or retail trader. Thefe are all the offences, which may properly be faid to refpect the public health.

V. The laft fpecies of offences which efpecially affect the commonwealth are thofe againft the public *police* and *oeconomy*. By the public police and œconomy I mean the due regulation and domeftic order of the kingdom: whereby the individuals of the ftate, like members of a well-governed family, are bound to conform their general behaviour to the rules of propriety, good neighbourhood, and good manners; and to be decent, induftrious, and inoffenfive in their refpective ftations. This head of offences muft therefore be very mifcellaneous, as it comprizes all fuch crimes as efpecially affect public fociety, and are not comprehended under any of the four preceding fpecies. Thefe amount, fome of them to felony, and others to mifdemefnors only. Among the former are,

1. The offence of *clandeftine marriages*; for, by the ftatute 26 Geo. II. c. 33. 1. To folemnize marriage in any other place befides a church, or public chapel wherein banns have been ufually publifhed, except by licence from the archbifhop of Canterbury;—and, 2. To folemnize marriage in

such church or chapel without due publication of banns, or licence obtained from a proper authority;—do both of them not only render the marriage void, but subject the person solemnizing it to felony, punished by transportation of fourteen years: as, by three former statutes, he and his assistants were subject to a pecuniary forfeiture of 100*l.* 3. To make a false entry in a marriage register; to alter it when made; to forge, or counterfeit, such entry, or a marriage licence; to cause or procure, or act or assist in such forgery; to utter the same as true, knowing it to be counterfeit; or to destroy or procure the destruction of any register, in order to vacate any marriage, or subject any person to the penalties of this act; all these offences, knowingly and wilfully committed, subject the party to the guilt of felony, without benefit of clergy.

2. Another felonious offence, with regard to this holy estate of matrimony, is what some have corruptly called *bigamy*, which properly signifies being twice married; but is more justly denominated *polygamy*, or having a plurality of wives at once. It is enacted, by statute 1 Jac. I. c. 11. that if any person, being married, do afterwards marry again, the former husband or wife being alive, it is felony; but within the benefit of clergy. The first wife in this case shall not be admitted as a witness against her husband, because she is the true wife; but the second may, for she is indeed no wife at all: and so, *vice versa*, of a second husband. This act makes an exception to five cases, in which such second marriage, though in the three first it is void, is yet no felony. 1. Where either party hath been continually *abroad* for seven years, whether the party in England hath notice of the other's being living or no. 2. Where either of the parties hath been absent from the other seven years *within* this kingdom, and the remaining party hath had no knowlege of the other's being alive within that time. 3. Where there is a divorce (or separation *a mensa et thoro*) by sentence in the ecclesiastical court. 4. Where the first marriage is declared absolutely void by any such sentence, and the parties loosed *a vinculo*. Or, 5. Where either of the parties was under the age of

consent at the time of the first marriage, for in such case the first marriage was voidable by the disagreement of either party, which the second marriage very clearly amounts to. But, if at the age of consent the parties had agreed to the marriage, which completes the contract, and is indeed the real marriage; and afterwards one of them should marry again; I should apprehend that such second marriage would be within the reason and penalties of the act.

3. A third species of felony against the good order and œconomy of the kingdom, is by idle *soldiers* and *mariners wandering* about the realm, or persons pretending so to be. But this sanguinary law is in practice deservedly antiquated (a).

4. Outlandish persons calling themselves *Egyptians*, or *gypsies*, are another object of the severity of some of our unrepealed statutes (b).

5. To descend next to offences, whose punishment is short of death. *Common nusances* are a species of offences against the public order and œconomical regimen of the state; being either the doing of a thing to the annoyance of all the king's subjects, or the neglecting to do a thing which the common good requires. The nature of *common* nusances, and their distinction from *private* nusances, were explained in the preceding book; when we considered more particularly the nature of the private sort, as a civil injury to individuals. I shall here only remind the student, that common nusances are such inconvenient or troublesome offences, as annoy the

---

(a) Such persons, however, shall by 32 Geo. 3. c. 45. be deemed rogues and vagabonds within the meaning of the said act.

(b) The statutes alluded to by the learned judge (and which in another place he justly observes were a disgrace to our statute book) I am happy to have an opportunity of remarking, have since been repealed, and gypsies are now subject only to the punishment inflicted by the last mentioned statute, on persons coming under the description of rogues and vagabonds, in which " all persons pretending to be gypsies, or wandering in the habit or form of Egyptians" are by that statute expressly included.

whole community in general, and not merely some particular person; and therefore are indictable only, and not actionable; as it would be unreasonable to multiply suits, by giving every man a separate right of action, for what damnifies him in common only with the rest of his fellow-subjects. Of this nature are, 1. Annoyances in *highways, bridges,* and public *rivers,* by rendering the same inconvenient or dangerous to pass: either positively, by actual obstructions, or negatively, by want of reparations. For both of these, the person so obstructing, or such individuals as are bound to repair and cleanse them, or (in default of these last) the parish at large, may be indicted, distreined to repair and amend them, and in some cases fined. And a presentment thereof by a judge of assise, &c. or a justice of the peace, shall be in all respects equivalent to an indictment. Where there is an house erected, or an inclosure made, upon any part of the king's demesnes, or of an highway, or common street, or public water, or such like public things, it is properly called a *purpresture.* 2. All those kinds of nusances, (such as offensive trades and manufactures) which when injurious to a private man are actionable, are, when detrimental to the public, punishable by public prosecution, and subject to fine according to the quantity of the misdemesnor; and particularly the keeping of hogs in any city or market town is indictable as a public nusance. 3. All disorderly *inns* or *ale-houses, bawdy-houses, gaming-houses, stage-plays* unlicenced, booths and stages for *rope-dancers, mountebanks,* and the like, are public nusances, and may upon indictment be suppressed and fined. Inns, in particular, being intended for the lodging and receipt of travellers, may be indicted, suppressed, and the inn-keepers fined, if they refuse to entertain a traveller without a very sufficient cause: for thus to frustrate the end of their institution is held to be disorderly behaviour. 4. The making and selling of *fire-works* and *squibs,* or throwing them about in any street, is, on account of the danger that may ensue to any thatched or timber buildings, declared to be a common nusance, by statute 9 & 10 W. III. c. 7. and therefore is punishable by fine. And to this head we may refer, (though not declared a common nufance) the making, keeping, or carriage, of too large a quantity of *gunpowder* at one time, or in one place or vehicle; which is prohibited by ftatute 12 Geo. III. c. 61. under heavy penalties and forfeiture.

6. Idlenefs in any perfon whatfoever is alfo a high offence againft the public œconomy. All idle perfons or vagabonds, are particularly defcribed by ftatute 17 Geo. II. c. 5, (a) and divided into three claffes, *idle* and *diforderly* perfons, *rogues* and *vagabonds*, and *incorrigble rogues;* all thefe are offenders againft the good order, and blemifhes in the government, of any kingdom. They are therefore all punifhed, by the ftatute laft mentioned; that is to fay, idle and diforderly perfons with one month's imprifonment in the houfe of correction; rogues and vagabonds with whipping and imprifonment not exceeding fix months; and incorrigble rogues with the like difcipline and confinement, not exceeding two years: the breach and efcape from which confinement in one of an inferior clafs, ranks him among incorrigble rogues; and in a rogue (before incorrigible) makes him a felon, and liable to be tranfported for feven years. Perfons harbouring vagrants are liable to a fine of forty fhillings, and to pay all expences brought upon the parifh thereby.

7. Next follows the offence of *gaming*. To reftrain this pernicious vice, among the inferior fort of people, the ftatute 33 Hen. VIII. c. 9. was made, which prohibits to all but gentlemen the games of tennis, tables, cards, dice, bowls, and other unlawful diverfions there fpecified, unlefs in the time of Chriftmas, under pecuniary pains and imprifonment. And the fame law, and alfo the ftatute 30 Geo. II. c. 24.

---

(a) And further by 28 Geo. III. c. 88, and 32 ibid, c. 53. by the firft of which ftatutes, all perfons having upon them any pick-lock or other implement or weapon, with an intent to commit any felonious act of houfebreaking or affault, as alfo perfons found in any dwelling houfe or appurtenant with an intent to fteal; and by the laft act, perfons charged on the oath of one witnefs to be of " evil fame, and reputed thieves, and who fhall not give a fatisfactory account of themfelves," are feverally declared to be rogues and vagabonds, and liable to be dealt with accordingly.

inflict pecuniary penalties, as well upon the mafter of any public houfe wherein fervants are permitted to game, as upon the fervants themfelves who are found to be gaming there. But this is not the principal ground of modern complaint : it is the gaming in high life that demands the attention of the magiftrate. When men are intoxicated with this frantic fpirit, laws will be of little avail; becaufe the fame falfe fenfe of honour that prompts a man to facrifice himfelf will deter him from appealing to the magiftrate. Yet it is proper that laws fhould be, and be known publicly, that gentlemen may confider what penalties they wilfully incur, and what a confidence they repofe in fharpers, who, if fuccefsful in play, are certain to be paid with honour, or, if unfuccefsful, have it in their power to be ftill greater gainers by informing. For by ftatute 16 Car. II. c. 7. if any perfon by playing or betting fhall lofe more than 100l. at one time, he fhall not be compellable to pay the fame; and the winner fhall forfeit treble the value, one moiety to the king, the other to the informer. The ftatute 9 Ann. c. 14. enacts, that all bonds and other fecurities, given for money won at play, or money lent at the time to play withal, fhall be utterly void; that all mortgages and incumbrances of lands, made upon the fame confideration, fhall be and enure to the ufe of the heir of the mortgagor: that, if any perfon at any time or fitting lofes 10l. at play, he may fue the winner, and recover it back by action of debt at law; and, in cafe the lofer does not, any other perfon may fue the winner for treble the fum fo loft; and the plaintiff may by bill in equity examine the defendant himfelf upon oath : and that in any of thefe fuits no privilege of parliament fhall be allowed. The ftatute farther enacts, that if any perfon by cheating at play fhall win any money or valuable thing, or fhall at any one time or fitting win more than 10l. he may be indicted thereupon, and fhall forfeit five times the value to any perfon who will fue for it; and (in cafe of cheating) fhall be deemed infamous, and fuffer fuch corporal punifhment as in cafe of wilful perjury. By feveral ftatutes of the reign of king George II. all private lotteries by tickets, cards, or dice, (and particularly the games of faro, baffet, ace of hearts, hazard, paffage, rolly-polly, and all other games with dice, except back-gammon) are prohibited under a penalty of 200l. for him that fhall erect fuch lotteries, and 50l. a time for the players. Public lotteries, unlefs by authority of parliament, and all manner of ingenious devices under the denomination of fales or otherwife which in the end are equivalent to lotteries, were before prohibited by a great variety of ftatutes under heavy pecuniary penalties. But particular defcriptions will ever be lame and deficient, unlefs all games of mere chance are at once prohibited; the inventions of fharpers being fwifter than the punifhment of the law, which only hunts them from one device to another. The ftatute 13 Geo. II. c. 19. to prevent the multiplicity of horfe races, another fund of gambling, directs that no plates or matches under 50l. value fhall be run, upon penalty of 200l. to be paid by the owner of each horfe running, and 100l. by fuch as advertife the plate (a). By ftatute 18 Geo. II. c. 34. the ftatute 9 Ann. is farther enforced, and fome deficiencies fupplied: the forfeitures of that act may now be recovered in a court of equity; and, moreover, if any man be convicted upon information or indictment of winning or lofing at play, or by betting at any one time 10l. or 20l. within twenty-four hours, he fhall be fined five times the fum for the benefit of the poor of the parifh. Thus careful has the legiflature been to prevent this deftructive vice: which may fhew that our laws againft gaming are not fo deficient, as ourfelves and our magiftrates in putting thofe laws in execution.

9. Laftly, there is another offence, conftituted by a variety of acts of parliament. That of deftroying fuch beafts and fowls as are ranked under the denomination of *game*. The ftatutes for preferving the game are many and various, and not a little obfcure and intricate. It is in general fufficient to obferve, that the *qualifications* for killing game, as they are ufual-

---

(a) "Unlefs," by the fame act, at "*Newmarket Heath*, in the counties of *Cambridge* and *Suffolk*, or *Black Hambleton*, in the county of *York*."

ly called, or more properly the *exemptions* from the penalties inflicted by the statute law, are, 1. The having a freehold estate of 100l. *per annum*; there being fifty times the property required to enable a man to kill a partridge, as to vote for a knight of the shire. 2. A leasehold for ninety-nine years of 150l. *per annum*. 3. Being the son and heir apparent of an esquire (a very loose and vague description) or person of superior degree. 4. Being the owner, or keeper, of a forest, park, chase, or warren. For unqualified persons transgressing these laws, by killing game, or keeping engines for that purpose, or even having game in their custody, or for persons (however qualified) that kill game, or have it in possession, at unseasonable times of the year, or unseasonable hours of the day or night, on sundays or on Christmas day, there are various penalties assigned, corporal and pecuniary, by different statutes; on any of which, but only on one at a time, the justices may convict in a summary way, (or in most of them) prosecutions may be carried on at the assises. And, lastly, by statute 28 Geo. II. c. 12. no person, however qualified to *kill*, may make merchandize of this valuable privilege, by *selling* or exposing to sale any game, on pain of like forfeiture as if he had no qualification.

## CHAPTER XIII.

### OF HOMICIDE.

IN the ten preceding chapters we have confidered, first, such crimes and misdemesnors as are more immediately injurious to God and his holy religion; secondly, such as violate or transgress the law of nations; thirdly, such as more especially affect the king, the father and representative of his people: fourthly, such as more directly infringe the rights of the public or commonwealth, taken in its collective capacity; and are now, lastly, to take into consideration those which in a more peculiar manner affect and injure *individuals* or private subjects.

The crimes and misdemesnors against private subjects are, principally, of three kinds; against their *persons*, their *habitations*, and their *property*.

Of crimes injurious to the *persons* of private subjects, the most principal and important is the offence of taking away that life, which is the immediate gift of the great Creator. The subject therefore of the present chapter will be the offence of *homicide*, or destroying the life of man, in its several stages of guilt, arising from the particular circumstances of mitigation or aggravation which attend it.

Now homicide, or the killing of any human creature, is of three kinds; *justifiable*, *excusable*, and *felonious*. The first has no share of guilt at all; the second very little; but the third is the highest crime against the law of nature that man is capable of committing.

I. Justifiable homicide is of divers kinds.

1. Such as is owing to some unavoidable *necessity*, without any will, intention, or desire, and without any inadvertence or negligence, in the party killing, and therefore without any shadow of blame.

2. Homicides, committed for the *advancement* of public *justice*, are, 1. Where an officer, in the execution of his office, either in a civil or criminal case, kills a person that assaults and resists him. 2. If an officer, or an private person, attempts to take a man charged with felony, and is resisted, and, in the endeavour to take him, kills him. 3. In case of a riot, or rebellious assembly, the officers endeavouring to disperse the mob are justifiable in killing them, both at common law, and by the riot act, 1 Geo. 1. c. 5. 4. Where the prisoners in a gaol, or going to gaol, assault the gaoler or officer, and he in his defence kills any of them, it is justifiable, for the sake of preventing any escape. 5. If trespassers in forests, parks, chases, or warrens, will not surrender themselves to the keepers, they may be slain, by virtue of the statute 21 Edw. I. st. 2. *de malefactoribus in parcis*, and 3 & 4 W. & M. c. 10. But, in all these cases, there must be an apparent necessity on the officer's side, viz. that the party could not be arrested or apprehended, the riot

could not be fuppreffed, the prifoners could not be kept in hold, the deer-ftealers could not but efcape, unlefs fuch homicide were committed: otherwife, without fuch abfolute neceffity, it is not juftifiable.

3. In the next place, fuch homicide, as is committed for the *prevention* of any forcible and atrocious *crime*, is juftifiable by the law of nature; and alfo by the law of England; for by ftatute 24 Hen. VIII. c. 5. If any perfon attempts a robbery or murder of another, or attempts to break open a houfe *in the night time*, (which extends alfo to an attempt to burn it) and fhall be killed in fuch attempt, the flayer fhall be acquitted and difcharged. This reaches not to any crime unaccompanied with force, as picking of pockets; or to the breaking open of any houfe *in the day time*, unlefs it carries with it an attempt of robbery alfo.

The law likewife juftifies a woman, killing one who attempts to ravifh her: and fo too the hufband or father may juftify killing a man who attempts a rape upon his wife or daughter; but not if he takes them in adultery by confent, for the one is forcible and felonious, but not the other. And I make no doubt but the forcibly attempting a crime of a ftill more deteftable nature, may be equally refifted by the death of the unnatural aggreffor. For the one uniform principle that runs through our own, and all other laws, feems to be this: that where a crime, in itfelf capital, is endeavoured to be committed by force, it is lawful to repel that force by the death of the party attempting.

In thefe inftances of *juftifiable* homicide, it may be obferved that the flayer is in no kind of fault whatfoever, not even in the minuteft degree; and is therefore to be totally acquitted and difcharged; with commendation rather than blame. But that is not quite the cafe in *excufable* homicide, the very name whereof imports fome fault, fome error, or omiffion; fo trivial however, that the law excufes it from the guilt of felony, though in ftrictnefs it judges it deferving of fome little degree of punifhment.

II. Excufable homicide is of two forts; either *per infortunium*, by mifadventure; or *fe defendendo*, upon a principle of self-preservation. We will first see wherein these two species of homicide are distinct, and then wherein they agree.

1. Homicide *per infortunium* or *misadventure*, is where a man, doing a lawful act, without any intention of hurt, unfortunately kills another: as where a man is at work with a hatchet, and the head thereof flies off and kills a stander-by; or, where a person, qualified to keep a gun, is shooting at a mark, and undesignedly kills a man: for the act is lawful, and the effect is merely accidental. So where a parent is moderately correcting his child, a master his apprentice or scholar, or an officer punishing a criminal, and happens to occasion his death, it is only misadventure; for the act of correction was lawful: but if he exceeds the bounds of moderation, either in the manner, the instrument, or the quantity of punishment, and death ensues, it is manslaughter at least, and in some cases (according to the circumstances) murder; for the act of immoderate correction is unlawful. Likewise, to whip another's horse, whereby he runs over a child and kills him, is held to be accidental in the rider, for he has done nothing unlawful; but manslaughter in the person who whipped him, for the act was a trespass, and at best a piece of idleness, of inevitably dangerous consequence. And, in general, if death ensues, in consequence of an idle, dangerous, and unlawful sport, as shooting or casting stones in a town, or the barbarous diversion of cock-throwing, in these and similar cases, the slayer is guilty of manslaughter, and not misadventure only, for these are unlawful acts.

2. Homicide in *self-defence*, or *se defendendo*, upon a sudden affray, is also excusable rather than justifiable, by the English law. The self-defence, which we are now speaking of, is that whereby a man may protect himself from an assault, or the like, in the course of a sudden brawl or quarrel, by killing him who assaults him. And this is what the law expresses by the word *chance-medley*. This right of natural defence does not imply a right of attacking: for, instead of attacking one another for injuries past or impending, men need only have recourse to the proper tribunals of justice. They cannot therefore legally exercise this right of

preventive defence, but in fudden and violent cafes ; when certain and immediate fuffering would be the confequence of waiting for the affiftance of the law. Wherefore, to excufe homicide by the plea of felf-defence, it muft appear that the flayer had no other poffible (or, at leaft, probable) means of efcaping from his affailant.

Under this excufe, of felf-defence, the principal civil and natural relations are comprehended ; therefore mafter and fervant, parent and child, hufband and wife, killing an affailant in the neceffary defence of each other refpectively, are excufed ; the act of the relation affifting being conftrued the fame as the act of the party himfelf.

III. Felonious homicide is an act of a very different nature from the former, being the killing of a human creature of any age or fex, without juftification or excufe. This may be done either by killing one's felf, or another man.

Self-murder, the law has ranked among the higheft crimes, making it a peculiar fpecies of felony, a felony committed on one's felf. And this admits of acceffories before the fact, as well as other felonies ; for if one perfuades another to kill himfelf, and he does fo, the advifer is guilty of murder. But what punifhment can human laws inflict on one who has withdrawn himfelf from their reach ? They can only act upon what he has left behind him, his reputation and fortune : on the former by an ignominious burial in the highway, with a ftake driven through his body ; on the latter, by a forfeiture of all his goods and chattels to the king : hoping that his care either for his own reputation, or the welfare of his family, would be fome motive to reftrain him from fo defperate and wicked an act. And it is obfervable, that this forfeiture has relation to the time of the act done in the felon's lifetime, which was the caufe of his death. As if hufband and wife be poffeffed jointly of a term of years in land, and the hufband drowns himfelf, the land fhall be forfeited to the king, and the wife fhall not have it by furvivorfhip. For by the act of cafting himfelf into the water he forfeits the term; which gives a title to the king, prior to the wife's title by furvivorfhip, which could not accrue till the inftant of her hufband's death.

The other fpecies of criminal homicide is that of killing another man. But in this there are alfo degrees of guilt, which divide the offence into *manflaughter* and *murder*. The difference between which may be partly collected from what has been incidentally mentioned in the preceding articles, and principally confifts in this, that manflaughter (when voluntary) arifes from the fudden heat of the paffions, murder from the wickednefs of the heart.

1. Manflaughter is therefore thus defined, the unlawful killing of another, without malice either exprefs or implied: which may be either voluntarily, upon a fudden heat; or involuntarily, but in the commiffion of fome unlawful act. And hence it follows, that in manflaughter there can be no acceffories before the fact; becaufe it muft be done without premeditation.

As to the firft, or *voluntary* branch: if upon a fudden quarrel two perfons fight, and one of them kills the other, this is manflaughter: and fo it is, if they upon fuch an occafion go out and fight in a field; for this is one continued act of paffion: and the law pays that regard to human frailty, as not to put a hafty and deliberate act upon the fame footing with regard to guilt. So alfo if a man be greatly provoked, as by pulling his nofe, or other great indignity, and immediately kills the aggreffor, though this is not excufable *fe defendendo*, fince there is no abfolute neceffity for doing it to preferve himfelf; yet neither is it murder, for there is no previous malice; but it is manflaughter. But in this, and in every other cafe of homicide upon provocation, if there be a fufficient cooling time for paffion to fubfide and reafon to interpofe, and the perfon fo provoked afterwards kills the other, this is deliberate revenge and not heat of blood, and accordingly amounts to murder. Manflaughter therefore on a fudden provocation differs from excufable homicide *fe defendendo* in this: that in one cafe there is an apparent neceffity, for felf-prefervation, to kill the aggreffor; in the other no neceffity at all, being only a fudden act of revenge.

The second branch, or involuntary manslaughter, differs also from homicide excusable by misadventure in this; that misadventure always happens in consequence of a lawful act, but this species of manslaughter in consequence of an unlawful one. As if two persons play at sword and buckler, unless by the king's command, and one of them kills the other: this is manslaughter, because the original act was unlawful; but it is not murder, for the one had no intent to do the other any personal mischief. So where a person does an act, lawful in itself, but in an unlawful manner, and without due caution and circumspection: as when a workman flings down a stone or piece of timber into the street, and kills a man; this may be either misadventure, manslaughter, or murder, according to the circumstances under which the original act was done: if it were in a country village, where few passengers are, and he calls out to all people to have a care, it is misadventure only; but if it were in London, or other populous town, where people are continually passing, it is manslaughter, though he gives loud warning; and murder, if he knows of their passing, and gives no warning at all, for then it is malice against all mankind. And, in general, when an involuntary killing happens in consequence of an unlawful act, it will be either **murder or manslaughter** according to the nature of the act which occasioned it. If it be in prosecution of a felonious intent, or in it's consequences naturally tended to bloodshed, it will be murder; but if no more was intended than a mere civil trespass, it will only amount to manslaughter.

Next, as to the *punishment* of this degree of homicide: the crime of manslaughter amounts to felony, but within the benefit of clergy; and the offender shall be burnt in the hand, and forfeit all his goods and chattels (*a*).

---

(*a*) But, by 19 Geo. III. c. 74. sec. 3. "it shall be lawful for the court, instead of such burning, to impose upon such offender a moderate pecuniary fine, or otherwise (except in the case of manslaughter) to order that such offender shall be publickly or privately whipt; and such fine and whipping shall have the like effect in all respects as to the party, as if the offender had been burned as aforesaid."

But there is one species of manslaughter, which is punished as murder, the benefit of clergy being taken away from it by statute; namely, the offence of mortally *stabbing* another, though done upon sudden provocation. For by statute 1 Jac. I. c. 8. when one thrusts or stabs another, not then having a weapon drawn, or who hath not then first stricken the party stabbing, so that he dies thereof within six months after, the offender shall not have the benefit of clergy, though he did it not of malice aforethought. But the benignity of the law hath construed the statute so favourably in behalf of the subject, and so strictly when against him, that the offence of stabbing now stands almost upon the same footing, as it did at the common law.

2. We are next to consider the crime of deliberate and wilful *murder*; a crime at which human nature starts, and which is I believe punished almost universally throughout the world with death.

Murder is thus defined, or rather described, by sir Edward Coke; " when a person, of sound memory and discre-
" tion, unlawfully killeth any reasonable creature in being,
" and under the king's peace, with malice aforethought, ei-
" ther express or implied." The best way of examining the nature of this crime will be by considering the several branches of this definition.

First, it must be committed by *a person of sound memory and discretion:* for lunatics or infants, as was formerly observed, are incapable of committing any crime : unless in such cases where they shew a consciousness of doing wrong, and of course a discretion, or discernment between good and evil.

Next, it happens when a person of such found discretion *unlawfully killeth.* The unlawfulness arises from the killing without warrant or excuse: and there must also be an actual killing to constitute murder; for a bare assault, with intent to kill, is only a great misdemesnor, though formerly it was held to be murder. The killing may be by poisoning, striking, starving, drowning, and a thousand other forms of death, by which human nature may be overcome. And if a person be indicted for one species of killing, as by *poisoning,* he cannot be convicted by evidence of a totally different species of death, as by *shooting* with a pistol or *starving*. But where they only differ in circumstance, as if a *wound* be alledged to be given with a sword, and it proves to have arisen from a staff, an axe, or a hatchet, this difference is immaterial. If a man does such an act, of which the probable consequence may be, and eventually is, death; such killing may be murder, although no stroke be struck by himself, and no killing may be primarily intended: as was the case of the unnatural son, who exposed his sick father to the air, against his will, by reason whereof he died; of the harlot who laid her child under leaves in an orchard, where a kite struck it and killed it; and of the parish-officers, who shifted a child from parish to parish, till it died for want of care and sustenance. So too, if a man hath a beast that is used to do mischief; and he knowing it, *suffers* it to go abroad, and it kills a man; even this is manslaughter in the owner: but if he had purposely *turned it loose*, though barely to frighten people and make what is called sport, it is with us (as in the Jewish law) as much murder, as if he had incited a bear or dog to worry them. If a physician or surgeon gives his patient a potion or plaister to cure him, which, contrary to expectation, kills him, this is neither murder, nor manslaughter, but misadventure; and he shall not be punished criminally, however liable he might formerly have been to a civil action for neglect or ignorance. In order also to make the killing murder, it is requisite that the party die within a year and a day after the stroke received, or cause of death administered; in the computation of which, the whole day upon which the hurt was done shall be reckoned the first.

Farther; the person killed must be " *a reasonable creature* " *in being, and under the king's peace*," at the time of the killing. To kill a child in it's mother's womb, is now no murder, but a great misprision: but if the child be born alive, and dieth by reason of the potion or bruises it received in the womb, it seems, by the better opinion, to be murder in such as administered or gave them. But, as there is one case where it is difficult to prove the child being born alive, namely, in the case of the murder of bastard children by the unnatural mother, it is enacted, by statute 21 Jac. I. c. 27. that if any woman be delivered of a child, which if born alive should by law be a bastard; and endeavours privately to conceal it's death, by burying the child or the like; the mother so offending shall suffer death as in the case of murder, unless she can prove by one witness at least that the child was actually born dead: but I apprehend it has of late years been usual, upon trials for this offence, to require some sort of presumptive evidence that the child was born alive, before the other constrained presumption (that the child, whose death is concealed, was therefore killed by it's parent) is admitted to convict the prisoner.

Lastly, the killing must be committed *with malice aforethought*, to make it the crime of murder. This is the grand criterion which now distinguishes murder from other killing: and this malice prepense, *malitia præcogitata*, is not so properly spite or malevolence to the deceased in particular, as any evil design in general; the dictate of a wicked, depraved, and malignant heart: *un disposition a faire un male chose:* and it may be either *express*, or *implied* in law. Express malice is when one, with a sedate deliberate mind and formed design, doth kill another: which formed design is evidenced by external circumstances discovering that inward intention; as lying in wait, antecedent menaces, former grudges, and concerted schemes to do him some bodily harm. This takes in the case of deliberate duelling, where both parties meet avowedly with an intent to murder: and therefore the law has justly fixed the crime and punishment of murder on them, and on their seconds also. Also, if even upon a sudden provocation one beats another in a cruel and unusual manner, so that he dies, though he did not intend his death, yet he is guilty of murder by express malice; that is, by an express evil design, the genuine sense of *malitia*. Neither shall he be guilty of a less crime, who kills another in consequence of such a wilful act, as shews him to be an enemy to all mankind in general; as going deliberately, and with an intent to do mischief, upon a horse used to strike, or coolly discharging a gun, among a multitude of people. So if a man resolves to kill the next man he meets, and does kill him, it is murder, although he knew him not; for this is universal malice. And, if two or more come together to do an unlawful act against the king's peace, of which the probable consequence might be bloodshed; as to beat a man, to commit a riot, or to rob a park: and one of them kills a man; it is murder in them all, because of the unlawful act, the *malitia præcogitata*, or evil intended beforehand.

Also in many cases where no malice is expressed, the law will imply it: as, where a man wilfully poisons another, in such a deliberate act the law presumes malice, though no particular enmity can be proved. And if a man kills another suddenly, without any, or without a considerable provocation, the law implies malice; for no person, unless of an abandoned heart, would be guilty of such an act, upon a slight or no apparent cause. No affront by words or gestures only, is a sufficient provocation, so as to excuse or extenuate such acts of violence as manifestly endanger the life of another. But if the person so provoked had unfortunately killed the other, by beating him in such a manner as shewed only an intent to chastise and not to kill him, the law so far considers the provocation of contumelious behaviour, as to adjudge it only manslaughter, and not murder. In like manner if one kills an officer of justice, either civil or criminal, in the execution of his duty, or any of his assistants endeavouring to conserve the peace, or any private person endeavouring to suppress an affray or apprehend a felon, knowing his authority or the intention with which he interposes, the law will imply malice, and the killer shall be guilty of murder. And if one intends to do another felony, and undesignedly kills a man, this is also murder. Thus if one shoots at A and misses *him*, but kills B, this is murder; because of the previous felonious intent, which the law transfers from one to the other. The same is the case where one lays poison for A; and B, against whom the prisoner had no malicious intent, takes it, and it kills him; this is likewife murder. So alfo, if one gives a woman with child a medicine to procure abortion, and it operates fo violently as to kill the woman, this is murder in the perfon who gave it. It were endlefs to go through all the cafes of homicide, which have been adjudged either exprefsly, or impliedly, malicious: thefe therefore may fuffice as a fpecimen; and we may take it for a general rule that all homicide is malicious, and of courfe amounts to murder, unlefs where *juftified* by the command or permiffion of the law; *excufed* on the account of accident or felf-prefervation; or *alleviated* into manflaughter, by being either the involuntary confequence of fome act, not ftrictly lawful, or (if voluntary) occafioned by fome fudden and fufficiently violent provocation. And all thefe circumftances of juftification, excufe, or alleviation, it is incumbent upon the prifoner to make out, to the fatisfaction of the court and jury: the latter of whom are to decide whether the circumftances alledged are proved to have actually exifted; the former, how far they extend to take away or mitigate the guilt. For all homicide is prefumed to be malicious, until the contrary appeareth upon evidence.

The punifhment of murder, and that of manflaughter, were formerly one and the fame; both having the benefit of clergy. But now, by feveral ftatutes, the benefit of clergy is taken away from murderers through malice prepenfe, their abetters, procurers, and counfellors. It is enacted by ftatute 25 Geo. II. c. 37. that the judge, before whom any perfon is found guilty of wilful murder, fhall pronounce fentence immediately after conviction, unlefs he fees caufe to poftpone it; and fhall in paffing fentence direct him to be executed on the next day but one, (unlefs the fame fhall be Sunday, and then on the Monday following) and that his body be delivered to the furgeons to be diffected and anatomized; and that the judge may direct his body to be afterwards hung in chains, but in no wife to be buried without diffection. And, during the fhort but awful interval between fentence and execution, the prifoner fhall be kept alone, and fuftained with only bread and water. But a power is allowed to the judge upon good and sufficient cause to respite the execution, and relax the other restraints of this act.

Petit treason, (which is an aggravated degree of murder) according to the statute 25 Edw. III. c. 2. may happen three ways: by a servant killing his master, a wife her husband, or an ecclesiastical person (either secular, or regular) his superior, to whom he owes faith and obedience. A servant who kills his master whom he has left, upon a grudge conceived against him during his service, is guilty of petit treason: for the traiterous intention was hatched while the relation subsisted between them; and this is only an execution of that intention. So if a wife be divorced *a mensa et thoro*, still the *vinculum matrimonii* subsists; and if she kills such divorced husband, she is a traitress. And a clergyman is understood to owe canonical obedience to the bishop who ordained him, to him in whose diocese he is beneficed, and also to the metropolitan of such suffragan or diocesan bishop: and therefore to kill any of these is petit treason. As to the rest, whatever has been said, or remains to be observed hereafter, with respect to wilful murder, is also applicable to the crime of petit treason, which is no other than murder in it's most odious degree: except that the trial shall be as in cases of high treason, before the improvements therein made by the statutes of William III. But a person indicted of petit treason may be acquitted thereof, and found guilty of manslaughter or murder: and in such case it should seem that *two* witnesses are not necessary, as in case of petit treason they are. Which crime is also distinguished from murder in it's punishment.

The punishment of petit treason, in a man, is to be drawn and hanged, and, in a woman, to be drawn and burned (*a*). Persons guilty of petit treason were first debarred the benefit of clergy, by statute 12 Hen. VII. c. 7. which has been since extended to their aiders, abettors, and counsellors, by statutes 23 Hen. VIII. c. 1. and 4 & 5 P. & M. c. 4.

---

(*a*) This barbarous law, in respect to the punishment of female criminals, is now repealed. See *ante*, p. 448. n. (*a*).

## CHAPTER XIV.

### OF OFFENCES AGAINST THE PERSONS OF INDIVIDUALS.

HAVING in the preceding chapter confidered the principal crime, or public wrong, that can be committed againſt a private fubject, namely, by deſtroying his life; I proceed now to enquire into fuch other crimes and miſdemeſnors, as more peculiarly affect the fecurity of his perfon while living.

Of theſe ſome are felonious, and in their nature capital: others are ſimple miſdemeſnors, and puniſhable with a lighter animadverſion. Of the felonies the firſt is that of *mayhem*.

I. Mayhem, was in part confidered in the preceding book, as a civil injury: but it is alſo looked upon in a criminal light by the law, being an atrocious breach of the king's peace, and an offence tending to deprive him of the aid and aſſiſtance of his ſubjects. By ſtatute 22 & 23 Car. II. c. 1. it is enacted, that if any perfon ſhall of malice aforethought, and by laying in wait, unlawfully cut out or difable the tongue, put out an eye, ſlit the nofe, cut off a nofe or lip, or cut off or diſable any limb or member of any other perfon, *with an intent to maim or to disfigure him;* ſuch perfon, his counſellors, aiders, and abettors, ſhall be guilty of felony without benefit of clergy.

Thus much for the felony of mayhem: to which may be added the offence of wilfully and maliciouſly ſhooting at any perfon, in any dwelling-houſe or other place; an offence, of which the probable confequence may be either killing or maiming him. This, though no fuch evil confequence enfues, is made felony without benefit of clergy by ſtatute 9 Geo. I. c. 22.

II. The fecond offence, more immediately affecting the perfonal fecurity of individuals, relates to the female part of his majeſty's ſubjects; being that of their *forcible abduction* and *marriage*, which is vulgarly called *ſtealing an heirefs*.

For by statute 3 Hen. VII. c. 2. it is enacted, that if any person shall for lucre take any woman, being maid, widow, or wife, and having substance either in goods or lands, or being heir apparent to her ancestors, contrary to her will, and afterwards she be married to such misdoer, or by his consent to another, or defiled, such person, his procurers and abettors, and such as knowingly receive such woman, shall be deemed principal felons: and by statute 39 Eliz. c. 9. the benefit of clergy is taken away from all such felons, who shall be principals, procurers, or accessories *before* the fact.

In the construction of this statute it hath been determined, 1. That the indictment must allege that the taking was for lucre, for such are the words of the statute. 2. In order to shew this, it must appear that the woman has substance either real or personal, or is an heir apparent. 3. It must appear that she was taken away against her will. 4. It must also appear that she was afterwards married, or defiled. And, though possibly the marriage or defilement might be by her subsequent consent, being won thereunto by flatteries after the taking, yet this is felony, if the first taking were against her will: and so *vice versa*, if the woman be originally taken away with her own consent, yet if she afterwards refuse to continue with the offender, and be forced against her will, she may, from that time, as properly be said to be taken against her will, as if she never had given any consent at all; for, till the force was put upon her, she was in her own power. It is held that a woman, thus taken away and married, may be sworn and give evidence against the offender, though he is her husband *de facto*, contrary to the general rule of law: because he is no husband *de jure*, in case the actual marriage was also against her will. In cases indeed where the actual marriage is good, by the consent of the inveigled woman obtained after her forcible abduction, sir Matthew Hale seems to question how far her evidence should be allowed: but other authorities seem to agree that it should even then be admitted; deeming it absurd, that the offender should thus take advantage of his own wrong, and that the very act of marriage, which is a principal ingredient of his crime, should (by a forced construction of law) be made use of to stop the mouth of the most material witness against him.

An inferior degree of the same kind of offence, but not attended with force, is punished by the statute 4 & 5 Ph. & Mar. c. 8. which enacts, that if any person, above the age of fourteen, unlawfully shall convey or *take away any woman child unmarried*, (which is held to extend to bastards as well as to legitimate children) within the age of sixteen years, from the possession and against the will of the father, mother, guardians, or governors, he shall be imprisoned two years, or fined at the discretion of the justices: and if he deflowers such maid or woman child, or, without the consent of parents, contracts matrimony with her, *he* shall be imprisoned five years, or fined at the discretion of the justices, and *she* shall forfeit all her lands to her next of kin, during the life of her said husband. But this latter part of the act is now rendered almost useless, by provisions of a very different kind, which make the marriage totally void, in the statute 26 Geo. II, c. 33.

III. A third offence against the female part also of his majesty's subjects, but attended with greater aggravations than that of forcible marriage, is the crime of *rape, raptus mulierum*, or the carnal knowlege of a woman forcibly and against her will. This, by statute 18 Eliz. c. 7. is made felony without benefit of clergy: as is also the abominable wickedness of carnally knowing and abusing any woman child under the age of ten years; in which case the consent or non consent is immaterial, as by reason of her tender years she is incapable of judgment and discretion. And the law holds it to be felony to force even a concubine or harlot, because the woman may have forsaken that unlawful course of life: for, as Bracton well observes, " *licet meret ix fuerit antea, certe tunc temporis non fuit, cum reclamando nequitiæ ejus consentire noluit.*"

These are all the felonious offences more immediately against the personal security of the subject.

IV. The inferior offences, or misdemesnors, that fall under this head, are *aſſaults, batteries, wounding, falſe impriſonment,* and *kidnapping.* With regard to the nature of theſe offences in general, I have nothing farther to add to what has already been obſerved in the preceding book of theſe commentaries; when we conſidered them as private wrongs, or civil injuries, for which a ſatisfaction or remedy is given to the party aggrieved. But, taken in a public light, as a breach of the king's peace, an affront to his government, and a damage done to his ſubjects, they are alſo indictable and puniſhable with fines and impriſonment; or with other ignominious corporal penalties, where they are committed with any very atrocious deſign.

## CHAPTER XV.

### OF OFFENCES AGAINST THE HABITATIONS OF INDIVIDUALS.

THE only two offences, that more immediately affect the *habitations* of individuals or private ſubjects, are thoſe of *arſon* and *burglary.*

I. Arſon, *ab ardendo,* is the malicious and wilful burning of the houſe or out-houſe of another man.

Our law diſtinguiſhes with much accuracy upon this crime. And therefore we will inquire, firſt, what is ſuch a houſe as may be the ſubject of this offence; next, wherein the offence itſelf conſiſts, or what amounts to a burning of ſuch houſe; and, laſtly, how the offence is puniſhed.

1. Not only the bare dwelling houſe, but all out-houſes that are parcel thereof, though not contiguous thereto, nor under the ſame roof, as barns and ſtables, may be the ſubject of arſon. The offence of arſon (ſtrictly ſo called) may be committed by wilfully ſetting fire to one's own houſe, provided one's neighbour's houſe is thereby alſo burnt; but if no miſchief is done but to one's own, it does not amount to felony, though the fire was kindled with intent to burn ano-

ther's. For by the common law no intention to commit a felony amounts to the same crime; though it does, in some cases, by particular statutes. However such wilful firing one's own house, *in a town*, is a high misdemesnor, and punishable by fine, imprisonment, pillory, and perpetual sureties for the good behaviour. And if a landlord or reversioner sets fire to his own house, of which another is in possession under lease from himself or from those whose estate he hath, it shall be accounted arson; for, during the lease, the house is the property of the tenant.

2. As to what shall be called a *burning*, so as to amount to arson: a bare intent, or attempt to do it, by actually setting fire to an house, unless it absolutely *burns*, does not fall within the description of *incendit et combussit;* which were words necessary, in the days of law-latin, to all indictments of this sort. But the burning and consuming of any part is sufficient; though the fire be afterwards extinguished. Also it must be a *malicious* burning; otherwise it is only a trespass: and therefore no negligence or mischance amounts to it. But by statute 6 Ann. c. 31. any servant negligently setting fire to a house or outhouses, shall forfeit 100l. or be sent to the house of correction for eighteen months.

3. The *punishment* of arson, and of all capital felonies is uniform, namely, by hanging.

II. Burglary, or nocturnal housebreaking. The definition of a burglar, as given by sir Edward Coke, is, " he that " by night breaketh and entereth into a mansion-house, with " intent to commit a felony." In this definition there are four things to be considered; the *time*, the *place*, the *manner*, and the *intent*.

1. The *time* must be by night, and not by day: for in the day time there is no burglary. We have seen, in the case of justifiable homicide, how much more heinous all laws made an attack by night, rather than by day; allowing the party attacked by night to kill the assailant with impunity. As to what is reckoned night, and what day, for this purpose, the better opinion seems to be, that if there be daylight or

*crepufculum* enough, begun or left, to difcern a man's face withal, it is no burglary. But this does not extend to moonlight; for then many midnight burglaries would go unpuniſhed: and befides, the malignity of the offence does not fo properly arife from its being done in the dark, as at the dead of night, when all the creation, except beafts of prey, are at reft; when fleep has difarmed the owner, and rendered his caftle defencelefs.

2. As to the *place*. It muſt be, according to fir Edward Coke's definition, in a *manfion* houfe. but the requifite of its being *domus manfionalis* is only in the burglary of a private houfe: which is the moſt frequent, and in which it is indifpenfably neceffary to form its guilt, that it muſt be in a manfion or dwelling houfe. For no diftant barn, warehoufe, or the like, are under the fame privileges, nor looked upon as a man's caftle of defence: nor is a breaking open of houfes wherein no man refides, and which therefore for the time being are not manfion-houfes, attended with the fame circumftances of midnight terror. A houfe, however, wherein a man fometimes refides, and which the owner hath only left for a ſhort feafon, *animo revertendi*, is the object of burglary, though no one be in it, at the time of the fact committed. And if the barn, ſtable, or warehoufe, be parcel of the manfion houfe, and within the fame common fence, though not under the fame roof or contiguous, a burglary may be committed therein; for the capital houfe protects and privileges all its branches and appurtenants if within the curtilage or homeſtall. A chamber in a college or an inn of court, where each inhabitant hath a diſtinct property, is, to all other purpofes as well as this, the manfion-houfe of the owner. So alfo is a room or lodging in any private houfe, the manfion for the time being of the lodger; if the owner doth not himfelf dwell in the houfe, or if he and the lodger enter by different outward doors. But, if the owner himfelf lies in the houfe, and hath but one outward door at which he and his lodgers enter, fuch lodgers feem only to be inmates, and all their apartments to be parcel of the one dwelling houfe of the owner. Thus too the houfe of a corpora-

tion, inhabited in separate apartments by the officers of the body corporate, is the mansion house of the corporation, and not of the respective officers. But if I hire a shop, parcel of another man's house, and work or trade in it, but never lie there, it is no dwelling-house, nor can burglary be committed therein: for by the lease it is severed from the rest of the house, and therefore is not the dwelling house of him who occupies the other part; neither can I be said to dwell therein when I never lie there. Neither can burglary be committed in a tent or booth erected in a market or fair, though the owner may lodge therein: for the law regards thus highly nothing but permanent edifices; a house, or church, the wall or gate of a town; and though it may be the choice of the owner to lodge in so fragile a tenement, yet his lodging there no more makes it burglary to break it open, than it would be to uncover a tilted waggon in the same circumstances.

3. As to the *manner* of committing burglary: there must be both a breaking and an entry to complete it. But they need not be both done at once; for, if a hole be broken one night, and the same breakers enter the next night through the same, they are burglars. There must in general be an actual breaking, not a mere legal *clausum fregit*, (by leaping over invisible ideal boundaries, which may constitute a civil trespass) but a substantial and forcible irruption. As at least by breaking, or taking out the glass of, or otherwise opening, a window; picking a lock, or opening it with a key; nay, by lifting up the latch of a door, or unloosing any other fastening which the owner has provided. But if a person leaves his doors or windows open, it is his own folly and negligence; and if a man enters therein, it is no burglary: yet, if he afterwards unlocks an inner or chamber door, it is so. But to come down a chimney is held a burglarious entry; for that is as much closed, as the nature of things will permit. So also to knock at a door, and upon opening it to rush in, with a felonious intent; or, under pretence of taking lodgings, to fall upon the landlord and rob him; or to procure a constable to gain admittance, in order to

search for traitors, and then to bind the constable and rob the house; all these entries have been adjudged burglarious, though there was no actual breaking: for the law will not suffer itself to be trifled with by such evasions, especially under the cloak of legal process. And so, if a servant opens and enters his master's chamber door with a felonious design; or if any other person lodging in the same house, or in a public inn, opens and enters another's door, with such evil intent; it is burglary. Nay, if the servant conspires with a robber, and lets him into the house by night, this is burglary in both: for the servant is doing an unlawful act, and the opportunity afforded him, of doing it with greater ease, rather aggravates than extenuates the guilt. As for the entry, any the least degree of it, with any part of the body, or with an instrument held in the hand, is sufficient: as, to step over the threshold, to put a hand or a hook in at a window to draw out goods, or a pistol to demand one's money, are all of them burglarious entries. The entry may be before the breaking, as well as after: for by statute 12 Ann. c. 7. if a person enters into the dwelling-house of another, without breaking in, either by day or by night, with intent to commit felony, or, being in such a house, shall commit any felony; and shall in the night break out of the same, this is declared to be burglary; there having before been different opinions concerning it: lord Bacon holding the affirmative, and sir Matthew Hale the negative. But it is universally agreed, that there must be both a breaking, either in fact or by implication, and also an entry, in order to complete the burglary.

4. As to the *intent*; it is clear, that such breaking and entry must be with a felonious intent, otherwise it is only a trespass. And it is the same, whether such intention be actually carried into execution, or only demonstrated by some attempt or overt act, of which the jury is to judge. And therefore such a breach and entry of a house as has been before described, by night, with intent to commit a robbery, a murder, a rape, or any other felony, is burglary; whether the thing be actually perpetrated or not. Nor does it make

any difference, whether the offence were felony at common law, or only created so by statute; since that statute, which makes an offence felony, gives it incidentally all the properties of a felony at common law.

Thus much for the nature of burglary; which is a felony at common law, but within the benefit of clergy. The statutes however of 1 Edw. VI. c. 12. and 18 Eliz. c. 7. take away clergy from the principals, and that of 3 & 4 W. & M. c. 9. from all abettors and accessories before the fact (*a*).

## CHAPTER XVI.

### OF OFFENCES AGAINST PRIVATE PROPERTY.

THE next, and last, species of offences against private subjects, are such as more immediately affect their property. Of which there are two, which are attended with a breach of the peace; *larciny*, and *malicious mischief*: and one, that is equally injurious to the rights of property, but attended with no act of violence; which is the crime of *forgery*. Of these three in their order.

I. Larciny, or *theft*, by contraction for latrociny, *latrocinium*, is distinguished by the law into two sorts; the one called *simple* larciny, or plain theft unaccompanied with any other atrocious circumstance; and *mixed* or *compound* larciny, which also includes in it the aggravation of a taking from one's house or person.

And, first, of *simple* larciny: which, when it is the stealing of goods above the value of twelvepence, is called *grand* larciny; when of goods to that value, or under, is *petit* larciny: offences, which are considerably distinguished in their

---

(*a*) Burglary in any house belonging to the plate-glass company, with intent to steal the stock or utensils, is by statute 13 Geo. III. c. 38. declared to be single felony, and punished with transportation for seven years. A.

## C. XVI. OFFENCES AGAINST PRIVATE PROPERTY. 513

punifhment, but not otherwife. I fhall therefore firft confider the nature of fimple larciny in general; and then fhall obferve the different degrees of punifhment inflicted on it's two feveral branches.

Simple larciny then is "the felonious taking, and carry-"ing away, of the perfonal goods of another." We will examine the nature of theft, or larciny, as laid down in the foregoing definition.

1. It muft be a *taking*. This implies the confent of the owner to be wanting. Therefore no delivery of the goods from the owner to the offender, upon truft, can ground a larciny. As if A lends B a horfe, and he rides away with him; or, if I fend goods by a carrier, and he carries them away; thefe are no larcinies (*a*). But if the carrier opens a bale or pack of goods, or pierces a veffel of wine, and takes away part thereof, or if he carries it to the place appointed, and afterwards takes away the whole, thefe are larcinies: for here the *animus furandi* is manifeft; fince in the firft cafe he had otherwife no inducement to open the goods, and in the fecond the truft was determined, the delivery having taken it's effect. But bare non-delivery fhall not of courfe be intended to arife from a felonious defign; fince that may happen from a variety of other accidents. Neither by the common law was it larciny in any fervant to run away with the goods committed to him to keep, but only a breach of civil truft. But by ftatute 33 Hen. VI. c. 1. the fervants of perfons deceafed, accufed of embezzling their mafter's goods, may by writ out of chancery (iffued by the advice of the chief juftices and chief baron, or any two of them) and proclamation made thereupon, be fummoned to appear perfonally in the court of king's bench, to anfwer their mafter's

---

(*a*) Unlefs the jury find that the horfe or goods were taken with an *intent* to convert to the perfons own ufe; in which cafe it is not the *pretence* or *avowed* purpofe for which they were taken, that will fcreen the offender. See the cafe of *Major Semple*, reported *Leach Cr. Law.* 355.

executors in any civil suit for such goods; and shall, on default of appearance, be attainted of felony. And, by statute 21 Hen. VIII. c. 7. if any servant embezzles his master's goods to the value of forty shillings, it is made felony; except in apprentices and servants under eighteen years old. But if he had not the possession, but only the care and oversight of the goods, as the butler of plate, the shepherd of sheep, and the like, the embezzling of them is felony at common law. So if a guest robs his inn or tavern of a piece of plate, it is larciny; for he hath not the possession delivered to him, but merely the use, and so it is declared to be by statute 3 & 4 W. & M. c. 9. if a lodger runs away with the goods from his ready-furnished lodgings. Under some circumstances also a man may be guilty of felony in taking his own goods: as if he steals them from a pawnbroker, or any one to whom he hath delivered and entrusted them, with intent to charge such bailee with the value; or if he robs his own messenger on the road, with intent to charge the hundred with the loss according to the statute of Winchester.

2. There must not only be a taking, but a *carrying away*: *cepit et asportavit* was the old law-latin. A bare removal from the place in which he found the goods, though the thief does not quite make off with them, is a sufficient asportation, or carrying away. As if a man be leading another's horse out of a close, and be apprehended in the fact; or if a guest, stealing goods out of an inn, has removed them from his chamber down stairs; these have been adjudged sufficient carryings away, to constitute a larciny. Or if a thief, intending to steal plate, takes it out of a chest in which it was, and lays it down upon the floor, but is surprized before he can make his escape with it; this is larciny.

3. This taking, and carrying away, must also be *felonious;* that is, done *animo furandi:* or, as the civil law expresses it, *lucri causa*. This requisite, besides excusing those who labour under incapacities of mind or will, indemnifies also mere trespassers, and other petty offenders. As if a servant takes his master's horse, without his knowlege,

and brings him home again: if a neighbour takes another's plough, that is left in the field, and ufes it upon his own land, and then returns it: if, under colour of arrear of rent, where none is due, I diftrein another's cattle, or feife them: all thefe are mifdemefnors and trefpaffes, but no felonies. The ordinary difcovery of a felonious intent is where the party doth it clandeftinely; or, being charged with the fact, denies it. But this is by no means the only criterion of criminality: for in cafes that may amount to larciny the variety of circumftances is fo great, and the complications thereof fo mingled, that it is impoffible to recount all thofe, which may evidence a felonious intent, or *animum furandi*: wherefore they muft be left to the due and attentive confideration of the court and jury.

4. This felonious taking and carrying away muft be *of the perfonal goods of another:* for if they are things *real*, or favour of the realty, larciny at the common law cannot be committed of them. Lands, tenements, and hereditaments (either corporeal or incorporeal) cannot in their nature be taken and carried away. And of things likewife that adhere to the freehold, as corn, grafs, trees, and the like, or lead upon a houfe, no larciny could be committed by the rules of the common law; but the feverance of them was, and in many things is ftill, merely a trefpafs: which depended on a fubtilty in the legal notions of our anceftors. Thefe things were parcel of the real eftate; and therefore, while they continued fo, could not by any poffibility be the fubject of theft, being abfolutely fixed and immoveable. And if they were fevered by violence, fo as to be changed into moveables; and at the fame time, by one and the fame continued act, carried off by the perfon who fevered them; they could never be faid to be taken *from* the *proprietor*, in this their newly acquired ftate of mobility, (which is effential to the nature of larciny) being never, as fuch, in the actual conftructive poffeffion of any one, but of him who committed the trefpafs. He could not in ftrictnefs be faid to have taken what at that time were the perfonal goods of another, fince the very act of tak-

ing was what turned them into perfonal goods. But if the thief fevers them at *one* time, whereby the trefpafs is completed, and they are converted into perfonal chattels, in the conftructive poffeffion of him on whofe foil they are left or laid; and comes again at *another* time, when they are fo. turned into perfonalty, and takes them away; it is larciny: and fo it is, if the owner, or any one elfe, has fevered them. And now, by the ftatute 4 Geo. II. c. 32. to fteal, or rip, cut, or break, with intent to fteal, any lead, or iron bar, rail, gate, or palifado, fixed to a dwelling-houfe or out-houfe, or in any court or garden thereunto belonging, or to any other building, is made felony, liable to tranfportation for feven years: and to fteal, damage, or deftroy underwood or hedges, and the like, to rob orchards or gardens of fruit growing therein, to fteal or otherwife deftroy any turnips, potatoes, cabbages, parfnips, peafe, or carrots, or the roots of madder when growing, are punifhable criminally, by whipping, fmall fines, imprifonment, and fatisfaction to the party wronged, according to the nature of the offence. Moreover the ftealing by night of any trees, or of any roots, fhrubs, or plants to the value of 5s. is, by ftatute 6 Geo. III. c. 36. made felony in the principals, aiders, and abettors, and in the purchafers thereof knowing the fame to be ftolen: and by ftatutes 6 Geo. III. c. 48. and 13 Geo. III. c. 33. the ftealing of any timber trees therein fpecified (a), and of any root, fhrub, or plant, by day, or night, is liable to pecuniary penalties for the two firft offences, and for the third is conftituted a felony liable to tranfportation for feven years. Stealing ore out of mines is alfo no larciny, upon the fame principle of adherence to the freehold; with an exception only to mines of black lead, the ftealing of ore out of which, or entering the fame with intent to fteal, is felony, punifhable with imprifonment and whipping, or tranfportation not ex-

---

(a) **Oak,** beech, chefnut, walnut, afh, elm, cedar, fir, afp, lime, fycamore, poplar, alder, larch, maple, and hornbeam. A.

C. XVI. OFFENCES AGAINST PRIVATE PROPERTY. 517

ceeding seven years; and to escape from such imprisonment or return from such transportation, is felony without benefit of clergy; by statute 25 Geo. II. c. 10. Upon nearly the same principle the stealing of writings relating to a real estate is no felony, but a trespass: because they concern the land, or (according to our technical language) *favour* of the *realty*, and are considered as part of it by the law; so that they descend to the heir together with the land which they concern.

Bonds, bills, and notes, which concern mere *choses* in *action*, were also at the common law held not to be such goods whereof larciny might be committed; being of no intrinsic value, and not importing any property in *possession* of the person from whom they are taken. But, by the statute 2 Geo. II. c. 25. they are now put upon the same footing, with respect to larcinies, as the money they were meant to secure. By statute 15 Geo. II. c. 13. officers or servants of the bank of England, secreting or embezzling any note, bill, warrant, bond, deed, security, money, or effects, intrusted with them or with the company, are guilty of felony without benefit of clergy. The same is enacted by statute 24 Geo. II. c. 11. with respect to officers and servants of the south-sea company. And, by statute 7 Geo. III. c. 50. if any officer or servant of the post-office shall secrete, embezzle, or destroy any letter or pacquet, containing any bank-note or other valuable paper particularly specified in the act, or shall steal the same out of any letter or pacquet, he shall be guilty of felony without benefit of clergy. Or, if he shall destroy any letter or pacquet with which he has received money for the postage, or shall advance the rate of postage on any letter or pacquet sent by the post, and shall secrete the money received by such advancement, he shall be guilty of single felony. Larciny also could not at common law be committed of treasure-trove, or wreck, till seised by the king or him who hath the franchise: for till such seisure no one hath a determinate property therein. But, by statute 26 Geo. II. c. 19. plundering or stealing from any ship-in distress (whether wreck or no wreck) is felony without benefit of clergy: in like manner as, by the civil law, this inhumanity is punifhed in the fame degree as the moft atrocious theft.

Larciny alfo cannot be committed of fuch animals, in which there is no property either abfolute or qualified; as of beafts that are *feræ naturæ*, and unreclaimed, fuch as deer, hares, and conies, in a foreft, chafe, or warren; fifh, in an open river or pond; or wild fowls at their natural liberty. But if they are reclaimed or confined, and may ferve for food, it is otherwife even at common law: for of deer fo inclofed in a park that they may be taken at pleafure, fifh in a trunk, and pheafants or partridges in a mew, larciny may be committed. And now, by ftatute 9 Geo. I. c. 22. to hunt, wound, kill, or fteal any deer; to rob a warren; or to fteal fifh from a river or pond, (being in thefe cafes armed and difguifed) alfo to hunt, wound, kill, or fteal any deer, in the king's forefts or chafes inclofed, or in any other inclofed place where deer have been ufually kept; or by gift or promife of reward to procure any perfon to join them in fuch unlawful act; all thefe are felonies without benefit of clergy. And the ftatute 16 Geo. III. c. 30. enacts, that every unauthorized perfon, his aiders and abettors, who fhall courfe, hunt, fhoot at, or otherwife attempt to kill, wound, or deftroy any red or fallow deer in *any* foreft, chafe, purlieu, or antient walk, or in any *inclofed* park, paddock, wood, or other ground, where deer are ufually kept, fhall forfeit the fum of 20*l.* or for every deer actually killed, wounded, deftroyed, taken in any toyl or fnare, or carried away, the fum of 30*l.* or double thofe fums, in cafe the offender be a keeper: and, upon a fecond offence (whether of the fame or a different fpecies) fhall be guilty of felony, and tranfportable for feven years. Which latter punifhment is likewife inflicted on all perfons armed with offenfive weapons, who fhall come into fuch places with an intent to commit any of the faid offences, and fhall there unlawfully beat or wound any of the keepers in the execution of their offices, or fhall attempt to refcue any perfon from their cuftody. Alfo, by ftatute 5 Geo. III. c. 14. the penalty of tranfportation for feven years is inflicted on perfons ftealing or taking fifh in any water within a

## C. XVI. OFFENCES AGAINST PRIVATE PROPERTY. 519

park, paddock, garden, orchard, or yard ; and on the receivers, aiders, and abettors: and the like punishment, or whipping, fine, or imprisonment, is provided for the taking or killing of conies by night in open warrens: and a forfeiture of five pounds, to the owner of the fishery, is made payable by persons taking or destroying (or *attempting* so to do) any fish in any river or other water within any inclosed ground, being private property. Stealing hawks, in disobedience to the rules prescribed by the statute 37 Edw. III. c. 19. is also felony. It is also said, that if swans be lawfully marked, it is felony to steal them, though at large in a public river ; and that it is likewise felony to steal them, though unmarked, if in any private river or pond ; otherwise it is only a trespass. But, of all valuable domestic animals, as horses and other beasts of draught, and of all animals *domitæ naturæ*, which serve for food, as neat or other cattle, swine, poultry, and the like, and of their fruit or produce, taken from them while living, as milk or wool, larciny may be committed ; and also of the flesh of such as are either *domitæ* or *feræ naturæ*, when killed. As to those animals, which do not serve for food, and which therefore the law holds to have no intrinsic value, as dogs of all sorts, and other creatures kept for whim and pleasure, though a man may have a base property therein, and maintain a civil action for the loss of them, yet they are not of such estimation, as that the crime of stealing them amounts to larciny. But by statute 10 Geo. III. c. 18. very high pecuniary penalties, or a long imprisonment and whipping in their stead, may be inflicted by two justices of the peace, (with a very extraordinary mode of appeal to the quarter sessions) on such as steal, or knowingly harbour a stolen *dog*, or have in their custody the skin of a dog that has been stolen.

Notwithstanding however, that no larciny can be committed, unless there be some property in the thing taken, and an owner ; yet, if the owner be unknown, provided there be a property, it is larciny to steal it ; and an indictment will lie, for the goods of a person unknown. This is the case of stealing a shroud out of a grave ; which is the property of those, whoever they were, that buried the deceased: but stealing the corpse itself, which has no owner, (though a matter of great indecency) is no felony, unless some of the gravecloths be stolen with it.

Having thus considered the general nature of simple larciny, I come next to treat of it's *punishment*.

In the ninth year of Henry the first, all persons guilty of larciny above the value of twelvepence were directed to be hanged; which law continues in force to this day. For though the inferior species of theft, or petit larciny, is only punished by imprisonment or whipping at common law, or by statute 4 Geo. I. c. 11. may be extended to transportation for seven years, as is also expressly directed in the case of the plate-glass company, yet the punishment of grand larciny, or the stealing above the value of twelvepence, (which sum was the standard in the time of king Athelstan, eight hundred years ago) is at common law regularly death. And, in many cases of simple larciny the benefit of clergy is taken away by statute: as from horsestealing in the principals, and accessories both *before* and *after* the fact; theft by great and notorious thieves in Northumberland and Cumberland; taking woollen cloth from off the tenters, or linens, fustians, callicoes, or cotton goods, from the place of manufacture (a); (which extends, in the last case, to aiders, assisters, procurers, buyers, and receivers) feloniously driving away, or otherwise stealing one or more sheep or other cattle specified in the acts (b), or killing them with intent to steal the whole or any part of the carcase, or aiding or assisting therein; thefts on navigable rivers above the value

---

(a) Stat. 18 Geo. II. c. 27. Note, in the three last cases an option is given to the judge to transport the offender; for *life* in the first case, for *seven years* in the second, and for *fourteen years* in the third;—in the first and third cases *instead of* sentence of death, in the second *after* sentence is given. A.

(b) These, by 15 Geo. III. c. 34. are bulls, cows, oxen, steers, bullocks, heifers, calves, and lambs.

C. XVI. OFFENCES AGAINST PRIVATE PROPERTY. 521

of forty shillings, or being present, aiding, and assisting thereat; plundering vessels in distress, or that have suffered shipwreck; stealing letters sent by the post; and also stealing deer, fish, hares, and conies, under the peculiar circumstances mentioned in the Waltham black act. Which additional severity is owing to the great malice and mischief of the theft in some of these instances; and, in others, to the difficulties men would otherwise lie under to preserve those goods, which are so easily carried off. And thus much for the offence of *simple* larciny.

Mixed, or *compound* larciny is such as has all the properties of the former, but is accompanied with either one, or both, of the aggravations of a taking from one's *house* or *person*. First therefore of larciny from the *house*, and then of larciny from the *person*.

1. Larciny from the *house*, though it seems (from the considerations mentioned in the preceding chapter) to have a higher degree of guilt than simple larciny, yet it is not at all distinguished from the other at common law: unless where it is accompanied with the circumstance of breaking the house by night; and then we have seen that it falls under another description, *viz.* that of burglary. But now by several acts of parliament the benefit of clergy is taken from larcinies committed in an house in almost every instance: except that larciny of the stock or utensils of the plate-glass company from any of their houses, *&c.* is made only single felony, and liable to transportation for seven years. The multiplicity of the general acts is apt to create some confusion; but upon comparing them diligently we may collect, that the benefit of clergy is denied upon the following domestic aggravations of larciny; *viz.* First, in larcinies *above the value of twelvepence*, committed, 1. In a church or chapel, with or without violence, or breaking the same: 2. In a booth or tent in a market or fair, in the day time or in the night, by violence or breaking the same; the owner or some of his family being therein: 3. By robbing a dwelling-house in the day time (which *robbing* implies a breaking) any person being therein: 4. In a dwelling-house by day or by night, with-

out breaking the fame, any perfon being therein and put in fear; which amounts in law to a robbery: and in both thefe laft cafes the acceffory before the fact is alfo excluded from his clergy. Secondly, in larcinies *to the value of five shillings*, committed, 1. By breaking any dwelling-houfe, or any out-houfe, fhop, or warehoufe thereunto belonging, in the day-time, although no perfon be therein; which alfo now extends to aiders, abettors, and acceffories before the fact: 2. By privately ftealing goods, wares, or merchandize in any fhop, warehoufe, coach-houfe or ftable, by day or by night; though the fame be not broken open, and though no perfon be therein: which likewife extends to fuch as affift, hire, or command the offence to be committed. Laftly, in larcinies *to the value of forty shillings* in a dwelling-houfe, or its out-houfes, although the fame be not broken, whether any perfon be therein or no; unlefs committed againft their mafters by apprentices under the age of fifteen. This alfo extends to thofe who aid or affift in the commiffion of any fuch offence.

2. Larciny from the *perfon* is either by *privately* ftealing, or by open and violent affault, which is ufually called *robbery*.

The offence of *privately* ftealing from a man's *perfon*, as by picking his pocket, or the like, privily without his knowlege, was debarred of the benefit of clergy, fo early as by the ftatute 8 Eliz. c. 4. But then it muft be fuch a larciny, as ftands in need of the benefit of clergy, viz. of above the value of twelvepence; elfe the offender fhall not have judgment of death. For the ftatute creates no new offence; but only prevents the prifoner from praying the benefit of clergy, and leaves him to the regular judgment of the antient law.

Open and violent larciny from the *perfon*, or *robbery*, the *rapina* of the civilians, is the felonious and forcible taking from the perfon of another, of goods or money to any value, by violence or putting him in fear. 1. There muft be a taking, otherwife it is no robbery. A mere attempt to rob was indeed held to be felony, fo late as Henry the fourth's time: but afterwards it was taken to be only a misdemesnor, and punishable with fine and imprisonment, till the statute 7 Geo. II. c. 21. which makes it felony (transportable for seven years) unlawfully and maliciously to assault another with any offensive weapon or instrument ;—or by menaces, or by other forcible or violent manner, to demand any money or goods with a felonious intent to rob. If the thief, having once taken a purse, returns it, still it is a robbery: and so it is, whether the taking be strictly from the person of another, or in his presence only; as, where a robber by menaces and violence puts a man in fear, and drives away his sheep or his cattle before his face. But if the taking be not either directly from his person, or in his presence, it is no robbery. 2. It is immaterial of what value the thing taken is: a penny as well as a pound, thus forcibly extorted, makes a robbery. 3. Lastly, the taking must be by force, or a previous putting in fear, which makes the violation of the person more atrocious than privately stealing. This previous violence, or putting in fear, is the criterion that distinguishes the robbery from other larcinies. For if one privately steals sixpence from the person of another, and afterwards keeps it by putting him in fear, this is no robbery, for the fear is subsequent : neither is it capital, as privately stealing, being under the value of twelvepence. It is enough that so much force, or threatening by word or gesture, be used, as might create an apprehension of danger, or induce a man to part with his property without or against his consent. Thus, if a man be knocked down without previous warning, and stript of his property while senseless, though strictly he cannot be said to be *put in fear*, yet this is undoubtedly a robbery. Or, if a person with a sword drawn begs an alms, and I give it him through mistrust and apprehension of violence, this is a felonious robbery. So if, under a pretence of sale, a man forcibly extorts money from another, neither shall this subterfuge avail him. But it is doubted whether the forcing a higler, or other chapman, to sell his wares, and giving him the full value of them, amounts to so heinous a crime as robbery.

This species of larciny is debarred of the benefit of clergy by statute 23 Hen. VIII. c. 1. and other subsequent statutes; not indeed in general, but only when committed in a dwelling-house, or in or near the king's highway. A robbery therefore in a distant field, or foot-path, was not punished with death, but was open to the benefit of clergy, till the statute 3 & 4 W. & M. c. 9. which takes away clergy from both principals and accessories before the fact, in robbery, wheresoever committed.

II. Malicious *mischief*, or damage, is the next species of injury to private property, which the law considers as a public crime. This is such as is done, not *animo furandi*, or with an intent of gaining by another's loss; which is some, though a weak, excuse: but either out of a spirit of wanton cruelty, or black and diabolical revenge. In which it bears a near relation to the crime of arson; for as that affects the habitation, so this does the other property of individuals. And therefore any damage arising from this mischievous disposition, though only a trespass at common law, is now by a multitude of statutes made penal in the highest degree.

By statute 22 & 23 Car. II. c. 7. maliciously, unlawfully, and willingly, in the night-time, to burn or cause to be burnt or destroyed, any ricks or stacks of corn, hay, or grain, barns, houses, buildings, or kilns; or to kill any horses, sheep, or other cattle, is felony; but the offender may make his election to be transported for seven years: and to maim or hurt such horses, sheep, or other cattle, is a trespass, for which treble damages shall be recovered. By statute 4 & 5 W. & M. c. 23. to burn on any waste between Candlemas and Midsummer, any grig, ling, heath, furze, gofs, or fern, is punishable with whipping and confinement in the house of correction. By statute 1 Ann. st. 2. c. 9. captains and mariners belonging to ships, and destroying the same, to the prejudice of the owners, (and by 4 Geo. I. c. 12. to the prejudice of insurers also) are guilty of felony without benefit of clergy. And by statute 12 Ann. st. 2. c. 18. making any hole in a ship in distress, or stealing her pumps, or aiding or abetting fuch offence, or wilfully doing any thing tending to the immediate lofs of fuch fhip, is felony without benefit of clergy. By ftatute 1 Geo. I. c. 48. malicioufly to fet on fire any underwood, wood, or coppice, is made fingle felony. By ftatute 6 Geo. I. c. 23. the wilful and malicious tearing, cutting, fpoiling, burning, or defacing of the garments or cloaths of any perfon paffing in the ftreets or highways, with intent fo to do, is felony. By ftatute 9 Geo. I. c. 22. commonly called the Waltham black-act, occafioned by the devaftations committed near Waltham in Hampfhire, by perfons in difguife or with their faces blacked, it is farther enacted, that to fet fire to any houfe, barn or out-houfe, (which is extended by ftatute 9 Geo. III. c. 29. to the malicious and wilful burning or fetting fire to all kinds of mills) or to any hovel, cock, mow, or ftack of corn, ftraw, hay or wood; or unlawfully and malicioufly to break down the head of any fifh-pond, whereby the fifh fhall be loft or deftroyed; or in like manner to kill, maim, or wound any cattle; or (*a*) cut down or deftroy, any trees planted in an avenue, or growing in a garden, orchard, or plantation, for ornament, fhelter, or profit; all thefe malicious acts, or procuring by gift or promife of reward any perfon to join them therein, are felonies, without benefit of clergy: and the hundred fhall be chargeable for the damages, unlefs the offender be convicted. By ftatutes 6 Geo. II. c. 37. and 10 Geo. II. c. 32. it is alfo made felony without the benefit of clergy, malicioufly to cut down any river or fea-bank, whereby lands may be overflowed or damaged; or to cut any hop-binds growing in a plantation of hops, or wilfully and malicioufly to fet on fire, or caufe to be fet on fire, any mine, pit, or delph of coal. By ftatute 11 Geo. II. c. 22. to ufe any violence in order to deter any perfon from buying corn or grain; to feize any carriage or horfe

---

(*a*) But to conftitute the offence of felony in regard to the maiming, &c. of cattle, it is held, that fuch maiming muft be committed out of fpite or revenge to the *owner* of the cattle. See *Shepherd's Cafe, Leach, Crown Law.*

carrying grain or meal to or from any market or feaport; or to ufe any outrage with fuch intent; or to fcatter, take away, fpoil, or damage fuch grain or meal, is punifhed for the firft offence with imprifonment and public whipping: and the fecond offence, or deftroying any granary where corn is kept for exportation, or taking away or fpoiling any grain or meal in fuch granary, or in any fhip, boat or veffel intended for exportation, is felony, fubject to tranfportation for feven years. By ftatute 28 Geo. II. c. 19. to fet fire to any gofs, furze, or fern, growing in any foreft or chafe, is fubject to a fine of five pounds. By ftatutes 6 Geo. III. c. 36 & 48. and 13 Geo. III. c. 33. wilfully to. fpoil or deftroy any timber or other trees, or roots, fhrubs, or plants, is for the two firft offences liable to pecuniary penalties; and for the third if in the day time, and even for the firft if at night, the offender fhall be guilty of felony, and liable to ttanfportation for feven years. By ftatute 9 Geo. III. c. 29. wilfully and malicioufly to burn or deftroy any engine or other machines, therein fpecified, belonging to any mine, or any fences for inclofures purfuant to any act of parliament, is made fingle felony, and punifhable with tranfportation for feven years, in the offender, his advifers, and procurers. And by ftatute 13 Geo. III. c. 38. the like punifhment is inflicted on fuch as break into any houfe, &c. belonging to the plate-glafs company with intent to fteal, cut, or deftroy, any of the ftock or utenfils, or fhall wilfully and malicioufly cut or deftroy the fame. And thefe are the principal punifhments of malicious mifchief.

III. Forgery, or the *crimen falfi*, is defined (at common law) to be "the fraudulent making or alteration of a writing "to the prejudice of another man's right:" for which the offender may fuffer fine, imprifonment, and pillory. And alfo, by a variety of ftatutes, a more fevere punifhment is inflicted on the offenders in many particular cafes, which are fo multiplied of late as almoft to become general. I fhall mention the principal inftances.

By ftatute 5 Eliz. c. 14. to forge or make, or knowingly to publifh or give in evidence, any forged deed, court-roll,

## C. XVI. OFFENCES AGAINST PRIVATE PROPERTY. 527

or will, with intent to affect the right of real property, either freehold or copyhold, is punished by a forfeiture to the party grieved of double costs and damages; by standing in the pillory, and having both his ears cut off, and his nostrils slit, and seared; by forfeiture to the crown of the profits of his lands, and by perpetual imprisonment. For any forgery relating to a term of years, or annuity, bond, obligation, acquittance, release, or discharge of any debt or demand of any personal chattels, the same forfeiture is given to the party grieved; and on the offender is inflicted the pillory, loss of one of his ears, and a year's imprisonment: the second offence in both cases being without benefit of clergy.

Besides this general act, a multitude of others, since the revolution, (when paper credit was first established) have inflicted capital punishment on the forging, altering, or uttering as true, when forged, of any bank bills or notes, or other securities : of bills of credit issued from the exchequer; of south-sea bonds, &c. of lottery tickets or orders; of army or navy debentures; of East India bonds ; of writings under seal of the hand of the receiver of the pre-fines, or of the accountant-general and certain other officers of the court of chancery ; of a letter of attorney or other power to receive or transfer stock or annuities; and on the personating a proprietor thereof, to receive or transfer such annuities, stock, or dividends : also on the personating, or procuring to be personated, any seaman or other person, entitled to wages or other naval emoluments, or any of his personal representatives ; and the taking, or procuring to be taken, any false oath in order to obtain a probate, or letters of administration, in order to receive such payments ; and the forging, or procuring to be forged, and likewise the uttering or publishing, as true, of any counterfeited seaman's will or power : to which may be added, though not strictly reducible to this head, the counterfeiting of Mediterranean passes, under the hands of the lords of the admiralty, to protect one from the piratical states of Barbary; the forging or imitating of any stamps to defraud the public revenue; and the forging of any marriage regifter or licence: all which are by diftinct acts of parliament made felonies without benefit of clergy. By ftatutes 13 Geo. III. c. 52. & 59. forging or counterfeiting any ftamp or mark to denote the ftandard of gold and filver plate, and certain other offences of the like tendency, are punifhed with tranfportation for fourteen years (*a*). By ftatute 12 Geo. III. c. 48. certain frauds on the ftamp-duties, therein defcribed, principally by ufing the fame ftamps more than once, are made fingle felony, and liable to tranfportation for feven years. And the fame punifhment is inflicted by ftatute 13 Geo. III. c. 38. on fuch as counterfeit the common feal of the corporation for manufacturing plateglafs (thereby erected) or knowingly demand money of the company by virtue of any writing under fuch counterfeit feal.

There are alfo certain other general laws, with regard to forgery; of which the firft is 1 Geo. II. c. 25. whereby the firft offence in forging or procuring to be forged, acting or affifting therein, or uttering or publifhing as true any forged deed, will, bond, writing obligatory, bill of exchange, promiffory note, indorfement or affignment thereof, or any acquittance or receipt for money or goods, with intention to defraud any perfon, (or corporation) is made felony without benefit of clergy. And, by ftatutes 7 Geo. II. c. 22. and 18 Geo. III. c. 18. it is equally penal to forge or caufe to be forged, or utter as true, a counterfeit acceptance of a bill of exchange, or the number or principal fum of any accountable receipt for any note, bill, or any other fecurity for money; or any warrant or order for the payment of money, or delivery of goods. So that, I believe, through the number of thefe general and fpecial provifions, there is now hardly a cafe poffible to be conceived, wherein forgery, that tends to defraud, whether in the name of a real or fictitious perfon, is not made a capital crime.

---

(*a*) Thefe offences are fince created felonies without benefit of clergy by 24 Geo. III. §. 2. c. 53.

## CHAPTER XVII.

#### OF TRIAL AND CONVICTION.

THE several methods of trial and conviction of offenders established by the laws of England, were formerly numerous; but that which is now in general use, is by jury. The trial by jury, or the country, is that trial by the peers of every Englishman, which, as the grand bulwark of his liberties, is secured to him by the great charter: "*nullus liber homo capiatur, vel imprisonetur, aut exulet, aut aliquo alio modo destruatur, nisi per legale judicium parium suorum, vel per legem terræ.*"

The excellence of this trial, for the settling of civil property, has before been explained at large. And it will hold much stronger in criminal cases; since, in times of difficulty and danger, more is to be apprehended from the violence and partiality of judges appointed by the crown, in suits between the king and the subject, than in disputes between one individual and another, to settle the metes and boundaries of private property. Our law has therefore wisely placed this strong and twofold barrier, of a presentment and a trial by jury, between the liberties of the people, and the prerogative of the crown. It was necessary, for preserving the admirable balance of our constitution, to vest the executive power of the laws in the prince: and yet this power might be dangerous and destructive to that very constitution, if exerted without check or control, by justices of *oyer* and *terminer* occasionally named by the crown; who might then, as in France or Turkey, imprison, dispatch or exile any man that was obnoxious to the government, by an instant declaration, that such is their will and pleasure. But the founders of the English law have with excellent forecast contrived, that no man should be called to answer to the king for any capital crime, unless upon the preparatory accusation of twelve or more of his fellow-subjects, the grand jury:

and that the truth of every accusation, whether preferred in the shape of indictment, information, or appeal, should afterwards be confirmed by the unanimous suffrage of twelve of his equals and neighbours, indifferently chosen, and superior to all suspicion. So that the liberties of England cannot but subsist, so long as this *palladium* remains sacred and inviolate; not only from all open attacks, (which none will be so hardy as to make) but also from all secret machinations, which may sap and undermine it; by introducing new and arbitrary methods of trial, by justices of the peace, commissioners of the revenue, and courts of conscience. And however *convenient* these may appear at first, (as doubtless all arbitrary powers, well executed, are the most *convenient*) yet let it be again remembered, that delays and little inconveniences in the forms of justice, are the price that all free nations must pay for their liberty in more substantial matters; that these inroads upon this sacred bulwark of the nation are fundamentally opposite to the spirit of our constitution; and that though begun in trifles, the precedent may gradually increase and spread, to the utter disuse of juries in questions of the most momentous concern.

This trial I shall consider; by following the order and course of the proceedings themselves, as the most clear and perspicuous way of treating it.

When a prisoner on his arraignment has pleaded *not guilty*, and for his trial hath put himself upon the country, which country the jury are, the sheriff of the county must return a panel of jurors, *liberos et legales homines, de vicineto;* that is, freeholders, without just exception, and of the *visne* or neighbourhood: which is interpreted to be of the county where the fact is committed. If the proceedings are before the court of king's bench, there is time allowed, between the arraignment and the trial, for a jury to be impannelled by writ of *venire facias* to the sheriff, as in civil causes: and the trial in case of a misdemesnor is had at *nisi prius*, unless it be of such consequence as to merit a trial at bar; which is always invariably had when the prisoner is tried for any capital offence.

In cases of high treason, whereby corruption of blood may ensue, (except treason in counterfeiting the king's coin or seals) or misprision of such treason, it is enacted, by statute 7 W. III. c. 3. first, that no person shall be tried for any such treason, except an attempt to assassinate the king, unless the indictment be found within three years after the offence committed: next, that the prisoner shall have a copy of the indictment, (which includes the caption) but not the names of the witnesses, five days at least before the trial; that is, upon the true construction of the act, before his arraignment; for then is his time to take any exceptions thereto, by way of plea or demurrer: thirdly, that he shall also have a copy of the panel of jurors two days before his trial: and, lastly, that he shall have the same compulsive process to bring in his witnesses *for* him, as was usual to compel their appearance *against* him. And, by statute 7 Ann. c. 21. all persons, indicted for high treason or misprision thereof, (except those respecting the coin and the royal seals) shall have not only a copy of the indictment, but a list of all the witnesses to be produced, and of the jurors impanelled, with their professions and places of abode, delivered to him ten days before the trial, and in the presence of two witnesses; the better to prepare him to make his challenges and defence. But no person indicted for felony is, or (as the law stands) ever can be, entitled to such copies, before the time of his trial.

When the trial is called on, the jurors are to be sworn, as they appear, to the number of twelve, unless they are challenged by the party.

Challenges may here be made, either on the part of the king, or on that of the prisoner; and either to the whole array, or to the separate polls, for the very same reasons that they may be made in civil causes: and the particular jurors must be *omni exceptione majores;* not liable to objection either *propter honoris respectum, propter defectum, propter affectum,* or *propter delictum.*

Challenges upon any of the foregoing accounts are stiled

challenges *for cause*; which may be without stint in both criminal and civil trials. But in criminal cases, or at least in capital ones, there is, *in favorem vitæ*, allowed to the prisoner an arbitrary and capricious species of challenge to a certain number of jurors, without shewing any cause at all; which is called a *peremptory* challenge: a provision full of that tenderness and humanity to prisoners, for which our English laws are justly famous. This is grounded on two reasons. 1. As every one must be sensible, what sudden impressions and unaccountable prejudices we are apt to conceive upon the bare looks and gestures of another; and how necessary it is, that a prisoner (when put to defend his life) should have a good opinion of his jury, the want of which might totally disconcert him; the law wills not that he should be tried by any one man against whom he has conceived a prejudice, even without being able to assign a reason for such his dislike. 2. Because, upon challenges for cause shewn, if the reason assigned prove insufficient to set aside the juror, perhaps the bare questioning his indifference may sometimes provoke a resentment; to prevent all ill consequences from which, the prisoner is still at liberty, if he pleases, peremptorily to set him aside.

This privilege, of peremptory challenges, though granted to the prisoner, is denied to the king by the statute 33 Edw. I. st. 4. which enacts, that the king shall challenge no jurors without assigning a cause certain, to be tried and approved by the court. However it is held, that the king need not assign his cause of challenge, till all the panel is gone through, and unless there cannot be a full jury without the persons so challenged. And then, and not sooner, the king's counsel must shew the cause: otherwise the juror shall be sworn.

The peremptory challenges of the prisoner must however have some reasonable boundary; otherwise he might never be tried. This reasonable boundary is settled by the common law to the number of thirty-five; that is, one under the number of three full juries.

But, by statute 22 Hen. VIII. c. 14. (which, with regard

to felonies, ſtands unrepealed by ſtatute 1 & 2 Ph. & Mar. c. 10.) by this ſtatute, I ſay, no perſon arraigned for felony, can be admitted to make more than *twenty* peremptory challenges. But how if the priſoner will peremptorily challenge twenty-one, what ſhall be done? The better opinion, as to this ſeems to be, that ſuch challenge ſhall only be diſregarded and over-ruled.

If, by reaſon of challenges or the default of the jurors, a ſufficient number cannot be had of the original panel, a *tales* may be awarded as in civil cauſes, till the number of twelve is ſworn, " well and truly to try, and true deliverance make, " between our ſovereign lord the king, and the priſoner " whom they have in charge; and a true verdict to give " according to their evidence."

When the jury is ſworn, if it be a cauſe of any conſequence, the indictment is uſually opened, and the evidence marſhalled, examined, and enforced by the counſel for the crown, or proſecution. But it is a ſettled rule at common law, that no counſel ſhall be allowed a priſoner upon his trial, upon the general iſſue, in any capital crime, unleſs ſome point of law ſhall ariſe proper to be debated. A rule, which (however it may be palliated under cover of that noble declaration of the law, when rightly underſtood, that the judge ſhall be counſel for the priſoner; that is, ſhall ſee that the proceedings againſt him are legal and ſtrictly regular) ſeems to be not at all of a piece with the reſt of the humane treatment of priſoners by the Engliſh law. And the judges themſelves are ſo ſenſible of this defect, that they never ſcruple to allow a counſel to inſtruct him what queſtions to aſk, or even to aſk queſtions for him, with reſpect to matters of fact: for as to matters of law, ariſing on the trial, they are *entitled* to the aſſiſtance of counſel. But, left this indulgence ſhould be intercepted by ſuperior influence, in the caſe of ſtate-criminals, the legiſlature has directed by ſtatute 7 W. III. c. 3. that perſons *indicted* for ſuch high treaſon as works a corruption of the blood, or miſpriſion thereof, (except treaſon in counterfeiting the king's coin or ſeals) may make their full defence by counſel, not exceeding two, to be named by the prisoner and assigned by the court or judge: and the same indulgence, by statute 20 Geo. II. c. 30. is extended to parliamentary *impeachments* for high treason, which were excepted in the former act.

The doctrine of evidence upon pleas of the crown is, in most respects, the same as that upon civil actions. There are however a few leading points, wherein, by several statutes, and resolutions, a difference is made between civil and criminal evidence.

First, in all cases of high treason, petit treason, and misprision of treason, by statutes 1 Edw. VI. c. 12. and 5 & 6 Edw. VI. c. 11. *two* lawful witnesses are required to convict a prisoner, unless he shall willingly and without violence *confess* the same. By statute 1 & 2 Ph. & Mar. c. 10. a farther exception is made as to treasons in counterfeiting the king's seals, or signatures, and treasons concerning coin current within this realm; and more particularly by c. 11. the offences of importing counterfeit foreign money current in this kingdom, and impairing, counterfeiting, or forging any current coin. The statutes 8 & 9 W. III. c. 25. & 15 & 16 Geo. II. c. 28. in their subsequent extensions of this **species of treason do also provide**, that the offenders may be indicted, arraigned, tried, convicted, and attainted, by the like evidence and in such manner and form, as may be had and used against offenders for counterfeiting the king's money. But by statute 7 W. III. c. 3. in prosecutions for those treasons to which that act extends, the same rule (of requiring *two* witnesses) is again enforced, with this addition, that the *confession* of the prisoner, which shall countervail the necessity of such proof, must be in *open court*. But in almost every other accusation one positive witness is sufficient.

Secondly, the mere similitude of hand-writing in two papers shewn to a jury, without other concurrent testimony, is no evidence that both were written by the same person.

Thirdly, by the statute 21 Jac. I c. 27. a mother of a bastard child, concealing its death, must prove by one witness that the child was born dead; otherwise such concealment shall be evidence of her having murdered it.

Fourthly, all prefumptive evidence of felony fhould be admitted cautioufly: for the law holds, that it is better that ten guilty perfons efcape, than one innocent fuffer.

Laftly, (contrary to the antient received practice) it was declared by ftatute 1 Ann. ft. 2. c. 9. that in all cafes of treafon and felony, all witneffes *for* the prifoner fhould be examined upon oath, in like manner as the witneffes *againft* him.

When the evidence on both fides is clofed, and indeed when any evidence hath been given, the jury cannot be difcharged (unlefs in cafes of evident neceffity) till they have given in their verdict; but are to confider of it, and deliver it in, with the fame forms as upon civil caufes: only they cannot, in a criminal cafe which touches life or member, give a *privy* verdict. But the judges may adjourn, while the jury are withdrawn to confer, and return to receive the verdict in open court. And fuch public or open verdict may be either general, guilty or not guilty; or fpecial, fetting forth all the circumftances of the cafe, and praying the judgment of the court, whether, for inftance, on the facts ftated, it be murder, manflaughter, or no crime at all. This is where they *doubt* the matter of law, and therefore *choofe* to leave it to the determination of the court, though they have an unqueftionable right of determining upon all the circumftances, and finding a general verdict, if they think proper fo to hazard a breach of their oaths; and, if their verdict be notorioufly wrong, they may be punifhed, and the verdict fet afide by attaint at the fuit of the king, but not at the fuit of the prifoner. Yet in many inftances, where contrary to evidence the jury have found the prifoner guilty, their verdict hath been mercifully fet afide, and a new trial granted by the court of king's bench: for in fuch cafe, as hath been faid, it cannot be fet right by attaint. But there hath yet been no inftance of granting a new trial where the prifoner was *acquitted* upon the firft.

If the jury therefore find the prifoner not guilty, he is then for ever quit and difcharged of the accufation, except he be appealed of felony within the time limited by law. And upon fuch his acquittal, or difcharge for want of profecution, he shall be immediately set at large, without payment of any fee to the gaoler. But if the jury find him guilty, he is then said to be *convicted* of the crime whereof he stands indicted. Which conviction may accrue two ways; either by his confessing the offence and pleading guilty, or by his being found so by the verdict of his country.

When the offender is thus convicted, there are two collateral circumstances that immediately arise 1. On a conviction, (or even upon an acquittal where there was a reasonable ground to prosecute, and in fact a *bona fide* prosecution) for any grand or petit larciny or other felony, the reasonable expences of prosecution, and also, if the prosecutor be poor, a compensation for his trouble and loss of time, are by statutes 25 Geo. II. c. 36. and 18 Geo. III. c. 19. to be allowed him out of the county stock, if he petitions the judge for that purpose; and by statute 27 Geo. II. c. 3. explained by the same statute 18 Geo. III. c. 19. all persons, appearing upon recognizance or *subpœna* to give evidence, whether any indictment be preferred or no, and as well without conviction as with it, are entitled to be paid their charges, with a farther allowance, (if poor) for their trouble and loss of time. 2. On a conviction of larciny in particular, the prosecutor shall have restitution of his goods by virtue of the statute 21 Hen. VIII. c. 11. And it is now usual for the court, upon the conviction of a felon, to order (without any writ) immediate restitution of such goods as are brought into court, to be made to the several prosecutors. Or, else, secondly, without such writ of restitution, the party may peaceably re-take his goods wherever he happens to find them, unless a new property be fairly acquired therein. Or, lastly, if the felon be convicted and pardoned, or be allowed his clergy, the party robbed may bring his action of trover against him for his goods, and recover a satisfaction in damages.

## CHAPTER XVIII.

### OF THE BENEFIT OF CLERGY.

AFTER trial and conviction, the judgment of the court regularly follows, unlefs fufpended or arrefted by fome intervening circumftance; of which the principal is the *benefit of clergy*; concerning which I fhall inquire, 1. To what perfons it is to be allowed at this day. 2. In what cafes. 3. The confequences of allowing it.

I. To what *perfons* the benefit of clergy is to be allowed at this day: upon which we may pronounce, that all clerks in orders are, without any branding, and of courfe without any tranfportation, fine, or whipping, (for thofe are only fubftituted in lieu of the other) to be admitted to this privilege, and immediately difcharged; and this as often as they offend. Again, all lords of parliament and peers of this realm having place and voice in parliament, by the ftatute 1 Edw. VI. c. 12. (which is likewife held to extend to peereffes) fhall be difcharged in all clergyable and other felonies, provided for by the act, without any burning in the hand or imprifonment, or other punifhment fubftituted in its ftead, in the fame manner as real clerks convict: but this is only for the firft offence. Laftly, all the commons of the realm, not in orders, whether male or female, fhall for the firft offence be difcharged of the capital punifhment of felonies within the benefit of clergy, upon being burnt in the hand, whipped, or fined, or fuffering a difcretionary imprifonment in the common gaol, the houfe of correction, one of the penitentiary houfes, or in the places of labour for the benefit of fome navigation; or, in cafe of larciny, upon being tranfported for feven years if the court fhall think proper.

II. The fecond point to be confidered is, for what *crimes* the *privilegium clericale*, or benefit of clergy, is to be allowed. Thefe have in general been mentioned under the particular offences to which they belong, and therefore need not be here recapitulated. But on this head of inquiry we may observe the following rules; 1. That in all felonies, whether new created or by common law, clergy is now allowable, unless taken away by express words of an act of parliament. 2. That, where clergy is taken away from the principal, it is not of course taken away from the accessory, unless he be also particularly included in the statute. 3. That, when the benefit of clergy is taken away from the *offence*, (as in case of murder, buggery, robbery, rape, and burglary) a principal in the second degree, being present, aiding, and abetting the crime, is as well excluded from his clergy as he that is principal in the first degree: but, 4. That where it is only taken away from the *person committing* the offence, (as in the case of stabbing, or committing larciny in a dwelling-house, or privately from the person) his aiders and abettors are not excluded ; through the tenderness of the law, which hath determined that such statutes shall be taken literally.

III. Lastly, we are to enquire what the consequences are to the party, of allowing him this benefit of clergy. And, we may observe, 1. That by his conviction he forfeits all his goods to the king ; which, being once vested in the crown, shall not afterwards be restored to the offender. 2. That, after conviction, and till he receives the judgment of the law, by branding or some of its substitutes, or else is pardoned by the king, he is to all intents and purposes a felon, and subject to all the disabilities and other incidents of a felon. 3. That after burning or its substitute, or pardon, he is discharged for ever of that, and all other felonies before committed, within the benefit of clergy, but not of felonies from which such benefit is excluded : and this by statutes 8 Eliz. c. 4. and 18 Eliz. c. 7. 4. That by the burning, or its substitute, or the pardon of it, he is restored to all capacities and credits, and the possession of his lands, as if he had never been convicted. 5. That what is said with regard to the advantages of commoners and laymen, subsequent to the burning in the hand, is equally applicable to all peers and clergymen, although never branded at all, or subjected to other punishment in its stead. For they have the same privileges, without any burning, or any substitute for it, which others are entitled to after it.

## CHAPTER XIX.

### OF JUDGMENT AND ITS CONSEQUENCES.

WE are now to confider the next ftage of criminal profecution, after trial and conviction are paft, in fuch crimes and mifdemefnors, as are either too high or too low to be included within the benefit of clergy: which is that of *judgment*. For when, upon a capital charge, the jury have brought in their verdict guilty, in the prefence of the prifoner; he is either immediately, or at a convenient time foon after, afked by the court if he has any thing to offer why judgment fhould not be awarded againft him. And in cafe the defendant be found guilty of a mifdemefnor, (the trial of which may, and does ufually, happen in his abfence, after he has once appeared) a *capias* is awarded and iffued, to bring him in to receive his judgment; and, if he abfconds, he may be profecuted even to outlawry. But whenever he appears in perfon, upon either a capital or inferior conviction, he may at this period, as well as at his arraignment, offer any exceptions to the indictment, in *arreft* or ftay of judgment: as for want of fufficient certainty in fetting forth either the perfon, the time, the place, or the offence. And, if the objections be valid, the whole proceedings fhall be fet afide, but the party may be indicted again. And we may take notice, 1. That none of the ftatutes of *jeofails*, for amendment of errors, extend to indictments or proceedings in criminal cafes; and therefore a defective indictment is not aided by a verdict, as defective pleadings in civil cafes are. 2. That in favour of life, great ftrictnefs has at all times been obferved, in every point of an indictment. Sir Matthew Hale indeed complains, " that this ftrictnefs is grown to be a blemifh and " inconvenience in the law, and the adminiftration thereof: " for that more offenders efcape by the over eafy ear given " to exceptions in indictments, than by their own inno- " cence." And yet no man was more tender of life than this truly excellent judge.

A pardon alfo, as has been before faid, may be pleaded in arreft of judgment. Praying the benefit of clergy may alfo be ranked among the motions in arreft of judgment.

If all thefe refources fail, the court muft pronounce that judgment which the law hath annexed to the crime, and which hath been conftantly mentioned, together with the crime itfelf, in fome or other of the former chapters.

When fentence of death, the moft terrible and higheft judgment in the laws of England, is pronounced, the immediate infeparable confequence by the common law is *attainder*.

The confequences of attainder are forfeiture and corruption of blood.

I. Forfeiture is twofold; of real and perfonal eftates. Firft, as to real eftates: by attainder in high treafon a man forfeits to the king all his lands and tenements of inheritance, whether fee-fimple or fee-tail, and all his rights of entry on lands and tenements, which he had at the time of the offence committed, or at any time afterwards, to be for ever vefted in the crown: and alfo the profits of all lands and tenements which he had in his own right for life or years, fo long as fuch intereft fhall fubfift. This forfeiture relates backwards to the time of the treafon committed: fo as to avoid all intermediate fales and incumbrances, but not thofe before the fact: and therefore a wife's jointure is not forfeitable for the treafon of her hufband, becaufe fettled upon her previous to the treafon committed. But her dower is forfeited by the exprefs provifion of ftatute 5 & 6 Edw. VI. c. 11. And yet the hufband fhall be tenant by the courtefy of the wife's lands, if the wife be attainted of treafon: for that is not prohibited by the ftatute. But, though after attainder the forfeiture relates back to the time of the treafon committed, yet it does not take effect unlefs an attainder be had, of which it is one of the fruits: and therefore if a traitor dies before judgment pronounced, or is killed in open rebellion, or is hanged by martial law, it works no forfeiture of his lands, for he never was attainted of treafon. But if the chief juftice of the king's bench (the fupreme coroner of

## C. XIX. JUDGMENT AND ITS CONSEQUENCES. 541

all England) in perfon, upon the view of the body of one killed in open rebellion, records it and returns the record into his own court, both lands and goods fhall be forfeited. But in certain treafons relating to coin, (which, as we formerly obferved, feem rather a fpecies of the *crimen falfi*, than the *crimen læfæ majeftatis*) it is provided by fome of the modern ftatutes which conftitute the offence, that it fhall work no forfeiture of lands, fave only for the life of the offender; and by all, that it fhall not deprive the wife of her dower. And, in order to abolifh fuch hereditary punifhment entirely, it was enacted by ftatute 7 Ann. c. 21, that, after the deceafe of the late pretender, no attainder for treafon fhould extend to the difinheriting of any heir, nor to the prejudice of any perfon, other than the traitor himfelf.

In petit treafon and felony, the offender alfo forfeits all his chattel interefts abfolutely, and the profits of all eftates of freehold during life; and, after his death, all his lands and tenements in fee-fimple (but not thofe in tail) to the crown, for a very fhort period of time: for the king fhall have them for a year and a day, and may commit therein what wafte he pleafes, which is called the king's *year*, *day*, and *wafte*. This year, day, and wafte are now ufually compounded for, but otherwife they regularly belong to the crown, and after their expiration, the land would naturally have defcended to the heir, (as in gavel-kind tenure it ftill does) did not its feodal quality intercept fuch defcent, and give it by way of efcheat to the lord. Thefe forfeitures for felony do alfo arife only upon attainder, and therefore a *felo de fe* forfeits no lands of inheritance or freehold, for he never is attainted as a felon. They likewife relate back to the time of the offence committed, as well as forfeitures for treafon; fo as to avoid all intermediate charges and conveyances.

Thefe are all the forfeitures of real eftates, created by the common law, as confequential upon attainders by judgment of death or outlawry. But I fhall juft mention, as a part of the forfeiture of real eftates, the forfeiture of the lands during life, which extends to two other inftances, befides thofe already fpoken of; mifprifion of treafon, and ftriking in Weftminfter-hall, or drawing a weapon upon a judge there, fitting in the courts of juftice.

The forfeiture of goods and chattels accrues in every one of the higher kinds of offence: in high treafon or mifprifion thereof, petit treafon, felonies of all forts, whether clergyable or not, felf-murder or felony *de fe*, petty larciny, ftanding mute, and the above-mentioned offences of ftriking, &c. in Weftminfter-hall. For *flight* alfo, on an accufation of treafon, felony, or even petit larciny, whether the party be found guilty or acquitted, if the jury find the flight, the party fhall forfeit his goods and chattels.

There is a remarkable difference or two between the forfeiture of lands, and of goods and chattels. 1. Lands are forfeited upon *attainder*, and not before: goods and chattels are forfeited by *conviction*. Becaufe in many of the cafes where goods are forfeited there never is any attainder, which happens only where judgment of death or outlawry is given, therefore in thofe cafes the forfeiture muft be upon conviction or not at all; and, being neceffarily upon conviction in thofe, it is fo ordered in all other cafes, for the law loves uniformity. ' 2. In outlawries for treafon or felony, lands are forfeited only by the judgment; but the goods and chattels are forfeited by a man's being firft put in the *exigent*, without ftaying till he is *quinto exactus*, or finally outlawed; for the fecreting himfelf fo long from juftice is conftrued a flight in law. 3. The forfeiture of lands has a relation to the time of the fact committed, fo as to avoid all fubfequent fales and incumbrances: but the forfeiture of goods and chattels has no relation backwards; fo that thofe only which a man has at the time of conviction fhall be forfeited. Therefore a traitor or felon may *bona fide* fell any of his chattels, real or perfonal, for the fuftenance of himfelf and family between the fact and conviction: for perfonal property is of fo fluctuating a nature, that it paffes through many hands in a fhort time; and no buyer could be fafe if he were liable to return the goods which he had fairly bought, provided any of the prior vendors had committed a treafon or felony.

Yet if they be collusively and not *bona fide* parted with, merely to defraud the crown, the law (and particularly the statute 13 Eliz. c. 5.) will reach them; for they are all the while truly and substantially the goods of the offender: and as he, if acquitted, might recover them himself, as not parted with for a good consideration, so in case he happens to be convicted the law will recover them for the king.

II. Another immediate consequence of attainder is the *corruption of blood*, both upwards and downwards; so that an attainted person can neither inherit lands or other hereditaments from his ancestors, nor retain those he is already in possession of, nor transmit them by descent to any heir; but the same shall escheat to the lord of the fee, subject to the king's superior right of forfeiture: and the person attainted shall also obstruct all descents to his posterity, wherever they are obliged to derive a title through him to a remoter ancestor. But, by the afore-mentioned statute of 7 Ann. c. 21. after the death of the sons of the late pretender, no attainder for treason will extend to the disinheriting any heir, nor the prejudice of any person, other than the offender himself; which virtually abolishes all corruption of blood for treason, though (unless the legislature should interpose) it will still continue for many them of felony.

## CHAPTER XX.

### OF REVERSAL OF JUDGMENT.

WE are next to consider how judgments, with their several connected consequences, of attainder, forfeiture, and corruption of blood, may be set aside. There are two ways of doing this; either by falsifying or reversing the judgment, or else by reprieve or pardon.

A judgment may be falsified, reversed, or avoided, in the first place, *without a writ of error*, for matters foreign to or *dehors* the record, that is, not apparent upon the face of it; so that they cannot be assigned for error in the superior court, which can only judge from what appears in the record itself.

⁋ Secondly, a judgment may be reverfed, *by writ of error:* which lies from all inferior criminal jurifdictions to the court of king's bench, and from the king's bench to the houfe of peers; and may be brought for notorious miftakes in the judgment or other parts of the record. Thefe writs of error, to reverfe judgments in cafe of mifdemefnors, are not to be allowed of courfe, but on fufficient probable caufe fhewn to the attorney-general; and then they are underftood to be grantable of common right, and *ex debito juftitiæ*. But writs of error to reverfe attainders in capital cafes are only allowed *ex gratia*; and not without exprefs warrant under the king's fign manual, or at leaft by the confent of the attorney-general. But the eafier and more effectual way, is,

Laftly, to reverfe the attainder by act of parliament.

The effect of falfifying, or reverfing, an outlawry is that the party fhall be in the fame plight as if he had appeared upon the *capias*: and, if it be before plea pleaded, he fhall be put to plead to the indictment; if after conviction, he fhall receive the fentence of the law: for all the other proceedings, except only the procefs of outlawry for his non-appearance, remain good and effectual as before. But when judgment, pronounced upon conviction, is falfified or reverfed, all former proceedings are abfolutely fet afide, and the party ftands as if he had never been at all accufed; reftored in his credit, his capacity, his blood, and his eftates: with regard to which laft, though they be granted away by the crown, yet the owner may enter upon the grantee, with as little ceremony as he might enter upon a diffeifor. But he ftill remains liable to another profecution for the fame offence: for, the firft being erroneous, he never was in jeopardy thereby.

## CHAPTER XXI.

### OF REPRIEVE AND PARDON.

THE only other remaining ways of avoiding the execution of the judgment are by a reprieve, or a pardon; whereof the former is temporary only, the latter permanent.

I. A reprieve, from *reprendre*, to take back, is the withdrawing of a sentence for an interval of time; whereby the execution is fufpended. This may be, firft, *ex arbitrio judicis*; either before or after judgment: as, where the judge is not fatisfied with the verdict, or the evidence is fufpicious, or the indictment is infufficient, or he is doubtful whether the offence be within clergy; or fometimes if it be a fmall felony, or any favourable circumftances appear in the criminal's character, in order to give room to apply to the crown for either an abfolute or conditional pardon. Thefe arbitrary reprieves may be granted or taken off by the juftices of gaol delivery, although their feffion be finifhed, and their commiffion expired: but this rather by common ufage than of ftrict right.

Reprieves may alfo be *ex neceffitate legis*: as, where a woman is capitally convicted, and pleads her pregnancy; though this is no caufe to ftay the judgment, yet it is to refpite the execution till fhe be delivered. In cafe this plea be made in ftay of execution, the judge muft direct a jury of twelve matrons or difcreet women to inquire the fact, and if they bring in their verdict *quick with child* (for barely, *with child*, unlefs it be alive in the womb, is not fufficient) execution fhall be ftaid generally till the next feffion; and fo from feffion to feffion, till either fhe is delivered, or proves by the courfe of nature not to have been with child at all. But if fhe once hath had the benefit of this reprieve, and been delivered, and afterwards becomes pregnant again, fhe fhall not be entitled to the benefit of a farther refpite for that caufe.

For she may now be executed before the child is quick in the womb; and shall not by her own incontinence evade the sentence of justice.

Another cause of regular reprieve is, if the offender become *non compos*, between the judgment and the award of execution: for regularly, as was formerly observed, though a man be *compos* when he commits a capital crime, yet if he becomes *non compos* after, he shall not be indicted; if after indictment, he shall not be convicted; if after conviction, he shall not receive judgment; if after judgment, he shall not be ordered for execution: for "*furiosus solo furore punitur*," and the law knows not but he might have offered some reason, if in his senses, to have stayed these respective proceedings. It is therefore an invariable rule, when any time intervenes between the attainder and the award of execution, to demand of the prisoner what he hath to alledge, why execution should not be awarded against him: and if he appears to be insane, the judge in his discretion may and ought to reprieve him. Or, the party may *plead* in bar of execution; which plea may be either pregnancy, the king's pardon, an act of grace, or diversity of person, *viz.* that he is not the same that was attainted, and the like. In this last case a jury shall be impanelled to try this collateral issue, namely, the identity of his person; and not whether guilty or innocent; for that has been decided before. And in these collateral issues the trial shall be *instanter*, and no time allowed the prisoner to make his defence or produce his witnesses, unless he will make oath that he is not the person attainted: neither shall any peremptory challenges of the jury be allowed the prisoner.

II. If neither pregnancy, insanity, non-identity, nor other plea will avail to avoid the judgment, and stay the execution consequent thereupon, the last and surest resort is in the king's most gracious *pardon;* the granting of which is the most amiable prerogative of the crown.

Under this head, of pardons, let us briefly consider, 1. The *object* of pardon: 2. The *manner* of pardoning: 3. The method of *allowing* a pardon: 4. The *effect* of such pardon, when allowed.

1. And, first, the king may pardon all offences merely against the crown, or the public; excepting, 1. That, to preserve the liberty of the subject, the committing any man to prison out of the realm, is by the *habeas corpus* act, 31 Car. II. c. 2. made a *præmunire*, unpardonable even by the king. Nor, 2. can the king pardon, where private justice is principally concerned in the prosecution of offenders: "*non potest rex gratiam facere cum injuria et damno aliorum.*" Therefore in appeals of all kinds (which are the suit, not of the king, but of the party injured) the prosecutor may release, but the king cannot pardon. Neither can he pardon a common nusance, while it remains unredressed, or so as to prevent an abatement of it; though afterwards he may remit the fine. Neither, lastly, can the king pardon an offence against a popular or penal statute, after information brought: for thereby the informer hath acquired a private property in his part of the penalty.

There is also a restriction of a peculiar nature, that affects the prerogative of pardoning, in case of parliamentary impeachments; *viz.* that the king's pardon cannot be *pleaded* to any such impeachment, so as to impede the inquiry, and stop the prosecution of great and notorious offenders. But, after the impeachment has been solemnly heard and determined, it is not understood that the king's royal grace is farther restrained or abridged: for, after the impeachment and attainder of the six rebel lords in 1715, three of them were, from time to time, reprieved by the crown, and at length received the benefit of the king's most gracious pardon.

2. As to the *manner* of pardoning. 1. First, it must be under the *great* seal. A warrant under the privy seal, or sign manual, though it may be a sufficient authority to admit the party to bail, in order to plead the king's pardon, when obtained in proper form, yet it is not of itself a complete irrevocable pardon. 2. Next, it is a general rule, that, wherever it may reasonably be presumed the king is deceived, the par-

don is void. Therefore any suppression of truth, or suggestion of falshood, in a charter of pardon, will vitiate the whole; for the king was misinformed. 3. General words have also a very imperfect effect in pardons. A pardon of all felonies will not pardon a conviction or attainder of felony; (for it is presumed the king knew not of these proceedings) but the conviction or attainder must be particularly mentioned; and a pardon of felonies will not include piracy; for that is no felony punishable at the common law. 4. It is also enacted, by statute 13 Ric. II. st. 2. c. 1. that no pardon for treason, murder, or rape, shall be allowed, unless the offence be particularly specified therein; and particularly in murder it shall be expressed, whether it was committed by lying in wait, assault, or malice prepense. Under these and a few other restrictions, it is a general rule, that a pardon shall be taken most beneficially *for* the subject, and most strongly against the king.

A pardon may also be *conditional:* that is, the king may extend his mercy upon what terms he pleases. Which prerogative is daily exerted in the pardon of felons, on condition of being confined to hard labour for a stated time, or of transportation to some foreign country for life, or for a term of years.

3. With regard to the manner of *allowing* pardons; we may observe, that a pardon by act of parliament is more beneficial than by the king's charter; for a man is not bound to plead it, but the court must *ex officio* take notice of it; neither can he lose the benefit of it by his own *laches* or negligence, as he may of the king's charter of pardon. The king's charter of pardon must be specially pleaded.

4. Lastly, the *effect* of such pardon by the king, is to make the offender a new man; to acquit him of all corporal penalties and forfeitures annexed to that offence for which he obtains his pardon; and not so much to restore his former, as to give him a new, credit and capacity. But nothing can restore or purify the blood when once corrupted, if the pardon be not allowed till after attainder, but the high and transcedent power of parliament. Yet if a person at-

tainted receives the king's pardon, and afterwards hath a son, that son may be heir to his father, because the father being made a new man, might transmit new inheritable blood: though, had he been born before the pardon, he could never have inherited at all.

## CHAPTER XXII.

### OF EXECUTION.

THERE now remains nothing to speak of, but *execution*; the completion of human punishment. And this, in all cases, as well capital as otherwise, must be performed by the legal officer, the sheriff or his deputy; whose warrant for so doing was antiently by precept under the hand and seal of the judge, as it is still practised in the court of the lord high steward, upon the execution of a peer: though, in the court of the peers in parliament, it is done by writ from the king. Afterwards it was established, that, in case of life, the judge may command execution to be done without any writ. And now the usage is, for the judge to sign the calendar, or list of all the prisoners' names, with their separate judgments in the margin, which is left with the sheriff. As, for a capital felony, it is written opposite to the prisoner's name " let him be hanged by the neck;" formerly in the days of Latin and abbreviation, "*suf. per coll.*" for "*suspen-datur per collum.*"

The sheriff, upon receipt of his warrant, is to do execution within a convenient time; which in the country is also left at large. In London indeed a more solemn and becoming exactness is used, both as to the warrant of execution, and the time of executing thereof: for the recorder, after reporting to the king in person the case of the several prisoners, and receiving his royal pleasure, that the law must take it's course, issues his warrant to the sheriffs; directing them to do execution on the day and at the place assigned. And in the court of king's bench, if the prisoner be tried at the bar, or brought there by *habeas corpus*, a rule is made for his execution; either specifying the time and place, or leaving it to the discretion of the sheriff. And, throughout the kingdom, by statute 25 Geo. II. c. 37. it is enacted, that, in case of murder, the judge shall in his sentence direct execution to be performed on the next day but one after sentence passed. But, otherwise, the time and place of execution are by law no part of the judgment.

And, having thus arrived at the *last* stage of criminal proceedings, or execution, the end and completion of human *punishment*, which was the sixth and last head to be considered under the division of *public wrongs*, the fourth and last object of the laws of England; it may now seem high time to put a period to these commentaries.

# INDEX.

## A.

ABatement of freehold, 350
   nusance, 309
Abbey-lands, 112
Abduction of child, 334
   heiress, 504
   ward, 334
   wife, 333
   women, 79
   or kidnapping, 507
Abeyance, 124
Abjuration, oath of, 455
Absolute property, 244
   rights and duties, 13
Acceptance of bills, 280
Account books, when evidence, 394
   writ of, 346
Act of bankruptcy, 284
   when pleaded, 546
  parliament, 9
   disobedience to, 455
   private, 10, 225
   public, 10
Action at law, 322
  *chose* in, 247
  property in, 247
Actual right of possession, 172
Adherence to the king's enemies, 444
Admeasurement of dower, 140
   pasture, 374
Administration, 292
  *cum testamento annexo*, 296
  *de bonis non*, 297
  *durante absentia*, 295
  *minore ætate*, 295
  limited or special, 297
Admission of a clerk, 60
Admittance to copyholds, 233
Advertising for stolen goods, 463

Adultery, 333
Advowson, 106
*Affectum*, challenge *propter*, 390, 531
Affinity, 73
Affray, 474
Age of consent to marriage, 74
  persons, how reckoned, 90, 424
Aggregate corporation, 94
Alehouses, 436
Alienation, 201
  forfeiture by, 101
Aliens, 48, 185, 193, 204
Alimony, 77
Allegiance, 48
Allowance of pardons, 548
  writs of error, 544
  to bankrupts, 288
Alteration of deeds, 210
Amendments at law, 408, 439
Ancestor, 176
Animals, larciny of, 518
  property in, 244
*Animus furandi*, 514
  *revertendi*, 246
Annuities, 117
  for lives, 275
Apparent heir, 175
  right of possession, 172
Appeal, proceedings in the nature of, 407
Appendant, advowson, 106
  common, 114
Appointment for charitable uses, 240
Apprenticeship, 482
Apprentices, 67
Appropriations, 57
  of commons, 115, 375
Approvers, compelling prisoners to become, 458

# INDEX.

Appurtenant, common, 114
Arbitrary confecrations of tithes, 108
Arbitration, 318
Archbishop, 53
Archdeacon, 56
Armed, being unusually, 476
Armour, &c. embezzling the king's, 452
Arms and ammunition, right of having, 18
Array, challenge to, 389, 531
Arrest of judgment, 403, 539
Arson, 507
Artificers, transporting or seducing them, 482
Asportation, 514
Assault, 323, 474
Assembly, riotous or unlawful, 474
*Assensu patris,* dower *ex,* 140
Assets, personal, 299
Assignees of bankrupt, 286
Assignment of bankrupts effects, 289
   dower, 140
   estate, 219
Assise, rent of, 118
*Assumpsit,* express, 342
   implied, 342
Assurances, common, 294
Attainder, 186, 540
Attainted persons, 202
Attestation of deeds, 210
   devises, 240
Attorney at law, action against, 349
Attorney-general, information by, 384
   warrant of, to confess judgment, 404
*Audita querela,* writ of, 408
*Auter vie,* tenant, *pur,* 132
Award, 318

## B.

Bailiffs, 34, 68
Bailiwick, 34
Bailment, 272
Banishment, 16
Bankrupt, 282
Bankruptcy, 282, 471, 200, 282
   fraudulent, 479
Banns, 76

Bar of dower, 140
Bargain and sale of lands, 221
Baron and feme, 72
Bastard, 84
  concealment of its death, 509, 534
  incapacity of, 86
  maintenance of, 86
  punishment for having, 437
Battery, 323
  of a servant, 335
Bawdy-houses, 427, 437, 487
Benefit of clergy, 537
Bigamy, 485
Bill for patents, &c. 225
  of exceptions, 398
  exchange, 279
  or note, forging, 528
  stealing, 517
Bishop, 53
Black act, 344, 470, 518, 525
Blasphemy, 434
Blood corrupted, 186, 543
  inheritable, 184
  of the first purchasor, 178
  whole and half, 180
**Body corporate and politic,** 93
*Bona notabilia,* 299
Bond, 223
  of arbitration, 319
Borough, English, 3
Borrowing, 273
Botes, 115
Bottomry, 274
Breach of close, 357
  covenant, 341
  peace, 467
  pound, 336
  prison, 459
Bribery in elections, 28
  magistrates, 466
Bridges, 42
  annoyances in, 487
  destroying, 524
Brothels, frequenting, 437
  keeping, 427, 437, 487
Burgage, tenure in, 119
Burgesses in parliament, their election 24

# INDEX.

Burglary, 508
Burning, malicious, 524
  the king's ships, 452
By-laws, 96

## C.

Cancelling deeds, 210
  wills, 295
Capacity to purchase or convey, 202
*Capias ad audiendum judicium,* 539
  *satisfaciendum,* 412
*Capita,* distribution *per,* 304
  succession, *per,* 178
Caption of indictment, 531.
Carnal knowlege of infants, 506
Carrier, action against, 347
Cart-bote, 115
Case, reserved at *nisi prius,* 400
Castigatory for vagabonds, 488
Cattle, malicious killing or maiming, 525
  owner answerable for, 339, 359, 499
*Caveat,* 377
Cause, challenge for, 531
Certificate for costs, 362
  of bankrupt, 288
  of poor, 46
Cession of a benefice, 62
*Cestuy que trust,* 221
  *vie,* 133, 288
  *use,* 221
Challenge of jury, 531, 589
  to fight, 476
Chance, 425
Chancellor, killing him, 445
  of a diocese, 55
Chance medley, 494
Charitable uses, 192, 240
Chastity, homicide in defence of, 493
Chattels, 244
Cheating, 480
Chief rents, 118
Children, duties of, 83
*Chose* in action, 244, 247
  how assigned, 266
  possession, 244, 247

Christianity, offences against, 428
  part of the laws of England, 434
Church, marriage in, 76
  offences against, 428
  or churchyard, affrays in, 474
Churchwardens, 64
Citizens in parliament, their electors, 24
Civil corporations, 94
  injuries, 307
  liberty, 13
Clergy, 52
  benefit of, 537
Clipping the coin, 446
Cloaths, malicious destroying of, 525
Close, breach of, 357
Cloth, stealing, from the tenters, 520
Coalmines, setting fire to, 525
Codicil, 293
Cognizance, *de droit, come ceo, &c.* fine *sur,* 228
  *tantum,* fine *sur,* 229
Cognizee of a fine, 228
  recognizance, 224
Cognizor of a fine, 228
  recognizance, 224
Coin, falsifying, *&c.* 445, 453
Collateral consanguinity, 174
  descent, 178
  warranty, 208
Collation to a benefice, 60
Collative advowsons, 107
Collecting the goods of the deceased, 299
Colleges, 94
  their visitors, 99
*Colligendum bona defuncti,* letters, *ad.* 296
Combinations, 481
*Commenda,* 62
Commission of bankrupt, 286
  the peace, 38
Commitment of bankrupt, 287
Common appendant, 114
  appurtenant, 114
  because of vicinage, 114

# INDEX.

Common, disturbance of, 373
 estate in, 170, 246
 farrier, &c. action against, 347
 form, proof of will in, 298
 in gross, 114
 informer, 345
 jury, 388
Common law, 1
 corporation by, 95
 dower by, 139
 guardian by, 88
Common nusance, 486
 of estovers, 115
 pasture, 113
 piscary, 115
 turbary, 115
 recovery, 231
 right of, 113
 *sans nombre*, 374
 surcharge, 373
 tenant in, of lands, 170
  of chattels personal, 248
 vouchee, 232
 utterer of false money, 450
 ways, 116
 without stint, 114
Commons, house of, 20
Commonwealth, offences against, 458
Compassing the death of the king, &c. 441
Competent witnesses, 396
Composition, real, for tithes, 109
 with creditors, 288
Compound larciny, 521
Compounding felony, 462
 other prosecutions, 464
Compulsion, 426
Concealment of bastard's death, 500, 534
*Concessit*, fine *sur*, 229
Conclusion of deeds, 209
Concord in a fine, 227, 342
Condition, 208
 breach of, 197
 estate on, 149

Condition, in deed, 151
 law, 151
 of a bond, 223
Conditional fees, 126
 pardon, 548
Confession by prisoners, 534
 of action, 404
Confirmation of bishops, 53
 lands, 218
*Congé d'eslire*, 56
Conies, taking, killing, or stealing, 518, 521
Conjuration, 434
Consanguinity, 173
Consecration of bishops, 53
Consequential damages, action for, 340
Conservators of the peace, 37
Consideration of contracts, 266
 deeds, 206
Conspiracy, 464
 action of, 328
Constable, 41
 lord high, 41
Construction of deeds and wills, 242
Constructive treason, 441
Contempt against the king, 454
Contingent legacy, 301
 remainder, 158
 trustees to support, 160
 uses, 221
Contract, 266
 express, 340
 implied, 343
 of marriage, 437
Contract, simple, 278
 special, 278
Conventional estates for life, 131
Conversion, 339
Conveyances, 203, 211
Conviction, 536
Coparceners, 168
Copper coin, counterfeiting, 451
Copy of indictment, 531
Copyhold, 120, 147
 for life, 121
 forfeiture of, 200

# INDEX.

Copyhold, not liable to *elegit*, 417
 inheritance, 121
Copyrights, 250
Corn, grain, meal, &c. destroying 525
Corn rents, 216
Corody, 116
Coroner, 35
Corporate name, 95
Corporation and test acts, 93, 259, 433
 its dissolution, 100, 187
 duties, 98
 incidents and powers, 96
 privileges and disabilities, 96
Corporeal hereditaments, 102
Corpse, stealing of, 258, 519
Correction of apprentices, 69
 children, 82, 494
 scholars, 82, 494
 servants, 69, 494
 wife, 80
Corruption of blood, 186, 543
Corseprefent, 256
Costs, 264, 406
 no more than damages, 407
Covenant, 341
 in a deed, 208
 real, 341
 to stand seized to uses, 221
 writ of, 227, 341
Coverture, 77
Counsel, action against, 349
 for prisoners, 533
Counterfeiting the king's coin, 445, 446
Counterfeiting the king's seals, 445, 446
Counterpart, 205
Country, trial by the, 387, 529
Credible witness, 396
Crimes, 420
Criminal conversation, 333
 law, 420

Cumberland, theft in, 520
Curate, 63
Cursing, 434
Curtesy, tenant by, 135
Custom, 189, 255
 assurances by, 235
 dower by, 139
 general, 2
 heriot, 255
 of London, how tried, 4
 particular, 2
 how allowed, 7
 when legal, 4
Customary freehold, 148
 tenant, 147
*Custos rotulorum*, 37

## D.

Damages to things personal, 340
Damage-feasant, 309
Damages, 264
*Darrien presentment*, assise of, 377.
Date of a deed, 210
Deacon, 56
Dead man's part, 305
Dean and chapter, 56
Deanry, 56
Debt, 378
Debt, action of, 341
 on amercement, 344
 on by-laws, 344
 on escape, 347
 on judgment, 343, 418
 on penal statutes, 344
Debt, information of, 384
Debtor refusing to discover his effects, 479
Debts, priority of, 300
Deceit, action for, 349, 408
Declaratory statutes, 10
*Dedimus potestatem*, 38, 228
Deed, 205
Deed-poll, 205
Deeds, stealing of, 517
Deer-stealing, 518, 521
 in disguise, 470

# INDEX

Default, judgment by, 404
Defeazance, deed of, 220, 224
*Defectum*, challenge *propter*, 390, 531
Deforcement, 351
Deforciant, 351
Degrees of consanguinity, 175
*Delictum*, challenge *propter*, 391, 531
Delivery of a deed, 210
Demolishing churches, houses, &c. 469
Denizen, 50, 185
Deprivation, 63
Derivative conveyances, 217
Descent of lands, 173
Descent, rules of, 175
Desertion, 452
Detainer, forcible, 476
   unlawful, 338
Determination of will, 145
Detinue, action of, 339
Devastation, 298
Devise, 239
Devisee, liable to debts of devisor, 242
Diminishing the coin, 446
Disabling a man's limbs or members, 504
   statutes of leases, 215
Disclaimer of tenure, 200
Discontinuance of estate, 351
Discovery by bankrupt, 288,
Disfiguring, 504
Disguise, 470
Disorderly houses, 487
   persons, 488
Dispossession, 350, 354
Disseisin, 351
Dissenters, protestant, 429
Distress, 309
   excessive, 314
   infinite, 371
   sale of, 316
   second, 314
Distribution of intestate's effects, 303
*Distringas*,
   detinue, 411
Disturbance, 372
   of common, 373
   franchises, 372

Disturbance of patronage, 376
   religious assemblies, 430
   tenure, 376
   ways, 375
Disturber, 195
Dividend of bankrupt's effects, 290
Divorce, 76
Doctrines illegal, asserting or publishing, 447, 455
Dogs, stealing them, 519
  &c. owner answerable for, 340
Dominion, 102
*Domitæ naturæ*, animals, 244
*Donatio mortis causa*, 302
Donative advowsons, 107
*Donis*, statute *de*, 127
Dower, 137
   *ad ostium ecclesiæ*, 139
   assignment of, 140
   bar of, 140
   by common law, 139
   by custom, 139
   *ex assensu patris*, 140
Draught for money, 279
Drunkenness, 425, 436
Duel, 474, 500
*Durante absentia*, administration, 295
   *minore ætate*, administration, 295
Duress, 203
   of imprisonment, 16

# E.

Earnest, 269
Ecclesiastical corporations, 94
Education of children, 82
Egyptians, 486
*Ejectione firmæ*, writ of, 355
Ejectment, action of, 355
Election of bishops, 53
   magistrates, 31
   members of parliament, 21, 26
Eleemosynary corporations, 94
*Elegit*, estate by, 156
   writ of, 415
Elopement, 78, 138

# INDEX. 557

Embassadors, violation of their privileges, 438
Emblements, 133, 144
Embracery, 466
Enabling statute of leases, 213
Endowment of widows, 140
Enemies, 444
Engrossing, 481
*Enlarger l'estate*, 218
Enquiry, writ of, 405
Entails, 128
Entry, 352
    tolled by descent, 352
    writ of, 354
Equity of redemption, 154
Error, writ of, 408, 544
    where prosecuted, 409, 544
Escape, 413, 459
    action for, 347
    assisting in, 460
Escheat, 418, 184, 453
Escrow, 210
Estate in lands, 122
Estovers, common of, 115
Estrepement, writ of, 369
Evidence, 393, 534
Examination of bankrupt, 287
    witnesses, 398
Exchange, bill of, 279
    deed of, 216
    or sale of goods and chattels, 268
    lands, 217
Excusable homicide, 493
Executed contract, 266
    estate, 156
    fine, 230
    remainder, 158
Execution, civil, 410
    criminal, 549
        plea in bar of, 546
        precept of, 549
        rule for, 549
        warrant of, 549

Execution, criminal, writ of, 549
    of devises, 240
    uses, 220
    process of, 410
Executor, 295
    *de son tort*, 298
    of his own wrong, 298
Executory contract, 266
    devise, 161
    estate, 156
    remainder, 159
Exemptions from tithes, 109
Expectancy, estates in, 156
Expenses of witnesses, 395
Exportation of wool, &c. 478
Express condition, 150
    contract, 266, 340
    malice, 500
Extent, writ of, 417
Extortion, 467
Eye, putting out, 504

## F.

Factors, 68
Fair or market, 363
False imprisonment, 328
    action of, 332
    judgment, writ of, 408
    news, 476
    verdict, 408, 466
Falsifying coin, 445, 449
    judgment, 543
Farrier, action against, 347
Favour, challenge to, 390
Fear, putting in, 523
Fee, 123
    farm rent, 118
    simple, 123
    tail, 127
*Felo de se*, 293, 495
Felon, 293
Felonious homicide, 495
Felony, 449
    compounding of, 462
    misprision of, 453
    punishment of, 449, 507, 508
Feme covert, 77, 203, 292
Feoffment, 211

*Feræ naturæ*, animals, 244
Ferry, 363
*Fieri facias*, writ of, 415
Final judgment, 405
Fine, in copyhold, 122,
    of lands, 226
        executed, 230
    reversal of, when levied of copyholds, 349
    *sur done, grant, et render*, 229
        *cognizance de droit, come ceo, &c:* 228
Fine *sur cognizance de droit tantum*, 229
    *concessit*, 229
Fire, negligence of, 71
Fire-bote, 115
Fire-works, 487
Fish, stealing, in disguise, 470, 518
    or attempting to steal, 518
Fishery, common of, 115
Fishpond, destroying, 525
Flight, 542
Foot of a fine, 228
Force, injuries with and without, 322
    when repellable by death, 493
Forcible abduction and marriage, 504
    entry and detainer, 476
Foreclosure, 158
Foreign bill of exchange, 279
    coin, forging it, 446, 449, 453
Forestalling, 481
Foretooth, striking out, 504
Forfeiture, 150, 191
    for crimes, 540
    of copyholds, 200
        goods and chattels, 254, 541
        lands, 191, 540
Forgery, 526
*Forma pauperis*, 406
Fornication, 437
Fortune-tellers, 434
Founder of a corporation, 98
Franchise, 116

Franchise, allowance of, 385
    disturbance of, 372
Fraud, criminal, 480
Frauds and perjuries, statutes of, 206, 240, 269, 278, 294, 342, 418
Fraudulent deeds, 206
    devises, 240
Free bench, 122
Freehold, 123
Funeral expenses, 298
*Furandi animus*, 513
*Futuro*, freehold, *in*, 143

## G.

Game, 247, 251
    destroying of, 490
    laws, 490
    selling of, 491
Gaming, 488
Gaming-houses, 487, 488
Gaol distemper, 35
Gaolers, 346
    compelling prisoners to be approvers, &c. 458
Gardens, robbing of, 515
Gavelkind, 3, 120
Gift of chattels personal, 265
Gift of chattels real, 265
    lands and tenements, 212
Gleaning, 360
God and religion, offences against, 427
Good consideration, 206
Government, contempts against, 455
Grand larciny, 512
Grants of chattels personal, 265
    real, 226
    lands and tenements, 213
    the king, 225
Great seal of the king, counterfeiting it, 445
Great tithes, 57
Guardian and ward, 87
    at common law, 88
    by custom, 89

# INDEX.

Guardian by nature, 88
    by statute, 89
    for nurture, 88
    in chivalry, 89
    in socage, 88
    testamentary, 89
Gypsies, 486

### H.

*Habeas corpus* act, 331
    the various kinds, 329
    *ad subjiciendum*, 330
*Habendum* of a deed, 207
Habitation, offences against, 507
Half blood, 180
Hand, burning in, 497
    disabling, 504
    loss of, 456
    writing, similitude of, 534
Hanging. 539
Hares, 518
Hawks, stealing, 518
Hay-bote, 115
Health, injuries to, 325
    offences against public, 483
Hedge-bote, 115
Hedge-stealing, 516
Heir, 173
    apparent and presumptive, 175
Heiress, stealing of, 504
Heir-looms, 257
Hereditaments, 103
Heresy, 427
Heriots, 121, 255
    seising of, 317
High constable, 41
High misdemesnors, 454
    treason, 440
    trials in, 531
Highways, annoyances in, 42, 116
    robbery in or near, 523
Hiring, 273
Hogs, keeping them in towns, 486
Holding over, 149, 358
Homicide, 491
*Honoris respectum*, challenge *propter*, 390, 531

Horse-races, 490
Horse stealing, 520
Horses, sale of, 271
Hospitals, 94
    their visitors, 99
House breaking, 508
    larciny from, 521
House-bote, 115
Hundred, action against, for robbery, &c. 344, 525
Hunting, 360
    by inferior tradesmen, 362, 407
    by night, or in disguise, 470
Husband and wife, 7z, 426
    injuries to, 333

### I.

Idiot, 202, 425
    marriage of, 75
Idleness, 488
Ignorance, 426
Imagining the king's death, 441
Imbezzling the king's armour or stores, 452
    public money, 454
    records, 458
Impeachment of waste, 199
Implication, 243
Implied condition, 150
    contract, 266, 342
Impostures, religious, 435
Incendiaries, 507
Inchantment, 434.
Inclosures, destroying, 526
Incorporation, power of, 95
Incorporeal hereditaments, 105
Incorrigible roguery, 488
Incumbent, 61
Indentures, 205
    of a fine, 226
Indictment, copy of, 351
Indorsement of bills and notes, 279
Induction to a benefice, 60
Infant, 90, 203, 292, 424
    carnal knowledge of, 506

# INDEX.

Infant, *in ventre sa mere*, 14, 159
    privileges and disabilities of, 91
Information compounding of, 464
Inheritance, 173
    estates of, 123
Injuries, civil, 307
    with and without force, 322
Innkeeper, action against, 347
Inns, disorderly, 487
Inquest of office, 383
Institution to a benefice, 60, 107
Insurance, 275
Interest of money, 273
    legacies, 302
    or no interest, insurance, 275
Interlineation in a deed, 210
Intestacy, 292
Intestates, their debts and effects, 299
Inventory of deceased's effects, 299
Investiture of benefices, 107
    lands, 212
Iron, stealing, 516

## J.

Joint-tenancy in lands, 165
    things personal, 148
Jointure, 141
Judges, assaulting them, 456
    killing them, 445
    threatening or reproaching them, 457
Judgment, 403
Judgment, action on, 343, 419
Jurors, fining or imprisoning, 535
Jury, trial by, 387, 529
Justice, offences against, 458

## K.

King, compassing or imagining his death, 441
    person and government, contempt against, 455
    levying war against, 442

## L.

Labourers, 68
Lands, property in, 102
Lapse, 193
Larciny, 512
    compound, 521
    from the house, 521
    from the person, 522
    grand, 512
    of things personal, 515
    petit, 512
    simple, 512
Law, common, 1
    divine or revealed, offences against, 427
    statute, 9
    unwritten, 1
    written, 9
Lazarets, escaping from, 484
Lead, stealing, 516
Lease, 213
    and release, 222
Legacies, 301
Lending, 273
Letter, demanding money, 472
    missive, for electing a bishop, 53
    threatening, 464, 472
Letters patent, 225
*Levant* and *couchant*, 312
*Levari facias*, writ of, 415
Lewdness, 437
Libel, immoral or illegal, 477
    malicious, 327, 477
Liberties or franchises, 116
    personal, 15
Life annuities, 275
    crimes against, 492
    estate for, 131
Limitation of actions, &c. 353, 379, 531
Linen, stealing from place of manufacture, 520
Lip, cutting of, 504
Literary property, 250
Liturgy, reviling of, 428
Livery of seisin, 212
Locks on rivers, destroying, 473
London, customs of, 3, 304
Lunaticks, 203, 425

# INDEX.

## M.

Madder roots, stealing them, 516
Magistrates.
    ——, oppression of, 467
    ——; subordinate, 30
Mainprize, writ of, 329
Maintenance of bastards, 86
    ———————— children, 81
    ———————— parents, 83
    ———————— suits, 69, 463
    ———————— wife, 77
Male preferred to female in descents, 170
    ——— stock preferred to female, 182
Malice express, 500
*Mandamus*, writ of, 386
Manor, 120
Manslaughter, 496
    —————, conviction of,
Manufacturers, seducing them abroad, 516
Mariners, wandering, 486
Market, 363
    ——, overt, 270
Marriage, 72
    ————; clandestine or irregular, 484
    ————, forcible, 504
    ————, licences and registers, forging or destroying 485, 527
    ————, proof of, 334
    ————, property by, 260
    ————, settlement, 45
Marriage, when good, 76
Master and servant, 66
    ————————, injuries to, 334
Mayhem, 324, 504
Memory, time of, 111
Menaces, 323
Menial servants, 66
*Mensa et thoro*, divorce, a 76
Merchants, custom of, 3
Merger, 164

Mines,
    ——, destroying their works, 526
    ——, stealing ore out of, 516
Mischief, malicious, 524
Misdemesnor, 420
Misfortune, 425
Misprision, 452
    —————, of felony, 453
    —————, of treason, 453
Mistake, 426
Mis-user, 150
Money,
    ——, counterfeiting, 445, 446
    ——, expended for another, action for, 345
    ——, received to another's use, action for, 345
Monopolies, 481
Monsters, 184
Mortgage, 152
Mortmain, 191
Mortuaries, 256
Moveables, 244
Murder, 498
    ———, pardon for, 547

## N.

Naturalization, 186
*Ne exeat regnum*, writ of, 455
Necessity, 426
    ————, homicide by, 492
Negligence of officers, 466
New trial, 401, 535
News, false, spreading, 476
Next of kin, 179
*Nihil dicit*, judgment by, 404
*Non compos mentis*, 292, 425, 546
    *sum informatus*, judgment by, 404
Non-claim of infants, 92
Nonconformity, 428
Nonjuror, 455
*Non user*, 150
Northumberland, theft in, 520
Nose, cutting off or slitting, 504

# INDEX.

Note of a fine, 228
    hand, 279
*Nudum pactum*, 267
Nuncupative wills, 293
Nufance, 309
    , affife of, 367
    , common, 486
    , private, 365

## O.

Obedience to parents, 82
Obligation or bond, 223
Obftructing of procefs, 459
Occupancy, 188, 249
Office found, 383
    , inqueft of, 383
Officers, killing them in executing their office, 500
Offices, 116
Oppreffion of magiftrates, 467
Orchards, robbing of, 515
Orders, holy, 57
Orphanage, 305
Overfeers of the poor, 43
Overt act of treafon, 441, 534
Oufter of chattels real, 354
    freehold, 350
Owling, 478

## P

Papifts, incapacities of, 204
    , laws againft, 430
*Paraphernalia*, 263
Parceners, 168
Pardon, 546
Parent and child, 8
    , injuries to, 334
Parents, &c. their confent to marriage 75
Parifh-clerk, 65
Parfon, 57
    imparfonee, 60
Particular eftate, 157
    tenants, alienation by, 193
Parties to a deed, 207
    fine, 230

Partition, 169
    , deed of, 217
Pafture, common of, 113
Patents, 225
Perjury, 464
Perfon, injuries to, 323, 492
Petitioning, right of, 18, 475
    , tumultuous, *ib.*
Piracy, 439
Pifcary, common of, 115
Pledge, eftates in, 152
Plough-bote, 115
Pocket-fheriffs, 32
Police, offences againft, 484
Policies of infurance, 275
Poll, deed, 205
Polls, challenge to, 389, 531
Polygamy, 74, 485
Poor, 44
Popifh prieft, 432
    recufants, *ib.*
Popular actions, 264, 344
*Poffe comitatus*, 33
    , neglecting to join, 454
Poffeffion, right of, 171, 353
    , eftates in, 156
Poffeffory action, 354
Poffibilities not affignable, 202
Pofthumous children, 14, 159
Pound, 315
Pound-breach, 336
*Præcipe*, common recoveries, 231
    , fines, 227
Prebendary, 56
Predial tithes, 108
Pregnancy, plea of, 545
Pregnancy, trial of, 84, 545
Premifes of a deed, 207
Prefcription, 189
    , corporations by, 95
    , time of, 111
Prefentation to benefices, 58, 107
Prefentment of copyhold furrenders, 237
Pretended titles, felling or buying, 463
Primogeniture, 177

# INDEX.

Princess of Wales, violating her, 442
Priority of debts, 300
Prison, breach of, 459
Privately stealing from the person, 522
Privies to a fine, 230
Probate of will, 298
Procuration-money, 479
Profaneness, 434
Promises, 342
Promissory note, 279
Prophecies, pretended, 476
Prosecution, malicious, 328
Protest of bills and notes, 280
Protestant dissenters, 429
Provisions,
, selling unwholesome, 484
*Pur auter vie*, tenant to, 131
Purchase, 183

## Q.

Qualification for killing game, 490
of electors to parliament, 21
jurors, 390
of justices of the peace, 38
members of parliament, 25
*Quantum meruit*, 345
*valebat*, ib.
*Quare impedit*, 377
Quarentine, widows, 140
of the sick, 483
Queen, compassing or imagining her death, 441
, violating her, 442
*Qui tam* actions, 345
Quit-rents, 118
*Quo warranto*, information in nature of, 101, 385
writ of, 385

## R.

Rape of women, 506

Rasure in deed, 210
Ravishment of children, 334
ward, 334
wife, 333
Reading of deeds, 209
Reasonable part, 304
Re-assurance, 275
Receiving stolen goods, 461
Recognizance, 224
Record, assurance by, 225
debt of, 278
imbezzling of, 458
Recovery, common, 231
Rector of a church, 57
Rectorial tithes, 57
Recusants, popish, 430
Regrating, 481
Release of lands, 218
Religion, offences against, 427
Remainder in chattels personal, 248
of lands, 157
Remitter, 320
Removal of poor, 45
Rent, 117
charge, 118
remedy for, 309, 371
substraction of, 370
Replevin, 316
action of, 336
bond, 337
Reprieve, 545
Reputation, 15
injuries to, 325
Rescue, 315, 457, 460
*Residuum* of intestates' effects, 303
Resignation, 55, 63
*Respondentia*, 274
Restitution of goods, 536
Reversal of attainder, 544
judgment, 409, 543
outlawry, 544
Reversion, 163
*Revertendi animus*, 246
Reviling church ordinances, 428
Revocation of devises, 241
uses, 222
will, 295

Rights,
    of persons, 13
    things, 102
Riot, 457, 467, 474
Riot-act, 467
Riotous assemblies, felonious, *ib.*
Rivers, banks of, destroying, 524
Robbery, 522
Rogues, 488
Roots, destroying of, 525
    stealing of, 516

### S.

Sabbath-breaking, 435
Sacrament, reviling of, 428
Sale, 268
Salvage, 275
*Scandalum magnatum*, 326
*Scire facias* against bail, 414
    in detinue, 411
    revive a judgment, 419
Scripture, scoffing at, 434
*Se defendendo,* homicide, 15, 494
Sea banks, destroying, 524
Sealing of deeds, 210
Seduction of women-children, 506
Seisin, 176
    livery of, 212
Self-defence, 308
    homicide in, 15, 494
Self-murder, 495
Servants, 65, 69
    battery or beating of, 334
    embezzling their master's goods, 513
    firing houses by negligence, 71, 508
    master when answerable for, 70
Settlements of the poor, 44
Severalty estates in, 164
Severance of jointure, 167
Sheep, &c. stealing or killing with intent to steal, 529
Sheriff, 30

Ships in distress, plundering them, 517, 520
    maliciously destroying of, 525
Shop-books, 394
Shrubs, destroying of, 525
    stealing of, 516
Shroud, stealing of, 258, 519
Signing of deeds, 210
Sign-manual of the king, forging it, 446
Similitude of handwriting, 534
Simony, 195, 435
Simple contract, debt by, 278
Slander, 325
Sluices on rivers, destroying, 473
Smuggling, 479
Soldiers wandering, 486
Specialty, debt by, 278
Squibs, 487
Stabbing, 498
Statutes, 10
Statutes, staple and merchant, 155
*Stirpes,* distribution *per*, 178, 304
    succession *in*, 178
Subornation of perjury, 465
Subscription of witnesses, 242
Substraction of rents and services, 370
Succession to goods and chattels, 259
Sufferance, estate at, 148
Suicide, 495
Supremacy, oath of, 432
Surcharge of common, 373
Surplus of intestates' effects, 303
Surrender, deed of, 219
    of bankrupt, 286
    copyholds, 235, 236
Surveyors of highways, 42
Survivorship, 167
    of things personal, 288
Swans, stealing of, 519
Swearing, profane, 434

### T.

Tail after possibility of issue extinct, 134

# INDEX.

Tail female, 129
    general, 129
    male, *ib.*
    special, *ib.*
    tenant in, 128
Taylor, common, action against, 347
Tenant to the *præcipe*, 231, 234
Tender of amends, 318
Tenement, 103
*Tenendum* of a deed, 207
Test-act, 433
Testament, 239, 292
*Teste* of writs, 28
Theft, 512
Theft, its punishment, 520
Theft-bote, 462
Threatening letters, 464, 472
Threats, 323
    of accusation to extort money, 464
Timber trees, stealing, 515
    destroying, 526
Tippling, 436
Tithes, 57, 108
Trade, offences against, 478
    offensive, 486
    unlawful exercise of, 68, 480
Traitors, 293, 441
Transportation, 16, 548
Transportation, returning from, 461
Treason, high, 440
    misprision of, 453
    petit, 503
    trials in, 531
Treasure-trove, concealment of, 454
Trees, destroying, 525
    stealing, 526
Trespass, costs in, 407
    on lands, 357
    on the case, action of, 325
    *vi et armis*, action of, 323
Trespassers *ab initio*, 317
Trial, new, 401, 535
Trover and conversion, action of, 339
Turbary, common of, 115
Turnips, stealing, 516
Turnpikes, destroying of, 473

## V. U.

Vagabonds, 488
Vagrants, 488
*Venire facias*, writ of, 530
*Ventre inspiciendo*, writ *de*, 84
    *sa mere*, children in, 14
Verdict, 400, 535
    false, 408, 466
Vicar, 57
Vicinage, common because of, 114
Visitor, 98
    of civil corporations, 99
    colleges, 99
    hospitals, 99
Umpire, 318
Undersheriff, 34
Underwood, stealing, 515
Voucher in recoveries, 231
Uses, covenant to stand seised to, 221
    deeds to lead or declare, 222, 234
    statute of, 220
Usurpation of franchises or offices, 385
Usury, 273, 479
Uttering false money, 446

## W.

Warrant of attorney, to confess judgment, 404
Warranty of chattels personal, 272
    goods sold, 348
    lands, 208
Warren, robbery of, 518
    in disguise, 470
Waste, 197, 367
Watch, 41
Ways, 116
    disturbance of, 375
Weights and measures, false, 480
Widow's chamber, 304

Wife, 77
    battery of, 334
Will, defect of, 424
    estates at, 145
    of the lord, 147
Wills and testaments, 239, 292
Witchcraft, 434
Witnesses, 396
    for prisoners, 535
    tampering with, 457
    their expenses, 395
    to deeds, 210
    wills, 294
Witnesses, two, where necessary, 396

Women, jury of, 545
Wool, &c. transporting, 478
Words, action for, 325
    costs in actions for, 407
    treasonable, 442
Wreck, 517
Writings, stealing of, 517
Wrongs, private, 307
    public, 420

## Y.

York, custom of the province of, 304

FINIS.

# LAW BOOKS,

*Lately Published by* W. CLARKE *and* SON, *Portugal-Street, Lincoln's-Inn.*

*In Two Volumes, Royal Octavo, Price* 18s. *in Boards,*

ANSTRUTHER'S REPORTS of CASES argued and determined in the Court of Exchequer, from Easter Term 32 George III. to Trinity Term, 35 George III. both inclusive.

\*\*\* *These Reports will be continued annually.*

*In Two neat Pocket Volumes, Price* 9s. *in Boards,*

BIRD'S NEW POCKET CONVEYANCER, or Attorney's Complete Pocket Book: comprising a choice Selection, and great Variety of the most Valuable and Approved Precedents in Conveyancing: in which the Modern Forms introduced by Conveyancers of the highest Eminence now in Practice are particularly attended to; and the Efficacy of them explained. To which are also added, Preliminary Observations, relative to the *Nature* and *Use* of each particular Species of Deed; an Introductory Discourse on the Subject of Deeds in general, and Conclusive Remarks on the Enurement and Construction of Deeds.

*In One neat Pocket Volume, being a Continuation to the above, Price* 3s *in Boards.*

BIRD'S ASSISTANT to the PRACTICE OF CONVEYANCING; containing Indexes or References to the several Deeds, Agreements, and other Assurances comprised in the several Precedent Books of Authority now in Print, from the Time of Sir *Orlando Bridgman*, to the present Period: with Short Remarks on the Distinguishing Qualities of each Precedent, and Cursory Observations on the Peculiar Merit of the Conveyancers by whom they were respectively prepared.

*In Octavo, Price* 5s. *in Boards, the third Edition, corrected & enlarged, of*

BOOTE'S HISTORICAL TREATISE of an ACTION or SUIT at LAW, and of the Proceedings used in the King's Bench and Common Pleas, from the Original Processes, to the Judgments in both Courts. The Third Edition, corrected and enlarged.

*In One thick Volume Octavo, Price* 9s. *in Boards.*

HULLOCK'S LAW of COSTS, in CIVIL ACTIONS and CRIMINAL PROCEEDINGS; with an Appendix, containing the Cases to Hilary Term, 1796, inclusive.

☞ *This Work shews particularly under what Circumstances Attornies may become personally liable to Costs; when they possess a Lien on Deeds, &c. in their Custody for their Fees; in what Cases their Bills are subject to Taxation, and when they ought to be delivered previously to bringing Actions thereon.*

*Law Books published by* W. Clarke *and* Son.

*In Quarto, Price* 10s. 6d. *in Boards.*

TURNER's COSTS and PRESENT PRACTICE of the COURT of CHANCERY; with Directions and Remarks for the Guidance of the Solicitor in conducting of a Cause, from the Commencement to its Close; and also in conducting other Proceedings in Matters under the Jurisdiction of the Court, or of the Lord Chancellor. *In a Manner entirely new.* Comprehending the Proceedings before the Master, in all the Inquiries usually directed to him, particularly in the Appointment of a Receiver, Sales of Estates, Appointment of Guardians for Infants, their Maintenance, &c. &c. With an Appendix, containing a Variety of Modern Precedents, in necessary Use during the Progress of a Cause. The *Second Edition*, with considerable Additions, Notes, and References, &c. Including the Costs and Practice in Proceedings under a Commission of Lunacy.

\*\*\* *This Work contains many Parts of the Chancery Practice, never before published, and forms a complete Practice in that Court.*

*In Octavo, Price* 5s. *in Boards,*

BARTON's HISTORICAL TREATISE of a SUIT in EQUITY, in which is attempted a Scientific Deduction of the Proceedings used on the Equity Sides of the Courts of Chancery and Exchequer from the Commencement of the Suit to the Decree and Appeal with Occasional Remarks on their Import and Efficacy.

*In Octavo, Price* 2s. 6d. *sewed, the Third Edition* of

BIRD's LAWS respecting LANDLORDS, TENANTS, AND LODGERS, laid down in a plain and easy Manner, and free from the Technical Terms of the Law. With many Practical Directions concerning Leases, Assignments, Surrenders, Agreements, Covenants, Repairs, Waste, &c. &c. Demand and Payment of Rent, Distress, and Ejectment, *up to the present Time.*

*Also, in Octavo, Price* 2s. 6d. *sewed, the second Edition,* of

The LAWS respecting WILLS, TESTAMENTS, and CODICILS, and Executors and Administrators, laid down in a plain and easy Manner. *To this Edition is added, an Abstract of the late Act imposing Duties on Legacies.*

*In Octavo, Price* 2s. *sewed.*

The LAWS respecting MASTERS and SERVANTS, Articled Clerks, Apprentices, Journeymen, and Manufacturers.

*In Octavo, Price* 2s. 6d. *sewed.*

The LAWS respecting PARISH MATTERS; Containing the several Offices and Duties of Churchwardens, Overseers of the Poor, Constables, Watchmen, Parish-clerk, Sexton, Beadle, &c.

*The above four Publications, for the Accommodation of those who take them together, may be had, done up in one convenient Volume, under the Title of* Law Selections, *Price* 9s. *in Boards, or* 10s. *bound.*

*In a neat Pocket Volume, Price* 3s. 6d. *bound, the Sixth Edition of*

NOY's GROUNDS and MAXIMS of the ENGLISH LAWS; with Notes by C. BARTON, Esq. Barrister at Law.

Printed in Great Britain by
Amazon.co.uk, Ltd.,
Marston Gate.